❖ The Last Water Hole in the West ❖

*The Colorado–Big Thompson Project and the Northern
Colorado Water Conservancy District*

Daniel Tyler

UNIVERSITY PRESS OF COLORADO

Copyright © 1992 by the University Press of Colorado
P.O. Box 849
Niwot, Colorado 80544

10 9 8 7 6 5 4 3 2 1

The University Press of Colorado is a cooperative publishing enterprise supported, in part, by Adams State College, Colorado State University, Fort Lewis College, Mesa State College, Metropolitan State College of Denver, University of Colorado, University of Northern Colorado, University of Southern Colorado, and Western State College.

Cover art: by Silvia Ruiz Tyler.

Library of Congress Cataloging-in-Publication Data

Tyler, Daniel.
    The last water hole in the west: the Colorado–Big Thompson Project and the Northern
  Colorado Water Conservancy District / Daniel Tyler.
        p. cm.
    Includes bibliographical references and index.
    ISBN 0-87081-268-8 (cloth). — ISBN 0-87081-277-7 (pbk.)
    1. Northern Colorado Water Conservancy District — History. 2. Colorado–Big Thompson
  Project (U.S.) — History. 3. Water-supply — Colorado — Management — History. I. Title.
  TD224.C7T95 1992
  333.91'15'09788 — dc20   92-26249
                                                                                                 CIP

The paper used in this publication meets the minimum requirements of the American National Standard for Information Sciences—Permanence of Paper for Printed Library Materials. ANSI Z39.48–1984
∞

To my children:
Daniel, Jr., Nicholas, Christopher, Alejandro, and Cristina,
with heartfelt thanks for their love and encouragement, which have sustained
me in the writing of this book.

Contents

Maps

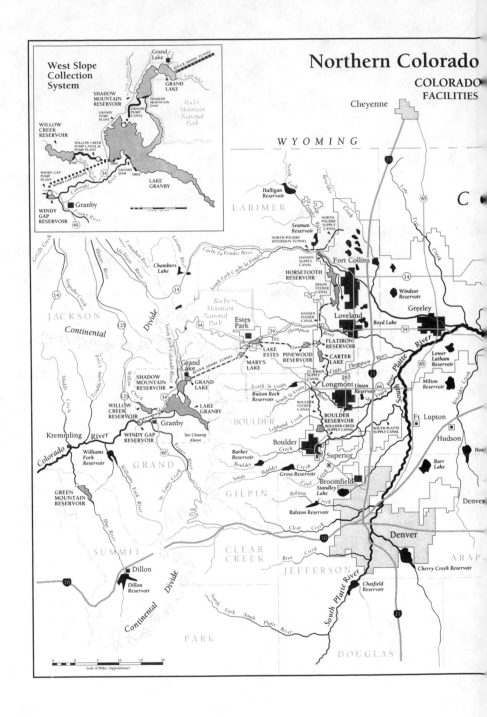

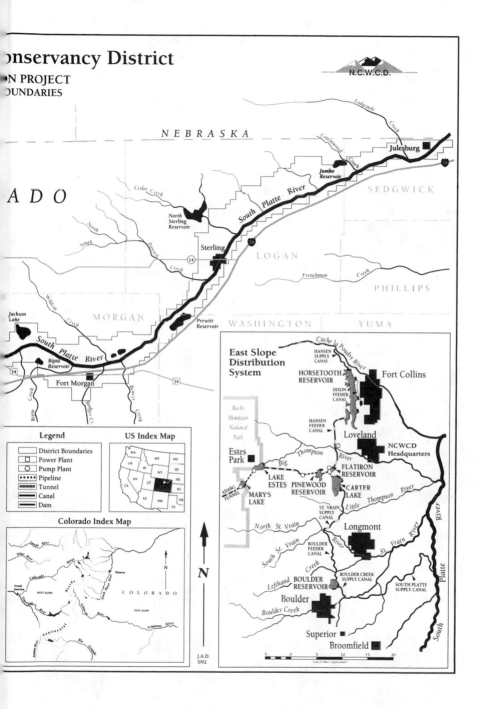

onservancy District

N PROJECT
OUNDARIES

N.C.W.C.D.

NEBRASKA

Lodgepole Creek

Julesburg

Cottonwood Creek

SEDGWICK

ADO

Cedar Creek

South Platte River

Jumbo Reservoir

North Sterling Reservoir

North

South

Darow Creek

Sterling

LOGAN

Frenchman Creek

PHILLIPS

Jackson Lake

MORGAN

Prewitt Reservoir

WASHINGTON

YUMA

White

Wildcat Creek

South Platte River

Bijou Reservoir

Fort Morgan

Bijou Creek

Beaver Creek

Badger Cr

East Slope Distribution System

Cache la Poudre River

HANSEN SUPPLY CANAL

HORSETOOTH RESERVOIR

Fort Collins

DIXON FEEDER CANAL

Rocky Mountain National Park

HANSEN FEEDER CANAL

Loveland

NCWCD Headquarters

Estes Park

Big Thompson River

FLATIRON RESERVOIR

LAKE ESTES

PINEWOOD RESERVOIR

CARTER LAKE

ADAMS TUNNEL

MARY'S LAKE

Little Thompson River

ST. VRAIN SUPPLY CANAL

North St. Vrain

Longmont

St. Vrain River

South St. Vrain

BOULDER FEEDER CANAL

River

Platte River

Lefthand Creek

BOULDER RESERVOIR

BOULDER CREEK SUPPLY CANAL

SOUTH PLATTE SUPPLY CANAL

Boulder

Boulder Creek

South Platte River

Superior

Broomfield

5   0   5   10   15   20

Scale of Miles (Approximate)

J.A.D. 5/92

Legend

District Boundaries
Power Plant
Pump Plant
Pipeline
Tunnel
Canal
Dam

US Index Map

WA MT ND
OR ID SD
WY
NV UT NE
CA IA
CO KS
AZ NM OK
TX

Colorado Index Map

River

Denver

Grand Junction

WEST SLOPE

Divide

COLORADO

EAST SLOPE

Continental

Arkansas River

Rio Grande

N

Acknowledgments

As with any such endeavor lasting more than five years, a great many debts have been incurred during the research and writing of this book. Among those who have read and critiqued various chapters of the manuscript, I especially wish to thank Donald Worster, Charles J. Bayard, J. R. "Bob" Barkley, W. D. "Bill" Farr, Larry D. Simpson, Gregory J. Hobbs, Jr., Bennett Raley, Lee Rozaklis, and Brian Werner. I have learned from their wisdom and am grateful for the time and energy they expended on my work.

The Northern Colorado Water Conservancy District's staff can now get back to normal. They have responded to my deadlines, endless questions, search for documents, and other chores with invariable good humor and kindness. In particular I want to mention Darell D. Zimbelman, John Bigham, Gene E. Schleiger, David Ayers, Brad Leach, Candee D. Werth, Joe K. Clark, Gordon N. Huke, Mike J. Carmon, Doris J. Farnham, Minerva G. Lee, Julie Danzl, Jean Maxwell, Cindy Barthlama, Jerry Westbrook, Marilyn L. Conley, Jim L. Struble, Dale Mitchell, John B. Budde, Chanda L. Johnson, Colleen M. Krabbenhoft, Lynn R. Raveling, Darwin W. Rutledge, Noble E. Underbrink, Roger A. Sinden, Jim Wooldridge, Dennis W. Miller, Denny Hodgson, Karl J. Dreher, Craig S. McKee, Eric W. Wilkinson, Jon Altenhofen, John Scott, Dennis J. Baker, Mike Fiscus, Mark A. Crookston, Gary Hoffner, Chris Anderson, Candys Arnold, Ken Whitmore, Bob House, and Harold Bower. Special thanks are due Debbie S. Goudie, who typed and retyped the entire manuscript, transcribed taped interviews, responded to a legion of related requests, and even gave birth to a son in the midst of everything. During most of the project her boss was June Moyes, who has since retired from the District. June provided unfailing support and good humor.

I could not have finished this book without the encouragement of my Colorado State University colleagues. History department chairman Mark Gilderhus showed great patience and arranged teaching schedules to benefit me. Susan Jones and Elva Flanigan invariably excused my preoccupation with water matters and helped me survive departmental crises.

Susan Boyle, Liston Leyendecker, James Hansen, Fred Enssle, Gene Berwanger, Harry Rosenberg, Lee Gray, and Bob Young kept me from taking myself too seriously. In the CSU Library, I am indebted to Doug Ernest, Judy Berndt, Emily Taylor, Marge Hill, Jennifer Monath, Evelyn Hayes, Barbara Branstad, Joan Beam, John Schmitt, Anna deMiller, Fred Schmidt, and John Newman, all of whom provided me with invaluable research assistance. But the compassion and good humor I needed most came from good friends Mims Harris and Christy Case, to whom I owe much more than I can ever repay. And I am most grateful to the College of Arts, Humanities and Social Sciences, which awarded me a grant for research assistance during the final year of manuscript preparation.

Others whose efforts contributed to this work include Roland C. Fischer, Don Hamburg, and Lee Harris of the Colorado River Water Conservation District; Peggy Ford of the Greeley Museum; archivist Larry Baum; attorneys John Sayre, Ward Fisher, Brian Blakely, Kenneth Balcomb, David Miller, George Vranesh, and Stan Cazier; lobbyist Fred Anderson; developer Craig Harrison; retired Bureau project manager Robert Berling; Colorado University economist Charles Howe; the Fort Morgan Historical Society; Cecil Osborne, Kish Otsuka, Don Hamil, Ival Goslin, Elton Watson, Bob "Smitty" Smith, John Eckhardt, Paul Schmelzer, Harlan Seaworth, Bob Stieben, Charles L. "Tommy" Thomson, Carl Breeze, Hatfield Chilson, and Sid Frier of the Salt River project; Jay Malinowski of the Metropolitan Water District in Los Angeles; the Imperial Valley Irrigation District; the Fort Collins Public Library; the Denver Water Board; the Colorado Water Conservation Board; the Colorado Water Resources and Power Development Authority; and the Colorado Endowment for the Humanities, which provided me with a grant to continue writing during the summer of 1991. I would also like to thank past and present members of the NCWCD Board who allowed me total freedom to pursue this research and to write my story without interference.

To Jody Berman of the University Press of Colorado, I owe more than can be measured in words. Her efficiency, common sense, tact, persistence, and good judgment have made the final production process a breeze. While I accept all the responsibility for any errors or inconsistencies in the final copy, Jody's professional direction simplified my tasks enormously.

My debt is greatest to a few key individuals. Brian and Wendy Werner never complained about my intrusions on weekends and even allowed one of their young daughters to sharpen her teeth on several chapters. To the Werner family I am enormously grateful. Bob Barkley and Bill Farr provided me with firsthand information that could not be found in the documents, and their professional demeanor won my uncompromising respect and admiration. Gordon Dyekman, NCWCD Board president from 1976 to 1991, died just before the manuscript was completed. He invariably showed genuine enthusiasm for the project and encouraged me to do my best. Larry Simpson deserves credit for seeing the need for a fifty-year history of the District. When I agreed to do it, he gave me all the support I needed without suggesting how the facts should be interpreted. Jeff Dahlstrom did the maps. His talents are obvious. Easy to work with and responsive to suggestions, Jeff has made this book easier to read. Jerry Leggate of the Bureau of Reclamation's regional office in Billings found many of the book's photographs. His contributions are most appreciated. Greg Silkensen worked with me during the final year of manuscript preparation. He prepared the bibliography, assisted in selection of photographs, helped prepare maps, and proofread much of the final draft. Apart from being a valuable assistant, Greg proved to have all the skills needed to become a professional historian. Editing assistance from Gail Reitenbach and Kim McGann kept me from making egregious mistakes. Finally, and with profound appreciation, I thank my wife, Silvia. She had legitimate reasons to wish I had never started this book, and she kept things running at home so I could concentrate on running water. Mil gracias!

Daniel Tyler

The Last Water Hole in the West

Introduction

When I was an assistant professor trying to make a mark in western history, I was invited to comment at the Texas State Historical Association's annual meeting on a paper that at the time seemed rather parochial. In my prepared remarks, I noted somewhat pompously that local history without links to regional, national, or world events had limited significance. The immediate response of Texas historian Nettie Lee Benson quickly put me in my place. She chastized me for implying that local Texas history was without merit and commended the paper's author for developing the building blocks on which she and other historians could base broader and more generalized interpretations of Texas history. A Coloradan in Alamo country, I decided on a full-scale retreat. I also made a mental note about the importance of discretion and humility if the Texans ever invited me back.

Since then I have been involved in my own parochial studies, but I have continued to believe that they should be set in some sort of larger context. Researching and writing the history of the Colorado–Big Thompson Project (C–BT) and the Northern Colorado Water Conservancy District (NCWCD) seemed to be a good extension of my previous experiences. The project lent itself to my interest in local history, and the history of water development intrigued me. I was somewhat aware of the anomalies of water, having used the working end of a shovel for several summers at my father's Crystal River Ranch on the West Slope of the Continental Divide. I had also set plenty of irrigation tubes for a sugar beet farmer in Burlington, Colorado, prior to deciding on a career as a western historian. Because of my familiarity with the Hispanic Southwest I was engaged as an expert witness by private and government entities in New Mexico and Colorado to testify in several trials dealing with Hispanic water rights. Because the NCWCD had an extensive archive and the Board and staff had given me carte blanche to write the fifty-year history as I saw it, there seemed to be few barriers in the way of getting the job done during a sabbatical year and two summers.

Tying the history of the C–BT and NCWCD into regional and national events took a good deal longer than I had anticipated. I began work shortly after the appearance of Donald Worster's *Rivers of Empire* (1985) and Marc Reisner's *Cadillac Desert* (1986), two volumes that are generally critical of water projects and that still evoke grumbling sounds from traditionalists in the water community. Both authors produced readable and provocative studies, and I am indebted to them for providing me with a better perspective. My own objective, however, was to create a history from the ground up, using primarily the minutes, correspondence, memoranda, reports, studies, speeches, legal opinions, and newspaper articles dealing with the C–BT, NCWCD, and the other regional organizations with which District staff and the Board of Directors had some relationship. I had no axes to grind, no preconceived idea of good guys and bad guys, and no philosophical or ideological models to follow. I did not know what I would find, but I knew that I did not want to write simply an institutional history.

Although one of my purposes had been to provide enough historical detail of the C–BT and NCWCD so that future Directors and District employees would have an adequate understanding of the role of their predecessors, I also wanted to incorporate these details into national events such as the Great Depression, World War II, the Cold War, the Korean and Vietnam wars, and the environmental revolution launched by the first Earth Day in 1970. The extent of the connection between NCWCD managers, their attorneys, and government officials needed clarification in order to explain the pace and direction of the District's maturity. Although this book provides a great deal of engineering, agricultural, demographic, and legal data, it also has vignettes of a more personal nature. I wanted to humanize the story in order to portray the occasional drama while making a very factual study more readable.

I make no pretense that this book is environmental history, but I have made a concerted effort to show how the combined pressures of federal legislation and popular activism caused conflict and policy changes at the District. The confrontation between water developers and environmentalists that began in the 1970s continues today, and so this book reveals the water community's sometimes unreasoning and stubborn adherence to the prior appropriation doctrine as well as environmentalist tendencies to neglect the social and economic value of water storage and the importance of private property rights to those possessing legitimate water decrees. I have tried not to take a position on either side of this debate, but I have attempted to show how progress has been attained, albeit at a snail's pace, through compromise and negotiation.

Anyone reading this book from beginning to end will want to remember some essential facts about Colorado. This is a state in which significant mountain ranges divide the watershed between the Atlantic and Pacific oceans. The West Slope of the Continental Divide receives between 65 and 70 percent of the state's moisture; the East Slope gets the balance. What is significant about this climatalogical fact is that 80 percent of the state's population resides on the Front Range between Trinidad and Fort Collins. The growth of this increasingly urbanized area has created demands for additional water, not for agriculture but for municipalities and industry. Under Colorado's prior appropriation doctrine as defined in *Coffin* v. *Left Hand Ditch Company* (1882), water may be diverted from one river basin to another if it is put to beneficial use and does not prejudice adjudicated rights of senior water users. The 1922 Colorado River Compact also endorsed the concept of water transfers out of the basin of origin. Under this principle, the East Slope has constructed thirty-seven transmountain diversion projects that collectively remove more than 650,000 acre-feet of water from the Gunnison, San Juan, and Colorado river basins. The C–BT is the largest diverter, but taken altogether, these projects threaten the future growth and development of the West Slope. They also raise questions about Colorado River salinity, the rights and obligations of all seven Colorado River basin states to each other, and the United States' treaty obligations to Mexico.

For more than fifty years, the C–BT Project has been inextricably involved in discussions involving not only metropolitan Denver's future but the future of the Colorado River basin. With the public trust doctrine's introduction into California courts, and wilderness water rights being litigated in other parts of the West, water management has attained a level of complexity that will require patience and outstanding leadership by all concerned about the future.

The narrative herein proceeds chronologically for the most part. Occasionally, I have seen the need for flashbacks as well as momentary anticipations of the future to put certain episodes in context. The five parts represent periods that seem to stand on their own. Part I deals with the birth of the C–BT idea and the battle between East and West Slopes to work out a mutually satisfactory plan of development. Part II details the impact of World War II and shows how District personnel adapted to political realities in competing for construction funds. Part III covers the completion of construction, the first water deliveries, and the emergence of District rules and regulations. Part IV introduces the relationship of the C–BT to other western water projects, the emergence of the environmental movement, and the District's plans to add water to the C–BT system through construction of the Windy Gap project. Part V brings to a head all of the challenges of the 1980s and presents some ideas for future consideration.

In reflecting on what has transpired in fifty years, I keep returning to the fact that the C–BT was designed and built by men who wanted to stabilize agriculture in northern Colorado by means of a supplemental water supply using construction money borrowed from the federal government under the 1902 Reclamation Act. In the Repayment Contract of 1938, the District obligated itself to pay a maximum of $25 million to the United States for a Project that eventually cost $163 million due to wartime inflation and design changes introduced by the Bureau of Reclamation. I have tried to explain the reasons why adherence to this contract was so important. Today, with money in the bank to retire its indebtedness and with adequate income from ad valorem taxes, water rentals, and the inclusion of new communities into the NCWCD and Municipal Subdistrict, the District finds itself with sufficient funds to pay its bills. The future, however, is fraught with potential problems. Not only has the importance of agriculture diminished, but the question of responsibility for point and nonpoint source pollution will fall squarely into the laps of future Directors. Furthermore, even though it is presently in excellent physical condition, the C–BT system is going to require constant and expensive repair and maintenance.

With the Two Forks project vetoed by the Environmental Protection Agency (EPA) and Denver's suburbs purchasing farmers' water rights in the Arkansas and South Platte River valleys, the challenges to NCWCD leadership are enormous. How water is to be managed, exchanged, and conserved; whether the Board should continue to be appointed by district judges or elected by the people; how rules and regulations should be amended to accommodate growing communities north of the City and County of Denver; and how much energy should be expended on environmental protection are issues that must be dealt with during the remainder of this last decade of the twentieth century.

I have no idea what role the NCWCD may play in the future, but if this history shows anything, it is that managerial flexibility will be needed to keep up with the fast-paced socioeconomic changes taking place in the West. Although their initial objectives may not be consistent with legitimate current concerns about the impact of transmountain diversion, the founders of the C–BT were dedicated and selfless men who believed in improving their community. They did not consider themselves heroes, but they were boosters who worked tirelessly to make northern Colorado a better place to live. With all due respect to those who view water projects as the work of evil megalomaniacs, I would ask readers to give some thought to the conditions that fostered the need for supplemental water in the 1930s and the vision of those men who believed they were taking risks for the betterment of their families, friends, homes, and businesses.

Part I: *The Formative Years (1933–1938)*

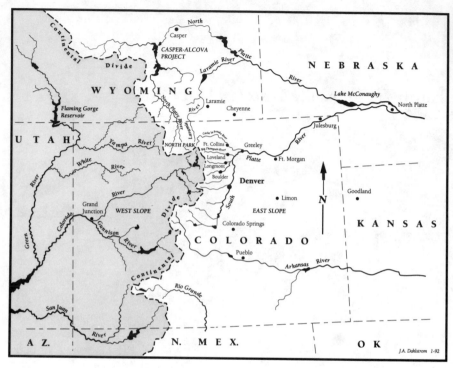

Central Rockies, Colorado, Neighboring States.

1

The Search for Supplemental Water: The North Platte River and the Casper-Alcova Project

On March 4, 1933, a gloomy, overcast Saturday, President-elect Franklin Delano Roosevelt shuffled slowly down a special ramp, leaning on the arm of his son James. FDR was eager and ready to take the oath of office from Chief Justice Charles Evans Hughes. Hundreds of thousands of people, gathered on the East Front of the Capitol, "blackened forty acres of park and pavement. They sat on benches. They filled bare trees. But for all the flags and music and ceremony, they were not a happy, carefree crowd. Their bank accounts were frozen. Many of them wondered how they could raise the cash to get home. Their mass spirits were as sombre as the gray sky above. Yet they remained doggedly hopeful."[1]

With his hand on a Dutch Bible that had been in the family for three centuries, Roosevelt broke precedent by repeating every word of the presidential oath and then turned quickly to the crowd before him.

My friends, this is a day of national consecration. . . . The only thing we have to fear is fear itself — nameless, unreasoning, unjustified terror which paralyzes needed efforts to convert retreat into advance. . . . Only a foolish optimist can deny the realities of the moment. . . . This nation asks for action, and action now. . . . Our greatest primary task is to put people to work. This is no unsolvable problem if we face it wisely and courageously. It can be accomplished in part by direct recruiting by the government itself, treating the task as we would treat the emergency of a war, but at the same time, through this employment, accomplishing greatly needed projects to stimulate and reorganize the use of our natural resources. . . . It is to be hoped that the normal balance of executive and legislative authority may be wholly adequate to meet the unprecedented task before us. But it may be that an unprecedented demand and need for undelayed action may call for temporary departure from that normal balance of public procedure. . . . In the event that the Congress shall fail to take [the proper] courses, and in the event that the national emergency is still critical, I shall not evade the clear course of duty that will then confront me. I shall ask the Congress for the one remaining instrument to meet the crisis — broad executive power to wage a war against the emergency as great as the power that would be given me if we were in fact invaded by a foreign foe.[2]

Hearing Roosevelt suggest the possible use of wartime powers, the crowd erupted.[3] Weary of Herbert Hoover's ineffectiveness and frightened by economic collapse and increasing signs of violence, citizens were ready to support a president who was willing to act, even if his actions might modify, albeit temporarily, the constitutionally mandated balance of powers.

The American people waited only days for Roosevelt to act on his first priority: to stop the run on bank deposits. Because bankers had no plan to save the banking system, and with Attorney General Homer Cumming's approval under the Trading With the Enemy Act, Roosevelt proclaimed a bank holiday (March 6–9) that closed all member banks in the Federal Reserve system, ended gold hoarding, and empowered the secretary of the treasury to authorize reopening financially solvent banks. When the House convened on March 9, it unanimously endorsed Roosevelt's proclamation, passing an Emergency Banking Relief Act in scarcely forty minutes. Few members even saw the legislation.[4] The Senate, more recalcitrant, got the job done in less than eight hours.

Momentum now belonged to the president. Seeing Congress in a mood of "unwonted acquiescence,"[5] he quickly struck again. Fully aware of the wartime grants of authority that Congress had made to Woodrow Wilson, one hour after signing the Emergency Banking Relief Act, Roosevelt proposed an economy bill designed to cut government spending by $500 million. Although the general objective was to work toward a balanced budget through general agency reorganization and reducing federal salaries and veterans' pensions, the Economy Act marked a "historic transfer of fiscal power from the Congress to the Presidency." Whereas Congress had previously appropriated specific sums to be spent as ordered on veterans and federal employees, the Economy Act appropriated a lump sum amount, leaving the president to spend under broad guidelines.[6] Thus began a fiscal process under which the president and his appointed New Deal agencies exercised significantly more fiscal control than before. Combined with the nation's desire to get the economy moving, Roosevelt's assumption of congressional authority played a key role in launching the construction of water projects designed by the Bureau of Reclamation (Bureau).

President Franklin D. Roosevelt was instrumental in passing legislation that provided funds to build water projects in the West. (Courtesy Denver Public Library, Western History Department.)

Though critics charged him with dictatorial tactics, Roosevelt calmly reassured the American people that Congress still retained its constitutional authority; it had "done nothing more than designate him as its agent in carrying out its will, all in keeping with U.S. tradition."[7] "Fireside chats" on the radio, open and frequent press conferences, and the undeniable sense of motion that had been so long absent in the White House combined to restore confidence in the federal government. Over the next three months — in what historians have referred to as the First Hundred Days — the president asserted his will, busying Congress with fifteen major laws while he met twice weekly with his cabinet, talked with foreign heads of state, sponsored an international economic conference, and "made all the major decisions in domestic and foreign policy."[8]

On June 16, 1933, the last of the Hundred Days, Congress passed the National Industrial Recovery Act (NIRA), providing both a system of industrial self-government (National Reclamation Association — NRA Eagle Plan) and a $3.3 billion public works program. With drought and economic depression undermining recovery hopes in the West, NIRA legislation came as manna from heaven. Title II created the Public Works Administration (PWA) to approve projects that would employ people on the construction of roads, buildings, dams, and other structures. From the standpoint of battle-weary Westerners, many of whom had fought each other in Congress for federal funding of water projects, the new PWA program appeared a godsend. Because $2 billion of the fund was supposed to be set aside for water conservation, reclamation, and flood control purposes, states that had been trying for years to interest Congress in reclamation projects now recognized that all they had to do was persuade the PWA's administrator, Secretary of the Interior Harold L. Ickes, of the merits of their plans; but convincing him proved difficult. Although he was honest, bold, energetic, and incorruptible, Ickes was also irascible. He trusted no one but himself and examined all projects with stingy, meticulous care. Although worthwhile water projects might win his support, especially those that included hydroelectric power, Ickes rejected those presented without proper documentation or those in conflict with his personal biases. For the moment, however, proponents of public works projects were greatly relieved to no longer beg Congress for funding.

For residents of the North and South Platte River basins, the 1933 creation of the PWA was a watershed event. Wyoming ended its thirty-year struggle to get funding for the Casper-Alcova project. Northern Colorado (the South Platte River and its tributaries), in its fifth year of drought, saw a new opportunity for federal money. If funds were to be used to preserve irrigated agriculture in the South Platte basin with supplemental water, regional leaders would have to plan, survey, and submit projects quickly, before Congress could reassert its fiscal authority. Too many frustrating years had already passed competing with Wyoming and Nebraska over ownership of water rights on the North Platte system. Additionally, some argued that another source of water might be available as a PWA project, lending new life to what was still the most productive irrigated farming region in the state. Could the Colorado River be tapped for the benefit of farmers in northern Colorado, whose ditches sometimes ran dry in the late summer months?

Marshaling the forces to prepare and forward proposals took time; thinking patterns changed slowly. While new opportunities for solving the five-year water crisis appeared obvious to some community and state leaders, others continued in their old ways, oblivious to national crises and new opportunities in recent legislation. Still, on the day Roosevelt took the oath of office, Fort Collins citizens were far more concerned about water shortages than bank failures, business foreclosures, and unemployment.

On the day after Roosevelt's inauguration, Colorado Governor Edwin "Big Ed" C. Johnson declared a three-day mandatory bank holiday. This act seems to have had little impact on local business because merchants continued to accept checks in payment for goods and extended credit "possibly even more liberally than usual."[9] Of far greater interest to community leaders was the reopening of water negotiations between Colorado and Wyoming.[10] The depression in agriculture, a fact of life since the end of World War I, and the general stagnation of economic growth were believed to be a result of unrelenting drought. Although New Deal programs were interesting enough, northern Colorado remained more concerned about its inability to import supplemental water from the North Platte River into the Poudre River basin. The agricultural boom of the early 1900s could not repeat without additional water.

In Larimer, Weld, Morgan, Logan, and Sedgwick counties — an area that would later compose most of the future Northern Colorado Water Conservancy District — economic growth was closely related to the availability of irrigation water. In the first ten years of the twentieth century, population grew by 57.8 percent. In the next decade the rate slowed to 28.2 percent, and from 1920 to 1930 growth fell to 17.5 percent. Stagnation now threatened a total population of 141,921.[11] The explosive rates of the first decades were a direct result of expanding irrigated agriculture. By 1929 significant growth had stopped. New sources of funding for reservoirs, tunnels for transmountain diversion, and distribution systems to farms and municipalities had run dry.

Agricultural data for the same five counties illustrate this relationship more dramatically. In 1899, 446,345 irrigated acres were being farmed, an increase of 85 percent over the previous ten years. By 1909 northern Colorado had increased its irrigated acreage by 68 percent to a total of 749,152 acres. In the next ten years the increase was only 7 percent, and by 1929 the total number of irrigated acres stood at 856,023 — a modest 8 percent rise from the previous decade.[12] The lively twenty-year trend of ditch and reservoir building in northern Colorado between 1890 and 1910 had slowed considerably; not only was the total dependable water supply being utilized, but junior appropriators were experiencing water shortages on the existing systems.

Drought was an additional factor. Contemporary observers disagreed on its duration, but all agreed that conditions had been especially acute since 1929.[13] By 1933 water in the irrigation network was insufficient to irrigate all the land under ditch. In fact, the Colorado drought had been on and off since the early 1920s. A 1922 study of the Poudre River documented an annual flow of 340,000 acre-feet. Foreign water brought into the basin from transmountain sources added another 35,000 acre-feet; but even with an additional 84,000 acre-feet of return flow, Robert G. Hemphill noted in 1922, many junior appropriations dried up, "chiefly in August," causing him to doubt the possibility of expanding irrigated acreage in the future.[14]

Eleven years later, engineer Royce J. Tipton observed that 390,000 acres of land under ditch lay fallow due to lack of water. Assuming a duty of 2 acre-feet per acre, he concluded that the Poudre River had an annual shortage of 140,500 acre-feet per year between 1914 and 1931. The Big Thompson River had also been short by an annual average of 126,200 acre-feet if the same duty were applied. Tipton also noted that attempts to fill reservoirs in the South Platte River basin faced nearly insurmountable odds, while efforts to catch spring runoff by building additional reservoirs raised the cost per acre-foot to as high as $300.[15] Although 47,000 acre-feet were being diverted into the basin from the Colorado and Laramie rivers in 1933 — all but a thousand of it destined for the Poudre River — the only viable supply of new water, Tipton concluded, was the Colorado River.[16]

What made water so crucial to Larimer, Weld, Morgan, Logan, and Sedgwick counties was the high percentage of row crops that required adequate and dependable irrigation throughout the growing season, not

The Great Western Sugar Company had seventeen processing plants in eastern Colorado by 1933. The company supported the search for supplemental water. (Photograph by Lew Dakan.)

just during the water-rich months of spring runoff. These croplands, representing 25 percent of the state's total irrigated land, had been the principal source of agricultural prosperity in northern Colorado and the reason why Colorado had been known since 1909 as the leading U.S. producer of sugar beets.[17] By 1933, however, the future of irrigated agriculture was grim. Just as all farm income in the state had declined 59.58 percent since 1929,[18] the sugar beet industry — on which 12,000 farmers, 20,000 field workers, and 6,200 processing plant people depended[19] — was in equally serious trouble. From a harvest valued at $27.6 million in 1920, sugar beet production had dropped to $22.8 million in 1930, $13.7 million in 1931, $8.2 million in 1932, $12.1 million in 1933, and $7.8 million in 1934. The 20 percent decline in acres planted to beets was also worrisome, but the most telling statistic for northern Colorado farmers was the market price, which slipped from $11.88 per ton in 1920 to $4.62 per ton in 1933.[20]

The one bright spot for sugar beet growers was the Great Western Sugar Company's large capital investment in its seventeen processing factories located throughout eastern Colorado. Since 1901, this company had increased its asset value to nearly $80 million, and rumors even suggested that after "declaring nice, juicy dividends" in 1933, the company had socked away $8–9 million in a holding company to avoid paying taxes.[21] Whether or not the rumors were accurate and the actions ethical, the fact remains that sugar beet farmers counted on the energy, capital, and political power of Great Western to support their search for supplemental water. Although farmers in northern Colorado planted a considerably larger area of irrigated land to alfalfa, wheat, oats, barley, dry beans, corn, and potatoes, sugar beets averaged 40 percent of the value of all irrigated crops.[22] The five counties most in need of water in 1933 were also the most agriculturally productive in the entire state.[23]

With a total population of 141,921, an assessed value of $203,955,540 (15 percent of the assessed value of all property in the state), an annual agricultural harvest worth $41,563,990,[24] and strong support from Great Western Sugar, northern Colorado was in a good position to garner public and private support for its water campaign. Until 1933, engineers, attorneys, and irrigation farmers directed their energies primarily toward the North Platte River. Hoping to augment existing transmountain diversion to the Poudre River by means of a negotiated agreement with Wyoming, Colorado saw neighboring Wyoming's proposed Casper-Alcova project as a threat to its plans for diverting additional water into the Poudre basin. Before 1933, when Congress exercised its fiscal responsibility to approve or disapprove reclamation projects, states sharing the same stream system had to effect legislative compromises to receive funding. After 1933, in part because of the PWA and other New Deal acts, federal funds were more readily available for physically and economically feasible projects that would also promise meaningful work to the unemployed.

In 1933 the Casper-Alcova project, already a long-standing proposal, was one of the first water projects advanced in Wyoming following passage of the Reclamation Act in 1902. Its objective was to store water on the North Platte River upstream from Casper, enabling development of 60,000 to 80,000 acres of unproductive land for irrigated agriculture. In 1904 the U.S. Reclamation Service (which officially became the Bureau of Reclamation in 1923) had surveyed the area to be serviced by the Alcova Dam and the Casper Canal, and by December of that year an "application for a permit authorizing the desired water appropriation for this canal was made. For the moment, no further action was taken."[25]

While Wyoming Senator John P. Kendrick promoted the Casper-Alcova project — which subsequently was named after him in 1937 — various federal agencies studied the plan thoroughly in the 1920s. Simultaneously, northern Colorado showed increased interest in diverting more water from the North Platte River to the irrigated fields of the South Platte River basin, hoping to lay claim through beneficial use to waters that originated in North Park. Wyoming, on the other hand, feared exhaustion

Alcova Reservoir in Wyoming was built as part of the Kendrick project. (Courtesy Bureau of Reclamation.)

of Casper's oil and gas economy, which threatened to leave the area a virtual wasteland unless the area developed an agricultural base. By 1926, construction of Casper-Alcova appeared increasingly likely. A special board of review, contracted by the secretary of the interior in 1920, made studies of the region, which were followed by reports from the Bureau of Reclamation in 1921 and the U.S. Department of Agriculture in 1922. Several bills had been introduced in Congress to authorize construction of the Casper-Alcova project.[26] Sensitive to the potential loss of additional water rights so soon after the Supreme Court's 1922 decision and the 1923 compact with Nebraska on the South Platte,[27] Colorado's powerful Representative Edward T. Taylor eagerly pursued some sort of agreement with Senator Kendrick prior to supporting the Casper-Alcova project in Congress. Even though Taylor knew how to play the compromise game, his political experience was no match for the administration's desire to put people back to work.

On April 29, with two Casper-Alcova bills awaiting congressional approval (H.R. 10356 and S. 3553), Taylor suggested an amendment safeguarding Wyoming and Colorado water rights "until such time as

Colorado and Wyoming or Colorado, Wyoming and Nebraska shall enter into and have approved by Congress . . . an interstate compact superseding the provisions of this agreement."[28] He agreed to building Casper-Alcova and to limiting Colorado's transbasin diversion from the North Platte to 30,000 acre-feet, provided that construction of the Wyoming dam and canals would not be considered a basis for a prior claim to North Platte water. Because of concurrent negotiations between Wyoming and Nebraska, Wyoming Representative Charles Edwin Winter, sponsor of House Report 10356, asked that the bill be passed over without prejudice and be debated properly at a later time. No one objected.

On June 7 Taylor returned to the debate with greater vigor. Without his proposed amendment, he said, carrying the bills in question on the legislative calendar was unjustified. Because 60 percent of the water destined for the Casper-Alcova project originated in Colorado and because that water was also needed for "further development in Jackson and Larimer counties," Taylor argued against making a "present of all that water to Wyoming. They make no provision whatever," he reasoned, "for the protection or safeguarding of any of the rights of my state to any use of any of the waters from this stream or any of its tributaries in Colorado at any time or in any way." Passage of the bill threatened to work "untold millions of dollars of unjust damage to my state throughout all future time."[29]

Putting teeth into his objection, Taylor entered two communications from former Secretary of the Interior Hubert Work into the *Congressional Record*. The first, dated January 16, 1926, concluded that the Casper-Alcova project would incur excessive costs and would require additional money to settle colonists on the reclaimed lands. The second, dated April 2, 1926, said that Work could not recommend construction "for administrative reasons" and that all money for this kind of project had already been committed for the next several years.[30] With this final blow, plus support from House sympathizers, who emphasized the importance of protecting each state's water rights, Congress temporarily derailed the legislation. Undismayed, Kendrick and Winter introduced identical bills (H.R. 5743 and S. 1136) in the next session.

For the next five years, legislators and others interested in Casper-Alcova's merits debated furiously. Proponents introduced evidence to show that water supply on the North Platte River was "sufficient for all existing rights and that there [was] some surplus available for further development without the construction of additional reservoirs."[31] Wyoming Governor Frank C. Emerson (formerly state engineer) expressed his opinion that since it "would be easy to make a compact with Colorado," his state was willing to concede to Colorado all use it could make of the North Platte River in the drainage area and "30,000 acre-feet out of the basin, which allowance, as far as we can ascertain at the present time, is considerably more than will ever be found practicable for Colorado to divert from the watershed."[32] Experts submitted land classification studies, feasibility studies, soil and climate analyses, and cost estimates to congressional committees while other proponents touted Casper as a city that had contributed $30 million in royalties to the Reclamation Fund through oil and gas production.[33] It deserved a future, they argued, when these resources were finally played out.

But questions remained, and Congress dragged its feet. Because it feared the legal consequences of approving a reclamation project on an interstate stream prior to the signing of an interstate water agreement, the House passed legislation (H.R. 7026 and H.R. 7027) that required Colorado to first sign compacts with both Wyoming and Nebraska regarding division of the North Platte waters. In western states the federal government owned the public lands, but each state controlled its waters. The Bureau expressed concern about Casper-Alcova, noting that "construction costs are expected to be so high as to require annual assessments two or three times as large as the lands can be expected to pay if repayment is to be effected in 40 years." Furthermore, fewer than 100 resident owners were expected to reclaim and live on the land, and none of them had made a concerted effort to urge construction. Bureau representatives concluded that the project was largely a promotional activity of the Casper Chamber of Commerce and the City of Casper, both of which might well offer to put up some money for construction. Further criticism revealed that river flows on the North Platte from 1895 to 1929 had been adequate for Wyoming farmers except for two out of the thirty-five years recorded.[34] Riddled with difficulties, Casper-Alcova failed once again, just at a time when acute drought in the region made the project more necessary than ever before.

The year 1931 "started the driest cycle or swing in the North Platte and [South] Platte river valleys of which there is any record." In Wyoming, the river measured only 55 percent of its mean flow as recorded between 1904 and 1940.[35] In Colorado the situation was equally dismal. According to figures released from the Colorado State Engineer's Office, the water available in Water Districts 1–6 and 64 (representing the region from Boulder to Fort Collins and east to the Nebraska line) declined 7.6 percent in 1930, 25 percent in 1931, and 5.3 percent in 1932. Given a minimum duty per acre of 1.25 acre-feet for the average crop, irrigation water available for these drought years was 1.20 (1929), 1.11 (1930), .83 (1931),

Senator Ed Johnson supported further development of Colorado's water resources, including the Grand Lake Project. (Courtesy Denver Public Library, Western History Department.)

and .79 acre-feet (1932).[36] In response to this serious shortage, the Bureau recommended enlarging the original Casper-Alcova project to include the Seminoe Dam, Reservoir, and Power Plant. President Hoover even approved $75,000 of supplemental funding, enabling the Bureau to investigate further the economic feasibility of the expanded project.[37]

Congressional approval was even harder to obtain now that depression stalked the land. Even though data on the western drought consistently pointed up the need for governmental assistance, the Hoover administration's reluctance to spend money on anything matched Congress's paralysis. The new secretary of the interior, Ray Lyman Wilbur, Bureau Commissioner Elwood Mead, and the House and Senate committees on Irrigation and Reclamation all favored the project; but unless the three states could agree on a division of water rights for the Platte system, Congress could persist forever in denying statutory authorization. For this reason, on the day of President Roosevelt's inauguration, Fort Collins and Greeley newspapers focused more on the progress of interstate water negotiations than on the changing of the guard in Washington.

Depressed by lack of progress on North Platte River negotiations, fears of water shortages, and evidence of continuing drought, Coloradans responded erratically. State Representative George Miller of Park County sponsored a bill authorizing Governor Johnson to order that water held for irrigation purposes be diverted to the cities and towns for domestic use. Denver, Boulder, and Colorado Springs outlawed lawn sprinkling.[38] State Engineer Michael C. Hinderlider incurred the displeasure of many irrigation and reservoir companies by issuing what some called an "arbitrary order" to terminate storage of water on the upper end of the Poudre and South Platte rivers so that water users in District No. 1 would have ample supplies for irrigation.[39] Accused of abusing his power and facing disobedience from northern Colorado reservoir companies, Hinderlider held his ground until April rains replenished the existing storage capacity and diffused criticism.

While Hinderlider's actions may have seemed irrational, his motives were clear. Irrigators on the upper end of the basin failed to understand why the state engineer was preventing them from storing water when their downstream neighbors were believed to be releasing it onto bare ground, but the state engineer, believing that he had the governor's support, was concerned about Colorado's South Platte compact with Nebraska. After almost a decade of negotiation, he felt that Nebraska was incapable of water conservation during dry years. Though he viewed Nebraska's claims for more water as "nebulous," he was determined to avoid further controversy by putting enough water into the South Platte River to honor the 1923 interstate agreement.[40]

In regard to Wyoming, Hinderlider's policy proved more demanding. That state offered up to 40,000 acre-feet of water for transbasin diversion from the North Platte River. Hinderlider insisted instead on a plan to divert 100,000 acre-feet from the North Platte River into the Poudre River basin via Cameron Pass.[41] Considered "impractical and visionary" by some and known locally as "Hinderlider's pipe dream,"[42] this plan disturbed Nebraska, whose state engineer, Roy Cachran, argued against "any diversion by Colorado of North Platte water," no matter how badly farmers might need it. The only solution for Colorado, he argued, was to build a "giant storage reservoir in Wyoming near the Nebraska border." If Colorado were to take the water without reaching an agreement with both Wyoming and Nebraska, he concluded, Nebraska would file suit to protect its rights.[43] Colorado was already engaged in a court battle over North Platte water. While its delegation was trying to block Nebraska's Sutherland and Tri-County projects at the Reconstruction Finance offices in Washington,[44]

State Engineer Michael C. Hinderlider incurred the wrath of many northern Colorado irrigators by requiring them to release water from storage. (Courtesy Colorado Historical Society.)

William R. Kelly was trying to defend the Laramie-Poudre Irrigation Company against Wyoming's charges of violating a 1922 Supreme Court agreement.[45]

As long as states depended on Congress to approve individual funding projects, legislative authorization could come only after politicians agreed to compromise. Until they settled differences, states could block each other's pet projects. The only means of modifying this pattern — one that had victimized the three states for thirty years — was a radical change in federal funding methods. On June 16, 1933, Roosevelt issued Executive Order No. 6174, creating a Special Board for the PWA with instructions to report directly to the president on how $3.3 billion allocated by Congress in the NIRA would be spent.[46] The Casper-Alcova project suddenly gained new life.

Reaction in Colorado, Wyoming, and Nebraska came immediately, revealing the extent of Wyoming's undisputed advantage in the battle for North Platte River water. The Colorado Engineering Council announced an immediate study of transmountain water diversion projects, "particularly those projects which may be undertaken in connection with the industrial recovery measure passed by Congress."[47] Simultaneously, the Cache la Poudre Water Users Association (CLPWUA) organized to combat Hinderlider's dictatorial policies and to take "part in transmountain diversion plans affecting the Poudre water supply."[48] Wyoming sent both its senators directly to the PWA's Special Board to request $15 million to construct the Casper-Alcova project. Without delay, Nebraska's Governor Charles W. Bryan sent a message to Colorado Governor Johnson asking for a tri-state conference.[49]

The three governors, along with their state engineers, irrigation experts, and attorneys, met in Denver on July 14, 1933. They parleyed for two days, collectively debating for the first time an agreement on distribution of North Platte River water. Colorado asked for rights to 180,000 acre-feet; Wyoming agreed to 30,000. Colorado argued that it was "economically infeasible" to build diversion works for only 30,000 acre-feet; Wyoming countered by refusing to finance Colorado's transmountain diversions. Responding to Nebraska's insistence that its "priorities of record" be protected, Colorado said that it had no money to pay for constructing a reservoir on the Colorado-Wyoming state line.[50] Stalemate.

Twelve days later, on July 28, Secretary Ickes announced that the administration had approved Casper-Alcova. On August 2 he stated that this approval omitted any reference to Colorado's and Nebraska's interstate water rights.[51] He refused to help the states solve interstate water problems or to provide the initiative in formulating interstate compacts.[52]

Coloradans were distraught. Rumors circulated that Governor Johnson had made a secret deal with Senator Kendrick; the governor accused members of the state delegation in Washington of political irresponsibility.[53] Johnson telegraphed the president to intervene to protect Colorado's water rights. Roosevelt responded by ordering the PWA to "reconsider approval" of Casper-Alcova.[54] While Ickes arranged for a hearing in Washington, the Colorado State Assembly, on a motion by Representative Wayne N. Aspinall, unanimously agreed to oppose Casper-Alcova "unless water rights of this state are amply protected."[55] Local interests also responded. The Fort Collins Chamber of Commerce ratified Aspinall's protest, and Larimer County treasurer C. S. Ickes wrote to his cousin the secretary, pointing out the expense of developing Wyoming farmland.[56]

The Washington meeting provided little satisfaction for Colorado. With Colorado Attorney General Paul P. Prosser representing Governor Johnson and threatening to go to the Supreme Court if Colorado failed to obtain a guarantee of 266,000 acre-feet of the North Platte River (40 percent of the flow of both the Laramie and North Platte rivers), Nebraska reacted characteristically by insisting that Colorado had no right to divert any water from the river. Wyoming's Senator Kendrick complained that Colorado was now trying to impose "unfair and unrighteous conditions" on his state.[57] Ickes, who was among Colorado's Washington delegation, intended to proceed with the project as planned with a federal allotment of $22.7 million, but old habits caused the Coloradans to continue seeking a deal with Wyoming. They were convinced that, one way or another, survival of North Platte River water and northern Colorado were inexorably linked.[58]

On November 24, 1933, the *Fort Collins Express-Courier* trumpeted victory. After deciding that Nebraska was too "selfish and unyielding" to be involved in further discussions,[59] the negotiators cabled home from Washington that they had reached an agreement including Colorado's endorsement of Casper-Alcova and Wyoming's willingness to provide the necessary rights-of-way, allowing Colorado to proceed with construction of the diversion works. The agreement also called for the accord to be brought home and signed by the governors with appropriate fanfare. By December 1933, however, local opposition had developed in both states.[60] Resolution of northern Colorado's water needs required more creative thinking. Many were now prepared to look beyond the North Platte River for supplemental water. Tired of the interstate fracas, some of northern

Colorado's leaders focused intently on the Colorado River as the last available water hole in the West. Depression, drought, New Deal policies, and the decision to build the Casper-Alcova project forced Coloradans to consider innovative plans for bringing supplemental water into the South Platte basin.

2
Shifting the Focus:
Grand Lake and the Colorado River

Although attorney William R. Kelly was not the only northern Colorado resident who understood the significance of the PWA's decision to fund the Casper-Alcova project in July 1933, he was one of the first to see that change in Washington demanded a shift of tactics in Colorado. If the state desired and needed federal monies to construct its water projects, Colorado would have to meet the requirements of New Deal agencies and their administrators. Cooperation among state officials, engineers, irrigators, and community leaders was essential; the old interstate battles must assume secondary importance while Colorado tried marching to the beat of the new drummer in the White House.

Kelly had set out his shingle as an attorney in 1901, the same year he graduated from high school in Greeley. While continuing his education at the University of Colorado, he slowly built his practice and a reputation as a knowledgeable attorney. Kelly knew both politics and water law. He served as water referee for Water Districts Nos. 1 and 2 from 1911 to 1925, as Greeley city attorney from 1916 to 1921, and as Weld County attorney from 1921 to 1928. In private practice, he represented the Cache la Poudre Irrigation Company for forty years and functioned as Colorado's special counsel in the U.S. Supreme Court in *Wyoming* v. *Colorado* and *Nebraska* v. *Colorado*.[1] His early enthusiasm for a Grand Lake transmountain diversion project marks him as a pioneer of a scheme many thought to be a technical and financial pipe dream.

When the *Greeley Tribune* reported on July 29, 1933, that the PWA had decided to fund Casper-Alcova, Kelly reacted with anger. This news would "sound the death knell of northern Colorado's plan to supplement river flow with the North Platte waters." The federal grant, he noted, "carries the danger that it will practically foreclose further development in Colorado of water from the North Platte."[2] Kelly hoped that the federal government would safeguard Colorado's interest before beginning the Wyoming project because to do otherwise would give Wyoming the "advantage of starting its irrigation works first and thus claiming priority over

William R. Kelly served as NCWUA
and NCWCD attorney from 1935 to
1956. His enthusiasm for the C–BT
Project is well documented. (Courtesy
NCWCD.)

<u>the waters of the stream</u>." Colorado irrigators had been developing their
land from Poudre, Platte, Michigan, Colorado, and Laramie River water
for forty years, he argued. At no time had Coloradans attempted to prevent
Wyoming from development. "Nebraska [is] taking the position that it will
agree to no [diversion] of water from the North Platte to Colorado and . . .
Wyoming [is] setting out to build works that will make such demand on
the river that after the Seminole [sic]-Alcova project is built, there will be
. . . [a] question as to how much water is left in the North Platte available
for appropriation in Colorado."[3] <u>Colorado, he concluded, was not getting
a fair shake</u>.

Equity was all Kelly wanted. Because "Colorado contributed 650,000
acre-feet[4] of water to the river . . . there should have been a reservation of
at least 100,000 acre-feet for future use, not in the North Platte watershed
alone, but as a supplemental supply for the proper irrigation of lands in
Weld, Morgan, Logan, Washington, and Phillips counties." Wyoming had
lost interest in negotiating, Kelly pointed out, and given the U.S. Supreme
Court ruling that "the first one getting works built shall have the first right
to the water regardless of the state lines,"[5] Colorado had but one choice:
to plan, organize, and survey its own project in order to recover its lost
advantage.

The unequal race resulting from the "federal bounty" to Wyoming was a wrong that Kelly believed could be righted only by construction of a project favoring Colorado irrigators and communities. Speaking to the Rotary Club of Eaton in August 1933, he urged that farmers, townsmen, and politicians unite to secure a federal grant for transmountain diversion into the Big Thompson River from Grand Lake and the Colorado River — what Delph Carpenter had referred to ten years earlier as "the last water hole in the West." If Colorado moved aggressively, the cost of the 12-mile tunnel, diversion works, and reservoirs would not exceed $12 million. An added incentive was the 30 percent of cost "awarded as a grant for reemployment relief, as [was] being done for Wyoming on the Casper-Alcova and for many municipal projects."[6] The estimated 180,000 acre-feet of supplemental water translated into a potential doubling of the Weld and Larimer counties' potato and sugar beet crops. In addition, the return flow would irrigate another 100,000 acres downstream on the South Platte River.

Kelly recognized that New Dealers were anxious to promote and subsidize reclamation projects as a means of putting the country's unemployed back to work. Arizona was benefiting from the Boulder Canyon project authorized in 1928, and Washington state had just been advised that construction was to begin soon on the Columbia Basin project (Grand Coulee Dam). Because Wyoming was about to receive $22.7 million for a project to provide irrigation on only one-half the acreage expected to benefit from a Grand Lake diversion project, Kelly argued that Colorado had a "strong claim for federal funds, and now is the time to act if further investigations confirm the supply and cost."[7] The problem was that in summer 1933, Colorado did not have a surveyed, tested, revised, or debated plan like Casper-Alcova. In order to qualify for federal funds, speed was of the essence. If Grand Lake were to become the focus of energies as Kelly hoped, then northern Colorado citizens would have to work and sacrifice. He believed, as one old-timer used to say, that "When you dream of running water, it is too late to wake up."[8]

Recollecting these worrisome times many years later, Kelly recalled that on the morning of July 29, 1933, he bumped into Fred Norcross and Weld County irrigation engineer L. L. Stimson at the Greeley Post Office. Faced with bad news from Washington, drought, and depressed agricultural prices, the three wondered collectively if technology had advanced sufficiently to justify building a tunnel from Grand Lake to the Big Thompson River. Stimson, who believed that skills developed during construction of the Metropolitan Aqueduct in California made the project feasible, was

Charles Hansen, editor of the *Greeley Tribune*, was a vocal supporter of the C–BT Project who earned the title "Godfather of the C–BT." (Courtesy NCWCD.)

willing to run a survey line between the two points to construct a map. Kelly and Norcross agreed to find money for him from Weld and Larimer county commissioners.[9] The three next looked up Charles Hansen, editor of the *Greeley Tribune*, hoping to convince this well-respected newspaper man and northern Colorado booster to help them. Hansen not only provided the promotion vehicle they needed but entered so vigorously into the organizational scheme of things that when Colorado River water finally flowed into farmers' ditches in the South Platte basin, he became known as "Godfather of the 'Big T.' "[10]

As the men of northern Colorado began the difficult task of gathering support for their project, they needed to know how much information was already available on transmountain diversion from Grand Lake. They engaged Royce J. Tipton to prepare a preliminary survey in summer 1933. Tipton had a limited amount of time to prepare his report, but he reviewed some early studies that had considered transmountain diversion from Grand Lake.

The first studies of Grand Lake had been ordered in 1889 when the Colorado legislature passed House Bill 161 "authorizing expenditure of $25,000 for the survey and construction of a canal along the Western Slope of the range, to cut across the range and augment the supply [of water] in South Boulder Creek."[11] In his *Fifth Biennial Report*, the state engineer had found such a canal "infeasible." He then changed the plan and ordered the

The first studies of a Grand Lake Project were conducted in 1889. (Courtesy Bureau of Reclamation.)

engineer in charge, George S. Oliver, to examine the "highest sources of water supply in the various branches of the Grand [Colorado River] from Grand Lake south to South Boulder Pass . . . [and] to make connection with all low passes of the range that might be used for diversion."[12]

After two months of work with twelve men at high altitudes in "stormy weather," Oliver concluded that because of the "broken and rocky nature of the ground," constructing collection ditches was impractical because the cost of building extensive flumes "along precipitous ledges and over rock-slides" would be prohibitive. If a new canal were constructed, a 3-mile tunnel would have to be built "through the range for the purpose of diversion." Oliver declined to recommend such a course of action. Instead, he abandoned the project and returned $23,443.32 of the appropriated funds to the state treasury.[13]

Pending the outcome of Oliver's survey, the Colorado Senate had appropriated $3,000 for its own study of the Grand, Laramie, and North Platte rivers. Although no teams were sent into the field, preliminary investigation revealed that private enterprise had already appropriated the most eligible canal sites; any project of material benefit to the East Slope must rely on "tunnels through the range that would cost in a single case, several times the [$10,000] appropriated [for construction]."[14]

Nothing more happened officially until after Congress passed the Reclamation Act in 1902. During hearings before the House Committee on Irrigation of Arid Lands, Elwood Mead, who would later give strong support to the C–BT in the 1930s, argued forcefully for federal assistance to irrigation farmers. A civil engineer with an 1882 degree from Purdue University, Mead had drawn up the constitutional provisions on water rights for Wyoming; he was an expert on irrigation and drainage investigations in the Department of Agriculture, and most people valued his testimony highly. Mead vigorously urged the government to build storage reservoirs on streams "as a means of further extending the reclamation of the irrigated area of public lands by permitting a larger use of the flood waters that now run to waste early in the season." Dams, he said, should be built by the government in large rivers "where the expense of diversion is at present prohibitive." On the North Platte, he noted, "it is not safe to attempt cultivation, because your crops will be started in the spring to be dried up in the summer." Build adequate storage, however, and the flood waters will be usable. Because private enterprise in the form of partnerships and corporations had proved unprofitable, he said, "we have practically reached the end of unaided development." He proposed that the government step in and build new storage facilities, allowing states to distribute water according to their own laws. In turn, the states must legislate against speculative acquisition of water stored at government expense.[15]

In 1904 and 1905 the newly formed Reclamation Service investigated a plan "involving enlargement of Grand Lake in connection with studies of potential reservoir sites in the Upper Colorado River Basin."[16] Under Reclamation Service direction, engineer Gerard H. Matthes made a reconnaissance of the north and south forks of the Grand River as well of the Fraser and Williams Fork rivers and Stillwater Creek. Matthes reported that although Colorado raised large amounts of hay in this area to winter feed cattle, very little land was irrigated, "and it is safe to say that no large amount of irrigation water will ever be used in this part of Grand County."[17] Future residents would certainly disagree.

After locating sites for reservoirs at Windy Gap and below the confluence of the north and south forks of the Grand, Matthes investigated additional water storage to Grand Lake "by means of a project including the diversion of the North Fork of Grand River into the lake." A dam that raised the height of Grand Lake 20 to 25 feet would result in 140,000 acre-feet of storage, but the lake would not be able to hold "even the annual discharge of the streams draining into it, not to mention water supply from other sources."[18] The Reclamation Service had earlier proposed tapping Grand Lake by means of a tunnel to the Big Thompson or St. Vrain River. Matthes estimated a tunnel about 12 miles long and urged special studies to determine cost feasibility. He also pointed out that Haberson Lake might receive North Fork water, thus allowing storage on Grand Lake to be "utilized to good advantage as an equalizing reservoir, and a probable flow of about 640 second-feet [to] be delivered on the East Slope throughout the entire irrigating season."[19] This plan, in very general terms, was the first official description of what would eventually become the Colorado–Big Thompson Project.

In the same year, district hydrographer Michael C. Hinderlider was establishing gauging stations to measure stream flow on the North Fork, the Grand Lake outlet, and on the main river near Hot Sulphur Springs and Kremmling. He also worked on the Fraser, Williams Fork, Troublesome, Muddy, and Blue rivers.[20] Little did he know then that as Colorado state engineer in the 1930s, he too would be an avid supporter of the C–BT.

Government agencies made no further studies of the project until 1916, when E. C. La Rue pioneered work on the Colorado River for the U.S. Geological Survey (USGS). His objective was to study flow control of the whole river by means of storage reservoirs "in order to avoid further danger of overflow to the Salton Sink [California] and to render available for profitable use the enormous quantity of water which now flows unused and largely unusable to the Gulf of California in the form of floods." He singled out Kremmling as the "largest and perhaps most valuable reservoir site in the Grand River Basin."[21] Raising the water level 230 feet there promised to produce a lake of 2.2 million acre-feet.

La Rue also reviewed transmountain diversion projects in operation and others still on the drawing board. He warned that if everything developed as planned, "the normal flow of Grand River during years of low run-off will barely meet the demands of irrigation" and that operation of the Central Colorado Power Company's hydroelectric plant on Grand River above Glenwood Springs might be affected by low water.[22] With his eyes on the future, La Rue concluded that the remedy for this shortage was to build a reservoir at the Kremmling site.

The next Department of the Interior report emerged in 1929 as a supplement to La Rue's study. The author, Robert Follansbee, noted that the six water diversions[23] across the Continental Divide were providing an annual average of 20,400 acre-feet to the East Slope. In his view, this represented about 4 percent of the mean annual discharge of the Colorado

River above the mouth of the Green River, constituting the present limit of transmountain diversion by means of open ditches.[24] To develop transmountain diversion to an annual total of 262,000 acre-feet per year, the system must extend collection ditches and build more tunnels. The only streams situated for further development, he argued, were the Blue, Eagle, Williams Fork, Fryingpan, and Fraser.

Water users on the East Slope were proposing diversions from both the Colorado and North Platte systems. Unfortunately, as Follansbee said, the Fraser and Blue River projects were on a scale that only a municipality such as Denver could undertake. Furthermore, in order to assure operation of the Shoshone Power Plant at Glenwood Springs, adequate water supplies for the Front Range would only be available between April 1 and September 30 each year.[25] The Grand Lake Project appeared viable, but Follansbee estimated that high construction costs would have to be borne by irrigation interests on the East Slope, which made this kind of project "extremely improbable" for many years to come.[26]

In 1931 the state engineer published a final Grand Lake report, whose objective was to evaluate both the water resource of the South Platte basin and the possibility of transmountain diversion. It noted that 15,585 acre-feet were currently coming into the South Platte drainage by way of "open cuts"[27] and that, except for possible extension of the Grand River Ditch, increased carriage along existing systems was unlikely. However, a readily available quantity of water for both power and irrigation on the East Slope originated in the Upper Colorado or Grand River watershed above Grand Lake. The most extensive scheme to make use of this resource involved a collection system to bring runoff water from Monarch Lake into Grand Lake by means of canals, either by an 11-mile tunnel to the Big Thompson or by one 14 miles long to the St. Vrain. Diking Grand Lake would permit "Western Slope storage of from 10,000 to 15,000 acre-feet for regulating the flow into the tunnel at times of excess run-off."[28]

The Shoshone Power Plant's 1,250 cubic feet per second (cfs) decree was critical in determining the amount of water available for diversion to the East Slope. From April to September, the Colorado River flowed far in excess of the plant's requirements and other decreed rights upstream. According to the state engineer's 1931 report, if these rights were protected for present and future needs, 178,000 acre-feet would be available for transmountain diversion based on 80 percent efficiency in the collection system.[29] Constructing a diversion tunnel large enough to take care of peak flows, which occasionally reached 3,000 cfs in June, was infeasible. Considerable storage would be necessary on the West Slope to regulate the runoff and achieve a reasonable tunnel capacity.[30] Nevertheless, the report concluded, diversion of larger amounts of run-off water "could be made without infringing on vested irrigation rights in Colorado, and without reducing the supply at the Shoshone Power Plant below its decree, except to the extent of about 3,700 acre-feet in September."[31]

Here at last was an endorsement, but proponents still needed further data to convince people that the Grand Lake Project was viable. After federal authorization of Casper-Alcova in August 1933, establishment of an organization to fund a new survey and generate cooperation among northern Colorado's citizens assumed paramount importance. Help came somewhat unexpectedly from George M. Bull, newly appointed PWA executive engineer in Colorado.

On Monday afternoon, August 14, 1933, Bull telephoned Weld County attorney Thomas A. Nixon to inquire whether he had any ideas about how to spend the $200 million available to the Rocky Mountain region for water development projects under PWA auspices.[32] Nixon agreed to call a meeting of the Weld County commissioners that evening. With little advance notice, the commissioners agreed to submit the Grand Lake Project. The next day, Chairman C. G. Carlson of Eaton, who was also a director of the Poudre Valley Water Users Association, wrote to Bull recommending a PWA project designed to bring water from Grand Lake to the Middle Fork of the Big Thompson River by way of a 12-mile tunnel. Such a project, he pointed out, "would make 100 percent productive farms that, for the past five years, [had] produced only partial crops." In addition, supplemental water from the Colorado River would put an end to yearly water shortages, which would mean greatly reduced unemployment figures and "the relief problem [would] practically cease to exist."[33]

His letter arrived in time for Assistant Interior Secretary Oscar L. Chapman's visit to Denver. A Coloradan himself, Chapman was on his way to an American Legion meeting in Durango, but he had planned to stop in Denver to meet with Bull's advisory board and receive Colorado's list of water projects. As eager as he was for his native state to share the federal largesse, Chapman detected a mood of resentment in the air over the Casper-Alcova decision. He urged Colorado to "quit arguing and ask for something for itself."[34]

Chapman and Bull were not alone in giving public support to the Grand Lake plan. After reading Carlson's letter, Governor Edwin "Big Ed" C. Johnson said that he was "favorably impressed," while N. R. McCreary, Colorado manager of Great Western Sugar, "heartily endorsed the plan" and agreed to "aid its progress in any way."[35] To many others, Grand Lake appeared to have obvious advantages over the North Platte diversion not only because it was not embroiled in interstate conflict but also because constructing a tunnel avoided the necessity of building costly collection ditches.

On August 18 the directors of the CLPWUA met to take a position on the project. After Carlson had outlined the main points, they decided to give tentative approval pending a "speedy investigation" of feasibility. A formal application was on file in Washington, the summer was already more than half over, and many demands were already being made on PWA funds. The association knew that it had to organize quickly and that it needed help from other counties, businesses, and municipalities to fund another survey.[36]

Organization came first. On August 22 the Chamber of Commerce named a new committee to deal with the Grand Lake Project. Chaired by Norcross and composed of Carlson, Charles Swink from Milliken, Hansen, Nixon, Kelly, Frank B. Davis, Claude Carney from Great Western, Harry Farr, and State Representative Moses E. Smith of Ault, this newly constituted Grand Lake Committee — the grandparent of the Northern Colorado Water Conservancy District Board — immediately conferred with a delegation from Fort Collins[37] to discuss how to finance a survey that had to be completed and sent to Washington within a month. Several spokesmen argued the urgency of the situation. Aware of the difficulties faced by northern Colorado farmers, Farr emphasized the need for supplemental water "if we are to survive," and Stimson explained the prospective benefits that would come to downstream users by the increase in return flows.[38] Shortly thereafter, Weld County commissioners gave their consent, agreeing to pay two-thirds of the estimated $3,000 cost of the survey. The Fort Collins delegation asked Larimer County to underwrite the other third.[39]

On August 28, the Grand Lake Committee sponsored a mass luncheon at the Independent Order of Odd Fellows (I.O.O.F.) hall in Greeley to introduce itself as a committee of the Greeley Chamber of Commerce and to begin soliciting community-wide support. On the following day the CLPWUA told its people to get behind the project.[40] With promised financial backing from Larimer, Weld, Morgan, Logan, and Sedgwick counties; plus the Chambers of Commerce of Brush, Fort Collins, Fort Morgan, Greeley, Loveland, and Sterling; Great Western Sugar; and the Burlington and Union Pacific railroads, Tipton and Stimson went into the field to begin their survey.[41]

In a report finished by December 1933, Tipton arrived at essentially the same conclusions that the state engineer had reached in 1931. He concluded that: the Grand Lake diversion could bring 285,000 acre-feet of water to the proposed district;[42] the "major conflict" would arise between the proposed diversions and the Shoshone Power Plant at Glenwood Springs; 46,000 acre-feet of storage would be necessary to protect the project against litigation from the power plant;[43] there would be no further problems stemming from the Colorado River Compact; and fifty-five years later, in 1988, the upper basin of the Colorado River would still have a "substantial surplus."[44]

With an organization in place, a formal request for funds in Washington, and a survey completed, the financial goal appeared near at hand; but the struggle for funding was just beginning. Coloradans had much to learn about New Deal politics and the liability of dissension between Colorado's East and West Slopes as they sought federal construction assistance.

3

Funding Frustrations: Congressman Edward T. Taylor Leads the Opposition

At the first meeting of the Weld County commissioners with the Grand Lake Committee in August 1933, George M. Bull had stated that his agency was looking for projects in Colorado. As executive engineer of all PWA projects in the state, Bull acted as "the final authority on all PWA regulations."[1] Before the meeting ended, the commissioners instructed attorneys Thomas A. Nixon and William R. Kelly to make a preliminary application and brief to the PWA, which was done and quickly forwarded to that agency. "A second prospectus and application to the President [of the U.S.] was prepared for the County Commissioners with the assistance of [Charles] Hansen and attorney Charles D. Todd in October 1933." Neither application brought tangible results.[2]

For a number of reasons, the PWA proved to be the wrong government agency for the Grand Lake Project. Organized under a state board, chairman Thomas A. Duke screened proposals and forwarded to Washington only those that he believed had merit.[3] Even though the PWA eventually spent more money in Colorado than in any other state in the trans-Mississippi West,[4] attorney Kelly discovered on one of his trips to Washington that PWA administrators spurned the C–BT Project because of its complex and extensive construction schedule.[5] Furthermore, the PWA expected state or local agencies to underwrite 70 percent (later 55 percent) of the costs. Obtaining such large amounts of matching funds was beyond the realm of possibility for an agricultural region already stressed to the breaking point by drought and depression.

Frustrations with PWA regulations led some to conclude that its chief administrator, Harold L. Ickes, was actually conspiring against Colorado. One report revealed that expenditures in Wyoming were twice those in Colorado. Much of this money was going into the Casper-Alcova project, which Ickes had supported since the PWA received a budget of $3.3 billion. Other reports described him as opposed to the principle of transmountain

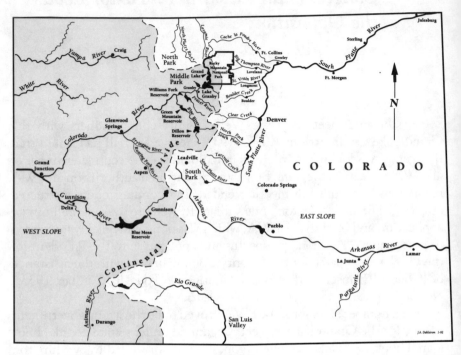

East-West Slope.

diversion.[6] But, even if Colorado had been able to raise matching funds, which is highly doubtful, the state constitution prohibited going into debt.[7] With his hands legally tied, Governor Edwin "Big Ed" C. Johnson also held to the philosophy that government, like a business, should be run with a balanced budget. Consequently, he found little to cheer about in the New Deal's trend toward deficit financing of large public works projects.[8]

While relations with the PWA were stagnating, Moses E. Smith went to Washington on behalf of the Grand Lake Committee to confer with Elwood Mead. Bull had sent a list of projects to Washington, endorsed by James Quigg Newton of Denver and D. W. Aupperle of the Western Slope Protective Association (WSPA), but Colorado was unable to erase its image of being divided on which water projects were most important, a reputation that made PWA reluctant to approve applications for construction funds.[9] As Kelly also learned on a trip to Washington, apart from the growing apathy in the PWA, the Reconstruction Finance Corporation (RFC), which had funded a transmountain diversion tunnel for the Twin Lakes project, did not want to get involved in another similar enterprise.[10] This left the Bureau as the best possible source of money because Commissioner Mead favored Colorado's objectives and believed in the future of the state's irrigated agriculture.

In 1883 Mead came to the faculty of Colorado State Agricultural College, where he pioneered a commitment to irrigation. After leaving Fort Collins in 1888, he gained national recognition by drafting Wyoming's constitutional provisions on water rights administration. Subsequently, he developed a water conservation and land settlement program for thirty-two irrigation projects in Australia.[11] Mead expressed to Hansen the hope that a workable plan would enable the Bureau to build a transmountain water diversion project into northeastern Colorado from the Colorado River.

> Your country, [he wrote Hansen,] has a special meaning to me. I made the first gauging of all the ditches in northern Colorado, working during vacations for the State Engineer. It was more of a job than it is now because they were running ties down most of the streams and the first step in gauging was to get down in the ditch and dislodge a tie. You have a great country and you need more water, and I feel a personal satisfaction in being able to work with you toward getting it.[12]

To this end, Mead met with the Grand Lake Committee in spring 1934. After preparing the way in Washington, he was finally able to write Colorado Agricultural College president Charles A. Lory with the good

Congressman Edward T. Taylor and Secretary of the Interior Harold L. Ickes. Taylor championed the protection of West Slope water rights while Ickes dealt with the difficult decision of whether to authorize funds to build the C–BT. (Courtesy Colorado Historical Society.)

news that Ickes had tentatively approved a survey of the "Northern Colorado Transmountain Diversion Water Project" by the Reclamation Service;[13] however, Mead, who was carrying a work load "that would stagger a man half his age,"[14] died in 1936 without seeing his objectives accomplished. Nevertheless, his efforts on Colorado's behalf had contributed significantly to federal approval of a supplemental water project built by the Bureau. By arguing that "most crops grown on Reclamation-irrigated lands were not in surplus and were consumed in local and regional markets," he had weakened the opposition of eastern politicians who held that more water for Colorado crops controverted administration goals of conserving the land and reducing agricultural production.[15] By September 1934, serious negotiations had begun between the Grand Lake Committee and the Bureau.[16] Concurrently, however, the West Slope was preparing to resist any federally funded transmountain diversion project. Congressman Edward T. Taylor's determination to protect the West Slope resulted in a legion of problems that took four years to resolve.

On September 27, 1933, two weeks after L. L. Stimson had begun his survey, Taylor arrived in Denver to attend a statewide meeting in George Bull's office to establish PWA priorities for Colorado water projects. Denver businessman Newton presided over this group, which represented irrigation interests on both sides of the Continental Divide. All hoped to win for Colorado a share of the federal funds being made available for public works. This "historic meeting," in the eyes of Congressman John Martin, was the first time that irrigation men with diverse points of view had sat down to adjust their differences over water conservation practices in the state.[17] According to Charles Hansen, the meeting was harmonious because "a fine spirit prevailed . . . [until] two special sessions of the legislature . . . upset all the good that had been accomplished."[18]

Taylor suggested that the state's different regions avoid throwing brickbats at one another because they all sought money for water conservation projects.[19] He then introduced a resolution, adopted by all in attendance, which he later claimed to be a "definite state policy."[20] As reported by the *Rocky Mountain News* in 1933 and recalled in 1938 by Taylor, this resolution stated that

> every transmountain diversion project out of the Colorado River Basin, other than the domestic projects for municipalities, shall include as an essential part of such project the construction of a compensatory reservoir on the Western Slope of sufficient capacity to hold an amount of water

) equal to the amount to be annually diverted by the transmountain
) diversion.[21]

Taylor's challenge became the first real road block to the men of the
Grand Lake Committee. If they wanted federal funding for a transmountain
diversion project, Taylor would use his considerable influence in the House
Appropriations Committee to help them, but only if the proposed project
included his proviso that an additional amount of water storage be built on
the West Slope equal to the amount of water diverted by the East Slope —
what soon became known as the acre-foot-for-acre-foot provision. Otherwise, Taylor warned, he could and would be a constant and resourceful
opponent of their plans in Washington.

None took Taylor lightly, but most felt that he would fall in line with
the Project once the proper surveys had been completed and all the data
were in. What they failed to appreciate was the relationship between Taylor
and his West Slope constituents, who held an almost reverent adoration
for their man in Washington.

Taylor's paternalism was born of more than his sense of political
responsibility. He had practiced law in Leadville and Aspen after receiving
his degree from the University of Michigan in 1884. In 1887 he had moved
permanently to Glenwood Springs. In addition to his terms as city and
county attorney, voters had elected him district attorney of Colorado's
Ninth Judicial District. During 1888 and 1889 he had helped adjudicate
irrigation rights for a large part of northwestern Colorado. In the eyes of
his constituents, "he led the fight both in and out of Congress to protect
the rights of the western twenty counties of Colorado to the future use of
seventy percent of all the flow of the Colorado River."[22] Taylor had also
earned the respect of irrigators on the Uncompahgre and Colorado rivers,
using his influence to oppose any attempts by the federal government to
control West Slope water. Not surprisingly, he looked with some suspicion
on the committee's plans to invade what he believed to be his proprietary
domain. This attitude created difficulties for advocates of the Grand Lake
Project.

When Moses Smith returned from Washington in spring 1934 after
delivering the Tipton Report, he announced that he had received encouraging consideration in Washington but that the united support of the
citizens of Colorado would be essential to achieve congressional funding
for a Grand Lake Project.[23] The Grand Lake Committee might well have
done more to ingratiate themselves with Taylor, but these men believed so
firmly in the righteousness of their cause that even the congressman, they

assumed, had to recognize sooner or later the inevitability of the Project when engineering reports showed its technical and economical feasibility.

Support from the recently organized Colorado State Planning Commission (CSPC) further strengthened their confidence. Established as a planning board by executive order on January 15, 1934, and given statutory life by the 30th General Assembly on June 18, 1935,[24] the CSPC was charged to assimilate and evaluate statewide needs for natural resources, highways and public buildings, public lands, recreation, sanitation, mining, and other programs that might require federal funding. As a coordinating agency at the state level, the commission set out to work with existing federal agencies — including the National Resources Committee (NRC) — that advised President Roosevelt directly on drought conditions in the Great Plains.[25]

The Colorado State Planning Commission owed a great deal to the leadership of its director, Edward D. Foster, who was convinced from the beginning that a transmountain diversion project from the Colorado River would benefit economies on both sides of the Continental Divide. Early in 1935 he began urging the Colorado delegation in Washington to seek a legislative appropriation for the purpose of completing surveys throughout the state. He also advised them to keep after the PWA to secure construction funds[26] and promised to "do anything we can" to promote an economic survey of the Platte River. When Governor Johnson bypassed the CSPC in a clumsy attempt to get federal funding for the Caddoa project on the Arkansas River, Foster urged Johnson to contact him in the future before endorsing special interests.[27] Because Foster was openly committed to the Grand Lake Project as one of the state's highest priorities, his energies in that direction made him somewhat suspect on the other side of the Continental Divide.

Despite Taylor's criticism of him for favoritism to the Front Range, Foster repeatedly assured the congressman that the CSPC promoted the interests of the entire state. Colorado River flood waters saved for irrigation use on the East Slope would alleviate the drought and help stay California's and Arizona's interests in acquiring more water from the Colorado River.[28] If Taylor would be willing to thrash out the "Grand Lake problem" in the presence of the CSPC, wrote Foster, "we might be able to arrive at some agreement to which he [Taylor] would stick at the next session of Congress."[29]

Foster was equally demanding about giving instructions to other Colorado delegates. He shared with them his conversations with Bureau representatives about the best way to construct projects for supplemental water

Colorado Senator Alva B. Adams was the son of a former Colorado governor. He played a major role in getting Congress to provide funding for C–BT construction. (Courtesy Denver Public Library, Western History Department.)

supplies, warned that the Bureau might require a lien on existing water rights and irrigation works, and pointed out the need for Colorado to write new laws enabling a water district to contract with the federal government. In a January 1936 letter, Foster urged the delegation to introduce authorization and appropriation bills giving the Bureau authority to construct the Project if there were "any possibility of success," but he also said that the door was open for any assistance that might be available from the Reconstruction Finance Corporation (RFC) or the PWA. All suggestions from the Colorado delegation to the CSPC, he concluded, would be most appreciated.[30]

For the most part, the state's delegation to Congress sprang from the 1932 Democratic revolution. Alva B. Adams, the new senator, was a Pueblo banker, son of former governor Alva Adams, and nephew of retiring Billy Adams. A Democrat described by Secretary Ickes as "on the conservative side,"[31] Adams voted against FDR on key issues, especially on fiscal matters. He was, however, an enthusiastic supporter of the sugar beet industry. When he realized what a federally funded transmountain diversion project meant to the industry's survival in Colorado, he modified his fiscal philosophy and strongly advocated the C–BT.

The House delegation included Taylor (Glenwood Springs), Fred Cummings (Fort Collins), John Martin (Pueblo), and Lawrence Lewis (Denver). Taylor had already served in Congress for twenty-five years. His seniority meant that he had power on committees; his support of FDR resulted in even greater influence in legislative matters. He was committed to the idea that the federal government must use its collective might to preserve the nation's lands (Taylor Grazing Act, 1934) and waters. He was also committed to protecting West Slope water rights from encroachment by outside forces. Taylor's resistance to the C–BT meant that the Colorado delegation lacked unity, and his lack of interest in compromise gave Congress more than one excuse to deny appropriations to Colorado when his support might have persuaded enough congressmen to follow his lead.

In contrast, Congressman Cummings openly and vigorously backed the Project; he was also Taylor's most outspoken critic. An enthusiastic proponent of the sugar beet industry and president of the Mountain States Beet Marketing Association, Cummings frequently revealed his impatience with his colleague's dilatory tactics during the four-year struggle to get federal funding.

John Martin was a loyal New Deal Democrat on most issues, and he generally supported Cummings on transmountain diversion. However, both he and Lewis, a frequent opponent of the New Deal, took a less active political role in the fight for the C–BT, preferring to leave the field of battle to Taylor and Cummings.

The only holdover from the Hoover administration was the old Progressive, Edward P. Costigan. Senator Costigan, a liberal Democrat in the New Deal, was philosophically attuned to Roosevelt's policies in regard to federal funding of public works.[32] While he chose to assert himself more in other political battles, he favored the C–BT as a means to get the unemployed back to work. In 1936, while seeking reelection, ill health forced Costigan to withdraw from the race and allowed his rival, Ed Johnson, an anti–New Deal Democrat, to win his seat. But by 1937, even Johnson recognized the importance of the C–BT. As "one of the most articulate politicians in Washington"[33] and a great favorite of Colorado voters, he soon gave the C–BT his unqualified support.

With Foster's urging, Colorado's congressional delegation began testing the legislative waters in 1935. When Michigan Representative Fred Crawford expressed the concern of legislators who opposed using tax dollars for water projects that were designed to increase agricultural productivity,[34] Senator Costigan countered by noting that farmers in his state were desperate for more water and favored federally funded relief acts to meet unemployment problems and to enlarge the public works program. While debating new legislation to provide $900 million for "public projects of states or political subdivisions thereof," Costigan asked for and received approval for an amendment that included "transmountain diversion" and "water conservation."[35] This inclusion appears to be the first formal effort by any member of the Colorado delegation to pursue federal funding in Congress for the C–BT.

The PWA, RFC, and other agencies of the New Deal administration had attracted the attention of the Grand Lake Committee because they came under executive — not congressional — control, had money, and approved projects without engaging in legislative debates. But after a year and a half of disappointments, Coloradans recognized that Congress still had the power of the purse. Its authorization of water projects and appropriation of funds appeared essential to the C–BT's success. At this point northern Colorado realized the need for a more purposeful organization. The Grand Lake Committee of the Greeley Chamber of Commerce gave way to the Northern Colorado Water Users Association (NCWUA), whose specific objective was to secure federal funding and win over adversaries on the West Slope.

The NCWUA came into being at a meeting in Greeley on April 6, 1934. As chairman of the Greeley Chamber of Commerce Irrigation Committee, Hansen called a gathering at the Weld County Court House of all interested people from the Poudre, St. Vrain, Thompson, and Platte valleys to devise plans for a Grand Lake water diversion project. His notice stated that promotion of the enterprise had reached the point at which full cooperation of all irrigation interests was essential. Survey reports now indicated that the Project could be built, but unless Colorado took united action soon, the state would lose an invaluable opportunity to solve its water problem.[36]

The day-long meeting evoked a ground swell of support for the proposed Project. Remarks by surveyors Stimson and Tipton confirmed the physical and financial feasibility of construction; Moses Smith, Michael C. Hinderlider, and Lory urged all interests to unite behind the Project; and Stimson moved to form a new committee to work on ways and means of getting a favorable hearing in Congress. Immediately after each water district had appointed a representative to serve on the new committee, the NCWUA held its first meeting.[37] On January 21, 1935, eleven new Board members signed the articles of incorporation, formally electing Hansen president.[38]

No one was better suited to lead the NCWUA through the struggles with Congress and the West Slope. As editor of the weekly *Greeley Tribune* in 1903, Hansen had succeeded in getting financial backing to consolidate and incorporate his paper and two rival dailies under the Greeley Republican Publishing Company.[39] His good fortune resulted in part from a close friendship with Dan A. Camfield, one of the most successful irrigation developers in northern Colorado. In addition to financing Hansen's newspaper, Camfield influenced Hansen's thinking about irrigated agriculture.[40]

Camfield had been a tenacious developer of farmlands. By increasing the water supply to new areas, he had raised the value of land in Weld County, adding to its water rights.[41] He believed in reclamation through greater water storage capacity. Practicing this belief, he gradually increased his projects' size "until it was thought possible for only the United States government to handle [them]."[42] In Hansen's own words, Camfield was "looking for new prairies to conquer [in 1908], after having virtually transformed the whole South Platte Valley from a barren waste to a splendid farming country." Camfield had moved into the Poudre Valley, backed by the prestige of many successes and unlimited capital. After he checked engineers' reports, made new surveys, measured available water, and explored new lands, he designed a plan to organize an irrigation district to pay for the reclamation of 125,000 acres with water diverted from the Laramie River to the Poudre River via a 3-mile tunnel. Hansen claimed that Camfield was running a "private reclamation service of wonderful efficacy," and that he would succeed in building "the greatest irrigation system ever constructed in Colorado."[43]

Hansen's praise of Camfield was written twenty-six years before the NCWUA was formed, but his remarks reveal lessons he had learned. Although Camfield died in 1914, Hansen continued to hold out hope for a transmountain water diversion project. In 1915 he was one of the advocates for the statutory provision in the act creating Rocky Mountain National Park stipulating that the park "should not interfere in any manner with the development of water resources for irrigation purposes."[44]

As president and publisher of the *Greeley Tribune*, past president of the Greeley Chamber of Commerce, community booster, friend of the irascible Congressman Taylor, and the man in charge of Weld County's public works projects, Hansen was in the best position to promote the C–BT with his experience and enthusiasm. Furthermore, his commitment to the Project was beyond criticism. He owned no farmland; he had no financial interest

in any ditch or reservoir company; and he could not profit directly from a
project bringing supplemental water into the community. At the same
time, he was positively motivated to support a program that would address
the appalling length of breadlines in northern Colorado and replace
wasteful government relief projects that encouraged men to dig useless
holes "only to dig another to get enough parched dirt to fill the first hole."
Manpower was readily available, Hansen concluded, but men could be far
more productively employed on a transmountain water diversion project.[45]
His mission in 1935 was to convince naysayers that transmountain diversion was feasible and good for northern Colorado. Often at his own expense
and with incredible patience, Hansen immersed himself in the world of
local, state, and national politics. This quiet evangelist of the C–BT soon
became a superb political strategist when, at age sixty and as president of
the NCWUA, he decided to take on the biggest battle of his life.

Hansen's first real challenge came in May 1935. Congressman
Cummings telegraphed from Washington that the National Park Service
(NPS) was putting up a bitter fight against a survey of the C–BT through
Rocky Mountain National Park.[46] The NCWUA Board authorized Hansen to go to the Capitol with attorneys Kelly and Nixon to discuss the
matter with the Colorado delegation, Commissioner Mead, and Secretary
Ickes. In correspondence from Washington, Hansen was optimistic. He was
able to speak with all the "big guns," but it was "Hell to mark time like
this." As he wrote home, "Progress is damn slow . . . [but] I think we are
moving in the right direction and hope to be definitely on the upgrade by
next week. When it does break, I think we will be pretty sure of our
construction fund, because they will not turn loose the survey fund without
being pretty sure that the project is to be constructed." He naively anticipated full cooperation from Congressman Taylor "because we are on very
good terms with him." Although Hansen worried about the power of NPS
officials to impede further progress on the survey, he counted on Secretary
Ickes to overrule them. "That is the main hurdle in sight," he concluded.
They have "fought like a bunch of wildcats, but I think we have them
licked." However, "this is not ready for publication yet."[47]

The NPS and its friends, however, proved worthy opponents right up
to beginning construction on the Continental Divide Tunnel. Established
in 1916, the NPS was first directed by the amiable Horace M. Albright,
who influenced Ickes profoundly toward a more aesthetic view of natural
resource management. When Albright resigned in 1933, the NPS was
"expansive, confident, vigorous, and effective," and "it was on the thresh-
old of an unprecedented expansion of its jurisdiction and bureaucratic

Thomas A. Nixon, along with William R. Kelly, was responsible for most of the legal work associated with creating the NCWCD. He is generally given credit for authoring the 1937 Water Conservancy District Act. (Courtesy City of Greeley Museums.)

structure."[48] Albright's successor, Arno B. Cammerer, had a bland style, a pat-on-the-back approach, and the annoying habit of chewing gum open-mouthed. Ickes just did not like him, but his primary focus was on remaking the Department of the Interior into a Department of Conservation that would combine the NPS and the United States Forest Service (USFS) under one director.[49]

When A. E. Demaray, NPS acting director, wrote to the Bureau in March 1935, denying the Bureau permission to enter Rocky Mountain National Park for the purpose of surveying for a proposed transmountain diversion project, he cited the Federal Water Power Act. Congress had designed this act, he said, to prevent the encroachment of "dams, reservoirs, power houses, transmission lines, or other works for the storage or carriage of water . . . within the limits . . . of any national park or national monument." Demaray further stated what would become a fundamental issue with the NPS: He did not want the survey to be an "opening wedge" in a hard-won wall of protection surrounding the national park system.[50] What Hansen and the NCWUA did not know was that Ickes had already expressed his sympathy for Demaray's objections.[51]

Two weeks later, NCWUA attorney Thomas A. Nixon noted that under the act creating the Rocky Mountain National Park, the Bureau was fully empowered to construct irrigation works; this right in no way negated the objectives of the Federal Water Power Act.[52] He might also have noted that the act had anticipated the possibility of reclamation activities by inserting the previously mentioned clause, "that the United States Reclamation Service may enter upon and utilize for flowage or other purposes any area within said park which may be necessary for the development and maintenance of a Government reclamation project."[53]

On April 15 the NCWUA called a special meeting to acquaint the Rocky Mountain National Park superintendent, Hedmond B. Rogers, and president of the Colorado Mountain Climbers Club, James Harvey, with a complete account of northern Colorado's acute need for water. Rogers, although "keenly sympathetic," made no commitment to a permit for the survey.[54] Two weeks later, Senator Adams told Hansen that Ickes had put the survey funds on hold because of the NPS contention that a tunnel through the park might damage Grand Lake.[55] Because of this snag, Hansen, Kelly, and Nixon headed for Washington in May. The results of their efforts were realized when Secretary Ickes, in July, finally authorized the Bureau to spend $150,000 on a preliminary engineering survey that got under way on August 1, 1935.[56]

Meanwhile, the CSPC was taking important steps to establish priorities for Colorado water projects. Relentless drought threats from lower basin states to take more Colorado River water and the persistent need for a unified approach in Washington prompted creation of a special Water Resources Advisory Committee. This "Committee of Seventeen," organized officially on June 3, 1935, held a most significant first meeting ten days later.[57] By the end of three days the committee had adopted nineteen resolutions, each representing distinct water projects. All were unanimously recommended to the CSPC. The most comprehensive of these was Resolution 1, the so-called "Delaney Resolution." Frank Delaney had become a leading figure on the West Slope soon after earning a law degree at the University of Colorado. In 1921 he moved to Glenwood Springs, where he worked as assistant district attorney for the Ninth Judicial District. Without a doubt, he was one of the most influential and respected citizens in his community and a fervent admirer of Congressman Taylor. Delaney's approach to the East Slope's plans for the C–BT reflected his close association with Taylor, a commonsense view of Colorado water law, and a commitment to negotiating solutions to water problems.[58]

At the Denver meeting, Delaney took a position similar to that expressed by Taylor on September 27, 1933, but with a subtle and important difference. Article 14 of his lengthy resolution stated that no construction of a major transmountain project could begin until a survey had shown its effect on West Slope water rights and future development. Further, a plan would have to be prepared, including compensatory storage "constructed as a part of the expense of the project, in the amount shown by such survey to be sufficient so that neither existing Western Slope rights nor probable future Western Slope development will be adversely affected by the proposed transmountain diversion." Article 2 of the resolution also stated that until a comprehensive survey settled the requirements of both slopes, "it is fair to assume that of the surplus water of the Colorado River which may be reasonably be [sic] expected to be allotted to the State of Colorado, the Western Slope will certainly need at least one-half."[59] Taylor had demanded an acre-foot of storage on the West Slope for every acre-foot delivered through the C–BT. Delaney agreed to this — *until* such time as a complete survey was made of the Colorado River. From that point on, transmountain diversion was acceptable to him as long as existing West Slope rights and compensatory storage equal to "probable future West Slope development" were properly accounted for and protected.

The NCWUA accepted the Delaney Resolution. Hansen even wrote to Walter Walker, editor of the *Grand Junction Sentinel,* to assure him that his people stood behind it. Likewise, Foster made clear that the CSPC "would oppose the Grand Lake, or any other, diversion which does not adhere strictly to the words and spirit of the Delaney Resolution." He later took umbrage when Taylor accused him of abandoning the earlier "agreement."[60]

While Taylor persistently refused compromise on the acre-foot-for-acre-foot principle, Delaney appeared significantly more reasonable. "I do not see how we can insist on any greater quantity of water," he wrote, "than a thorough survey shows is sufficient to protect our present appropriations and reasonable future needs arising from further probable development. . . . We cannot ask for more than we need."[61] He was also convinced that the C–BT Project had an excellent chance of implementation despite the West Slope's protests. Until economic and technical studies were completed, of course, surplus (unappropriated) waters would have to be shared fifty-fifty. To this extent, Hansen and Taylor were saying the same thing; however, Delaney was willing to negotiate after proper surveys were executed, and Taylor remained adamant in adherence to his 1933 pronouncement.

Resolution 17 described the "Grand Lake Transmountain Project." Hansen made a number of revisions before the Committee of Seventeen gave approval. In final form, this resolution urged immediate release of survey funds ($150,000) to determine "present and probable Western Slope requirements for water" and also recommended construction of the project at an estimated cost of $15 million so long as it was found

> feasible, economically sound, and not in any way interfering with the present needs and future requirements of the Western Slope . . . and provided further that all the terms and conditions set forth in Resolution No. 1 with respects [sic] to transmountain diversion projects, shall apply to this resolution and the project herein mentioned, and shall have been approved by the Western Slope Protective Association and the Western Slope members of this Committee.[62]

Although awkwardly worded, Resolution 17 plainly revealed how anxious the East Slope was to cooperate with its counterparts across the mountains. Hansen concluded, "We want to try to leave your water situation in better shape than we found it";[63] in this spirit, he was able to negotiate with considerable success.

A total of $33.6 million in federal loans and grants was finally requested in the nineteen resolutions proposed by the Water Resources Advisory Committee. Endorsed by the CSPC and sent on to Washington, these projects, in Taylor's eyes, demanded many times the amount of money that Colorado could ever expect, and the committee had failed to identify the more important projects, thus asking Congress to make the choice.[64] Taylor had a point; but because of his known opposition to the Grand Lake Project, along with his powerful position as chairman of the House subcommittee that reviewed Interior Department appropriations, the NCWUA regarded Taylor's criticism of the Colorado resolutions as a smokescreen and thought that he alone was responsible for killing the funding possibilities in 1936.[65] Suspicion of Taylor's negative role increased when Lory wrote from Washington with the news that Congress had appropriated $100 million for western irrigation projects, but "Colorado was left off the list."[66] This omission was probably not Taylor's doing. Senator Adams even believed that the West Slope congressman would soon use his connections to secure an appropriation for the C–BT. Still, to the NCWUA, Taylor had become the Project's bête noire. The time had come, they believed, to enlist Roosevelt's support.

Governor Johnson joined the Colorado delegation to seek intervention from the White House. On January 7, 1936, FDR responded that these kinds of projects were customarily under reclamation law and required "a repayment of cost in 40 years without interest and that allotments of money for such irrigation developments are not made without showing willingness and ability to repay the cost." Additionally, "in order to secure further consideration of the Colorado projects, it will be necessary to supplement the statement submitted [by the CSPC] by a showing of repayment conditions and the contribution to be expected from beneficiaries of the development." Compliance with reclamation law now became the sine qua non of success.[67] Through battles in Congress over Casper-Alcova, interstate conflicts with Wyoming and Nebraska, and short-lived expectations from New Deal agencies, northern Colorado had learned that future water development was tied to a formal relationship with the Bureau.

Hansen was delighted. The NCWUA, he said in a letter to Taylor, represented eighty irrigation companies in six counties and "is duly incorporated as a mutual irrigation company . . . fully qualified by law to do any and all things necessary to negotiate with the U.S. Bureau of Reclamation for construction of the Northern Transmountain diversion." He expressed his faith in securing water at a reasonable cost, even with compensatory storage for the West Slope. The NCWUA, he added, was ready at any time to enter into negotiations with the Bureau, and every effort would be made to comply with the reclamation law and FDR's letter to the state delegation.[68]

Taylor, however, was in no hurry. While he urged Foster to woo the Bureau[69] and noted the NCWUA's resolution to contract with the Bureau for construction and repayment purposes,[70] he advised his West Slope constituents to read and reread FDR's letter. "This is the route we have got to take," he wrote the West Slope's D. W. Aupperle, "and the sooner we commence the sooner we will get somewhere." While Colorado milled around, said Taylor, other states had complied with the law and had received the money. Ickes made clear that the Department of the Interior planned no free grants for irrigation. Because of this and threats from California and Arizona to thwart transmountain diversion in Colorado, constituents ought to insist on compensatory reservoirs. For any project taking water out of the Colorado basin, "storage must be equal to the amount diverted. . . . Those compensatory reservoirs must be built and maintained by and at the expense of the transmountain diversions."[71] In other words, Taylor was willing to work with the Bureau but unwilling to abandon his acre-foot-for-acre-foot condition.

Meanwhile, in Washington, Senator Carl Hayden of Arizona, a ranking member of the Senate Appropriations Committee, requested an amendment to H. R. 10630, the Department of the Interior Appropriations Bill for the year ending June 30, 1937. The amended bill authorized construction of a "Grand Lake–Big Thompson transmountain diversion project [and others] . . . *Provided,* That said project will include the construction and permanent maintenance of adequate compensatory or replacement reservoirs, necessary feeder canals, and other incidental works, at the most suitable sites within said State." The bill also stipulated that water users pay all compensatory and diversion costs to deliver water outside the drainage basin and that the entire system operate in such a way as to maintain the water in Grand Lake at normal levels.[72]

Hayden was looking for political allies in his fight for Arizona's Gila River project. He hoped that his efforts on behalf of Colorado would produce mutually beneficial results.[73] What he failed to take into consideration was Taylor's ongoing recalcitrance, manifested through his position as chairman of the Interior subcommittee in the House Committee on Appropriations. Hayden's amendment omitted the acre-foot-for-acre-foot stipulation. Furthermore, opponents in the House attacked H.R. 10630 following its return from the Senate with a host of new reclamation projects attached. Congressman John Taber, one of Taylor's close friends and the ranking minority member of the House Appropriations Committee, argued forcefully against any increase in government expenditures. He noted that H.R. 10630 had been increased by $62 million and that most of the increase was for reclamation projects that Taylor had refused to consider because they were "useless and unnecessary." Worse than that, Taber continued, the Senate had added authorizations for projects, the worst of which was Grand Lake–Big Thompson, "a $22 million project to dig a canal for 13 miles under a mountain 10,000 feet high to irrigate a lot of land many miles away. . . . This is one of the most ridiculous things I have ever heard of," he raged. "We ought not to have unsound reclamation projects when we have an agricultural surplus."[74]

On March 5, 1936, Taylor made his position very clear. In a telegram to Foster he insisted that "this matter [the acre-foot-for-acre-foot business] must be settled here and enacted into law before there is any further progress made towards transmountain diversions with my consent." In his presentation in Denver on September 27, 1933, he had pressed for a definite state policy, and "I understand the same principle was again agreed to on June 15 last year in the Delaney Resolution."[75] Taylor either did not understand the Delaney Resolution or he had not read it carefully. In any case, while progress was gradually being made in Colorado to harmonize the interests of the NCWUA and the WSPA and while the rest of the state's delegation in Washington was trying to secure authorization and funding legislation, Taylor was using his influence to block progress until the acre-foot-for-acre-foot principle could be agreed to and signed into law.

Congressman Cummings was so frustrated with Taylor that he wired Hansen: "We will never get water from [the] Western Slope under [the] present congressional setup — stop — suggest you wire Ed [that] we are considering redistricting the state for congressional purposes."[76] While Cummings vented his own frustration, the Colorado legislature on March 28 made its own views known to Taylor by approving House Joint Resolution 1, introduced by A. C. Tinsley of Delta County and Charles W. Lilley, who represented Jackson and Larimer counties.

Intended for the Congress in Washington, the secretary of interior, and the president of the United States, this resolution pointed out that Colorado needed to develop irrigation works to prevent its waters from escaping across its borders; that lands already under cultivation were in desperate need of water; and that additional storage was necessary "to impound the flood stages of the rivers for use during the irrigating seasons, when supplies now available are wholly inadequate." What the state needed was federal assistance to complete the surveys and to construct the works to "aid the dominant industry of Colorado" (farming) and relieve the "menace of recurrent floods on the lower rivers."[77] Although Congressman Taylor was in no way singled out for criticism, the resolution sent a clear message to him that the folks back home were united in favor of transmountain diversion.

By June, however, the C–BT authorization bill was "definitely dead."[78] Congressman Lewis did his best to counter views that transmountain diversion projects "[were] novel and of doubtful economic soundness," contending that "no definite national policy concerning such projects had been established by the federal government." Each project deserved evaluation on its own merits, he argued. In a speech to the entire House, he traced the evolution of the Colorado Doctrine of prior appropriation and its adoption by neighboring states. He further outlined the eight court cases that sanctioned the principle of transmountain diversion under the prior appropriation system and reviewed the Reclamation Act of 1902, the Colorado River Compact of 1922, and "repeated acts of Congress" that showed a national policy allowing Bureau construction of transmountain diversion projects.[79]

Lewis's speech had little effect on Taylor or uninformed congressmen. In July 1936 the Grand Lake Project became known as the Colorado–Big Thompson Project,[80] but this did not signify official acceptance in Washington. When the Budget Committee approved $1 million for "Grand Lake," Taylor made a hurried trip to Washington to put pressure on this committee and other departments to nullify the funding.[81] As reported by

Senator Adams, he might even have "bombard[ed] the National Resources Committee with letters threatening to cut off appropriations from that body if it report[ed] favorably on the Grand Lake Project. . . . If my correspondent's information is correct," Adams warned, "Congressman Taylor is threatening to use his position as a member of the House Appropriations Committee to cut off appropriations . . . unless that Committee acts in accordance with his wishes."[82]

At this point in fall 1936, congressional legislation for the C–BT was clearly beyond reach unless its proponents weakened Taylor's influence. That was possible only if Colorado presented a united front, if the Bureau's report found the idea possible, and if a better organization developed in northern Colorado to contract with the federal government and assure the reimbursement of construction funds forty years after completion — as provided in the reclamation law. These matters required prompt attention.

NCWUA Directors had already made some progress. On September 19, 1936, Hansen reported that the Bureau had finished its survey, which had been approved by Acting Director John C. Page, that both Ickes and the National Resources Committee had signaled their approval, and that the only opposition was coming from Taylor and the NPS. NCWUA's work, Hansen said somewhat critically, was six months behind the engineering and, "if we are to continue our efforts, immediate steps should be taken to set up a real organization to dispose of the water and sell the ditch companies on the idea."[83] His sense of urgency might have been heightened even further had he known that on February 22, 1937, James P. Buchanan, chairman for the House Appropriations Committee, would die, leaving his gavel in the hands of the ranking Democrat, Edward T. Taylor.[84] Congressman Cummings was not pleased by the Washington scene. In his opinion, Taylor had become an unreconciled obstructionist whom he would be inclined to tell "to go to H——," he wrote Hansen, "but the poor fellow is not very well, and I suppose it is best to humor him."[85] The NPS was equally guilty of opposition, he said, and the wave of economy that had become noticeable in Congress during spring 1937 augured poorly for C–BT funding. Cummings concluded: "I think sometimes there are more damn fools working for the government than in any other organization in the United States, and I am not excepting Congress [or] . . . those poor mutts in the Park. . . . You couldn't pry that Park away from them. . . . You will probably notice that whenever the weather gets right hot in Washington, a bunch of those fellows come west to see how the Parks are getting along."[86]

Northern Colorado had to convince Congress that its organization was capable of entering into a contractual relationship with the Bureau once Congress appropriated funds. At this time, the state's water *conservation* district law was inadequate to allow for retiring debt obligations incurred in a reclamation project constructed jointly with the federal government. Further, Congress remained wary of approving a project that appeared to divide Colorado between East and West Slopes. What President Hansen needed to accomplish, therefore, was enactment of a *conservancy* district law in the state legislature and detente between Taylor's supporters on the West Slope and the NCWUA. As of 1937, these were his principal objectives.

4

Progress at Last:
West Slope Cooperation and the 1937
Conservancy District Act

During most discussions of Colorado's 1935 water conservation district law, doubts were usually expressed about the authority of conservation districts to contract between mutual irrigation companies and the federal government. The law was passed to give groups of irrigators the right to act as public bodies in securing funds from the PWA.[1] It provided the statutory assistance that farmers needed by authorizing district organization by a petition of citizens that was to be filed in the office of the secretary of state and to include the district's name, its metes and bounds, and a statement of the number of elected board members who represented each of its three subdivisions.[2] Districts could

> own, construct, reconstruct, improve, purchase, lease, or otherwise acquire, extend, manage, use, or operate any Irrigation Works, as defined in this Act . . . [with] the right and power to enter into any contract . . . with the government of the United States, or with any officer, department, bureau or agency thereof, or with any corporation organized under federal law including the Public Works Corporation.[3]

The law also empowered districts to borrow money, pledge revenues as security, accept bids for construction contracts, and collect rents for water service, but under no circumstances could they "levy or collect taxes for the purpose of paying, in whole or in part, any indebtedness or obligation . . . incurred by the district."[4]

Coloradans organized eight conservation districts under the 1935 law. Spencer L. Baird, district counsel for the Bureau, held that the law was perfectly valid and would enable water users associations to contract with the United States "for the construction of irrigation works and payment therefore in pursuance of the Reclamation Law." However, in Baird's view, Congress had to amend federal laws before the government and an association such as the NCWUA signed a contract.[5]

Since January 21, 1935, when the NCWUA incorporated, Charles Hansen had held that this organization qualified as a mutual irrigation company with every right to negotiate with the Bureau for construction of a water project. His only concern was that the NCWUA included eighty different irrigation companies in seven counties.[6] Therefore, to contract with the Bureau under the 1902 Reclamation Law, "joint liability contracts [would be] required from all ditch companies . . . on their present works and present water rights."[7] To Edward D. Foster, this provision would require owners of the water rights and works to mortgage their properties to a water users association, which in turn would contract with the Bureau for repayment of the costs. Repayment would then be financed wholly through the sale of water to voluntary purchasers, denying the association the right to levy a tax for this purpose.[8] The association's inability to raise funds through taxes made the 1935 law inadequate for a more complex and costly transmountain diversion project.

By 1937 the NCWUA clearly understood that water sales alone would be insufficient to repay debt obligations if a transmountain diversion contract were signed with the Bureau of Reclamation. Furthermore, as Charles Hansen wrote to Carl Gray, president of the Union Pacific Railroad, when the time came to contract with the government, some of the many irrigation companies might "absolutely refuse to enter into a deal." What was needed, he said, was a conservancy district with taxing powers.[9] Like his colleagues, however, Hansen at first felt uncertain about how to persuade the state legislature that Colorado agriculture needed a new law.

NCWUA attorneys Thomas A. Nixon and William R. Kelly began work on two separate bills in January. With assistance from Hansen and fellow NCWUA Director, J. M. Dille, conferences with state legislators, plus "valuable legal help from experienced Reclamation Counsel J. A. Alexander of Salt Lake City and Spencer L. Baird of Denver,"[10] they began looking for precedential legislation in Colorado and in other states for a water conservancy district with general taxing powers. They borrowed sections of the Colorado Irrigation District Act of 1901 (amended in 1935); the Conservation Act and the Moffat Tunnel Improvement District Act, both of 1922; and the Internal Improvement District Act of 1923.[11]

Other sections came from court-tested legislation in California and Utah. In both of these states, public agencies generally analagous to the water conservancy districts under consideration were judicially designated "quasi-municipal" corporations.[12] This characterization seemed appropriate and adaptable to the Colorado situation. A water district could avoid the definition of a true municipal corporation — having powers of local government — by becoming an "agency of the state vested with some of the powers and attributes of a municipality."[13] Furthermore, the metropolitan water district acts of both California and Utah provided precedents for merging several communities into a corporation formed for a publicly stated purpose with authority to raise funds through an ad valorem tax. The emphasis here on taxation for a *public purpose* differed from an "assessment for benefits as in the case of irrigation and drainage districts, the Moffat Tunnel Improvement District, and flood control districts formed under the 1935 Conservation Act."[14] Kelly and Nixon disputed whether the act, in final form, should create only a northern Colorado district or apply more broadly to the entire state.

Kelly's more specific bill proposed the legislative creation of one northern Colorado water conservancy district with boundaries clearly defined. The alternative bill, written by Nixon with assistance from Dille and Hansen, was accepted by the NCWUA Board of Directors, approved by the legislature, and signed into law by Governor Teller Ammons on May 13, 1937. The new law proposed the formation of districts throughout the state by petition of the taxpaying electors to a district court and vested a district with taxing power exercised by a court-appointed board of directors. This plan, although more cumbersome, appeared to its authors to be more acceptable statewide because citizens would have a chance to testify locally whenever a district might be proposed in their area.[15]

As finally written, House Bill 714 comprised forty-three sections extending over fifty pages in the *Session Laws of Colorado*. Described as "an Act to provide for the organization of water conservancy districts and to define the purposes and powers thereof," its stated objective was "to provide for the conservation of water resources of the State of Colorado and for the greatest beneficial use of water within the state, the organization of water conservancy districts and the construction of works as herein defined by such districts."[16]

Among the more important provisions were stipulations that initially required a proposed district to have no less than $20 million of assessed value in irrigated lands. Petitions for organization had to be filed in the office of the clerk of the district court, "signed by not fewer than fifteen hundred (1500) owners of the irrigated lands situated within the limits of the territory and no fewer than five hundred (500) owners of non-irrigated lands and/or lands embraced within the incorporated limits of a city or town, all situated in the proposed district."[17] The district court, "sitting in and for any county in this state," was vested with the jurisdiction, power, and authority to establish water conservancy districts "for conserving, developing and stabilizing supplies of water for domestic, irrigation, power, manufacturing and other beneficial uses as herein provided."[18] The court would set a hearing date on the petition, with notices mailed to the county commissioners whose territory fell within the proposed district. Protests were allowed under certain rules, but if such petitions were dismissed, the court could rule that a district had been duly organized as a "political subdivision of the State of Colorado and a body corporate with all the powers of a public or municipal corporation."[19] The only challenge would come through a writ of *quo warranto* commenced by the attorney general within three months of the district's organization.[20]

The Water Conservancy District Act further stated that the court was to appoint a district's board of directors. The decision to have directors appointed by the district court, rather than elected by taxpayers, was a reflection of the source materials and precedents Kelly and Nixon used to draw up the rest of the Water Conservancy District Act. Utah's 1935 Metropolitan Water District Act stated that directors would be appointed by municipal authorities, who would retain the power of recall. Likewise, California's Golden Gate Bridge Act and a 1935 Street and Highways District Act specified that directors would be appointed by county boards of supervisors. In Colorado the 1922 Conservancy District Act (S.B. 2, Chap. 1) provided that district courts would appoint board members who were residents of the counties in which the district was situated. Although a number of other Colorado districts were run by elected boards (water works, roads, schools, etc.), the authors of the Water Conservancy District Act opted for the appointment process to keep directors out of politics and to free them from costly campaigning. Thus constituted, water conservancy district boards were theoretically more independent to exercise their responsibilities. They could own "water, water works, water rights and sources of water supply" and other forms of real and personal property on behalf of the district and could exercise the power of eminent domain, contract with the federal government, allot, appropriate, acquire, and store water, invest surplus money, organize subdistricts, levy and collect taxes, and sell, lease, or otherwise dispose of the use of water "by contracts for the perpetual use of such water to persons, mutual ditch companies, water users' associations and other private corporations for irrigation or commercial use as shall be provided by contracts."[21] With the passage of the 1937 Water Conservancy District Act, Hansen's first objective was accomplished fairly easily, but his second proved far more trying and required all of his skills of personal diplomacy.

C–BT proponents would have had a far more difficult time with this 1937 state legislation if relations between the NCWUA and the sometimes bitter and antagonistic West Slope had not gradually improved. The threat of losing federally funded relief projects because of intrastate disunity worried East Slope negotiators. Their West Slope adversaries were already suspicious of the 1935 Conservation District Law, which they believed the legislature had enacted "to probably effect some of the transmountain diversion projects which were proposed at that time."[22] They had become convinced that Front Range interests were selfish and acquisitive, and for their own protection they rallied around Congressman Edward T. Taylor. When he promised to use his prestige and power in Congress to secure compensatory reservoirs "before the government puts any money into those blue sky transmountain diversion schemes," they felt more at ease in negotiating with the NCWUA.[23] To fully appreciate the intensity of the West Slope's attitudes as well as the ongoing conflict between both slopes over various water projects requires a review of the origins and activities of the West Slope Protective Association (WSPA) during its first five years.

On June 19, 1933, one month before Congress approved the Casper-Alcova project, the WSPA was born with a stated objective to protect western Colorado from loss of water from transmountain diversion to the east "and demands of Arizona and California to the West, according to President D. W. Aupperle."[24] Already convinced that "those Eastern Slope fellows" were in league with "the big sugar corporations" and that their man "Friday," Michael C. Hinderlider (state engineer), was blocking surveys of the Colorado River watershed, western Coloradans had organized into a protective association even before the Grand Lake Committee announced its formation.[25] Threatened by both the lower basin states and fellow Coloradans on the Front Range, as well as by the suspected inadequacy of their own water decrees on the Colorado River,[26] the WSPA had assumed a defensive posture toward northern Colorado's appeals for cooperation. From 1934 to 1937, however, this overt resistance and hostility gradually shifted to a more amicable spirit. Without the selfless leadership of Charles Hansen and Frank Delaney, detente would have been impossible.

Hansen knew all along that transmountain diversion from the Colorado River would require West Slope cooperation. Since the September 27, 1933, Denver meeting in George M. Bull's office, which several West Slope representatives attended, he had recognized the need to determine the effects of a C–BT Project on West Slope water users. He had asked engineer Royce J. Tipton to include this information in the study he launched the summer of 1933.[27] By the time the NCWUA was organized formally on April 6, 1934, reports from Tipton and his field man, L. L. Stimson, had already concluded that the Project was technically feasible. Hansen regretted not having maintained better contact with the WSPA during the interval since the Denver meeting,[28] but he remained sensitive to West Slope fears. The notice he drew up calling for a meeting of interested irrigationists at the Greeley Court House also pointed out that, before May, it would be necessary "to have some discussion with water users in the Grand Valley."[29]

Hansen's first overture was an inquiry letter to Walter Walker, publisher of the *Grand Junction Daily Sentinel*. "As one newspaperman to another," he wrote, the time had come to speak frankly about the proposed "diversion of some water out of the Colorado River into the territory of northern Colorado." Although it was a "touchy subject" when viewed politically, Hansen urged Walker to scrutinize the proposal from the standpoint of potential benefits to the West Slope. Plans were in the works, he said, to build a "storage reservoir of sufficient capacity to take care of any present needs for late water in the Grand Valley, and for future needs insofar as this can be determined by the most competent engineers that may be engaged." After requesting a meeting at an early date to work out a plan "mutually agreeable to both sides," he warned that delay would allow "other states" to appropriate currently unused waters of the Colorado River. He assured Walker that the East Slope's irrigation farmers wanted an "honorable and fair deal" with the West Slope; they harbored no unfriendly feelings. Personally, he desired to "heal the foolish breach that has existed for some time among certain elements on both sides of the Continental Divide."[30]

A few days later, Walker wrote to Aupperle, enclosing a copy of Hansen's letter. "You can follow up on this correspondence any way you want to," Walker advised, "but I must say that no newspaper man [sic] and no paper [*Greeley Tribune*] in northern or eastern Colorado have been more active through the years in fanning the very sentiment which he condemns." Unable to give personal time to the matter, Walker promised to continue in the future, "as I have in the past backing up the movement for the protection of western Colorado's interests."[31]

To Hansen, Walker expressed appreciation for the confidence placed in him and the "personal friendship manifested by your action in writing to me." He agreed that the building of internal strife and prejudices between the two slopes was unjustified, but he also revealed his feeling that both contingents shared the blame for present animosities. Although Walker accepted the idea of a meeting, he warned against too large a role for the state engineer, who was not trusted among men of the West Slope and who may have "on more than one occasion juggled statistics to suit the arguments of diversion proponents."[32]

After Aupperle received the Walker-Hansen correspondence, he wrote to Congressman Taylor that the "northern Colorado people" had agreed among themselves "that they must provide reservoir storage to replace such water as the West Slope needs for its protection." He had visited the designated site in the Williams Fork basin, with its 75,000 acre-foot capacity. He believed that it would "probably fully protect our interests in all the territory that can be affected by storage at that point." Furthermore, he pointed out to Taylor that, because the Twin Lakes Company had plans to increase its demand from the Roaring Fork River to 20,000 acre-feet and because several sites for reservoirs were available to protect existing water rights, the time was ripe to establish a precedent affecting all transmountain diversion. In fact, he concluded, "If a general plan can be worked out now to cover the entire water diversion question . . . we can well afford to give favorable consideration."[33]

On the same day, Aupperle wrote Hansen that the West Slope was already on record as willing to cooperate with the people of the East Slope "on any fair basis," as long as full protection of its water rights was an established fact. He was disappointed that northern Colorado had "followed the lead of an official and a few exploiters in attempts to put something over on us," and he suggested that this same leadership had gotten them into trouble with Wyoming. Aupperle was optimistic that "our Western Slope people will readily and heartily join in any sane sensible plan or program for conserving and using all available water within the state," but all plans, he noted, had to conform to the Colorado River Basin Compact.[34] Grand Junction was a fine place to hold a meeting.

In response, Hansen assured Aupperle that his people did not want to "deprive anybody of any rights or privileges now held or that they need for their future development." They wanted only to divert the water otherwise wasted down the Colorado River if not "employed" in Colorado. He expressed willingness to compensate West Slope people "to a reasonable extent," but if they asked too high a price, "then of course that will end the story." With united effort, Hansen said, and the cooperation of Congressman Taylor, the two slopes could and should work together to promote each other's economic development; the East Slope would buy West Slope cattle and fatten them on the grain and beet pulp produced with an adequate water supply, and both slopes would take advantage of cheaper electric rates from hydroelectric power. "Whatever has been in the past," he said, "should not be repeated, because other states are fattening on our dissension."[35]

While both sides expressed the need to meet, between the lines of their correspondence and implied in the subtle warnings they exchanged intruded a posture of defiance unameliorated by courteous and ingratiating phrases. If the East Slope constructed a transmountain diversion project, it must be prepared for the West Slope to exact its duty. Planted solidly behind one of the most powerful men in Congress, West Slope negotiators were dealing from a position of strength. Demands for compensatory storage, although not yet fully formed, had to remain the keystone of the West Slope's strategy. On the other side of "the hill," the northern Colorado people believed fervently that what they wanted was best for the entire state. They were so convinced of this that they occasionally showed impatience with what often appeared to them as West Slope provincialism. They planned to use every effort to obtain what they considered a fair agreement, but if the West Slope demanded too much in return, they would find ways to accomplish by force what they preferred to effect by negotiation.

The first meeting of the WSPA and the NCWUA took place in Grand Junction on April 27, 1934. Hansen made the arrangements, grumbling that it would take a day and a half to get there because "so much of the way [was] mountain roads."[36] Thus began a series of negotiations that continued off and on for more than three years.

The first session was introductory in nature. Although Hansen felt that the hosts treated his committee well, he was concerned that the West Slope people looked on the Project as a "promotion scheme by which some individuals may make a lot of money."[37] He assured them otherwise, pointing out that, except for the engineers, no one was being paid for his work. He also noted that Wyoming and Nebraska were planning to produce power out of North Platte water and sell it back to Colorado — all the more reason to support transmountain diversion with its hydroelectric possibilities. When the meeting ended, Hansen visited Grand Lake and Hot Sulphur Springs, where he found "no particular opposition to the Project so long as Western Slope water users were amply protected."[38]

Back in Greeley, Hansen suggested that NCWUA secretary J. M. Dille make direct contact with the West Slope water users, and he provided the names of people to see in Glenwood Springs and Grand Junction.[39] To Aupperle, Hansen expressed hope that the NCWUA and the WSPA could join together as one committee to "work out the details of the whole plan." He also urged that they "submit the whole question to the experts of the

Reclamation Service before much money is spent by anyone, or before we enter into obligation for a huge sum from the U.S. government."[40]

While Hansen was the primary negotiator with the West Slope, Dille used his talents and experience on the East Slope. Prior to his appointment as secretary of the NCWUA (later secretary-manager of the Northern Colorado Water Conservancy District [NCWCD]), he had been superintendent of both the Riverside and Bijou irrigation districts on the South Platte River. Water was his life. Those who knew him were aware of his toughness. Quiet, for the most part, Dille was known as an able, devoted, and conservative leader. He became a persuasive spokesman for the C–BT, argued with the Bureau over engineering details, spoke confidently to groups about the need to support the Project, and shunned public recognition. He was a practical man, self-educated, optimistic about finding solutions to problems, and a good delegator. With Hansen the public leader and strategist, Dille could be the master diplomat and craftsman. Although he tended to be autocratic at times and did not like to be crossed, he had few enemies. From the formation of the NCWCD in 1937 until his resignation as its first manager in 1958, Dille was identified with "the Northern." To many he was the District.

In 1934, however, Hansen was the principal diplomat with the West Slope. He and Aupperle became involved in planning for the upcoming Four States Water Conference (Upper Colorado River basin states), scheduled for June 29–30 in Denver. Aupperle wrote Taylor, urging him to attend and assuring him that the WSPA would not enter into any kind of agreement regarding transmountain diversion before this meeting and that they would "prepare well for the conference." "Working with the Bureau of Reclamation," he said, was acceptable, "but we made no suggestion about leaving the matter entirely in the hands of a Reclamation engineer . . . and confidentially, we have no intention of doing so. This, of course, is between us." Aupperle further added that finding local experts capable of determining water supply, water rights, and other engineering data was preferable to total dependency on the Bureau. For the moment, he concluded, a trip to Delta, Gunnison, and Montrose was necessary "to get our people up to speed and get things moving rapidly"[41] and to make sure that his constituency developed a proper sense of urgency about the delicate but vital negotiations.

A day before the four-state meeting, the Colorado delegation caucused to discuss its position. Tipton informed them of an arrangement worked out by the state engineer in 1929 concerning possible use of Colorado River water in the state. When Taylor arrived for the afternoon session, he urged state representatives to unify. Nonetheless, he pointed out that although the West Slope was receptive to sharing its water with Denver "the only way transmountain diversions for agricultural purposes could be safely done was to build compensatory reservoirs on the Western Slope equal in capacity to the amount of water to be diverted." He further reminded them that before the federal government would allow any money to be spent on transmountain diversions, a four-state compact had to be signed. The delegates then passed a resolution stipulating that "no transmountain diversions [would be] contemplated without fully protecting Western Slope users to the extent of their present and future needs."[42]

When state delegations met the next day, they adopted another resolution, part of which urged the federal government to appropriate $1 million "to complete the plan for the comprehensive development of the lands of the Colorado River Basin." Delegates asked the government to address both extra- and intra-basin uses of water in its survey.[43] Congressman Taylor and representatives from both slopes signed this document.

None of these developments promised a speedy resolution to northern Colorado's water problems. In November Hansen met with Aupperle to explain the seriousness of the domestic water shortage in Greeley, Fort Collins, and other towns. Asking for another conference, Aupperle suggested that the NCWUA "draft an outline of what they want[ed] in the matter of an agreement" to be sent to the WSPA in time for its board meeting.[44] Hansen agreed.

On November 27 the WSPA attempted for a second time to convene a quorum. Their officers had failed on November 22, and five days later they were still short several members. Determined to go ahead anyway, the assembled group addressed the matter of an "unnamed document purporting to be a tentative and suggested agreement between the Northern Colorado Water Users' Association and the Western [Slope] Colorado Protective Association."[45] After reviewing it item by item, directors B. M. Long and F. I. Huntington argued that the content was too indefinite and that the intent implied that eastern Colorado only wanted the WSPA's cooperation to obtain federal funding for that region's own benefit. Engineer F. C. Merriell doubted the power of the parties to contract; even if agreement were possible, he reminded the directors, in determining compensatory water storage, northern Colorado still had to absorb evaporation and loss by transfer. He warned that "western Colorado should take proper measures to protect itself against eastern Colorado's securing water power rights requiring a flow in addition to such period of flow as would be required for irrigation."[46]

Following several other objections, the participants decided to amend the draft agreement to say that if surplus waters existed in the Colorado River basin in the state, that part in excess of the "present and prospective needs" of the West Slope should be put to beneficial use on the East Slope. The amendments further stated that West Slope water rights remained guaranteed, that East Slope officials could request a Bureau survey of available water and probable diversion costs, and that until the Bureau study was completed, application for construction funds would be "based upon the building of replacement reservoirs of ample capacity at suitable locations to protect and supply present and future needs" of the West Slope. Finally, when a binding agreement was signed determining the amount of compensatory storage and protecting the "present and future needs" of western Colorado, the West Slope would render all assistance possible toward securing the funds required for Project development.[47]

The WSPA accepted a motion to send a copy of the draft to the East Slope, "with the understanding that the tentative agreement has not yet been submitted to all the directors of the Western [Slope] Colorado Protective Association, [and is being furnished] for the study and further comment of the Northern Colorado Water Users' Association."[48]

Three weeks later President Aupperle tactfully expressed his concern about the WSPA's apathy, pointing out that the East Slope was uniting "in dire need of water and desperate" to secure it from the West Slope. Because he believed that the NCWUA represented the entire South Platte basin and that Congress was about to set aside "a liberal sum" for public works, especially conservation projects, he reasoned that northern Colorado could get what it wanted.[49] In addition, he said, the Bureau seemed favorably disposed to build the Project. In Aupperle's eyes, the diversion of West Slope water was a matter of David confronting a powerful Goliath. If West Slope interests failed to unite energetically to negotiate with the imposing might of the Front Range giant, defeat seemed inevitable. His constituents had shown a lack of interest in the November 27 draft agreement; county commissioners had been equally unsuccessful in getting water users to fix their water rights "at the highest possible duty." Legislative sessions were about to begin in Washington and Denver with much at stake. If Aupperle failed to secure the assurance of "reasonable compensation, financial assistance for emergencies, and cooperation from the best minds in our territory to cope with the problems just ahead of us," he would feel compelled to resign as president of the WSPA.[50]

Aupperle got the board's attention. At the next scheduled meeting on December 28 in Grand Junction, six of the nine WSPA directors attended, as did a great many county commissioners and interested observers. After discussing the impact of several other diversion projects and the need to have a representative from the West Slope in the National Reclamation Association (NRA), a question surfaced about joining the East Slope in its $150,000 request for a Bureau survey of the proposed Grand Lake Diversion Project. Consensus favored the idea, even though Frank Delaney pointed out that endorsement of an individual project before a survey of the entire Colorado River basin was completed ran contrary to the agreement adopted at the Four-States Water Conference in Denver.[51]

Finally, after agreeing to compensate President Aupperle and Secretary Silmon Smith for their time at $25 per month[52] plus some expenses, the board of directors selected a committee made up of Judge E. M. Nourse, Delaney, and Smith to redraft the tentative agreement with the East Slope. Their efforts resulted in a significant amendment to paragraph 6, which reflected the pervasive influence of Congressman Taylor's insistence on acre-foot-for-acre-foot compensation:

> Sixth. IT IS TENTATIVELY AGREED That until the said survey is completed, the application for funds for the construction of the transmountain diversion projects shall be based upon the building of replacement reservoirs of ample capacity at suitable locations to protect and supply present and future needs of western Colorado, and, until such time as the United States Bureau of Reclamation submits a final report with detailed information as to the present and future requirements of the Western Slope of Colorado, IT IS UNDERSTOOD AND AGREED That all applications for funds for the initiation or construction of transmountain diversion projects shall be based upon a plan, or plans, which call for sufficient replacement reservoir capacity to store and permit to be released for use on the Western Slope *the same quantity of water stored for and/or diverted to the Eastern Slope.* After said report is submitted, it is declared to be the intention of the compacting parties hereto to enter into a further agreement as provided in paragraph seven hereof.

Leaving the NCWUA little time to review the revised tentative agreement, Aupperle went to Denver on January 1, 1935, where he met with Hansen, Moses E. Smith, Charles A. Lory, Nixon, Dille, Ben Wright, and others. Hansen told Aupperle in no uncertain terms that northern Colorado "could not accede to the plan of an acre-foot of compensation for an acre-foot of diversion; that it was both physically and financially impossible."[53] On his return to Grand Junction, Aupperle reported these views to the board, noting that after several phone calls and telegrams to

Charles Lory, president of Colorado A&M (Colorado State University) and NCWCD Board member from 1940–1954. (Courtesy Colorado State University Office of Instructional Services, Photographic Services.)

Washington, Taylor had agreed to the $150,000 survey, which would begin immediately and would "consume one year." Aupperle also reported that the NCWUA had wanted to finance the Project by establishing a conservancy district, "making all taxable property, farm, business, and home subject to the cost on the theory that the matter is of general interest and an economic necessity."[54] WSPA board members were becoming aware of subtle changes in the negotiations.

By early 1935 both committees had made some movement toward rapprochement. WSPA board members were more receptive to the East Slope's possible use of surplus Colorado River water because of renewed fears that Arizona and California were about to resolve their differences and unite against all the upper basin states.[55] They also wanted the Bureau to complete its review of water resources in the Colorado River basin before making further agreements with the NCWUA. True to his word, Taylor worked to this end, reminding Ickes that such a study had legislative authority under Section 15 of the 1928 Boulder Canyon Project Act.[56] Hinderlider echoed these sentiments when he urged participants in the Four-States Water Conference to put pressure on Ickes to complete the survey work.[57] Implementation took time, however, which sharpened East Slope impatience.

During the remainder of 1935, the WSPA and NCWUA remained preoccupied with their own concerns. While survey parties worked on the Grand Lake Diversion Project in August, both organizations used the time to consolidate their respective positions. For its part, the NCWUA was relieved to learn that the solicitor general had found no legal obstacle in running the survey through Rocky Mountain National Park.[58] Although the battle was far from over, the NCWUA was sufficiently encouraged to begin talks in August about a more general economic survey of all the lands "under the proposed Northern Colorado Transmountain Diversion."[59] To nourish grass-roots support for the C–BT Project on the East Slope, the Great Western Sugar Company instructed its field men to talk to growers, "making it a special point to bring up the subject with the thought . . . of getting as much interest aroused throughout the entire district . . . as we possibly can."[60]

In the meantime, Aupperle was busy strengthening his organization. As new counties showed interest in participating in the WSPA, he encouraged them to join. He attended meetings around the state where he felt the West Slope should be represented, and he expressed hope that WSPA directors would "take more definite action." Aupperle again raised the question of salary compensation and was gratified to have his stipend raised to $100 per month.[61] At the end of the year he received a congratulatory letter from Foster, expressing pleasure that Aupperle had made a plea for state unity at a Greeley meeting.[62] This was a good sign. It was supported by comments expressed at a second statewide water conference held in Grand Junction in early 1936. A spirit of cooperation was gradually beginning to develop.

In February 1936 a third statewide water conference convened in Grand Junction. A large number of people from both slopes attended, including water users; city, state, and local officials; attorneys; and interested citizens. Minutes indicate that the meeting was held under the auspices of the Colorado State Planning Commission (CSPC).[63] The Colorado delegation in Washington sent supportive telegrams and letters to urge conferees to cooperate in seeking hard information, thus easing the task of guiding legislation through Congress. Conference speakers urged cooperation with the CSPC, the agency responsible for formulating a state water program. Before the meeting adjourned, participants adopted resolutions that reflected the ever-present fear that a water grab by California and Arizona was imminent. Specifically, Resolution 8 protested against

federal aid for the Gila project in Arizona and for the Pilot Knob project
in California. Conferees opposed the former because Arizona had yet to
sign the Colorado River Compact. They objected to the latter on grounds
that a power plant close to the international border with Mexico might
enable that country to expand its irrigated acreage and make a claim against
the United States for more water.

In a lengthy letter to conference delegates, Taylor brought up another
dimension of the problem: the possibility that California would make "vast
appropriations" of water before construction of a transmountain diversion
project in Colorado and then would join with Arizona "in an injunction
proceeding to restrain . . . transmountain diversion unless we can show that
we are prior to them."[64] He had spotlighted one touchy question and
implied another: What would happen if the C–BT were built and the lower
basin states in a drought year made a call under the Colorado River
Compact for more water? Would the C–BT water be the first called?

For the moment no one had a clear answer, even though WSPA
members had been thinking about this possibility since 1934. In that year
a resolution prepared for the NCWUA suggested that if it were necessary
to deliver water "to fulfill any of the terms of the Colorado River Compact
which is in excess of the actual delivery of the Colorado River and its
tributaries at that time, then such water shall be supplied from the water
then being diverted or held for such transmountain diversion, and, if
necessary, the full extent thereof."[65] The agreement was never signed, but
when the Bureau prepared Senate Document 80 for approval by both slopes
in 1937, the "Manner of Operation," Section 5 {i}, included a statement
that protected the West Slope: If an obligation were created under the
Colorado River Compact "to augment the supply of water from the State
of Colorado to satisfy the provisions of said Compact, the diversion for the
benefit of the Eastern Slope shall be discontinued in advance of any
Western Slope appropriations."[66]

The "Manner of Operation" section of Senate Document 80 also
defined the several "purposes" of the Project, how Green Mountain Reservoir was to be operated, what compensation would be provided to Grand
County, and the operational role of the secretary of the interior. The three
critical pages of Senate Document 80 were finalized in Washington by East
Slope and West Slope representatives. As recalled by Silmon Smith
twenty-five years later, the "Manner of Operation" section was the only
part of Senate Document 80 created by both the NCWUA and the WSPA.
The rest of the document had been compiled by the Bureau. "When it came
time to put our thoughts on paper," Smith remembered, "there was no one

who seemed very keen to start dictating. . . . We appealed to John C. Page, who at this time was Commissioner of Reclamation, and with whom most of us were acquainted, for suggestions." Page agreed to help, and a stenographer was called to take down what these men had agreed to after four years of argument. "From time to time there would be suggestions and corrections," recalled Smith, "but the plan of dictation was that organized by John C. Page."[67]

Senate Document 80, unquestionably the most important document for construction and operation of the C–BT, has survived more than fifty years with relatively few modifications. Essentially written by Bureau staff, it represented agreements with the West Slope that Hansen said he would honor "to the best of my ability and conscience." Largely because of its agreed-upon stipulations, mutual respect gradually emerged as representatives of both slopes came to know and trust each other. Even Delaney — recognizing himself in March 1936 as a one-time extremist who still threatened to form a "protective alliance" with the lower basin states if the East Slope were to break faith — used his leadership to persuade colleagues that their demands should be moderated in favor of compromise. In a letter to attorney Dan Hughes of Montrose, he said, "I do not see how we can insist on any greater quantity of water than a thorough survey shows is sufficient to protect our present appropriations and reasonable future needs arising from further probable development of Western Slope agriculture, mining, and industry. We can not [sic] ask for more than we need."[68] At the very time that Congressman Taylor was insisting on acre-foot-for-acre-foot compensation and recommending that the WSPA protest to Secretary Ickes against further surveys for transmountain diversion until all upper basin states had the opportunity to review the Bureau's final report,[69] Delaney was leading his followers toward a compromise position that resulted in a written agreement with the NCWUA.

The basis for this agreement was partially finalized in Denver at the Shirley-Savoy Hotel in January 1937. Delaney asked Hansen to bring advisors to Denver to work out "some amicable and satisfactory compromise upon which we can proceed with some degree of assurance as to the future use of waters of the Colorado River."[70] Hansen arrived on January 3 with Dille, Nixon, and Kelly from the NCWUA and Porter Preston and Mills E. Bunger from the Bureau. After insisting that a call by lower basin states under the Colorado River Compact must first be met by Grand Lake or the Big Thompson Project, West Slope representatives Silmon Smith, Clifford Stone, Dan Hughes, Judge Clyde H. Stewart, and Delaney tentatively agreed to pay one-third of the cost of storage reservoirs in exchange for one-third of the profits from the power sales.[71] However, the WSPA had to consult with West Slope water users before any agreement could be formalized. To this end, a meeting was called for March 24, 1937, in Grand Junction.

At last, with a good turnout at the Grand Junction Court House, Delaney had a chance to speak his mind. He advised the gathering that this meeting, which was primarily for citizens, had been called to provide direction to the WSPA. The Bureau had completed its surveys, and that agency had already recommended going forward with construction. While the State Legislature still had to enact a law to create water conservancy districts, the new legislation was pending. Taylor, who had defeated Project appropriations in 1935 and 1936, could not hold the line forever. "In my opinion," he said "[C–BT] is coming, if not this year or a year from now, undoubtedly within five years."[72] "I am in favor of compromise," Delaney argued, "because the only thing that stands in the way of this project going forward without our having any say at all is the power and prestige of Mr. Taylor in Washington." From a legal standpoint, he continued, the waters of Colorado belong to the public; the state Supreme Court has already approved diversion of Colorado's waters to other basins. Furthermore, legislation in the Colorado Assembly to create conservancy districts, if enacted, would give these districts "tremendous and far-reaching powers." The West Slope would then be faced with an organization that has "the wealth and population to build this project even without the assistance of the federal government." According to the Bureau's figures, by holding the streamflow of the Colorado River at 1,250 cfs at the Shoshone Power Plant, "all rights could be met, and this could be done with a reservoir holding 152,000 acre-feet. Locating this reservoir at the right place would provide a much better stream, and a more valuable stream to the people who are using that water than at the present time."

In summary, Delaney said, northern Colorado "is now quite willing to cooperate with us to see that the cost of construction of that reservoir" is paid by some other entity. If WSPA allows the East Slope to divert 310,000 acre-feet, and if they build us our reservoir, Delaney said, northern Colorado will be meeting the West Slope on a fairer basis "than they will ever offer should there be a change of circumstances along the line that might be possible. I believe this thing is coming because it is feasible and can't be stopped."

As Delaney spoke, Taylor's shadow cast a spell over some of his listeners. Hansen knew that Taylor might use his influence to "wiggle" the Grand Junction meeting by remote control; Dille felt that even if Taylor were absent, "the reflected power from the ghost of the savior of the West Slope" was a powerful presence, capable of undermining logic and a spirit of compromise.[73] But, except for a few diehards, most participants were favorably inclined toward Delaney's reasoning. Judge Stewart of Delta County reminded delegates that Taylor was an aging representative who, when he died, would be the last member of the Appropriations Committee to thwart C–BT funding. What was proposed to northern Colorado by the WSPA was

> not so much what was desired as what we thought we could get. . . . No matter how much we talk of our rights, in population and political authority the Eastern Slope outnumbers us 10:1. We can't stop them. . . . It is not a question here of whether we want to see our house burn down or not, but what we can get out of it while it is burning; whether we are going to take what we can get — and I am in favor of getting all we can — or whether we should say, "No, they haven't any business to set fire to our house," and sit here and let it burn.[74]

Silmon Smith, WSPA secretary, supported Stewart's views. He pointed out that Taylor was in a hot spot. "He started out on a foot-for-foot, acre-for-acre compensation basis, [but] you can't justify that position from an engineering standpoint." That was why Smith had suggested forming a committee to deal with the NCWUA. Made up of Delaney, Hughes, Stone, and Smith, this group "sweat a lot of blood," and tensions were so high during the first meetings that "we could not say goodbye when we got through with the conference." In the last few months, however, "we have concluded that these people are not out to harm us. We even have dinner with them. . . . It didn't used to be that way." In addition, argued Smith, the Bureau had no designs to "cheat or double-cross western Colorado." The new commissioner, John C. Page, "grew up here. He knows western Colorado . . . is an able and fair man, and he wouldn't be party to anything that would be improper for western Colorado." Because northern Colorado apparently had agreed to build and pay for a reservoir to contain enough water for the West Slope's future development, and because the NCWUA had made clear that nobody's present rights were going to be interfered with and that the West Slope would have "better than the natural flow" during the entire irrigation season, the WSPA should not let an opportunity such as this pass by, leaving it with nothing.

The loudest protest came from Kremmling banker Carl Breeze, who argued that negotiators had overlooked the people of Grand County. He

Representative Edward T. Taylor (left) and Commissioner John C. Page (right). This gavel was presented to Taylor by the National Reclamation Association in appreciation of his interest in water conservation in the arid West. (Courtesy Colorado Historical Society.)

pointed out that Denver had already dried up the Williams Fork; the C–BT would dry up the Colorado River, leaving only Muddy Creek untouched. He estimated the annual loss of $15,000 to $18,000 in tax revenue with the building of Green Mountain Reservoir, which, in its contemplated location, would provide no benefit at all to Grand County. His conclusion: block the C–BT. "We don't intend to sit still and not be heard from over here."[75]

At this point, Delaney rose for the last time. He told the Grand County delegates that there had never been any attempt to double-cross them. "If I overlooked the situation in which Grand County is, it was unintentional." He had previously suggested hiring an engineer to establish the facts regarding the best reservoir site; nothing had happened. County leaders had failed to call meetings that he had hoped to convene in Grand County. His objective at this point was to implement a survey that would clearly locate a reservoir site beneficial to Grand County. Almost immediately, participants moved and adopted a motion to this effect.

Still, said Delaney, "our situation is that we have to say something to these fellows [NCWUA]. We can't indefinitely say, 'Well, let's wait.' They are not going to wait. They are going to try to pass [the Water Conservancy District Act]." Delaney begged the assembly to reach a decision. "You can talk about compensating us [WSPA], but it is too late for that. What you have got to talk about is what you want us to say to those people. Do you want us to say that we are going on with these things and try to work it out, or do you want us to say, 'No, stop it!' If we can stop it, we will and call all bets off and just go down the hill." Referring to the WSPA, he admonished, "Do you think any set of men are [sic] going to keep sticking out their necks to have their heads cut off? Especially when you haven't any cooperation and you can't get any cooperation?"[76]

Delaney's threats brought action. At the March 24, 1937, meeting, H. F. Lake from Gunnison proposed a motion to empower and back the committee composed of Stone, Stewart, Delaney, Hughes, and Smith "to go ahead and negotiate in future dealings" and to make arrangements that members deemed necessary. The motion, seconded by Roy Sisac of Grand Junction, met with no objections. An additional motion by Alfred M. Sloss, Eagle County commissioner, seconded by engineer F. I. Huntington of Hot Sulphur Springs, was also approved. It authorized WSPA directors to approve or disapprove the actions of the ad hoc committee. The record reveals no objections.

Delaney was now able to proceed with some sense of legitimacy. For the next three months, committees from the WSPA and the NCWUA worked toward the final agreement while Grand County continued to advance demands for financial compensation and for additional water to be added to the Colorado River between the Fraser River and the proposed dam site.[77] Both sides continued the dialogue. By April Grand County's only complaint was sufficient minimum streamflow for Colorado River fishermen.[78] Grand County protests had an annoying effect on the NCWUA. The usually demure and diplomatic Hansen suggested that the governor telephone Carl Breeze to tell him that "this is a state project and is going through whether they consent or not."[79] Such arrogance was born of four years' hard work and frustration.

The Bureau's final report and the Water Conservancy District Act of May 13, 1937, prompted Governor Ammons's inviting representatives of both slopes to sign an agreement in Washington that could be submitted with the Bureau's recommendations and Taylor's approval. Unfortunately, the congressman was not well. In April doctors had confined him to his apartment with a bad cold; by May he was in a sanitarium.[80] Taylor was in a key position to kill the Project even at this stage. Hansen, already in Washington, knew this only too well. Writing to Dille, he said that "regardless what his people may want or say," he has "left word with his committee to kill Grand Lake if it showed." Meanwhile, Congressman Lewis and Senator Johnson were fighting hard as "pitcher and catcher," but "just what the batter [Taylor] will do to them," mused Hansen, "is something else again."[81]

Taylor's ill health was a blessing for C–BT proponents. While Hansen complained that heat in Washington "even without a controversy" caused sweat in his pajamas at 5:30 A.M., Taylor was isolated. When Delaney, Stone, and Moses Smith joined Hansen and Nixon in the capital, they were able to discuss their differences without feeling his pressure. The only irritant they faced was Grand County's A. C. "Doc" Sudan, who continued to insist on what was to Hansen an exorbitant amount of water to satisfy fishermen in the Colorado River.[82] While these discussions continued, two significant developments occurred in Colorado: organization of the Colorado Water Conservation Board (CWCB) and creation of the Colorado River Water Conservation District (CRWCD).

House Bill 6, "An Act Relating to the Waters of the State of Colorado; Providing for the Control, Protection and Development Thereof; and Making an Appropriation Therefore,"[83] created the CWCB. It was to consist of twelve members, including the governor, attorney general, state engineer, director of the CSPC, an overall director to be appointed, and seven members chosen by the governor — three from the West Slope and four from the East Slope and the San Luis Valley. The board's duties resembled those of the Committee of Seventeen of the State Planning Commission: to promote the conservation of waters in Colorado in order to secure the greatest utilization and prevention of floods; to promote irrigation projects and conservancy districts; to assist such agencies in getting financing; to gather data; to cooperate with the United States in making surveys; to prepare legislative drafts; and to protect the rights of Colorado in interstate matters. The act, which was approved by the Assembly and signed by the governor on June 1, 1937, went into effect immediately.

Six days later House Bill 504 passed as "An Act to Provide for the Creation of a Water Conservation District, to be called the 'Colorado River Water Conservation District' [CRWCD]." Designed to unite Mesa, Garfield, Pitkin, Eagle, Delta, Gunnison, and Summit counties, the district's purpose was to conserve the Colorado River for "storage, irrigation, mining, and manufacturing purposes, and the construction of reservoirs, ditches and works for the purpose of irrigation and reclamation of additional lands not yet irrigated as well as to furnish a supplemental supply for lands now under irrigation."[84] Delaney had previously recommended this kind of organization to the West Slope, and on June 7, 1937, it became an accomplished fact. The WSPA continued to operate until August 11, 1938, when the CRWCD took over with considerably expanded duties.[85]

During that same week in Washington, all concerned with the C–BT were taking final steps toward an agreement. On June 6 Nixon wrote, "We will probably agree with the West Slope tomorrow, but it looks doubtful about Grand County. If we cannot agree, the Bureau will write the document and send it to the Senate anyway."[86] Five days later, negotiators reached an accord. On June 12 Hansen telegraphed triumphantly to Dille: "Taylor approved East/West Slope settlement today. Hurrying necessary documents and other matters to Senate early in the week. Looks now like project [to] go through without much trouble. Asking for $1 million to start."[87] He had attained his second objective. Although Taylor, the NPS, Grand County, environmentalists, and a host of other critics were still planning to derail the Project that Hansen had fought so hard to launch, for the time being, victory was his. Taylor had approved letters of agreement from both slopes that he had sent to Secretary Ickes along with the Bureau's final report by Mills E. Bunger, constituting what eventually became Senate Document 80. But Hansen failed to foresee the political shoals that would force his protracted stay in Washington. Back home, Dille fought a different set of battles with small but vocal groups who vehemently opposed inclusion in the newly formed NCWCD. The four-year fight had been long and difficult. Considerable progress had been made, but many battles still lay ahead for proponents of supplemental water for northern Colorado.

5

Appropriation, Authorization, and Organization: C–BT Finds a Window of Opportunity

History-making events sometimes occur when a myriad of related and unrelated forces converge at precisely the right moment. At any other time, no matter how holy or logical the cause, results will be different. In the case of the C–BT Project, congressional appropriations were obtained when a window of opportunity appeared. If East and West Slopes had delayed signing their agreement a little longer, if Congressman Edward T. Taylor had not been hospitalized early in the summer of 1937, and if President Roosevelt's Supreme Court-packing plan had not distracted Congress from its newly found desire to economize and balance the budget,[1] northern Colorado's four-year struggle for supplemental water from the Colorado River might have ended in failure. Instead, the hard work of Charles Hansen, J. M. Dille, and others paid off in the form of a congressional appropriation, approval of the NCWCD by eligible voters, and a Repayment Contract signed with the Bureau of Reclamation. All of this happened very quickly.

Since April 1937, Congressman Fred Cummings had been warning Hansen that prospects were still uncertain in Washington. "There seems to be a wave of so-called economy, or rather an effort to curtail expenses, seizing the Capitol at present," he wrote. "Just how it will affect us will be hard to say," but members of Congress "have just about wakened up to the fact that we have been spending a lot of money, and they seem to think that it can be paid back by cutting every appropriation that is suggested."[2] Senator Edwin C. Johnson also saw a mood change in Congress that signaled difficulties ahead for approval of a C–BT appropriation.[3]

Both men had sized up the situation correctly. Although the C–BT was not yet victimized by increasingly frequent demands to balance the budget, everyone in Washington was aware that New Deal spending had yet to produce the promised economic recovery. With elections coming in 1938, congressmen were increasingly outspoken about the need to return to more

Fort Morgan's John M. Dille, the
NCWCD's first manager from 1937–
1958, worked tirelessly to get the C–BT
built. (Courtesy NCWCD.)

conservative economic policies. All through summer and fall 1937, members who had previously accepted pump-priming federal expenditures
without question, took more critical looks at bills needing their votes.[4]
Hansen and the Colorado delegation knew that the proper legislation for
authorization and funding must be introduced with dispatch before the
window of opportunity closed forever.

Senator Alva B. Adams took the lead. While Hansen prepared the
"necessary documents and other matters"[5] as quickly as possible, the
senator first asked unanimous consent for printing the Bureau's "Synopsis
of Report" as Senate Document 80. Approved and ordered into print on
June 15, this document contained Mills E. Bunger's final report on how the
C–BT Project was to be built and operated, the assignment of costs to the
NCWCD and the United States, and the integration of power and pumping systems with the delivery of irrigation water on the East Slope. It also
included a letter of transmittal from the Bureau's senior engineer, Porter J.
Preston, to the Bureau's chief engineer, R. J. Walter, along with letters of
submittal dated June 11, 1937, from both the WSPA and the NCWUA.[6]
Worked out with great care during the previous four years, Senate Document 80 became the governing authority for construction and maintenance of the C–BT system; its viability today speaks to the wisdom of those
who first negotiated C–BT terms and conditions.

Three days after the acceptance of Senate Document 80, Senator Adams introduced Senate Bill 2681, "A bill (S. 2681) to authorize construction of the Grand Lake–Big Thompson transmountain water diversion project as a Federal reclamation project; to the Committee on Irrigation and Reclamation."[7] Congressman Cummings explained that "due to the fact that essential legislation had not passed in the Colorado legislature, and the agreement between Eastern Slope and Western Slope people in Colorado was not completed until after the Interior Department bill had been passed in the House,[8] it was necessary to present this [authorization] measure first in the Senate."[9] Cummings might also have noted that in the past, Congressman Taylor had treated similar bills with little respect. Adams knew that the Senate was more tractable; he also knew that if senators passed an authorization bill, he would have the right to add an appropriation item to the Department of the Interior appropriation bill. Referred to the Senate Committee on Irrigation and Reclamation, Senate Bill 2681 received a favorable report with only the suggestion that it be debated as the "Colorado"–Big Thompson Project instead of the "Grand Lake"–Big Thompson Project.[10] After a quick hearing before the Senate Subcommittee on Appropriations, where Bureau Commissioner John C. Page gave his solid support,[11] the bill was sent to the House, where once again it passed unscathed through the Committee on Irrigation and Reclamation. This committee recommended approval by the whole House.[12]

Hansen began to sense imminent victory. While awaiting debate on Senate Bill 2681 by the full House, he received word that the Interior Department appropriation bill, with $900,000 allocated for the C–BT, had passed the Senate and arrived June 30 in the House from the conference committee.[13] Although frustrated by delays from July 4 festivities, Hansen told Dille back in Greeley that he felt optimistic. Dille responded euphorically that the Chamber of Commerce was planning to meet him with a band when he stepped off the train, "so you better have the porter brush you off well."[14]

But patience had become increasingly necessary. As Hansen baked in the muggy heat of Washington in July, he realized that almost anything could happen to either the authorization or appropriation bills pending before Congress. The Colorado delegation was also nervous. Representative Lawrence Lewis appealed to the House to concur with the Senate amendment to the Interior Department appropriation bill, arguing that this request for reclamation funds was Colorado's first for the "eastern part of our state," that it would not bring new acreage under cultivation, and that it would supplement existing and presently insufficient water supplies.[15]

Every effort would be required to convince Congress that the C–BT would not put new acreage under production or increase the harvest of surplus agricultural products. Congressman Cummings, meanwhile, blitzed his colleagues with letters that described the real purpose and expected benefits of the C–BT.[16]

Controversy continued to stall progress of both bills. Apart from congressional concerns about overspending, C–BT funding came under criticism because members of the Colorado delegation had not voted unanimously in the past for New Deal programs, behavior they might now regret.[17] Additionally, key congressmen were under acute pressure from the National Parks Association and from the National Resources Board to vote against the C–BT. Both groups represented powerful conservation lobbies that feared the C–BT tunnel under Rocky Mountain National Park would damage the environment and serve as an opening wedge for reclamation projects in other national parks.[18] With Secretary Harold L. Ickes in the hospital and other business of greater urgency demanding attention, the House was not able to vote until July 22 on the Department of the Interior appropriation bill carrying $900,000 in Amendment 90 for the C–BT.

Pennsylvania Congressman Robert F. Rich felt angry. Why appropriate more money for a reclamation project, he asked, when the Department of Agriculture is trying to reduce production? "This is the time of economy, not additional expenditures."[19] Representative John Taber of New York agreed and recommended rejecting C–BT funding "because of the fact that it is inadvisable economically to go ahead with more reclamation projects with the present agricultural situation in this country."[20] Others presented similar objections while stressing the possibility of real damage to Rocky Mountain National Park. The Colorado delegation fought back. Cummings reviewed the national importance of their state's agriculture, further warning that Colorado River water left unused in Colorado would flow to Mexico; Mexicans would raise cheap cotton, which would then travel to Japan to be made into cheap clothes to be marketed eventually in the United States.[21] Colorado Congressman John Martin noted that the Project, which was practical and acceptable to both slopes, would get the "landless water to the waterless land."[22] Lewis, making an impassioned appeal to his colleagues, said that Colorado was in fact "fighting for life. In this vote today, there is involved the future existence of northern Colorado." Not only was the Project necessary, Lewis said, but the very man (Taylor) who had opposed it "for good and sufficient reasons," had expressed his hope that "the House would concur in the Senate amendment to the Interior Department appropriation bill which provides $900,000 for

Rocky Mountain National Park was created in 1915, although lands for a potential transmountain diversion project were withdrawn in 1905. This view is looking SE from Trail Ridge Road with Forest Canyon below. (Courtesy Bureau of Reclamation.)

beginning construction of this project."[23] The House concurred, but the margin of victory was small: 174 yeas, 154 nays, and 103 not voting.

On August 9, 1937, by signature of the president, House Report 6958 became Public Law 249. One small part of this act appropriated construction money to the C–BT, "*Provided,* That no construction thereof shall be commenced until the repayment of all costs of the project shall, in the opinion of the Secretary of the Interior, be assured by appropriate contracts with water conservancy districts, or irrigation districts or water users' associations organized under the laws of Colorado, or other form of organization satisfactory to the Secretary of the Interior."[24] Money had been appropriated, but Congress had not yet formally authorized the C–BT.

The authorization bill, Senate Bill 2681, suffered an ignominious fate; it never arrived on the House floor for debate. After extensive hearings before the Committee on Irrigation and Reclamation on June 30 and July 2, resulting in the committee's recommendation for passage, the House took no further action. However, the bill had served two purposes. Senate approval had made possible the inclusion of Amendment 90 in the Department of the Interior appropriation bill,[25] providing the C–BT with the first funding allocation; and all arguments against the C–BT had been aired in the House hearings, thereby exposing the national parks people as its most vocal critics.

The act that created Rocky Mountain National Park (RMNP) on January 26, 1915, provided in part that the "United States Reclamation Service may enter upon and utilize for flowage or other purposes any area within said park which may be necessary for the development and maintenance of a Government reclamation project."[26] Nevertheless, organizations and individuals remained convinced that a project such as the C–BT violated the letter if not the spirit of national park legislation and were determined to use their collective power to prevent transmountain diversion of water under or out of RMNP. Throughout summer and fall 1937, Senator John Bankhead, chairman of the Senate Irrigation and Reclamation Committee, received anti–C–BT protest letters. Most claimed that a tunnel under the park threatened to "destroy the primitive quality [of the Parks] . . . [as well as] the Congressional precedent upon which the entire primeval system depends."[27] Questioning the removal of water from a public park for the benefit of a particular locality, they pressed their previously stated position — the "opening wedge" argument — that approval of Senate Bill 2681 would damage the natural scenery and result in additional raids on other national parks.[28]

At the House hearings on Senate Bill 2681, a variety of groups voiced related concerns. G. H. Collingwood, chief forester for the American Forestry Association, reiterated his organization's opposition to building reservoirs for irrigation purposes in any of the national parks. Despite denials of this, he spoke of the "grave danger that some of the lakes within the park [might] be drained as a result of fissures that [might] be developed."[29] M. D'Arcy Magee, national vice-president of the Izaak Walton League, objected "emphatically" to the bill because of the possible encroachment of the tunnel into the park. In his view, this degradation of the park would negatively affect tourism in Colorado.[30] Dora A. Padgett, librarian for the American Planning and Civic Association, read a telegram from Frederic A. Delano, relative of President Roosevelt and chairman of the National Resources Committee, who based opposition to the bill on his personal aversion to depriving one region of water to benefit another. She also introduced into the record an "editorial" by Horace M. Albright, former director of the NPS, who questioned adding irrigation facilities to the Big Thompson area "or for that matter in any area under present conditions of agriculture." To him this was a "backward step."[31]

Backward step or not, Secretary Ickes became sufficiently concerned about the protests to call a meeting for November 12 in Washington so that "protestants and proponents of the Colorado–Big Thompson Project [could] present their views." Because Ickes had the power to approve reclamation projects without congressional authorization, he wanted to know "first hand" the reasons for and against the Continental Divide tunnel.[32] For proponents of the C–BT, this meeting was of enormous importance.

Ironically, negotiations between the NPS and Bureau had focused since early July on the problems identified by opponents of the C–BT. The two departments had reached a temporary solution. On July 3 Hansen wrote Dille that the NPS would be satisfied if it could receive some free water and electricity from the Project. The "wildlifers, who just don't know what they are talking about," he said, would have their pins knocked entirely out from under them if this could be accomplished.[33] A week later, Commissioner Page wrote Congressman Cummings that the Bureau would, in fact, "furnish not to exceed three cubic feet of water per second to offset losses in existing rights occasioned by the consumptive use of an equivalent amount for park purposes." The park would also receive free power for its own use, plus power to sell to other interests in the park, while trails and roads of the C–BT Project would be built to meet the approval of the secretary of the interior.[34]

Ickes faced a dilemma. He loved both the Bureau and the NPS, although they were still on opposite sides of this issue. He was troubled by his own conflicting desire for power (personal and hydroelectric) on the one hand and his empathy — inherited from Horace Albright — for the protection of natural resource aesthetics on the other. Ickes came to the November 12 meeting with every hope that his dilemma would be resolved by the participants, knowing full well that one of his options was to nullify the $900,000 appropriation that Congress had made a few months earlier.

Ickes asked Page to speak first. Page pointed out that Colorado would not have approved cession of land to RMNP had there been no provision in the enabling legislation that authorized reclamation projects for irrigation. He noted that the Project would cost $44 million, that this estimate would increase by 50 percent if a tunnel were located around the southern border of the park, and that, with Ickes's approval of an existing interdepartmental agreement, the park was going to get free water and electricity.[35]

The next speaker, NPS director Arno B. Cammerer stated that the NPS respected both the law that created RMNP and the congressional appropriation made to the C–BT. At the same time, he argued, Congress had established the national parks "to conserve the scenery and natural and historic objects and wildlife therein by such means as will leave them unimpaired for the enjoyment of future generations." He feared that debris from the eastern side of the main tunnel would be dumped into an area that had been authorized as a future addition to the park. Similarly, at the West Portal, where another section was destined for inclusion, Cammerer anticipated flooding by an artificial reservoir. If the C–BT were built, he concluded, supervision under very strict controls was essential.[36]

Other speakers echoed comments from hundreds of letters and testimonials sent to House and Senate committees, mostly well-worn emotional themes. Ickes's final statement asked the audience to empathize with his position as both secretary of the interior and as a conservationist. "I am not convinced that there should be the taking of water from one watershed to another," he began. "I am opposed to it, — but, it goes further than the National Park Service." Rocky Mountain National Park came into existence with a condition unique to that park alone, he said: the inclusion of a reclamation project for irrigation. The United States accepted this condition — a condition as good in 1937 as in 1915. Likewise, the $900,000 appropriation was "the most recent declaration of policy" by Congress, which can change and unmake laws, but the law of the moment must be obeyed. Ickes concluded, "I cannot follow my own will in the matter before us. I have to follow the law and I tell you very frankly that between the Bureau of Reclamation and the Park Service, I am for the Parks, but I am sworn to obey the law. . . . I wish the baby had not been laid at my doorstep, but it is there. . . . Pray for me!"[37]

All that remained under the Reclamation Act was for Ickes to present a finding of feasibility on the C–BT Project to President Roosevelt for his signature. Understanding that the congressional appropriation mandated beginning the Project, he felt that he would not be performing his duty were he to arrive at a finding of infeasibility for some "trivial reason." At the appropriate moment, therefore, he sent a "letter of justification" to Roosevelt, who approved the finding of feasibility on December 21, 1937.[38]

The responsibility for advancing the Project now lay with the people of northern Colorado, who had to organize a conservancy district (already authorized by a state law of May 13, 1937) and to draw up a satisfactory Repayment Contract as called for in Amendment 90 of the Interior Department Appropriation Act for fiscal year 1938. As Hansen had provided essential leadership in Washington, Dille now exercised his own talents to bring about NCWCD organization at home. His job was to get voter approval of a district under terms of the Water Conservancy District Act, which vested the district courts "in and for any county [with] jurisdiction, power and authority . . . to establish water conservancy districts."[39]

Before forming a district, however, Project leaders had to file a petition in the office of the clerk of the court.

Dille's task was to circulate petitions for the proposed district and to establish its boundaries. He had prepared hundreds of petitions "containing the name of the proposed District, the purpose, detailed description of the area, the assessed value, designation of divisions, and number of Directors for each and the prayer to the court for organization."[40] That job alone was extremely time consuming. Complaining to Hansen about how much "pushing and nagging" was necessary to get the required signatures, Dille expressed gratitude to the "Sugar Co. men" at Fort Collins and Loveland who were doing the bulk of the work.[41] At one time he estimated that they had collected 1,487 verified signatures plus 163 still circulating. He later agonized over county assessors' disqualification of so many signatures for technical reasons, concluding that there would not be very many to spare when the final tally was made.[42]

Dille's aides and volunteers held petition meetings in all population centers where publicity would do some good. Dille later singled out the work of Charles A. Lory, Harry Farr, and Moses E. Smith as exemplary.[43] But the biggest obstacle to rapid district organization came from some ditch and reservoir companies, whose owners feared that the proposed C–BT Project jeopardized the sale of their water at the same high margins of profit. Bob Wykert, for example, waged "a strenuous campaign" against the proposed district, calling it a "speculative scheme," whose taxing authority threatened the loss of farmers' property.[44] State Representative Moses E. Smith put down this "insurrection" when he spoke in favor of the Project at several meetings held in Ault, Wykert's backyard.[45]

A far more lengthy battle took place with Platteville farmers, led by Roy Briggs, who headed a delegation that came storming into Dille's office in Greeley. This group, upset that its land was included in the proposed district, "demanded that it be taken out right now or they would start a protest petition."[46] Dille responded that he was unable to comply immediately, explaining the procedure for withdrawing lands at a later date, but Briggs continued on the attack, sarcastically criticizing the "whole theory of indirect benefits and seem[ing] very anxious to talk [the] crowd into trouble which would give him a job and a place in the limelight."[47] Dille, who assured him that no one would be forced into the proposed district against his will, expressed complete conviction that Briggs's problems could be worked out if they did not get into a big rush. Briggs promised to wait a while "before starting the fireworks," and Dille, in an airmail letter to

Washington, implored NCWUA attorney Thomas A. Nixon to find some way to "allay their fears of being rendered destitute by the mill taxes."[48]

Nixon telegraphed that whatever the NCWUA Board decided suited him, while Hansen, in a separate and "confidential" telegram, urged Dille to stonewall the Platteville protesters. Protesting petitions, he emphasized, could not be circulated under the terms of the Water Conservancy District Act until petitioning for approval was complete. He urged delay and suggested that Dille speed up his search for supporting signatures.[49] In a letter written on the same day, Hansen released some of his own frustrations, suggesting to Dille several counterattacks. He noted that changes in district boundaries were inevitable, and the Platteville problem could be considered along with others of a similar nature "in the proper time. Meantime," he advised,

> If Briggs wants to be the leader of a movement to wreck the Project, let him have the honor. The best defense against him is to push the signing of petitions for the District so hard and fast that he can't get up a protesting petition. They will try to scare people by misrepresentations. Don't answer them directly through the papers, but keep on putting out true statements about every phase of the Project and plan of financing. In other words, create such a surge of opinion in favor of [the Project], that the opposition cannot be heard.

He urged making "full use" of the Great Western Sugar Company, along with a commitment "to see that no injustice is done to anyone. If such a promise is insufficient, and they are [still] determined to fight, let's give them all we have."[50] Taking his cue from Hansen, Nixon wrote Dille two days later that "if Briggs comes up with some more objections, be sure and tell him where to get off."[51]

Meanwhile, the Platteville delegation took its case to a June 5 meeting of the NCWUA Board and obtained a resolution excluding the Platteville district from the proposed NCWCD.[52] True to Hansen's predictions, an additional number of exclusion petitions surfaced in the weeks and months that followed, mostly from landowners in Boulder County. The Board dealt with many of these at its February 5, 1938, meeting.[53]

The boundary question still required Dille's attention. The Board instructed him to drive through the irrigated district for the purpose of establishing temporary boundaries.[54] His biggest problem proved to be the Boulder Creek area, because the feasibility of routing a ditch into that area and from there to the Platte River had not been studied.[55] The Board wanted to include the city of Boulder, "but most of the city officials doubted the feasibility of the C–BT and were opposed to inclusion. It was finally decided to include only the lower Boulder valley which could be served directly by a canal from the St. Vrain to Boulder Creek. The south line was located on section lines following the course of the Lower Boulder and Coal Ridge Ditches."[56] Other lines were drawn "at the closest section line to the established ditches and irrigated areas," finally including 2,316 sections totaling 1,481,600 acres.[57]

With a sufficient number of signatures, NCWUA attorneys entered a formal petition for organization with the clerk of the District Court of Weld County on July 19, 1937, three days before Congress debated and approved the $900,000 appropriation measure. The document listed the name of the proposed district, described the property within the seven counties, and detailed its purpose of conserving, developing, and stabilizing the supplies of water for domestic, irrigation, power, manufacturing, and other beneficial uses.[58] As required by the Water Conservancy District Act, the court set a hearing for September 20, 1937, when Hansen, Lory, engineer Porter Preston, and others would present testimony before the Honorable Judge Claude C. Coffin concerning the plans and purpose of the proposed district. Dille introduced the required petitions "signed by more than the required number of taxpayers." Because opponents had not filed protest petitions, the judge signed the decree in Proceeding Number 9454 on the docket of the court, declaring the NCWCD organized.[59]

On September 28 Judge Coffin appointed the members of the NCWCD Board as follows: Boulder County — William E. Letford and Ray Lanyon; Larimer County — Robert C. Benson, Ed F. Munroe, and Ralph W. McMurry; Weld County — Charles Hansen, Moses E. Smith, and William A. Carlson; Morgan and Washington counties — J. M. Dille; Logan County — Robert J. Wright; and Sedgwick County — Charles M. Rolfson. At its first meeting the newly elected Directors took the prescribed oath of office and executed a corporate surety bond as required by law.[60] Hansen was elected president and chairman of the Board, and Dille was appointed secretary of the Board and manager of the District. An official seal was approved, and an agreement was reached to raise operating funds by a tax levy of three-tenths of one mill of assessed valuation on real and personal property within the District. Before adjourning, the Board gave a "rising vote of thanks to Dr. Charles A. Lory in appreciation of his services in advancing and establishing the Colorado–Big Thompson Project and for his advice and assistance in bringing to a successful conclusion the organization of the Northern Colorado Water Conservancy District."[61]

The NCWUA continued to function with a slightly different group of Directors. After providing the NCWCD Board with additional monies to meet expenditures for a few months, it became inoperative in July 1938, when a Repayment Contract was signed with the United States.[62] Securing voter approval of this contract — the official promise to retire a federal construction loan (the $900,000) — as dictated by Amendment 90 to the Department of the Interior appropriation bill served as the final step in preparing the District for C–BT construction.

Although NCWUA leaders had discussed the question of repayment many months earlier when they were drawing up the Water Conservancy District Act, the newly formed NCWCD Board first addressed a draft Repayment Contract at its meeting of March 21, 1938. Directors and attorneys agreed to meet with the Bureau in Denver for further discussion on March 28 and 29. At this meeting, the Board authorized Dille to employ engineer Royce J. Tipton to prepare any material "that might enable the Board of Directors to make the most favorable decision concerning the construction features and concerning the allocation of costs between the power features and the irrigation features."[63]

The problems were nothing if not complex. The Bureau had not previously contracted with a water district to provide supplemental water; past projects had provided new water to unreclaimed lands. In its agreement with the NCWCD, the Bureau was breaking new ground. Its officials also had to consider the results of a recently formed Repayment Commission that had spent fifty-seven days studying repayment provisions in fifteen western states.[64] Among other loose threads in negotiations, the NCWCD Board knew that a Repayment Contract had to be approved in a special election. Voters would need the security of a fixed obligation that was reasonable in terms of production expectations and consistent with the terms of the Water Conservancy District Act.

Known as "The Colorado Plan,"[65] the NCWCD Repayment Contract was ultimately hammered out at conferences in Colorado and Washington in which Hansen, Nixon, and Tipton played leading roles. On May 8, 1938, Tipton sent Hansen an outline of the understanding reached the day before "by the Bureau and your committee with respect to change in allocation costs between power and irrigation and a clearer outline of the manner in which the Project shall be operated." Tipton noted the allocation of one-half the Project cost to power facilities and one-half to irrigation. In regard to operations, he said, "the need of water for irrigation shall have preference over the demands and need of water for power," but to assure a minimum quantity of firm electrical energy, a minimum of 225,000 acre-feet was to be delivered through the tunnel.[66]

Problems remained. On May 23 the NCWCD Board met to discuss a draft of the contract revised on May 14. Directors reviewed each of the articles, approving operation of the Project primarily for irrigation and accepting allocation of construction costs on a fifty-fifty basis to power and irrigation works. The Board also approved a tentative estimated construction obligation of $22 million with a "total obligation of the District under this contract for construction" not to exceed $25 million.[67] All parties fully accepted this last provision; when questioned a year later, as estimated costs began rising, Tipton reminded Hansen that the Bureau had agreed "to make a finding of feasibility based upon a payment of $25 million by the District and the assuming of the balance of the cost up to the present estimated cost by power."[68] At the conclusion of the May 23 meeting the Board adopted a motion to approve the contract.

In final form the Repayment Contract also described, among other things, the thirty-four features to be constructed, the forty years without interest to repay construction costs, operation and maintenance of "joint features" used for both power and irrigation, and the tax levies and assessments allowed the District.[69] On June 28, 1938, the twenty-two-page document with its fifty-eight articles[70] was submitted to the voters. All the daily papers had printed it previously as a "Resolution," along with explanatory articles and announcements of special meetings to inform property owners about what they were being asked to approve. By combining existing voting precincts, the District was divided into twenty-four separate entities for voting. When judges had finished counting the returns, the NCWCD Repayment Contract had passed with 7,510 votes for and 439 against (with twelve spoiled ballots).[71]

On July 5 the NCWCD Board passed a resolution ordering President Hansen to execute and deliver the contract and charging Secretary Dille to affix the district seal attesting to the contract as in fact that of the District. Dille promptly complied and then noted that insufficient funds were on hand to pay for the cost of the special election ($4,881.96). In response, the Board passed another resolution authorizing an additional loan from the Great Western Sugar Company ($6,000 had already been borrowed) in the amount of $20,000 at 5 percent interest due December 1, 1938. With this business completed, the meeting ended.[72]

Apart from the excellent terms and adequate publicity that the Repayment Contract had received, much of the credit for victory at the polls must go to the Colorado delegation in Washington for its legislative success

NCWCD Board president Charles Hansen signs the 1938 Repayment Contract with the United States, allowing construction of the C–BT to begin. Seated (left to right) Thomas Nixon, Charles Hansen, J. M. Dille. Standing (left to right) Fred Norcross, Burgis G. Coy, Robert J. Wright, Robert C. Benson, William A. Carlson, Ralph W. McMurray, Ray Lanyon, Ed F. Munroe, Moses E. Smith, William E. Letford, Charles M. Rolfson. (Courtesy NCWCD.)

in separating the C–BT Project from the 1902 Reclamation Act's requirement that only agricultural units of 40 to 160 acres were eligible to receive Project water. On May 16, 1938, Senator Adams had introduced Senate Bill 4027, which stated that the excess land provisions in the Reclamation Act would not apply to "certain lands that will receive supplemental water supply from the Colorado–Big Thompson Project." After approval by the Senate Committee on Irrigation and Reclamation, this bill passed on June 7.[73]

An identical bill, introduced in the House by Congressman Cummings, moved quickly through committee and was laid on the table on June 10. At this point it was suggested that the approved Senate bill be considered in lieu of the House version. After acceptance of this option, Senate Bill 4027 was ordered read a third time and passed. On June 15 President Roosevelt signed what became Public Law 665.[74]

Exaggerating the importance of this act is difficult. So many of the productive lands in the District were in excess of 160 acres that if the Reclamation Act had been strictly adhered to, the Repayment Contract might never have been passed by the voters. The C–BT would not have been built. But because of Adams's and Cummings's political perspicacity, many respected farmers in the District perceived the real benefits they would receive from a supplemental water supply, and their leadership persuaded most of the smaller operators to join the bandwagon. On October 12, 1938, one year to the day after Secretary Ickes wrote President Hansen, asking him to come to Washington to discuss the pros and cons of the C–BT Project, the Bureau of Reclamation opened bidding for the first of the construction projects: Green Mountain Dam, the West Slope's sine qua non for participation in the C–BT.

Because this reservoir and power plant resulted from Representative Taylor's hard bargaining, did he feel totally satisfied with the Project as construction was about to begin? No, his enthusiasm was still measured. Although his activities had been somewhat curtailed by advancing years and declining health, he continued to doubt the C–BT's merits and thus remained a threat to its proponents. Cummings told Hansen in February 1938 that Taylor was still in a position "to scuttle the Project and I am really afraid that he is going to do this."[75] He also noted that Taylor was sending wires to the West Slope and was "raising all the Hell he possibly can."[76]

Congressman Cummings had every reason to be skittish. Taylor, as chairman of the House Appropriations Committee, had waged a pretty good fight against the C–BT in its early stages, even though evidence does not show that he was trying to kill it after accepting the agreement between East and West Slopes the previous summer. What he did repeatedly was to remind everyone that he opposed transmountain diversion without building compensatory reservoirs. He had fought this battle for a long time, especially during the previous six years, and he still saw it as a "constant nightmare" and "tragic menace." When the Moffat Tunnel District petitioned to obtain a right-of-way to bring water through the Continental Divide from the Colorado River, he lectured his colleagues loudly on the need for West Slope storage.[77]

In the long run, Taylor had earned his opponents' respect. At age eighty-three, he responded to a letter from Hansen thanking him for "going down the line so nobly for the appropriation for the Big Thompson Project."[78] Taylor said that he was pleased to have worked so "loyally" in helping secure the Project. He also asked Hansen to be a watchdog over

Senate Document 80 so as to protect the rights of the West Slope in the future under that agreement.[79]

Providing protection for the West Slope was precisely what Hansen and Dille planned to do. Agreements had been achieved through hard work by honorable men who had compromised many of their own principles. As Hansen said in a letter to the WSPA's D. W. Aupperle soon after Congress authorized the $900,000 appropriation, the four years of negotiation represented "the finest of cooperative effort." With attorneys and laymen working on both sides trying "their best to work for the efforts of all . . . friendships . . . have been formed that I hope may last as long as any of us shall live. . . . How much we'uns now think of you'uns."[80] Hansen might also have noted how many times they had almost had their efforts negated by forces beyond their control when Congress was becoming increasingly illiberal with federal money. As Commissioner Page told representatives of the WSPA and NCWUA in Washington, "You got the last nickel."[81] The window of opportunity closed rapidly. With war clouds forming on the horizon, the long struggle for authorization and appropriation appeared once again to jeopardize northern Colorado's dream for supplemental water. Was construction really possible in a world at war?

Part II: *The District During War (1938–1947)*

6

Green Mountain Dam
and an Unexpected Labor War

Fall 1938 was an uncertain time for construction of a multimillion-dollar reclamation project. Although the NCWCD had signed a Repayment Contract with the United States and money was available to begin work immediately, the C–BT design was complex enough to require constant explanation in Washington, where funds had to be requested well in advance of actual need. With a deteriorating world situation and nagging domestic problems, proponents of the C–BT were eventually placed in a position of defending the Project as part of a national defense program; that they were successful is testimony to their persistence, flexibility, and diplomacy.

The gravity of the global situation was hard to deny. As of 1938, war had already broken out in Asia and was threatening to do so in Europe. Japan, fighting in China against both communist and nationalist forces, declared allegiance to Italy and Germany while voicing hostility to the United States' traditional "Open Door" policy in China. Germany, which had occupied the Rhineland, annexed Austria, and provided military aid to General Francisco Franco in Spain, was poised to invade the Czechoslovakian Sudetenland.

President Roosevelt had publicly described the world crisis a year before, warning of an "epidemic of world lawlessness." Totalitarian dictators threatened the foundations of civilization, he said, and advocated breakdown of international law and order. Quarantine of the culpable nations seemed the only recourse "to protect the health of the community against the spread of the disease." He was determined to avoid war, but insisted that the United States could not have "complete protection in a world of disorder in which confidence and security have broken down."[1] In September 1938 Roosevelt appealed to disputing nations to solve their problems through peaceful means. A few days later, Neville Chamberlain returned "triumphantly" from the notorious meeting in Munich where he, Edouard Daladier of France, and Benito Mussolini of Italy had agreed to accede to Adolph Hitler's demands for a German occupation of the

Sudetenland and all Czech fortifications. They had averted war for the moment, but the Czechs lost their only dependable frontier, their richest industrial area, and their right to exist as a free nation. World stability was severely threatened.

"Peace in our time," bragged Chamberlain when he returned to London. According to a Gallup poll conducted in the United States, nervous Americans were greatly relieved that the German dictator had been appeased. Yet, when actor Orson Welles presented a radio play, "Invasion from Mars," on the night of October 30, 1938, describing a landing of Martians on the New Jersey coast, the ensuing panic was at least partially a result of war fears that isolationist America had endured for two years. Even though Welles ended his program by wishing everyone a Happy Halloween, tense listeners were so caught up in the drama of the moment that CBS had to pepper the airwaves with assurances that the show had been fictional.

Additionally, the economy was unhealthy. Since August 1937, recession had shadowed the land, causing Roosevelt to ask Congress for more funds to stimulate economic activity; but Congress was weary of this formula. By fall 1938 southern conservative Democrats had already jumped ship to join ranks with the Republicans; in midterm elections, Republicans gained seven Senate and eighty House seats, their first numerical increase since 1928. The president was still able to get a $3 billion relief and recovery program, an expansion of Works Progress Administration (WPA) rolls, and a "loose money" policy authorized by the Federal Reserve Board, but his opponents enacted a revenue statute without his signature, lowering taxes on large corporations and modifying tax provisions on capital gains and losses.

In letters to the president, critics began to express their frustrations more directly. Roosevelt was urged to throw out the National Reclamation Association (NRA) and the Agricultural Adjustment Act (AAA), to stop being a "stooge" for his advisors, and to disassociate himself from the "crooked crowd" that had joined him in Washington.[2] Even labor groups were fomenting trouble for the administration. Under the leadership of John L. Lewis, the Congress of Industrial Organization (CIO) broke away from the American Federation of Labor (AFL) to form its own union. Attacking first the automobile industry, where it won recognition after a forty-four day strike against General Motors, the CIO then took on the steel industry. U.S. Steel was quick to sign a contract, but its competitors resisted, resorted to violence, and eventually forced the union to return to work without an agreement. The setback was less meaningful than the fact that by 1938 union organization was increasingly successful, with over 7 million workers boasting contracts with their employers, guarantees on wages and hours, and safety requirements in the work place. In addition, the public had grown tired of company violence, vigilantism, and Pinkerton detectives. In some parts of the country, the national mood supported union gains; in Colorado, however, anti-union prejudice still flourished, especially on the West Slope.

All of these events — world war, economic depression, rising hostility toward the New Deal, industrial strife — affected the newly formed NCWCD as it began to fulfill its responsibilities under the Water Conservancy District Act, Senate Document 80, and the Repayment Contract with the United States. The NCWCD Board was composed of experienced and dedicated men, but these national and international crises made their job far more difficult.

The first Board members reflected the dominant agricultural interests of northern Colorado, but these eleven men, appointed by District Judge Claude C. Coffin, were not exclusively farmers. Representing Boulder County, William E. Letford was a bank president and landowner, and Ray Lanyon was a newspaper publisher-editor and attorney. Representing Larimer County were Ed F. Munroe, rancher and stock feeder; Robert C. Benson, a farm owner-manager; and Ralph W. McMurry, a farmer and stock feeder. From Weld County came Charles Hansen, newspaper publisher-editor; William A. Carlson, farm owner; and Moses E. Smith, farm owner-manager and former state legislator. Washington and Morgan counties were represented by J. M. Dille, irrigation company superintendent, who resigned as Director in 1938 to become the District's first secretary-manager. He was replaced by H. W. Clatworthy, a landowner and merchant. From Logan County came Robert J. Wright, irrigation company superintendent, and from Sedgwick County, Charles M. Rolfson, attorney and landowner.[3] All but three had been members of the NCWUA.[4] They were strongly motivated to assist the Bureau of Reclamation in beginning construction even as they focused on encouraging farmers to sign up for water allotment contracts.

The Board soon learned that more operating monies were needed because the mill levy authorized by the Water Conservancy District Act would not produce revenue until county tax assessors made it available in June 1938. The Directors had to borrow operating funds from Boulder County, which issued a $500 warrant to the District to be used toward expenses. An additional $20,000 came from Great Western Sugar Company, which agreed to repayment by the end of 1938.[5]

Meanwhile, Secretary Dille ran announcements in local newspapers to solicit petitions from landowners for Class D agricultural water allotments. Under Section 125 of the Water Conservancy District Act, petitioners were eligible for an amount of supplemental water that, "in the judgment of the Board, together with the present supply of water for irrigation purposes on such lands, [will] make an adequate water supply for irrigation purposes on such lands."[6] In other words, farmers with a base supply of water, who showed need for supplemental water to properly irrigate their crops throughout the entire growing season, had a good chance of having their petitions approved. Their main concern was the probable cost of this water.

The 1902 Reclamation Act dictated a forty-year repayment period without interest for Bureau-built projects. Based on a maximum of $25 million for the irrigation features of the C–BT (one-half of the estimated total cost of the Project), the Board calculated a need of $600,000 per year annually for forty years to meet Reclamation Act requirements. Because a charge of $2 per acre-foot on 310,000 units seemed excessive, the Board decided to charge $1.50 per acre-foot unit (1/310,000 of the annual supply) "to be attached to, used upon and transferable with said lands by deed, but such use shall not be limited to the above described lands."[7] The balance, it was believed, approximately fifty cents, would be generated by an ad valorem property tax.

Fearing that the Department of the Interior might not approve a Repayment Contract unless the District showed demand for a large percentage of the 310,000 acre-feet of Project water,[8] the Board "urged" all potential Class D water applicants to present their requests by April 1, 1938.[9] Quickly it became apparent that this amount might soon be oversubscribed. North Poudre Irrigation Company's request for 40,000 acre-feet in December 1937 and the rapid rate at which the Loveland, Berthoud, and Fort Collins offices received applications in January and February led to early optimism. By mid-February 1938 individuals and ditch companies had petitioned for one-third of the water; a week later the total amount subscribed had reportedly reached 60 percent.[10] By late April enough water had been petitioned to enable the Department of the Interior to authorize construction of Green Mountain Dam on the Blue River.[11]

Before moving earth, the District and the Bureau signed the NCWCD Repayment Contract on July 5, 1938. Working out construction details with Bureau representatives provided NCWCD Directors opportunities to draw on the collective wisdom and experience of two men, Judge Clifford Stone and Royce J. Tipton, who had already given valuable service to the

Judge Clifford Stone of Gunnison was the first director of the Colorado Water Conservation Board, serving in that capacity from 1937 until his death in 1953. One of Colorado's leading water authority's, Stone was an enthusiastic supporter of the C–BT Project. (Courtesy Patricia Tretick.)

Project and whose usefulness to the District became even more apparent in the years ahead.

Judge Stone of Gunnison was nominated by Dille for the position of director and secretary of the Colorado Water Conservation Board (CWCB) at its first meeting in Denver in summer 1937. Although he had once been a bitter critic of transmountain water diversion along with other West Slope leaders (Dan Hughes of Montrose, Silmon Smith of Grand Junction, and Frank Delaney of Glenwood Springs), he gradually softened his opposition and gave unstinting support to the C–BT. Known for complete dedication to his work, Stone was also gifted with an ability to reduce complicated subjects to their essentials.[12] He was fully aware of the CWCB's diverse responsibilities to promote all kinds of water development within the state, to orchestrate cooperation among competing project proponents, and to participate in interstate litigation. CWCB minutes make no mention of the C–BT until January 15, 1941,[13] but Stone maintained a close relationship with Dille and the NCWCD's Board. His involvement with the C–BT from 1938 on was constant, enthusiastic, and immensely important to the Project's success.

Tipton also figured importantly in the District's early history. In addition to the December 1933 engineering report on the Grand Lake Project, he continued to provide constructive advice to the NCWUA as well as to the state engineer. His opinions were so highly respected that when negotiations began with the Bureau over the Repayment Contract, the NCWCD Board hired him as consultant to "prepare any material that might enable the Board of Directors to make the most favorable decision concerning the construction features and concerning the allocation of costs between the power features and the irrigation features."[14] Tipton's major contribution was to underscore the contractual obligation of keeping the District's financial obligation limited to $25 million. In 1938 Bureau Commissioner John C. Page had strongly opposed any "limitation of costs" for the District and had argued for reopening discussions on cost allocation between power and irrigation by the secretary of the interior during a period commencing ten years after completion of the first power plant and ending five years thereafter.[15] Tipton, resisting this proposal, accused the Bureau of overemphasizing the power aspects of the Project while denying the priority of irrigation and the importance of a fluctuating water supply for irrigation purposes. He then recommended that the Board send a committee to Washington to negotiate the matter with Secretary of the Interior Harold L. Ickes. In May 1938 Tipton's final draft of the yet unsigned Repayment Contract required that the Project be operated "primarily for irrigation," with a total financial obligation to the District limited to $25 million.[16] This document was especially favorable to the District given the inflation that occurred nationally in the postwar period.[17]

Tipton's role as consultant also enabled him to keep a close eye on the Bureau's design and construction cost estimates. Because Senate Document 80 required completion of Green Mountain Reservoir prior to delivery of any water to the East Slope,[18] this feature was the number one construction priority. The Bureau, which sent engineers to the site in May 1938 for a two-day field study, announced that bidding would be accepted for construction of the dam and power plant the following August. The Warner Construction Company of Chicago, Illinois, entered the lowest bid and was awarded a contract.

Actual construction at Green Mountain did not begin until December,[19] but Tipton had already warned the Board that cost estimates were rising. The Directors immediately formed a special committee to report on the situation. They found that the Bureau had revised its figures upward by 26 percent. According to the Bureau, unit prices of materials had risen; original estimates had been erroneously prepared "in haste" just to meet

Washington deadlines, and peculiar engineering and climatological problems required more realistic cost estimates. However, the Bureau concluded, extra costs at Green Mountain could be offset by savings on other Project features.[20]

The Board's committee pointed out that higher cost estimates might adversely affect water allotment contract deals and recommended rejection of all Green Mountain bids. Tipton advised a more cautious approach that resulted in a Board resolution urging preparation of final cost estimates as soon as possible on Lake Granby, Shadow Mountain Reservoir, and the Continental Divide Tunnel, prior to letting additional contracts. The Board also requested the Bureau to confer with the District regarding costs before opening bidding on additional features in the future, and it expressed a desire that the Bureau make every effort to absorb the extra Green Mountain costs in the construction of other features without exceeding original estimates for the entire Project.[21] In effect, the Board put the Bureau on notice that the District was very sensitive to any changes in Senate Document 80. Tipton had been instrumental in establishing a policy that proved crucial in future relations between the District and the Bureau.

For these and many other kinds of problems, the Board realized the need for a full-time attorney. Thomas A. Nixon, who had contributed significant work to the Water Conservancy District Act and to many Washington negotiations, became the unanimous choice. He was officially appointed the District's attorney on November 1, 1938, at a salary of $600 a month.[22] Although his health was beginning to fail, Nixon was greatly respected by Board members and was remembered by Greeley farmer W. D. "Bill" Farr as the dean of lawyers — the quiet, astute person who could bring together people of differing views. Nixon was very much like Charles Hansen. He worked hard, had everyone's respect, and was a good listener. He was high quality and not the least bit selfish.[23] Unfortunately, Nixon only worked with the Board until June 1941, when sickness forced him to resign. He was replaced by William R. Kelly. During his tenure, Nixon was known as a gentleman and superb lawyer who steered the Board around many legal difficulties and who fought hard for his beliefs. Along with the Directors, he insisted that C–BT contractors on West Slope facilities use unemployed laborers residing within District boundaries. These men, he argued, were paying for one-half of the Project, and they were entitled to some of the construction work. Nixon also fought for the corollary view that job sites should remain open for nonunion labor — the "open shop" argument. Unfortunately, he lost both battles, earning the resentment of unions for his insistence that the District be represented at all labor negotiations. He traveled widely, however, during the first year of C–BT construction, to represent his and the Board's views on labor issues.

For better or worse, organized labor was enjoying a period of protection and prosperity as a result of new federal laws. The amended Davis-Bacon Act, for example, required the Bureau to forward suggested wage rates — accompanied by information on the prevailing scales for various kinds of employment in the Colorado area — to the Department of Labor for approval before releasing bid specifications on any one of the C–BT features. After making an initial ruling on July 29, 1938, the secretary of labor received contradictory information on the Green Mountain project, leading him to suggest an on-site hearing among concerned parties that was held in Greeley August 26–28.[24]

Referee Ben Grodsky from the Department of Labor listened to both sides' arguments. Representatives from the Colorado State Federation of Labor, an AFL affiliate, insisted that the Denver wage scale, used on other West Slope projects, should apply to C–BT construction. Contractors denied this, even as NCWCD representatives insisted that Denver labor rates would add $2.5 million to the cost of the Project.[25] Grodsky, returning to Washington with this information, sent a revised ruling to Commissioner Page on October 4. In essence, he bowed to the union's wishes, raising the rates for skilled labor from $1.10 an hour to $1.25 an hour, semi-skilled labor from $.70 an hour to $.80 an hour, and common labor from $.50 an hour to $.65 an hour.[26] In November the Bureau announced publicly that because "more than enough local unskilled labor" was available for the work at hand, workers would be advised against traveling to the Green Mountain job site in hope of employment.[27]

The District Board, already concerned about escalating cost estimates at Green Mountain, worried that unemployed District residents would not get the construction jobs. On December 3 the Board organized a labor committee made up of Moses Smith, Lanyon, and Dille. In February 1939 this committee reported on conferences with the Bureau, the State Industrial Commission, and the Warner Construction Company, noting that "Mr. Warner indicated [a willingness] to cooperate . . . in securing employment for residents of the District."[28] Regrettably, Warner could not keep his word. He agreed to use the State Employment Service that had offices in Denver, Fort Collins, Longmont, and Greeley, as well as contact offices in Hot Sulphur Springs and Estes Park, but he could not prevent the unions from pressuring for a "closed shop" on the job site.

Labor organizations first moved on March 14, 1939, when members of the Mine, Mill, and Smelter Workers Union (a CIO affiliate) went on strike, picketing the outlet tunnel that had been constructed to divert waters of the Blue River around the proposed Green Mountain Dam. Union president Reid Robinson called the strike to protest Warner Construction Company's unwillingness to negotiate collectively. Additionally, he charged violation of state mining laws regarding internal combustion machinery in the tunnel.[29] Approximately 120 men armed with pick handles walked the picket line, but no violence erupted because nonunion workers made no attempt to return to work.[30]

The Bureau's position was that the union and the contractor should settle this matter.[31] District officials, however, contended that union domination threatened serious increases in the total cost of the Project; that of the 400 men on the job site, District residents had not received their share of positions; and that the trouble at Green Mountain appeared to be a "test of strength." Both Dille and Hansen were outspoken about maintaining an open shop.[32] With the hint of violence, Summit County officials asked Governor Ralph Carr to send in the militia. He refused but suggested a meeting of all parties before the State Industrial Commission and resumption of work at the dam site. The union accepted his proposal.

At this meeting, union attorney Charles Mahoney petitioned against the presence of NCWCD representatives. Over Nixon's response that the District was keenly and properly interested in the construction of Green Mountain Reservoir and opposed to "certain labor groups" taking over the Project, Mahoney argued that the union, the Bureau, and the Warner Construction Company were the only parties of legitimate interest. Ray H. Brannaman, commission chairman, denied the petition and immediately organized an advisory committee to effect a compromise. The District was represented by Lanyon and Dille.[33] Mahoney, who was furious, charged the committee with being nothing more than a "company union" and accused Dille of threatening to close down the whole C–BT Project if a union were organized at Green Mountain. Brannaman agreed to take Mahoney's comments "under advisement."[34] On April 5, after receiving advice from the committee, he rendered a decision stating that employees and employer must cooperate to avoid difficulties. He directed the Warner Company to observe the forty-hour week and to pay full wage scale, but he left unsettled the question of collective bargaining.[35] This issue, along with the unresolved matter of an open or closed shop, precipitated a more violent outburst at Green Mountain three months later.

The Board was shocked by this labor violence. In April 1939 the labor committee had reported tranquility on the job site. About forty union agitators had left, and a Green Mountain unit of the Workers Association had formed to provide representation and bargaining power to all men involved in construction.[36] In May the Board traveled to Kremmling to attend a mass meeting organized by the AFL. The District's June minutes indicate that the Directors lacked sympathy for the union position and remained committed to the open shop principle.[37] When a strike was called on the afternoon of July 12 by AFL affiliates, the news reached Greeley in conjunction with a Bureau announcement that the total cost estimate of the Project had risen 23 percent to $54 million. Furthermore, the Bureau reported, none of the bids for construction of the Continental Divide Tunnel were low enough to justify awarding a contract. With a major labor problem developing at Green Mountain and Project cost estimates rising, the Board urged the Bureau to consider tunnel construction by government forces.[38]

Meanwhile, the Green Mountain situation was deteriorating. Dille feared that if the AFL successfully forced a closed shop on the Warner Construction Company, organized labor would be well on its way to sewing up all jobs on the Project. "The District's position," he said, "is that union control would work to the disadvantage of workers within the District who are entitled to jobs."[39] The State Industrial Commission declared the strike illegal and ordered the men back to work, but the union was adamant that Warner Construction Company sign an agreement to hire construction workers through the unions, not through the State Employment Service. J. L. Warner, caught in the middle, responded that the NCWCD objected to his signing a closed shop agreement with the unions.[40]

Negotiations between the unions and the construction company continued with no progress throughout July. By August, Kremmling citizens grew impatient with union obstructionism. Without money or credit and with families to feed, a group of nonunion men met and decided to break the strike. According to *The Middle Park Times*,[41] local businessmen from Granby, Hot Sulphur Springs, and Kremmling first called on J. A. Walther, AFL chief in Kremmling and told him to leave town, after which a caravan of fifty cars headed for the work site at Green Mountain. After removing structural steel from the boundary perimeter, the men roared through the gates, forcing union pickets to surrender. By August 3, 175 nonunion men were back at work, while 225 armed "deputies" patrolled the gates and the roads leading into the project, "watching for any attempt to bring in strike sympathizers from Denver." Official headquarters of the nonunion "back-

MASS MEETING

Kremmling --- Town Hall

Sunday, May 7

11:00 A. M.

ALL CITIZENS WHO ARE VITALLY INTER-
ESTED IN THE BIG THOMPSON PROJECT SHOULD
ATTEND THIS MEETING AND HEAR PROMINENT
COLORADO CITIZENS SPEAK.

COLORADO STATE FEDERATION OF LABOR
By JAMES BROWNLOW, Secretary.

Flyer, mass meeting, Kremmling Town Hall. (Courtesy NCWCD.)

Governor Carr called in the National Guard to control the labor situation at Green Mountain Dam. Photograph shows tank entering dam area while dump trucks in background are used to barricade the bridge. (Courtesy Bureau of Reclamation.)

to-work" group were established 2 miles from the Hennyville gate at a tavern frequently referred to as the "Bucket of Blood."[42]

Wild rumors flew, but all remained peaceful until a report reached Kremmling that "dozens of cars and trucks carrying an estimated five hundred Mexicans, Negroes, and hard cases" had passed through Empire, headed for Kremmling and Green Mountain. Telephone lines were cut later in the afternoon. When a carload of deputies went to investigate on Highway 9, they encountered a barricade defended by fifty armed AFL pickets who were trying to surround and isolate nonunion workers. Later in the afternoon, union men who had approached the work site were told that the road was dynamited, but they proceeded anyway. Nonunion workers set off the charges, and in response, the "Denver mob" opened fire on "deputies" guarding the gate. The fire was returned and both sides saw casualties. Besieged workers called for reinforcements, which arrived over back roads with high-powered rifles. By midnight, more union men had arrived in the area, the Bucket of Blood was under their control, and several hundred shots had been fired.[43] Governor Ralph Carr finally called out the National Guard. Soldiers arrived in the early morning of August 4, equipped with rifles, machine guns, gas guns, and two tanks to enforce martial law in Grand and Summit counties. As they took charge and began to collect weapons, strikers and their sympathizers cheered. In Kremmling the commanding officer disarmed the town marshal while soldiers confiscated weapons from townspeople. With order restored, work began again at Green Mountain. Company vice-president Warner announced that he was willing to discuss any disagreement with employees or union representatives at a meeting to include the State Industrial Commission, but the union denied the commission's authority in this matter and dragged its feet. Another stalemate.

Tension mounted again. A dynamite blast in a canyon 5 miles north of Dillon cut off electricity to the dam site and to Kremmling. Officials prohibited the sale of liquor after 9 P.M. in the troubled area. While state officials feared that strikes might spread to other construction sites in Colorado, Governor Carr worried about the $1,000-a-day cost of maintaining the National Guard at Green Mountain.[44]

By August 15 Nixon announced a meeting before the Industrial Commission with representatives from Grand and Summit counties, Kremmling businessmen, nonunion workers, union representatives, and the Warner Construction Company. Two days earlier, he had served notice that the District would also be represented.[45] These talks almost failed. The union again insisted on a closed shop and demanded that all men employed on the job join one of the AFL unions within seven days of starting work. It threatened damage suits against Summit and Grand counties on behalf of the wounded men and boldly refused to back down on any demands.[46] The Associated Workers, meanwhile, asked for a vote of the laborers to determine the kind of union they wanted. Residents of the two counties, joined by the NCWCD, made a final pitch for an open shop. After all views had been expressed, negotiators finally reached agreement on August 22.[47]

The union made substantial gains. For ending the strike and accepting the presence of troops at the job site for several weeks more, AFL negotiators won permission to sign a closed shop agreement with the Warner Construction Company. The agreement stated that residents of the District and Summit and Grand counties were to receive work preference, but everyone knew that the union was now in a position to use whatever hiring practices it desired.[48] Nixon questioned the legality of Warner's signing a closed shop agreement with the union when the union lacked a majority of workers on the job, but his concerns proved academic. The closed shop agreement, also signed on August 22, became effective on September 15, 1939.[49] According to P. W. Chappel, U.S. Department of Labor conciliator, it was the *"first of its kind* ever made between a contractor and unions in the West." The NCWCD Board was so angry at Warner Construction Company that it voted to bill the company for the cost of sending men to Green Mountain to participate in negotiations.[50]

Two days before the commencement of World War II, Governor Carr ordered withdrawal of troops from Green Mountain, where they had preserved order for twenty-seven days. District officials were decidedly unhappy with the outcome of their struggle with organized labor, but Secretary of the Interior Ickes bluntly announced his contempt for their attitude. "After all," he told a press conference,

> when the dam is built and there is water on the land, the water users will have a benefit out of all proportion to the wages that the workers can earn in building the Project. The Northern Colorado Water Conservancy District favored an open shop policy to encourage hiring of workers from the area . . . an area of chiefly unorganized labor. I don't agree with that attitude. This is strictly federal money. Local people who come in and ask for such a development as we are undertaking there . . . are likely to assume that it is their money being invested and that it is their private property. The proposition that non-urban labor should have first call on the jobs appears unfair to me in the face of the great unemployment in labor in the larger cities.[51]

By the end of 1939, work was progressing smoothly on the West Slope without any hint of further strikes. The earth and rock-fill dam at Green Mountain was about "27.8% completed with winter operations limited to stripping the dam foundation and excavating for the powerhouse and spillway."[52] The outlet tunnel for the Blue River diversion was "holed through." Concrete lining was placed in the tunnel, and on December 13 water was diverted so that work could be started on a permanent cofferdam. The contractor had also begun excavating the powerhouse and switchyard area, expected to be completed during the winter.[53]

Government forces worked on other elements of the project: Kremmling to Green Mountain telephone lines; base camps at Green Mountain, Shadow Mountain, and Estes Park; water supply and sewage systems; and a switching station at Dillon to bring power to the job site. They cleared a right-of-way for a transmission line between Green Mountain and Grand Lake, built warehouses along the railroad tracks, and constructed several electrical substations to bring power to the West Portal of the Continental Divide Tunnel and to the future Shadow Mountain work camp. At Estes Park government forces cleared rights-of-way from Loveland to the East Portal for transmission lines, constructed buildings for a headquarters camp, and hired Civilian Conservation Corps (CCC) labor for various landscaping projects.[54]

Work had not yet started on drilling the 13.1 mile Continental Divide Tunnel, a delay that disappointed District Directors, who had already endorsed Tipton's suggestion that federal government agencies undertake the work.[55] Although government specifications for construction were written to reassure timid contractors — eliminating many of the risks and providing in detail methods to be adopted by them in various formations and conditions — only three companies responded to the bid invitation by June 1939. The lowest bid of $10.7 million from the Shasta Company was $2.5 million above the Bureau's estimate. By January 1940 the Bureau debated constructing the tunnel with government employees or readvertising the job with amended specifications and contracts for smaller segments.[56] Aware of the ominous world situation, NCWCD Directors found themselves worrying that the Continental Divide Tunnel, the main artery of the C–BT system, might be delayed indefinitely.

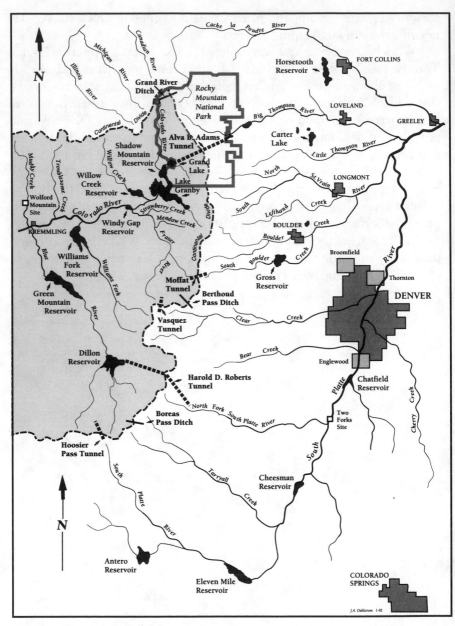

Central Colorado and West Slope.

7 Wartime Priorities: Board Policies and Construction Funding

To NCWCD Directors, construction progress seemed interminably slow during winter 1940. Work on the Continental Divide Tunnel still had not begun, although the AFL appeared to be organizing in northern Colorado with the announced plan of placing workmen somewhere on the C–BT Project. Meanwhile, the Board began to address the dozens of details that required attention. With few precedents for their many responsibilities, the Directors continually looked to the future, trying to imagine what would be best for the District once supplemental water was flowing through the C–BT system. Because of their wide-ranging experience and successful resolution of problems at hand, most Directors were reappointed for as long as they wished to serve. Although this pattern of long terms has continued to the present day, Weld County Judge Claude C. Coffin had hoped to impose more frequent rotation.

The Water Conservancy District Act provided for the appointment of directors by the court in whose jurisdiction the conservancy district functioned. This provision was included not only to save the expense of general elections but "principally to assure that the selection of Directors of the District should never become involved in politics or be made the subject of partisan controversies."[1] Coffin believed that rotation was advisable to accomplish "wider representation, diversity of judgment, and public confidence,"[2] a view he articulated in 1937 and again the next year. When he recognized the experience accumulated by the Directors and received no complaints about their work, he reappointed all five when their terms expired. In 1940, however, Coffin reverted to his earlier position, that of bringing in "new blood" each year. In letters to new appointees, he noted that "to maintain public confidence and interest, it is deemed advisable, where all other considerations are near equal balance, to make such changes in the personnel."[3]

Unquestionably, the judge had in mind the best interests of the District; however, the complexity of the C–BT Project led some insiders to believe that rotation on the Board was inadvisable just for the sake of "new blood." In fall 1948, for example, Charles Hansen requested Coffin to reappoint all members "since it takes several years of membership on the Board before anyone can become familiar with the many ramifications of the C–BT Project, enough to be of any independent value to the District."[4] No one had complained about the appointment system at that time, but Hansen had no interest in training new Directors in everything that had happened since the Project's inception.

Although critics of the appointment process became increasingly vocal with the passage of time, the first Directors' ability to deal responsibly with the ad valorem tax revealed something of their sense of duty to District residents. The Water Conservancy District Act authorized a tax of up to 1/2 mill on the dollar before water was delivered "and thereafter shall not exceed one mill on the dollar of valuation for assessment of the property within the district, except in the event of accruing defaults or deficiencies when an additional levy may be made as provided in Section 37-45-126."[5] By October 1 each year, the Board had to prepare a budget and set the mill levy needed for District operation and expenses. The first levy was set at 3/10 of a mill in 1937. Based on a property valuation of $120 million in the District, income from the tax was $36,000. The Board believed that the District was also eligible for a share of the revenue from the motor vehicle tax. When the money was not forthcoming, the Directors authorized Nixon to bring an action against the county treasurers of the seven counties within the District "to obtain a declaratory judgment on the right of the District to participate in the special ownership tax."[6] Ultimately, the case was appealed to the Colorado Supreme Court, where the judge ruled that, because the District was not in the same classification as a city, county, town, or school district, it was therefore not entitled to a portion of the tax.[7]

Anticipating this decision and aware that the Water Conservancy District Act obligated the District to make right-of-way purchases for all construction features of the C–BT,[8] the Board raised the mill levy to 4/10 in September 1938, but the income was still inadequate to make costly land purchases. Consequently, the Bureau negotiated rights-of-way and closed deals directly.[9] In 1940 the mill levy was reduced to 2/10 because expenses were lower than anticipated.[10] The following year, the assessment was again raised to 3/10 of a mill, anticipating a three-fold increase in right-of-way expenses and the obligation to make the first of ten annual compensation payments to Grand County in the amount of $10,000 as required by Senate Document 80.[11] It remained at 3/10 of a mill throughout the war.

By the 1940s the Board of Directors had also established policies in regard to water allotments. President Hansen reported completion of allotment contracts totaling 206,726 acre-feet of water by January 1940. He noted that each petition had been checked for accuracy and that every farm had been inspected in the field. The Directors planned to act slowly regarding the remaining one-third of the 310,000 acre-feet units of supplemental water because of the many possible uses assigned to the balance. Hansen estimated that eventually C–BT water would be oversubscribed by at least 50,000 acre-feet. The Board also considered Class B petitions for municipal water in the following allotments: Greeley, 15,000 acre-feet; Longmont, 5,000 acre-feet; Loveland, 5,000 acre-feet; Fort Collins, 1,000 acre-feet; Berthoud, 300 acre-feet; and Mead, 100 acre-feet.[12] Boundary questions focused on Boulder County, where some residents wished to be excluded from the District. Other water users wanted the District to construct "canals" from St. Vrain Creek to Boulder Creek and then to the South Platte "at a point south of the headgate of Evans No. 2 Ditch." In 1940 the Board approved construction of the St. Vrain–Boulder Creek Canal[13] — a plan that was delayed by the war as well as by the Bureau's postwar reluctance to increase Project costs.

Legal matters occupied considerable time and up to 10 percent of the annual budget. In addition to condemnation proceedings,[14] Thomas A. Nixon and William R. Kelly were involved in several matters of great significance to the District's future. The question of title to return flows from supplemental Colorado River water was one such issue. In January 1938 the Board had directed Nixon and Director Charles M. Rolfson to draft a policy statement in regard to return-flow waters.[15] Article 19 of the Repayment Contract provided that supplemental water brought to the East Slope from the Colorado River was reserved by the United States for exclusive use by the District. Although the Bureau agreed that return flows were to be administered by the state engineer, confusion emerged over the fact that the federal government made the original filing on return flows "as protection against possible claims . . . by new claimants, such as Nebraska."[16] After a meeting on September 30, 1938, representatives from the NCWCD, the Bureau, and the state engineer's office agreed to treat return flows from the C–BT just as any other return-flow water from existing irrigation ditches.[17]

Another legal problem developed when water users in Water District No. 4 protested a U.S. and District claim to unused water on the Big Thompson River. Such a claim threatened to prevent the second filling of their reservoirs from undecreed water. Nixon cited several cases to show that reservoir owners were only entitled to one filling of their reservoir during a single season. Bureau counsel Spencer L. Baird supported him on this point.[18] To keep the peace, however, Nixon agreed to allow water users of the Big Thompson to "apply for a decree for an original filling and a second filling of certain reservoirs," with the understanding that these decrees were senior to those of the District and the United States.[19]

The most important legal issue emerging in this early construction period involved Denver's claims to rights on the Blue River. Taylor had warned Hansen in 1941 that confirmation of Denver's claims across the Continental Divide could destroy the basis on which the East and West Slopes had agreed to transmountain diversion. Taylor saw that

> the [main] consideration of that agreement [Senate Document 80] was really the construction of Green Mountain Reservoir to stabilize the flow of the waters in the Colorado River. Now Denver, a lot of promoters, real estate men, engineers, and lawyers are trying to promote a scheme to take all of the water of the Blue River at a point above that reservoir. . . . While the whole matter is such a preposterous and brazen conception, nevertheless, its backing is very dangerous for the West Slope. . . . I would like to have you people give notice to that Denver bunch that you are interested in having that Blue River water conserved for our benefit. I understand they have a report . . . which says that there is a large quantity of water that they can take without injury to us, but anybody with any sense knows that the diversionists up the stream have a very big advantage over those down the stream. . . . Of course, you realize all of this without me mentioning it, but I do want you to know that I feel perturbed about that scheme which apparently has the enthusiastic support of the *Denver Post* and I suppose naturally a large part of the people of that entire region. They are concerned not at all about our welfare on the Western Slope.[20]

Taylor's fears were well-grounded. The *Denver Post* did indeed support the Denver Water Board (DWB) and Chamber of Commerce in promoting transmountain diversion of water from the Blue River through a tunnel into the North Fork of the South Platte River, a project eventually realized by building the Roberts Tunnel and Dillon Reservoir. Preliminary investigations were made in 1940 under the direction of Mayor Ben Stapleton and George Cranner, manager of Denver's Parks and Improvements Department. Meanwhile, a subcommittee headed by George M. Bull, former regional engineer for the PWA, and composed of Assistant City Attorney Glenn G. Saunders, Chapman Young, Dr. R. D. Elmore, and Adolph Zang, began to plan construction. Proponents of the Blue River project estimated four years to build a hydroelectric system that would generate more power than the C–BT. They had hoped to begin construction in 1940 with the assistance of the United States promoting the project as a "national defense measure."[21]

Denver's designs on the Blue River, as well as its plans to compete for increasingly scarce federal funds, angered NCWCD officials. By June 1940 the "Phony War" in Europe had ended, the German *Blitzkrieg* had broken France, Norway and Denmark were under Nazi control, and the German *Luftwaffe* had begun the Battle of Britain. Fears of global war were building in Washington, where both legislators and the president questioned the wisdom of spending money on reclamation programs unrelated to national defense. As the presidential campaign heated up in the fall, Republican challenger Wendell Willkie appealed for western support by assuring Governor Ralph Carr that if elected, he would complete the C–BT as planned.[22]

From the Board's point of view, the Project needed a boost in Washington to cope with the changing circumstances, something that would identify it with national defense. In a speech made in June 1940 to celebrate the beginning of tunnel construction at the West Portal, Director Charles A. Lory noted the importance of the power that the C-BT would produce when completed. He stressed the value of supplemental water to northern Colorado farmers, the primary purpose of the C–BT as stated in Senate Document 80, but he also spoke of the excess power ultimately available for commercial purposes.[23] The following month, Royce J. Tipton began a study to detail the importance of the C–BT as a power project.[24] Power quickly became the key word to unlock doors for federal funding, and Washington seemed suddenly receptive.

Following his expected reelection, Roosevelt publicly announced in December a policy of holding down nondefense expenditures. CWCB director Clifford Stone, accompanied by Hansen and J. M. Dille, presented a six-point proposal to the Bureau of the Budget that urged continued funding for C–BT construction at no less than existing levels.[25] A week later, Stone concluded that appropriations to reclamation projects would be related to the amount of power that each produced for national defense. After discussions with Director of the Budget Harold D. Smith, he became aware that "the attitude of Washington officials, both legislative and budgetary, was that power production, as a backlog for industrial expansion in the safe interior, loomed uppermost in their thoughts as they contemplated future courses of action on the project."[26]

Noting this change in emphasis, a 1941 Colorado newspaper reported that, even though the C–BT culminated fifty years of work to obtain supplemental irrigation water for northern Colorado farmers, "power production has recently assumed an important role in the nation's defense plans. . . . Normally a by-product of reclamation work . . . electric energy has suddenly become a major factor in strengthening the nation, and power plants are being enlarged to meet the demand."[27] Secretary Ickes was directly behind this promotion of power. In February 1941 he supported accelerated construction of power projects in the West and expanded capacity to bring them into operation as quickly as possible for national defense purposes.[28] Stone confirmed this thinking with the head of the Federal Power Commission, who specified the need for nearly 200,000 kilowatts of extra capacity in the "Colorado District over the next six years."[29]

In June, Roosevelt designated the C–BT one of five projects vital to national defense that would receive immediate "anti-sabotaging policing."[30] The following month, John C. Page announced to the Colorado River Water Conservation District (CRWCD) that during the national emergency government agencies would regard irrigation projects as secondary in importance, with work on them greatly curtailed. He declared that "power is the only thing that is important" and expressed hope that the Bureau would make strenuous efforts to obtain a preferential rating for the C–BT, freeing work from unwanted impediments.[31]

About the same time, Hansen was surprised to learn that a participant at a session of the Public Lands Committee in Washington had proposed building a steam electric power plant of 110,000 kilowatt capacity as part of the C–BT. Hansen wrote Senator Ed Johnson that the District Board held fast to the $25 million obligation for the irrigation part of the Project; if a steam plant were needed, the federal government would be responsible for construction and payment.[32] Seven months later, in a letter to Dille, Senator Eugene D. Millikin revealed that Ickes supported the idea, and that construction of the plant would be "an important firming element [adding] to the reservoir of power for defense purposes which the authorities are eager to build up at interior points."[33]

By December 1941 Dille optimistically estimated completion of the Continental Divide Tunnel by early 1944 if sufficient money were available. Other parts of the Project could also be completed, he added, "so that a large amount of power could be made available for defense and industrial purposes."[34] The *Tipton Power Report*, published in January 1942, also projected power production by early 1944 if the Bureau pursued an intensive construction program.[35] Obviously, District officials had become aware of an exceptional opportunity to advance the C–BT, even at the risk of temporarily redefining its original purpose. Although they had no interest in shifting the primary mission of the Project to power, they were uninhibited about emphasizing its power potential to improve prospects for annual appropriations. After years of struggle with Washington, this turn of events provided an unexpected but a well-deserved shortcut in a long journey to the ultimate goal. When the power factor faded in 1942 and the government worried about having enough food for the war's duration, District officials vigorously returned to their original argument that the C–BT's primary purpose was to provide supplemental water for agriculture, thus enabling the government to meet wartime quotas of food production.

Even with adaptations to Washington's shifting moods and fears, the District was repeatedly frustrated by the C–BT's financial dependency on the Reclamation Fund. Late in 1938 Ickes had projected depletion of the Bureau's funds by the end of fiscal 1941; either the administration had to increase the fund from the Treasury's general fund or finance some of the more costly projects from other sources. When Congress passed the Reclamation Act in 1902, as Ickes pointed out, the Bureau was to receive 52.5 percent of the income from sales of public lands. By 1938, however, the vastly reduced income from land sales left the Bureau dependent on oil royalties and repayment of construction costs for completed projects.[36] Reclamation Fund resources were simply inadequate for the many authorized projects.

Hansen, who was acutely aware of the problem, wrote to Senator Alva B. Adams in December 1940, puzzling over "how to get this Project completed in the shortest possible time." With drought continuing in northern Colorado and the pressing need for power, he wanted to reduce the estimated completion time for the Project from seven to four and one-half years, requiring an additional $8–10 million per year of funding. Total Project appropriations by the end of 1940 were only $8,050,000.[37] "Possibly the best hope," Hansen concluded, "is to try to get future appropriations directly from Treasury funds as several other of the larger reclamation projects are doing."[38] Dille concurred. After one of his many trips to Washington, he reported to the Board that the Senate had initiated plans to transfer the C–BT and other reclamation projects to the general fund,[39] a move that was successful. For fiscal 1942 and for each year thereafter up to 1958, the C–BT received funding from the general fund of the U.S. Treasury.[40] This adjustment did not move construction forward as rapidly as Hansen and the Board had hoped. By the end of December

1941, with the United States at war after the Japanese surprise attack on Pearl Harbor, the Board was able to report significant progress only at Green Mountain Dam and the Continental Divide Tunnel.

At the beginning of 1941, 44.2 percent of Green Mountain Dam and Power Plant were completed. Blue River water flowed through the outlet tunnel, upstream and downstream cofferdams had been constructed, excavation for the power plant had begun, and 353,000 cubic yards of earthfill had been placed in position on the dam. During 1941 the Warner Construction Company not only stripped and shaped dam abutments but increased the amount of compacted earthfill in the dam itself to 55 percent of the final configuration. All excavation required for spillway construction was completed, as was concreting for the powerhouse structure and the trash rack. By the end of 1941, with 65 percent of the work at Green Mountain complete, Dille predicted that the power plant would be ready in spring 1943.[41]

After rejecting the first bids for the Continental Divide Tunnel construction, Ickes sent out new invitations, hoping for lower cost estimates. Prospective contractors welcomed a second chance to bid on labor, materials, and all construction work for excavation of the first 8,000 feet from the East Portal. The S. S. Magoffin Company, which submitted the lowest of thirteen bids, signed a contract on April 25, 1940.[42] By June the East Portal area was fully electrified, roads were built, and the Estes Park headquarters was well underway.

On June 23, 1940, while 2,500 spectators cheered under a blazing Colorado sun, Hansen closed an electric switch that touched off dynamite in thirty-six holes, beginning construction of the world's longest tunnel for irrigation purposes. "A series of heavy but muffled booms together with vivid flashes visible from the tunnel entrance showed that the dedicatory shot was successful." All Directors attended, as well as many dignitaries, such as Frelan D. Stanley, the man who drove the first automobile to Estes Park.[43] Although invited to attend, Ickes declined because of pressing business in Washington. Instead, he sent a letter praising the C–BT as an example of the "resourcefulness" and "tenacity" of democracy:

> Here and now in this lofty spot you are taking an important step to save a living segment of that democracy. Right here on the rooftop of this country, a mile and a half above sea level, you are beginning a job that may take seven years to complete. . . . Through the aid of the federal government you are enabling 175,000 persons . . . to continue to live and grow and develop and add their contribution to the country's welfare,

Dedication ceremony at the East Portal of the Alva B. Adams Tunnel, June 23, 1940. Twenty-five hundred spectators attended. (Courtesy NCWCD.)

forbidding their communities to choke and die for lack of a supplemental water supply. This is your great project and your great work. You are democracy exercising its most influential function: self-preservation. The Department of the Interior is merely the instrument of that expression, but I take pride in being a part of that instrument. Especially do I, because all of you, farmers and townspeople, are bearing the cost of this Project. All of you will get its benefits. All of you are paying for them. It is a cooperative democratic endeavor.[44]

By the end of 1940 construction had driven the Continental Divide Tunnel 6,555 feet from the East Portal. Magoffin had reluctantly signed a closed-shop agreement with unions affiliated with the AFL. Except for a one-week labor dispute in November, excavation proceeded smoothly through stable granite. Workers received more than the minimum wages established by the Bureau of Labor, as well as travel time from the East Portal to the heading. Apart from what they considered the high cost of living in Estes Park, union men had no complaints.

Platt Rogers of Pueblo, Colorado, which won the contract for beginning the first 8,000 feet of construction at the West Portal, fired the first

Frelan O. Stanley (center), who built the landmark Stanley Hotel in Estes Park, attended the tunnel dedication ceremony. With him are Geo. A. Hodgson (left) and Abner Sprague (right). (Courtesy NCWCD.)

round of shots on August 20, 1940. By the end of the year workers had penetrated only 2,145 feet through unstable gneiss and schist that hampered progress on the west side of the Continental Divide. A unique track-mounted "jumbo," designed to serve as both a drilling and mucking machine, slowed work through numerous breakdowns in a tunnel "of small bore and heavy ground."[45]

In 1941 the Magoffin Company received a second contract and successfully drove the tunnel heading to a point 20,196 feet into the mountain. Even with delays resulting from delivery of the second contract, Magoffin Company made such good progress that Dille predicted completion of tunnel excavation by April 1943. At the end of the year he reported: "The progress made by S. S. Magoffin, Inc. has changed the picture regarding the time necessary to complete the project and furnished the basis on which a much faster construction schedule can be founded if Federal approval and the necessary appropriations can be secured."[46]

In January Platt Rogers addressed problems at the West Portal heading. When crews abandoned the "jumbo," the company replaced it with a drill carriage and a Gardner-Denver shovel mucking machine that experienced

This track-mounted mucking machine lifted rock and debris up and over to a waiting car behind. (Courtesy Bureau of Reclamation.)

fewer mechanical breakdowns.[47] In another change on June 5, Stiers Brothers Construction Company of St. Louis offered the low bid for the second section of 8,000 feet of excavation. While Platt Rogers and Stiers Brothers were changing places, work came to a standstill, but the hiring of well-known John Austin as superintendent moved West Portal construction along rapidly.[48] By the end of 1941 workers had penetrated to 7,835 feet but still lagged behind the Magoffin Company. Forty percent of the total tunnel construction was now completed.[49] Had world and national circumstances not intervened, Dille's optimistic predictions might have been realized.

Work also progressed at Granby Dam and Reservoir, structures that were essential before water could be delivered through the Continental Divide Tunnel. Storing Colorado River water behind Granby Dam required a collection system built at the head of a narrow canyon to trap additional waters from Stillwater Creek and the South Fork of Arapahoe Creek. After construction of the dam and dikes, plans were to fill the

"Long Tall" John Austin was a well-known tunnel construction superintendent who worked on the C–BT Project. Shown here with Bureau project engineer J. C. Howell. (Courtesy NCWCD.)

reservoir from which the stored water would be pumped up approximately 96 feet to Shadow Mountain Reservoir. Shadow Mountain was to act as a shock absorber, keeping the level of Grand Lake constant while water was diverted at different times and seasons through the Continental Divide Tunnel.[50] Because initial bids on Granby Dam and Reservoir had been higher than expected, the Bureau delayed signing a contract with Platt Rogers for the diversion and outlet tunnel until November 1, 1941. Not until December was proper equipment in place and tunnel excavation started; only 11 percent of the tunnel was finished by the end of the year.[51]

Even if labor problems, severe weather, and administrative obstacles had not slowed construction, the C–BT faced almost certain delays as a result of the national defense program. In September 1941, three months before the Japanese attack on Pearl Harbor, Dille wrote a worried letter to Senator Adams concerning the Bureau's application for a "Project Preference Rating" from the Priorities Board in Washington. A low numerical rating indicated a high defense priority in delivery of construction materials such as steel, copper, and cement; a high numerical rating meant that vital construction materials might be unavailable during the crisis.[52] Adams responded that a high priority A–3 rating had been approved for the Green Mountain Dam and Power Plant, with a lower priority A–10 rating for the C–BT in general.[53] When Congress declared a state of war on December 8, 1941, reclamation projects were suddenly vulnerable — unless backers proved their indispensable function in the newly established national defense program. Proponents of the C–BT now needed different, convincing arguments to secure construction funds.

Unfortunately, three of the most effective and influential C–BT wheelhorses died in 1941. Congressman Taylor, who died on September 3, had stood in the way of transmountain diversion in 1933 and had pestered NCWUA and NCWCD officials to protect West Slope interests; yet he had been a constant and effective supporter of Colorado and the West. The chairmanship of the powerful House Appropriations Committee would no longer be held by anyone who understood so well the C–BT's complexities. Having served in Congress from 1909 to 1941, Taylor was one of only six individuals ever to win election to Congress sixteen consecutive times.

Attorney Nixon died two months later. After resigning from the Board in June 1941, his health steadily worsened until he suffered a heart attack and never recovered. As a knowledgeable water lawyer who commanded the respect of officials in both Colorado and Washington, Nixon's loss was a blow to the District. As Robert G. Smith wrote in a 1938 letter urging the University of Colorado to award Nixon an honorary degree, Nixon "had no superiors and few equals at the Bar in this County. . . . Morally and ethically he is as outstanding as he is in legal ability."[54]

Senator Adams died on December 1, 1941. Elected to the Senate in 1932 and again in 1938, he had been chairman of the Public Lands and Surveys Committee and had served on the important Deficiency Appropriations Committee and the Irrigation and Reclamation Committee. Although an outspoken critic of Roosevelt's spending policies, Adams had strongly supported the C–BT and fought hard for adequate legislative funding on more than one occasion.[55] In comments to the Board, Dille noted that Adams's loss would "have a serious effect on the prospects of completion of plans that had been made."[56] Had he known how difficult the year ahead would be, Dille might have expressed his grief more forcefully, not just for the loss of Adams, but for the deaths of a trio of capable men.

8

Food for Defense: New Life for C–BT and a Modified Construction Plan

In 1942, a bleak war year for the United States, the Japanese overran valiant forces at Bataan and Corregidor in the Philippines; Wake Island collapsed; aircraft carriers *Lexington, Yorktown*, and *Wasp* were sunk; and a Japanese submarine caused panic in California by shelling an oil refinery north of Santa Barbara. Meanwhile, Germany's field marshal, Erwin Rommel, defeated the British at Tobruk, and German armies surrounded Stalingrad for what they expected to be the last battle in Russia. Matters became even more depressing at home when the Office of Price Administration announced food rationing, as Congress responded to the increasing need to supply the Allies with nonmilitary foodstuffs. The U.S. commitment to a "Food for Defense Program" — from victory gardens to regional production quotas — inspired the District's Board of Directors to press for more rapid construction by emphasizing the C–BT's potential for expanded food production if supplemental water were made available through the Continental Divide Tunnel.[1]

As early as March 1941, District officials had recognized the need to vigorously promote the C–BT as an irrigation project. Harold L. Ickes urged the Bureau to bring western federal power projects into capacity use for energy production, but Director Leland Olds of the Federal Power Commission advised Clifford Stone that foreseeable regional power needs were insufficient to recommend accelerated appropriations for the C–BT. He advised framing the primary emphasis for construction funds in the context of the Project's irrigation capability.[2] In response, Stone authorized the CWCB staff to make two studies of northern Colorado agriculture and a third of the C–BT's power features,[3] all of which proved invaluable when legions of special interests competed in Washington for legislative attention. As Charles Hansen noted, hotels were so filled with lobbyists that visitors were limited to one-week stays.[4]

The December 1941 agricultural report, submitted by E. Herbert Dyer and J. R. "Bob" Barkley, provided current information for Stone and Hansen on the agricultural potential of northern Colorado. Responding to the U.S. Department of Agriculture's (USDA) war production goals for the District, the authors argued that excess food production could best be obtained from areas where diversified agriculture already existed. If the government were fully committed to completing the C–BT, supplemental water would be available from the Poudre and South Platte rivers by 1944, allowing the District to meet USDA quotas.[5] The report also pointed out that, while northern Colorado was uniquely adaptable to sugar beet production, meeting 1942 goals was unlikely without supplemental water.

An additional report, dated March 1942, reemphasized Colorado's importance as a sugar beet area, noting that the District was capable of harvesting beets from approximately 193,000 acres (almost twice the 104,000 acres planted in 1941) and that the thirteen existing refineries were adequate to process the harvest. Farm operators were already equipped with the necessary tools and machinery; no vital war materials were needed; "Spanish-American" labor was available; and the by-products (tops, pulp, and molasses) would actually augment the production of fat livestock to meet wartime needs.[6] The report concluded, however, that "if a stable and sustained production . . . is to be maintained, and if future goals call for further production increases, the development and utilization of [a] supplemental water supply will be imperative."[7] Surveys indicated above average water supply for the 1942 season, but the record of the past ten years strongly suggested that moisture availability was erratic at best. Given the wartime food crisis, could the United States afford *not* to build the C–BT as rapidly as possible?

The 1942 Power Report, a companion to the agricultural reports, described the expected cost and amount of energy on line when the C–BT was completed. Although the estimated total cost of the entire Project had already escalated to $65 million, this report echoed the need for "vigorous" action on all phases of construction to make water available by the end of fiscal year 1944, with power on line one year later. To accomplish this, congressional appropriations of $54 million were needed during the next three years, a substantial increase in the average annual funding to date.[8]

While District officials presented these reports in Washington to garner greater congressional support, Bureau Commissioner John C. Page also supported the need for increased food production.[9] Although the power argument was still very persuasive among House subcommittee members in charge of Department of the Interior appropriations, Page continued to stress the agricultural importance of water diversion to Colorado's East Slope.[10] In Denver for a short visit, he spoke about the effects of Lend-Lease food demands by the Allies and the possibility that

Sinclair O. Harper, chief engineer for the Bureau during the 1940s. (Courtesy Denver Public Library, Western History Department.)

the United States might face a shortage "in many essential farm products before this war is over." Given this possibility, he toured twenty western reclamation projects to determine what resources were needed to facilitate a rapid increase in food production.[11]

The powerful War Production Board (WPB) had other ideas. After granting a high priority for materials to complete the Green Mountain Dam and Power Plant,[12] the WPB refused to reconsider the relatively low A-10 rating for the rest of the C–BT. Contractors reported enough supplies on hand to continue existing work projects for the duration of 1942, but they foresaw trouble ahead. The Bureau's chief engineer, Sinclair O. Harper, noted difficulties in obtaining rubber accessories for machinery and hauling equipment at the Continental Divide Tunnel. Other contractors complained about the shortage of skilled labor and the need to pay overtime and bonuses in order to keep men on the job. The Bureau even reported uncertainties of finding a "crew of men suitable for the work" on its own jobs.[13] The war was taking its toll on C–BT construction.

On October 27, 1942, the WPB suddenly revoked construction priorities of seven reclamation projects, including the C–BT. Except to maintain safety and health standards and to prevent damage to structures, it suspended further construction and prohibited contractors from accepting delivery of construction materials.[14] Green Mountain Dam and Power Plant was the only exception to this ruling. Senators Ed Johnson and Eugene D. Millikin and Congressman William S. Hill filed protests immediately, asking for a stay of the WPB's order pending appeals from the District. In a letter to Roosevelt, Hill pointed out that if construction stopped, water would enter the Continental Divide Tunnel, causing damage and creating the necessity of high-cost pumping. With support from Ickes, Hill said that completing the final 2.5 miles would be cheaper than pumping water out of the tunnel.[15]

Tunnel construction continued despite the WPB's stop-work order while Johnson reasoned with the WPB. He argued that the government gained very little labor and few materials from shutting down construction; furthermore, the C–BT, as an irrigation project, promised a major contribution to the war effort.[16] He failed to convert WPB officials, who ranked the C–BT in the same category as "hundreds of other projects" and responded that the tunnel would not be used until after the war even if it were finished. Fearful of "setting a precedent," the WPB concluded that tunnel excavation would cease for good on December 31, 1942.[17]

Millikin refused to yield to the bureaucracy. Believing that a completed C–BT was an important contribution to national defense, he pressed J. M. Dille for additional information to bring to Washington, including summaries of the ideas contained in the "1941 Agricultural Report." Millikin planted in Dille the seed that eventually produced a modified construction program when he wrote:

> My own feeling is that the closing down of irrigation projects which can be finished without due consumption of needed materials is a mistake that will rank in magnitude and seriousness with the original reduction of our synthetic rubber program. The demands of our armies and Allies for food are constantly increasing. The nation has had almost miraculous fortune in having favorable conditions for crops during the past year or so. But give us a drought year, and no prudent man can leave that out of his calculations, and we may have a hell of a situation in this country. The decision to drop seems final at the moment, and although this may not be halted by presidential or any other intervention yet, we should not let it get out of mind that such matters are not static, that they are in a constant state of flux and that a go-ahead order sometime in the future is not out of the cards, although at this writing, the odds seem to be long against it. Let's keep the flag flying. We are right, and we have nothing to lose and everything to gain by continuing to fight.[18]

Dille agreed totally. He knew that the Bureau had already begun studies to modify East Slope features of the Project, but he had some questions about its motivation.[19] After a quick trip to Washington to warn the WPB's Facilities Review Committee of the harm from shutting down construction, he prepared a memorandum entitled "Project Water Delivery" for the Board, which expressed preliminary concerns about the Bureau's modification of the original plan and closed with an appeal that the Bureau consult with the District before making drastic changes.[20] Dille also reported that he and Stone were working with the Bureau to remove the WPB's stop order. The general opinion in Washington, he reported, was that while they must obey the WPB's decision, "food conditions of the nation may soon develop to an extent where reconsideration of the matter may well result in reinstatement of the project in the construction program of the nation."[21]

Dille recognized that, while the District was pursuing its agriculture-for-defense argument to secure sufficient appropriations for completing the tunnel and Shadow Mountain Dam, the Bureau was altering the original water delivery plan to generate more power and revenue to pay off mounting construction costs. Although the two organizations were working at cross purposes, both had sympathetic ears in Washington, and both achieved their objectives.

The pressing task of the District and the CWCB was to convince Congress that water could be delivered to the East Slope without completing all the works of the C–BT. They argued for building Shadow Mountain Dam and spillway to allow water from the North Fork of the Colorado River to flow backward through the present Grand Lake outlet, through the lake, and into the Continental Divide Tunnel by gravity. Lack of reservoirs on the East Slope would necessitate temporarily conveying water from the tunnel down the Wind River to the Big Thompson River and thence to the irrigated areas that served approximately 322,000 of the District's 675,000 acres. Water could be available for the 1944 crop year if work on this modified plan began without delay and with diligence.[22]

While the Facilities Review Committee of the WPB challenged this conclusion, recommending no change in status for the C–BT, the War Food Administration (WFA) reacted quite differently. Urged by Ickes to cooperate in developing an optimum five-year plan for producing certain critical war foods,[23] the WFA joined the Interior Department to remove the WPB's construction restrictions. They were aided by the USDA and Senator Carl Hayden's special committee, organized to move western reclamation projects to completion as quickly as possible.[24] After a conference with the USDA, Millikin wrote to Stone in April that he saw "encouraging signs" to position the C–BT as one of the first projects to be restored to construction activity.[25] The continuing wartime food crisis proved him right. Dille reported to the Board that the Bureau continued to work closely with the USDA while preparing data for the WPB that showed how the West could grow food to meet the emergency.[26] Simultaneously, western congressmen and the National Reclamation Association (NRA) aided Millikin by pointing out that, even after the war, the United States would have to feed other nations.[27]

The WPB officials were stubborn. Responding to an inquiry from Roosevelt, their chairman, Donald M. Nelson, wrote that he was only following the president's directives: A construction project "requiring critical materials and manpower should not be permitted at the present time unless it will make a contribution to the war effort sometime during the calendar year 1944." Because the C–BT could not begin to produce additional food until 1945 at the earliest, the stop order had not been revoked; nevertheless, the WFA had recently recommended reinstating the C–BT. Even though it was "one of the least essential of the group" (one of eight projects that the WFA recommended for funding), Nelson agreed to review its status.[28] As Roosevelt wrote Colorado Governor John C. Vivian: "It does not look very promising, but we are keeping the door open."[29]

While Dille worried about the availability of steel and adequate labor to finish the tunnel, he also filed written statements with the House Subcommittee on Interior Appropriations that anticipated a resumption order from the WPB.[30] On June 15, 1943, Stone received and reported to Dille a "very confidential" letter from Millikin, noting that members of the Appropriations Committee were certain to provide supplemental funding for the C–BT soon. Three days later, Millikin telegraphed Dille that the C–BT had been awarded an appropriation of $3.6 million.[31] Ironically, the stop order was still in effect. Not until July 24 did the WPB authorize the deputy war food administrator to resume construction, appending a new provision that the War Manpower Commission must determine that "employment for construction of the Project will not unduly impair other essential employment in the region directly related to the war program."[32]

District officials now had another wartime agency to deal with, but they were optimistic. Hansen gave credit to Millikin for his role in lifting the stop-work order. He admitted difficulty deciding which was better news, authorization to resume tunnel work or the resignation of Italian dictator Benito Mussolini.[33] In either case, northern Colorado farmers were

Workers leaving the East Portal of the Adams Tunnel. The Mancha Electric Mules were used to transport men and materials. (Courtesy Bureau of Reclamation.)

ecstatic. The WFA had accepted Dille's modified plan for 400,000 acres to receive supplemental water, resulting in an estimated 15,000 extra tons of alfalfa, 1,500,000 extra bushels of potatoes, 360,000 extra cubic weight of beans, and 180,000 extra tons of sugar beets. Time was allowed for training new crews, which meant that the bore should be holed through in 240 days from the time work resumed.[34] Supplemental water through the Continental Divide would not be far behind.

The construction estimate proved fairly accurate. When work ceased in December 1942, crews had excavated a total of 55,444 feet from both ends of the Continental Divide Tunnel, representing 80.5 percent of the total distance.[35] With approximately 2.5 miles of tunnel work remaining, Stiers Brothers Construction began digging again from the West Portal on August 24, 1943, and the S. S. Magoffin Company resumed work from the East Portal on September 17.[36] Enough labor was temporarily available for two and three eight-hour shifts; however, to keep men on the job, contractors had to pay higher wages already approved by the secretary of labor.[37]

View of the S. S. Magoffin Company shop near the East Portal of the Adams Tunnel. Magoffin's men constructed the eastern segment of the Adams Tunnel. (Courtesy Bureau of Reclamation.)

Despite congressional authorization to hire American-born Japanese on reclamation jobs, Bureau officials dismissed this plan due to possible hostility from labor unions and a belief that the *Nisei* would refuse to work underground.[38] Excavation progress was interrupted when Stiers Brothers's superintendent John Austin and forty-two of his men were called off the job to fight a fire and cave-in at Tunnel 10 of the Denver and Salt Lake Railroad (the Moffat Line), where they stayed until the end of November. By the time crews returned to the West Portal, they were able to advance the heading only 1,290 feet for the year while the East Portal heading moved ahead 2,976 feet.[39] By Christmas 1943 a little less than 2 miles remained to be holed through.

At Green Mountain Dam and Power Plant, Warner Construction Company completed work under the original contract. The Bureau chose two new contractors to relocate State Highway 9, which would be inundated by water from Green Mountain Reservoir. Meanwhile, government forces installed turbines and generators in the Green Mountain Power

Plant, completed clearing of the reservoir area, and resumed clearing work in the area that would be flooded by Shadow Mountain Lake.[40] On December 3 the J. F. Shea Company of Los Angeles contracted to build the Shadow Mountain Dam and dikes, with construction scheduled to start on April 16, 1944.[41] Dille's modified plan was now taking shape before planners' and workers' eyes.

With only 9,030 feet of Continental Divide Tunnel to be excavated, excitement mounted. In January Stiers Brothers began working three shifts a day for six days a week. By March 31, with the two headings less than a mile apart, men claimed they heard shots fired at the West Portal heading. For safety's sake, S. S. Magoffin Company stopped work on June 7,[42] and Stiers Brothers completed excavation from the west heading. Before they left work on June 9, workers drilled a 25-foot pilot bore into the remaining rock to prepare for the final holing through. Although the Board had agreed not to hold any public ceremony "on account of war conditions,"[43] the Directors arranged for publicity of the long-awaited event.

Dille planned the ceremony, which excluded women because of a long-standing superstition against women in tunnels. On June 10, 1944, at 12:24 P.M., the Bureau's chief engineer, Sinclair O. Harper, closed a switch that ignited nine charges of dynamite. Within seconds, 150 guests, the entire NCWCD Board, and Assistant Secretary of the Interior Oscar Chapman heard the dull, heavy detonations. A blast of warm wind whipped back along the shaft, blowing spectators' hats and cigarettes all around. Workers on the east end started air blowers, while those at the West Portal cranked up suction fans. Less than twenty minutes later, clear air flowed through the 10-foot wide tunnel, and debris from the blast was removed so that men on both sides could meet face to face. Bureau engineers Arthur C. Link and Frank Matejka met in the opening, accompanied by cheers from crews on both sides.[44] A check on the center line and grade revealed the former off 1/16 of an inch and the latter 3/4 of an inch.[45] Six months later, on December 21, 1944, Roosevelt signed legislation that officially named the tunnel after the late Senator Adams, a fitting tribute to a man who had worked so hard to persuade his colleagues to support the C–BT.

Having Adams's name thus commemorated on one of the C–BT's principal features did not come about easily. Early in 1942, Senator Johnson wrote Hansen that a movement had begun to have the late senator's name attached to the new "cantonment" (Camp Carson) in Colorado Springs. Johnson had spoken with the Adams family and had learned that they preferred having the C–BT renamed in his honor. He asked Hansen if the Board had any objection,[46] and Hansen replied patiently that he would discuss the matter at the next meeting. He personally felt that getting the C–BT into people's minds had taken some time, especially in some of the Washington bureaus, and he did not relish reeducating Congress, who might be unfamiliar with the Project. Furthermore, Hansen noted, with only 20 percent of the Project completed and the rest possibly shelved for the war's duration, renaming it now might prove no honor at all for the Adams family. After the Board met, Hansen reported that everyone expressed a great regard for Adams but that their unanimous opinion was to wait until Project completion before renaming it.[47]

Johnson persisted. Somewhat perturbed, he told Hansen that he disagreed with the Board's point of view. Because Congress was familiar with Adams's work, it would have a harder time reducing appropriations for the "Alva B. Adams Project"; however, he wondered if the Board would agree to renaming the Continental Divide Tunnel in Adams's name,[48] an alternative that Hansen proposed at the April meeting. After unanimous adoption,[49] Hansen told Johnson: "It had been the hope of some of us that this naming ceremony might have been carried on at the tunnel itself in a year or so, but if it fits in better now, that is the thing to do."[50] The name change was made public at the memorial service for Adams and became official in December 1944.

By then the Alva B. Adams Tunnel was already holed through, but completion of the remainder of the modified plan faced the possible threat of manpower shortages. Crews had lined only 3 percent of the tunnel with concrete by the end of 1944. Shadow Mountain Dam and dikes were 58 percent complete; the connecting channel between Grand Lake and Shadow Mountain Reservoir, designed to maintain Grand Lake at a constant level, was complete except for foot and automobile bridges. After local citizens and members of the Grand Lake Yacht Club petitioned the Board of County Commissioners of Grand County to close Shadow Mountain Reservoir to motor and sailboats so that fishing might prosper, the channel contractor decided to install rigid spans that had been omitted in the original order. On November 11, 1944, excavating operations halted until these new bridges were ordered.[51]

The final link in Dille's modified plan was the delivery system from the East Portal to the Big Thompson River by way of a proposed 54-inch wood stave pipe, which the Bureau carefully studied in spring 1943. At that time, Page had ordered construction teams to use wood in order to save steel for the war effort.[52] The Bureau was more concerned about the carrying capacity of the Big Thompson River channel. The modified plan called for annual interim deliveries of 90,000 to 100,000 acre-feet through the Adams

Construction workers inside the Alva B. Adams Tunnel. Installation of 69 Kv line at top. (Courtesy NCWCD.)

Tunnel into the Big Thompson. Although experts concluded from historical records that the river channel could safely carry 500 cfs of additional flow (362,000 acre-feet per year), Bureau officials conducted their own studies to determine potential risks to Highway 34 and local residents.[53] They never arrived at any definite conclusions, and they never showed much interest in building the conduit. What became apparent to both the Bureau and the District, however, was the serious labor shortage that was about to delay lining the Adams Tunnel. It would make the whole modified plan irrelevant.

The first hint of difficulties appeared in summer 1944. Work at Shadow Mountain Reservoir and preparation of the Adams Tunnel for concrete lining became problematic because contractors' authorizations for construction omitted a special classification permitting referrals of labor by the United States Employment Service.[54] In November the Bureau filed a statement with the War Manpower Commission (WMC) in Washington, stating that unless enough men were allowed for a full three-shift operation, the modified plan would not be completed on time to deliver water in 1945.[55]

State and regional offices of the WMC contacted Stiers Brothers and S. S. Magoffin Company for data on current manpower needs. They also announced a meeting of the WMC Priorities Committee on December 4, 1944, to determine the number of workers allowable on the Project. Meanwhile, the War Food Administration, C–BT Project engineer C. H. Howell, and Dille urged the WMC to approve a work force of 350 men whose labor would permit supplemental water to reach the East Slope during the critical summer months of 1945.[56] Their efforts were unsuccessful. The Priorities Committee decided that the U.S. Employment Service should interview all men currently working on the Adams Tunnel, referring those qualified to "high priority jobs where their services [were] desperately needed in the immediate war effort." If enough men were left to permit work on a one-shift basis, tunnel maintenance would continue just to prevent deterioration of existing facilities.[57] As a result of these interviews, nearly 107 men at the Adams Tunnel accepted "priority jobs" or referrals to the U.S. Employment Service offices for further information. The Bureau complained that they had been "intimidated" into accepting jobs in war plants, but there was little redress against the powerful WMC.[58] Regional director E. B. Debler, who reminded the WMC that both the WPB and the WFA had approved the modified plan, announced that the Bureau would appeal the decision and request a minimum of 125 men for each tunnel bore;[59] but the WMC had clout.

On January 9, 1945, the WMC placed ceilings on the number of men allowed to work at the Adams Tunnel — forty on the West end, fifteen on the East end, effective 12:01 A.M., Monday, January 14, 1945[60] — and sent men to Grand Lake to "inspect" the tunnel to check obedience to its orders. While the Bureau objected to this invasion of authority, the District accepted the decision reasonably well "with the idea that when war conditions allowed, the force could be increased and the tunnel then [could] be made ready for use in 1946."[61] Once again, the Project stalled. Labor ceilings remained until March 1945, one month before Roosevelt's death and two months before the war's end in Europe. Although District officials were frustrated that supplemental water would not come through the tunnel in 1945 as planned, they had other issues to consider, not the least of which was the Bureau's interest in making major changes in the original contracted plans and in water delivery locations of several East Slope features.

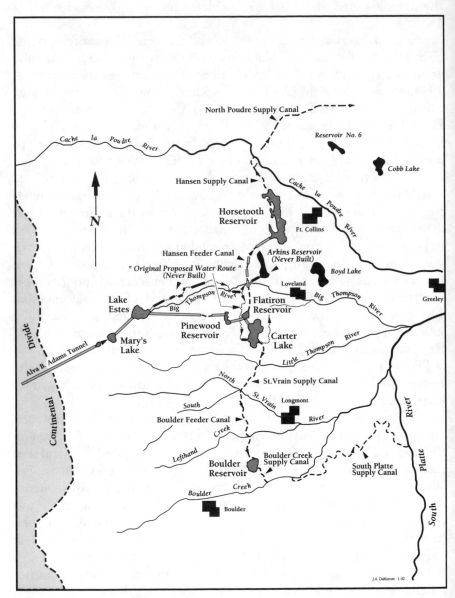

C–BT Project, East Slope Facilities.

Water at Last: Interim Deliveries to the Big Thompson River

In 1942 Bureau engineers began conducting extensive surveys and studies to determine whether better routes or locations existed for C–BT features on the East Slope.[1] Motivated by the uncertainties of war, fears of postwar inflation, and the District's insistence that $25 million was the limit of its contractual obligation to the United States, the Bureau began to seek cheaper ways to meet its own responsibilities without violating terms of Senate Document 80 and the Repayment Contract.

J. M. Dille, who was fully aware of the implications of the Bureau's actions, submitted a November 1942 memorandum to the Directors that explained Bureau concerns about the three East Slope reservoirs mentioned in Senate Document 80. Carter Lake appeared too large for its service area; Horsetooth Reservoir was too small for the expected Poudre River demand; and Arkins Reservoir, to be located just below the junction of Buckhorn and Redstone creeks, seemed too expensive "to justify any probable benefit for irrigation storage purposes on the Big Thompson River."[2] Dille reported that his office had "definitely placed" 208,476 acre-feet of Project water, and the District was holding petitions for an additional 53,000 acre-feet that he expected to allot; however, the best place for the remaining 102,000 acre-feet was in the four upper water districts (Nos. 3, 4, 5, and 6), "where most of the present Class D allotments are located and where the need for additional supplemental water still exists." About half of the lands in these districts had already received water allotments, but owners of the other 110,000 acres were still undecided about the future success of the Project and whether or not to assume an assessment lien. Dille estimated that even if these farmers did not want the water, entitled allottees might make supplemental petitions because of increasing awareness that they had underestimated their needs.[3]

Dille's challenge was to approximate the percentage of future supplemental water to be petitioned from each stream system. For this reason, any modifications that the Bureau made in East Slope features were critical. Of the 208,476 acre-feet allotted as of 1942, 57 percent was destined for the Poudre River (including 40,000 acre-feet to the North Poudre Irrigation Company), 26.5 percent for the Big Thompson, 1.5 percent for the Little Thompson, and 15 percent for the St. Vrain River. Determining destinations for the remaining 102,000 acre-feet would strengthen the District's case for reservoirs of predetermined capacity in predetermined locations.[4]

Regarding the District's south end, Dille noted that the Bureau had studied the feasibility of constructing conduits from St. Vrain Creek to Boulder Creek and the Platte River. The line to Boulder Creek seemed feasible and necessary due to known water shortages in farmlands located in Left Hand Valley, whose irrigation water came from Boulder Creek. However, the District Directors saw no necessity for a canal to the South Platte River because few petitions had arrived from Water District No. 2. If Denver's proposed Blue River project were completed, Dille argued, enough water would come from the West Slope to satisfy any shortages in that area.[5] Building the Project as originally contemplated would mean that the three storage reservoirs were positioned correctly to deliver water to the Poudre, Big and Little Thompson, and St. Vrain systems, but if the Bureau developed a "cheaper or better plan for irrigation storage . . . it [would] create some problems of delivery to avoid claims of preferential treatment in points of delivery measurements."[6] In other words, Dille concluded, if the Bureau felt obligated to revise the original plan, supplemental water for irrigation must still be considered the first priority of the C–BT. The District Board had approved petitions for allotments of two-thirds of the 310,000 acre-feet units with the understanding that the Bureau would follow, or improve on, stipulations already laid out in the Repayment Contract. Rumored modifications in Project design unnerved District officials, but the Bureau was determined to effect changes that would produce additional revenue.

Dille soon became resigned to having the Bureau make "numerous changes" in the plan for the East Slope system.[7] In summer 1943 he noted that the Bureau was working on a plan to convey C–BT water directly east from Estes Park through a series of tunnels and reservoirs in order to generate more hydroelectric power. This new plan, he said, was "almost entirely different" from the original plan provided by the Repayment Contract.[8] In October the Board met with Bureau officials during an all-day trip to the newly proposed sites: Flatiron and Rattlesnake reservoirs, a canal from Flatiron to the Poudre River, and new reservoir sites further east.[9] In the 1943 annual report, Dille again expressed concern that Bureau engineers still misunderstood the "practical requirements of the irrigation features of this project."[10] The new route, he concluded, undoubtedly proposed a better power system and, in some aspects, better service for irrigationists, but in other ways it was unsatisfactory to the District as a whole.[11]

The Bureau, however, defended its plan, which included a 7.3-mile tunnel from Estes Park to Rattlesnake Reservoir, five power plants, and the necessary penstocks and additional works. From the Flatiron Power Plant tailrace at a 5,360-foot elevation, canals would diverge south to St. Vrain and Boulder Creeks and north (28 miles) to the Big Thompson and Poudre rivers. Because of the elevation and location of these canals, the Bureau's new arrangement eliminated the cost of constructing Horsetooth and Carter reservoirs and part of Arkins Reservoir. Instead, the system would store water in No. 6 Reservoir and Cobb Lake near Wellington, as well as in Boyd Lake northeast of Loveland[12] — reservoirs that were already in place and owned by local irrigation companies.

Dille saw flaws in this plan. Because of their low altitude and shallow depth, all three plains reservoirs identified by the Bureau would have limited value for "hold-over" purposes. Furthermore, the proposed system limited upstream exchange possibilities, compromised benefits from return flows, and risked development of heavier seepage and evaporation problems. Project water, Dille insisted, *should be delivered into the streams above all existing ditches as was originally planned.*"[13] The Bureau's changes seemingly provided only 105,000 acre-feet as the *"extreme limit"* of the amount of storable water available to the District. "Any additional capacity," he observed, "will be useful only for occasional 'hold-over' to keep the power plants in operation." The remaining 205,000 acre-feet would have to be delivered from Flatiron and Rattlesnake during the irrigation season, requiring a discharge of 1,400 to 2,000 cfs through the Adams Tunnel for seventy-five days and a capacity of 1,000 cfs in the 28-mile canal from Flatiron to the Poudre River.[14]

Dille suggested modifications to the Bureau's plan. Although he rejected the premise of some critics, that the Bureau wanted to force changes on the District that might detract from the Project's original benefits, he did feel that the "economics" of the new plan required study. He also wanted assurance of postwar resumption of an "all-out construction program [to] . . . finally bring into being a back-log of stored water [to] start a new and more stable era for irrigated farming in Northern Colorado."[15]

Dille's immediate concern, however, was restoring Horsetooth Reservoir as a key element of East Slope features and taking water out of Flatiron at a higher elevation so that a feeder canal would run a shorter distance of

12 miles into Horsetooth Reservoir.[16] Senate Document 80 provided that Horsetooth Reservoir would have a capacity of 96,000 acre-feet. Properly operated, Horsetooth could convey 70,000 acre-feet of storage water to Reservoir No. 6, while Boyd Lake would store 35,000 acre-feet of "useful water," leaving approximately 110,000 acre-feet "to be delivered from Flatiron outlet on direct irrigation demand." This scheme, Dille concluded, compared roughly with what he had calculated as the "probable total [allotment] requirements of the Thompson, St. Vrain and Boulder District."[17]

This fair compromise with the Bureau's plans conformed East Slope features with expected demands for supplemental water on the three rivers that were foremost in Dille's mind. He also believed that his plan allowed diversion of a large part of the 310,000 acre-feet of Colorado River water "and its use to some advantage on all District lands in the shortest possible time," further allowing two of the power plants to start operations on a "firm power basis" when completed. While recognizing that engineers had to finalize details, Dille remained certain that "some such program offer[ed] the only hope of any irrigation benefits, or of any East Slope power production, in any reasonable period of time." He hoped to secure irrigation benefits and part of the power production without waiting for energy demands to reveal a need for the full power project.[18] His time schedule called for completing the modified plan first — the Adams Tunnel, Shadow Mountain Reservoir, and the interim delivery system from the East Portal to the Big Thompson River. Lake Granby and Pumping Plant and the Estes Park Power Plant (No. 1) should also reach completion as rapidly as possible. Then, instead of proceeding east with the Mt. Olympus Tunnel, crews would build irrigation storage facilities and distribution works in the foothills while water flowed on an interim basis into the Big Thompson River.[19] Flatiron Reservoir, St. Vrain and Boulder canals, the North Poudre Canal, and enlargement of Boyd Lake and No. 6 Reservoir would soon follow. The balance of East Slope power features were to be built "as demand for power justifie[d] [them]."[20]

Although consistent with the District's priority for delivery of supplemental water to irrigated agriculture, Dille's compromise plan revealed that the Bureau and the District had begun to head in different directions. The District's goal was to support the war effort through increased agricultural production, but from 1944 on, and especially after the war's end, the Bureau became so concerned about congressional criticism of rising construction costs that every means of cutting corners and advancing revenue-producing power capability was followed to neutralize criticism. For the moment, however, the Bureau and District Board resolved their differences in a friendly manner, even though the Bureau was undergoing major organizational changes.

Reorganization had been in the planning stages for several years. Harold L. Ickes, who was convinced that the time had come to adapt the Bureau's mission to a New Deal philosophy that stressed water resource development along drainage basins, opposed establishing independent regional entities similar to the Tennessee Valley Authority but supported regional decentralization to preserve responsibility for reclamation and flood control of western rivers in the Department of the Interior.

Approved by Ickes in 1942, the reorganization plan was activated by Commissioner Harry Bashore on September 9, 1943, and established six regional offices in the seventeen western states. The chief engineer's office in Denver undertook the dual role of designing works and supervising construction, with resultant management problems. Construction engineers had two bosses, the regional director and the chief engineer. In many cases they were responsible for carrying out conflicting instructions. Denied complete control over a project, they felt handicapped in efforts to hold down costs. This attempt to centralize technical control machinery clashed with the Department of the Interior's commitment to decentralize water resource development.[21]

NCWCD Directors became concerned about the six-region plan at the July 1944 Board meeting. Region 6 at Billings, Montana, was to assume responsibility for C–BT construction, and Mills E. Bunger, assistant director of Region 5 at Amarillo, Texas, author of much of Senate Document 80, was coordinator for the six regions.[22] The Board found this arrangement awkward. At the August meeting Directors passed a resolution requesting the Bureau to create a seventh region with headquarters in Denver. The Bureau responded favorably. Region 7's newly appointed director, E. B. Debler, immediately spoke to the Board about whether the District or the Bureau should control plans for the distribution of C–BT water. The Board informed Debler politely and forcefully that water delivery was the responsibility of the District "and should be left entirely in our hands."[23] As chief of all project investigation work for the Bureau, Debler was familiar with the C–BT and was thought "capable and energetic," with every intention of presiding over rapid conclusion of the Project.[24] But District leadership balked at allowing him or anyone else to intrude in administrative matters that had been clearly spelled out as District responsibilities in Senate Document 80. Debler got the message.

Another "authority" issue on an even larger scale surfaced at the same time. With the 1940 completion of Fort Peck Dam on the Missouri River, both the Bureau and the Army Corps of Engineers proposed plans for basin-wide development of their own particular interests. The Corps's Pick Plan emphasized flood control and navigation, while the Bureau's Sloan Plan stressed irrigation and hydroelectric power. Both scenarios endorsed multipurpose improvements by all interested federal and state agencies.[25] As with other regional water matters, the federal government's plans for Missouri River development were of considerable interest to the NCWCD Board. The 1944 Flood Control Act reconciled the two proposals by charging the Corps to build downstream dams and reservoirs for navigation and flood control, while the Bureau would work on power and irrigation at upstream sites. The Missouri River basin project was "the most comprehensive water resource program envisioned to that time";[26] its potential impact on South Platte River water users caused considerable consternation among District officials.

Dille, expressing his concern to the Board in August 1944, reported on a meeting with upper (Missouri) basin states representatives, where he had supported the view that these states had "prior rights to the use of water for irrigation and consumptive purposes as against the program of navigation interests in the lower states."[27] When the Missouri Valley Authority (MVA) formed the following year, the CWCB prepared 500 pamphlets entitled "The Authority Issue" that described how Colorado and the District felt threatened by the establishment of such regional authorities. The Board then passed a resolution in September 1945 decrying the formation of the MVA; "as American citizens," Directors strenuously opposed the plan as "destructive of our democratic system of government."[28]

Conversely, the CWCB gave enthusiastic blessing to a proposed treaty with Mexico involving the Colorado River. The 1922 Colorado River Compact divided the waters of the Colorado River between upper and lower basin states. No specific provision was made for Mexico, but both basins were expected to contribute to Mexico's allotment if a formal international agreement were found necessary in the future. In June 1942 the CWCB announced that its "principal business" was to effect an allocation of this system's waters between Mexico and the United States.[29] The Committee of 14, a voluntary association of representatives from the seven states of the Colorado River basin, had taken this matter under consideration in 1941. A subcommittee prepared engineering studies for the CWCB, which reviewed these reports, estimated the availability of between 4 and 7 million acre-feet of water at the U.S. border in any given year, and composed a statement of policy. Among other things, settling Mexico's right to water was provided for as soon as possible; allocation was based on principles of "comity and equity" because all waters of the Colorado River could be easily developed in the United States; any treaty was required to recognize the Colorado River Compact; infringement of water deliveries on waters already appropriated by the upper basin states was precluded; 500,000 acre-feet were committed to Mexico annually; any amount in excess appropriated by the Mexicans was not to be used as a basis for an increased demand in future years; and Mexico was to have no right to this water unless for agricultural and domestic purposes.[30]

A year later, however, the CWCB approved a formula that reflected the State Department's concern about water shortages in dry years, guaranteeing Mexico 2 million acre-feet for undefined purposes related to beneficial use, except in the event of U.S. drought, when proportionately less water would flow across the border.[31] On February 3, 1944, Mexico and the United States signed a treaty that awarded 1.5 million acre-feet to Mexico plus an additional 200,000 acre-feet if enough river water were available. The guarantee was for a quantity of water, not quality water. In the event of a drought, Mexico would accept a reduction in water in the same proportion as the reduction of consumptive uses in the United States.[32]

While California prepared to fight ratification of the treaty, Colorado Governor John C. Vivian and the CWCB urged Washington officials to sign. The board telegraphed both the State Department and the president and passed a resolution recommending Senate ratification. It argued that a "definite determination of the apportionment of water of the Colorado River to the Republic of Mexico [would] be a protection to the C–BT."[33] Because Clifford Stone and Royce J. Tipton had played such prominent roles in the extended negotiations and final plan for the treaty and because both were close allies of the District, Dille recommended that the Board pass this resolution unanimously.[34]

By ratification of the Mexican treaty on April 18, 1945, NCWCD officials could again focus on C–BT construction. The War Manpower Commission had lifted the labor ceiling, allowing work to continue on the modified construction plan. The Colorado State Manpower director wrote contractors at the Adams Tunnel and Shadow Mountain Reservoir, urging them to raise the employment ceiling to "100 male workers" to ensure no loss of completed work and to retain the possibility of supplementary irrigation water through the tunnel for the 1946 crop season.[35] Walker Young, the Bureau's chief engineer, appealed to Commissioner Harry

After holing through the Adams Tunnel in 1944, workers began preparing the tunnel for concrete lining. (Courtesy NCWCD.)

Bashore to secure the highest labor priority rating possible for the C–BT. To bring water through the tunnel in 1946, he said, construction must be completed at Shadow Mountain Dam and dikes, Colorado River diversion improvements, and at most of the Adams Tunnel's inlet structure by September 1, 1945. He also recommended completion of the "wood stave pipeline" from the East Portal of the tunnel to the Big Thompson River as well as initiation of concrete arch lining on a three-shift basis with 175 men at each end of the tunnel. He recognized that completion by spring 1946 was "at best somewhat of a gamble," but he believed it was possible and would thereby enable delivery of 90,000 acre-feet annually to the East Slope. If Bashore did not approve the plan, he recommended termination of all contracts as soon as practicable;[36] fortunately, Bashore cabled to Young that he approved of the Project and that it should be prosecuted with all speed.[37]

Labor shortages plagued construction during April and May. Although wage rates increased 75 percent from the 1940 average, contractors had difficulty finding enough skilled and semi-skilled workers.[38] As Dille reported to the Board, the Bureau was trying to complete the modified plan on schedule,[39] but the Directors were questioning the merits of interim water delivery to the Big Thompson River in the face of rapidly rising construction costs. Because ample moisture was available by summer 1945, Directors wondered if foregoing construction of a conduit down Wind River to the Big Thompson River might not be wiser. Construction of this temporary delivery system might delay "rapid completion of the total project."[40] Though they took no action, this shift in focus indicated how both advocates and opponents of water projects could be influenced by the abundance or shortage of snow and rainfall.

Simultaneously, Bureau officials reported good news. They had finally consented to construct Horsetooth Reservoir and to abandon plans for using three other lakes for storage. Studies showed that proper materials were available at the chosen site; with some additional expense, they even wanted to increase the reservoir capacity from 96,000 to 146,000 acre-feet. The only unresolved question concerned the final location and the capacity of the outlet from Horsetooth to the Poudre River. Debler also informed the Board that his department had omitted Arkins Reservoir but authorized construction of Carter Lake to a capacity of 110,000 acre-feet as originally planned.[41] Dille, although pleased, worried that the Bureau had insufficient interest in the Boulder Creek–South Platte area. His letter to Debler underscored the Bureau's obligation to provide water to this part of the District "regardless of the possibilities of the Blue River Project." If Debler had any other ideas, Dille urged him to consult the District.[42] From 1942 to 1946 Dille had become convinced that the Bureau would have to construct some conduits to provide adequate service to the south end of the District.

Given the inflationary situation and the Bureau's pressure to cut costs, it is not surprising that the two agencies disagreed about what was best for the District's south end. Article 4 (Section ff) of the Repayment Contract specified only that conduits from the St. Vrain River to Boulder Creek and to the South Platte River were "now being studied." Dille blamed this imprecision on funding limitations imposed when the 1937 Bunger Report was prepared.[43] The District had neglected an early effort to solicit water allotments from this area because it lacked hard information on methods of delivery. When some landowners in the south end petitioned for 11,000 acre-feet of C–BT water, Dille began searching for some way to give these people their entitled benefits. Following 1943 Bureau studies, he proposed several options under which the government might authorize construction of a conduit from St. Vrain to Boulder Creek, accompanied by an enlargement of the lower Boulder and Coal Creek extension ditches following the District's southern boundary.[44]

On Christmas Eve 1945 Dille invited Debler to the January 1946 Board meeting to discuss these options. Debler accepted. He had decided to follow the original Bunger Plan and to place the Poudre River outlet at the north end of Horsetooth Reservoir, favoring a gravity-feed canal for the North Poudre Irrigation Company.[45] Although Debler wanted to give the matter of south end deliveries additional study, he promised to work with the District to develop a suitable plan and authorized the District to proceed with allotments of water in that area. The Board expressed its pleasure.[46]

The war ended when Germany surrendered in May and Japan followed suit in August 1945. While the Bureau worked as quickly as possible to complete the modified plan on schedule (by June 1945),[47] the end of hostilities with Japan resulted in the Board's formal suggestion to the Bureau that this plan be dropped and that "all efforts be concentrated on completing the entire Project as rapidly as possible."[48] The CWCB also gave highest priority to the acceleration of C–BT construction consistent with Senate Document 80.[49] Because the Bureau had almost finalized plans for all the East Slope features, its officials agreed. They officially dropped the modified plan — at least for the moment.

By the close of 1945 enough federal funds became available to allow pouring concrete at both ends of the Adams Tunnel. Progress slowed due to continuing labor shortages. Workers finished part of the intake structure from Grand Lake to the West Portal and completed 95 percent of Shadow Mountain Dam and dikes. Although the government had appropriated only $800,000 in response to the Bureau's request for $2 million in fiscal year 1946, the House Appropriation Committee at the war's end approved another $5,575,000 in supplemental appropriations, bringing total funding for the Project to $29,633,070.[50] With ample appropriations, gradually increasing manpower and materials, and a reasonably harmonious relationship between the Bureau and the District, everything seemed right for construction to move ahead rapidly on all features of the C–BT. The modified plan had apparently been defeated by consensus. Even Tipton argued it "impractical" to think about bringing water through the Adams Tunnel "at this time."[51]

However, early indications of inadequate moisture on the East Slope in spring 1946 gave the Board second thoughts about abandoning the interim diversion plan. At almost the same time, alarming cost estimates[52] and renewed pressure from Congress to reduce expenditures forced the Bureau to urge the District to renegotiate the Repayment Contract. In short order the District found itself once again at odds with the Bureau. If the East Slope really needed water for the immediate future, the NCWCD Board might have to consider renegotiating the Repayment Contract.

Tipton warned of the Bureau's dilemma at the June 1946 Board meeting, describing Congress's concern about public power projects and suggesting that Directors prepare for negotiations.[53] As predicted, Debler attended the next meeting to explain why he favored adjusting the District's repayment obligation. He argued that postwar inflation meant farmers were receiving higher prices for their crops and should be willing to pay more for C–BT water. The Directors listened but agreed unanimously that Debler's suggestion lacked sufficient merit for serious consideration.[54]

Dille and Debler were again moving in opposite directions. Dille met with stockholders of the Greeley-Loveland Irrigation Company in September, where he discussed reactivating the modified plan to divert water for three or more years via the Adams Tunnel and the Big Thompson River. Harry Farr and others in attendance favored this interim diversion with the largest flow possible, characterizing the construction costs as "cheap insurance and a sound investment." They voted to contract for a minimum of 35 percent and maximum of 75 percent of the 200 cfs that Dille estimated could be added to the Big Thompson. They also approved construction of a 38-inch steel pipe conduit, in lieu of a wood stave pipe, from the East Portal to the Big Thompson River.[55] Dille hoped that speedy implementation of this operation would save some crops then suffering from abnormal moisture conditions in Water District No. 4.[56] Debler still wanted to renegotiate the Repayment Contract. He appeared to be putting obstacles in the path of District officials, who wanted assurance of water diversion through the Adams Tunnel before the Project's completion. To remove some Bureau objections, the Board agreed to authorize an expenditure of $2,500 for improving West Slope ditches that would protect Colorado River ranchers in the event of an interim diversion,[57] but the Bureau was not satisfied. It wanted to revise the Repayment Contract. Two critical meetings in July and October 1946 resulted in a showdown.

Meeting in Greeley with the NCWCD Board and CWCB's Clifford Stone, Debler energetically argued the Bureau's view that the power side of the C–BT should not be expected to pay more than three-quarters of the total cost. Farm prices were holding strong and were not expected to drop to 1934 levels. Why couldn't irrigation farmers pay more? Stone was not sure about Debler's conclusions. Economic conditions were in fact quite unsettled, he replied, and it was not a good time to renegotiate the Repayment Contract. Furthermore, he told Debler, "you don't have enough facts on which they [farmers] or anyone else can base an opinion."

Debler responded angrily, "I didn't come up here to be told that I don't know what I'm talking about, or to get your personal opinion, Judge. . . . What I'd like to have is the opinion of the Board." He then suggested extending the repayment period to fifty years at $1.50 per acre-foot, although he admitted to not knowing how this could be done.

Charles Hansen and Dille denied any interest in renegotiating the Repayment Contract. They pointed out that some farmers in the District were still skeptical about the Project's viability. Public discussion of contract renegotiation could seriously jeopardize the allotment process. Debler agreed, but he was already planning to apply additional pressure at the NRA annual meeting in Omaha, Nebraska. Newly appointed Bureau Commissioner Michael Straus would be there.[58]

When NCWCD Board members and Bureau officials convened in Omaha on October 10, 1946, Straus told the Board that he knew of their interest in obtaining water delivery through the Adams Tunnel during the next spring. He asked whether the Board had reviewed the Bureau's proposal for interim water deliveries, an issue that would be addressed on the following day. Straus felt displeased with the Directors' opposition to Repayment Contract renegotiation. He was especially "disturbed" because of the Bureau's need to justify the *"excessive"* cost increase on the C–BT Project to the House Appropriations Subcommittee. He indicated that the total cost now approximated $128 million, adding that the Appropriations Subcommittee "would require a lot of explanation on the increase from 44 to 128 millions." He asked the Board how to explain this increase to Congress.[59]

Hansen replied directly that his people had entered into the Repayment Contract in good faith, submitting it to a vote by property owners in the District. The Repayment Contract formed the basis of nearly 2,000 "bona fide contracts" with water users; consequently, there was no way that the Board "could or would be willing to voluntarily increase the obligation of the District." If Straus wanted the District to submit the question of renegotiation to property owners, many of whom had already contracted for water at $1.50 an acre-foot, Hansen would willingly comply, but he predicted unfavorable results for the Bureau.[60] Straus noted that 58 percent of the increased costs was due to a rise in prices, with the balance from changes in plans and designs and unforeseen conditions. Although he admitted that the District was not directly consulted regarding these changes, he predicted real uncertainties in securing future appropriations from Congress. Possibly, he warned, "work would have to stop until prices adjusted themselves." How rapidly did the District want the job finished?

Faced with this not-so-subtle threat to their plans, Dille and Hansen stood firm. Even though other Bureau representatives complained that the Board had shown "an attitude of unwillingness to be cooperative" and that the Colorado delegation had been "even less than cooperative in relation to certain matters relating to power aspects of the Project," they professed an inability to change the present contract. If the Bureau wanted to shut down the Project, so be it, but the Board would maintain hopes of finishing the C–BT without delay. The meeting adjourned on this discordant note.

On the following day, Directors met with Stone, who endorsed the position taken by Dille and Hansen and urged the Board to accept the Bureau proposal for interim diversion in order to strengthen their position "in any later attempt by the Bureau to re-negotiate repayment." Some Directors expressed fears about the cost to the District of delivering water to the Big Thompson River; others worried about the plan's fairness relative to other stream systems within the District. But Hansen, Dille, and J. Ben Nix underscored the experiential advantages and psychological effects of having at least some water delivered as soon as possible. Their view was persuasive. By unanimous vote, the Board accepted the Bureau's proposal for interim deliveries.[61]

One week later, Dille and his recently hired engineer-assistant, J. R. "Bob" Barkley,[62] met with directors of the Big Thompson Mutual Pipe Line and Irrigation Company, a mutual stock company formed by water users to build a conduit to the Big Thompson River and to receive interim diversion water. With advice from their attorney, Hatfield Chilson, they subscribed to 65 percent of the deliverable water and agreed to contact other ditch boards to underwrite the remaining 35 percent.[63] In November the NCWCD Board signed a contract between the District and the Bureau for water delivery to the East Portal of the Adams Tunnel; in January Ickes permitted the District to execute a contract with the Big Thompson Mutual Pipe Line and Irrigation Company that provided water delivery to the ditches along the Big Thompson River.[64] Based on an annual estimate of required water, the District agreed to pay the Bureau in advance for the supply of Colorado River water at the rate of $1.50 per acre-foot. The Big Thompson Mutual Pipe Line and Irrigation Company assumed all costs and responsibilities for construction of the pipeline and for conveyance and delivery of the water.[65]

Not unexpectedly, the Bureau continued to remind District officials that Repayment Contract renegotiation was not "a dead issue as yet."[66] In a January 1947 memorandum to the District, Debler noted that construction costs between 1937 and 1947 had doubled while the annual value expected of agricultural production by Project water had risen an estimated 186 percent; but his tone was more conciliatory than it had been in Omaha. Appraising the C–BT as a "greatly improved" project, he assured the Board that the Bureau was willing to discuss future modifications with the District while fully protecting its interests.[67]

For their part, both Dille and Stone supported legislative efforts to ease the Bureau's repayment obligations. The Rockwell Bill (H.R. 2873) offered the best hope. Sponsored by Colorado Congressman Robert F. Rockwell, who assumed Edward T. Taylor's seat in December 1941, this bill extended the repayment period to seventy-eight years and lowered the interest rate on construction funds to 2.5 percent. After a favorable report from the Committee on Public Lands, the bill stalled in open debate. California congressmen protested the extended repayment period as a "dangerous provision," arguing that atomic power would soon be used to generate electricity, thus superseding hydroelectric plants in twenty-five to fifty years. The bill died on the floor of the House.[68]

Not until Project completion did the Bureau find a significant scheme for alleviating repayment obligations; an Interior Department solicitor's opinion in the 1950s provided the answer. Offering a broad interpretation of Section 9 of the 1939 Reclamation Project Act, this opinion recommended a bookkeeping maneuver that would allow the Bureau to allocate $100 million of the final Project cost ($163 million) to irrigation. The District was responsible for $25 million; the balance of $75 million was technically the Bureau's responsibility. The allocation of this amount to irrigation features meant that the Bureau avoided paying 3 percent annual interest on $75 million, a bookkeeping maneuver resulting in an annual savings of $2.25 million. The Bureau paid interest on only $63 million.[69] One might ask if this savings was passed on to the customers to whom the Bureau sold its power.

None of this fiscal maneuvering had much impact on C–BT construction. Appropriations were still adequate in 1946 and 1947, even though Congress had become increasingly vocal about increasing the cost share of taxpayers and water users who expected to benefit from reclamation projects. For fiscal year 1947 C–BT funding was $7,504,075, about half what the Bureau recommended but more than what the House Appropriations Committee had originally approved. As a Project deemed capable of providing irrigated farms for veterans, the C–BT held a slight advantage in competition for federal money during these inflationary times.[70]

By the end of 1946 Shadow Mountain Dam and Reservoir were finished. S. S. Magoffin Company and Stiers Brothers Construction Company had

Workers inside the Adams Tunnel after concrete lining. (Courtesy NCWCD.)

completed lining the Adams Tunnel, and most work on the West Portal inlet and East Portal outlet was finished. Lowdermilk Brothers won the contract to construct the Rams Horn and Prospect Mountain tunnels as parts of the Bureau's new route to Flatiron Reservoir. The company also completed Rams Horn Tunnel and had dug 1,600 feet of the Prospect Tunnel bore by the end of the year. Work also proceeded at Granby Dam and Reservoir, and a cofferdam and channel for diverting the Colorado River were completed. Dikes were about 40 percent finished, and clearing and burning of the reservoir site were well under way.

In spite of labor, material, and housing shortages, construction was under way at Horsetooth Reservoir. Contracts were let for Horsetooth, Soldier Canyon, Spring Canyon, and Dixon Canyon dams. By the end of 1946 work crews had completed the earth fill of Satanka Dike, cutting much of the channel for the Horsetooth outlet and almost finishing a new highway at the south end of the reservoir. Bureau officials reported with pleasure that Horsetooth Reservoir's lower construction costs resulted because stripping on all dam sites involved much less yardage than estimated.[71] When weather permitted in spring 1947, excavation began on the pumping plant and discharge conduit at Granby Dam and Reservoir. On the East Slope, construction started on Estes and Mary's Lake power plants, Mary's Lake penstock and spillway, and the Horsetooth Feeder Canal.[72] While contractors fulfilled these jobs for the Bureau, the Big Thompson Mutual Pipeline and Irrigation Company finalized work on a 2-mile-long, 38-inch steel pipeline from the East Portal to the Big Thompson River. Seven ditch companies financed this construction.[73] Because attorney Hatfield Chilson encountered some difficulties in securing a contract between Thompson Pipe and Steel Co. and the Mutual Pipeline and Irrigation Company, he arranged an informal agreement based on mutual trust: the Mutual Pipeline and Irrigation Company deposited in escrow the $109,560 construction bid, and Thompson Pipe and Steel Co. wrote a letter guaranteeing completion of the project by a predetermined date.[74] Both sides were satisfied when the conduit was finished in June 1947.

Now for the great moment: the meeting of East and West, the wedding of two oceans. Although the total C–BT Project was still less than half finished, delivery of water through the Adams Tunnel represented a signal event, an inspiration to planners and developers, and the harvest of fourteen years' work. Commissioner Straus, who knew the importance of the occasion, asked the Board to plan a proper celebration, one that would be undiminished by the serious business of war that had tempered the holing-through experience three years earlier. When the Bureau's representatives passed through Loveland June 23 on their way to the East Portal celebration, the fire department blew its whistle for fifteen minutes while local residents cheered. Nothing dampened everyone's enthusiasm to witness another great victory.

Even West Slope people celebrated the event. Representing Colorado River water users at the West Portal, one-time opponent Carl Breeze spoke eagerly about this new chapter of irrigation history. Formerly a feisty and persistent critic of the C–BT Project, Breeze now became conciliatory, praising the "meeting of minds and understanding between two different groups in order that both mutually benefit so that the state and nation will benefit." He hoped that the occasion would be precedent-setting and that the gunfights "of our pioneers" for water rights would end, just as the

Kremmling resident and early C–BT opponent, Carl Breeze later recognized its benefits for both slopes. (Courtesy Carl Breeze.)

conflict between nestors and cattlemen and sheepmen had. Breeze predicted that an "even and constant flow of water" would benefit West Slope agriculturists, that a new source of power would bring industry to the area, and that mineral resources would be developed and utilized along with recreational opportunities that would benefit Colorado's tourist trade. An impressive and conciliatory speech, it set the tone for Breeze's introduction of Colorado Governor William Lee Knous,[75] who had the honor of releasing water from the West Portal into the Adams Tunnel.

At 11:00 A.M. Knous had been waiting expectantly for a phone call from Harry S. Truman that never came; the Bureau had forgotten to tell the governor that they had canceled the president's call. By 11:16, however, he turned a valve at the West Portal that released 75 second-feet of water through the Adams Tunnel, which flowed three hours later into a 200-yard-long reservoir just outside the East Portal. For two hours it flowed until the sump filled.[76] A big cloud of dust preceded the water. W. D. "Bill" Farr recalled, "You have never heard cheering equal to what was heard that day. No one, not even the fans of the Denver Broncos in more recent times were as excited as those conservative businessmen and farmers when they saw that water."[77] While first delivery into the pipeline to the Big Thompson was not made until August 11, the sight of water flowing under the Continental Divide caused soaring emotions among the thousand people gathered at the East Portal.[78]

Governor William Lee Knous pushes button releasing first water through the Alva B. Adams Tunnel on June 23, 1947. (Courtesy Colorado Historical Society.)

Undersecretary of the Interior Oscar L. Chapman was the featured speaker at the noon luncheon. He shared the crowd's enthusiasm, recalled his small part in the early planning stages as executive secretary of the Public Works Administration Board, and reminded everyone that the Adams Tunnel was not only the longest ever constructed from two portals but the longest ever constructed for irrigation purposes. Chapman estimated that the gross net income to District farmers would increase by $21.5 million annually and that the District's population would soon increase by 50 percent.[79]

At the evening banquet in Loveland, Commissioner Straus, the main speaker, delivered a more ominous message. At this final phase of the celebration, in front of more than 400 officials and community residents, Straus described the C–BT as part of the Bureau's plan to develop the entire

The first Colorado River water reaches the East Portal almost three hours after being diverted into the Adams Tunnel on June 23, 1947. (Courtesy Colorado Historical Society.)

Missouri River basin area. He also reminded the audience that continued funding faced difficulties resulting from the House Appropriation Committee's recent requirement that the Bureau seek renegotiation of the Repayment Contract.[80] Taxpayers and water users must increase their share of construction costs, he said, to convince a chary Congress to be generous in future appropriations.[81] Once again, Hansen responded, echoing what he had told Straus in Omaha. Although Straus was an honored guest that night because of his long, selfless commitment to the Project, Hansen refused to allow Straus's remarks to pass without comment. "The federal government would be acting with poor grace," he said, "if it pressed the District for additional construction funds." Nine years ago property owners had approved the Repayment Contract after considerable soul searching. They would not appreciate the federal government's breaking faith with them.[82]

Ironically and somewhat menacingly, the *Fort Collins Coloradoan* reported the next day that President Truman had just signed a bill that increased by 50 percent the construction repayment obligation of the Mancos Water Conservancy District in southwestern Colorado. Theirs was a smaller project approved in 1940 to irrigate 10,000 acres, but the message was clear to District officials: pressure to renegotiate the Repayment Contract would continue.

What mattered for the moment, however, was that available water would benefit irrigators in the Big Thompson Valley. During four years of operation, the interim delivery system would provide water as follows to the Big Thompson River: 6,009 acre-feet in 1947, 8,819 acre-feet in 1948, 15,160 acre-feet in 1949, and 25,683 acre-feet in 1950. Most went to farmers, but some was used for Loveland's hydroelectric plant. The four-year cost per acre-foot to the water users, including capital invested in the pipeline, was about $3.50.[83] Considering the returns, the interim diversion of water proved highly successful. District officials, however, had also fought off enough challenges to the Project in ten years to know how essential a good public relations program would be for future progress and goodwill in northern Colorado.

10 Public Relations and Legal Problems

The Bureau, in its first *Project History*, published in 1938, recognized the "outstanding" need for a continuous program of education "to inculcate in communities, organizations, and individuals a full appreciation of the values and benefits to be derived from the [C–BT] Project." Even with past efforts to secure the approval of Congress and the public, Bureau officials were aware of the "surprising lack of understanding among the people of the Western and Eastern Slopes, and in surrounding cities, as to the purposes of the Project and the nature of the benefits which [would] accrue to the state and nation through its construction." They recommended establishment of a public relations bureau, frequent newspaper articles, addresses before representative groups, and personal contacts with the affected communities. Of many Bureau predictions about the C–BT, none has proved more appropriate for every phase of development than this. To promote the beginning of construction, the Bureau contracted with the newly formed Air Corps Technical School at Lowry Field to take seventy "official" photographs of the "natural and artificial features of the project."[1]

The following year, demand for general and specific information required that the Bureau assign an office employee to public relations.[2] With construction under way, interest in the Project steadily increased. In addition to articles in newspapers and construction magazines, the Bureau prepared a model of the C–BT to be displayed at various educational organizations, the Stanley Hotel in Estes Park, U.S. Customs in Denver, and the 1940 convention of the American Society of Civil Engineers.[3] For the duration of the war, problems with appropriation requirements, labor shortages, and the Washington bureaucracy eclipsed the Bureau's sense of urgency about public relations, but J. M. Dille and Charles Hansen filled in where the Bureau left off. In 1943 Dille arranged to have a movie made of C–BT construction. With the Board's permission, he hired Thomas J. Barbre of Denver, who made two copies of a 16mm sound and color film entitled "Green Fields," which dealt largely with construction of the Adams Tunnel and cost the District $1,254.30.[4] Although Eastman Kodak ruined two sections of the film in the development process, this "rush job" was finally previewed at the February 1944 Board meeting. Dille wanted to improve the film for educational purposes and to show it that year at the annual NRA convention.[5]

Other groups soon asked to see "Green Fields." Requests came in from the Westwood Methodist Church in Cincinnati, Ohio; the Engineering Department at Texas Technological College, Lubbock, Texas; the Ohio Public Service Company of Mansfield, Ohio; the Board of Education of Akron, Ohio; and the Bureau. In 1947 J. R. "Bob" Barkley asked the Bureau in vain to return the one remaining copy because he had been unable to fill several requests. Two years later, because of its fragile condition, the Bureau agreed to replace the film at its own expense, but by 1953 the whereabouts of "Green Fields" was unknown. Possibly, speculated Dille, "it [was] still somewhere in the Bureau's office in Denver."[6]

"Green Fields" had extensively and successfully explained the engineering marvel of the Adams Tunnel. Unfortunately, the film had little influence on District residents, who remained cautious about subscribing to supplemental C–BT water. As NCWCD Director William Bohlender (NCWCD president in 1991) recalled many years later, even the people who stood to benefit most had doubters in their midst. While examining some of Greeley's historical records, he discovered that voters almost recalled the Greeley City Council because it supported the Project. Some officials just refused to believe that the region needed the water.[7] Environmental and growth issues were not part of the debate. Even early enthusiasts began questioning the C–BT during wartime delays. A group representing the Greeley Chamber of Commerce asked the Board of Directors to reduce the amount of C–BT water for which the city had contracted because of fears that it would cost too much. Hansen made it clear that no reduction in the 15,000 acre-feet contracted would be allowed "for the present at least."[8] Doubts about the affordability of C–BT water demanded public relations skills from the District's hard-pressed staff. With ample evidence and bitter recollections of damage done to northern Colorado's irrigated agriculture in the thirties by drought and economic depression, the $1.50 per acre-foot of water charge plus an ad valorem property tax appeared risky to farmers still trying to recover from hard times.[9] Additionally, both rural and urban District residents had difficulty grasping the enormity of the Project. Many wondered if it would ever be built.

To assuage doubters' fears, Dille started publishing "Progress Reports" in 1938. Printed during most years of the construction phase and mailed to both individuals and organizations within the District, these reports were designed to boost confidence in the viability of the C–BT Project and to keep people informed of its headway while the nation was engaged in fighting a two-ocean war. They included updates on appropriations, water allotments, plan modifications, Bureau construction activities, repayment plans, Project statistics, Board members, District finances, and future plans and developments. Articles, which were equally informational and motivational, countered criticism that occasionally surfaced in Denver newspapers after construction began.[10] Dille also organized occasional tours, letting District residents see firsthand the features being built.[11]

Little was said, however, about legal complications that had begun to take increasing amounts of Board time and District money. Litigation was not unexpected because of the size and complexity of the Project, but few had any idea how extensive and involved legal problems would be or what District costs would be in the future to defend itself from attack. Initially, attorneys' fees and costs were modest. According to the District's year-end balance sheets, annual legal expenses between 1939 and 1947 averaged $3,500. This figure excluded an attorney's monthly salary, but the amount was still reasonable — three times less than that spent on "Office Salaries" and frequently less than amounts disbursed for "Office Travel" and "Directors' Per Diem Reimbursement."[12] Between 1939 and 1947 the principal concerns of NCWCD attorneys Thomas A. Nixon and his replacement William R. Kelly were: (1) negotiating rights of way purchases and delivering satisfactory titles to the Bureau; (2) initiating condemnation suits in the event land purchases and easements were not otherwise obtained; and (3) assisting the Bureau in establishing C–BT water rights for the federal government.

Up to 1947 necessary property easements and rights-of-way rights were acquired with relatively little resistance. A few pieces of land in Green Mountain and Shadow Mountain Reservoirs required the District to proceed with litigation under its right of eminent domain, but in no case did the courts make awards that compared unfavorably with what the Bureau's board of appraisers had set as proper value. What developed as a far more complex and extended legal difficulty arose in Water District No. 36, where the City and County of Denver filed suit on November 16, 1942, in Summit County District Court for 1,600 cfs of Blue River water. Because it claimed 1914 as a priority date, Denver's suit threatened the August 1, 1935, priority date of Green Mountain Reservoir. Both the Bureau and the District were understandably concerned by this challenge.

Many meetings and much correspondence were devoted to resolving this matter. Both sides assembled data in support of their respective positions, but they were unable to reach any agreement. When Denver announced that it was proceeding with depositions in order to establish a conditional decree on the Blue River, the United States filed a petition on January 15, 1944, for adjudication of all water rights on the river, which was executed and sent to the clerk of Summit County District Court for filing. The court issued a letter of continuance on November 2, 1944, and continued the hearings each year until litigation was initiated in the U.S. District Court for the District of Colorado on June 10, 1949.[13]

Attorney Kelly made regular reports to the Board regarding the status of this litigation. In spring 1946 his impatience with Bureau policies resulted in an indiscretion that nearly caused censure from the very people he was paid to represent. At a March meeting in Denver to discuss the adjudication of water rights on the Colorado River, Kelly argued that building the Green Mountain Reservoir had removed any obligation of the East Slope to recognize the superiority of the West Slope's right to water for "present and future use." While asking for written instructions from the Board on how to proceed, Hansen expressed complete opposition to Kelly's argument. He reminded Kelly that "such had never been the policy of the District as he understood it." Furthermore, said Hansen, Kelly's position, "contrary to the agreements entered into with the State and with the Western Slope people," constituted a repudiation of spoken and written obligations of the District, including Senate Document 80. A "calamity" threatened if Kelly's course were pursued.[14] Dille concurred. All of the studies and discussions with the West Slope, he said, led to agreement that the Project "would not interfere with present or future uses of water on the Western Slope."

The Board was upset with Kelly's hard line. Director Charles M. Rolfson moved that Kelly "be directed to recognize the agreement that our transmountain diversion should not interfere with present or future uses of the Colorado River." Kelly, of course, opposed this motion during subsequent discussion. The Board finally agreed to defer the matter to a later meeting.

In April the subject surfaced again in relation to possible litigation in Water District No. 51. This time Hansen reported on a conference with the Bureau in Denver where it was agreed that District policy should be to secure water rights for the Project in state courts as soon as possible. The Board feared injurious effects from the conditional decree awarded the Moffat Tunnel and Development Company on March 3, 1941. At the Denver meeting, Hansen and the Bureau jointly concluded that procedures "should be in strict conformity with previous agreements with the West Slope interests and that the final decree should be made subject to the provisions of Senate Document 80 of the 75th Congress."[15] Kelly agreed to follow this policy but remained convinced that his interpretation was right. As will be seen in Chapter 12, the matter came to a head in 1948.

In establishing other legal precedents with considerably more confidence, Dille kept the Board informed of numerous discussions with the CWCB. High on the CWCB's agenda was the protection of all rivers whose waters were involved in transmountain diversion projects. In 1940 the CWCB formally resolved that basins of origin "must be fully protected in [their] present and future use of water before . . . interstate exportation [is] made."[16] Other discussions involved protection of underground water in the South Platte drainage and an amendment to Section 13 of the Water Conservancy District Act, which removed the maximum limitation of "320,000 acre-feet that could be transported out of any watershed subject to the Colorado River Compact and the Boulder Canyon Act."[17] In postwar Colorado, the C–BT Project officially became the CWCB's number one priority.[18]

As interim allotments of water flowed into the Big Thompson River, the District's foremost concern was still continuation of work on East Slope features so that all water users would be provided with an adequate supply and an efficient system of operation. Plans for delivery to the North Poudre Irrigation Company and to water users in the Buckhorn Creek area around Masonville were still incomplete. Further study was also necessary to determine how to deliver water to Boulder Creek and to the South Platte River. Dille predicted that if the Bureau completed studies as efficiently as possible and if Congress provided the $25 million needed to accomplish the next stage of construction, the irrigation delivery features of the C–BT could be ready by summer 1950.[19]

Matters concerning the remaining allotments of water needed more study time. As already noted, by November 1942, 208,476 acre-feet had been "definitely placed." The NCWCD held petitions for an additional 53,000 acre-feet. Of the amount allotted, 119,335 acre-feet were destined for the Poudre River, 55,202 acre-feet for the Big Thompson River, 3,055 for the Little Thompson River, and 30,884 for the St. Vrain River.[20] Dille's only real worry materialized when the Federal Land Bank expressed support of the Reclamation Act as related to the 160-acre limit. Many farms in the District were mortgaged to the Federal Land Bank, whose administrators pointed out a potential conflict to C–BT officials. Dille's willingness to supply all requested data and his confidence that Congress would overturn this restriction allowed the District and the bank to proceed harmoniously with water allocations.[21]

During the mid-1940s and early 1950s, Dille and Barkley worked continuously at the multitude of details required to develop a water distribution system, including the plat records of water allotments and land ownership. Ultimately, these plats assumed great importance because they constituted the District record that county assessors used to make assessment certifications for correct application of ad valorem taxes. Because Dille expected complications to arise from the division of tracts, he planned for field examinations, transfers, and reallocations of water.[22] He also asked the Board to organize a legal committee to study the impact on tax liens when property was divided.[23]

Aware that every decision established a precedent for future water users, the Board moved slowly and conservatively to form new policies. Even in 1948, the only additional water allotment approved was 3,000 acre-feet to the City of Fort Collins; 98,554 acre-feet still remained to be allotted.[24] There was still plenty of time to find allottees as each construction achievement underscored the viability of the C–BT Project. But problems and obstacles were never far away. In the postwar period, progress was threatened by rifts with both the Bureau and the City of Denver.

Part III: C–BT Construction and Water Delivery
(1947–1957)

Postwar Adjustments With the Bureau

The euphoria of having Colorado River water flow into the Big Thompson River was shared far beyond the immediate confines of the NCWCD. Widely hailed as a measure of engineering skill, the Project also heralded federal cooperation with local water users and Secretary Harold L. Ickes's model New Deal policies. Even before water reached expectant farmers in the Big Thompson Valley, two unidentified New Yorkers, grasping the significance of the moment, asked permission to make the first water crossing of the Continental Divide on a raft through the Adams Tunnel. Singling out cold water temperatures and insufficient oxygen in the tunnel as deterrents, Bureau officials denied their request even as they called attention to the magnificent structure bored 13.1 miles through the bowels of the earth.[1] Undoubtedly, the New Yorkers were disappointed with this technical and unsympathetic response. They were not the only people frustrated with the postwar Bureau. District officials had their own concerns about the Department of the Interior's priorities during the early years of the Truman administration.

Ickes was no longer around. Having resigned from the Truman cabinet in 1946, when the president felt he was getting "too big for his britches," Ickes had been determined to establish river basin authorities in both the Columbia and Missouri valleys.[2] During the war years the Bureau had compiled numerous surveys for large-scale projects similar to the Tennessee Valley Authority (TVA), "showpiece of the New Deal's resource program," and when Roosevelt began to feel that a military victory was close, he asked Congress to approve "regional conservation authorities" for several other rivers, including the Missouri and the Columbia.[3] Opponents railed against this "socialist" and "communist" trend in government, but proponents argued that such river basin authorities would "act as a countervailing force to the increasing consolidation of private corporations in the nation's economy."[4]

Immediately after Roosevelt's death, Truman made expanding regional water power projects "a primary domestic goal of his administration." With all the other problems he faced, the new president intended to "resume the course set by Roosevelt by seeking congressional authorization of programs outlined in the Bureau of Reclamation's wartime surveys."[5] His disagreement with Ickes, however, stemmed from a conviction that river basin control should be in the hands of local entities. Ickes had been accustomed to having his way with President Roosevelt. Furthermore, his interest in power, both personal and hydroelectric, made it impossible to give up administrative control of an entire river basin in favor of state and local interests. When Truman refused to pamper him, he resigned. In 1946 Julius A. Krug replaced Ickes as the new secretary of the interior.

Krug was a good appointment. He was handsome, genial, and a staunch supporter of many of Ickes's policies. He had entered federal service as a staff member of TVA and became chairman of the War Production Board during the war. His undersecretary was a Coloradan, Oscar Chapman, and his commissioner of reclamation was Michael Straus, whom Ickes had recommended to Truman as a man of "vision, enthusiasm, and a full appreciation of the necessity for sound planning."[6] Consistent with the views of President Truman, Krug made water and power a priority of his administration (1946–1949) while adhering to the principles of a public power policy that Ickes had outlined in January 1946.[7] He was dedicated to the idea of multipurpose reclamation projects in which both power and water would have the widest possible distribution. Such programs, he believed, should only be administered by river valley authorities. Straus agreed,[8] but the NRA and NCWCD officials did not.

Reflecting the views of the NCWCD and Judge Clifford Stone of the CWCB, J. M. Dille argued that creation of a Missouri Valley Authority (MVA) would threaten existing state and federal laws and administration. Because he saw the MVA as a centralization of power under one political agency, he feared subordination of the Bureau's role in reclamation to this new authority.[9] After returning from appropriations talks in Washington in March 1946, Dille expressed a fear that Krug's appointment would involve a "radical departure from some of the recent policies of that department" (Interior).[10]

What seemed radical indeed was the rapid shift of political winds in fall 1946 and the extent to which a changed Congress had affected the operations of Straus's Bureau. Because of inflation fears at home, deteriorating relations with Russia, homeless refugees, and a host of other unsolved problems, the 1946 congressional elections were held amid charges of "To err is Truman" and "Had Enough? Vote Republican." Many voters stayed away from the polls, but those who voted elected 245 Republicans and 188 Democrats to the House — the first Republican-controlled House since

Herbert Hoover's presidency. With his popularity rating at 32 percent, Truman faced a crisis of confidence.[11] The Republicans, meanwhile, took aim at what they viewed as waste, mismanagement, and corruption in the federal bureaucracy.

Reclamation took a big hit. The new leadership in Congress laid plans to cut every aspect of the Truman water development program. The House Interior Appropriation Subcommittee "slashed away at the department's budget for reclamation projects and transmission lines." Funds requested by the Bureau were trimmed because western Republicans thought they would further promote the river valley authorities.[12] As expected, the District felt the results of congressional penury.

In Omaha in October 1946 Straus had demanded that the District renegotiate its Repayment Contract. The Board, which held firm to its $25 million obligation, knew the price for stonewalling the Bureau at a time when budgets were so carefully scrutinized by a Republican Congress. Two months after this meeting, Dille counseled that any project with a power component would be very carefully reviewed. Congress, he said, "will insist on a satisfactory solution to the power controversy before appropriating more money to multiple-purpose projects."[13] He was referring to two contentious situations, the first, an ongoing conflict between public and private power proponents in which eastern congressmen were determined not to subsidize any more of what they called "cheap western power."[14] The second conflict, related more specifically to the C–BT, dealt with the Bureau's interpretation of the 1939 Reclamation Act, which — if authorized by statute — would allow a sizeable part of Project construction costs to be designated for payment without interest to the government. As everyone waited for Congress to pass legislation on these matters, District consultant Royce J. Tipton and Dille frequently traveled to Washington in fear that the House might cut the C–BT budget up to 50 percent.[15]

By spring 1947 the future of continued funding for the C–BT was enmeshed in partisan politics and in complex bills aimed at finding a new approach to the Bureau's financial dilemma. The situation in Washington became increasingly "complicated and baffling," but by the end of April Dille felt optimistic that congressional wrath seemed aimed more at the Bureau than at the District. Even under the existing economy drive and the president's January 1947 freeze order on the expenditure of reclamation funds, Dille surmised that the House Interior Appropriations Subcommittee, which appeared "friendly toward our project," would not oppose an increase in funding if so voted by the Senate.[16]

Regardless of this optimism, Straus's Bureau was still being chastised for profligacy. Region 7 officials had to find subtle or not-so-subtle ways to squeeze more money out of the District while they redesigned the C–BT to generate more income-producing power. As Congress loosened its purse strings over the next few years, Bureau officials divided Region 7 into four districts to permit placement of personnel as close to the scene of operations as practicable. The South Platte River District — all of the area drained by the South Platte River and tributaries from its headwaters to Paxton, Nebraska — was designated the watchdog of the C–BT. Almost simultaneously, the Bureau announced a restudy of all C–BT features not yet built in order to provide Congress with up-to-date information on which to base more intelligent funding decisions. A restudy would analyze available water supplies, construction features, reasons for design changes, and power rates. Region 7 director Avery Batson, who requested the Board's cooperation, promised that everyone would benefit from such a study.[17]

District officials, however, feared that the true purpose of the restudy was to justify ways the Bureau might reduce contractual obligations and thereby prove to the Congress that it was not a spendthrift organization. For this reason, the two organizations soon disagreed over the real factors that had contributed to an exponential increase in construction costs. The District Board, which agreed to cooperate in the restudy, passed a resolution saying that it did not "thereby agree to any modification of the contractual relations between the District and the United States."[18] Furthermore, the staff and some Directors seriously questioned the reasons why C–BT Project costs had escalated exponentially since 1937.

The Bureau's answer was straightforward. In October 1947 Batson identified four circumstances that led to the 192 percent increase in construction costs: (1) inadequate cost estimates in the 1937 Bureau report; (2) development of "desirable" changes to improve Project services that would assure its permanency or increase its efficiency; (3) discovery of unforeseen conditions necessitating design changes in various works; and (4) increased costs due to construction delays during the war and high prices during the postwar years.[19] Batson noted that the House Interior Department Appropriations Subcommittee had formally stated that "prewar repayment contracts on projects under construction must now be amended in consideration of increased construction costs. Future appropriations for projects in Colorado," warned the Committee, "will depend on the willingness of beneficiaries to assume additional repayment obligations."[20] In Batson's eyes, the District should have no problem with a contract amendment because the 192 percent increase in construction costs was balanced by a 186 percent increase in the annual value of agricultural projects to be produced with the use of C–BT water "plus increased security and economy in operation throughout the life of the project" as a result of a $1.1 million increase in gross power revenue.[21] In an eight-page explanation of why so many modifications had been made in the original C–BT design, most of which were executed without consulting the District, the Bureau concluded that the completed project would now cost $128,110,120. Supplemental water quantities delivered to the District would remain the same, enabling farmers to increase their productivity from a prewar average of $7 million annually to an average of $20 million based on "present day prices." Additionally, changes in C–BT power features would increase power production from 560 million kwh to 600 million kwh of firm power, while other modifications would increase the recreational value of the entire system.[22]

Dille knew that congressional and economic pressures on the Bureau required the District's immediate attention. Although he saw high construction costs as essentially the federal government's problem, he advised the Board to analyze whether, "when the proper time comes," there would be any way to contribute toward the extra costs "within the limits of the agreements which they [the Feds] are bound to uphold." Still, he questioned the Bureau's figure of $128 million for total Project construction, accused the Bureau of tripling the costs of its hydroelectric power system, and wondered if the increased power revenue would be sufficient to enable the Bureau to pay off the construction debt. As solutions to the dilemma, he suggested extending the Bureau's repayment period[23] and having the District take over a larger part of C–BT operation and maintenance when construction was completed. The latter possibility, he noted, would have to be covered by an additional 1/2 mill tax allowed to the District to cover defaults and deficiencies.[24]

J. R. "Bob" Barkley, formally designated the District's assistant secretary-manager in October 1947, believed that the Bureau should have exercised better control over escalating costs. In 1946 he pointed out that construction costs, including both labor and materials, had already risen by 167 percent over 1937 figures, with design change the major influencing factor. In comparing 1937 and 1946 Project estimates, he showed that 62 percent of the increase was due specifically to design changes.[25] He also lamented the Bureau's more recent tendency to over-design expensive features in laboratory situations, without much consideration for their cost and practicality. He blamed the Bureau for an overloaded bureaucracy that, combined with a postwar empire-building philosophy, produced the duplication and waste that Congress had criticized.[26]

This dichotomy between the Bureau and the District with regard to a Project originally estimated at $44 million that now was nearly three times as expensive, underlay much of the friction that surfaced during the remaining years of construction. Because the Bureau was reluctant to discuss Project-related power modifications with District officials,[27] the NCWCD entered most negotiations suspicious that Bureau changes might affect the C–BT system's ability to accomplish its primary objective: to supply 310,000 acre-feet of supplemental irrigation water to northeastern Colorado. One such negotiation concerned Strawberry and Meadow creeks on the West Slope. Senate Document 80 stated that these two streams, along with Walden Hollow Creek, would be diverted "whenever practicable" to offset evaporation and seepage losses in excess of "present losses" from Lake Granby and Shadow Mountain Reservoir.[28] In comparing 1937–1947 costs, the Bureau noted that the plan for utilization of Strawberry and Meadow creeks had been "inadvertently omitted from the summary of project costs as reported in S.D. 80."[29] Consequently, field surveys and designs for these diversions had not yet been completed by 1947.

The following year, James H. Knights, manager of the South Platte District of Region 7, told NCWCD officials that Bureau studies of these two streams indicated that too little water was available to justify development. Furthermore, Knights stated, a land classification study of the downstream end of the NCWCD area would determine whether District irrigation capabilities required the full 310,000 acre-feet. Not long thereafter, Batson informed the Board that the "present average yearly water supply of the C–BT [would] amount to 245,000 acre-feet per year. Ways and means of increasing this yearly supply to 310,000 acre-feet [were] being investigated."[30] Had the Bureau decided to cut costs by reducing the contracted scope of water delivery in the C–BT system? Was there any connection between the Bureau's position vis-à-vis the C–BT and Denver's interest in expanding its collection system on Meadow Creek and nearby Ranch Creek for delivery through the Moffat Tunnel?[31] These questions had no ready answers, but District officials were clearly agitated by the possible loss of Strawberry and Meadow creek water.

Dille, Barkley, and Hansen expressed dissatisfaction to Knights in the District office. They told him that complete elimination of Strawberry and Meadow creeks should neither be proposed by the Bureau nor accepted by the Board.[32] Even though the Bureau presented detailed studies showing that it would be uneconomical to divert the "small amount of water available in these streams due to existing prior rights,"[33] NCWCD leaders could not let the matter rest with simple elimination of these features. After several months of wrestling with this and related problems, the Board responded with a letter and resolution that it would not object to postponing "at this time" construction of the Strawberry and Meadow Creek features. "But in view of the value of the water for both power and irrigation purposes in the future, [the Board] assume[d] that when more information [was] available and the final determination made, the District [would] be consulted."[34]

These diversion structures were never built. In 1956 District officials signed off the completed system without insisting that the Bureau comply with Senate Document 80. As Barkley later recalled, it would have been politically inexpedient to jam Strawberry and Meadow creeks down the Bureau's throat. Everyone knew that the Bureau's chief hydraulic engineer, E. B. Debler, had made the best possible estimate in 1937 when he calculated that the C–BT would produce 310,000 acre-feet on the average. But as things turned out historically, "we know it didn't pan out. About 240,000 to 250,000 acre-feet was all it could hack."[35] Another 10,000 to 12,000 acre-feet from Strawberry and Meadow creeks would have helped, but the entire system needed a Windy Gap project before it could produce its contracted 310,000 acre-feet. More about this in Parts IV and V. For the moment, it is important to recognize that the Strawberry–Meadow Creek discussion was symptomatic of building tensions between the District and the Bureau as the latter continued reeling from attacks by Congress and the public on its objectives and fiscal policies in the West.

Harry Truman's surprise victory in 1948 was seen by many as a positive means to alter the Republican Congress's policy of pruning every aspect of the Truman water development program. During the presidential campaign, both Truman and Straus toured the West with the message that even more devastating cuts would come if a Republican president and Congress were elected. As Truman loved to say, every appropriation that affected the West had been "slashed with malice aforethought."[36] Although the charges might not have been completely accurate, the tactic worked — at least politically. Ten out of the eleven western states voted for Truman and Democratic representatives to Congress. In Colorado, Republican Congressman William S. Hill defended his party's record on reclamation projects and warned that a Democratic victory would further strengthen the Soviet menace.[37] From a purely accounting standpoint, the first part of his statement was defensible. One month before Hill's pronouncement,

Congress approved for the C–BT the largest amount of money ever granted in any one year. But memories of C–BT supporters were more affected by the many budget uncertainties of the past two years when construction progress had actually been curtailed due to a shortage of funds.[38] The threat of additional delays to the Project was hard to accept after a slow start and a long war. Better to vote for the party whose track record favored government spending.

The return of a Democratic majority to Congress, however, did not ensure tranquility for the Bureau. Criticism of government waste was just as pronounced. Because of charges that too many "leeches" worked for him, Straus was forced to remove 2,882 of his 18,000 employees, with a cut of 202 people in Region 7.[39] In May 1949 the *Saturday Evening Post* ran an article by the former governor of Wyoming, Leslie Miller, who had been appointed chairman of the Natural Resources Committee of the Hoover Commission. Established by Truman to investigate charges of waste, duplication, and inefficiency in both the Bureau and Army Corps of Engineers, the Hoover Commission recommended elimination of the Department of the Interior, replacement by a Department of Natural Resources, merger of the Bureau and the Army Corps of Engineers, and centralization of all water projects in a Water Development Service.[40]

Miller's hard-hitting article grew out of information made available to the Hoover Commission that charged both the Bureau and the Corps with: (1) senseless competition; (2) underestimating project costs in their zeal to outdo one another; (3) deceiving Congress; and (4) pernicious lobbying. In addition, he described the C–BT as another example of "malodorous planning" and stressed the importance of a Water Development Service to take over the function of both agencies. Finally, Miller recommended establishing a Board of Coordination and Review in the president's office to pass on the feasibility of any proposed water project.[41] The *Denver Post*, echoing these sentiments, called attention to C–BT cost overruns and the Bureau's recent pronouncement that the completed Project would be unable to deliver a full 310,000 acre-feet of water.[42] Others jabbed the Bureau for being empire builders, for thinking only of their engineering skills and little of the social and economic consequences of what they designed,[43] and for trying to usurp the traditional role of the Extension Service in matters of farmer education.[44]

Straus remained nonplused by the attack. While admitting that estimates of C–BT costs had now escalated to $144 million, he blamed the war, the revision in plans to improve operation and maintenance, and the over 200 percent increase in construction costs over the life of the Project.

He also faulted Miller for not admitting his bias against public power. In an article in the *Denver Post*, entitled "It's Your Dam Money," Straus maintained that the Bureau had kept the wheels of wartime industry turning with its power, even as crops grown with federal reclamation water over the past forty-six years had increased in value to $4 billion, or three times what taxpayers had invested. In response to accusations of waste and inefficiency, Straus noted that the Bureau was dedicated to rewarding those who found ways to reduce costs. The laboratories in Denver alone, he stated, had made possible savings of $20 million.[45]

Straus remained eager to build projects. In summer 1949 he predicted that Congress would approve $350 million for reclamation in its next appropriations, "but you haven't seen anything yet." In his view, the entire nation was calling on the Bureau to deliver a program beyond anything ever attempted. In addition to multiple-basin projects that would bring water from the Columbia River to southern California, he foresaw construction of Bridge Canyon Dam in the Grand Canyon. In the next twelve months, he said, the Bureau would accomplish more than in its first thirty years of existence.[46] Straus defended the Bureau's need to organize the West into large river basins in order to pool resources and to provide electric power for the 14 million people expected to expand the West's population in the next twenty-five years.[47]

Straus was, in fact, the West's leading reclamation booster, but he had two major flaws. First, he made plenty of enemies. When he tried to crack down on the big California growers "who were setting up dummy corporations and trusts in order to farm tens of thousands of acres illegally with Bureau of Reclamation water," he put powerful political forces in motion that called for his removal.[48] By pinning an obscure rider on the 1949 Public Works Appropriations Bill, Straus's critics in the Senate deprived the commissioner of his salary. But Straus was independently wealthy. He stayed on the job without pay, boasting that he had accomplished what the Republicans had failed to do: unite the party around a single issue. They wanted Straus fired, but the commissioner survived until the end of the Truman administration.

Second, Straus was unconcerned about the economic feasibility of projects that the Bureau considered. Marc Reisner, author of *Cadillac Desert*, tells the story of the commissioner's visit to Billings, Montana, where he informed employees that their area included the greatest concentration of "physically possible but economically unfeasible projects." In his address, Straus said that he didn't give a damn whether a project was feasible or not. "I'm getting the money out of Congress and you damn well better spend it. And you better be here early tomorrow morning ready to spend it, or you may find someone else at your desk."[49]

Although Reisner does not document this specific incident, his book supports others' views that Straus's modus operandi was often pushy and abrasive. In the upper basin states of the Colorado River, however, his developmental mania was seen as cheerleading for projects that were needed to put 7.5 million acre-feet of Colorado River water to beneficial use. The 1922 Colorado River Compact had provided equal distribution of water between the upper and lower basin states, but if the rapidly growing lower basin began "borrowing" what was unused upstream above Lee's Ferry, the upper basin might never get its full allotment back. As much as Straus wanted to submit upper basin reclamation projects to Congress, however, he refused to approve them until Wyoming, Utah, Colorado, and New Mexico agreed to a state-by-state distribution of its 7.5 million acre-feet.[50] The resultant compact was of no small interest to the NCWCD.

Because Colorado frequently pointed out its production of 72 percent of the Colorado River water, the other upper basin states viewed the state as "Uncle Shylock" during the early stages of negotiation. They repeatedly tried to reach agreement in 1946 and 1947, but ill will prevailed. The total amount of water requested by each far exceeded the stated allotment authorized by the Colorado River Compact.[51] Agreement seemed out of reach, but the Bureau's insistence on accord before Project authorization and California's attempt to undermine the process by scaring West Slope representatives with fears of future water robberies by the East Slope finally brought all parties together.

At Vernal, Utah, in July 1948, after fifteen days of meetings and threats to go home, the four upper basin states plus Arizona signed a draft agreement. Colorado was represented by Stone of the CWCB, Tipton, and the District's J. M. Dille. Together they managed to get 51.75 percent of the 7.5 million acre-feet for Colorado. Other apportionments were Utah, 23 percent; Wyoming, 14 percent; New Mexico, 11.75 percent; and Arizona (although not an upper basin state), 50,000 acre-feet above Lee Ferry. While California stepped up attempts to sow discord in Colorado by telling West Slope delegates to the State Assembly not to ratify the agreement, California Senators Sheridan Downey and William Knowland were working toward a plan to force the upper Colorado apportionments into the U.S. Supreme Court if the five states failed to ratify the signed compact;[52] but California's plans failed. All the states ratified the compact, and President Truman signed a bill on April 6, 1949, that had been passed by both houses of Congress. Theoretically, the Bureau could now proceed with construction of projects in the upper Colorado River basin.

Officials from the District soon learned, however, that the Bureau was still very much affected by charges of empire building and irresponsible management of existing projects. Exemplary of this situation were the nearly four years of argument between the Bureau and the District over the North Poudre gravity canal. Senate Document 80 called for a pump plant to be installed on the banks of the Poudre Valley Canal. The cost of two 75 cfs vertical single-stage pumps was estimated at $200,000. A canal costing $128,889 was to be constructed from the pressure outlets of the pump plant 9.98 miles to the North Poudre Canal.[53] Early in 1946 Debler wrote Dille that he was considering replacing the pump plant with a gravity canal.[54] Sometime before this, Dille, Barkley, and Board member Ed F. Munroe (president of the North Poudre Irrigation Company) had discussed their concern that a pump plant would be far more expensive to the District in the long run than a one-time higher cost of a gravity-feed canal. Although the matter had been mentioned briefly in 1947, the Board did not learn until 1948 that a gravity-feed system would cost an extra $900,000.[55] Seven months later the Bureau's South Platte project office quoted the change at $1.4 million.[56]

Tension appeared in subsequent discussions between the two agencies. At first Dille and Barkley told the Board that the gravity-feed system could be built for $970,000. In spring 1949 the Board resolved to go ahead with the project.[57] Avery Batson felt that the Board's resolution was sufficient authority for the Bureau to design a change that could be incorporated into a supplemental contract as provided in Article 8 (c) of the Repayment Contract.[58] But the harmonious agreement turned sour during execution. While the Bureau responded to fears of inflation and worries about renewed criticism from Congress, the District poised to pounce on any indicator that the Bureau's engineering plans might be impractical, overdesigned, or cost ineffective. Neither side wanted to be pushed around.

Dille fired the first blast when he told Knights that letters he and attorney Kelly had received in regard to the proposed new contract "were phrased in a manner we did not like." He told Knights to tell Batson that "we are not going to be pushed around in that manner."[59] Clarence J. Eynon, the Bureau's regional counsel, fanned the flames when he told Kelly that the District's rejection of a service contract in favor of an amendment to the Repayment Contract was totally unacceptable.[60] Both he and Batson spoke against amending the Repayment Contract because the amendment would have to go before Congress. Barkley believed that the Bureau's real paranoia stemmed from the threat of opening up before Congress the numerous Project changes initiated and made by the Bureau without secretarial approval as specified in Article 4 of the Repayment Contract.[61] The two sides finally executed a supplementary construction and repayment contract, but bureaucratic obstacles created new challenges. During the first six months of 1950 Bureau officials began to contend that its financial obligation be limited to a fixed sum, because they did not want to risk unanticipated construction difficulties and possible cost overruns on another phase of the C–BT Project.[62]

In Washington, meanwhile, leadership of the Department of the Interior was now in the hands of Oscar Chapman, an Ickes disciple. Some said that Krug had been forced to resign because he had so aggressively pushed for projects,[63] but Chapman was just as supportive of the Bureau's goals. When he took the oath of office in December 1949, Chapman was already a competent and seasoned politician. He was also vulnerable to the attacks of those who associated the federal reclamation program with "communism" and "socialism." He was personally attacked for being a member of several communist front organizations and for crossing out the loyalty portion of his oath.[64] He assumed leadership of a department that was suffering from internal power struggles and external attacks.

When Dille went to Washington in spring 1950 to testify to Congress on appropriations matters, he found that Chapman had been advised by Regional Counsel Eynon not to sign the North Poudre contract. The Bureau's objection now focused on submitting the contract to a voter election in the District.[65] Chapman wanted to sign the contract but he could not because the department solicitor's opinion confirmed the views of Bureau attorneys. The only way out of the dilemma was a confirmation proceeding in the district court under provisions contained in Section 36 of the Water Conservancy District Act. If Judge Claude C. Coffin in Greeley approved the action taken by the NCWCD Board in regard to the North Poudre contract, the secretary would sign the document.[66] At Coffin's hearing on June 12, no objectors appeared in court, and the following day he sent a decree on the North Poudre contract to the Bureau's Region 7 office for approval. From Denver, it was forwarded for Chapman's signature, and by September Dille was able to present a signed and executed copy of the contract to the District Board.[67]

End of story? Not quite. Delays had brought on further fears of inflation. By early 1951 Knights had estimated a $172,000 overrun if the gravity canal were built as designed. He asked the Board to pass a resolution that would bind the District to accept additional costs if construction work exceeded the estimate, now calculated at $3,144,000. The Board refused. The District staff, which had made an effort to help the Bureau reduce costs, now urged the Bureau to get on with the task of soliciting bids without further delay.[68] Two months later Knights reported that construction costs would exceed the contract bid by $321,600 and again suggested that the Bureau cover these costs with a resolution. He further pointed out that Batson was under pressure from Straus to get more money out of the District. In fact, Knights warned, if the District did not comply, the commissioner might just refuse to award the contracts.[69]

Dille doubted that the Board would agree to the proposed resolution and, he countered, if the commissioner refused to award contracts, the District might be forced "to take appropriate action through Congress." Barkley expressed his feelings more directly. He was "frankly disgusted" with the Bureau's request, for in his view the greater part of the discrepancy occurred in the Bureau's overhead. He complained that the whole history of the North Poudre project involved changing estimates, and the Board of Directors was now particularly "disgusted" that the latest cost revision had come out after the contractors' bids were known. He reminded the Bureau that the contract called for them to build the system until $3,144,000 had been exhausted and then to take up the matter with the District if necessary.[70] The conflict over construction never really ended. Charges and countercharges continued until the Bureau finally completed work on the gravity-feed system, which was finally dedicated as the Ed Munroe Canal in July 1953.[71] Each side had responded to a different set of local, regional, and national pressures. At times, the principals doubted the outcome, but compromises eventually emerged from expert leaders on both sides who felt that nothing would be gained by halting the Project.

North Poudre was only one of the problems that had to be worked out in 1950; a new water rental contract had to be drawn up. The temporary one, originally signed by the District and the Department of the Interior in 1947, enabled farmers to receive C–BT water only from the Big Thompson River. By 1950 more water was available in the C–BT system from completed storage facilities on the West Slope as well as from East Slope features that could now receive delivery at Horsetooth Reservoir and Carter Lake. Negotiating a new contract, however, required an exchange of letters and contract drafts between the Bureau and the District that was almost as tedious as the struggle over the North Poudre gravity canal.

Meanwhile, an ugly international situation had developed in June 1950 when North Koreans overran the 38th parallel to enter South Korea. Many, Dille included, now believed that early completion of power plants was essential to national defense.[72] But both Dille and Barkley stood their ground against the Bureau's attempts to make changes that might only add to the District's future debt burden. The Willow Creek Pumping Plant was a case in point. The Bureau had decided that a pump system would be more reliable on a year-round basis than a gravity flow into Lake Granby; however, Dille countered that the District should not have to bear half the pumping cost because it had not been a party to the plan change.[73] Shortly thereafter, the Bureau pressed for a new water rental contract, but District staff showed displeasure by opposing the plan on a number of technicalities. The District was finding it increasingly difficult to figure out who was calling the shots in the Bureau's bureaucracy. Barkley noted that disagreement between Region 7 and the South Platte project office was evident on several matters.[74]

This friction became more obvious during the year. The commissioner pressured the regional office to squeeze more money out of the District;[75] however, Knights was much closer to District officials and more sympathetic to their point of view. He had conceived the idea that both sides should formulate their positions in letters regarding the proposed new water rental contract, the conflicts on Willow Creek, the St. Vrain-Boulder–South Platte conduits, and other matters that resisted successful negotiation.[76] Thus was born a "single package" approach in which "the project works required to be constructed for service of the entire District were agreed upon and, by the contract, the method of dividing revenues from water rental during an interim period was established."[77]

Knights and Barkley deserve credit for breaking the log jam in negotiations. The Willow Creek conflict could be resolved quite easily. Even though Barkley had faulted the Bureau for making a design change beneficial only to its own power system, he urged the Directors in April 1950 not to protest the government's plan. The possibility of larger amounts of firm power and diversion of a "somewhat greater annual water supply" were advantages that the Board should support.[78] Two months later, after several meetings and exchanges of letters, and after Dille had visited Commissioner Straus in Washington, the Board resolved to accept the pumping plant along with the responsibility of paying half of operation and maintenance costs (calculated at approximately $10,000 annually) on the completed Willow Creek system.[79]

The St. Vrain-Boulder–South Platte conduit discussion had deeper roots. When Bureau officials began recognizing in 1946 how cost estimates were accelerating, they looked critically at the language of Senate Document 80, hoping to find a way to deny responsibility for extending the

Willow Creek Reservoir. Additional water is collected here and pumped up into Lake Granby. The pump canal is shown middle right with Willow Creek in center. (Courtesy NCWCD.)

Project south of the St. Vrain River.[80] Debler had already proposed serving the Boulder area with the South Platte–Blue River project, if built, and Dille had responded pointedly that the Bureau had an "obligation" to deliver water to this area if people wanted it, "regardless of the possibilities of the Blue River Project."[81] In 1949 Bureau officials at group meetings in Boulder said that there were still some questions as to whether the District would provide service to water users in the Boulder Creek area.[82]

By 1950 the Boulder community had still not formally decided to apply for admission into the District. Water users on the Little Thompson River were in dire straits, and Boulder's city manager, having just been denied 500 acre-feet of water by the City of Denver, knew that his municipality desperately needed a supplemental supply.[83] The stalemate revolved around how much water would be needed, who would pay the increased costs, and whether the Bureau still planned to contest its obligation to build the conduits. Director Charles A. Lory wrote Hansen that he favored an

Willow Creek Pump Plant lifts water 175 feet to a canal, where it flows into Lake Granby a quarter mile away. (Courtesy Bureau of Reclamation.)

election to determine what water users wanted. Hansen replied that getting assurances from the Bureau about conduit construction was most important. "If we must pay something of a price in money or pride," he said, "this must be of secondary consideration." The worst that could happen would be for the Bureau to decide against building the St. Vrain, Boulder, and South Platte conduits.[84]

On both June 15 and 21, 1946, the Bureau and District had exchanged letters in draft form that stated their respective positions. The Bureau noted that because the conduits were not specifically mentioned in the Repayment Contract (or in S.D. 80), constructing them must be based on the "feasibility of extending the Project features to serve a great area." Barkley responded that even though the obligation of the United States was not clearly defined in the existing Repayment Contract, the decision "must be based on the intent of the Repayment Contract and upon the necessity for constructing those Project features required to serve the lands within the Conservancy District boundaries."[85] Batson agreed to Barkley's wording;

Signing of the Interim Water Rental Contract on December 15, 1950. Seated (left to right) J. R. "Bob" Barkley, William R. Kelly, J. M. Dille, Charles Hansen, Avery Batson, James H. Knights, Ben King. Standing (left to right) Robert J. Wright, Hatfield Chilson, Jacob S. Schey, Joe Howell, Carl Metzger, Olin Venable, J. Ben Nix. (Courtesy NCWCD.)

however, assumption of financial responsibility was still a matter to be worked out. The commissioner continued to remind Batson that the Bureau needed better assurances in regard to repayment, along with more money for any contemplated canal enlargements. Straus was committed in principle to the idea that the District should pay whatever improvement costs might be.[86]

Over the next few months, these letters were revised and reworked along with an interim contract defining the new water rental policy and the Bureau's construction obligations to complete the Project. NCWCD relations with Boulder, south-end ditch companies, and the Bureau were far from finalized, but agreement had been reached by 1950 to extend the C–BT system to the South Platte River.[87] On September 27 Hansen provided drinks for a celebration. Chapman approved the contract on November 10, and Knights wrote the District on December 11 to express his appreciation of the "close and considerate cooperation" of District staff and Board members.[88]

The Interim Water Rental Contract of December 15, 1950 (amended April 8, 1953), providing for partial operation of the Project and utilization of completed features in coming irrigation seasons, was expected to remain in effect from five to seven years. In the early spring it provided for sale of a variable amount of what was known as "future" water, the amount determined by supply and demand and the price fixed after discussions with

District officials. From the Bureau's point of view, this "future" water was what would be released from Project reservoirs to provide space for power water or to prevent a spill out of Lake Granby.[89] The District would have to pay for water in advance, but it could also collect from water users in advance and could charge them something extra for operations, maintenance, and administration. Ten percent of the gross revenue received by the United States was credited to the District "as advances by the District of its share of operation and maintenance costs required during the early years of operation in the second period of operation as defined in Article 9(d) of the existing [Repayment] Contract."[90] In other words, the more water the District used, the more power revenue the Bureau would generate and the larger the operations and maintenance (O&M) credit account would grow for use after Project completion.

What would happen in wet years when East Slope reservoirs were already full? Would the District successfully persuade the Bureau to deliver greater quantities of water in dry years to save crops in northern Colorado? These and many other unknowns continued to test Bureau-District relations while Project construction was being completed. Meanwhile, the District became embroiled in controversies involving the Blue River, the City of Denver, and its own attorney, William Kelly.

12 Breach of Faith or Law?
Front Range Growth Causes Dissension Over Senate Document 80

Less than two months after President Truman signed the Upper Colorado River Basin Compact into law on April 6, 1949, the United States filed suit in Federal District Court to seek a declaratory judgment in regard to its rights and obligations pertaining to C–BT water. The suit asked for determination of the government's priority dates, amounts of water, points of diversion, and places of storage in the Colorado River, the Blue River, and other tributaries of the Colorado River in connection with the C–BT Project.[1]

Although a similar situation was developing in California, where state and federal authorities were in conflict over water rights on the Santa Margarita River,[2] the Justice Department's decision to file suit in Denver sprang from the C–BT's extensive geographical location in several different river basins. It was also inspired by the realization that postwar growth and recent drought along the Front Range had caused the Denver Water Board (DWB) and its allies to seek supplemental supplies of water on the Blue River with renewed vigor. Because Denver's actions appeared to threaten the West Slope and to raise questions about the jurisdiction of Senate Document 80, especially in regard to Green Mountain Reservoir, the Federal District Court became the most appropriate forum to litigate the many water rights issues involving Denver, Colorado Springs, Englewood, the CRWCD, the Public Service Company (PSC), the South Platte Water Users Association, and the NCWCD.

Several years of planning and discussion between the Justice Department and the Bureau preceded the suit's actual filing in 1949. Most of the litigants knew that it was coming. What troubled Colorado water officials was that the suit might set a precedent capable of undermining the long-established rights of states to adjudicate water rights in state courts. Additionally, the suit was opposed by those who associated the Justice Department's decision with what they labeled "creeping socialism."

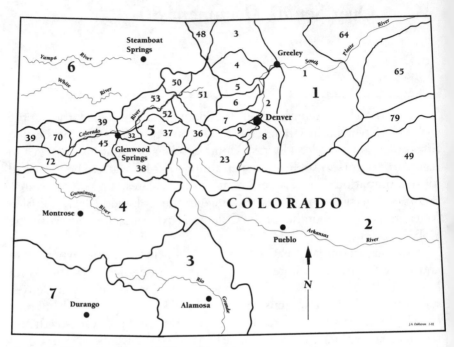

Colorado Water Divisions and Water Districts.

The government's strongest argument for a suit in Federal District Court was that the completed C–BT Project would function as a single, integrated unit. Parts of the Project were located in Water District Nos. 36 and 51 on the West Slope, while other features were at that time in Water District Nos. 3, 4, 5, and 6 on the East Slope. Due to the several courts and the multiplicity of suits in which adjudication proceedings would be conducted under state laws, the Department of Justice became convinced that one class action suit was the simplest, most expeditious means of resolving conflicts involving Front Range cities, the C–BT, and the West Slope's increasing sensitivity to further transmountain diversion.

On the other hand, government critics expressed outrage at further evidence of an overweening federal presence in natural resource development. In protest, states' rights advocates generated fiery complaints, including letters and editorials to warn Coloradans that the United States was about to set aside the Colorado system of water rights and to undermine the state engineer and his water commissioners. While one angry citizen suggested that all government bureaucrats either take a vow of celibacy or be reduced to the status of eunuchs, others saw a great conspiracy in which the Bureau was actually pushing vast, multipurpose irrigation projects as a first step to gain control over the nation's economy.[3] Governor Ralph Carr and DWB attorney Glenn G. Saunders also opposed these adjudication proceedings by strongly supporting organization of an Association of Water Users for State Control.[4] On the West Slope, where suspicion of Denver's water plans was never far below the surface, the CRWCD prepared for battle, urging the NCWCD to support adjudication of C–BT water decrees in state courts and authorizing a large increase in legal expenses to fight Denver's claim to the Blue River.[5]

The Justice Department was determined to proceed with the suit. By 1949 U.S. attorneys recognized that Front Range growth following World War II would force Denver to double its efforts to find additional water. While Summit County District Court slowly and methodically considered Denver's claim for a 1914 water right on the Blue River,[6] the old frictions and jealousies, temporarily patched up by East and West Slope leaders in 1937, resurfaced to obstruct East Slope transmountain diversion plans. What was ultimately at stake in this suit was not only water rights of the C–BT Project but the future plans of Denver, Englewood, Colorado Springs, and the entire West Slope. Given the demographic and economic changes that occurred on the Front Range between 1945 and 1950, it is now evident why the East-West Slope conflict was renewed with such energy and why the NCWCD could not avoid being drawn into this struggle.

Census data for 1940 and 1950 revealed the alarming nature of new demographic trends. While Denver's population had increased 28 percent, and northeast and southeast Colorado had grown by 25 percent and 8 percent respectively, the West Slope actually lost population.[7] In the 1940s Colorado's overall population had increased 17.3 percent to 1,325,089, but a major shift had occurred in distribution of residences: Jefferson and Adams counties each reported an astonishing 80 percent growth, while Arapahoe, El Paso, Boulder, Larimer, and Pueblo counties tabulated increases of 20 percent to 60 percent. In 1950 nine of the ten most heavily populated counties in Colorado were located on the Front Range, and 42.5 percent of the state's population was concentrated in Denver, Adams, Arapahoe, and Jefferson counties. Meanwhile, the West Slope was losing population and jobs.

Other data indicated the existence of increased economic power on the East Slope as well. Record cash receipts for agriculture and livestock in 1948 and 1949 were accompanied by reports that the state's farm population was actually shrinking, even as bigger mechanized farms on the East Slope successfully planted large acreages to wheat. Colorado ranked seventh nationally in bushels of wheat harvested and tenth in cattle on feed. Most of these profitable enterprises were located east of the Continental Divide. In wholesale and retail trade, manufacturing, construction, and service industries, payrolls had risen an average of 57 percent. More than half the state's employees in commerce and industry worked in Denver, while another 25 percent were employed in the other Front Range counties, meaning that 82 percent of all jobs relating to commerce, manufacturing, and industry were located on the Front Range. Furthermore, banks holding the majority of the state's deposits were concentrated in Denver, El Paso, and Pueblo counties.

These developments were particularly evident to the DWB. Following reports of record-breaking service connections and total water use in 1946, the DWB decided to embark on a five-year construction program to expand its storage, distribution, and water treatment systems. Part of the plan included beginning work on a tunnel designed to bring Blue River water into the South Platte River.[8] Again in 1948 the DWB reported a record distribution of water, with high demand resulting from an increased number of users and a drought year in which rainfall was below normal.[9] DWB board members met with committees from Adams, Arapahoe, and Jefferson counties to discuss zoning conditions under which these outside areas could be annexed to the City and County of Denver to secure a definite supply of water. They also announced that water users outside Denver would have to pay approximately one-third more for water delivered to them by the DWB.[10]

Because the U.S. Census showed a population of approximately 500,000 in the Denver metropolitan area by the end of 1950, with record numbers of water taps for new residents, the DWB accelerated plans to expand all water facilities, including the Blue River Tunnel, Gross Reservoir on South Boulder Creek, and the Fraser River collection system, used for diversion via the Moffat Tunnel.[11] Predicting the same growth rate for the future, DWB leaders, aided by city and county officials, embarked on an aggressive program to acquire new supplies. As demand for filtered water continued to escalate in 1951 and 1952, the DWB concluded that additional water facilities would be needed for 725,000 people in the Denver urban area by 1963. Given past growth patterns and future projections, and because the South Platte River supply had already been developed to capacity, the needs of the next ten years would have to be met "by prompt expansion of available facilities located on the headwaters of the Colorado River."[12] This thinking paralleled what the Bureau was saying about population growth and future power demands. In a report based on "years of field study," which constituted part of a survey of the entire Missouri River basin, the Bureau concluded that power demands on the South Platte would triple by 1970. If enough water could be diverted from the Blue River to the South Platte, these energy demands could be met by hydroelectric plants constructed in a number of highly recommended sites, not the least of which was the Two Forks location at the confluence of the North and South forks of the South Platte River.[13]

From the CRWCD's vantage point on the West Slope, Denver and the Bureau were pursuing a common objective that lacked any consideration of previous commitments to protect present and future water requirements in the basin of the Colorado River. The NCWCD was also concerned about what Denver's plans for the Blue River might mean to C–BT water rights at Green Mountain Reservoir.[14] Both districts became increasingly alarmed as Denver launched the Blue River project by initiating a 23-mile tunnel to carry water from the Dillon area to the South Platte River.[15] Such transmountain diversion had first been contemplated in 1940, when the DWB and Chamber of Commerce joined forces to seek construction funds for the project as a "national defense measure." Glenn G. Saunders, then assistant city attorney, promoted the project as one that would produce more power than the C–BT and that could be built in four

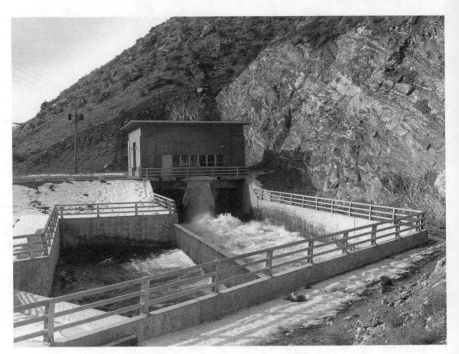

Outlet portal of the Harold D. Roberts Tunnel. This Denver Water Department facility was completed in 1964 and transports water 23.3 miles from Dillon Reservoir to the South Platte River. (Courtesy Bureau of Reclamation.)

years.[16] Ground breaking did not begin, however, until June 24, 1946 — the date that Summit County Judge William Luby recognized as Denver's priority date for the Blue River — when work began on the East Portal of what was then called Montezuma Tunnel (Harold D. Roberts Tunnel after 1955). With budgets that allocated from $100,000 to $250,000 per year to the project, the DWB engaged in a modest amount of excavating during the next few years while continuing to develop West Slope collection systems to increase flows through the Moffat Tunnel.[17] By the end of 1948 the Montezuma Tunnel had been driven forward only several thousand feet.

What particularly upset the CRWCD and the NCWCD was not so much the small amount of work that Denver had pursued on the Blue River project but the arrogance of city officials, who claimed immunity from previous commitments to the West Slope, especially Senate Document 80 stipulations. As noted by CWCB Director Clifford Stone, Senate Document 80 had been adopted into Colorado law, but "the Denver Water

Glenn G. Saunders, long-time Denver Water Board attorney, differed with NCWCD attorneys over the use of water from Green Mountain Reservoir. (Courtesy Denver Water Board.)

Board had seen fit to claim that it would not recognize these principles, especially as they appl[ied] to prospective Western Colorado development."[18] Furthermore, Stone pointed out, Denver's unilateral approach to satisfying its own water needs was playing into the hands of California, which wanted to keep the state divided so that the legislature would never ratify the 1948 Upper River Basin Compact on the Colorado River. If Stone could persuade Saunders to change his views, a statewide agreement on Blue River diversion might be possible.[19] Moreover, Stone, CRWCD attorney Frank Delaney, and the NCWCD wanted to convince Denver to recognize and affirm Senate Document 80. Because the adjudication of water rights in Water District No. 36 (Summit County) was still pending after several years of delay, and because the United States had filed suit in Federal District Court to establish the integrity and binding effect of Senate Document 80, Delaney proposed a resolution asking Denver to agree in principle to protect the "present vested rights" and "reasonable future development" of the West Slope as a basis for further discussion of Denver's transmountain diversion plans.[20] The CRWCD passed this resolution unanimously.

In Denver, however, it was rebuffed. At a meeting with Saunders and A. P. Gumlick, president of the DWB, Stone and Delaney presented a memorandum pressing for Denver's recognition of existing West Slope rights and probable future development as well as the integrity of Senate

Document 80 "in so far as the same is necessary for the protection of Western Colorado." Specifically, they wanted assurance of the priority rights to the 52,000 acre-foot replacement pool and the 100,000 acre-foot power pool in Green Mountain Reservoir.[21] Saunders and Gumlick, who had been counting on a 1914 Blue River priority from the Summit County District Court, saw no reason to prematurely guarantee water rights or water storage to the West Slope. A few months later, however, Denver modified its rigid position by confining claims on the Blue River "to an amount required for future domestic use" and promised to inform all concerned when the precise calculation was made.[22] This promise was followed by another that Denver would put in writing to the effect that "storage at Green Mountain [Reservoir] would not be interfered with and no calls would ever be made to release water from [Lake] Granby."[23]

As J. M. Dille observed, a reasonable probability existed in 1948 that Denver might be willing to make compromises. Chances for amicable settlement on Blue River matters seemed "very good," he told the Board, and he was optimistic that extensive litigation could be avoided by mutual understanding. Even the Bureau, he pointed out, was anxious to help all parties find a common ground;[24] but Dille had trouble keeping his own house in order. The Blue River discussions only emphasized that the seminal issue between East and West Slopes was the interpretation of the "present or future" clause in the "Conclusions" section of Senate Document 80. Over this very issue, strong disagreements existed at the NCWCD between attorney William R. Kelly and President Charles Hansen. The opinions of their respective followers revealed a substantial rift between those concerned by a potential breach of Colorado law (Kelly and his supporters) and those who worried more about a breach of faith with the West Slope (Hansen and his supporters). The details of this dispute illuminate the District's dilemma vis-à-vis the West Slope, a dilemma exacerbated by Denver's determination to provide for future growth by establishing priority rights to water in the Colorado River basin.

Kelly had attempted clarification of his position in 1947 after learning of the Justice Department's interest in entering water adjudication proceedings in Federal District Court. In a lengthy memorandum to the Board, he noted the probability that the United States could not be compelled to enter state water adjudication proceedings. Kelly preferred state adjudication, but U.S. attorneys had persuaded him of the efficacy of litigation in Federal District Court. As owner of legal title to all C–BT water, Kelly concluded, the United States was subject by contract "to give the perpetual right to irrigation, domestic, and municipal uses to the District on completion of payment." The federal government had a duty "as trustee, to enter some proper adjudication proceeding and to protect the priorities of all these rights, those of power for the United States, and those for irrigation and domestic uses for the District."[25] Apart from arguing that the District should cooperate in the U.S. plan to adjudicate C–BT water rights in Federal District Court, Kelly insisted that the obligation of the District, the United States, and East Slope appropriators was "satisfied and performed, as to works constructed, for all time" by construction of the Green Mountain Reservoir at no cost to the West Slope. Except for this concession, Kelly concluded, "no other West Slope works [were] affected and priorities for diversion to the East Slope [would] naturally go, under the Constitution of Colorado, according to dates of initiation, provided application [were] made to beneficial use within a reasonable time."[26] In other words, Kelly reasoned, the NCWUA (predecessor of the NCWCD) had voluntarily yielded its superior priority right to let Green Mountain Reservoir step ahead in the line of appropriators when, by ordinary application of the laws, Lake Granby and the Adams Tunnel would have been eligible for earlier decrees.[27] Thus, he concluded, the District's obligations to the West Slope under Senate Document 80 had been fulfilled.

In January 1948 the NCWCD Board authorized Kelly to join the District as co-plaintiff in the Justice Department's suit in Federal District Court. Dille pointed out that C–BT water rights decreed in this court would have higher standing in any interstate case between Colorado and the lower basin.[28] While Denver, the Justice Department, and the CWCB agreed to delays in the Summit County District Court proceedings, Kelly continued to meet with the U.S. attorneys. In July 1948 he reported to the Board that "he was not prepared to stipulate that all Western Slope decrees [would] be considered senior to Project water rights."[29] Nothing he might have said could have done more to awaken the moral sensibilities of seventy-five-year-old NCWCD President Hansen. Kelly's words brought back a flood of memories of hard-nosed negotiations and of compromises and commitments with the West Slope in 1937. As one of the last living members of the original East Slope group that had finally earned the trust of Edward T. Taylor, Delaney, and the WSPA, Hansen responded with moral outrage at what he viewed as Kelly's misunderstandings. He responded just as Taylor had requested of him in 1941, three months before the late congressman's death.[30]

As Kelly later recalled, Hansen summoned him to the Greeley office, where he bluntly stated his desire to stipulate "that the future, as well as the existing appropriations on the Colorado River would be ahead of the

District's rights. I counseled against this step," Kelly reported, "and told him I thought that was going further than the Western Slope representatives were asking." Hansen was adamant. He was convinced that Kelly's interpretation of Senate Document 80 would undermine the mutual respect and confidence that he and others from both slopes had fought so hard for during the 1930s. They had agreed in 1935 not to interfere in any way with "present needs and future requirements of the Western Slope" and to the terms and conditions set forth in the Delaney Resolution. Hansen's sense of moral obligation to the West Slope was further buttressed by a letter from engineer Royce J. Tipton.[31]

Tipton wrote Hansen on July 24, one week after Kelly had announced his unwillingness to stipulate in favor of seniority for all West Slope water decrees. The tone of the letter implied that Hansen specifically requested Tipton's support in his confrontation with Kelly. As the engineer responsible for the 1933 report on the feasibility of the Grand Lake Project, Tipton had concluded that there was such an abundance of water in the Colorado River basin and such limited potential for West Slope development that the Grand Lake Project could not possibly interfere with prior West Slope rights, as long as 46,300 acre-feet of storage were provided to satisfy the decree of the Glenwood Power Canal and Pipeline (Shoshone Power Plant) during drought years.[32]

Fifteen years after these investigations, Tipton's clients included the South Platte Water Users, a group directed by the City of Denver, which, in 1948, was heavily involved in developing its own transmountain diversion project from the Blue River.[33] Even if he recognized a potential conflict of interest, Tipton wrote his old friend as if nothing had changed in Colorado since 1933.

> I am firm in my conviction that the Colorado–Big Thompson Project was authorized on the basis that it would divert only surplus water from the Colorado River. . . . The fact that storage has been provided [Green Mountain Reservoir] in my opinion does not relieve the District of the obligation embodied in the *original intent* [emphasis added] that all future potentialities in Colorado which could be interfered with by the operation of the Project shall be protected.

From a "moral standpoint," Tipton argued, if that replacement storage at Green Mountain Reservoir proved inadequate, "it would be the obligation of the District to provide the required additional storage or to forego the use of that water which would interfere with the future projects as they go into operation. For the District to take any other position at this time I believe would be very unwise and would border on the unethical."[34]

Tipton had spoken just the words Hansen wanted to hear. He cited the Delaney Resolution as proof that transmountain diversion should in no way adversely affect "existing Western Slope rights [or] probable future Western Slope development"; however, he said nothing of Denver's moral and ethical obligations or of the fact that his 1933 report assumed that Blue River water not captured by Green Mountain Reservoir would be available downriver for future West Slope uses.[35] Tipton's communication with Hansen drew more on nostalgia and his own reputation as a civil engineer than on the reality of Colorado water law as manifested by Denver's challenge to the C–BT on the Blue River.

Energized by the Tipton letter, Hansen delivered an ultimatum at the August 14, 1948, Board meeting. First he reviewed Kelly's opposition to stipulating in the adjudication proceeding "that all present and future use of water on the Colorado River would have priority over Project diversions to the Eastern Slope." Such a position, Hansen explained, "was contrary to the historic agreements with the people of the Western Slope as outlined in the Delaney Resolution and Senate Document No. 80 and to the previous policy of the District. It would be a breach of faith," he said, "that could do untold damage to the Project. . . . He must insist that the Board determine a definite policy of the District in this matter at this meeting."[36] Hansen, spoiling for a showdown, saw his leadership, based on agreements worked out between East and West Slopes from 1934 to 1937, being severely tested.

After lengthy discussion, the Board addressed a resolution reiterating its

> well established policy to adhere to and be bound by the provisions and conditions of Senate Document No. 80 . . . in the spirit and understanding of the parties interested therein at the time of its promulgation. . . . That no technical interpretation shall be adopted that will nullify the accepted interpretation thereof at the time; namely, that the diversion of water from the Colorado River to the Eastern Slope shall at no time interfere with the right of the people of the Western Slope to the present or future use of water in the basin of the Colorado River in Colorado.[37]

Following a vote, Hansen declared the resolution approved unanimously. Kelly agreed that the District should be bound by Senate Document 80, but he reiterated that Green Mountain Reservoir had absolved the District of further obligations to the West Slope and stressed the need to regulate additional uses of Colorado River water by priority dates under state laws, "regardless of the commitments made when the Project was being developed." He disagreed with other sentiments expressed by the Board and advised against the Directors' interpretation of its obligations as expounded; however, he would be bound by any policy specifically directed by the Board.[38]

Deep down, Kelly seethed. His extensive experience as a water attorney convinced him that the Board was making a huge mistake. Furthermore, he had recently been disturbed to learn that the CWCB and the Bureau were discussing "adjudication of water rights of [the] Project and [were considering] dividing the waters of the Colorado River [on some basis] other than on the priority of appropriation rule."[39] The plan, as he described it, was to allow Green Mountain Reservoir one annual filling, with Denver receiving the rest of the Blue River's natural flow. Kelly's eight-page memorandum to Hansen and the NCWCD Board lamented what was happening. Senate Document 80, he said, was based on a "continuance of the natural flow of the Blue River" into the Colorado River. If Denver preempted this flow, releases from Granby Dam would have to be made, in violation of Senate Document 80, to satisfy downstream priorities. The impact on District water users would be significant. Their $25 million investment would be jeopardized by a failure to guarantee the 310,000 acre-feet of water for which they had contracted. "Possibly we should remind ourselves," concluded Kelly, "of some elementary principles of rights to [the] use of water in Colorado. The water of the natural streams belongs to the state."[40]

Kelly's thinking was not lost on the man responsible for appointing or reappointing NCWCD Directors, District Court Judge Claude C. Coffin. Although no direct evidence shows that Kelly specifically sought his collaboration, the judge sent a letter to Hansen two days after Kelly's memorandum saying that he would delay announcement of appointments to the NCWCD Board to enable the sitting Directors to have "the opportunity, if it be so advised and desired, to reconsider that certain resolution passed and appearing on its minutes under date August 14, 1948." He wondered "whether the resolution should not be modified or expunged." He also questioned whether an "assumed policy to make the District's priorities subservient to future use on the Western Slope" might be "contrary to long settled rules of law pertaining to priorities of right to appropriated water." Would such an "assumed policy," he asked, be in accordance with Senate Document 80?[41] These questions clearly echoed

The completed Green Mountain Reservoir became a focal point of contention following Denver's construction of Dillon Reservoir in 1963. (Courtesy Bureau of Reclamation.)

Kelly's own concerns. Hansen addressed Coffin's letter immediately at "the urgent request of *some* [emphasis added] members of the NCWCD Board of Directors. . . . I have been too deeply stirred by your recent letter," he said, "to care for myself. Certainly there must have [been] some misinformation come to you from persons who lack knowledge of the situation or who have deliberately misused the facts."[42] Was he referring to Kelly?

Hansen was angry and hurt. He told Coffin that no apology was necessary for himself or for "any of the men with whom I have talked" regarding the August 14 resolution. "Senate Document 80 is to the Colorado–Big Thompson Project what the Bible is to the Christian religion. Men may interpret it differently, but its moral interpretations remain intact." After four years of acrimonious discussion with the West Slope, minds finally met "in amicable agreement in this instrument. I took part in every one of these discussions, in fact carried the brunt of the battle for our people. At any time during the four years, if I had faltered or quit, we would not have had our Project. . . . My name . . . is on that document and . . . I will defend its terms to the last ounce of my ability."[43] Noting that Green Mountain Reservoir was constructed "for the sole benefit of the Western Slope people," with 52,000 acre-feet for replacement and "100,000 acre-feet for power and security for any future needs on the Western Slope," Hansen explained to Coffin that "the controversy seem[ed] to be about the words 'present and future needs' along the Colorado River in Colorado." Conflict had begun more than two years earlier, when the Bureau stated that West Slope people had the first right to appropriation for present and future use of water from the Colorado River under terms of Senate Document 80. Kelly "took strong issue" with the Bureau. When the matter came before the NCWCD Board, Hansen clashed with Kelly, stating "that his position violated the terms and spirit of Senate Document 80." Kelly then acquiesced to the document's validity regarding West Slope rights in Green Mountain Reservoir, rights that guaranteed present and future water uses by West Slope residents.

The matter had come up again, explained Hansen, because in recent months Kelly had been involved in discussions with U.S. attorneys to start adjudication proceedings in state or federal court. Because the government attorneys took the same position as the Bureau had two years earlier, Kelly immediately opposed them and erroneously pronounced his views as official Board policy. Because he refused to alter his position after discussions with Hansen and because he felt that he was only responsible to the Board, Hansen had asked the Directors to state their policy in an August 14 resolution drawn up by attorney Charles M. Rolfson of Julesburg, "himself a lawyer who has been identified with the Project from its earliest inception. . . . In conclusion," wrote Hansen, "I wish to reiterate that I feel that even though we have made the Western Slope triply secure in their water rights by physical works, there is still a *moral* obligation on us to help them retain those rights, and whether or not I am a member of the Board of Directors of Northern Colorado Water Conservancy District, I shall carry out these *moral* obligations to the best of my ability and conscience" (emphasis added).

Coffin replied immediately that he did not want to give the impression that he was dictating Board policies; furthermore, he recognized that it was not his right or responsibility "to pass on the propriety of Board action." However, because this was the only action in the entire history of the Board "that had made even an adverse ripple," he would gladly give the Board opportunity for reconsideration. He was also responding to protests, presumably from some NCWCD Directors, that the August 14 resolution provided a basis for "literally selling our rights down the river."[44]

Shortly thereafter, Dille announced a Board meeting for October 9, 1948, and attached a memorandum providing information on the dispute that now involved the West Slope, Senate Document 80, and the claims of Denver, Colorado Springs, and Englewood to the Blue River. He noted that the "crux" of Senate Document 80 "and all of the agreements, personal statements and official records is that the Project is to be constructed and operated without interference with the 'vested and future rights in irrigation' on the Colorado River in Colorado." On the basis of "exhaustive studies" by Bureau engineers, Dille noted, "it was decided" that "such an agreement could be made without any danger to the Project, provided a 'replacement' reservoir was built on the Blue River. With all the *theoretically possible* future development of irrigation on the Colorado River and with the shortest possible yearly water supply," Dille concluded, "only 52,000 acre-feet would be needed to replace full diversion of all water available to the Project."[45] Though provisions were made in Senate Document 80 to protect the C–BT from any injury, "the obligation remain[ed] of record for whatever it may be considered to mean or be worth, and any indication that this District contemplat[ed] repudiating the agreement [would] surely be considered by Western Slope people, and all others whose good will and help we still need, as a flagrant and totally uncalled for breach of faith." Nothing could be gained by "repudiating the historic agreement and there [was] everything to lose in the respect, confidence, and good will of the Western Slope people, and of all others who may hear about it in general."[46]

When the Directors convened the October Board meeting, Hansen reviewed negotiations that had preceded the 1937 agreement with the West Slope. He then outlined Kelly's view that the District's obligation to the West Slope had been fulfilled by construction of Green Mountain Reservoir and that "all future appropriators should be junior to the Project." By contrast, Hansen argued, his "own interpretation was based on the intent of the parties at the time of agreement, namely that the right of Western Slope people to present and future use for irrigation would never be interfered with by the operations of the Colorado–Big Thompson Project."[47]

Furthermore, Hansen stated, that part of Senate Document 80 providing protection for future appropriators was made for two reasons: (1) because Congressman Taylor would have blocked the Project without such statements; and (2) because engineering studies by the Bureau and by Tipton, the District's consulting engineer, had shown that any possible future development of the West Slope along the Colorado River would not endanger full diversion by the C–BT.[48] Kelly then reasserted his view that the District should not concede any superiority of right to future appropriators on the Colorado River.

A lengthy and animated discussion ensued, with Directors expressing contradictory views. The Board was divided, and Hansen felt betrayed. When asked to confirm their convictions on the August 14 resolution, five Directors now voted in favor, three against, and two abstained.[49] What had gone wrong? Where was the Directors' sense of history? What choice did

Hansen have but to terminate his association with these men? He must resign immediately.

The Board, however, refused to accept his resignation. To solve the crisis, Vice President Ray Lanyon appointed a committee under Charles A. Lory to work out a compromise agreement with Coffin. In November this committee reported to the Board a "very satisfactory conference" with the judge, at which time everyone agreed on a new resolution with this revised wording:

1. The integrity of Senate Document 80 must be maintained.
2. In any and all determinations of the water rights of the Colorado–Big Thompson Project, Senate Document 80 must be recognized and given effect.
3. The officers and attorneys of the District are hereby directed to carry into effect this Resolution.
4. This Resolution is for the purpose of more clearly stating the intent of the Resolution of the Board of August 14, 1948, and shall be taken as superseding and rescinding such Resolution.[50]

Kelly and Hansen approved the new resolution, and the Board accepted it unanimously. The crisis was over. The meaning of Senate Document 80 and how it would be implemented in court decrees and decisions would await another day. In December Coffin presented the Board with a court order reappointing all Directors whose two-year terms had expired. The reconvened Directors promptly reelected Hansen to the presidency. Peace was restored. But what had been learned, and what was the long-range impact of this contretemps among the Directors, NCWCD officers, and the Board's attorneys?

The new resolution no longer made any reference to the "right of the people of the Western Slope . . . to the present or future use of water in the basin of the Colorado River."[51] Hansen had lost this round to Kelly. Established principles of Colorado water law prevailed. At the same time, the West Slope was assured of the District's determination to preserve the supremacy of Senate Document 80. Individuals might question whether existing surveys were adequate to determine the West Slope's future water needs for industry, oil shale development, municipal growth, and irrigation, but clearly the NCWCD was committed to defending the 152,000 acre-feet of water in Green Mountain Reservoir for the sake of harmony between the two slopes. If Denver wanted to continue its claims on the Blue River, it would find the NCWCD and the CRWCD united against any tampering with the priority of Green Mountain Reservoir and the authority of Senate Document 80.

The dispute also left visible scars that surfaced on many occasions before Kelly finally stepped down as NCWCD attorney in 1956; however, he should not be seen as a villain. Hansen's moral commitment to the West Slope became involved with legal interpretations of water rights under the province of the judicial system. Had his views prevailed, C–BT operation would have required compensation to the West Slope for Denver's Blue River diversions. The DWB had no plans to compensate the West Slope for diverting Blue River water through the Roberts Tunnel. Under Hansen's interpretation of East-West Slope arrangements, the C–BT could only operate if all West Slope users were satisfied, regardless of who took their water. Coffin recognized the dangers inherent in Hansen's emotional view, which would have made the District the guarantor of water delivery to West Slope users beyond Green Mountain Reservoir's capacity to serve them. Meanwhile, through a policy of divide and conquer, Denver would have gotten water free of charge. The Board's November 6, 1948, resolution underscored the importance of Senate Document 80 and Colorado water law to secure a water supply and maintain stable relations with the West Slope, an importance they still hold today. Hansen's moral stance cemented the relationship between East and West Slopes by committing the United States, the CRWCD, and the NCWCD to ensure that Green Mountain Reservoir's priority date would remain senior to Denver's Blue River claims. Both Kelly and Hansen, therefore, contributed to the principles that have guided the NCWCD over the past forty years.[52]

Kelly finally received a salary increase in January 1949. Though he had asked for it nine months earlier, the Board's finance committee had not responded to his request during the tumultuous summer of 1948. Lory noted that most Directors showed their confidence in Kelly and his judgment "by not taking the time to read [his] carefully prepared opinion[s] on . . . involved legal matter[s]. . . . We cannot afford to lose his services," he wrote, "and must not risk doing so."[53] Most probably agreed, but over the course of the next eight years they tired of Kelly's occasionally outspoken and confrontational approach to legal matters.[54] Attorney-client relations were further strained by Kelly's tendency to present drawn-out legal reports and redundant factual data to the Board.[55] Because of inflation and the steadily increasing work load of Kelly's firm (Kelly was now in partnership with Jack Clayton), the Directors raised Kelly's salary in 1953 and again in 1955 but insisted that he attend all Board meetings and present monthly reports.[56]

The latter request reflected a lack of confidence in Kelly, exacerbated by a worrisome physical infirmity: he had begun to lose his hearing and refused to use a hearing aid. He attended a great number of meetings where the District's representation was essential. As Barkley later recalled, the problem became especially noticeable in September 1955, when he and Kelly went to Washington to meet with Justice Department officials in a compromise effort related to Denver's Blue River objectives. After long work sessions with many individuals, Barkley found himself briefing Kelly in the evenings on everything that had transpired during the day.[57] When they returned to Colorado, Kelly appeared less frequently at Board meetings. President J. Ben Nix finally reminded him that both he and Clayton had promised to attend regularly, but Kelly did not comply, possibly out of embarrassment over his hearing condition. Nix, angry and frustrated with Kelly's stubbornness, discussed with the Directors their fear that Kelly might no longer be able to represent the District effectively. In July 1956 the Directors moved to terminate his services.[58] A month later Kelly and Clayton dissolved their partnership, and Kelly transferred District files to the new firm of Clayton and [Robert M.] Gilbert, whom the Board immediately recognized as the District's legal counsel. At the same meeting, the Directors passed a resolution of appreciation for Kelly's "many years of valuable service."[59]

This was hardly an emotional parting. Kelly had indeed provided the District with dedicated service; no attorney ever worked harder on behalf of a client. But during the final seven or eight years of his employment, he became increasingly irascible and difficult. His positioning on issues was frequently reactionary. Although Kelly was respected he was not always appreciated. Because his modus operandi seemed anachronistic at a time when the District sought compromise in Blue River adjudication proceedings, NCWCD Directors concluded that his usefulness had been substantially diminished. He was hurt by the abrupt termination, but the Board clearly saw how his obstinacy and hearing problems were affecting negotiations with Denver, Colorado Springs, the West Slope, and the federal government. Kelly remained the District's attorney during the critical years of negotiation that led to the Blue River decree of 1955, but that landmark agreement was reached almost in spite of rather than because of him.

13 Conflict and Compromise: Negotiating the Consolidated Cases and the Blue River Decrees of 1955

By late 1949 intrastate competition for the Blue River had become entwined in interstate concerns about Colorado's role in securing congressional enactment of the Colorado River Storage Project (CRSP). State leaders on both sides of the Continental Divide favored building dams on the Colorado River, but they did not know how to unify East and West Slopes over the contentious matter of transmountain diversion. As long as the state remained divided, the CRSP had little chance of success in Congress; however, accord would bring the CRSP funding from which all of the upper basin states would benefit. The consolidation of three cases in Federal District Court, along with the out-of-court settlement referred to as the 1955 Blue River decrees, provided the necessary proof of unity. Within months of this historic agreement, Congress passed the CRSP Act.

The West Slope was determined to resist Denver's Blue River plans and all other transmountain diversions until the Bureau completed adequate water and land surveys with data necessary to estimate probable water needs for future growth and development in the Colorado River basin. The CRWCD argued that significant amounts of information were necessary to determine how the proposed Fryingpan-Arkansas and Blue River–South Platte projects would affect the West Slope's future. Until then, the CRWCD would block any plans by East Slope communities to export additional water from the Colorado River or any of its tributaries, a stance that the CRWCD Board believed was more than justified.

To comprehend the NCWCD's role in the Blue River decrees requires understanding the nature and depth of the West Slope's hostility to transmountain diversion. The 1922 Colorado River Compact, the 1928 Boulder Canyon Act, and at least two resolutions of the Colorado State Planning Commission (CSPC) (1935, 1936) authorized surveys for appraisal of probable consumptive uses of all water in the State of Colorado.[1] In 1943 the Colorado State Assembly passed an act in preparation for constructing a transmountain project to the Arkansas River. Any project built by any district created under the 1943 act in which water would be exported out of the Colorado River basin would have to be constructed so that the "present appropriations . . . and . . . prospective uses of water . . . including domestic, mining, and industrial purposes" would not be impaired "nor increased in cost at the expense of the water users within the said natural basin."[2] This statute appeared to reaffirm earlier agreements.

By 1950, however, West Slope anxieties became intensified by the CWCB's declared support for the Fryingpan-Arkansas and Blue River projects, the Bureau's backing of a transmountain diversion to the South Platte, and the state's official sanction of the CRSP.[3] With the real possibility of additional water needed in the Colorado River basin for oil shale development, West Slope leaders felt like "political orphans" who were falling behind in the race for federal funds.[4] From their vantage point, the Bureau had to complete the heretofore authorized surveys with an eye to the likelihood of coal, oil shale, and other forms of industrial development[5] in the Colorado River basin.[6] When the Bureau did not get the job done, West Slope leaders interpreted this failure all the more ominously. In 1951 they approved the Fryingpan-Arkansas project but only with the understanding that "there would be no more federally financed transmountain diversions approved unless and until surveys of water resources and needs of Western Colorado had been completed."[7] When the CWCB approved the Fryingpan-Arkansas project, it agreed to the West Slope's stipulation.[8] But when Denver pressed the CWCB to support the Blue River project without waiting for surveys now estimated to take nearly five years,[9] West Slope feelings of abandonment mounted. As the *Grand Junction Sentinel* pointed out, the hour had arrived to decide whether the West Slope would remain an exploited country colony of Denver or defy the capital city and seek development in its own right.[10]

To Frank Delaney and his colleagues, the CWCB was bowing to Denver's relentless pressure while ignoring promises made to the West Slope regarding basin-of-origin protection for inhabitants of the Colorado River basin.[11] Growing anger first manifested itself in a plan by Grand Junction's Preston Walker to divide the state into two water conservancy districts, one for the East Slope and the other for West Slope. In this way, Walker explained, agreements would be mutually binding. He contended that Denver officials were trying to "crucify" the West Slope. He singled out Glenn G. Saunders, CWCB attorney Jean S. Breitenstein, and John Geoffrey Will as the most irresponsible East Slope leaders and criticized Dan Thornton as a "playboy, headline hunting governor."[12] Delaney joined this movement to rally the West Slope against Denver's use of "power politics" to get whatever water the city wanted.[13] In a more strident vein, West Slope Senator D. Lou Williams of Norwood announced his plan to seek the CWCB's abolition because members were not supplying leadership and were "running around like blind dogs in a butcher shop."[14] The Grand Junction Chamber of Commerce, which supported Williams, summed up West Slope frustration with a sixteen-point proposal to reorganize or eliminate the CWCB, establish harmony between both slopes and the other upper Colorado River basin states, encourage the Bureau to complete river basin studies, and reaffirm the policy "adopted in 1935 by the Colorado State Planning Commission" that the basin of origin has first call on water use.[15]

Given the bitterness and pervasive animosity of West Slope officials during the early fifties, how did these outspoken opponents of transmountain diversion finally join a compromise agreement with the federal government, Denver, Colorado Springs, Englewood, and the NCWCD on the Blue River? A first step toward settlement of differences grew out of a Colorado statute authorizing the CWCB to make the surveys that the Bureau had failed to complete, with $100,000 allocated for this purpose. The University of Colorado's Bureau of Business Research contracted for an industrial and economic survey of the West Slope, and the Los Angeles engineering firm of Hill, Leeds and Jewett agreed to do a water survey of the same area.[16] Findings of both organizations allayed some West Slope fears and lent some credibility to Denver's contention that plenty of water was available to meet not only the obligations of Green Mountain Reservoir but future agricultural and industrial needs of Colorado River basin residents. Surveys alone, however, were not enough to effect agreement between East and West Slope rivals. Saunders kept tensions high by claiming that Senate Document 80 protected vested rights of water appropriators on both slopes, including Denver.[17] He also riled the West Slope by accusing their leaders of obstructionism and of a transparent policy to oppose any project presented to the CWCB that included transmountain diversion.[18] His consistently antagonistic manner in regard to the complex Blue River issues caused Governor Thornton to label him and his sidekick, Allen P. Mitchem, "Denver's two trouble-making water agitators."[19] When Summit County District Court finally issued a conditional decree in 1952 that provided Denver and Colorado Springs, respectively, with 1946 and 1948 priority dates on the Blue River — rather than the 1914 and 1927 dates for which the cities had vigorously argued — Saunders appealed the decision to the State Supreme Court. Recognizing that the Blue River fight was vital to Denver's interests and would probably be long and costly, the DWB established for the first time a budget category specifically earmarked for legal expenses in the coming year.[20]

Late in fall 1951 Judge William Luby of the Summit County District Court issued a "proposed decree" regarding the Blue River litigation that was submitted to attorneys for study and reaction. Simultaneously, he announced another hearing in January 1952 to present the final decree for signing and for any objections. In addition to the priority dates awarded Denver and Colorado Springs, the proposed decree established Green Mountain Reservoir's priority ahead of Denver, with an August 1, 1935, date. Following the January hearing, Luby announced that he would sustain his proposed decree, meaning that Denver would have a 1946 priority to 788 cfs and Colorado Springs a 1948 priority to a maximum of 400 cfs from the Blue River. Because both the United States and the NCWCD had withdrawn from these Summit County proceedings in 1949, everyone concerned with the Blue River realized that the final legal battle would take place in Denver's Federal District Court, where the Justice Department had filed a quiet title suit on June 10, 1949 (Civil Action No. 2782).[21] Attorneys for Denver maintained that the Federal District Court had no jurisdiction in state water adjudication proceedings, but Judge William Lee Knous had already ruled in 1951 to accept the case. Meanwhile, both Denver and Colorado Springs appealed to the State Supreme Court to overturn Judge Luby's ruling. While awaiting his decision, attorneys for both cities used delay tactics to slow down proceedings in Knous's court.[22]

The State Supreme Court took nearly two years to review all the evidence in Denver's appeal of the decrees entered in general adjudication proceedings in Water District No. 36 (Civil Action Nos. 16881 and 16888). Denver and Colorado Springs tried to join the United States as a defendant in the Colorado Supreme Court suit, but that court granted the United States' motion to dismiss in March 1953. Five months later the two cases were removed to Federal District Court and renumbered Civil Action Nos. 5016 and 5017. A comprehensive pretrial order was filed to formulate issues in the case, but no further action was taken pending outcome of the appeal in the State Supreme Court. On October 18, 1954, Chief Justice Mortimer Stone announced a 4–3 decision, upholding Judge Luby's priority dates. The majority opinion affirmed the trial court judgment in awards of conditional decrees to Denver and Colorado Springs and denied a decree to the South Platte Water Users Association.[23] Two months later the Court denied Denver and Colorado Springs a new hearing by unanimous vote, thus closing the door on attempts to keep alive the controversial Blue

River water case in state court.[24] Because it was becoming clear that the C–BT Project and Green Mountain Reservoir would be senior to Denver's Blue River water rights, Saunders's response was defiant. "It is hard to say what the total effect of the ruling is," he said, "but one thing we know: Denver must have that water from the Blue River."[25] Three months later a DWB spokesman stated that Denver would get what it needed from the Blue River one way or another.[26]

By the end of 1954 Denver's sense of urgency had grown even more acute. Continued high levels of growth and a drought that devastated the streams and reservoirs caused the DWB to make dire predictions. Unless Blue River plans were approved as the "center" of an expanding program of water collection and distribution, it would not be able to provide water to present and expected future customers.[27] Based on 83 years of climatological history recorded by the U.S. Weather Bureau, 1954 was one of the worst precipitation years in Colorado. Compared to an annual average of more than 14 inches, less than 7 inches had been measured along the Front Range that year. The drought had begun with a typical pattern: a warm, dry autumn in 1953 followed by a warm, dry winter in 1954. Under limited mountain snowpack, the soil was dry and was expected to absorb much of the moisture from the streams as spring runoff. By March the U.S. Weather Bureau, Soil Conservation Service, and Colorado A&M researchers predicted that, although surface flows in the South Platte Valley would eventually reach an historical average, they would remain insufficient for the many acres under cultivation.[28] The Bureau was forced to release C–BT water three months earlier than planned, and the City of Boulder, already short of water by May, appealed to Denver for whatever surplus might be available for rental.[29] In early summer Barkley noted that the annual stream flow on the East Slope was 50 percent of average. By October he was convinced that even a wet winter would not end the drought because below-average precipitation had been a fact of life for the past five years. In addition, he lamented, pumping from wells had made deep inroads into underground storage and return flows.[30]

By every standard the drought was a disaster, coming on the heels of the setback Denver had experienced while waiting for the State Supreme Court to rule on the Blue River claims. At the January 30, 1953, meeting of the Upper Colorado River Commission in Cheyenne, Wyoming, a Denver delegation, headed by Saunders, petitioned for inclusion of its Blue River project in the CRSP. Attorney Breitenstein, Colorado's official representative to the commission, suggested that Denver's request was inappropriate because the CWCB had not approved it. Not only did

Saunders fail, he aroused a storm of protest in Colorado among West Slope members of the CWCB and in the delegations from the other states of the upper Colorado River basin.[31] These states had met specifically to settle disagreements that had so far prevented them from obtaining congressional authorization for the CRSP. Even though Interior Secretary Oscar Chapman had already submitted a $1 billion budget for five dams and eleven associated irrigation projects, Congress had not yet authorized CRSP funding.

Because the Korean war was dragging on, military expenditures were still a priority even though President Eisenhower called for a balanced budget. The Bureau, however, exploited national and international conditions to urge funding of the CRSP. It warned of war with Russia, argued that dams and power plants should be funded for patriotic reasons, and declared that the CRSP "would open the way for the expansion of one of America's few remaining [economic] frontiers."[32] In spite of these appeals, Congress continued to use the disunity of the upper basin states in general, and Colorado in particular, to table CRSP legislation. President Eisenhower had endorsed it, but Congress remained penurious until the upper basin states could show indisputable evidence of unity favoring such an expensive project[33] — a déjà vu attitude for those who remembered the C–BT's problems in 1937. Unity was achievable if all interested factions could compromise on how Blue River water rights should be adjudicated. But coming together would not be easy. Egos were inflated and old feuds had surfaced. Furthermore, Denver was driven by the drought to double its efforts to achieve success in its stated transmountain diversion plans.

Meanwhile, the CRWCD postured in defiance of the University of Colorado and California survey results. The former concluded that the West Slope would show no significant future increase in population and that the actual amount of irrigated acreage had declined between 1920 and 1950. The latter report, prepared by Raymond A. Hill, revealed enough of a surplus in the Colorado River to allow Denver to take 550,000 acre-feet of water annually in the Blue River project without infringing on senior priorities.[34] This was not what the CRWCD had wanted to hear. Furthermore, since CWCB Director Stone's death in 1953, the CRWCD had distanced itself from the one state agency that had promised to protect its interests. In Greeley, the NCWCD Board and staff favored the Federal District Court's handling of Blue River litigation and C–BT water rights, but the Directors wanted to loosen attorney William R. Kelly's rigid view that any implementation by Denver of Judge Luby's 1946 Blue River decree would harm the District.[35] Finally, the CWCB, whose job it was to plan and protect Colorado water projects, was under pressure from the governor to end the discord between East and West Slopes. Lacking Stone's leadership, however, the board was in disarray and under fire from all quarters. A committee was appointed to study possible plans for reorganization, but simultaneous resignations of consultants Royce J. Tipton and Breitenstein[36] only exacerbated the CWCB board's difficulties.

While Judge Knous prepared for trial, a meeting in December 1954 at the Pepper Pod restaurant in Hudson, Colorado, which appeared relatively insignificant, ultimately led to an out-of-court Blue River settlement. The juxtaposition of good timing and attendance by representatives from all interested parties made this attitude change possible. As important as this meeting was, however, the drought, pending legislation on the CRSP, and anticipation of an expensive battle in Federal District Court added considerable motivation to the participants. Nor should the importance of Saunder's removal as the DWB's special counsel be underestimated. His replacement by Harold Roberts from the firm of Holme, Roberts, Moore and Owen immediately resulted in a far less adversarial situation, allowing all concerned to seek agreement in the true spirit of give and take.[37]

All parties with legal interests in the Federal District Court case were invited to the Pepper Pod meeting by the Henrylyn Irrigation District, one of the leading proponents of a Blue River–South Platte Conservancy District.[38] Earl L. Mosley, project engineer for the DWB, who represented Denver, remarked on several conversations with the NCWCD's J. M. Dille "in which they had agreed that there should be no real difference [of opinion] between Denver and Northern Colorado."[39] In fact, Dille had been optimistic for some time about a compromise with Denver. Just ten days before this meeting, consultant Tipton had advised NCWCD Directors to influence "other transmountain diversion proposals." Tipton and Dille believed that projects such as Denver's Blue River plan would help develop the Front Range and contribute to the utilization of Colorado's full share of Upper Basin Compact allotment.[40] Dille responded to Mosley that "Denver could do just about as she pleased without interfering with the District's ability to obtain its replacement storage at Green Mountain [Reservoir]."[41]

This was not an insouciant remark. Engineer J. R. "Bob" Barkley's preliminary studies indicated that even in a drought year like 1954, the District's replacement obligations at Green Mountain Reservoir could have been met if Denver had taken 94,000 acre-feet out of the Blue River.[42] Roberts responded that Denver's own studies came to the same conclusions. Would it not be proper, therefore, to request that Kelly stop opposing

Denver so that the city could focus on its real disagreement with the United States over use of the Green Mountain Power Plant? "Frankly," Roberts stated, "Denver needs all the help it can get."[43] Dille also understood that negotiation was the only sensible approach. He felt that the District Board would agree with him, but Kelly remained adamant. "In order to go along [with Denver]," he said, "he would have to be given the Board's authority, backed by engineering opinion."[44] The meeting adjourned on this discordant note, but the seeds of compromise had been sown.

Over the next few months Denver and Colorado Springs pressed their case against the United States and tried to remand the unresolved Blue River cases back to Summit County Court. They claimed that Senate Document 80 had no legislative authority, that the Constitution of Colorado recognized a preference right for domestic use of water, and that the federal government should be bound by the principles and procedures of Colorado water law. The city did not seek water stored at Green Mountain Reservoir for West Slope users, but it wanted rights of the power features subordinated to Denver's municipal needs. An unidentified Denver spokesman said that the city "objected to having the spring run-off course through the power plant merely to generate electricity. The run-off, averaging about 200,000 acre-feet annually, is unappropriated water," he said, "water which we badly need over here for domestic purposes."[45] Denver objected to the federal government's generation of power to pay off C–BT construction debt at the expense of the city's right to surplus flow in the Blue River.

After hearing all sides, Judge Knous ruled that the proceedings initiated against the United States were properly removed and that Federal District Court was the only court that could grant relief in the three cases. Knous's determination was placed on solid ground by the 1951 California decision (Fallbrook Case) and the McCarran Amendment to the 1953 Justice Department Appropriation Act that authorized entities such as the NCWCD to join the federal government as defendants in administration and adjudication of water rights cases. Attorneys J. Lee Rankin and William H. Veeder then petitioned the court to consolidate the cases and proceed to an early trial.[46] The West Slope was also ready to litigate. They scoffed at Denver's arguments and suspected ulterior motives. Denver had not shown any great sensitivity to West Slope needs, and Roberts had even stated at the Hudson meeting that those concerns were invalid "from both a legal and practical viewpoint."[47] The city's real objective, from the West Slope point of view, was most likely the appropriation of Blue River water for sale to agricultural interests, something to which the CRWCD would most vehemently object.

By late summer 1955 conciliation appeared as unattainable as ever, but the Justice Department in Washington suddenly decided on a new tactic. Disputing factions were invited to send one attorney and one advisor each to the capital to explore the possibility of common grounds that might eliminate the need for a formal trial. Judge Knous had already ruled in May that he would hear the Blue River case in Federal District Court, but he had also chosen to limit the issue to adjudication of Bureau water rights for generating electricity at Green Mountain Dam. Trial was scheduled for October 1955.[48] The two cases from Summit County District Court were renumbered and consolidated into one case, thus the frequently used reference to the "Consolidated Cases." The District Board authorized Kelly and Barkley to make the Washington trip. Before departure, they scheduled a meeting with the DWB to explore how the District could sustain Denver's designs on the Blue River. Kelly still favored settling all water adjudication matters in state courts, and he felt that Denver's objectives threatened the District's rights under Senate Document 80; however, the Board instructed him to cooperate with Denver and to seek an operating agreement "to provide for the highest beneficial use of the waters of the Blue River."[49] Kelly chose to ignore these instructions.

When Roberts pleaded that Denver was a "lone wolf" against both the United States and the West Slope, Kelly stated that "any diversions from the Blue River would increase the chances of the District having to release from Granby [Dam] for replacement purposes" in violation of Senate Document 80.[50] Roberts disagreed and requested that the District not oppose Denver. Tipton, who backed Roberts, reiterated his previous statement that Denver could take all the divertible water above Dillon without impairing the ability of Green Mountain Reservoir to make C–BT replacements. Dille and Barkley sided with Tipton. Roberts closed the meeting with the assurance that Denver would accept the position of junior appropriator on the Blue River in recognition that the Green Mountain decree had to be protected. He also hoped that Kelly would not present further legal obstacles. With this admonition, Kelly and Barkley headed for Washington — Kelly by plane, Barkley by train. As Barkley recalled later, the District's principal concern at the meeting was that the United States obtain decrees that matched commitments made in the Repayment Contract. This objective was achieved, but not before an encounter with Veeder resulted in the City of Englewood receiving water rights under very unusual circumstances.

Barkley recalled that Englewood's attorney, Mark Shivers, came to Washington interested in the Blue River situation. At a meeting chaired by Veeder, Shivers mentioned that Englewood had purchased water rights from the Moffat Tunnel and Development Company. Veeder jumped all over him, claiming that not an ounce of due diligence had ever been done on those rights and that "in all honesty he couldn't understand how anybody had the intestinal fortitude to come before the Justice Department" with such a feeble claim. Shivers, who had to be restrained from attacking Veeder, got his revenge almost immediately from other representatives of the Colorado delegation. As they walked back to the Washington Hotel, Kelly, Barkley, Delaney, and John Barnard, Sr., from the West Slope expressed outrage at Veeder's remarks. They agreed to stipulate Englewood into the Consolidated Cases, stating that "no party has any objection to granting the decrees to the City of Englewood as a result of their purchase of the old Moffat Tunnel Water and Development Company." In such a manner, Veeder got his due and Englewood got rights to a decree that has never been developed.[51]

While participants were returning to Colorado, the *Rocky Mountain News* reported that Denver and Colorado Springs had agreed to take Blue River water for municipal purposes only. Barnard, a West Slope rancher and water attorney who had openly fought Denver's Blue River plans, commented that this new proposal "seemed to express a reasonableness which we on our side have not detected before in the Denver attitude."[52] Kelly told the District Board that he now hoped to make an amicable settlement with Denver, Englewood, and Colorado Springs, and Barkley reported that U.S. Assistant Attorney General Rankin favored the Denver proposal as a "very fair basis" for compromise.[53]

The stage was set for a watershed event. Not for twenty years had Colorado celebrated an intrastate water agreement. Following a two-day session in Denver under the direction of attorneys Rankin and Veeder, Judge Knous announced that a "milestone" out-of-court settlement had been reached. Unfortunately, Roberts was absent from the formal signing. He had suffered a heart attack on the very night agreement was achieved. Hudson Moore, president of the DWB, credited Roberts with making an "indispensable contribution" to Colorado, the impact of which was expected to "grease the wheels" for passage in Congress of the CRSP legislation.[54] The Blue River decrees, signed by Knous on October 12, 1955, recognized Senate Document 80 as the controlling instrument in C–BT and Blue River operations. It placed an obligation on Denver, Colorado Springs, and Englewood to guarantee the filling of Green Mountain Reservoir, whose decreed capacity was increased to 160,000 acre-feet. Storage rights for the 52,000 acre-foot C–BT replacement pool and 100,000 acre-foot "power pool" dedicated to West Slope beneficiaries were formally recognized as having a priority of August 1, 1935. C–BT diversions through the Adams Tunnel were awarded the same priority date. Both were senior to the June 24, 1946, priority given to Denver's Roberts Tunnel and Dillon Reservoir.[55]

Denver and Colorado Springs were limited to diverting for municipal purposes only, bound to pay the Bureau for any lost power revenue caused by their taking of Blue River water, and obligated to employ due diligence in conserving return flows. Denver's biggest concession was to recognize the right of the federal government to generate power at Green Mountain Dam as senior to Denver's municipal needs. The West Slope surrendered direct flow rights on the Blue River junior to Green Mountain Reservoir.[56] The District kept faith with the West Slope by defending Green Mountain Reservoir and gave up nothing. The long and bitter Blue River feud was temporarily ended.

A few months later, opponents of the CRSP agreed to a truce. On March 28, 1956, a House-Senate conference report was approved and the CRSP became Public Law 485 on April 11. In June the DWB announced bids for construction of the Blue River project's key feature — the Montezuma Tunnel, whose name was changed to honor Harold D. Roberts's successful negotiations. The District could now concentrate more fully on the final phases of construction, operation, and maintenance of its own C–BT Project.

14 The Bureau Completes C-BT Construction

On the cloudy afternoon of August 11, 1956, a large crowd gathered at the new headquarters of the NCWCD in Loveland, Colorado, to celebrate the Bureau's completion of C–BT construction.[1] Minute Men of the Colorado National Guard (Chili Pepper Air Force) streaked over the assembled throng in four shiny F-80 jets, and a seventy-eight-piece championship band from Ottawa, Illinois, entertained with a variety of rousing tunes. Following dedication of a monument and Reclamation Commissioner W. A. Dexheimer's announcement renaming the Horsetooth Feeder and Poudre Supply canals in memory of Charles Hansen, Governor Ed Johnson, Congressman William S. Hill, and Assistant Secretary-Manager J. R. "Bob" Barkley gave short speeches. The principal address was assigned to President Dwight D. Eisenhower's newly appointed secretary of interior, Fred A. Seaton. As he rose to speak, the heavens poured rain. While people darted for cover, Seaton paid special tribute to the Bureau and to the far-sighted vision of northern Colorado's agricultural leaders. "You people and the Bureau brought water to this land," he declared, "and if it can be said that the Secretary of the Interior brought a single rain, that will be enough." The C–BT, he proudly noted, was the largest project ever completed by Bureau engineers,[2] ample cause for a major celebration.

Not everyone shared in the secretary's prideful enthusiasm. Roscoe Flemming of the *Denver Post* found immediate fault with the proceedings for not crediting Mills E. Bunger, Clifford Stone, Harold L. Ickes, FDR, and others who had made the vision a working reality. Republicans, he noted, were too concerned about "creeping socialism" to give Democrats proper credit for their pioneering efforts.[3] Another writer known to *Post* readers, Philip Wylie, had a different axe to grind; he worried about potential salinization and pollution of water systems from reclamation projects in semi-arid environments. The C–BT, he suggested, was indeed a grand engineering feat, but the land it watered should have been left alone. His views would be echoed a decade and a half later during what came to be known as the environmental movement. Other newspapers accused the *Post* of using a big-name writer for propaganda purposes.[4]

The criticism might have been expected. Due to cost overruns, shortfalls in congressional budgets, suspicion of centralized government during the Cold War, and the inchoate environmental movement, reclamation's opponents had become increasingly vocal since the end of World War II. In 1949 Leslie Miller, former governor of Wyoming, had published an article in the *Saturday Evening Post*, noting that the tax burden on every U.S. citizen would amount to $1,500 per capita if all Bureau and Army Corps of Engineers construction projects were actually completed. He charged both agencies with senseless competition, underestimating project costs, deception before Congress, and pernicious lobbying. The C–BT, he concluded, exemplified more "malodorous planning."[5] Two months after this article, Bernard DeVoto, guru of western environmentalists, expressed outrage at the Bureau's plans to build Echo Park Dam on the Green River as part of the CRSP. He accused the Bureau and the Corps of using tax money to despoil public lands, and he deplored the Bureau's 1943 withdrawal of land from Dinosaur National Monument so that dams and power plants could be built within its boundaries. DeVoto also questioned other Bureau projects for the Colorado and Missouri River basins at a time when agricultural surpluses cost the government hundreds of millions of dollars a year and when agricultural methods were becoming more productive.[6]

Critics of reclamation were in plentiful supply, their presence a fact of life with which the District Board and staff had to contend. Some of their concerns were legitimate, but many ignored the context in which the C–BT had been planned and built. The earliest promoters — men who belonged to the NCWUA — wanted to stabilize northern Colorado agriculture with a supplemental water supply at a time when environmental and economic damage was a direct result of severe drought and the Great Depression. Twenty years later, Colorado reclamation supporters claimed that projects like the C–BT not only contributed to the revitalization of the West's economy but also added population to urban oases when western leaders were looking for greater political clout in Washington and investment from both industry and government. Viewed from this perspective, and with the knowledge that the C–BT system had been well built, the celebration of August 11, 1956, was fitting and appropriate. Those Bureau stalwarts who had designed and supervised construction of the Project deserved the accolades that Seaton and Dexheimer bestowed on them that day. In fact, they had done their job so well that critics often chastised the Bureau for deliberately exceeding acceptable standards for engineering quality. Elaborate models of flumes, surge tanks, canals, and dams — successfully tested at Region 7 headquarters in Denver — appeared overly complicated, impractical, and excessively costly to field contractors. But Bureau employees had purposefully built a cadillac system, intended to endure the capricious nature of Colorado's mercurial weather, changing seasons, and the erosive impact of running water. In J. M. Dille's words, the result was "the highest standard of construction perfection."[7] The final years of construction seemed to bear him out.

With Colorado River water collected at Shadow Mountain Reservoir and deliveries being made via the Adams Tunnel through a temporary steel pipeline into the Big Thompson River, the Bureau turned attention to four areas of C–BT construction: (1) Granby Dam, Reservoir, dikes, and Pump Plant; and Willow Creek Reservoir, Canal, and Pump Plant; (2) Estes Park Aqueduct and power system; (3) Foothills power system to Flatiron Reservoir and Carter Lake; and (4) Horsetooth Dam, Reservoir, and Feeder Canal. While Bureau and District discussions regarding the extension of the system southward from Carter Lake continued intermittently, work proceeded on the features awaiting completion.

GRANBY DAM / RESERVOIR / PUMP PLANT AND WILLOW CREEK

Construction progress in the Granby area depended largely on cooperative weather. Heavy winter snows and late spring rains slowed work on Granby Dam and dikes, but by fall 1949 the reservoir site was cleared and dam construction was sufficient to plug the bypass of the Colorado River and to begin water storage. Workmen executed a temporary closure of the dam on September 14 and put the final touches on all four dikes.[8] The only problem occurred when seepage was noticed below dikes 1 and 2. By drilling holes and pouring cement into these dikes, the flow was reduced from a maximum of 7.15 cfs to 3.16 cfs. The Bureau also constructed water gauging stations and a drainage ditch to divert ongoing seepage into the Colorado River.[9]

At the north end of Lake Granby work was started on the pump plant and canal that were designed to deliver stored Colorado River water into the already completed Shadow Mountain Reservoir. The pump plant contract was awarded to Granby Constructors, a consortium of six companies that had also contracted for Granby Reservoir. The Vinell Company began work on the canal between the two reservoirs. By the end of 1948 work on the pump plant was 70 percent complete, but a high groundwater

Lake Granby following completion, view looking northward. (Courtesy NCWCD.)

table and ancient peat bog along some sections of the canal hampered the Vinell Company's progress. Quicksand in the excavated area required special stabilization work in the canal, including drainage and backfill with coarse rock. Granby Constructors took over this work, and the completed canal was inspected and accepted by the government by the end of the year.[10]

The pump plant structure was finished in 1949, with the installation of pumps, motors, hydraulic pipelines, and a variety of electrical equipment the following year. Final pump completion and testing followed during spring and summer 1951, and the Bureau dedicated the pump plant in July. Governor Dan Thornton's wife christened the $9.7 million edifice with a bottle of champagne. Bureau Commissioner Michael Straus described the pumps as the "beating heart" and the Adams Tunnel as the "jugular vein" of the C–BT. "Without the throb of these pumps," he said, "over 700,000 acres of our good land could not make their full contribution to our dynamic national economy and the feeding of this hungry world." He paid tribute to Edward T. Taylor and Wayne N. Aspinall and, after finding fault with

Granby Pump Plant under construction, September 1948. Intake structure is in foreground. (Courtesy Bureau of Reclamation.)

the critics of the proposed Echo Park Dam, Straus urged his listeners to stick together, to avoid the kinds of fights engaged in by California and Arizona, and then "come Hell or high water or drought [to] drive on for new projects." Only in this way, he concluded, could the West emerge from colonial status.[11]

Power to the Granby Pump Plant, generated by water passing through Estes Park Power Plant turbines, was delivered back through the Adams Tunnel by a 69,000 Kv transmission line. Early in 1948 the Bureau had suggested the tunnel route as an alternative to crossing the Continental Divide at Buchanan Pass,[12] but fear of high cost and difficulty locating an appropriate submarine cable delayed the decision for another year. Estes Park citizens also affected the Bureau's determination to go with the tunnel route. Led by Mrs. Enos A. Mills, wife of the famous RMNP conservationist, they protested that the use of Buchanan Pass violated the sanctity of the park. When the Bureau finally found the necessary material and established a tunnel route cost of $500,000 — less than a Buchanan Pass route — they won approval. Estes Park people were delighted.[13] The high-pressure, gas-filled power conduit was assembled outside the East Portal of the Adams Tunnel in lengths of 2,700 feet, each composed of three conductor cables

Cutaway view of Granby Pump Plant. Referred to as the heart of the C–BT system, the Granby Pump Plant is sixteen stories high, although only three of those are visible above ground. (Courtesy NCWCD.)

encased in a 5-inch, enamel-coated steel pipe. Assembled sections, pulled into the tunnel with specially designed equipment, were suspended from the tunnel ceiling in the previously installed pipe. Ferrule plates were placed at the end of each section. Air was then drawn out of the pipe. After a test at 400 psi, a positive charge of dry nitrogen was introduced to fully protect the cable from moisture damage. When all sections were in place, power generated at the Estes Park power plant flowed through the cable to drive Granby pumps, the "heartbeat" of the C–BT.[14]

Construction of Willow Creek Reservoir, Pump Plant, and Supply Canal to Lake Granby was the last major phase of the C–BT's West Slope collection and storage system. Because the lake was already filling in 1950, the Bureau first contracted L. J. Hesser Construction Company to begin work on a concrete chute at Dike 4, to be completed before the water level reached the outlet area. With this part of the feature constructed, Peter Kiewit Sons' Company of Omaha, Nebraska, was contracted to complete the rest of the Willow Creek system. The dam, reservoir, and supply canal were constructed in 1951, while work on the pump plant was not completed until 1953.[15] The finished system's reservoir featured a storage capacity of 10,553 acre-feet and a 400 cfs feeder canal extending 2 miles from the reservoir to a pumping plant forebay. From this point, the pump lifted water 171 feet into a conduit that continued about 1.5 miles, passing under Highway 34 before entering the Willow Creek chute and stilling pool in Lake Granby.[16] In December 1953 approximately 3,000 acre-feet of water were delivered to Lake Granby from Willow Creek, signifying the end of construction on all major Project features on the West Slope.[17]

ESTES PARK AQUEDUCT AND POWER SYSTEM

Across the Continental Divide work had progressed since 1947 on the Estes Park Aqueduct and power system. Bureau officials felt that the route from the East Portal of the Adams Tunnel should utilize the topography so that water could be stored and regulated to provide peaking power ability for the Estes Park, Mary's Lake, and Pole Hill power plants.[18] Thus, they authorized construction of a buried siphon 1.3 miles long to carry water from the East Portal under Aspen Creek into the horseshoe-shaped Rams Horn Tunnel, also 1.3 miles in length. From the tunnel, water flowed through a short penstock into Mary's Lake Power Plant. This facility, designed for remote operation from Estes Park, was located on the western shore of Mary's Lake, a natural basin enlarged to provide sufficient pondage

Mary's Lake and Power Plant. To avoid ice buildup, the inlet structure to the conduit was submerged 5 feet below minimum reservoir elevation. (Courtesy Bureau of Reclamation.)

for regulating flows to the Estes Park Power Plant. From Mary's Lake, water was directed into a conduit running 3,143 feet to Prospect Mountain Tunnel. To avoid problems with ice build-up at Mary's Lake, the inlet structure to the conduit was submerged 5 feet below the minimum tailwater elevation of the power plant.[19] Both the conduit and the tunnel (completed in 1948) were designed for pressure operation with a capacity of 1,300 cfs. About 200 feet from the outlet portal of the Prospect Tunnel, on the way down to the Estes Power Plant, a surge tank 50 feet in diameter by 100 feet high was constructed, which provided protection for 1.67 miles of upstream aqueduct when power demands caused the system to be suddenly shut off. It also functioned as a readily available storage supply that enabled the Estes generators to pick up load quickly.[20]

By 1949 the only remaining incomplete portions of the link between the Adams Tunnel and the Big Thompson River (the point initially designated as the repository of C–BT water) were the two power plants. Concrete work on both superstructures was finished late in the year. At

Lake Estes and Olympus Dam. From this location water is diverted into either the Big Thompson River or into a series of pipelines and the power system heading down to Flatiron Reservoir. (Courtesy Bureau of Reclamation.)

this time the Flora Construction Corporation began electrical and mechanical installations — slow and meticulous work; but by October 1950 Estes turbine 1 was in place and tested, and preparations were made in December to test the other two turbines. The single turbine at Mary's Lake was installed but untested.[21] During 1951 generating units in both power plants were successfully operated as part of the Bureau's integrated Colorado-Wyoming power system.[22]

Olympus Dam and Lake Estes were not specifically contemplated in either Senate Document 80 or the Repayment Contract. In order to reregulate imported Colorado River water to provide a controlled rate of outflow for the newly designed Estes Park-Foothills power system, the Bureau decided that a functional afterbay for the Estes Park Power Plant would require a 70-foot-high earth and rock-fill dam on the Big Thompson River. Denver-based contractors began construction of Olympus Dam in summer 1947. By fall 1948 virtually all work was finished, including relocation of Highway 66 from Estes Park along the Big Thompson River. On November 30, 1948, the Bureau ordered 1 foot of water to be skimmed off Lake Granby for partial filling of dead storage behind Olympus Dam. Water flowed through the Adams Tunnel for a day and a half.[23] On June 5, 1949, the body of water behind the Olympus Dam was officially named Lake Estes. Three thousand people gathered at the lake for dedicatory ceremonies. Undersecretary of the Interior Oscar L. Chapman spoke of the benefits expected from electricity generated at Mary's Lake and Estes Park. He also promoted the Interior's objective of "basin-wide development of our western rivers . . . so that we can add 17 million acres of irrigated land and realize increased yields on 9 million more acres [through the application of] supplemental water."[24]

J. R. "Bob" Barkley's remarks focused on the Bureau's remarkable construction achievements. He noted, for example, that Colorado River water emerging from the Adams Tunnel had to flow through almost every known type of hydraulic conduit before reaching Lake Estes. He paid tribute to the construction crews for their "creditable physical accomplishment" and to the "technical excellence" of the engineers who successfully fulfilled the Bureau's responsibilities. With a tip of his hat to Hansen and other NCWCD Directors for their vision, Barkley also expressed pleasure at the good relations the NCWCD enjoyed with the Bureau, the West Slope, and the CWCB.[25] At this harmonious moment, at a time for conciliation, Barkley was the consummate diplomat. He knew that the Project still had a long way to go and that farmers on the St. Vrain and Little Thompson rivers would be clamoring for water if the drought of 1948 were repeated. From Olympus Dam eastward, another 16 miles of waterways and at least two more power plants remained to be built before C–BT water could be conveyed along a permanent route to the foothills area. Always conscious of the need for good public relations, Barkley deliberately flattered everyone concerned but reserved his strongest praise for the Bureau, on whom the District depended for prompt and efficient construction of the remaining features.

FOOTHILLS POWER SYSTEM, FLATIRON POWER SYSTEM, AND CARTER LAKE

Up to 1948 the Bureau had conducted extensive studies on alternate power routes between Estes Park and the foothills, together with various combinations of features, to determine what would be required to tie

Flatiron Reservoir and its aptly named bathtub spillway. C–BT water enters through the Flatiron penstocks shown at upper right. Carter Lake is at top left. (Courtesy Bureau of Reclamation.)

together the power and irrigation systems where they joined west of Loveland.[26] Having arrived at a plan the District accepted, government officials authorized new construction contracts immediately following the Lake Estes dedication. Nearly 25 percent of funds allocated by Congress were earmarked for four new tunnels for water to flow from Lake Estes to Flatiron Reservoir: Olympus (1.8 miles), Pole Hill (5.4 miles), Rattlesnake (1.7), and Bald Mountain (1.3 miles). Dille estimated that at least three years would be needed before water could be delivered to Carter Lake, then southward into the Little Thompson and St. Vrain rivers, and finally into Boulder Creek.[27] His estimate proved only partially correct. Although water was not pumped from Flatiron into Carter Lake until February 26, 1954, Little Thompson ditches received over 18,000 acre-feet in 1953 from the Bureau's decision to dump water out of the Pole Hill Canal into Hell Canyon just above the Pole Hill penstock line.[28] Water users on Boulder and Left Hand creeks and the St. Vrain River waited longer for C–BT water due to many construction challenges and shortages of construction materials delayed during the Korean War. Fortunately, Congress viewed the Project as vital to national defense, so the average annual appropriations from 1948 to 1953 actually increased.[29]

Excavation and concrete lining of the four tunnels were finished on schedule. The Bureau now had enough experience to know what to expect in the area of funding problems, and contractors had learned to read Bureau specifications and to plan for contingencies. Thus, in 1949, the Wunderlich Contracting Company of Omaha, Nebraska, successfully bid the contract on both Olympus and Pole Hill tunnels, agreeing to drive both shafts from a common point in Noel Gulch, accessed from Highway 34. With portals of both tunnels separated by only 130 feet, drilling and shooting crews first worked in one tunnel while mucking crews worked in the other. Shifts completed, they swapped locations until each bore was sufficiently long to justify an entire work crew in each tunnel.[30] In 1950 Gibbons and Reed Company of Salt Lake City submitted the low bid for the Rattlesnake Tunnel, and Winston Brothers Company of Monrovia, California, won the contract to construct Bald Mountain Tunnel and surge tank. By the end of 1951 tunnel work was nearly complete, including the 5,890-foot pressure tunnel between the Flatiron Pumping Plant conduit and Carter Lake. By year's end, Winston Brothers had completed 65 percent of the work on Carter Lake and dams.[31]

Few new construction contracts were awarded in 1952. The Bureau concentrated its energies on linking the many features in the Foothills power system. This meant finishing the connecting conduit between the Olympus and Pole Hill tunnels at the common point, digging and lining the Pole Hill Canal, and installing the Pole Hill and Flatiron penstocks. Although most of this work ran according to plan, workers at the Pole Hill penstocks experienced some excitement in July when the hoist on the gantry crane failed, causing the entire machine to somersault out of control down the steep slope.[32]

Flatiron Dam and afterbay, Carter Lake pressure conduit, and Carter Lake were all completed by the end of 1952. All that the system required to operate up to that point was completion of the two power plants and their respective penstocks, which were finished in 1954. The Pole Hill Power Plant went into service in January, and Flatiron started pumping water up to Carter Lake in February. About 200 spectators lined the banks to witness the first stream of water flow into the reservoir. A luncheon was arranged for interested parties, but no ceremony was planned. Local newspapers recorded only one event, the result of a bet by Berthoud barber, Leo Schultz, who became the first man to catch a fish in Carter Lake. He had

First C–BT water enters Carter Lake on February 26, 1954. First fish "caught" here. (Courtesy NCWCD.)

wagered a friend that he would catch the first fish in the new reservoir. To assure his win, Schultz brought a rod and reel — and a frozen rainbow trout — thus earning himself some money and a page in local history.[33]

Although not considered part of the Foothills power system, the St. Vrain Supply Canal, the only delivery system for C–BT water from Carter Lake to the St. Vrain River, was put into operation shortly after Carter Lake began filling, This 9-mile canal was specifically stipulated in both Senate Document 80 and the Repayment Contract, but neither document mentioned service to the District's southern limits. Dille had located the boundary line approximately 12 miles south of the St. Vrain River on section lines following the northeast course of the Lower Boulder and Coal Ridge ditches. Problems arose in 1949 and 1950 that delayed construction of the St. Vrain Supply Canal. The Bureau became increasingly worried about rising Project costs, while the District argued the need to develop a delivery system to provide ample amounts of Project water to the south end of the NCWCD. When these issues were resolved in an interim contract signed December 15, 1950, the Bureau proceeded with construction.[34]

Most of the tunneling, excavating, and canal lining were finished in 1953, with the first Project water delivered south to the St. Vrain basin on May 30, 1954.

HORSETOOTH DAM, RESERVOIR, AND FEEDER CANAL

From Flatiron, water would also be directed north to Horsetooth Reservoir and the Poudre River, a procedure that was not possible before completion of the Horsetooth Feeder Canal (renamed the Charles Hansen Feeder Canal in 1956). The Bureau had been working at Horsetooth Reservoir since 1946. After three years (at approximately the time when Lake Estes was dedicated), four dams (Horsetooth, Soldier Canyon, Dixon Canyon, and Spring Canyon) had been completed except for plugging the construction bypass conduits under Spring and Dixon Canyon dams. Satanka Dike, located just west of Horsetooth Dam, was also finished according to Bureau specifications and later modified, as will be noted in the following chapter.

Because plans for Horsetooth Reservoir did not include replacing water rights below the reservoir, a canal became necessary from the Soldier Canyon outlet to Dixon Canyon Reservoir, to be served by a pressure outlet in Horsetooth Reservoir. This 8 cfs canal, approximately 3 miles long, was completed in December 1950.[35] Horsetooth Reservoir received some C–BT water on January 11, 1950, through the completed section of the Horsetooth Feeder Canal, but it only filled the required 10,000 acre-feet of dead storage. Construction of the Poudre Supply Canal (renamed Hansen Supply Canal in 1956) was necessary before any C–BT water could be directed into the Poudre River. While Horsetooth Reservoir continued filling in 1951, Peter Kiewit Sons' Company put the finishing touches on a Poudre Supply Canal. Realization of this 6-mile link was celebrated as a long-standing dream shared by fathers of the C–BT and most of northern Colorado's farmers.

Representing their cooperative role in this important phase of the Project, Dille and the Bureau's district manager, James H. Knights, flicked a switch on July 21, 1951, that opened twin circular steel gates beneath Horsetooth Dam, allowing water to flow "with a roaring rumble" from the reservoir into the Poudre River. Commissioner Straus reminded the 500 celebrants that the eyes of the world were on the C–BT and that if this Project succeeded, other proposed transmountain diversions in Colorado would also have an excellent chance. Hansen noted that the so-called

View of Horsetooth Reservoir construction from Soldier Canyon Dam with Horsetooth Dam in background. (Photograph by Skeets Calvin.)

Grand Lake Project, considered by some a Jules Verne idea in the 1930s, would in reality help solve employment problems and provide much needed irrigation water. Fred Cummings, member of the Colorado delegation in Washington when the Project had won approval in the thirties, pointed out that July 21 was the fourteenth anniversary of the first congressional appropriation for the C–BT.[36] Not much water was allowed to run into the Poudre that summer day because 1951 was a wet year and ditch company reservoirs were full. But Horsetooth Reservoir already held 37,500 acre-feet, about 25 percent of active capacity, and experienced water users knew that that water would eventually be needed to save their crops. Three years later, during the worst drought since the thirties, the C–BT delivered 301,500 acre-feet of supplemental water to seventy irrigation systems in the District, the difference between an almost total crop failure and a "fairly profitable season on over 4,000 farms."[37]

To get C–BT water into Horsetooth Reservoir prior to completion of the Foothills power system, the Bureau had to complete work on those parts of the Horsetooth Feeder Canal that extended north from the Big

Hundreds of people attended the ceremony marking the first release of water from Horse-tooth Reservoir to the Poudre River on July 21, 1951. (Courtesy NCWCD.)

Thompson River. This work started in 1947 with boring and excavation of four tunnels, but a cave-in in May 1948 at the west portal of Tunnel 5 killed three men. Accidents were not common. This one had happened when men were setting steel supports in the tunnel, thus indicating no lack of caution by work crews or their supervisors. Delays in tunnel completion could be attributed more to a 9-inch rainstorm that occurred during the same month. The quick deluge created a powerful flood that washed an 8-ton electric locomotive downstream a quarter of a mile.[38] Cleanup from this disaster took several weeks.

Late in 1949 the Bureau contracted with the Western Paving Company of Denver to construct that portion of the Horsetooth Feeder Canal from a point just south of the Big Thompson River to Horsetooth Reservoir. The work included crossing the river with a siphon and connecting about 10 miles of canal sections with the previously constructed tunnels. The Bureau also signed with the G. L. Tarlton Company of St. Louis, Missouri, to build a nearly 1-mile tunnel from the Big Thompson River to the Horsetooth Feeder Canal. This so-called Tunnel 1 (Horsetooth Supply Conduit), later renamed the Dille Tunnel, formed the inlet from the river to the Horse-tooth Feeder Canal to make partial filling of Horsetooth Reservoir possible

Aerial view of the 6.5-mile-long Horsetooth Reservoir. (Courtesy Bureau of Reclamation.)

prior to completion of the entire delivery system from Flatiron. The District had urged construction of this diversion when the Bureau rerouted East Slope water deliveries from the Big Thompson Canyon to Flatiron by way of Olympus, Pole Hill, and Rattlesnake tunnels. The Bureau agreed to the plan, because water could be delivered sooner to the Poudre River while productively generating electricity at the Mary's Lake and Estes Park power plants.[39] Work on the Big Thompson Siphon required construction of an inclined tunnel section from a trifurcation point south of the river,[40] a steel pipe to span the river, and a cut-and-cover section north of the river.

Digging the south bank tunnel proved costly and dangerous to workmen due to rock instability in a plane nearly vertical to the ground and at an angle of 55 degrees to the tunnel centerline. A special canopy of 6-inch steel was built to protect drillers working on the outlet portal of the tunnel, though they finished the job in 1950 without incident. Workmen then constructed two concrete piers for support of the 108-inch steel pipe being prepared to carry C–BT water over the river and highway. When concrete in the piers had cured, the pipe was raised onto a temporary scaffold and

Outlet works at Horsetooth Reservoir. When opened completely, these hollow jet valves are capable of discharging 1500 cfs of water. (Courtesy NCWCD.)

welded into place. To keep automobile traffic delay in the canyon to a minimum, the three sections of pipe were welded together on the ground before being raised into position.[41]

Construction of the mile-long unlined Dille Tunnel, which began in late October 1949, was considered complete on December 19, 1950. A week later, the Bureau announced that the Horsetooth Feeder Canal from the outlet of the Dille Tunnel to Horsetooth Reservoir was ready for water. As previously noted, this portion of the system began operation in January 1951 with the filling of Horsetooth Reservoir. In summer 1951 Winston Brothers contracted to complete the final portion of the Horsetooth Feeder

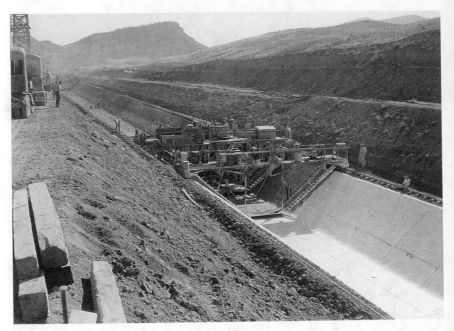

Construction of the concrete-lined Hansen Feeder Canal between Flatiron Reservoir and the Big Thompson River. (Courtesy Bureau of Reclamation.)

Canal by building from Flatiron to the outlet of the Dille Tunnel. The contractor first excavated Dry Ridge Tunnel, a 625-foot bore through a ridge north of Flatiron afterbay. Workmen completed canal excavation in 1952, trimmed canal edges preparatory to concrete lining, and poured most of the canal concrete before year's end. All that remained in 1953 was to pour the final sections of a siphon beneath Cottonwood Creek and the transition structure below the works of Flatiron Dam, all of which was finished by mid-summer.

What appears most obvious after reviewing construction of East Slope features is that, in addition to technical competence in design and construction, the Bureau scheduled the Project building in such a way that major segments, separately contracted, came together to benefit water users in the least amount of time. Completion of the Flatiron section of the Horsetooth Feeder Canal, for example, occurred only six months prior to inaugurating the Flatiron Power Plant for water delivery to Carter Lake and the St. Vrain Supply Canal. Coordinating construction of the northern sections of the Horsetooth Feeder Canal with Horsetooth Dam and Reservoir and the Poudre Supply Canal further illustrates a level of construction

Hansen (Horsetooth) Feeder Canal winds its way over 13 miles from Flatiron Reservoir to Horsetooth Reservoir. Horsetooth Mountain is the prominent feature in the background. (Courtesy Bureau of Reclamation.)

The original Big Thompson Siphon being placed across Highway 34 and the Big Thompson River. It was later washed out in the 1976 Big Thompson flood. (Courtesy Bureau of Reclamation.)

management that merits applause for those who designed, built, and supervised construction of C–BT features.

Considering all the potential for postwar labor problems, accidents, funding complications, and material shortages, construction proceeded with remarkably few interruptions. When the volume of construction work dropped off markedly by the close of 1953, the Bureau could boast of few labor difficulties. Average wage rates had risen gradually from $1.84 an hour in 1947 to $2.23 an hour in 1953. Only a few short-lived strikes of minor consequence slowed construction progress.[42] Four fatalities occurred in 1948, two in 1949, and three more in 1950. Causes ranged from cave-ins and machinery malfunction to electrocution. Disabling injuries were also a fact of life, but safety precautions and lengthening on-the-job experience gradually meant that contractors improved the injury record. All in all it was a commendable performance on a Project in which the Bureau wrote up to fifty different contracts a year and contractors employed thousands of men to work long hours at high-risk tasks.

Between 1950 and summer 1956 coordination and timing of the final phase of Project construction were integrally related to the outcome of discussions between the Bureau, the District, and Boulder. In dozens of formal and informal sessions, representatives met to deliberate what quantity of water to deliver to the south end and how Boulder's increasingly persistent request for supplemental water would affect the Bureau's construction plans. Following more than three years of negotiations, NCWCD Directors passed a resolution on February 7, 1953, authorizing a contract with Boulder to include the city and its immediate lands in the District with a C–BT water allotment.[43] Almost immediately, the District opened an office in Longmont to take allotment petitions from all potential water users along Boulder Creek and the South Platte River, anticipating completion of all District water allotments by the end of construction.[44] In July 1953 Bales and Kite Construction Company of Kansas City, Missouri, started work on the Boulder Creek Supply Canal. To understand why construction of south end conduits and other features became so controversial, the objectives and concerns of the entities involved — Boulder, the Bureau, the District, and the Boulder Creek and South Platte River water users — must be reviewed.

Electing exclusion from the NCWCD in 1937 on the basis that its water supply from Arapahoe Glacier would be sufficient, Boulder reevaluated its position when faced with exponential postwar growth. The District never had any doubts about delivering water to Boulder Creek and the South Platte River, even though Article 4(ff) of the Repayment Contract only vaguely referred to conduits extending south from the St. Vrain River. The only issue for staff and Board members was how large the south end allotments would be in order to determine the size of the conduits. Furthermore, if Boulder were to be allowed into the District, the size of the conduits would also have to reflect the city's needs; the Bureau clearly would not absorb the extra costs of a more extensive delivery system to the south end. Because Dille had purposefully refrained from soliciting allotments in the south end until he knew how much water could be delivered, all interested parties waited for the District to address the apparent dilemma. Dille first met with the Bureau during the 1948 drought, but neither side presented a specific proposal.[45] In 1949 and 1950 some Bureau officials intimated that they were under no obligation to build any conduits, but Regional Director Batson agreed with the District that eliminating Boulder Creek and the

South Platte would be a "terrible mistake." He hoped that they might soon be able to work out a compromise solution.[46]

In an exchange of letters beginning in summer 1950, with final drafts accompanying the interim contract of December 15, 1950, the Bureau formally consented to build the conduits. The District agreed to underwrite some of the added cost of increasing the capacity of the St. Vrain Supply Canal from 300 cfs to 625 cfs. Boulder's precise objectives remained unknown, though it was learned that the city had again applied for and been denied use of Denver water, that plans were being discussed by some city officials to form a subdistrict within the NCWCD, and that the city viewed the situation as "desperate."[47] Dille told the Board in December 1950 that Boulder officials were "increasingly interested in securing a water supply from the Project."[48]

More accurately, Boulder's city council was becoming impatient.[49] The federal government announced in April 1951 that the city had been selected for a $45 million atomic energy plant and two new laboratories. Feeling some panic as to future water supplies, the council immediately hired engineer Royce J. Tipton to do a feasibility study to determine the best possible plan for the city. Some of the District's Board members, along with attorney William R. Kelly, were prepared to resist any move by Boulder to request Project water,[50] but preliminary discussions with the District remained noncommittal pending Tipton's completion of a detailed report. The main questions concerned how and when Boulder might pay back taxes it would owe to the District (about $65,000), how the Bureau and the state would respond to the District's increased assessed valuation with Boulder's inclusion (estimated by Charles A. Lory at $21 million), and who would pay the cost of a much-needed storage reservoir.

These and other matters were discussed with greater intensity in 1952. At the April NCWCD meeting in Greeley, a Boulder delegation arrived, led by Bert W. Johnson, city manager; Alfred H. Allen, acting mayor; and city attorney John M. Sayre. Collectively, they made Boulder's position clear: the city "definitely" wanted Project water, it was willing to pay back taxes, and a committee would be organized to work out details with the District.[51] The Board agreed to name a corresponding committee. During the summer months both sides explored the pros and cons of a regulating reservoir in the Dry Creek Valley. The Bureau estimated a cost of $1.4 million. While the Boulder group appeared willing to construct the reservoir if it could be excused from paying back taxes, Dille suggested that the District might assume one-third of the cost if Boulder would pay up to $2 per acre-foot for C–BT water.[52] With Tipton's report now in hand, which

The former Twin Lakes Reservoir was enlarged to allow storage of Boulder's C–BT water shortly after the city was included in the NCWCD in 1953. When completed in April 1955, it became known as Boulder Reservoir. (Courtesy NCWCD.)

concluded that inclusion in the District was the most feasible way for the city to satisfy future water needs, the Boulder contingent submitted a formal proposal to the District, and Kelly drew up a resolution for the Board's consideration.

After extensive discussion, and following modifications by attorneys Kelly and Sayre, the Directors voted unanimously on January 10, 1953, to authorize a second unit of the District in which assessment for C-BT water would be paid at the rate of $2 per acre-foot unit.[53] Boulder would join the District as the second unit; pay an estimated $70,000 in back taxes; and finance construction of a Twin Lakes (Boulder) Reservoir, one-third of the cost to be paid by the District in forty equal payments not to exceed a total of $450,000. The District would operate, maintain, and repair Boulder Reservoir at its own cost and would retain a right to one-third of the operating capacity. Boulder would maintain control of recreation use of the reservoir.[54] Based on maximum annual deliveries of 12,700 acre-feet, net water to Boulder would be 8,466 acre-feet and to the District, 4,234 acre-feet. The question was whether the people of Boulder would approve a bond issue at a special election on June 9, 1953.

Unquestionably, the dry spring worked in favor of the city's proposal. Although it was still too early for anyone to predict one, a severe drought was already on the horizon.[55] The $2 million bond issue would be used to build the reservoir. To put this in perspective for voters, the city explained that water bills for an average five-room house on a 50-foot lot would jump 65 percent, from $23.50 to $39. Even with this increase, voters approved the bond issue by a four-to-one margin, not only because the cause seemed worthy but because water rates had remained unchanged since 1918.[56] At the same time, proponents of the city council's plan successfully solicited the required number of signatures on inclusion petitions enabling District Judge Claude C. Coffin to set a formal hearing for August 31. When no one protested, Coffin set September 8 as the date for the final inclusion decree, thus allowing the District sufficient time to approve a water allotment petition. At the September 4 meeting the Board officially allotted 12,700 acre-foot units to Boulder. Four days later, Coffin signed the decree to annex 32,640 acres of land in Boulder County to the NCWCD. The final step required Secretary of the Interior Donald McKay to give written approval, but his blessing was nothing more than a formality. The deed was done! The only people in the south end who were still uncertain about how their C–BT water would be delivered were those served by Lower Boulder and Coal Ridge ditches.

The Bureau expected to secure an easement to enlarge Lower Boulder and Coal Ridge ditches. The new conduit with increased capacity would be named the South Platte Supply Canal, carrying C–BT water from Boulder Creek to the South Platte River. Specific Bureau plans and designs were not available until March 1953. With these documents in hand, negotiations with the ditch companies stalled over how much the District would pay for the easement. Ditch companies asked for $15,000 plus a two-thirds assumption of operations and maintenance by the District; Dille countered with $10,000 and one-half the operation and maintenance expenses. Stockholders voted to stand fast; they wanted adequate protection from claims that might come from damage associated with widening their ditch.[57] The Platte Valley Irrigation Company caused additional problems by its objections to the design and cost of Sand Hill Reservoir, which it planned to build and use as a regulating reservoir for its own water users.[58]

Gradually, disputants agreed to allow the Bureau to contract for the construction of a water delivery system south of Boulder Reservoir. Construction on the Boulder Creek Supply Canal, which started in late 1953, was finished by Burks and Company of Denver in 1954. In the meantime, a supplemental contract between Boulder and the District permitted enlargement of Boulder Reservoir to 13,100 acre-feet with an operating capacity of 12,800 acre-feet. Boulder let the construction contract for $773,861, though total costs exceeded $1 million after all work was completed.[59] Within a month after completing the reservoir in April 1955, enough Project water was stored to allow the first delivery into Boulder Creek.[60]

Widening of existing ditches, installation of siphons and turnouts, and concrete work on the Erie, South Platte, Coal Ridge, and Firestone sections of the South Platte Supply Canal were completed and approved by the Bureau in May 1956.[61] The South Platte Supply Canal was turned over immediately to the District for operation and maintenance. The first Project water reached Sand Lake Reservoir (Sand Hill Lake or Coal Ridge Waste Lake) in April.[62] For all intents and purposes, the construction phase was over. As a result of negotiation and execution of a supplemental agreement with the Bureau, the District was allowed to start full delivery of Project water in 1957, according to "second" period specifications found in the 1938 Repayment Contract.[63] The long "first" period of construction and development had taken nearly twenty years. With East Slope reservoirs still showing the effects of three years of reduced moisture and South Platte tributaries running at 75 percent of normal,[64] completion of the C–BT was welcome news to NCWCD farmers.

Coincidentally, historian Walter Prescott Webb published a 1957 article in *Harper's Magazine*, warning Coloradans that they lived in the heart of a depressed region, a desert like the guest who came to dinner but never went away. Placing Colorado at the center of a large, arid area, he compared the land to a place where a slow fire had been burning for a million years and where the absence of significant population and wealth suggested a lower level of civilization than that normally found in more humid regions. With aid from the federal government, he noted, an oasis civilization had developed, an urban society frequently used by others as a place to discard what was unwanted elsewhere. Like a musician playing a stringed instrument with missing strings, the 1957 westerner and future residents would have to compensate for their environmental handicap "by ingenuity, agility, and improvisations for the missing strings."[65] He made no mention of the C–BT or other reclamation projects, and he said little about agriculture; but District staff, the Board, and all those who could already see how Project water was stabilizing northern Colorado's economy considered his desert analysis at best puerile and at worst offensive. Construction of the C–BT was viewed in 1956 as a commendable engineering feat that provided northern Colorado with water and hydroelectric power at a time when Front Range growth was spectacular. The real problem faced by District staff was how to operate and manage the new water supply in such a way that the benefits of twenty years' construction would be judiciously distributed among all District taxpayers. To this end, the District had to formulate fundamental administrative policies and procedures during the final years of construction. Operation and management of the Project demanded closer relations between the NCWCD and local and regional communities.

During the final years of C–BT construction, the District's Board and staff faced a host of administrative decisions that determined the NCWCD's direction in the "second" period.[1] Although such challenges might have been anticipated, most required inventive solutions by individuals aware of the potential impact of precedents they were establishing. The District had to complete allotment allocations, process transfer applications, deal with unhappy water commissioners, establish adequate operation and maintenance procedures, respond to public perceptions of possibly unsafe features, and plan for future financial stability. Those responsibilities forced the District to mature rapidly as a major force in the economic, social, and political life of the northern Front Range. Pressures to add additional staff and to professionalize salary and benefits policies increased. As the District entered ineluctably into this period of greater responsibility and greater public visibility, many of the water profession's old guard were no longer available for guidance and counsel.

Death took Delph Carpenter in 1951. Although he had not been directly involved with C–BT plans and development, the Board knew too well that his farsighted provision in the 1922 Colorado River Compact regarding transbasin diversions "constituted the first foundation stone" in the C–BT idea.[2] Carpenter, not Herbert Hoover, had conceived of the Colorado River Compact when the Boulder Canyon project appeared to threaten the rights of upper basin states of the Colorado River. He was "directing counsel" in interstate disputes between Colorado and Wyoming and Colorado and Nebraska and was referred to by Governor Ralph Carr as "the father of interstate river treaties."[3] As one who had become familiar with his work, CWCB Director Clifford Stone spoke of Carpenter's brilliant mind and the frequency with which others referenced his verbal and written statements.[4]

Stone died the following year. Considered by many to be Colorado's foremost water authority, he had guided the CWCB through the first fifteen years until his sudden and unexpected death in New Orleans at the age of sixty-four.[5] Through his involvement in the Upper Colorado River Basin Compact, the Rio Grande Compact, and the Republican River Compact, Stone followed Carpenter's path. A man who lived for his work, he was known as a patient and able negotiator, whose ability to achieve compromise among disparate groups was sorely missed. The Board passed a resolution to recognize his long service to the state and his valued assistance to the NCWCD.[6] His especially close friendship with J. M. Dille had been nurtured by Dille's continuous appointment to the CWCB since 1937.

Fred Cummings and Moses E. Smith also died in 1952. Cummings had been a leader among beet growers of northern Colorado and one of the members of the Colorado delegation who fought for C–BT authorization in 1937. Smith was remembered as one of the Directors of the NCWUA when it submitted the first C–BT plans to Secretary of the Interior Harold L. Ickes. Both men played a vital role in promoting water development during the District's early years. Ickes also died in 1952.

Next to go was the "Godfather of the C–BT," Charles Hansen, who died at the age of eighty on May 24, 1953. Twenty years earlier, at a point in life when most men consider retirement, Hansen had been the principal energizer of the group that promoted what was then called the Grand Lake Project. Publisher of the *Greeley Tribune* and president of the Greeley Tribune Republican Publishing Company, Hansen was first elected chairman of the NCWUA and then president and chairman of the NCWCD Board. Known for his hard work, leadership, patience, fairness, modesty, and devotion to public service, Hansen's loss was deeply felt by those with whom he had worked. A superb strategist, he had talents that complemented those of Dille, the craftsman of organization and administrative detail. When he resigned in spring 1951 the Board relieved Hansen of responsibility while retaining him in association with the Project that he had fathered. Directors agreed unanimously that he should be made lifetime honorary president and chairman of the Board; in this capacity, Hansen continued to serve actively until two weeks before his death.[7]

His personal commitment to the NCWCD had long been a matter of record: Hansen never accepted per diem or Director's fees, and he allowed the NCWCD to rent space in the *Greeley Tribune* headquarters for $50 a month. When District staff began to modernize the accounting system in 1953 to prepare for operation and maintenance of Bureau-constructed features, Hansen requested that $2,396 on the books in his name be written off and that no further credits be accumulated.[8] When his long-standing friend and associate on the Board, Charles A. Lory, persuaded the Directors to combine this money with $841 owed to the NCWUA and to establish an irrigation scholarship in Hansen's name,[9] William R. Kelly found this a perfectly legal memorial to Hansen. Kelly's litigious side forced him to say, however, that "although its wisdom as a matter of public relations as to an act of a taxing body is another question seriously to be considered."[10] Some also wanted to rename the Adams Tunnel or Horsetooth Reservoir for Hansen, but the simple flow of water along the Horsetooth Feeder and Supply Canal into the Poudre River from Flatiron Reservoir seemed a more appropriate way to recognize his "quiet evangelism" on the Project[11] — thus, the designation of the Charles Hansen Feeder Canal flowing into Horsetooth Reservoir and the Charles Hansen Supply Canal heading from there into the Poudre River.

Boulder County's Jacob S. Schey was elected NCWCD president following Hansen's death. He inherited a strong Board and an experienced staff, but additional changes were in the wind. Judge Claude C. Coffin, who died in August 1954, had been senior judge of the Eighth Judicial District for as long as the NCWCD had existed, and he was in no small way responsible for the Board's composition and direction in crucial matters of policy.[12] He was succeeded by William E. Buck of Boulder, who replaced wheelhorse Lory with John G. Nesbit and Ray Reynolds with Dudley Hutchinson, Sr. The Board voted to give emeritus status to Lory, and Schey asked that he continue to head a committee charged with possible renaming of Project features.[13]

Dille's health was another question mark. He had been sick with encephalitis in spring 1948, causing the Board to reduce his salary and to name J. R. "Bob" Barkley as acting manager.[14] In 1955 Barkley again reported to the Board that Dille was ill and might not be able to leave his Fort Morgan home for awhile. The same month in 1955 that J. Ben Nix was elected president to replace Schey, the Board decided to reduce Dille's salary once again. Dille expressed confidence that Barkley was more than capable of carrying on the District's management duties.[15] From this point, Barkley accepted a much heavier responsibility for District affairs. His role in establishing final allotment, transfer, and reallocation policies gave early evidence that Dille's confidence in him was well placed.

Following execution of the Repayment Contract in 1938, the District undertook a program to allot only a part of the 310,000 acre-foot units of Project water "in order to get the Project firmly established and to definitely demonstrate its repayability."[16] By 1948, 208,476 acre-foot units had been allotted in contracts as follows: Class D (1,732), Class C (7), Class B (1), and Corporate Contracts (25).[17] Each allotment had been carefully checked by field survey to verify needs for supplemental water. Petitions, when approved, became contracts that were recorded in the District's "Allotment Record" books.[18] By 1948 some 400 petitions were on file requiring action. The District had decided not to continue evaluating allotments until the Bureau determined the location and construction of a distribution system to the south end, specifically the Left Hand Valley, Boulder Creek, and the South Platte River basin. While this matter was being negotiated, Barkley was faced with an increased number of requests for both transfers and reallocations of allotments by original allottees.[19] This situation arose from two causes. First, a number of farms had been divided and subdivided since original allotments had been contracted ten years earlier. Second, as Barkley later recalled, a large number of farmers north of Fort Collins on the Pierce Lateral Ditch got their water from the Water Supply and Storage Company (WSSC), whose rules enabled them to limit the quantity of delivered C–BT water. After occasionally receiving only half of the C–BT water for which they had contracted during the drought years from 1948 to 1954, many farmers objected to paying the C-BT assessment. Because they were able at that time to transfer their water for the same price they had paid ($1.50 an acre-foot unit), they flooded the District with requests for transfers.[20]

The Board established a policy that transfer of allotments would not be permitted until all Project water had been allotted and the Project placed in operation.[21] It also ruled that an allotment could be reallocated to different tracts on the originally described land or transferred at some later date to another owner but never returned to the District for reissue. In other words, an allotment could never be canceled.[22] Differences of opinion on these policies pitted Kelly against Dille and brought Barkley to prominence as a peacemaker. Disagreement on allotment transfers had existed between the two men since 1946. At a meeting in July 1948, Dille had complained that Kelly had refused to discuss their differences during the previous two years. Kelly had responded that his main concern was procedural and that he saw no reason why both reallocation and transfer petitions could not be handled by a single form. Somewhat testily, he concluded that there was no further need for discussion; if staff wanted to ask him any questions, they could do so in writing, and he would respond with a written opinion.[23]

To assuage bruised egos, Barkley worked on Dille while Jack Clayton softened up his partner, Kelly. Their objective was some form of compromise even while making the disputants feel that they were initiating their own compromise solution. This minor uproar indicated that both Kelly and Dille had reached a point in life when valuable experience frequently turned into stubbornness. A temporary truce was arranged, but the simplified change of application form that Barkley wanted could not be introduced for some time.[24] The crisis passed but returned again when the District was finalizing water allotments. Barkley soon learned that in managing District affairs his diplomatic talents would be just as important as his expertise in civil engineering.

Once the Bureau and District decided how the south end facilities would be constructed, whether or not Boulder would be included in the NCWCD, and how much water would flow south from Flatiron, the District announced its readiness to receive applications for the remaining 100,000 acre-foot unit allotments of C–BT water. While attorneys John M. Sayre and Kelly were working out final details of Boulder's inclusion, the District opened a temporary branch office on January 7, 1953, in Longmont for the convenience of water users in the south end. Earl F. Phipps informed interested petitioners that the office would remain open six days a week for several weeks to accept applications for Project water.[25]

In June Dille told the Board that 215,076 acre-foot units[26] had been formally contracted throughout the District and that petitions were on file for "a large part" of the remaining water.[27] Henceforth, he announced, petitions would be handled according to the date received, and allotments would be made on a date priority basis. With the Board's approval of 12,700 acre-foot units to Boulder, 82,224 acre-foot units remained to be allotted. Dille wondered if it might be wise to set a final date for receipt of petitions.[28] This proved unnecessary, but the Board agreed on April 15, 1955. In conformance to the Water Conservancy District Act, the NCWCD published notices in two issues of six different newspapers, announcing a February 24 hearing for any objections against allocation of 960 Class D allotments. None were made.[29] Two weeks later, at the February 24 Board meeting, Dille announced that a balance of 64,894 acre-foot units still remained for further action. The Directors immediately approved all petitions dated between June 6, 1953, and February 1, 1954. Voting on any other petitions was delayed until April 15, 1955.[30]

Meanwhile, the transfer and reallocation controversy between Kelly and Dille resurfaced. Kelly tried to persuade the Board that each petition for C–BT water should contain a legal opinion that the applicant owned the land for which water was sought. Following Dille's response that the difficulties and expense of such an investigation could not be justified, the Directors voted against Kelly's suggestion.[31] With Dille absent frequently due to various illnesses, resolution of this ongoing controversy fell once again to Barkley. In summer 1955 he noted the continuing high volume of transfer requests at the District. There was still no policy, he told the Board, except to allow transfers from lands being platted for industrial or domestic uses.[32] Eight months later the Board addressed the matter once again, this time on a request by Farr Farms to reallocate its C–BT water. Kelly argued that the Board should insist on a security lien of sufficient quality and that the land offered as security qualified for supplemental water.

Barkley countered that complex issues had arisen out of ownership changes. Even though Kelly did not consider these serious, Barkley felt that "ownership problems would be a great concern to management in advance of any necessity for assessment certification."[33] At issue was his experience with situations when several allotment owners could not agree voluntarily on reallocation of their C–BT water. What Barkley wanted was a policy whereby the District would recognize primary concern with the "character of the right which attaches to a water allotment and the power and ability of the Board to retain control of the use of the water and the placement of allotments and liens." Kelly, he believed, was overly caught up in the procedural aspects of transfers and reallocations.[34] At its April 13, 1956, meeting, the Board followed Barkley's lead. It adopted supplemental rules and regulations for reallocation and transfer of water allotments. Kelly, who still saw no reason for these rules, stated that the Water Conservancy District Act already stipulated that liens could be removed from a property only if the water contract were breached or if the lien holder were in default of payments. The Board, however, agreed with Barkley that the rapid urbanization taking place in an agricultural area made it incumbent upon the District to adopt an amended policy. The six supplemental rules required certification of all owners of record who might have an interest in an application for reallocation or transfer of C–BT water. Notice of a hearing date before the Board had to be sent to all parties of interest. The Board would decide based on the merits of each case and, in the event of objections, would decide in the District's best interest.

Over the next few months the Board had many opportunities to test the new policy. By year's end Clayton noted that much of the attorneys' time was consumed by work on *involuntary* reallocations and transfers.[35] Clearly, Barkley's instincts had been correct. He had recognized that an increasingly large number of requests for transfers were submitted by farmers who wished to transfer their C–BT water from agricultural land to municipalities.[36] These change applications, as much as any other available data, revealed the significance of District policy decisions at a time when diverse trends in water use were manifest. Because the Front Range was undergoing enormous economic, political, and demographic transformations,

NCWCD policies were going to affect future water users in ways not readily discernible in the 1950s.

The time had also come to think about a new headquarters closer to the C–BT physical works. In addition to facilitating operation, maintenance, and management of C–BT water, such a move promised better cooperation with the Bureau, which had been considering for some time a branch office nearer C–BT features. In June 1953, less than a month after Hansen's death, Dille and Barkley officially recommended that the Board consider moving permanent headquarters to a new location. The Directors selected Nix to head a study committee to determine the best location.[37] Nix reported in August that the "large majority" of the Board favored the Loveland area. Dille, who stressed the "urgency" of responding as quickly as possible, requested that the committee propose a specific site.[38] Two days later, after inspecting several properties, the committee recommended purchase of two acres west of Loveland on the south side of U.S. Highway 34. Owned jointly by Edward J. Nugent and his son, the property was easily reached by municipal utilities, was on high ground with excellent drainage, and was easily accessible to C–BT canal structures. Positioned only a mile west of the major Fort Collins–Loveland-Denver highway, the land could be reasonably bought for $1,500 an acre.[39] At the September meeting, the Board agreed to purchase 2.6 acres and made a downpayment of $500.

The *Greeley Tribune* expressed disappointment at losing the NCWCD headquarters for "personal and sentimental reasons" and for a "certain loss of prestige," but the move was not entirely unexpected. Loveland was centrally located both to the C–BT's water delivery points and to the three principal county seats and their assessors, with whom the District dealt on a regular basis. In fact, concluded the *Tribune's* editor,

> Charles Hansen himself saw the advantage of placing the operational and maintenance headquarters at the same point and regarded as an eventuality the move decided upon by the Board in its session here Friday. From a personal and sentimental standpoint, Charles Hansen certainly did not contemplate with pleasure the prospects of the headquarters being moved from Greeley. However, in conversation he made it clear that he was aware of the practical value to the District of the Loveland location. The *Tribune* today comments upon the District's moving its headquarters because people have asked, what is the *Tribune* going to do about it? This is it.[40]

Architect James M. Hunter of Denver drew up plans for a one-story building 72 feet long by 37 feet wide with approximately 2,500 square feet.

First headquarters of NCWCD located in basement of Charles Hansen's *Greeley Tribune* building. NCWCD name is lettered on two basement windows. (Courtesy City of Greeley Museums.)

He sited the building on the northeast corner of the purchased land, selected native stone for the north side of the building and locally made contrasting tinted brick for the rest of the building's exterior, and designed offices and meeting rooms for maximum utility.[41] Twelve companies responded to the request for construction bids. On December 8, 1953, the Board accepted the lowest bid from a Greeley firm, John Brass and Sons, for $33,261. On May 27, 1954, after seventeen years in Greeley, District personnel moved into the nearly completed building.[42] Although Kelly had personally objected to the move, he agreed to petition changing the NCWCD's principal place of business from Greeley to Loveland. The District Court set a hearing date of June 11, at which no one entered a protest. The Board held its first meeting in the new quarters on June 12. Though landscaping, adequate storage space, and a garage were not complete, the building was operational. The Board transferred District funds from the First National Bank in Greeley to the First National Bank of

NCWCD personnel moved into their new Loveland headquarters building on May 27, 1954, to be closer to water distribution facilities. (Courtesy Bureau of Reclamation.)

Loveland and designated the Farmer's National Bank of Ault as depository for funds to be invested in U.S. Treasury issues.[43] One month after the move to Loveland, the Bureau announced plans to build a South Platte project office staffed by 155 people close to the new District headquarters.[44]

Compared to the Bureau's adequately staffed operation, the District was shorthanded. In 1948 Lory had urged the Board to find additional employees to collect, record, and maintain data on water supply, allotments, and other matters. His fellow Directors authorized a search for new employees, but they were cautious about money.[45] Dille and Barkley went to considerable trouble to find and interview three engineers, but the Board refused to act.[46] Two years later Lory again pointed out that work loads borne by Dille and Barkley left no time for conferences with water officials and water users.[47] Not until February 1951 did the Board agree to hire additional office staff.[48] Phipps, a 1951 agronomy graduate from Colorado A&M in Fort Collins, was hired following graduation to staff a branch office in Loveland during the water season.[49] Recipient of the Distinguished Flying Cross, Air Medal, and Purple Heart for his service in World War II, Phipps was thirty-one years old when he began his long association with the District. In 1951 Dille believed that the District could no longer wait to expand staff further. Purchase of new equipment for operation and maintenance purposes was also overdue.[50]

Hansen appointed a committee to design the upgrade for all aspects of NCWCD operations. In November 1952 they reported that a professional salary schedule must provide annual raises at each grade. In addition, the committee recommended that the secretary-manager advise the Board regarding manpower needs for assuming Project operation and maintenance and that a retirement system be instituted to supplement Social Security.[51] A tentative organizational chart, which accompanied this report, divided employees into two sections: field operations and office administration. Field operations called for a superintendent and assistant superintendent, two foremen, three ditch riders, and three maintenance men. Heavy maintenance would be contracted out. New office administrators would include an accountant and a records clerk. All told, the 1953 organizational plan called for a staff of fifteen individuals.[52]

The same chart established new wage scales and stipulated $75,000 as a maximum allowable salary budget for all employees. As part of the modernization and professionalization of staff operations, Lory accepted the responsibility of writing to stenographer Sadie Johnson, who had served the District for many years, to ask whether she would like a $25 a month raise and retirement at the end of twelve months. Her reply revealed that the District's maturation and professionalization had unpleasant side effects. It is reproduced in part to reveal how District affairs were proceeding rapidly into an era of specialization. After explaining that she had worked for the District since its inception, Johnson answered Lory's question as follows:

> Will you please tell me what I would do with tweedle-dee and tweedle-dum after all these years of active life? I have been secretly hoping that I would be able to continue my work (so long as I am able) for that always has been and is my "life." . . . I have never been under Social Security, so you can very readily see there is nothing there for me. I would simply be down and out if I should lose this position. . . . I have full charge of the books in the office, no one else ever making an entry of any kind, unless, of course, something unforeseen should happen. I am now juggling around anywhere from $170,000 to $200,000 a month, so perhaps my work is not all "play work" after all. There are so many angles to it all that you sometimes wonder where you are coming out, but the auditors tell me that they have yet to make their first scratch or change a figure. . . . Folks have no idea of the duties that fall upon me. In fact, I have not taken a two-weeks vacation since 1941 because I have had no "under-study" since

then and cannot afford to let "Tom, Dick, and Harry" take the books where I perhaps could not find the error for six months. . . . Another thing, we have had a Scrap Book ever since the District was organized and that has taken time, both night and day, to keep up with that. I am now only about three months behind with pasting articles and perhaps a half month in catching up with reading. So when you see me reading, that is not always play work either. . . . Just because I am a woman is no reason I should be holding the "sack." Women in positions similar to mine are receiving anywhere from $300 to $500 per month. I have never made any complaint because I have always been so happy that I have my work. It keeps me contented and out of mischief and I sincerely hope that I may be allowed to continue the same. I have always tried to give satisfaction, many times working over-time when it was necessary. . . . I did not intend to give you a life's history when I started out, but it has just come along so I hope it is all right. I hope after reading this, the Salary Committee may have more consideration for my services.[53]

Sadie Johnson worked eighteen months longer. In May 1954 the Board instructed Dille to write to her, thanking her for long, faithful service and advising her that when the District moved to the new offices in Loveland, she would be terminated with an extra month's pay.[54] This must have been a difficult moment for a woman who took so much pride in her work, but changes in District organization and operation were coming so rapidly that the Board and staff felt she might not adapt at age seventy-eight. Tracking water operations and maintaining newly acquired features would require new routines, new skills, and enormous amounts of energy.

Under terms of the Repayment Contract, the District assumed responsibility for operation and maintenance of the North Poudre Supply Canal, the St. Vrain conduits, and Project works that were "appurtenant and incidental" to these features, following written notice from the secretary of the interior "any time after the beginning of the second period."[55] By signing the interim contract on December 15, 1950, the District agreed to begin these duties prior to the onset of the second period. With the addition of Dennis Walker to the Loveland branch office in 1953, two men now handled the water delivery and whatever maintenance they could do without heavy equipment. The Bureau turned over the Poudre Supply Canal, the Windsor Extension, and the Dixon Feeder Canal to the District. Walker and Phipps accomplished required operation functions by frequently working late into the night and on weekends. Because they had only one vehicle between them, they did some of the ditch riding in their own cars at "lower-than-cost per mile reimbursement," which meant personal losses combined with ten- to twenty-hour days. By year's end, O&M costs totaled $12,118. For 1954 the District increased the budget 58 percent to $24,500 in anticipation of taking over the St. Vrain Supply Canal with its 20 miles of maintenance roads and recommended purchase of two pickup trucks and the addition of another maintenance man.[56]

Most operational tasks in these first years of water delivery focused on learning how to satisfy the allottees requirements. The small O&M staff functioned like a close-knit family, each person convinced that the District's principal task was to serve the water users — even if this meant working overtime.[57] Maintenance was minimal, but the District soon added a road grader and dump truck to the fleet to improve canal bank roads and to replace the many wire fence gates with cattle guards. The men also worked with the Bureau on solving algae build-up problems in the canals. Copper sulphate was used extensively to cut down on flow restrictions; but until they had experimented with different chemical proportions, treatment was inconsequential. Some slides occurred in the bentonite area along the St. Vrain Supply Canal, and weeds occasionally plugged siphons and trash racks in the reservoirs. Overall, however, maintenance problems were dispersed enough to allow the small O&M staff to cultivate excellent relations with neighboring landowners and to develop an efficient manner of water delivery and record keeping that earned respect from state water commissioners as well as the Bureau.

During the final years of the first period (mid-1950s), the O&M budget grew in proportion to the features that the District serviced in the south end. With the Boulder Creek Supply Canal, Boulder Reservoir, and the South Platte Supply Canal placed under District control, total O&M costs jumped rapidly to $32,495 in 1955 and $55,967 in 1956.[58] Addition of a short-wave radio communication system for the office in Loveland, field personnel, and water commissioners in Water District Nos. 3 and 6 eliminated many communication problems encountered earlier by saving time, telephone calls, and many miles of vehicle travel. With a newly purchased tractor and flatbed truck, graveling canal bank roads and adding riprap at the structure transitions of all canals was greatly simplified. By the end of 1956 all C–BT physical works relating to water distribution were completed and turned over to the District for operation and maintenance. The entire system worked according to design; however, water commissioners, whose job it was to regulate all water deliveries on the state's rivers and streams, were unhappy administering a volume of water increased by C–BT units with no increase in monetary compensation from the state. Their efforts to get help from the District lasted ten years with the same results. Barkley showed some concern in 1948, when he spoke to the state engineer about how stream measurements would be taken once the C–BT was in operation.[59] They reached no known agreement. Two years later the state engineer wrote Dille, specifically requesting assistance to state officials (water commissioners) in covering the cost of Project water deliveries.[60] At this time the water commissioners were not only concerned with the impact of interim water deliveries on their work load; they worried even more about the effect of a fully operational C–BT Project. They requested a meeting with the Board to find out how the District planned to compensate them for the added work and mileage in handling Project water.[61] Deputy State Engineer C. C. Hezmalhalch explained the need for supplemental salaries on their behalf.

The Board was willing to cooperate but failed to agree on a specific plan. Some Directors felt that, because the water commissioners were state employees under civil service, the legislature would be the appropriate forum for salary appeals; others believed that the need for good rapport with the water commissioners dictated that the Board should make a compromise agreement with the state engineer as soon as possible. Meanwhile, two of the local water user associations sent bills to the Board because Kelly had stated that the Board could properly contribute to the water users associations but not directly to the commissioners.[62] The stalemate continued for several years. Dille negotiated an agreement with the state engineer that the District would contribute $2,300 annually to five different water user associations, but the money was never paid.[63] Kelly persuaded the Civil Service Commission to recommend salary improvements to the legislature, but the legislature was slow to respond. Finally, Clayton reminded the Board that if the Directors voted to provide any additional compensation to the water commissioners, they would be in violation of their individual performance bonds.[64] He even noted that an amendment to the Water Conservancy District Act would be nullified by provisions in the Criminal Code.[65]

What could be done? A harmonious relationship between the water commissioners and the District became increasingly essential as the Project neared completion. Rebuffed by the State Assembly, the water commissioners hired a Fort Collins attorney, Alden T. Hill, to represent them before the Board. He focused on the legality issue, on which Clayton and Kelly had based most of their arguments, and suggested that if this were the real stumbling block, the dispute could be submitted to the courts. After hearing Clayton's presentation, however, the Directors instructed him to write Hill that the District could not provide additional compensation.[66]

The finality of this decision upset State Engineer J. E. Whitten, who informed the Directors that if they remained adamant, he would be forced to draw up a set of operational guidelines that reflected their position. In March 1957 the Board received new rules that required ditch companies to give water orders directly to the District, which would in turn forward them to the state engineer, who would send them to the water commissioners. Though the Board expressed concern at the unwieldy process, they approved it by resolution.[67] In terms of future relations with the water commissioners, it was too soon to determine whether the Board's position was appropriate. The staff had made efforts to help the water commissioners with their problem, but the Board in the last analysis decided to heed the advice of counsel. Many of their decisions in the mid-fifties made the Directors increasingly aware that management of the completed C–BT system required choices much more complex and far-reaching than during the long construction phase.

With water flowing through the C–BT, principally for agricultural and domestic purposes, and the 1 mill ad valorem tax about to be levied on all District property owners, both the Bureau and the Board found themselves more squarely than ever in the public eye. What they did, why they made certain decisions, and how they managed tax monies required a good public relations program. Some people had already complained about condemnations of land for Project rights-of-way, awkward transfer procedures, and delays in construction. Residents in Water District No. 64 (Logan and Sedgwick counties) grumbled that their water tables had dropped, that they needed a regulating reservoir, and that they had not received the return flows they expected from the Project. They felt abandoned and even talked of removing Logan County from the District.[68]

To address the need for better publicity about Project objectives and limitations, the Bureau constructed a large model of the entire system, which was completed in June 1952 and displayed in Gunter Hall at Colorado State College in Greeley. Built to scale, the model measured 20 by 37 feet and comprised twenty-two different pieces all bolted together.[69] The Bureau's public relations officer also announced production of a twenty-eight-minute documentary color film that they hoped to have for celebration of the Project's completion.[70] Unfortunately, Bureau officials in Washington delayed approval of the film for almost a year. Finally authorized in 1957, "The Barrier Between" informed general audiences who had little knowledge of the Bureau's role in water and hydroelectric projects.[71] The film was more to celebrate the Bureau's accomplishments than a documentary of the NCWCD's role in making water deliveries, but it was a beginning in what would become a continuous effort to better inform the public about the Project's origins and operation. District and Bureau employees showed it in schools, at public meetings, and at service clubs until the partisan message began to appear dated. In 1976 a more balanced film was made entitled "The Green Echo of Snow" that addressed both environmental and recreational aspects of the Project.[72]

No matter how well the District promoted its mission, the organization's widening impact on people and institutions required constant vigilance to avoid misunderstandings, uninformed criticism, and misconceptions. The group's financial condition was always fair game for critics concerned about waste of tax dollars by an appointed Board of Directors. For example, postwar economic growth in northern Colorado caused District income from assessed property valuations to advance faster than the 5 percent per annum permitted by law. Almost every year from 1947 to 1957 the District requested special permission from the Colorado Tax Commission to exercise the 3/10 mill levy, because application of this levy normally increased revenues to the District by more than 5 percent.[73] When Boulder was added to the District in 1954, this inclusion added over $34 million in total taxable property; but instead of being rich and affluent, as some contended, the District had to ask the Colorado Tax Commission to increase the mill levy to 1/2 mill to meet contractual obligations to the Bureau and to the city of Boulder. The District's total estimated taxable value in 1954 was $300 million, which grew to $334 million in 1957, at the beginning of the second period.[74]

Public perceptions of the District also depended on how capably the Board and staff responded to safety concerns. James H. Knights, the Bureau's South Platte River district manager, spoke to the Fort Collins Rotary Club, where he was asked why Satanka Dike had not been built to the same elevation as Spring, Dixon, and Soldier Canyon dams. Located on a saddle just west of Horsetooth Dam, Satanka was 14 feet high with a crest elevation 4 feet lower than the other dams. Knights replied that, in the event of an extreme storm over Horsetooth Reservoir, Satanka Dike would act as a spillway.[75] This truthful reply shocked his audience, who feared that Fort Collins could be washed away by a severe storm.

Director Lory brought the matter to the attention of the Board.[76] He noted that Guy Palmes, Fort Collins city and utilities manager, felt justifiably upset. Lory had also spoken with a close friend, R. L. Parshall, who expressed another concern. "Should this matter be aired in the press," he ventured, "the communities would be needlessly abused and also would put the Bureau in a bad light." Parshall believed that the combination of a filled reservoir and an unprecedented storm from the southwest "would without a doubt create a condition that would overtop the dike . . . and once the water started over the dike there [was] nothing man [could] do to prevent destruction."[77]

While Royce J. Tipton and Bureau employees studied the problem, a committee of concerned citizens announced at a NCWCD Board meeting that, with the backing of the NRA, they would ask the state engineer to stop filling Horsetooth Reservoir until a safe spillway could be added.[78] Although Barkley argued that the suggested maximum storm and 60 mph southwest wind could never occur simultaneously, the Board agreed with the Bureau that public confidence in the Project warranted expenditure of additional funds to raise construction standards of Satanka Dike to those of other dams. After this work was completed in fall 1954, Lory wrote Bureau Commissioner W. A. Dexheimer to express his appreciation for restoring public confidence in Horsetooth Reservoir and in the District's Board of Directors.[79]

From 1955 to 1963 the Board acquired a singular personality that reflected Judge Buck's commitment to appointing informed and dedicated men who represented the multitudinous interests and professions within the District.[80] He drove to cities in all District counties to inquire about the people he contemplated appointing to the Board. As a result of his extensive investigations, Buck was able to bring diversity to the Board at a time when its responsibilities were becoming more extensive and complex. He knew that the Project could only be managed well by Directors with a broad view of northern Colorado's needs and a dedication to hard work.[81] Like Coffin, he was always reluctant to deny reappointment to men who were capable and who had served well, but both he and Coffin placed great importance on the principle of rotation in office, in the best tradition of appointed boards.[82] As the District approached the second period, this policy paid off. The range of issues requiring deliberation demanded individuals with business experience and community service. Preserving good relations with residents in the District's east end was a case in point.

In 1955 farmers in Water District No. 64, clamoring for more water, formed a Water Users Protective Association that demanded 50,000 acre-feet annually and objected to paying taxes for the 164,000 acre-feet of return flows, which Knights assured them they would receive from the proposed Blue River and C–BT projects.[83] Others in the Sterling area favored construction of Narrows Dam and urged the Board's support.[84] Narrows Dam, however, proved controversial even for people living along the South Platte. Fort Morgan residents stood in opposition because the project would inundate 15,000 acres of farmland, displace 250 families, and cover the towns of Weldona, Goodrich, and Orchard, as well as 22 miles of Union Pacific Railroad tracks. Faced with countervailing opinions, the Bureau bought time with feasibility studies while the District demurred. The Board finally decided that "some plan for mainstream storage on the South Platte River was desirable," but high-altitude storage made more sense to the Directors.[85]

A dam site on Elkhorn Creek in Poudre Canyon 32 miles west of Fort Collins appeared ideal. Governor Ed Johnson and Fort Collins Mayor C. H. Alford, who bluntly admitted that he was interested in "nailing down" all available water rights in order to meet the city's future needs,[86] supported the plan. Director Lory saw Elkhorn Dam as the "last big water hole for the people in the Cache la Poudre Valley," but when rain returned to the area in 1957, urgency to build a storage reservoir temporarily vanished.

Board members also had concerns about how recreation on Project reservoirs would be administered. They agreed that the Bureau should enter into understandings with the Bureau of Land Management (BLM), NPS, counties, and towns, as long as the District incurred no liability.[87] They wrestled with Water Supply and Storage Company (WSSC) requests to carry Grand River ditch water through the Adams Tunnel so that the ditch company would not have to face the annual expense of opening its high-altitude ditch in the spring. Because carrying this water into the C–BT system would take space in Horsetooth Reservoir, the Board denied the ditch company's request.[88]

The Directors pioneered as they planned for the present and the future. On the advice of Directors Hatfield Chilson and Barkley, they marked surplus funds for investment in U.S. Treasury notes to establish a fund that would meet the obligations of the last ten years of the repayment schedule.[89] They changed their accounting system from calendar to fiscal year beginning November 1, 1957.[90] They set water quotas, discussed growing needs of municipalities, commented on proposed amendments to the Water Conservancy District Act, and debated their position on congressional legislation for other water projects. Sizable numbers of foreign visitors inspected the Project annually. They asked about operational details that tended to obscure the twenty-year struggle to get the system built.

To record those events, Dille took it upon himself to write a brief history of the C–BT and the NCWCD.[91] It was an appropriate task for a man whom the *Greeley Tribune* called the "ramrod" of the C–BT. At a testimonial dinner three months before the August 11, 1956, celebration of Project completion, the Department of the Interior presented Dille with its highest award. Commissioner Dexheimer recognized his "patience, persistence, wisdom, energy, tact, and diplomacy" in formulation and construction of the C–BT. R. J. Walter, Bureau director of Region 7, paid tribute to his "staunchness, perseverance, and courage" in the long battle to tap the "last water hole in the West."[92] At eighty years old, Dille announced his intention to retire in 1957, and the Board selected Barkley to replace him as secretary-manager in 1958. This watershed event for the District signaled the end of Dille's era; the next stage, 1958 to 1974, belonged to Barkley.

Part IV: *Urbanization and the District's Response to Water Projects (1958–1974)*

16 *Dealing With the Impact of Growth*

Speaking to the Four States Irrigation Council in January 1959, J. R. "Bob" Barkley described how a conservancy district manager should exercise authority. An intimate observer of J. M. Dille's strengths and weaknesses during their long association — from the end of World War II until Dille's retirement in 1958 — Barkley revealed that he had been a perceptive and sensitive student of the man who had guided the District from inception through completion of C–BT construction. With the Board of Directors, he said, a manager must "suggest and advise" so they have every opportunity to "see it his way"; however, he quickly admitted that the Board had every right to disagree with management. With the staff, two-way communication was essential so that free exchanges of ideas could develop. "I would much rather have a few good men working *with* me than to have several hundred working *for* me," he said. With the water users, he concluded, a manager must always be prepared to deal with their unpredictable wrath, most frequently provoked by misunderstood or erroneous water measurements. The only way to avoid unpleasantness was to insist on scrupulous attention to detail when measuring water into the District's streams.[1]

Over the next fifteen years, until he retired in fall 1974, Barkley had ample opportunities to test these basic theories and develop new ones. Many of the demands and challenges he faced had not been foreseen by Dille or addressed specifically in Senate Document 80, the Water Conservancy District Act, or the Repayment Contract. With the Project entirely constructed, Barkley turned his attention to regional and national water issues, many of which directly affected C–BT management. He was forced to deal with exponential urban growth along the Front Range, the gradual transfer of water from agriculture to municipal use, rural domestic water associations, water quality laws, environmental concerns, and state water law reform. He represented the District in Washington at numerous congressional hearings, including the one on the Colorado River Basin Project Act; traveled to the Yukon to investigate water importation to the Colorado River basin; and played a leading role in the National Reclamation

J. R. "Bob" Barkley came to work for
the District in 1945. In 1958 he became secretary-manager, a position he
held until his retirement in 1974.
(Courtesy NCWCD.)

Association at a time when the NRA was adjusting to reclamation's
apparent fall from grace. Throughout his tenure Barkley increasingly
involved the NCWCD in matters of general interest to Colorado and the
West. Flexible and compromising, rarely confrontational, he led the Board
toward policies that reflected dramatic demographic changes throughout
the District. With an eye to the future, Barkley warned about consequences
of ongoing urbanization and industrialization, supported CWCB policies
that protected Colorado's rights in the upper Colorado basin, and positioned District finances so that obligations under the Repayment Contract
during the last ten years were met without fail. His highest priority was to
see that the District met every term of that contract, knowing full well that
a single deviation or violation would result in demands for renegotiation.

During the last years of Eisenhower's presidency, the Bureau of Reclamation was subjected to intense pressure to justify dam-building and power-
generating activities. Following heavy military expenditures in the Korean
War, a special Republican study group had recommended that the federal
budget be pruned by 20 percent and that water resource development be
cut by $400 million. Furthermore, no new projects were to be authorized
between 1954 and 1957 "unless defense needs [were] clear and compel-
ling."[2] Eisenhower agreed with this budgetary philosophy mainly because
he was horrified by the big, centralized nature of federal government. He

Bureau of Reclamation commissioner Floyd E. Dominy defended reclamation to the end.
NCWCD manager Bob Barkley listens to Dominy address the Four States Irrigation Council
in Denver in 1960. (Courtesy Bureau of Reclamation.)

too wanted to cut federal expenses, but he believed that cuts could be made
in defense spending if he were effective in lowering tensions in the Cold
War; unfortunately, that crisis worsened during the Eisenhower administration's last years. Because he felt a growing responsibility to resource
development and conservation, his plan was to encourage local government and private initiative as well as to promote increased state sharing in
the cost of water project development. The Bureau, however, continued
lobbying Congress for large-scale planning and construction funds. Commissioner W. A. Dexheimer, who quietly refused the so-called partnership
policies,[3] doggedly fought against criticism that federal support for irrigation farming was adding to escalating crop surpluses in the nation. His
principaled firmness eventually led to resignation in 1959, but his replacement, Floyd E. Dominy, defended reclamation with even greater fervor.
The Bureau would not back down without a fight.

Results of the policy conflict between the Bureau and Eisenhower were mixed. To the end of his second term, the president remained committed to reducing federal spending, but the Bureau managed overall to do pretty well in the annual budgets. What may have done more damage in the long run was the constant maligning of the Bureau's leadership role.[4] Forced to defend its historical mission and indicted by critics for contributing to the "farm crisis," the Bureau looked for any actions that might temper criticism that it was irresponsibly spending the taxpayers' money. Regional and national officials alike continued to view renegotiation of the District's Repayment Contract as an objective worth pursuing. Under Barkley's commitment to meet all payment conditions of this contract, however, the Bureau never found an opening to exploit. In fact, fifteen months after becoming manager, Barkley presented the Board with a plan to raise funds that would meet the large payments owed to the United States in the last ten years of the District's forty-year contract (1962–2002).[5] Barkley explained that rising operation and maintenance costs of the District's portion of the Project and the joint features were likely to sabotage the District's ability to meet anticipated contract obligations. Therefore, he recommended that water allotment contracts be opened for a new rating whenever an original owner transferred or reallocated an allotment to another party.[6] Assessed valuations were predicted to continue their rise in the seven counties of the NCWCD; however, the 1-mill limitation, fear of inflation, and the mistaken belief that most of the District's revenue would always come from contracts with water users led Barkley and his staff to conclude that open-rating contracts would best meet the District's future financial responsibilities.[7]

In 1964 Barkley conceived another way to prepare for the $1.1 million annual payments owed to the United States from 1992 to 2002 by investing excess revenue in an escrow account so that interest could accrue to the District's benefit; however, because the Repayment Contract stipulated that excess revenue would be deposited in the U.S. Treasury without earning interest, an amendment was required if Barkley's plan were to take effect. The only options available to the District, aside from open-rating water allotment contracts, were to increase the levy by 1/2 mill under the default provision of the Water Conservancy District Act or acquire additional financing through an election-approved bond issue, both of which the Directors opposed. By a resolution of April 3, 1959, they agreed to set new rates on an annual basis for those contracts that thenceforth were open-rated by transfer or reallocation of C–BT water.[8] The Board's action in no small way responded to alarming growth statistics that revealed increasing amounts of agricultural water being transferred to municipalities. The intent was not to penalize farmers with Class D allotments but rather to capitalize on postwar urbanization and industrialization that was reaching boom proportions north of metropolitan Denver.[9]

From the late fifties to the middle of the seventies, nearly 500 new rural subdivisions were recorded in the plains area of Boulder, Larimer, and Weld counties.[10] Census data from 1960 showed that the Denver metropolitan area (Denver, Adams, Arapahoe, and Jefferson counties) had increased 116 percent since 1950, an average for the four counties that included a modest 18.8 percent gain for Denver itself. Within the District, Larimer and Weld counties had grown by 22.5 percent and 7.2 percent respectively, while Boulder County registered a 53.7 percent increase. Eastward along the South Platte River, Morgan County increased 17.3 percent, Logan County was up 18.1 percent, while both Washington and Sedgwick counties registered declines.[11] Manufacturing, which had quadrupled since the end of the war, was growing twice as fast as agriculture and was drawing people to the Front Range corridor, where domestic and industrial water needs were rising.

Those who observed this phenomenon believed that rapid growth had to be accepted and planned for; no one argued consistently that the trend might be short-lived. While Barkley recommended flexible policies that could be adjusted in future years, attorney Glenn G. Saunders of the DWB interpreted the data to mean that Denver would *never* have enough water.[12] Judge William E. Buck wanted to transfer the District's court case from Weld County District Court to Boulder County because of the heavy case load in that area.[13] Bureau Commissioner Dexheimer and other federal officials warned of the need to conserve water and urged further development of the West's water resources to meet a 250 percent population expansion by the end of the century.[14] When the Senate Select Committee on Water Resources reported that one-third of the nation would be short of water by the twenty-first century and Secretary of the Interior Stewart Udall warned that the nation's population would increase by nearly 90 percent in the same time period, local water people became convinced that a water shortage was imminent. Acquisition of new supplies and the development of facilities to treat the urban-industrial wastes became twin necessities born of the West's population explosion.[15] Few voices protested.

As discussions commenced on how to finance new engineering studies and expansion of existing delivery systems, the NCWCD focused on the appearance of newly formed rural domestic water districts, composed of farmers and other rural residents who were willing to assume further debt to secure a clean and reliable domestic water supply. Farmers, long accustomed to importing water from towns in tank trucks because of fertilizers leaching into the groundwater and contamination from septic systems, believed that their organization in rural domestic districts, associations, or companies would enable them to build the necessary reservoirs and conduits to qualify for purchase of transferred C–BT water.[16] For some of the early rural domestics, the opportunity to buy C–BT shares occurred shortly after WSSC limited the amount of "foreign" water it would carry for each share of stock. For farmers in the area of Ault and Pierce, who relied on supplemental C–BT water delivered through the Pierce Lateral, the company announcement was a blow. They held more C–BT shares than the company would honor, and their only recourse was to put them on the District's open market. Most found willing buyers in the rural domestics. Others, who panicked at paying another year of special taxes, returned their shares to the District, where they were offered on a first-refusal basis to petitioners placed on a list after 1955 allotments were filled.[17]

Making an exception to the standard criteria for obtaining C–BT units, the District Board did not require rural domestics to show proof of a base water supply. All they needed was a workable arrangement to store and distribute water purchased on a free-market basis from within the District. This free-market system, although not foreseen in the Water Conservancy District Act, began operation in the early sixties, when the Bijou Irrigation Company of Fort Morgan offered 3,000 acre-foot units to three newly formed rural domestics at $30 per acre-foot;[18] thenceforth, as municipal demands for water increased, the price of C–BT units gradually rose. The Board saw the free-market system as an extension of water rental procedures followed in pre-District days when one South Platte tributary basin supplied another with surplus water. The Bureau had no objections to the free-market transfer of C–BT units, but others asked some hard questions. Even attorney Clayton questioned the ethics of allowing original allottees to make profits on water partly subsidized by taxpayers. The Board countered that those who first signed contracts for C–BT water had placed an additional lien on their lands at a time when many farms were unable to pay any property taxes at all. Those who agreed to buy C–BT water obligated themselves financially with little more than a promise of future Project construction. Directors felt that these pioneers were entitled to just compensation for their risk.[19]

Law professor Joseph L. Sax of the University of Michigan, expressing an opposing opinion, described C–BT water rights as a "public subsidy" "held and sold, under current practice, as a private asset." With more than

11,000 acre-feet transferred during 1963–1964, Sax concluded that farmers realized enormous profits from "incremental value" increases in their property. Although Sax recognized that ongoing water transfers to municipalities meant that the incremental value would remain within Project boundaries, he concluded that "the money for which a reclamation-project water right is sold . . . should be recovered by the irrigation conservancy district . . . to be held in trust and used for the benefit of the present project community."[20] Barkley and the Board, which totally supported the free-market system, did not agree. Barkley did wonder, however, if the resulting rapid growth of industry, municipalities, and rural domestics might indeed create a need for year-long water deliveries.[21]

From the 1957 inception of the quota system, the District operated on the basis of an April through October delivery period. The quota, which was announced in April of each year (with the exception of a March 1958 announcement), depended on existing water supplies, agricultural needs of farmers, forecast weather conditions, and available soil moisture. Fully aware of Mother Nature's unreliability and the C–BT's present inability to deliver 310,000 acre-feet on an annual basis, Barkley counseled the Board to set quotas that would allow the system to function like a bank account: Lake Granby and Willow Creek Reservoir were the savings accounts for runoff "deposits," and Horsetooth and Carter were the checking account from which "payments" were made to water users during delivery season. This scheme would satisfy the supplemental water needs of allottees without depleting the savings accounts in high-altitude storage. The initial quota could be set very conservatively, with the option of adding a supplemental distribution later if conditions warranted.[22] In a wet year, the District could set a low quota and build up storage, but it could not go below 50 percent, because it was obligated to furnish the Bureau with water to generate electricity.[23]

The quota system was far more precise than the rule of thumb used by old-timers before the C–BT. Easily visible for over 100 miles to the east, Long's Peak had always been the perfect farming barometer. If the entire front face of the peak were covered with snow when planting time arrived, farmers were optimistic; they planted a greater acreage to cash crops — sugar beets, potatoes, dry beans — and cut back on small grains. If the peak's Notch remained white through the Fourth of July, farmers felt sure that runoff would be adequate for the remainder of the irrigation season; if the Notch lacked snow by early July, they ceased irrigation of hay and grain immediately and used the remaining water supply judiciously to finish cash crops.[24]

Irrigated farmland stretches out as far as the eye can see below snowcapped Long's Peak. Farmers have long used this landmark as a barometer for the water season. (Courtesy NCWCD.)

Although C–BT water was provided precisely to address mid- and late summer water uncertainties, the Board's quota policies still provoked criticism. Some farmers complained that they did not know what crops to plant and how much early water to use for germination; the vague possibility of a second quota created uncertainty for them. Others accused the District of holding back water or failing to use it to develop new lands within the District.[25] Even Directors occasionally differed on how high the quota should be. By and large, however, they adhered to a conservative policy, depleting the bank account only to the extent necessary to meet water users' needs. In the event of drought, like those of the thirties and fifties, supplemental water would be available to sustain farmers through the arid cycle. Although Barkley had expressed some concern about what District urbanization would mean to criteria for setting quotas, he concluded that all the transfers to municipalities ultimately had no effect on the Board's underlying principles.[26] This bank account philosophy survived the criticism and continued to guide future Directors.

What seemed to cause some discontent, at least from the standpoint of water users at the District's east end, was that return flows from the C–BT did not arrive as expected because of the increased amount of groundwater pumping in the South Platte basin. Availability of cheaper electricity through the Rural Electrification Administration (REA), supplies of natural gas, a new type of turbine pump that withdrew water from deeper aquifers, and the absence of restrictive state laws all made it economical for farmers to expand their underground water withdrawal operations in Morgan and Logan counties.[27] The District's involvement in this development emerged from its obligation to taxpayers as well as to statewide interest in bringing groundwater regulations in line with Colorado water law.

When underground pumping began to proliferate during the 1954 drought, statutory control was limited (under the 1953 act) to the CWCB's authority to establish groundwater districts and determine their regulations. This action could not, however, "affect priorities to the use of any well producing water." Emergency districts were established in the event of excessive groundwater depletion, but a survey of Morgan County farmers indicated that between 50 and 60 percent opposed any legislation to restrict their pumping rights.[28] The Colorado Ground Water Act of 1957 gave the state engineer authority to issue permits for the "drilling of [and] increased use of wells," but regulation of nontributary groundwater remained outside the prior appropriation system. This act also established the Colorado Ground Water Commission, which was authorized to designate tentatively critical groundwater districts where withdrawal of water approached or exceeded the normal replenishment rate. A restriction on drilling could then be implemented.[29] However, the act proved virtually useless. In January 1958 the commission designated the Bijou alluvial basin in Morgan and Adams counties a critical water area. Under terms of the 1957 act, residents were empowered to elect a local advisory board that could overturn the designation if they so desired. In spite of threats to disrupt the election, voters selected a five-man board, which promptly reported to the commission that they had dissolved the district.[30] Reenforcing the proprietary nature of nontributary groundwater, the Colorado Supreme Court held that groundwater was not subject to the appropriation doctrine. The purpose of the 1957 act, said the court, was "to provide administration facilities to control reasonable use and to provide a record of facts upon which such reasonable use can be determined."[31] Ten years later the state legislature repealed the toothless law, reenacting it as the Colorado Ground Water Management Act of 1965. The new law not only applied the

Greeley attorney Jack Clayton began his NCWCD association in partnership with William R. Kelly. He served the Board until his untimely death in 1964. (Courtesy NCWCD.)

appropriation doctrine to groundwater in designated groundwater basins but gave the state engineer power to shut down well owners where conditions of injury existed.[32]

Questions raised by the struggle over groundwater rights extended into the general area of Colorado's water law administration. More than once the District's attorneys argued that the system needed modernization. Alluvial groundwater, for example, should have been subject to administration of water rights priorities along the surface streams to which the groundwater was hydrologically connected, but state law did not yet provide for an integrated system of conjunctive use of both surface and tributary groundwater.

Relationships between water users and state-appointed officials also needed streamlining. Jack Clayton urged the state to put water commissioners under civil service, specify their authority, and pay them better. He urged Colorado to join with the other sixteen states of the West and to develop a statewide water users' association.[33] As a member of the Colorado Bar Association's committee to recodify Colorado water law, Clayton reported frequently to the Board, noting sentiment to abolish the old water districts, prepare a master index for all water decrees, and require the state

John M. Sayre became NCWCD legal counsel in 1964 and served the Board until 1989. He then was appointed as the Department of the Interior's assistant secretary for water and science. (Courtesy NCWCD.)

engineer to report every four years at a general water adjudication hearing on the actual water use under existing decrees.[34] Meanwhile, Barkley chaired the Colorado Water Investigation Commission (CWIC), whose purpose was to make recommendations to the CWCB regarding recodification and revision of Colorado water laws. He testified at hearings of the state legislature and supported funding for the Department of Natural Resources for recodification studies.[35] After Clayton's unexpected death in 1964, John M. Sayre, his replacement, and Barkley supported the 1965 Ground Water Management Act and served on the Colorado River Advisory Committee with the same group that was involved in legislation to revise the entire Colorado Water Code.[36]

The principal connection between the District and the recodification process was the newly formed Colorado Water Congress (CWC), the roots of which were multiple. In a stereotypical argument with John Barnard, Sr., of Granby, the DWB's Glenn G. Saunders claimed that Colorado needed a statewide organization to present facts on water problems to Colorado residents.[37] In contrast, Barnard and other West Slope residents, who had recommended against formation of a CWC, favored closer relations with neighboring states.[38] After nearly a year's

Felix "Larry" Sparks was executive director of the Colorado Water Conservation Board from 1958 to 1979. (Courtesy Felix Sparks.)

planning by a committee organized by Governor Stephen McNichols, the CRWCD finally agreed to participate in a CWC without fear of bullying by Denver and the East Slope.[39] McNichols wanted to end feuding between the two slopes through the CWC. He knew, as governors before him, that such controversy damaged the state's chances of congressional support for water projects. Since Clifford Stone's death, the CWCB had been ineffective. In both inter- and intrastate water matters, Colorado was also ineffective and essentially leaderless until Felix "Larry" Sparks took over as CWCB director. A CWC was desperately needed to address a number of pressing issues: California's opposition to continued funding for the Colorado River Storage Project, problems associated with unrestricted groundwater pumping, lack of congressional support of the Fryingpan-Arkansas project (Fry-Ark), the possibility of a federal wilderness preservation law, a need for studies of water supplies in Colorado's major river basins, and interest in alerting Colorado citizens to Colorado's water problems.[40]

The organizational meeting, jointly called by Governor McNichols and Attorney General Duke Dunbar for June 4, 1958, brought out 450 delegates who gave overwhelming approval to the CWC's bipartisan charter document, prepared after "considerable time and effort" by Barkley and Clayton.[41] The document called for an executive committee composed of one representative from each of nineteen districts — eighteen men and Mrs. Hestia Wilson of Nucla, a Democrat and the only woman in the state senate;[42] the governor and attorney general appointed ten additional persons. The executive committee then created the CWIC, composed of representatives of the state's major water entities. With Barkley as chairman, the CWIC was asked to suggest special water studies to be made by the CWCB and to promote investigations for a "sweeping" reform of the state's water code.[43] The CWC, as a voluntary organization, asked no financial help from the state and charged individual members only $10. Organizations with larger budgets were expected to contribute more; for instance, the NCWCD Board initially agreed to pay $500 annually. The Directors also approved the time that Barkley and Clayton spent on CWC matters.[44]

Within five years the CWC was asked to lead the promotion of water law reform. John B. Barnard, Jr., the CWC's first chairman, recognized the almost impossible task of determining who owned what water.[45] By early 1960 the CWC went on record to end the piecemeal approach to solving Colorado's groundwater problems.[46] At the annual meeting in 1961 delegates discussed the "horse and buggy nature of Colorado water laws" and proposed that the seventy water districts be abolished, that the state establish an organization to oversee administration of a projected new law to curb waste of water, that a state administrative body be established to represent the public interest in administration and adjudication of water rights decrees, that tributary groundwater and surface water be administered similarly, and that general adjudication of all water rights be made easier in the courts.[47] Major reform was effected in 1969 when seven judicial water divisions were established as jurisdictions over Colorado's primary river basins. Until then Barkley reported with regularity to the NCWCD Board regarding his activities with the CWC. The state's rapid growth, urbanization, and changing patterns of water use were finally causing state legislators to modernize state statutes. With such a large Project to administer, the District had a special interest in any bills that might affect C–BT operation, including legislation to divide the judicial district where the NCWCD case was assigned.

Early in 1960 Democratic state legislators introduced a bill to divide the Eighth Judicial District into three parts. Rapidly changing growth patterns in Boulder, Larimer, and Weld counties indicated the need for revision of judicial district boundaries, although the three existing Republican judges at first staunchly opposed what they viewed as a purely political move.[48] The bill died for lack of support, but the seed of reform had been planted in the legislature. In fall 1962 electors voted on an amendment to the state constitition that gave the general assembly power to change the boundaries of judicial districts and relegated to each district's voters the right to elect judges for a six-year term.[49] This amendment passed and went into effect in 1965. Almost immediately, the general assembly addressed problems in the Eighth Judicial District, where three judges were responding to a growing population and a work load in Boulder County alone that demanded 50 percent of their time. Following recommendations of the Weld County Bar Association, legislators divided the Eighth into three districts, the new Eighth to include Larimer and Jackson counties and the Nineteenth and Twentieth to represent Weld and Boulder counties, respectively. Because the presiding judge of the Eighth Judicial District had chosen the NCWCD Board since 1938, a new appointment system was called for to assure all counties in the NCWCD fair representation in the selection process. Once this district was formally divided, the only voters who would elect the presiding judge, in whom resided the power of appointment to the District Board, were residents of Weld County.[50]

Attorney Ward H. Fischer of the Cache la Poudre Water Users' Association (CLPWUA) had already recognized the need for better voter representation. Under his direction, the association passed a resolution in 1963 to request judges of the Eighth Judicial District "to reassign the case having jurisdiction of the NCWCD from a single judge of said district to three judges of said district sitting *en banc*, which judges shall be selected one from each of Boulder, Weld, and Larimer counties."[51] A cover letter to these judges urged endorsement of this plan prior to a Legislative Council on Water committee hearing scheduled for July 26 in Fort Collins and warned that, without a united front, the legislature might "set up a non-judicial board or commission to administer the district, which we all wish to avoid."[52] After Fischer explained his proposal to the NCWCD Board, the Directors "seemed to agree" that the *en banc* idea was a legitimate option. At the Fort Collins meeting the Legislative Council on Water approved the *en banc* plan and pledged to place the proposed amendment to the Water Conservancy District Act on the governor's call for the legislature.[53] One committee member suggested electing conservancy district directors; though the committee took no action, others began to voice the same concern: that the NCWCD Board should more directly represent the constituency it served.[54]

In January 1965 the new judicial districts were effected with presiding judges newly appointed by the Colorado Supreme Court: Donald A. Carpenter (Nineteenth); Dale E. Shannon (Eighth); and William E. Buck (Twentieth). Francis L. Shallenberger presided over the Thirteenth Judicial District, representing Morgan, Logan, Washington, and Sedgwick counties. From this point on, the four judges who met *en banc* were expected

Judge Donald A. Carpenter was the presiding judge in the Nineteenth Judicial District from 1964 to 1979. (Courtesy Donald Carpenter.)

to appoint or reappoint the District's Directors; if they disagreed, the amendment stipulated that "the presiding judge of each judicial district shall appoint the directors from each eligible county within his judicial district." This plan was not democratic enough for some critics. Although state officials were generally satisfied with the Water Conservancy District Act,[55] the Legislative Council on Water was asked in 1966 to consider a proposal for electing conservancy district directors like school board members, who were chosen in May of uneven years.[56] This bill never appeared on the floor for debate, but the following year another bill (S.B. 145) was drawn up that required election of Board members by a majority vote of county commissioners.[57] Representative Tom Farley, one of the bill's sponsors, explained that, because judges were to be appointed and not elected, the electorate would in effect lose control of accountability from conservancy district boards. The District responded with no position on the proposed legislation, "but if testimony were to be given at any legislative hearing, the procedural difficulty should be noted and the committee advised of the fact that th[e] District had found the present system to be totally satisfactory over a period of 29 years of operation."[58] State Senator James Thomas's later attempt to obtain the Legislative Council on Water's support for an election plan also failed. Thomas predicted that conservancy districts would play an increasingly important role in the state but would suffer from lack of communication with the people.[59]

NCWCD President J. Ben Nix presided over a special meeting to discuss District operations held March 26, 1963, in Greeley. He was a Director and then Board president from 1955 to 1976. (Courtesy NCWCD.)

New growth patterns along the Front Range, particularly the large numbers of immigrants settling in the area, meant that telling the C–BT story so that present and future generations might comprehend its complexity, its value to northern Colorado, and the circumstances of the thirties — when plans, contracts, and agreements had been made — gained incremental importance. Barkley, who recognized the need for an informational publication to follow in the tradition of Dille's biannual progress reports, told the Board that he had no time to prepare materials and recommended that the District contract with a Denver public relations firm. The Board agreed. At a cost of $5,500, White and White agreed to publish a single-page flyer with statistical information, booklets on Project operation for allottees and others interested in more detail, and a brief summary of the annual report.[60]

The need to explain its mission required even greater efforts from the District. As demographic patterns continued to shift rapidly within District boundaries, Barkley called on the Directors to explain NCWCD history and workings to an invited group of professionals who represented new businesses, industries, banking and public sectors, as well as the water users themelves. At a special meeting held in Greeley on March 26, 1963, Barkley introduced District staff and the Board to over two hundred participants and then turned the meeting over to President J. Ben Nix and

The U.S. Park Service, which managed nearby Rocky Mountain National Park, established the Shadow Mountain Recreation Area in 1953. Management for recreation facilities was transferred to the U.S. Forest Service in 1978 with the creation of the Arapahoe National Recreation Area. (Courtesy Bureau of Reclamation.)

Directors W. D. "Bill" Farr, Gordon Dyekman, Sayre, and Clyde Moffitt. After each spoke on some aspect of the District's operation, Nix expressed thanks for the good attendance and indicated the possibility of additional meetings.[61] Regretfully, none were held, even though public education became more urgent. Farr suggested mailing the annual report to mayors of all cities and towns and to city councils of towns with water allotments; others wanted to include high school libraries on the mailing list.[62]

Even with Barkley's interest in better public relations, by 1975, the end of his managerial term, he realized that much more needed doing. Because of the immigration of "new people" into Boulder, Larimer, and Weld counties, he saw the need for "periodic releases" of information and "stories of interest" in relation to District activities. Operations and maintenance superintendent Robert G. Smith told of "considerable confusion" regarding the Bureau's and the District's activities. Director Kiyoshi Otsuka, representing Sedgwick County, said that "not one in 50 persons in the lower part of the river valley knew the purposes of the District or how its activities

Fishing at Shadow Mountain Reservoir with Mount Baldy in the background. A connecting channel allows boats to travel between Shadow Mountain and Grand Lake. (Courtesy Bureau of Reclamation.)

were carried forward." With two negative votes from Directors, the Board approved a motion for some form of service designed to publish releases of an "informational nature."[63] A few months later, Barkley presented a letter from newspaperman Merritt Lewis, a life-long resident of the South Platte Valley, who was interested in telling the District's story from a journalistic point of view. The Board accepted his suggestion of a $1,200-a-year retainer in return for ninety hours of work;[64] however, his wife's illness forced Lewis to leave the state. By this time, Barkley had retired, and the problem of how best to explain the District's mission and activities was as pressing as ever.

So much needed saying because so much was changing. From the beginning of Barkley's tenure, C–BT features took on a recreational importance the founders had never dreamed of.[65] Following completion of the entire Project, lake water recreation began to provide an unexpected boon to local communities. In 1958 the Board approved a memorandum of

A portion of the crowd attending the Grand Lake Icy Autocrossy in March 1966, indicating the increased use of the C–BT reservoirs for winter recreation. (Courtesy Bureau of Reclamation.)

understanding with the Bureau, the NPS, and the Estes Park Metropolitan Recreation District in which the District withdrew from supervisory or monetary interest in recreational activity.[66] As fishing opportunities at Lake Granby gained wide recognition, citizens of Granby and Grand Lake organized the Shadow Mountain National Recreation Area, hoping to develop a golf course, ski lift, skating rink, and other amenities.[67] On the East Slope a similar agreement was signed with the Larimer County Recreation Commission and the National Park Service.[68] Within a few years visitor use statistics revealed what a big business recreation had become. Operating on a bare-bones budget drawn from license fees and donations, the Larimer County Parks and Recreation Commission administered Horsetooth, Carter, Flatiron, and Rattlesnake (Pinewood) reservoirs and encouraged local service clubs to provide additional facilities for adjacent recreational areas.[69] In 1960 over 400,000 visitor days were recorded at these facilities, and three years later the number of visitors was up 20 percent.[70]

Horsetooth Reservoir rapidly became a recreational playground following completion in the early 1950s. This picture taken in 1972 attests to its popularity. (Courtesy Bureau of Reclamation.)

Across the country outdoor recreation exploded as the national pastime. President Lyndon B. Johnson's budget for 1965 included requests for $3.2 billion in recreational facilities for the Colorado River storage projects. Secretary of the Interior Udall warned that future outdoor recreation needs could inundate public park areas unless public and private agencies joined in a common control effort.[71] The NCWCD staff's challenge was maintaining the height of reservoirs at suitable recreational levels while preserving and protecting the primary purpose of the C–BT — providing supplemental water for farmers and municipalities.[72]

As federal interest in outdoor recreation branched out into preservation of rivers for their "wild and scenic" values, Farr spearheaded an effort to build a storage reservoir on the upper Poudre River. Sixty-four rivers were designated for study under the Wild and Scenic Rivers process; the Poudre River was one of these.[73] Farr's interest stemmed from the same conviction held by water men who watched helplessly as annual spring runoff disappeared across the state line into Nebraska. They believed that it made sense to build storage reservoirs as high as possible, where they would be of greatest value to all users and where evaporation would be at a minimum. Because discussion of a dam at the Narrows site near Fort Morgan was taking place at the same time, Farr began to push for a Poudre River project in 1959.

The initial plan was to build one reservoir at Idylwilde, a second at the confluence of the Poudre with Elkhorn Creek, a dam on the Little South Poudre, a holding reservoir on the North Poudre in the Livermore area, and enlarge Halligan Dam on the North Poudre.[74] Farr first formed a steering committee from representatives of the cities of Greeley and Fort Collins and the irrigation companies of the Poudre River basin. He announced in fall 1961 that a 250,000 acre-foot reservoir would be necessary to take care of municipal and agricultural needs. The Bureau, he reported, supported the project[75] because of possibilities for power revenue. Secretary Udall had already indicated that the newly elected administration of John F. Kennedy would vigorously support a program of public power "to meet the nation's growing demands."[76] Farr had already indicated that a considerable portion of project costs could be absorbed by power revenue, with the balance paid by municipal and agricultural water users.[77] Bureau officials supported a feasibility study because they saw the possibility of selling the project's peaking power.

As Director Moffitt saw it, the Poudre Storage project was the last phase of water development needed in northern Colorado.[78] Although the Bureau's feasibility study would take three years to complete, he and Farr were optimistic. They urged District employees to help coordinate efforts of the Poudre River water users and the Bureau because the feasibility study involved making positive arrangements with cities and irrigation companies for storage and use of impounded water.[79] The study also considered markets for the sale of peaking power. By early 1963, however, momentum on the project had been lost, which Farr explained as a result of the Bureau's preoccupation with the Fry-Ark project. Barkley and Clayton flew to Washington to pull some strings with Commissioner Floyd E. Dominy and his assistant Gilbert G. Stamm,[80] but the Bureau seemed to drag its feet. By mid-1963 the Bureau was suggesting a two-stage project over an eight-year period. The first stage was construction of Idylwilde Reservoir; the second stage involved building terminal storage at Grey Mountain, near the mouth of Poudre Canyon, and a power system between the two storage sites. Total cost was estimated at $111.1 million for 28,000 acre-feet of salable project water.[81] Farr reported that test drillings would begin in the fall and that the CLPWUA was discussing the type of district or subdistrict that might prove feasible for development and further cooperation with the NCWCD.[82]

But in spite of a regional drought and rumors of a national water shortage, the Poudre Storage project proceeded no further. It was shelved with the CWCB's endorsement of the Narrows project in fall 1964, ongoing interest in the Fry-Ark project, and the Bureau's belief that the Poudre River's flow was too minimal to generate substantial hydroelectric power.[83] Reintroduction of the Poudre project in the 1980s would be far more costly and complicated due to concerns about the impact of reclamation projects on the environment.

17 Response to Other Water Projects: The Narrows, Fryingpan-Arkansas, and Four Counties Water Association

The NCWCD's intense interest in the Narrows, Fry-Ark, Crown Zellerbach, and Four Counties Water Association projects reveals how closely the District had become connected to other water enterprises throughout the state. As further noted in Chapter 18, this involvement grew especially intense when Denver or the lower basin states tried to alter conditions or agreements relative to the Colorado River and its tributaries. When J. R. "Bob" Barkley took over as NCWCD manager in 1958, however, his attention was first drawn to a dispute that had been brewing for some time in Morgan, Logan, and Sedgwick counties and that promised to have a considerable impact on the District's overall plans for management of the South Platte drainage.

Director W. D. "Bill" Farr's enthusiasm for building storage on the upper Poudre River was shared by everyone who believed in water storage for future droughts, controlled spring runoff, preparations for floods, and better management of water releases to Nebraska. The Poudre facility was designed to be located in an area favorable to growing Front Range cities and least susceptible to evaporation losses. A dam on the lower South Platte River east of Greeley was equally desirable to reduce the danger of flood damage while providing better management of return flows for NCWCD taxpayers and water users in that area. Both projects were widely discussed, but neither has been built.

In 1931 the Army Corps of Engineers reported on the feasibility of a flood-control dam at the Narrows site near Fort Morgan. Because of the need for further studies and the intervention of World War II, the project remained unfunded. The Bureau of Reclamation, as part of its policy of creating river basin authorities after the war, took over the Narrows for inclusion in the Missouri River basin project, authorized in 1944 as one of more than 300 projects in the 1944 Pick-Sloan Act. While planning additional surveys, Bureau officials promoted this area for both flood

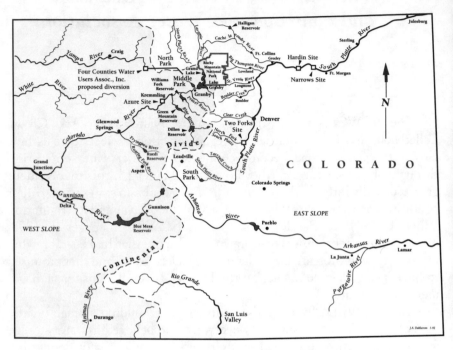

East-West Slope, 1960s.

control and irrigated agriculture. In 1949 it became part of President Harry S. Truman's flood control program, but the proposed location proved problematic to local interests, the state engineer, and the CWCB.[1] The ensuing dispute has continued to the present. Aware of certain hydrological difficulties, the Bureau planned to investigate the Narrows site more carefully. Long before the C–BT and the Roberts Tunnel were completed, the Bureau calculated that the lower South Platte River would be affected by approximately 164,000 acre-feet of new water coming from transmountain diversions,[2] but engineers did not know how to evaluate the impact of these return flows on existing distribution systems. By 1958 groups had already organized to support and to protest the Narrows project; the Bureau's reaction was to delay construction due to the "enormous cost" involved.[3]

Opposition was indeed well organized. The Weldona Valley Association meeting in Fort Morgan complained that the Narrows site would wipe out 15,000 acres of farmland and 250 farm families. Water backed up from the dam would inundate the towns of Weldona, Goodrich, and Orchard and would require rerouting of 22 miles of Union Pacific Railroad tracks.[4] Others pointed out that the Bijou and Riverside irrigation companies, both allottees of the NCWCD, would lose some of their service area and that the dam, as planned by the Bureau, appeared vulnerable to soil instability in the area designated for the right abutment.[5] But from Sterling to Julesburg such arguments fell on deaf ears. To these residents, the alternate Hardin site appeared equally flawed. Although it was an area of grazing and pastureland, not farmland, the Hardin location on the main river channel presented much higher construction costs due to the need for expensive sealing work and because the dam itself would stretch nearly 3 miles. After hearings on both sites, the CWCB concluded that the Fort Morgan and Sterling groups were too radically opposed for the board to make a recommendation; instead, the project was held in abeyance indefinitely.[6]

Paradoxically, most river basin residents strongly favored a storage reservoir somewhere on the lower South Platte River. Many hoped the NCWCD would take the lead toward compromise, but they waited in vain. Under J. M. Dille's administration, proponents of the Narrows site received little sympathy. While he delayed in publicly declaring himself against a dam at this location, Dille was known to oppose any project that would not benefit the Riverside and Bijou irrigation companies, with which he had invested a large portion of his professional life. When NCWCD Directors William Blair (Logan County) and Carl H. Metzger (Sedgwick County) pointed out that water tables were dropping, return flows were not getting

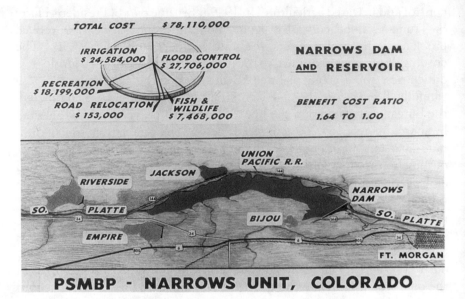

The Bureau's proposed Narrows project. (Courtesy Bureau of Reclamation.)

down river, and that Water District No. 64 wanted conduits for future delivery of 50,000 acre-feet of C–BT water, the NCWCD Board simply took no action. Dille referred them to Article 19 of the Repayment Contract, which established United States ownership of return flows and the District's right to determine the uses thereof.[7] When Blair tried to discuss his letter, which urged involvement, the Board responded with caution "to preclude financial obligation for such surveys and studies."[8] Following the disastrous drought years of the mid-fifties, Director J. C. Howell of Morgan County reintroduced the Narrows issue for NCWCD discussion. Dille noted that the Bureau had decided to develop its own proposal for a dam. The Board went on record as supporting "some plan for main stream storage on the South Platte River" and even discussed the possibility of initiating project development.[9]

The District's supposed lack of initiative frustrated water users on the lower South Platte. With Barkley as Board manager and Dille as consultant, proponents of the Narrows assumed that NCWCD staff would unilaterally oppose their project in meetings with the Bureau, Congress, and the CWCB;[10] their assumptions, however, were only partly correct. True, Dille and Barkley favored a reservoir upstream from the Bijou and Riverside diversions as well as an off-channel reservoir near the state line to permit controlled water releases to satisfy the South Platte River Compact with Nebraska. The Hardin site would be so superior in service, Barkley argued, that the higher cost was negligible,[11] but he consistently took the position that the District should not work for either site until the Fort Morgan and Sterling groups agreed on what they wanted. At the CWCB's request, Barkley chaired a steering committee, held meetings in both cities, and eventually concluded that even his group was divided on a site recommendation.[12] Consequently, he wanted the District to maintain neutrality until the Bureau entered into a complete study of return flows, water exchange possibilities, repayment plans, and engineering problems. Instead of unilaterally opposing the Narrows, as critics expected, the District was reserving judgment until more information was available. Meanwhile, the Bureau and the CWCB moved closer to endorsing the Narrows site.[13] Dille's death on February 24, 1963, may have seemed incidental to further developments in lower South Platte storage plans, but everyone knew that a powerful and respected Narrows opponent had left the struggle. During his last days Dille had been working on an article, published posthumously in the *Fort Morgan Times,* in which he argued that if the Bureau officially designated the Narrows site, a dam would never be built for a divided community in an area that would flood good farmland.[14]

By now, however, the Bureau was singularly focused on cost; the Hardin site estimate required $23 million more than the Narrows site.[15] Weldona valley residents indicated their willingness to cover some of the increased expense, but the Bureau's sensitivity to cost-benefit ratios precluded any investigations into arguments favoring Hardin. Late in the year, against opposition from the Fort Morgan Water Users Association, Narrows proponents formed the Lower South Platte Water Conservancy District (LSPWCD) to create an organization with which the United States could sign a construction contract.[16] Simultaneously, while opponents of the LSPWCD threatened opposition locally and in Congress, the CWCB formally voted to approve construction of the Narrows Dam. Felix "Larry" Sparks, CWCB director, said that they intended to ask the secretary of the interior to approve construction as soon as possible.[17] The CWCB's position as the state's official mouthpiece in water matters might have assured a simple, happier conclusion, but such was not the case. Over the next ten years the Bureau became increasingly reluctant to fund further studies on the impact of a Narrows Dam.

As the Fry-Ark slowly became the pet project of state officials, construction of the more controversial Narrows Dam appeared less urgent. In 1965, however, the South Platte River experienced a devastating June

The devastating June 1965 South Platte River flood forced the Bureau to focus again on providing flood control for the lower river. (Courtesy Bureau of Reclamation.)

flood, which caused the Bureau to focus attention once again on flood control for the lower part of the river. By this time though, the Two Forks site southwest of Denver attracted more interest for flood control and storage. Dam construction at the confluence of the Platte's north and south forks could have prevented the nearly $2 million in damage caused by the flood. More importantly, Two Forks was gradually becoming a central part of Denver's overall water expansion plans.[18] The flood also proved to the Bureau that the plan for a Narrows Dam was flawed; Bijou Creek, which had been expected to flood into the designated Narrows site,[19] widened in places to more than a mile and ravaged the very area where the Narrows Dam would have been located.

Undeterred by Bureau apathy, the LSPWCD continued to fight for construction of the Narrows Dam and appealed directly to the District to use its considerable political influence with the Bureau. Because Barkley was also the Colorado director of the National Reclamation Association (NRA), Eric Wendt, secretary-manager of the LSPWCD, wrote to ask for endorsement of the project. Although the CWCB was about to give its blessings to the Narrows as part of the grander Missouri River basin project, Barkley replied that the NRA had a tradition of avoiding endorsements or opposition to projects prior to congressional authorization. Once again the District's Board remained uncommitted.[20] This lack of response angered the LSPWCD. Already upset by the District's opposition to their claim for a 1931 decree on the Narrows site, LSPWCD officials requested that NCWCD representatives testify with them before the Interior and Insular Affairs committees of Congress in support of Narrows. When the Board declined, Wendt and LSPWCD attorney Monte Pascoe personally appealed to the Board for District support. Pascoe argued that the LSPWCD was willing to subordinate its decree to that of the NCWCD; because both the CWCB and the Bureau had endorsed the project, he could see no reason for the District not to add its blessing. Board members agreed to endorse a statement for downstream channel storage, but they would go no further.[21] Project endorsement moved ahead anyway. By summer 1970 Department of the Interior officials had recommended congressional action, Governor John Love had voiced his support for construction, and Senate and House committee hearings had begun.[22] Incredibly, Sparks testified that opposition to the Narrows had been converted into support. By the end of summer both houses of Congress had passed a compromise bill that President Richard M. Nixon signed into law.[23]

Construction never began. The Nixon administration provided funds for preconstruction planning in 1972, but economy measures wiped out further appropriations in 1973 and 1974.[24] The LSPWCD had successfully allotted 75 percent of the 138,000 Narrows units at $5.49 per unit and had agreed to annual payments to the federal government of $525,000 per year for fifty years. Even with top priority designation by the CWCB, not a shovelful of dirt was moved.[25] The Colorado delegation in Washington urged the administration to appropriate construction funds, yet the Narrows project got caught in fallout from the Watergate scandal, escalating cost estimates, and the clamor for studies of environmental impact. In 1974 the Bureau reported to the Morgan County Planning Commission that construction would be launched in 1977 and would last four years.[26] Unfortunately, no one anticipated President Jimmy Carter's anti-reclamation "hit list." Hopes for the Narrows were dashed again in 1978.

Looking back at the District's role in the Narrows situation, its "neutral" role clearly played a part in the outcome. Although the District was probably not the power broker the LSPWCD thought, its growing opposition to the Narrows site did influence state and federal agencies in the location dispute. When the LSPWCD organized, Barkley felt that if they wanted to absolve the District of further responsibility, that was fine.[27] But delays and indecision were also caused by the lower river's inability to overcome legitimate fears about the dam's impact and by territorial squabbles over site location. The Bureau never completed comparative studies of the Hardin and Narrows sites. When Congress finally voted appropriations for the project, a combination of politics, national events, and growing concern about reclamation boondoggles provided a hostile reception. Even in 1990 both the LSPWCD and the Central Colorado Water Conservancy District (CCWCD) continued to work for an on-channel reservoir, with filings on both sites but no hint of federal funding. As NCWCD manager Larry D. Simpson has recently suggested, the District might best build a reservoir along the lower South Platte River without federal participation. "Better to do it ourselves," he noted, "than to belly up to the pork barrel."[28]

The Board was prepared to play a much more active role regarding the Fry-Ark project. Transmountain diversion plans of the Southeastern Colorado Water Conservancy District (SECWCD) created a pronounced ripple effect on the West Slope and in Denver. Ultimately, the NCWCD's relations with the DWB, the CRWCD, and the CWCB were affected by plans to take an annual average of 69,200 acre-feet from a Colorado River tributary (Fryingpan River) to the East Slope. In July 1958, three months after the creation of the SECWCD by the Pueblo District Court, the CRWCD registered anxiety about yet another plan to take West Slope water for use on the Front Range. The CRWCD already suspected that a Narrows project might facilitate additional diversion through the C–BT. With official formation of an organization to build the Fry-Ark project, West Slope leaders worried that they would have insufficient water for future development of an oil shale industry.[29] The real issue, however, emerged from their sense of betrayal.

When the CWCB passed a resolution in 1951 to approve the Fry-Ark project, the unanimous vote included adoption of an important quid pro quo introduced by representatives of the CRWCD: no additional transmountain diversions authorized and financed by the federal government until West Slope water needs were adequately surveyed.[30] Specifically citing 1943 statutory language, the resolution reiterated that water exportation from the West Slope would be subject to provisions of the Colorado River Compact and the Boulder Canyon Project Act. Further, any works or facilities "shall be designed, constructed and operated in such a manner that the present appropriations of water, and in addition thereto, prospective

Ruedi Reservoir was built on the West Slope near Aspen as part of the Fry-Ark project. (Courtesy Bureau of Reclamation.)

uses of water for irrigation and other beneficial consumptive purposes, including consumptive uses for domestic, mining, and industrial purposes within the natural basin of the Colorado River . . . will not be impaired or increased in cost at the expense of the water users in the said natural basin." Finally, in the event of a compact call from lower basin states, "the diversions by the project for use in eastern Colorado shall be curtailed before there is any curtailment of the right to store water in Aspen Reservoir in a quantity not in excess of the capacity of that reservoir."[31] Understanding West Slope expectations that this agreement would be honored by Colorado is critical to an appreciation of succeeding events.

When Frank Delaney learned in 1953 that the Bureau had not completed the agreed-upon surveys and had estimated at least five more years to do the job, he vented his feelings. The occasion was Denver's request to the CWCB to have the Blue River project included in the Colorado River Storage Project (CRSP) package. A fair decision, he said, had been made in 1951 to which every party was bound unless good reasons showed that it should be rescinded. If Denver's transmountain plans for the Blue River were to be approved by the CWCB as part of the CRSP legislation prior to completion of West Slope surveys, the West Slope would make trouble for the Fry-Ark project. This might cost the West Slope some water, he concluded, but [we] "would like to say to posterity that [we] tried to save the water which may be needed for oil shale development."[32] Delaney's warning was not an idle threat. When the CWCB approved Denver's Blue River project as part of the CRSP and the Bureau of Reclamation and Bureau of the Budget endorsed the Fry-Ark project, West Slope representatives went to Washington, sided with California opponents, and testified against pending legislation. Preston Walker of the *Grand Junction Sentinel* fanned the flames of a new East-West Slope dispute by accusing the CWCB of betrayal. He charged Denver officials with trying to "crucify" the West Slope.[33]

Whatever the East Slope's motive, West Slope wrath was sufficient to halt congressional authorization. Colorado learned very slowly that a penurious Congress was happy to delay expensive reclamation projects when the region to derive benefit was divided. After representatives of twelve West Slope counties told the Bureau that they would oppose any further transmountain diversion to protect their water for future oil shale development,[34] the Fry-Ark project lost support in Congress. Frustrated, Director Sparks asked the CWCB to approve a two-year study of "all present and future West Slope water requirements." He also agreed to convene CRWCD and SECWCD representatives to iron out differences, and he requested $15,000 from the state legislature to help his staff survey the present and future water needs of the West Slope.[35] Sparks's talented leadership produced almost immediate results. As of August 1958 an agreement allowed for a better compensatory reservoir on the Fryingpan River (Ruedi Dam) and also recognized decreed water rights on both the Fryingpan and Roaring Fork rivers as senior to the Fry-Ark project. The following year, all parties signed a "peace pact" in what Governor McNichols called "a historic foundation for unity."[36] Colorado's congressional delegation was now prepared to reintroduce Fry-Ark legislation.

Congressman Wayne N. Aspinall, chairman of the powerful House Committee on Interior and Insular Affairs, who guided the bill through preliminary phases, was reluctant to bring it to the floor for full debate until he could be certain of votes for passage. President John F. Kennedy recognized Aspinall's efforts and fully endorsed the Fry-Ark project in a letter to *Denver Post* editor, E. Palmer Hoyt.[37] The usual anti-reclamation forces were marshalled in opposition; however, JFK's assistant secretary of the interior, Kenneth Holum, promoted Fry-Ark as a "duplicate of the C–BT Project, one, if you please that has certainly changed the economic dimensions of northern Colorado."[38] The SECWCD turned to the

NCWCD for help in an effort to overcome hostile opponents in Washington, especially those who consistently opposed reclamation projects as a matter of principle and who now branded Fry-Ark as the "Rube Goldberg of the Rockies."[39] The District Board agreed to provide whatever aid possible.[40] Now that the West Slope had been mollified, support for the project could in no way jeopardize relations with the CRWCD.

Within months congressional opposition had ceased. Both the House and Senate approved the Fry-Ark bill in summer 1962, and President Kennedy signed it as "an excellent example of full development of our water resources to provide maximum benefits for all our people."[41] Two years later construction crews broke ground at the site of Ruedi Dam and Reservoir. East-West Slope harmony seemed evident at this point; however, when a large newsprint company declared its intention to build a pulp mill in the Kremmling area, the old jealousies and suspicions regarding Colorado River water rights resurfaced. This time the central role of Green Mountain Reservoir caused the NCWCD to threaten a lawsuit against the Bureau of Reclamation. Had it been filed, legal action might have prevented the Fry-Ark project from receiving congressional approval.[42]

In fall 1959 the chief industrial engineer of Crown Zellerbach Corporation met with CRWCD attorney John Barnard, Jr., to discuss a possible plant near Kremmling on the Colorado River. Five months later company representatives told Barnard of their interest in building up to four plants, each of which would require a constant 15 cfs flow of water for plant operations, 5 cfs of which would be consumed. Barnard told Crown Zellerbach that the CRWCD board would be interested in promoting this development of western Colorado's resources.[43] With cooperation from the West Slope assured, Crown Zellerbach attorneys specifically requested from both the Bureau and the CWCB a constant and guaranteed supply of water from Green Mountain Reservoir. While the Bureau delayed response, the CWCB endorsed Crown Zellerbach's plan at the August 1960 meeting. Sparks requested the secretary of the interior to contract with Crown Zellerbach for delivery of 5,000 acre-feet of water a year from Green Mountain Reservoir.[44]

Almost immediately the DWB announced to the Bureau its desire to be involved in any new interpretation of how Green Mountain water could be used. During the previous fall Denver and Colorado Springs had been interested in "replacement releases" at Green Mountain Reservoir. When Crown Zellerbach announced its objectives, DWB chief counsel Glenn G. Saunders argued that the 100,000 acre-feet power pool at Green Mountain had been established for the benefit of both East and West

Slopes. Although he stated Denver's intention of "scrupulously [giving] recognition to the prior claims" of the NCWCD in the 52,000 acre-feet at that reservoir, he told the Bureau that Denver "wanted to have an opportunity to bid and negotiate for use of all or any part of the capacity of Green Mountain Reservoir not committed to the Colorado–Big Thompson Project."[45] Any operation modification at Green Mountain Reservoir concerned the NCWCD. In response to Denver's proprietarial interpretation of that water, attorney Jack Clayton wrote the secretary of the interior that the "District must be party to any negotiations involving the operation of said reservoir and a party to any contract which might arise therefrom."[46] The District, however, made this same argument with less success during subsequent negotiations with Crown Zellerbach, whose plans they only learned of in August 1960, when Barkley received the CWCB's agenda for the August 1960 meeting in Alamosa. Attached to the agenda were copies of letters from Crown Zellerbach's attorney, John P. Akolt, and Philip P. Smith, secretary-engineer of the CRWCD. Smith's letter stated that the CRWCD supported Crown Zellerbach's proposal because it "complied fully with the provisions and intent of the operating principles for the Colorado–Big Thompson Project as set forth in Senate Document 80."[47]

Barkley and Clayton, who could not agree with this contention, argued that Senate Document 80 stipulated that anyone who benefited from the C–BT should share construction as well as operation and maintenance costs. Furthermore, they insisted, the District had to be involved in any contract signed between the Bureau and other parties. Finally, any new contract must stipulate that the contracting party "discontinue their diversions and storage in advance of the discontinuance of the diversions and utilization of water by the Colorado–Big Thompson Project or any of its components or units on the eastern or western slopes of Colorado."[48] But the District had difficulty being heard. Region 7 director John N. Spencer simply acknowledged that Clayton and Barkley's seven-page letter had been sent to the Bureau's regional solicitor. Meanwhile, he noted, the commissioner was giving attention to the Crown Zellerbach proposal. Clayton and Barkley were not pleased with this response, which they considered somewhat patronizing. In spite of their formal and reasoned request to be included in contract negotiations, they felt excluded from active participation. In fact, they received the first contract draft from the Bureau without any request for District opinions. In two letters to the Bureau, Clayton and Barkley expressed their disappointment that the District was a "contractual partner with the United States in the use, operation, and maintenance of any or all features and facilities of the

Project. We see no reason why we should not be treated as such." The NCWCD had no objections, they said, to the sale of Green Mountain water to Crown Zellerbach "so long as the reservoir operations will provide the replacement necessary for maximum trans-mountain diversion of water by our Project, and so long as the manner of Green Mountain operation does not require additional releases from Granby or Willow Creek reservoirs."[49]

An issue of even greater concern to Crown Zellerbach, the CRWCD, the NCWCD, and the Bureau was what this water should cost. The company complained that a charge of $8.50 per acre-foot was "absolutely prohibitive" and warned that if the Bureau insisted on this figure, "that in itself might be a sufficient deterrent to cause Crown Zellerbach not to come into Colorado with its new industrial enterprise."[50] On behalf of the CRWCD, Barnard agreed. Citing the historical basis for Senate Document 80 and construction of Green Mountain Reservoir, as well as the original objectives of Congressman Edward T. Taylor, he advised Spencer that the Bureau was entitled to income from power generation at Green Mountain, but the water that entered the Colorado River was then available for "future agricultural, industrial and municipal development in Western Colorado." If the Bureau insisted on selling "this compensatory storage for all or more than the traffic will bear," Barnard warned, "it is my conclusion that we in Western Colorado can 'write off' the Green Mountain Reservoir as an asset to our area."[51]

The District, meanwhile, insisted that the proposed $8.50 per acre-foot charge was "ridiculous and preposterous," but on the low side.[52] Again the Bureau appeared disinterested but made some revisions in the contract without consulting the NCWCD and sent the revised draft to all concerned parties. Clayton and Barkley tried once more to get the Bureau's attention. They "assumed" that approval of any contract by the NCWCD Board was necessary. Having just signed a contract with a municipal corporation (City of Englewood) for carrying an independent water supply at the rate of $10 per acre-foot, they lamented the low price demanded of Crown Zellerbach; however, they concluded, the Board had instructed them "to work with you in every way possible way to reconcile the existing divergent views."[53] When Spencer returned another draft of the contract, noting Crown Zellerbach's acceptance and that it had been sent to Washington for approval, Barkley decided to make the District's position even clearer. Apparently, he wrote Spencer, "no cognizance has been given to the views and suggestions of our Board of Directors." Under these circumstances, "it seems most doubtful that District approval of the presently proposed contract can be expected. If the contract is executed without District approval, the Board may take such action as is appropriate to have the contract set aside."[54] Spencer replied that the Bureau "appreciated having the suggestions and views of your District on this contract . . . [but] we do not believe it necessary to ask the District to be a party to the Crown Zellerbach contract or to have a resolution of approval of the contract by the Board."[55]

The Department of the Interior executed the contract on June 28, 1962, basing prerogative on the assumption that the United States retained dominion and control over water released from Green Mountain Reservoir.[56] Two weeks later the District received copies of the contract from the Denver office. Crown Zellerbach never built the pulp plant — a blow to the West Slope — but the Bureau had established a principle that continued to cause friction for another twenty years. As the shale oil industry began to grow in the mid-sixties, the Bureau announced plans to sell water from the 100,000 acre-foot pool in Green Mountain Reservoir.[57] District representatives reiterated that their position had not altered since the conflict over Crown Zellerbach. An impasse, with the real threat of litigation, pointed to the fact that increasing demands on Project water from both sides of the Continental Divide, as well as requests to use the C–BT system to carry foreign water, now required increased NCWCD vigilance to avoid precedents that could injure present and future District residents.

Consulting engineer John P. Elliott presented this kind of challenge to the Board when he asked to use the Adams Tunnel for water delivery from the Yampa River to East Slope municipalities. His proposal seemed bizarre in 1958 when he first described it in a letter to Barkley; however, his earlier plans for the Homestake project had so benefited Aurora and Colorado Springs that a proposal to bring 50,000 acre-feet of water from the Yampa River to Lake Granby demanded the Board's serious attention. Whether or not the District could benefit legally from Elliott's purchase of unused Adams Tunnel capacity, the Board declined to discuss the matter further until Elliott presented full details of his plan.[58]

After a two-year hiatus, Elliott again contacted Barkley. If he successfully secured a conditional decree to Yampa River water, he would transport a like quantity to the headwaters of Willow Creek through a series of exchanges involving the Big Grizzly and Illinois rivers, both tributaries of the North Platte. In view of the District's operation and maintenance obligations, Barkley replied that the Board could not consider a carriage contract through the tunnel without some proportional cost sharing.[59] Enter the City of Englewood. Several years earlier, the attorney for Englewood, Mark

Shivers, had been publicly ridiculed by U.S. Attorney William H. Veeder during attempts to negotiate settlement of the Blue River decrees in Washington, D.C. What prompted Veeder's outburst was the city's purchase of Moffat Tunnel Water and Development Company's water rights on several tributaries of the Fraser River. Veeder mocked Englewood's contention that the city would someday use these decrees. The other parties to these negotiations were so appalled by Veeder's insensitive actions that they agreed to stipulate Englewood's rights to this water in the final Blue River consent decree. Englewood had to find a way to get the decreed water to the East Slope.[60]

Shivers visited the NCWCD Board in summer 1960 to explain his efforts to work out a carriage contract with the DWB to bring water through Denver's Moffat Tunnel system. Saunders, who had proved obstinate, was threatening Englewood with astronomical charges. If the District would agree to carry his water through the C–BT system, Englewood would build the necessary reservoirs and canals to reach Lake Granby. The Board immediately decided to begin discussions and studies with both Englewood and the Bureau to determine the legal, physical, and financial feasibility of such a project. Board members and District staff knew that the facilities would probably never be built, but successful negotiation of a contract with the District would allow Shivers's return to Denver with an improved bargaining position.[61] Coincidentally, the Board evaluated Elliott's second request to use C–BT facilities for carriage of Yampa River water, and the Directors approved $3,500 for a feasibility study.[62] They also invited Elliott to explain his plan at the December 1960 Board meeting. Elliott assured the Directors that 55,000 acre-feet of water were potentially available from the Yampa River. Although he was still negotiating to secure conditional rights, his objective was to furnish this water to Westminster, Broomfield, and other incorporated municipalities north of Denver. Because he understood that his Four Counties Water Association (later determined to be Elliott's private company) could not receive a perpetual right to utilization of the C–BT's unused capacity, he was willing to accept a term contract. Following this presentation, the Board voted to inform Elliott that its position would remain undetermined until after the Bureau completed the feasibility study.[63]

While the Bureau simultaneously engaged in negotiations with Crown Zellerbach, the District concentrated on executing a carriage contract with Englewood for the remainder of 1961. The first-draft agreement indicated that the Bureau was willing to incorporate the District's opinions. The Bureau recognized that both the NCWCD and the United States might profit from carrying approximately 6,000 acre-feet of water for Englewood through the C–BT system.[64] Within a week a District staff memorandum stated unequivocally that "the District does have power to transport other than Project water for all uses within the District."[65] On July 19 the secretary of interior approved the carriage contract in final form. The next month, NCWCD Directors voted a formal approval resolution, and the Englewood City Council passed an ordinance approving the carriage contract.[66] Although attorney William Kelly immediately expressed reservations,[67] Barkley argued that the arrangement enhanced the District's water supply at Lake Granby and provided unexpected revenue to help meet District financial obligations under the 1938 Repayment Contract.[68] For Shivers, the tactic paid off. Denver agreed to a water rental contract allowing Englewood to pump 6,000 acre-feet of exchange water from the South Platte River into a reservoir specifically built to store Fraser River rights delivered through the Moffat Tunnel.[69] Elliott felt encouraged by Englewood's success and increased his efforts to negotiate a similar contract.

Within weeks of the secretary of interior's signature on the Englewood contract, Elliott requested carriage of water through the South Platte Supply Canal to Westminster. He hoped that the Englewood contract would set a precedent for his project, but the District did not agree. To Clayton, the two plans differed because Elliott wanted C–BT facilities to deliver water outside the NCWCD area; on the other hand, Englewood "understood that sometime in the future it might be necessary for them to become part of the Northern Colorado Water Conservancy District."[70] The Board of Directors' additional concern was that any policy statement that implied support for plans of the Four Counties Water Association would probably reopen the controversy between East and West Slopes. Although the Directors had not closed the door on Elliott, they would wait until the Fry-Ark legislation was enacted before further consideration.[71] That occurred in summer 1962. The following year the District prepared a draft contract for conveyance of Elliott's water through the District's works. District courts in Grand and Routt counties, however, denied the application for a conditional decree for surplus waters in the Yampa River basin. Furthermore, the CWCB had taken the position that further diversion of water from the West Slope through C–BT facilities violated Senate Document 80.[72] In the long run, Elliott's failure proved of immense benefit to northern Colorado because the excess carriage capacity of the C–BT system was later fully subscribed for the Municipal Subdistrict's Windy Gap project.

Against the advice of attorney John M. Sayre, who conveyed the Board's concern over using C–BT facilities for private profit,[73] Elliott continued to solicit the support of Front Range municipalities while he appealed to the State Supreme Court to overturn the district courts' denial of a conditional water decree. His optimism was rewarded. Following an appearance before Directors with his attorney, Monte Pascoe, when he noted that both Boulder and Fort Collins were interested in water he could deliver,[74] the Supreme Court ruled in his favor, seemingly removing the last obstacle to a carriage contract with the District. But events worked against Elliott. Even with Front Range cities convinced that his plan would resolve their predicted future water shortages, success depended on complete support and participation by the NCWCD, which was now uninterested. In addition to a variety of legal and contractual concerns that had not surfaced during negotiations with Englewood, the District saw serious problems with the West Slope. CRWCD anger over the Supreme Court's decision combined with a West Slope anxiety over potential "raids" on the Colorado River by Denver and other Front Range entities.[75] The *Grand Junction Sentinel* urged the District to oppose Elliott and to deny him use of the C–BT. "To take any other stand," the paper said, "is to break faith with Western Colorado men who negotiated the agreement settling the big transmountain water diversion battle of the mid-1930s."[76] Such NCWCD action proved unnecessary because Elliott unexpectedly suffered a fall at his home during Easter week. A blood clot developed on his brain; on May 20 he underwent surgery, but the damage had been done. He died on June 16, 1966.[77]

Although the project was defunct, Elliott's seven-year efforts to bring water to East Slope municipalities left an important legacy that came to fruition almost immediately as the Windy Gap project. Boulder, Estes Park, Longmont, Loveland, and Fort Collins soon met with the Four Counties Water Association to discuss possible acquisition of Elliott's conditional water rights. Because the DWB also bid for these rights, the five cities (joined shortly by Greeley) did not pursue further negotiations.[78] Instead, they met with the Bureau and NCWCD representatives to discuss water importation to their communities through the C–BT system to East Slope reservoirs from a reservoir at Windy Gap, just below the mouth of the Fraser River. Through formation of a NCWCD subdistrict, the Six Cities wanted to use some of the C–BT's unused carriage capacity to bring more than 30,000 acre-feet of water through the Adams Tunnel;[79] thus began in 1966 the planning phase of a project that owed its intellectual roots to John P. Elliott.

Two other requests came into the District to use the Adams Tunnel's unused carriage capacity to deliver "foreign" water to East Slope entities. Both met with resistance but for different reasons. WSSC made several inquiries about shutting down its costly Grand River Ditch and using the C–BT to carry Colorado River water rights to the East Slope. Even though Bureau Commissioner John Page had promised in 1937 that WSSC could route its water through the C–BT system "if and when . . . [they] so desire,"[80] the District declined the company's request for two reasons. First, the C–BT's delivery point on the Poudre River necessitated a very complicated exchange that might jeopardize North Poudre Irrigation Company's water rights during a drought year. Second, the District was uncertain about sufficient storage space in Horsetooth Reservoir for WSSC's decreed rights; on this basis, WSSC's request for a carriage contract had to be denied.[81]

Fort Collins's request for a carriage contract precipitated a more violent outburst. In May 1963 the city met with the Bureau to discuss purchase of water rights for the Mitchell Ditch, north of Grand Lake. The city wanted to transport .625 cfs (452.4 acre-feet per year) through the Adams Tunnel.[82] H. P. Dugan, Region 7 director, asked the city to get opinions from the CWCB and the NCWCD. After reviewing Senate Document 80 and considering the possibility of injury to West Slope water users, Sparks recommended approval to the CWCB.[83] Under a contract similar to Englewood's, the NCWCD told Fort Collins to first file for a change in point of diversion with Grand County District Court to determine its right to transfer water to the East Slope.[84] By implication, the Board apparently felt that a contract could be negotiated subject to District Court approval. A heated exchange between Barkley and William H. Nelson, associate editor of the *Grand Junction Sentinel* and a West Slope CWCB representative, exposed the real issues in what seemed a simple contractual matter. Nelson wrote to Sparks that the Fort Collins request and Sparks's facile approval thereof were symptomatic of long-standing difficulties between East and West Slopes. He chastised the CWCB for what he called an "emerging pattern." The West Slope was asked to negotiate, "when it is necessary to grease the political skids in Congress. . . . Then, when we have lost our political leverage and when the facilities are a physical fact, the Water Board, in your opinion as expressed in the [September 11, 1963] memorandum, should allow the courts to decide the issue." He strongly opposed the "piggy-back contract" with Fort Collins, or Elliott, unless the West Slope participated in negotiations.[85]

Although Barkley did not receive a copy of Nelson's letter, he soon became aware of its contents. He told Nelson that transport of Mitchell

The NCWCD Board of Directors and staff in 1963. Seated (left to right) R. J. Lamborn, J. M. Dille, J. Ben Nix, Ed F. Munroe, and Clyde "Red" Moffitt. Standing (left to right) Bob Barkley, James C. Nelson, Herb Vandemoer, John Moore, George Deines, Gordon Dyekman, Robert M. Gilbert, W. D. Farr, Jack Clayton, Dennis Walker, John M. Sayre, Earl F. Phipps, and Kish Otsuka. (Courtesy NCWCD.)

Ditch water to Fort Collins would have no impact on West Slope water users because of the location and the date of decree. Furthermore, he "resented" the implication that the District had "ignored," "violated," "tossed aside," or "made worthless" agreements "to which we sincerely committed ourselves in Senate Document 80." The transfer of water, he said, falls under the jurisdiction of the Grand County District Court, not the CWCB. Approval would not violate Senate Document 80 or the 1955 Blue River consent decree in either letter or spirit.[86] Nelson replied with equal fervor on the "emerging pattern." He called Barkley's attention to Elliott's plans, those of the "bungling Bunglers," the Fry-Ark project, and Denver's bullish approach to Green Mountain Reservoir. He reiterated the West Slope's position that all parties should be involved in amendments or modifications to contracts for federally funded projects. He urged Barkley to take a "broad look" at the West Slope's position.[87]

The exchange of correspondence might have continued indefinitely. Both men represented fundamental positions that they believed in and that were justified by history and the facts as they saw them. In a sense, the argument proved academic, for Fort Collins never signed a carriage contract; however, Barkley, the NCWCD Board, and the CWCB realized that even the smallest request for transmountain diversion of Colorado River water would cause West Slope hackels to rise. Nevertheless, Barkley was as convinced as Charles Hansen had been in the 1930s that the Colorado River — "the one last water hole" for the state — was not being utilized to the fullest. Believing that Colorado's water needs were growing faster than the existing means to fulfill them, he saw no reason to retreat from plans and policies to further develop the resource that the West Slope wanted so vigorously to protect.[88]

18 New Challenges From the Colorado River Basin

When East and West Slope representatives agreed on Senate Document 80, one issue was tabled for future resolution: the amount of water that the Project would release to the Colorado River to preserve an adequate fishery ("live stream") between Lake Granby and the mouth of the Fraser River. In 1937 Grand County's special representative, A. C. "Doc" Sudan, had insisted on a minimum release of 18,000 to 24,000 acre-feet a year, but Charles Hansen and J. M. Dille argued that 1,000 acre-feet per month was sufficient. Because neither side wanted to sacrifice the entire C–BT Project over this impasse, and at the suggestion of Commissioner John C. Page, they consented to an article in the "Manner of Operations" section that authorized the secretary of the interior to make a final determination after the Project was in full operation.[1]

The secretary established a temporary schedule for releases from Willow Creek Reservoir and Lake Granby in 1951, but the District grew increasingly frustrated with an inflexible arrangement that required a minimum of 7 cfs monthly from Willow Creek Reservoir. Attorneys and staff pointed out that before the C–BT was built, Willow Creek had dried up from decreed irrigation diversions during summer months; they also complained that an inflexible release schedule for both reservoirs deprived the Project of valuable storage water in wet years.[2] Efforts to revise the temporary schedule and to make a final determination took almost ten years. The Colorado Game and Fish Department pressed for settlement in 1958, a year of abnormally high water supplies on the West Slope; but fixed terms of the temporary schedule required releases of over 36,000 acre-feet for irrigation needs and fish releases from the two reservoirs. J. R. "Bob" Barkley and Dille queried former Board member — then undersecretary of the interior — Hatfield Chilson, about the District's chances for a final decision. Chilson recommended a trip to Washington to meet personally with Secretary Fred A. Seaton. Barkley and attorney Jack Clayton departed immediately[3] but were unsuccessful. The secretary, who was having a

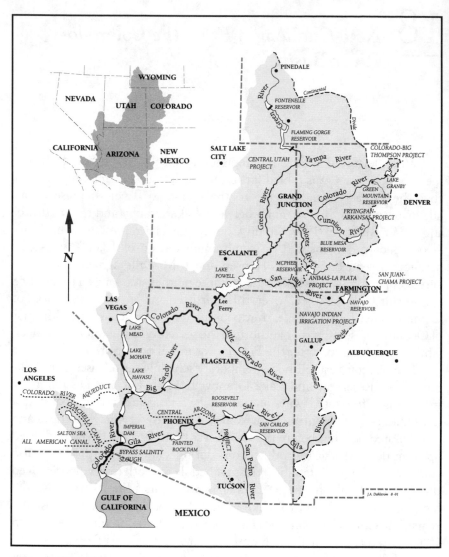

Colorado River Basin.

similar problem on Idaho's Snake River, was unwilling to make a determination for the C–BT at that time.

Barkley persisted, and by late summer he had persuaded the secretary to meet with the four interested parties: NCWCD, Colorado Game and Fish Department, U.S. Fish and Wildlife Service (including the Bureau of Sports Fisheries and Wildlife [BSFW]), and the Bureau. Edward Fischer, associate solicitor of the Interior Department, convened the meeting and heard all proposals. Although he was not empowered to decide, Fischer promised to relay the opinions and data to the assistant secretary of the interior for final determination.[4] Still nothing happened. Barkley and Clayton returned to Washington in 1959, at which time they became aware of Interior's extreme sensitivity to the fish-release issue. Environmental organizations were now sufficiently active to begin questioning Eisenhower administration policies.[5] Acting Secretary of the Interior Elmer Bennett wrote that he was considering a District proposal, but the year ended without further action.[6]

Nineteen sixty proved equally disappointing. Environmental causes were popular as Washington focused on the November elections. Following John F. Kennedy's victory, Barkley pushed one final time for a permanent fish-release schedule before the inauguration of Democrat Kennedy on January 20, 1961.[7] He and Clayton returned to the capital to find success, but not without struggle. Exasperating talks with the BSFW became even more uncomfortable under pressures of pre-inauguration events. Hotel officials made it clear to Barkley and Clayton that rooms were reserved only for celebrants. To achieve an agreement that would allow fish releases from both Granby and Willow Creek reservoirs, the BSFW insisted on only one gauging station below Lake Granby on the Colorado River. Reluctantly, Barkley and Clayton agreed in order to salvage the rest of the proposal. With their bags packed and waiting in the hotel lobby, they finally obtained approval from federal agencies on January 19, 1961.[8]

The agreement meant a savings of 8,000 to 12,000 acre-feet a year in water spilled for fish releases, depending on the type of water year.[9] Although, in retrospect, the District would have been better off accepting Sudan's demands in 1937, Barkley felt satisfied with the final settlement. He was reminded of the unpleasant negotiations with the Bureau of Sports Fisheries and Wildlife several years later when Region 7 director John N. Spencer called him to Denver to explain why Willow Creek was dry and fish were dying. Barkley reminded Spencer that his own BSFW had specifically denied the District the option of releasing water from Willow Creek Reservoir. Because the C–BT system now needed as much water as it could pump from Willow Creek Reservoir to Lake Granby, the fish would pay the consequences of bureaucratic rigidity. Case closed. Barkley left the meeting and returned to Loveland.[10] Such obdurate behavior, which occurred infrequently under Barkley's direction, reflected the immense amounts of time and energy the District expended in negotiations to protect a water supply provided for and protected in Senate Document 80. When Denver suddenly declared its right to Green Mountain Reservoir water under this same agreement, the District found itself engaged in another battle over rights to water in the upper Colorado River basin, this one with much higher stakes.

Denver insisted that Senate Document 80 provided for "replacement releases" from Green Mountain Reservoir in favor of Denver's Williams Fork Reservoir. In other words, Denver claimed that the required releases from Williams Fork and the Fraser rivers could be made from the 100,000 acre-foot pool in Green Mountain Reservoir so that Denver might store water for future use in its own Williams Fork Reservoir.[11] Denver's interest in accumulating additional water rights, while simultaneously developing greater flexibility in its West Slope collection system, was nothing new. The city had been buying up ranches in the Green Mountain area since 1951 to acquire the appurtenant water rights. Summit and Grand counties objected to losing the tax revenue, but land acquired by municipalities for water supply reasons was tax exempt under Colorado law.[12] Denver also expanded the storage capacity of its Williams Fork Reservoir, a move that NCWCD officials supported. They recognized that the enlargement would be "beneficial to the area served by [the] District in future years by assuring additional protection of [the] contractual obligations and responsibilities to the water users of the Colorado River basin."[13] Little did they imagine how Denver would attempt to amplify water storage at the expense of the C–BT and in violation of Senate Document 80 and the 1955 Blue River decrees.

DWB attorney Glenn G. Saunders was determined to stretch the meaning of Senate Document 80 to fit the needs of his principal client. During meetings of the CWCB, he infuriated West Slope representatives by insisting that the 100,000 acre-foot pool in Green Mountain Reservoir "may find its highest and best use for the people of Colorado in Eastern Colorado." He represented about half the water users in the state, Saunders argued, and he agreed with CWCB Director Felix "Larry" Sparks that Senate Document 80 was one of the worst operating documents he had ever seen. Perhaps, he concluded, even the remaining "50,000" acre-feet commitment of the C–BT in Green Mountain Reservoir could be better met out of some other [unspecified] resource."[14] John Barnard, Sr., attorney for the CRWCD and president of the Colorado River Water Users Association, responded to his ploy as an attempted "bastardization" of the Blue River Pact. "We still stand unprotected," he lamented, and forced "to watch every gopher hole . . . to see that it is not used for transmountain diversion." What bothered Barnard most was that Denver's water supply appeared adequate to furnish a population more than twice its size, but the DWB under Saunders's urging continued "crying to this board [CWCB] and to the general public and to everyone who will listen that Denver . . . and the adjacent areas are drying up." To the best of his knowledge, Barnard said, the West Slope had never attempted "to deny the City of Denver the water it needed for its municipal use at the present time and those [needs] which will come into existence in the reasonable future." He believed that the Queen City was really interested in acquiring water to rent or sell to the highest bidder in the South Platte Valley. Consequently, and in response to Denver's recent petition to the secretary of the interior to bid on the uncommitted portion of Green Mountain Reservoir,[15] Barnard stated emphatically that Green Mountain Reservoir was built for western Colorado alone, and that "there ain't going to be no more Blue River stipulations with the City of Denver as far as I am concerned."[16]

Conflict was on the rise once again between East and West Slopes. While DWB officials opened bids for construction of Dillon Dam and Reservoir, the secretary of the interior called all parties to the Blue River decrees to Washington to settle the controversy out of court. The meeting took place before Assistant Secretary of the Interior Fred G. Aandahl. The Department of Justice was annoyed with Denver for trying to reopen the 1955 decrees;[17] Barnard, representing the West Slope, stirred the pot even more by accusing Denver of secret, "ambitious, comprehensive, and entirely ruthless" plans to use Dillon Reservoir and the Roberts Tunnel "to take water wherever she can find it for irrigation and other purposes in the South Platte basin." Saunders countered that Denver had to plan for future growth. The legal structure under which Green Mountain Reservoir had been established, he said, provided that water be made available for future use and domestic purposes on "both [emphasis added] slopes of the Continental Divide."[18]

Clayton and Barkley, representing the District, said they did not object to Denver receiving "incidental benefits" from Green Mountain Reservoir "[as] long as any operation of the reservoir did not compromise the ability of the District to make replacements for maximum Project diversions and as long as such operations did not require additional releases from Granby or Willow Creek reservoirs."[19] In the worst drought year of 1954, Barkley noted, 80 percent of the 52,000 acre-foot pool had been released to fulfill C–BT commitments at the Shoshone Power Plant and only 38 percent of the 100,000 acre-foot pool had been released to fulfill the demand at Cameo, east of Grand Junction.[20] Aandahl, who was not impressed with Denver's logic, rejected the city's request to use Green Mountain Reservoir for replacement releases. Because Crown Zellerbach Corporation was negotiating for a contract to *purchase* Green Mountain Reservoir water, Denver next proposed a similar contract. The secretary of the interior invited comments from interested parties. Barkley repeated the District's earlier position but also stipulated that any third-party beneficiary would have to "share an equitable portion of construction [costs] and perpetual operation and maintenance costs of [Green Mountain] Reservoir."[21]

Undisturbed by rejection from Washington, Saunders tenaciously pursued his objectives and presented the same replacement release plan directly to the NCWCD to promote a bilateral agreement. Clayton noted that the Denver attorney now claimed his client's rights under Senate Document 80, after he had previously denied that the city could be controlled in any way whatsoever by its terms. But Denver's inconsistency was not the District's greatest concern; both Clayton and Barkley feared that if Denver obtained Green Mountain Reservoir water, the city would apply this replacement release theory to Dillon Reservoir, thus possibly cutting off upstream Blue River flows.[22] Late in 1960 other litigants, similarly preoccupied with Denver's actions, filed motions in Federal District Court for a determination of all parties' rights to utilization of Green Mountain Reservoir. Although Barkley and Clayton hoped to avoid litigation, Judge Alfred A. Arraj was forced to set a hearing date for January 19, 1961.[23] Testimony and the court's deliberations, which continued off and on for a year and a half, finally resulted in denial of Denver's motion. Although Clayton argued that Denver had no right, title, or interest in benefits derived from release of water from Green Mountain Reservoir, he also advised the court of the future advantage to all parties "if Denver were permitted some benefit from the release of water for exchange replacement purposes." Barkley agreed. Flexibility was a hallmark of his administrative leadership. Instead of a binding court decree, he saw more advantage in a system that would allow the exchange of water between the transmountain systems, including the C-BT, Denver, and others.[24]

Still preferring to go it alone, DWB members voted to petition the secretary of the interior for purchase of the entire Green Mountain Reservoir and Power Plant and to assume all contractual obligations between the United States and the District. As expected, the Department of the Interior replied that the United States had no intention of surrendering these facilities; if the DWB wished to pursue the matter, it could do so by means of comprehensive legislation;[25] thus, Denver's drive to expand its water collection and distribution system advanced on all fronts. The Colorado Supreme Court upheld its claim to conditional rights on the Eagle River. In a 6–0 ruling the decision overturned District Court Judge William Luby's earlier finding that West Slope water should remain in the basin of origin.[26] In May 1962 the DWB celebrated completion of the Roberts Tunnel, a project that had taken six years to complete at a cost of $51 million. Fourteen months later Dillon Dam was completed at a cost of $18.7 million.[27] By early spring 1963 the DWB was urging city residents to approve a $152 million expansion of the city's water system over a seven-teen-year period. In a special report prepared for the DWB, the Kansas City engineering firm of Black and Veatch noted that by 1980 Denver would be serving 1.1 million people, whose average daily consumption under drought conditions would reach 268 million gallons. Better yields from collection systems, more water rights, and construction of improvements on existing facilities would all be required, the report concluded, if Denver were to meet water distribution obligations.[28]

Many outspoken officials had issued similar warnings since the 1960 Census showed exponential growth rates in the West. Although Denver's plea for funding to provide water for this predicted population explosion has been viewed by critics as a tactic to expand empire and power, the consensus among most Front Range water providers in the mid-sixties was that growth would continue unabated and that water supplies would soon be inadequate without drastic measures. Gilbert G. Stamm, then chief of the Bureau's Division of Irrigation and Land Use, predicted that the West's water supplies would not meet population needs by the year 2000 "even if additional developments proceed at all possible speed."[29] Governors of the seventeen western states urged President Kennedy to recognize and act on these growth patterns.[30] Colorado Congressman Wayne N. Aspinall worried about the food needs of an expanding population, and the Chicago Daily News warned that if the present rate of migration to the West continued, "the desert dwellers, like desert animals may need to eat certain foods that reduce the need for water."[31] From Pueblo to Fort Collins the water community focused on preparations for the future. Denver was not alone in anticipating a demographic nightmare. While construction was being completed on Dillon Reservoir and the Roberts Tunnel, cities like Arvada, Aurora, Englewood, and Westminster, along with three ditch companies,

Congressman Wayne N. Aspinall represented the West Slope for years. As a disciple of Edward T. Taylor, he staunchly defended and supported water projects to provide this section of Colorado with more water. (Courtesy Denver Public Library, Western History Department.)

pledged $10,000 to study Two Forks Dam on the South Platte River.[32] Greeley, Longmont, and Fort Collins began to question the adequacy of existing municipal water systems. In a move that captured everyone's attention, two opportunist businessmen formed a company and filed a claim to the Ogallala Aquifer underlying parts of Elbert and El Paso counties.[33]

As if the general expectancy of exponential growth were not enough to fuel the race for additional West Slope water, a severe drought in 1963 meant that spring and summer months were some of the driest on record. Water supplies entering the NCWCD area were 56 percent of normal.[34] On the West Slope, the Colorado River watershed was 41 percent of average in the Williams Fork area; the Yampa, White, and North Platte rivers were 65 percent of normal; and the Gunnison River was flowing 57 percent of average.[35] Under more than 140 contracts with distributors outside the city, the DWB recorded the highest consumption rates in Denver's history.[36] Small wonder, then, that Denver water officials decided to test their strength again. On September 3, 1963, Dillon Dam was closed, sealing off the water flow down the Blue River into Green Mountain Reservoir. Three days later, the U.S. Justice Department charged in Federal

Dillon Reservoir was completed in 1963, making possible the transportation of Blue River water to Denver through the Roberts Tunnel. (Courtesy Bureau of Reclamation.)

District Court that the DWB was violating the 1955 Blue River decrees and that water storage in Dillon Reservoir would interfere with the government's obligations to provide water to the NCWCD. Attorney Saunders replied that the DWB's action had nothing to do with the 1955 decree; the Water Board was only transferring water by exchange into the Colorado River through releases from Williams Fork Reservoir.[37] Although some may have accepted this reasoning, the *Grand Junction Sentinel* described Denver as "financially and morally bankrupt. . . [whose] leaders don't care about right and wrong. They care nothing about the rights of others just so Denver's needs are taken care of. Glenn Saunders, in riding roughshod over everyone, is a fair example of all Denver's official family."[38]

Battle lines were drawn once again, but this time the West Slope was more unyielding. By contrast, Denver's actions did not initially worry the NCWCD. Barkley noted that the present flow into Green Mountain Reservoir was sufficient off the Gore Range to meet downstream water rights. He and Clayton recognized that the District's interest in Green

Mountain Reservoir storage was limited to the 52,000 acre-foot pool and that the possibility of this amount not being in the reservoir "was more hypothetical than real." Of greater concern to the District was the Federal Court's need to rigidly clarify the reservoir's operation.[39] Barkley, who believed strongly in the virtues of flexibility and common sense, took this approach to Washington when Ramsey Clark, assistant attorney general of the United States, called together all interested parties for resolution of the conflict. Several years of operating experience with both Dillon and Green Mountain reservoirs, he argued, would provide the best basis for settlement of all legal questions as well as development of "flexible operating criteria" for changing conditions.[40] Denver and West Slope representatives, however, were in no mood to negotiate. With no indication that an out-of-court settlement was in the making, Federal District Judge Arraj set a trial date for December 9, 1963, on four primary points of law: (1) whether Denver and Colorado Springs had any right to exchange Williams Fork for Dillon water; (2) whether Denver and Colorado Springs could take water that might interfere with direct-flow rights at the Green Mountain Power Plant; (3) whether Denver and Colorado Springs were entitled to require releases from the 100,000 acre-foot pool referred to in the 1955 Blue River decrees; and (4) whether the Federal District Court had authority to enjoin and restrain Denver from proceeding in several cases that might have an impact on the Colorado River storage project.[41]

Saunders and his lieutenant, Jack Ross, stated Denver's position in a pretrial order. The federal government's appropriation of water for Green Mountain Reservoir, they said, "was for the primary purpose of preserving, insofar as possible, the rights and interests dependent on the waters of the Colorado River which existed at the time of the appropriation, on *both slopes* [emphasis added] of the Continental Divide in Colorado, including the rights of Denver." Green Mountain Reservoir existed to preserve Denver's rights to domestic and sanitary water from the Colorado River. The secretary of the interior was obligated to see that Denver received equitable treatment, especially "so that the 100,000 acre-feet of the capacity of Green Mountain Reservoir shall be available without charge for the benefit and stabilization of water rights of Denver existing as of the day of appropriation attributable to said Green Mountain Reservoir."[42] Denver had been expounding this same theory, one that the NCWCD could not accept, for several years. However, if Denver had guaranteed the 52,000 acre-foot pool annually, the District would at least have supported the city's plan for exchange releases.[43] Failing to obtain agreement on this issue, the District filed a pretrial brief stating that Senate Document 80 prevented

Denver from exchanging water from its own system to compensate down-stream water users on the Colorado River.[44] While attorneys agreed to a trial postponement until April, Denver stopped storing water in Dillon Reservoir on November 20, 1963. The West Slope showed no interest in any out-of-court settlement.

Forces for compromise still hoped to avoid litigation. Working harder than he probably should have, Clayton looked for a way that both reservoirs could operate prior to fixing procedural details. Assistant Attorney General Clark, who had the same objective, encountered West Slope resistance in the form of a storage facility planned for development at Parshall, below Denver's Williams Fork Reservoir. Denver's exchange plans appeared to threaten the Middle Park Water Conservancy District's scheme to build Ute Mountain Reservoir about 18 miles upstream from Denver's reservoir. Clark asked Denver what concessions the city might be willing to make.[45] Meanwhile, the CWCB also tried to bring everyone to the discussion table through a task force of all principal litigants coordinated by State Engineer C. J. Kuiper.[46] With a trial set for Monday, April 13, 1964, Clark remained optimistic about some form of agreement, but disaster struck on Friday, April 10, when Clayton fell over at his desk from an apparent heart attack. One of the most knowledgeable and committed participants in the case, Clayton had been a prime force for negotiated settlement. Barkley lost a colleague and close friend at a critical point in the negotiations. With only a weekend to prepare, he brought in Board member John M. Sayre to represent the District.[47]

Everyone believed the trial would be long and costly, and no one showed any willingness to make any last-minute, out-of-court settlement. The CRWCD's manager, Philip P. Smith, and attorney Frank Delaney began a lengthy presentation before Judge Arraj by covering the wall with maps of many proposed West Slope projects. As Barkley later recalled, Arraj just lost patience. He told Delaney that someday, instead of coming to the Continental Divide, laying a shotgun up there, and pulling both triggers hoping to hit something, "you'll come into this court and tell me precisely what it is you want. Until you're ready to do so, I think we have heard enough for today." Following the West Slope's retreat, Saunders made Denver's case with a long, convoluted statement about the prior appropriation doctrine. "Mr. Saunders," the judge said,

> I'm a Colorado native. I have been in the water business myself and I don't think I need your review of the appropriation doctrine, so let me make a suggestion. There's a conference room upstairs. All of you

participants go up there and sit down at the table. When you have come to some agreement, you come back and tell me. I'll be glad to listen. Until then, this Court stands adjourned.[48]

The tactic worked. Denver offered to relinquish claims to the 100,000 acre-foot pool in Green Mountain Reservoir in return for the right to substitute water from the Williams Fork system when storing water in Dillon Reservoir. The United States and the NCWCD signed the agreement, but the West Slope at first refused, contending that Denver and Colorado Springs had asserted an illegal interest in Green Mountain Reservoir.[49] On April 16, 1964, Judge Arraj imposed a final solution: a consent decree addressing the first three of the four contested issues of law. All parties signed.

These results defined with more exactness the Blue River decrees of 1955. Denver and Colorado Springs would be allowed to store water in Dillon Reservoir and to exchange water from Williams Fork Reservoir into Dillon Reservoir when the secretary of the interior determined that there was sufficient water to fill Green Mountain Reservoir to capacity. The court also determined that Denver and Colorado Springs had no right, title, or interest to Green Mountain Reservoir or the water stored therein. Denver and Colorado Springs could use the direct flow from Green Mountain Reservoir, provided they replaced the power losses or compensated the federal government for loss of power from the use thereof. Finally, Denver and Colorado Springs were not entitled to any water from the 100,000 acre-foot pool.[50] Within a fortnight Sayre suggested to Barkley that they summarize what was accomplished in the consent decree, and Barkley agreed. In a letter to the Board, Sayre predicted that if 1964 turned out to be a poor water year, all parties could be back in court by September.

> As Denver begins its attempt to acquire new appropriations or to pursue certain courses contemplated under the Decree, I feel sure that a new Complaint will be filed with the Federal Court by the Western Slope interests and we will all be back in Federal Court again. . . . There is no secret that Denver would ultimately like to acquire Green Mountain Reservoir and our only interest in this matter would be to make sure that if this were ever done we would still be able to deliver our replacement water to the Colorado River at such places, and at such times, and in such amounts as would fully satisfy the provisions of Senate Document 80.[51]

Sayre's sense that the agreement was fragile proved accurate, but the consent decree remained unchallenged until 1977, when Denver unilaterally refused to release water to Green Mountain Reservoir. The Bureau went back to Federal District Court, where Judge Arraj ordered Denver to comply with the 1964 stipulation. No further problems developed until 1986, when Denver again made claims on Green Mountain Reservoir.

While both District and West Slope officials kept a close eye on Denver's transmountain diversion plans, a more serious threat to the entire state developed in the lower basin of the Colorado River. As a result of postwar growth and an agricultural boom that caused rapid depletion of underground aquifers, Arizona decided to launch a major effort to utilize its share of water authorized by the 1922 Colorado River Compact. First in the Supreme Court and then in Congress, Arizona's relentless pursuit of the Central Arizona project (CAP) reawakened fears that a future call for water from the upper basin states could develop during drought years. The implications of this threat to the C–BT demanded the District's closest attention. Arizona, which had refused to sign the Colorado River Compact in 1922, fought California's water developments for the next twenty-two years. In 1944 the state ratified the compact and contracted with the Department of the Interior for a feasibility study on ways to utilize its 2.8 million acre-foot share of Colorado River water.[52] The CAP's basic design would divert water from the Colorado River at Lake Havasu and lift it over 900 feet to an aqueduct extending 240 miles to the farmlands of central Arizona. The Bureau's study, completed in 1947, noted that the project would "sustain the agricultural economy of the area."[53]

Following a short-lived attempt to persuade the state legislature to fund the CAP in 1947, veteran Arizona Senator Carl Hayden took up the cause in Congress. The first CAP bill visualized repayment of most construction costs through generation of hydroelectric power at a dam built at Bridge Canyon on the Colorado River. Because most power would be sold to California, users in that state objected both to paying for the CAP and to setting a precedent for upper basin states to follow.[54] Although Hayden and his cohort, Senator Ernest McFarland, warned that "our farmers will have to move off the land, and ground once fertile and productive will go back to desert waste," California's opposition shut down Senate committee hearings. Similar legislative attempts in 1950 and 1951 survived the Senate but were prevented from committee consideration in the House by the California delegation's strength. California was now using considerably more than its allocated 4.4 million acre-feet of Colorado River water; Arizona, embittered by its long struggle with California, filed suit in August 1952 in the U. S. Supreme Court. Five months later the Court formally granted Arizona's motion, thus beginning a case that lasted twelve years, cost $5 million, involved fifty lawyers and 340 witnesses, and produced forty-three volumes of testimony.[55]

Barkley was fully aware that the struggle between California and Arizona could significantly affect C–BT operations. Soon after being appointed NCWCD manager, he advised that Board members take "considerable interest" in events in the lower basin states.[56] In spring 1960 Special Master Simon H. Rifkind issued a 387-page draft report recommending that when the Colorado River had 7.5 million acre-feet of consumptive use available below Lee Ferry, the Bureau would have to release 2.8 million acre-feet to Arizona, 4.4 million acre-feet to California, and 300,000 acre-feet to Nevada. If surplus water were available, 50 percent would go to Arizona and 50 percent to California; in case of a shortage, each state would receive a reduced portion in the same percentage stipulated for a full river.[57] After hearings on the draft report and a denial of California's motion to reopen the case, Rifkind mailed his final report to the Supreme Court. Oral arguments began in January 1962.

The Californians fought with every conceivable weapon. If Rifkind's recommendation were allowed to stand, rapidly growing southern California would lose about 1 million acre-feet of water. Northcutt Ely, special counsel for California, told the Court that the Rifkind Report projected a hybrid system of water rights "never before seen in the jurisprudence of this country." The 5.1 million acre-feet being used by California, he said, were entitled to legal protection under the doctrine of prior appropriation.[58] On most issues, however, the Supreme Court sided with Rifkind. In a June 3, 1963, decision, the Court ruled that California was entitled to only 4.4 million acre-feet of the Colorado River. The very next day Senators Hayden and Barry Goldwater reintroduced CAP legislation in the Senate while the three Arizona congressmen offered similar bills in the House. California asked the Court to reconsider, asserting errors of fact and law, but the Court refused. Many thought the decision would launch a water grab on the Colorado River.[59]

What happened during the next four years was different than most expected. Although clashes between representatives of the upper and lower Colorado River basin were frequent and intense, the seven states compromised differences, won approval of their own regional projects, and developed an overall basin unity not possible in the contentious atmosphere of the previous forty-five years. For the C–BT specifically, President Lyndon B. Johnson's signature on the Colorado River basin project bill (which included the CAP) on September 30, 1968, resulted in clarification of District obligations to lower basin states in the event of a Colorado River

Compact call. The reappearance of this touchy but vital question can best be explained by certain problems that affected the Colorado River in the 1960s.

Water quality had suddenly become an international issue. The 1944 treaty with Mexico for 1.5 million acre-feet a year had made no specific guarantee of water quality, but the Mexican government after World War II almost doubled the land under irrigation in the Mexicali Valley. Cotton became king, but the rising percentage of dissolved salts — a partial result of upstream irrigation in the United States — drastically reduced yields south of the border.[60] Highly polluted drainage waters were dumped into the river from the Wellton-Mohawk drainage district a few miles east of Yuma, Arizona. Farmers in this valley relied increasingly on wells to irrigate their crops, but the deeper the water, the saltier it became. A Bureau project brought fresh supplies of water from the Gila River, but "a basaltic plug, a virtual underground dam at the head of the valley, prevented the ground water from flowing back to the Colorado River. The underground water table rose, pushing up with it the accumulation of salts that had been buried in the aquifer after many years of irrigation."[61] The Bureau responded by building a drainage channel into the Colorado River. More than a hundred wells pumped salty water from the Wellton-Mohawk drainage district in the United States through the channel into the Mexicali Valley of Mexico via the Colorado River. Mexicans were justifiably angry. Crowds marched on the U.S. Consulate in Mexicali. The powerful State League of Mexican Farmers demanded immediate action or they would stop work on the Rio Grande Friendship Dam.[62] The Mexican foreign minister hinted that his country might no longer cooperate with the United States in finding locations for space-tracking stations. President Adolfo López Mateos simply noted that the salinity issue was the greatest diplomatic problem confronting the two countries.[63]

Because of international tension, upper basin states officials worried that President Johnson might sign an agreement reducing their entitlement to water from the Colorado River. For this reason Barkley recommended to the CWCB that the problem be resolved without any amendments to the 1944 Mexican Treaty. He favored construction of a new drainage channel to extend around the Mexican-built Morelos Dam.[64] Governor John Love, who supported this view, urged President Johnson to make no commitments to Mexico that might include any guarantee of water quality or of any increase in the volume of water delivered to Mexico.[65] Dilution as a solution to pollution was not favored in a state that had not yet fully developed its share of water under the Colorado River Compact. A short-term fix, arranged with the new President Gustavo Díaz Ordaz in 1965, extended the drainage channel so that Mexicans could at least determine for themselves where they would take the saline water. Nothing was done, however, to improve water quality. Consequently, the Mexicans threatened to take their case to the World Court. During the four-year negotiations on the Colorado River basin project bill, the very real possibility of the U.S. government making major concessions to Mexico caused Barkley and the District Board to support plans for a water importation program from Canada, Alaska, or the Columbia River basin to the Colorado River.

To deal with such legislative complexities and to keep peace between East and West Slopes, the CWCB organized a special advisory committee in 1965 that represented all major water entities of the state, the Bureau, Colorado Springs and Denver, and the Public Service Company of Colorado. Barkley was elected chairman. This committee's first task was to review resolutions of the CWCB and the Upper Colorado River Commission, both of which urged Congress to investigate Northwest water importation plans. CWCB Director Sparks pointed out that the lower basin states were in accord on this issue.[66] The next task would be to protect and guarantee upper river basin storage, the Colorado River Compact, certain West Slope projects, and financial commitments for studies of water importation.[67] This accomplished, the committee noted that the Colorado objectives were for the most part accepted by the other basin states. For the first time in the history of the Colorado River basin, all seven states agreed that water importation should be a quid pro quo of legislation authorizing the CAP.[68]

Schemes for transbasin importation of water were not in short supply. Engineers from the Ralph M. Parsons Company of Los Angeles urged a Senate subcommittee to consider a $50 billion joint United States–Canadian venture in which surplus water would be collected in Alaska, British Columbia, and the Yukon for delivery to Lake Superior. A canal dug from Vancouver to Duluth, Minnesota, would carry water to the Great Lakes, thus increasing the St. Lawrence River flow so that power production would be enhanced by 50 percent at Niagara Falls. Another feature of this plan was a 500-mile-long reservoir called the Rocky Mountain Trench, designed to stretch northward from Flathead Lake in Montana.[69] Incredibly, the Senate was interested in this plan. Experts predicted a water crisis of "alarming proportions" in the West. With estimates that demand for water would double by 1980 and triple by the year 2000 and "with farmland being lost at the rate of 700,000 acres annually" to urbanization and erosion,

Tapping the Northwest.

the subcommittee favored detailed studies of all projects, no matter how bizarre.[70]

Unfortunately, Northwest congressmen, whose votes would be needed to pass CAP legislation, were unequivocally opposed to water exportation from the Columbia River basin to the Southwest. Caught unaware by the Colorado River basin states' unity, they had no studies to show a need for surplus water. In fact, a U.S. Geological Survey report showed that only 9.4 million acre-feet of the 138 million acre-feet flow of the Columbia River had been put to use in 1960. Worse still, the report predicted that fifty years later, the maximum use would reach only 18.3 million acre-feet.[71] Barkley was well aware of the political opposition led by Senator Henry Jackson of Washington, but the unresolved Mexican situation and the fear that the CAP would eat into the 7.5 million acre-feet allotted to the upper basin states drove Barkley to search for supplemental water supplies for the Colorado River. Noting that the alternative — sea water desalinization — was too costly under existing technology, he favored legislation that authorized some type of transbasin diversion. Even Texas indicated an interest in imported water.[72]

Although the Columbia River was the most often mentioned source of supply, more creative thinkers, as well as those who recognized the growing resistance of northwestern members of Congress, considered icebergs a solution for the Southwest's water shortage. With National Geographic Society encouragement, the Department of the Interior's Geological Survey section and the Army's Cold Regions Research and Engineering Laboratory estimated that an iceberg towed from Antarctica to the California coast would cost $1 million and would provide $5.5 million worth of water. The cost of super tugs, built with power sufficient to haul giant mountains of ice 6 miles long, a mile wide, and 800 feet deep, seemed inconsequential compared to $1.2 billion to desalinate an equivalent amount of sea water.[73]

Barkley told the House Subcommittee on Irrigation and Reclamation that whatever plan was selected, authorization of the CAP must include simultaneous approval of supplemental water deliveries to the Colorado River in sufficient quantities to guarantee U.S. obligations to Mexico, annual consumptive use of 7.5 million acre-feet by both the upper basin and lower basin states, and adequate additional water for new projects.[74] In addition to CAP construction, Barkley kept in mind certain West Slope projects that Congressman Aspinall insisted on including in the same legislative package.

Aspinall's position as chairman of the House Interior and Insular Affairs Committee was critical to the fate of the Colorado River basin project bill. He delayed bringing the measure to the floor until all components were agreed upon and passage assured. As Aspinall's biographer points out, he functioned as a water Solomon, "able to cope not only with two mothers who wanted one child but with seven Colorado River basin states all wanting one river."[75] What he objected to in early legislative proposals was emphasis on building an Arizona project at Colorado's expense. Since the 1956 passage of the Colorado River storage project, Colorado had been authorized projects that allowed the state to store only 95,000 acre-feet of more than 800,000 acre-feet remaining to the state under provisions of the 1922 Colorado River Compact and the 1948 Upper Colorado River Basin Compact. Because both the Upper Colorado River Commission (UCRC) and the Bureau had reports that showed Colorado's need to further develop its allotment, Aspinall consulted with Sparks to determine which projects might stand the best chance; the five selected were Animas–La Plata, Dolores, San Miguel, Dallas Creek, and West Divide. Even with these projects built and storing water, Colorado would still have 400,000 acre-feet to be utilized from its share of the Colorado River.[76]

Aspinall's problem was to persuade the Bureau to complete feasibility studies in sufficient time for the Bureau of the Budget to recommend congressional authorization. They soon found the Animas–La Plata and Dolores projects feasible but rejected the others on grounds of "high cost per acre and investment per farm."[77] Aspinall threatened to discontinue further discussion on the Colorado River basin bill until all five Colorado projects were found feasible.[78] Known for compromise, Aspinall's obstinacy was uncharacteristic. He even argued that each project was qualified by cost-benefit ratios;[79] but what really drove him was the conviction that if Colorado failed to develop its water in the near future, the lower basin would grab it and claim prior appropriation against any compact or statute, past, present, or future. Compared to a cost of $779.9 million for the CAP alone and an estimated $1.2 billion for the entire Colorado River basin project, $392 million seemed reasonable for Colorado's five projects.[80]

Over objections from several of his own committee members, Aspinall won approval to include the five projects in the Colorado River basin project bill. Many of his Colorado associates sensed that they would never be built, that they were "dogs," and that their inclusion in legislation only satisfied Aspinall's West Slope constituency.[81] Despite there being some truth to these allegations, Aspinall strongly believed that water projects were integral to western growth and — in the tradition of his mentor, Edward T. Taylor — that he was protecting the best interests of his people. What he did not anticipate was the West Slope's insistence that these projects be given senior priority to East Slope projects already drawing Colorado River water through the Adams and Roberts tunnels.[82] This repeated demand convinced Barkley of the need to clarify, once and for all, the C–BT's rights and obligations in the event of a compact call on the Colorado River by the lower basin states. The Colorado River basin project bill was the perfect place to do this.

At issue was paragraph 5 (i) of the "Manner of Operation of Project Facilities and Auxiliary Features," Senate Document 80, which stated in part: "if an obligation is created under said compact [1922 Colorado River Compact] to augment the supply of water from the State of Colorado to satisfy the provisions of said compact, the diversion for the benefit of the eastern slope shall be discontinued in advance of *any* [emphasis added] western slope appropriations."[83] This passage, which reflected Charles Hansen's strong feelings of commitment to his West Slope counterparts, was based on specific stipulations in the 1935 Delaney Resolution that were fully accepted by the NCWUA, both in the 1935 Grand Lake Resolution 17 and at a meeting of East and West Slope representatives at the Shirley-Savoy Hotel in Denver on January 3 and 4, 1937.[84] Obviously, the West Slope promoted a literal interpretation of paragraph 5 (i). CRWCD attorney Kenneth Balcomb argued that Senate Document 80, as a contract, did not require contextual interpretation.[85] CWCB member and city editor for the *Grand Junction Sentinel*, William H. Nelson, further insisted that paragraph 5 (i) clearly referred to all water rights on the entire West Slope and that both Denver and the NCWCD would have to accept priorities junior to the five projects in the event of a compact call.

Nelson became the West Slope's spokesman on this subject. When the Colorado Supreme Court determined that promoter John P. Elliott should receive a conditional decree for his Four Counties Water Association, Nelson editorialized that every drop of water removed from the West Slope to eastern Colorado reduced the amount available for commitments to Colorado River users of both upper and lower basins.[86] In the event of a call, he wrote, the West Slope would feel the pinch unless paragraph 5 (i) were interpreted as written. He was suspicious of Denver's power and believed that the capital city had stored ample water for the future. He anticipated municipalities of northern Colorado planning to take more water through the C–BT. The Fry-Ark project was under construction; Colorado Springs and Pueblo were angling to recover some water from

Ruedi Reservoir; and new federal legislation was locking up other lands and water courses through establishment of wilderness areas and wild and scenic stream systems — all at a time when the West Slope was on the verge of an oil shale boom. How could growth take place, Nelson asked, unless developers were assured that "diversion for the benefit of the eastern slope shall be discontinued in advance of *any* [emphasis added] western slope appropriations?"[87]

Barkley threw his energy into answering the West Slope. As chairman of the Colorado River Advisory Committee, he repeated to the CWCB what he and Sayre had told the NCWCD Board: the language of the Colorado River basin bill had to place future West Slope projects junior to the C–BT and Denver's Blue River project.[88] Both men persistently said that the word "any" in paragraph 5 (i) referred only to appropriations in the segment of the Colorado River and tributaries that were covered in Senate Document 80. In the event of a compact call, therefore, the C–BT should not be shut down as long as Green Mountain Reservoir could contribute a proportional share to the river. That was one of the expected uses of the 100,000 acre-foot pool. Other rivers on the West Slope not affected by Green Mountain Reservoir and not included in Senate Document 80 — such as Yampa, White, Gunnison, and Dolores — would constitute the rest of Colorado's portion of any call. In January 1966 the Colorado River Advisory Committee unanimously approved a revised version of the Colorado River basin project bill. Because the West Slope still wanted to make the Adams and Roberts tunnels junior to the five new projects, the CWCB went into executive session with Governor Love before approving the amended legislation.[89]

Balcomb, who remained hostile, submitted a statement of opposition to Aspinall's committee regarding key wording in Title V, Section 501 (e) of the revised bill. This section said:

> In the diversion and storage of water for any project or any parts thereof constructed under the authority of this Act or the CRSP Act within and for the benefit of the State of Colorado only, the Secretary is directed to comply with the constitution and statutes of the State of Colorado relating to priority of appropriation; with State and Federal court decrees entered pursuant thereto; and with operating principles, if any, adopted by the Secretary and approved by the State of Colorado.[90]

This endorsed the District's interpretation of Senate Document 80 and restated the applicability of prior appropriation vis-à-vis transmountain diversions. During final hearings in Washington, Balcomb threatened to testify against the amended legislation, now referred to as House Report No. 3300. As the incident was recalled by Barkley many years later, Balcomb had a sudden change of mind. Barkley and Sayre invited Balcomb and CRWCD manager Philip P. Smith to dinner the night before Aspinall's committee met for the final hearing. Both Barkley and Balcomb had placed their names on the witness list for the next day. During dinner, Balcomb said he would oppose the language in Section 501 (e), whereupon Barkley threatened to oppose the five West Slope projects. When Aspinall called on witnesses the next day, both Balcomb and Barkley passed. The hearing ended with no further discord between East and West Slopes.[91]

Although the Colorado River Basin Project Act became reality in September 1968, the West Slope had little to cheer about over the next five years because its projects did not receive funding to begin construction while Denver, CWCB, and NCWCD interests drew closer together. Saunders boasted that the act proved Congress's support for Colorado's prior appropriation doctrine in transmountain diversions.[92] NCWCD president J. Ben Nix proudly noted that CWCB director Sparks lauded Barkley and Sayre for getting the Colorado River Basin Project Act through Congress. A letter from Barkley to Governor Love, commenting on Sparks's "very competent performance," [93] further detailed the NCWCD's close relations with the CWCB. These developments were not lost on the West Slope when the District began discussions with six Front Range cities over a proposed Windy Gap project designed to bring additional water through the C–BT system from the Colorado River. Barkley's last five years as NCWCD manager were entangled in these negotiations, made even more complex by state and national concerns over water quality and the environment.

19 Conservation and Progress: Environmental Challenges and Economic Growth

National environmental concerns intruded on NCWCD management almost immediately after J. R. "Bob" Barkley became secretary-manager in 1958. This is not to say that C-BT construction and operation were originally conceived without consideration of potential impact on the natural environment; but the political climate for water projects changed so dramatically following the 1956 defeat of Echo Park Dam on the Green River that Barkley had to address a host of new challenges unforeseen by Charles Hansen and J. M. Dille in the 1930s. The new environmental movement, which could not be disregarded, garnered coast-to-coast support during the 1960s and 1970s and appeared especially threatening to District officials who were planning expansion of the existing C-BT system to meet the needs of municipal, industrial, and agricultural growth.

Due to the focus on preservation of wilderness areas, water quality questions, land- and water-use planning, conservation, and the dedication of water courses to fish and wildlife functions, the District also saw this national movement as a possible threat to Colorado's long-standing water laws. The challenge became apparent when additional features became necessary on the West Slope to deliver the 310,000 acre-feet of water promised by the Bureau in Senate Document 80. With booming agricultural productivity and growing municipalities, a real potential for conflict existed between the environmentalists' intentions to restrict water development and the NCWCD's perceived necessity to increase C-BT deliveries. The threat of federal and state regulations on water quantity and quality, land-use planning, and recreational opportunities drew NCWCD officials into the maelstrom of environmental debates.

Designation of Colorado wilderness areas directly challenged traditional ways of thinking. The Wilderness Act of 1964, considered the "jewel in the preservationists' crown," clashed "glaringly with the laws and popular philosophy that had directed the treatment of the western lands from

Jamestown to the opening of the twentieth century."[1] Eight years of lobbying were required before the Wilderness Act became law. During this time most Colorado water officials, including District leaders, expressed dissatisfaction with the plan to "lock up" millions of acres of national forest lands. In 1959 attorney Jack Clayton warned the Board that proposed wilderness legislation would prohibit development of water projects on government lands. Barkley was concerned that the Department of the Interior had already become overly sensitive to the nationwide political strength of fish and wildlife enthusiasts. Although Director Clyde Moffitt noted that the general public opposed the legislation, for those who did not understand it, he recommended an explanation that stressed economic loss to the average taxpayer through nondevelopment of wilderness lands.[2]

By the end of the year, however, citizen opposition to wilderness legislation had begun to soften.[3] Even though the CWCB, the Colorado Cattleman's Association, and the NRA remained opposed to establishment of wilderness areas,[4] the broad range of national support and the bill's sponsorship by eighteen senators convinced opponents that sooner or later Congress would pass a law. The only question was how to amend the legislation so that Colorado could preserve control of its watersheds. DWB attorney Glenn Saunders was outspoken against any wilderness bill that did not permit collection of information on water supplies and construction of tunnels underneath designated wilderness areas.[5] In spring 1962 Governor Stephen McNichols advised Congress that Colorado could support wilderness legislation. Though only five areas in the state were contemplated for wilderness at that time, he reminded legislators to take a hard look at potential effects of designation on the "stringent problems of water supply and conservation as well as upon economic . . . and industrial development."[6] By 1964 Governor John Love, Saunders, the CWC, and the Colorado Game and Fish Department supported compromise legislation that enabled Congress to classify wilderness lands with a provision for certain types of multiple use.[7] Eight years after Senator Hubert Humphrey first introduced a wilderness bill, and after sixty-six separate revisions, President Johnson signed the Wilderness Act on September 3, 1964.

Some delays were attributable to Congressman Wayne N. Aspinall's role as chairman of the House Interior and Insular Affairs Committee. Aspinall had always considered himself a conservationist, but he supported the Gifford Pinchot–Teddy Roosevelt school, which viewed conservation both as an ideology and an action program based on "wise use" of natural resources.[8] He was reluctant to see the nation's natural resources locked up forever, and he feared that legislation would jeopardize future water projects. But Aspinall's main objection to wilderness bills was their ten-dency to leave selection of designated areas to the executive branch of government. When the 1964 bill assigned this responsibility to Congress, while still allowing the president to authorize construction of new water facilities in designated wilderness areas if such projects were in the public interest, Aspinall agreed to compromise, but he worried about West Slope constituents. He knew that the 9.1 million acres approved by President Johnson were an opening wedge for Congress to make additional designa-tions in future years.[9] He wondered if the Wilderness Act might eventually cause new water wars to start up between East and West Slopes.

Barkley had the same worry. The Gore–Eagle's Nest Wilderness desig-nation preoccupied DWB officials. Full utilization of Lake Dillon and the Roberts Tunnel depended on the right to divert water from Blue River tributaries. If these boundaries were extended too far, Denver's plans for the Eagle-Piney collection system would be compromised.[10] Along with Directors W. D. "Bill" Farr and Charles Hallenbeck, Barkley attended a meeting called by the DWB to form a coalition of cities to work toward size reduction of wilderness areas proposed for Colorado. Everyone agreed that unless something of this sort were accomplished, Denver, the Rocky Mountain Power Company, the CRWCD, and other entities could not begin future water projects. Barkley returned to the District and persuaded the NCWCD Board to pass a resolution urging officials in Colorado and in Congress to oppose the designation of wilderness areas containing "renewable natural resources susceptible of economic development for fulfillment of vital human needs."[11]

In 1974 the House Public Lands Committee held additional hearings on the Gore–Eagle's Nest proposal. While Denver and wilderness advo-cates agreed to compromise, the West Slope again felt like the victim. Although expansion of Denver's water system appeared assured, no agree-ment provided the West Slope with compensation for water diverted to the Front Range. While gubernatorial candidate Richard Lamm advocated that water diversion from the West to the East Slope had to stop, and Governor John Vanderhoof declared opposition to Denver's proposed Two Forks Dam, West Slope officials geared up for another defense of the Colorado River basin with some assurance that they no longer stood alone.[12]

West Slope anxiety over East Slope water raids deepened with the federal government's claim in State District Court to a reserved water right on six types of federal reservations. The United States invoked these claims while simultaneously arguing for protection of its rights under the Colorado doctrine of prior appropriation.[13]

East Slope interests began fighting wilderness areas because they feared that lands withdrawn around watersheds would impede development of future water projects. By 1972 apprehension on both sides of the Continental Divide intensified when the U.S. Forest Service used the reserved rights doctrine to claim senior water rights in the Gore–Eagle's Nest Wilderness area.[14] With planning for the Windy Gap Dam and Power Plant well along, NCWCD officials now faced the unpleasant prospect of a major court battle with both the West Slope and the federal government over water rights in the Colorado River.

At a 1972 meeting attorney John M. Sayre explained to concerned NCWCD Directors that the United States had wilderness water rights claims in State District Court in Glenwood Springs that affected two water divisions and four water districts and that involved thirty-five attorneys. The District had to be represented, he said, to protect both the C–BT decrees and those of the newly formed Municipal Subdistrict.[15] Additionally, Sayre noted, the United States argued that it was not subject to interstate compacts. If the court sustained the U. S. position, both District and Subdistrict water rights would be vulnerable. Thirty thousand dollars of supplemental legal costs would be necessary, he said, to participate in the case, a burden the Board agreed to bear.[16]

A compromise had been worked out within a year regarding the Gore–Eagle's Nest Wilderness boundaries.[17] When the House Public Lands Subcommittee threatened new hearings in response to requests from wilderness advocates, it became obvious that environmental activists would continue to increase their impact on plans for future water developments. In fact, by the time Barkley retired from the District in 1974, wilderness was only one of several environmental issues facing the NCWCD.

Water quality issues had a long history and demanded even greater attention. Following World War II, a national crisis developed over sewage and industrial wastes discharged into increasingly polluted streams and lakes. Although little information about the impact of this pollution on public health and aquatic life was available, President Kennedy's administration began to provide funds to address what was fast becoming a national tragedy.[18] Prior to the Clean Water Act of 1972, however, legislation did not keep pace with national outrage. During the 1960s predictions by private and public officials underscored the need for cooperative planning between federal, state, local, and private water entities to clean up the nation's waterways. Warnings stressed the need for more efficiently irrigated agriculture and state construction of more waste treatment plants to prevent rivers from turning into open sewers. While predictions of industrial and population growth continued in the West, newspapers reminded readers that industrial cooling gluttonously consumed water. Furthermore the average family of four consumed up to 660 gallons of water per day (an exaggerated estimate), while excessive deployment and use of garbage disposals, dishwashers, washing machines, air conditioners, extra bathrooms, and car washes would result in no clean water for the West by the year 2000.[19]

The Water Pollution Control Act of 1961, which set up a federal program with authorization to spend $570 million to help communities build new waste water treatment plants, was hardly a drop in the bucket. President Kennedy tried on three occasions to improve the federal government's role in regional water planning, but Congress proved uncooperative. In 1965, with mounting evidence that polluted waterways were rapidly becoming a national disgrace, President Johnson transferred responsibility for water pollution control from the Department of Health, Education and Welfare to the Department of the Interior. In the same year, Congress passed the Water Resources Planning Act, which established a Cabinet-level Water Resources Council and allowed the president to appoint river basin commissions at the request of state governors. Additionally, this act authorized the government to provide $20 million in matching funds to states that requested assistance to solve local water pollution problems,[20] but the contamination continued. While the Atomic Energy Commission was praised for a "good job" of preventing pollution in the Colorado River basin, studies of the Animas and San Miguel rivers showed that uranium mill tailings and slag piles were increasing radioactivity in aquatic life by nearly 100 percent.[21] Farther east, Lake Michigan was dying. Three hundred towns, several of the nation's largest industries, four states, and ten federal agencies were desperately trying to save the lake. For the sake of national survival, President Johnson urged increased federal aid to states to build waste treatment plants, but his influence was short-lived when he chose not to run for the presidency in 1968.

Johnson's successor, Richard M. Nixon, did not immediately understand the impending crisis. He named Alaska's Walter Hickel as secretary of the interior, knowing that Hickel was a strong promoter of development and an opponent of environmental causes. Nixon recommended budgetary increases to fight water pollution, but the government's ability to attack polluters was not approved by statute until passage of the Clean Water Act

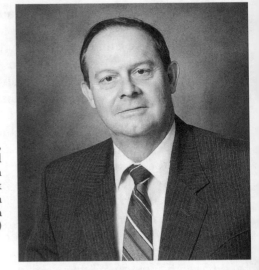

Larry D. Simpson grew up in Colorado, graduated from the Colorado School of Mines, and then went to work in California. In 1971 he was lured back to Colorado and the NCWCD. In 1982 he became the District's fourth general manager. (Courtesy NCWCD.)

(CWA) of 1972, which proclaimed a new goal: to "restore and maintain the chemical, biological and physical integrity of the nation's waters."[22] As with earlier acts that described federal guidelines for clean air, the CWA insisted on strong federal leadership to set standards and deadlines for state compliance and also authorized $18 billion to assist states in building municipal waste-water treatment facilities to meet the goals defined by law. This act became the largest single public works project ever created by Congress.[23]

As environmental groups began to pressure the Environmental Protection Agency (EPA) to pay more attention to the *source* of pollution, state and local concerns in Colorado recognized that every entity distributing and administrating water would be affected by the new regulations, and the NCWCD was no exception. While the State Assembly worked furiously to pass a state water-quality control act, Larry D. Simpson, recently hired as the District's planning coordinator and Windy Gap project manager, noted that the EPA had set a 1975 deadline for a regional water-quality management plan; unless that deadline were met, the federal government could refuse requests for subsequent water and sewer treatment grants.[24] Environmentalist's discussions of *nonpoint source* pollution during the next few years clearly indicated that irrigated agriculture would be targeted by the EPA. Attorney Sayre warned that waste discharge permits for agriculture might soon be required, and Professor Norm Evans, director of the Environmental Resources Center at Colorado State University, estimated that more than $400 million would be required in the next five years for

In the mid-1970s the Environmental Protection Agency began targeting agricultural water users for nonpoint source pollution. (Courtesy NCWCD.)

construction of water treatment plants if state waters were to meet federal standards.[25]

Barkley was annoyed by the federal imposition of clean water standards, but he also knew that increases in population and industrialization could create water-quality problems in Colorado just like those in California.[26] He conferred with representatives of the Public Health Service and the Department of Health, Education and Welfare. He visited Utah communities to learn about cooperative arrangements between local governments and water districts to prevent water pollution. He counseled the Board that the public's concern over environmental matters meant that a dialogue had to be established between the CWC and those active in promoting water-quality issues.[27] Despite Barkley's hopes for conciliation with environmental groups, fear that water-quality controls could stifle water project development dominated the thinking of most water officials, who believed that conservationists were primarily interested in reducing the *amount* of water in use. In semi-arid lands, they argued, irrigation farmers and

Secretary of the Interior Stewart Udall.
(Courtesy Bureau of Reclamation.)

municipalities should restrict water application and consumption to reduce contamination of streams, lakes, and underground aquifers.[28] In spite of research on water pollution at Colorado State University, however, the state legislature did not address this issue as a conservation problem until 1965.

In that year legislators discussed the creation of a special state water control commission to designate areas of industrial and municipal water pollution. Over the next year, strong opinions were voiced about how to enforce such a bill and what liability polluters would have for cleaning up the rivers.[29] With three different bills considered in 1966, a compromise statute apparently could not be passed unless an environmental crisis occurred or new federal regulations demanded state action.

Meanwhile, evidence of statewide water pollution increased. Nebraska and Kansas clamored for cleaner water from Colorado. Mexico complained about heavy salinity in the Colorado River. Chemical analyses of the South Platte River produced evidence of unacceptable amounts of fecal coliform agents from raw sewage in towns as far away as Longmont. Shadow Mountain Reservoir and Lake Granby were considered so polluted that they were described as "dead lakes."[30] The Federal Water Pollution Control

Commission pressured the state to buy land along the Arkansas River to reduce damage from irrigated farming, but CWCB director Felix "Larry" Sparks responded by urging all state water agencies to recognize the statewide crisis and to unite for protection of Colorado from similar "unreasonable" demands and pressures.[31]

In the seven years prior to Colorado's successful passage of effective water pollution legislation, water quality in the state deteriorated rapidly. Under federal guidelines every state was required to set water-quality standards by July 1967, but Governor Love told Secretary of the Interior Stewart Udall that the federal government asked too much too fast.[32] At the same time, experts prepared citizens for the probability of drinking their own treated sewage. Others noted that every stream in the state was polluted, unable to provide a clean drink of water. The crisis at hand was survival.[33] One year after the CWA of 1972, Colorado passed the Colorado Water Quality Control Act to provide a Water Quality Control Commission (CWQCC) that would develop policies to prevent further stream pollution. Its declared legislative purposes included the need to achieve the maximum degree of water quality in Colorado, to conserve water resources, and to abate water pollution; however, the CWQCC also stressed that interpretations of the act should have no effect on the doctrine of prior appropriation. Water rights had to be protected, and the Water Quality Control Commission could not "require minimum stream flows or minimum water levels in any lakes or impoundments."[34] Although written to conform with federal statutes, whose goal was to eliminate discharge of all pollutants by 1985 and to "restore and maintain the chemical, physical and biological integrity of the Nation's waters,"[35] the legislation contained, in attorney Sayre's words, "very broad definitions."[36]

For the moment at least, the District felt no obligation to change extant policies or future plans. Barkley, who warned about "highly emotional obstructionist attitudes" prevalent among environmentalists, also saw 1972 as the year in which environmental issues took precedence over water supply and resource development.[37] He might even have agreed with William Gianelli, director of California's Department of Water Resources, that the environment had clearly replaced sex, night baseball, the economy, and the Vietnam War as the most popular topic of conversation in America.[38] Even while the Bureau engaged in water-quality studies on the Colorado River and various federal, state, and local agencies launched at least six similar projects along the Front Range, Barkley knew that new EPA water-quality standards were still a long way off. Except for ongoing concern about pollution in Granby and Shadow Mountain reservoirs —

the only water-quality issue of real significance to the District during the late sixties and early seventies — Barkley and the Board were pleased that northern Colorado's ample water supplies continued to attract industry and population to the Front Range.[39]

At the May 10, 1968, Board meeting, an attorney who represented the Caribou Water Company explained that his client, a subsidiary of a principal company, was looking for a clean and reliable water source in order to locate a major industry on the Front Range. He would not identify this company because the need for substantial space would result in immediate inflation of land values. Over a forty- to fifty-year period, he noted, the company wanted to acquire rights to 4,000 acre-feet of water.[40]

As Barkley later recalled, his first acquaintance with this project occurred when two bright and dapper individuals, identifying themselves only as "Bob" and "Bruce," came to inquire about availability of a clean water supply. They had scouted the Front Range from Canada to Mexico and were interested in purchasing land from the Great Western Sugar Company. Great Western had been slowly going out of business for a variety of reasons, including the estimated high costs associated with cleaning up the water pollution caused by their ten processing factories.[41] The Windsor plant had closed; consequently, about 3,000 acres of sugar beet land were available for purchase. "Bob" and "Bruce" assured Barkley that they were neither secret service agents nor federal examiners; but they did represent a major U.S. company that needed large amounts of land and high-quality water. Recalled Barkley, "They were two sharp guys who knew what the company wanted."[42] They disguised their identity so well that no one guessed what company they represented until Governor Love called Barkley to a reception in the Brown Palace Hotel where they joined the governor in announcing that the Eastman Kodak Company would locate a processing plant in Windsor. Barkley then understood why they had placed so much emphasis on the availability of high-quality water.

Soon after plant construction, however, Kodak began having film processing problems. The culprit was dirty water provided by the Greeley Water Department. In spring 1970 this water turned a yellowish-brown color due to aspen leaves and pine needles in snowmelt and adhered to photographic materials. Greeley built another water line from the Boyd Lake system to Kodak, but Windsor, still miffed by Greeley's unwillingness to allow more water taps in the late fifties, argued for an expanded water supply and delivery program. Predictions of industrial and municipal growth for northern Colorado were already so alarming that Barkley proposed a more comprehensive solution for Kodak, Windsor, and every other water-using entity. He suggested a long-term regional approach that would consolidate water districts along both the Big Thompson and Poudre rivers, and he committed the District to this organization if cities, counties, and industries were interested in dealing with water distribution and sanitation on the basis of regional cooperation.[43]

Although the idea seemed ahead of its time, Barkley was aware of the rapid organization of planning groups that focused on controlling land use and water quality. He had hired Simpson as planning coordinator to keep the District abreast of developments and to ascertain how the growth of municipalities stimulated the water-use shift from agriculture to industrial and urban purposes. Simpson, who had grown up in Eaton, Colorado, had to take a considerable cut in salary when he came to the District, but his family wanted to leave California and return to Colorado.[44] Beginning work in May 1971, he immediately became acquainted with three active environmental groups that were trying to curtail growth in Boulder County — "Plan Boulder County," "People United to Reclaim the Environment," and "Zero Population Growth." These groups advocated everything from flood plain regulation to restrictions on water and sewage extensions. They supported growth control and urged policies that would make growth pay for itself.[45] Similarly, the Larimer-Weld County Regional Planning Commission focused on the impact of growth on future quality of life.

Simpson attended group meetings and met with other county planning commissions; became acquainted with municipal and county staff members, utility and zoning boards, members of the CWQCC, and the Denver Regional Council of Governments; and reported back to District Board members. Barkley was pleased with his work, relieved to attend fewer meetings, and happy that Simpson learned quickly. Understanding the desires and accomplishments of so many planning agencies would facilitate regional planning and would ultimately lead to orderly growth in the District area.[46] This is what Barkley had had in mind when he proposed a regional organization to Windsor's mayor in 1970. Increasingly, Simpson's reports mentioned the evolution of a statewide movement, supported at many levels, in which water planning was the ultimate tool to restrict and redirect population growth along the Front Range. Only six months after he began work with the District, the Colorado Environmental Commission published its second interim report, suggesting coordination of water resource management and land-use planning. The report criticized Colorado's water laws because they "treated water as a negotiable commodity separate from the land through which it flows." Tying water to statewide planning, the commission concluded, would end the policy of sending West

Slope water to the Front Range to further complicate its population problems.[47]

Once again the underlying premise of Colorado water law, the prior appropriation doctrine, was being challenged. A state water plan appealed to many in the political arena who deplored transmountain diversion, urban sprawl, water waste, and ignorance of conservation methods. Governor Love endorsed a state water plan in his state-of-the-state message in January 1972. Three months later, he asked the legislature to study the state's water laws.[48] In the 1972 Democratic primary, Alan Merson defeated veteran Congressman Aspinall by urging an end to transmountain water diversion and by calling for changes in Colorado water law.[49] Lieutenant Governor John Vanderhoof described the state's appropriation doctrine as "not adequate" and urged all Colorado water groups to daringly propose innovative ideas and new techniques.[50]

Merson was narrowly defeated by Republican James P. Johnson in the November elections. Conservational and environmental groups made their power felt in other races in 1972 and again in 1974. Youthful voters, many of whom had recently settled in Colorado, felt that the old guard had not watched over the state's natural treasures with sufficient zeal. Voters were saying "that possibly their patrimony was being expended too rapidly, too recklessly, and sometimes for the wrong reasons."[51]

When Barkley, Simpson, and Board members were asked about the District's position on land- and water-use planning, they replied that the District should not be involved in land planning or zoning and that the allocation or transfer of water should follow patterns established by government bodies with appropriate authority.[52] Colorado State University professor Henry Caulfield, formerly a close associate of Secretary Udall, believed that land-use controls proved more effective in the guidance of growth than any attempt to limit development through control of water supplies.[53] The CWC, which also supported this position and which was even more concerned that the federal government might override Colorado's water laws with new legislation, passed a resolution opposing any statute seeking to use control of water rights as a planning or zoning tool.[54]

In sum, the environmentally backed attempt to revolutionize Colorado water law when growth was creating demographic chaos on the Front Range was a logical expression of frustration with a legal system that appeared to favor only the affluent and powerful. The clash between those who insisted on the proven efficacy of the prior appropriation system and those who cynically saw all water flowing to money could have no simple resolution. When Barkley retired in 1974, however, criticisms of the prior appropriation doctrine were becoming increasingly vocal. While Barkley remained firmly opposed to a state water plan, he did favor some form of integrated conjunctive use of the state's water supplies. As indicated by his proposal to Windsor's mayor, he preferred a stream basin management system administered to benefit both urban and rural users, but he predicted a "change in the present system of water law before the concept could be developed." As is, he said, "the Colorado water system cannot operate to maximize beneficial use of water when everyone can be cut off to supply a single priority user."[55]

This threat of being cut off, or called out, presented an ironic twist for the District on a much grander scale when environmental activists coalesced to oppose the Bureau's planned developments on the Colorado River. Throughout the long political struggle to win congressional approval of the CAP, the Sierra Club had used increasing influence to help defeat plans to construct Marble and Bridge Canyon dams in the Grand Canyon. As chairman of the Colorado River Advisory Board, Barkley had also opposed the dams.[56] When the same groups filed suit in 1970 against the secretary of the interior to halt the filling of Lake Powell because of potential danger to Rainbow Bridge, his response immediately reflected the District's fear that such a limitation might have serious implications for C–BT water storage on the West Slope. Friends of the Earth and the Sierra Club objected to filling Lake Powell to the designed level of 3,700 feet. Water at this level would invade the 160-acre national monument, established in 1910 to protect the world's largest natural arch. Although the concern of these and other environmental groups was genuine, Sayre and Barkley argued that unless Lake Powell were filled to the intended capacity, existing and future water projects planned for the upper basin states would be permanently handicapped. They noted that in the likelihood of four to five drought years, the lower basin states would exercise their right to call water from the upper basin states, thus requiring water already stored in Green Mountain Reservoir, Lake Granby, and a planned Windy Gap project.[57]

Ival Goslin, executive secretary of the Upper Colorado River Commission (UCRC), agreed with their assessment. Restricting the fill level of Lake Powell would diminish its use as a long-term bank account. With water consumption on the upper Colorado River expected to increase due to population and industrial growth, Goslin concluded that water to meet Colorado River Compact obligations would have to come from Granby, Blue Mesa, Flaming Gorge, and other reservoirs located above Lee Ferry.[58] In the history of C–BT operations, nothing had been more threatening to

Constructed as part of the 1956 Colorado River Storage project, Glen Canyon Dam and Lake Powell were created amidst controversy, much of which centered around Rainbow Bridge. (Photograph by Randy Werth.)

the NCWCD staff and Board members than having to spill water collected and stored at Lake Granby. Sayre recommended that the District intervene directly in the case, but the Board preferred the role of *amicus curiae* while the CWCB, CWC, and UCRC carried the brunt of the litigation. When the directors of the Metropolitan Water District of Los Angeles adopted a resolution supporting Colorado's position and when the Lower Colorado River Board of California indicated likewise, the entire Colorado River basin manifested a unity rarely enjoyed in the twentieth century.[59] The environmentalists had proved that in matters of water, political alliances can be unpredictable.

The case was assigned to Salt Lake City Federal District Judge Willis W. Ritter, who noted that the CRSP Act of 1956 specifically instructed the secretary of the interior to "take adequate protective measures to preclude impairment of the Rainbow Bridge National Monument." The defendants alleged "sovereign immunity," but Ritter rejected their claim and found in favor of the plaintiffs.[60] In April 1973 he ordered the secretary of the interior to prevent water in Lake Powell from rising to the 3,700-foot level. Opponents appealed to the 10th Circuit Court of Appeals. By a 5-2 majority, the appeals court overruled Judge Ritter, stating that if Lake

Powell were only filled to 3,600 feet, as requested by Friends of the Earth, total storage would be 12.2 million acre-feet less than the 27 million acre-feet of designed capacity. Because storage in Lake Powell was considered essential to successful agreements between upper basin and lower basin states and to the treaty with Mexico and because restricted storage would impair operation of existing and future projects, the appeals court reasoned that Judge Ritter's decision had to be "vacated and set aside."[61] Environmentalists appealed to the U.S. Supreme Court but were denied a hearing. The Court voted 6-3 not to review the circuit court's decision. On August 2, 1973, water was allowed to enter Rainbow Bridge National Monument.[62]

Colorado water officials breathed a relieved sigh; they considered the court's decision a victory. But the growing influence of other environmental activities threatened to have an impact on both agricultural and municipal life along the Front Range. Even though Congressman Aspinall persisted in seeing agitation by environmentalists as nothing more than an "emotional binge,"[63] state agencies by the 1970s were becoming conscious of the need to address a number of water-quality issues. The Wild and Scenic Rivers Act, considered an extension or corollary the Wilderness Act, passed Congress in 1968 after six years' deliberation. Its objective was to preserve components of certain rivers in their natural state because of their wild, scenic, or recreational uniqueness. The statute initially designated eight river segments — none in Colorado — and outlined procedures for the inclusion of other streams or rivers in the Wild and Scenic River System. In the mind of its principal sponsor, Senator Frank Church, this legislation was planned to "complement the policy of building dams and other control structures"[64] and to preserve the natural and pastoral nature of the nation's rivers.[65]

Not until the 1980s did NCWCD officials become concerned with how the Wild and Scenic Rivers Act might affect the C–BT.[66] In the seventies, however, the nation had made so many commitments to environmental matters that Colorado could not escape the impact of other laws. On the first day of 1970, President Nixon signed the National Environmental Policy Act (NEPA), assuring a worried citizenry that the federal government would consider any and all deleterious effects of its actions on the environment. Three months later, the nation celebrated the first Earth Day with teach-ins, garbage collection campaigns, and other demonstrations of practical concern for a livable environment. Judged from the vantage point of the 1990s, 1970 appears the "single most important year in this country's environmental history."[67]

This was also the year that Colorado state agencies responded with action. The CWQCC conducted hearings at Fort Morgan to consider reclassification of the Poudre and South Platte rivers to warm-water fisheries. Hoping to dilute existing pollution by establishing year-round flow conditions, the CWQCC ran into strong objections from the District, which urged instead construction of additional channel storage on the South Platte.[68] The CWC then resolved to oppose dilution of pollution to meet new water-quality standards, but the resolution's tone implied a new interest in establishing dialogue with environmentalists.[69] Meanwhile, researchers at the University of Colorado worked to turn sewage effluent into potable water while the state senate drafted legislation to impose a weekly $5,000 fine on South Platte polluters.[70] With newspapers urging state officials to raise water-quality standards because of pollution in all Front Range streams, some of which was said to be arriving through the Adams Tunnel from Grand County, legislators addressed a bill (S.B. 97), introduced by Senator Fred Anderson, to establish minimum stream flows as a beneficial use of Colorado water. The controversial Senate Bill 97 gave the CWCB authority to obtain water rights for the sole purpose of maintaining a minimum level in flowing streams. Although Governor Love believed that such an amendment to Colorado water law could only be legitimized through a constitutional amendment, he signed the legislation on April 23, 1973.[71] The CRWCD later sued the CWCB to prevent the board from holding minimum stream flow rights on segments of the Crystal River and one of its tributaries,[72] but Senate Bill 97 at the time of its passage received support from the NCWCD, DWB, CWCB, and all environmental organizations. As CWCB director Sparks noted, a new era had arrived. With large project developments in the state essentially complete, the CWCB could now reorient activities toward improved use of existing water supplies.[73]

Environmentalists had indeed made their mark. Their nationwide warnings were issued when agriculture was enjoying considerable economic success within the District, much of this prosperity attributable to regular C–BT water deliveries and to the open-market policy espoused by NCWCD staff. As Ralph Nader's task force blasted the Bureau and its projects for damaging the environment, wasting billions of dollars, and subsidizing unproductive irrigation farming at the expense of the nation's taxpayers,[74] the economy was booming in northern Colorado. NCWCD payments on C–BT obligations to the government were on schedule, and an escrow account had been established to meet the large balloon payments of the last ten years of the Repayment Contract (1992–2001). In addition

Monfort feedlot near Greeley fattened thousands of cattle in their pens and also provided the impetus for expanding corn and silage planting in the NCWCD area. (Courtesy Bureau of Reclamation.)

to a healthy agricultural economy, 1970 found the District enjoying harmonious relations with the people, businesses, and institutions it served. These positive features of the C–BT Project seemed to belie harsh criticisms of "Nader's Raiders." The first Earth Day, therefore, was celebrated at the same time that the District was providing water to maintain a healthy agricultural and industrial economy in northeastern Colorado.

Exemplifying the area's prosperity was the successful partnership between farmers and livestock feeders. In the first five years of full C–BT operation, 1957 to 1962, alfalfa and sugar beets ranked as favored crops. Beginning in 1963, however, farmers doubled their plantings of ensilage and corn, a dramatic change due to postwar mechanization of agriculture, development of new kinds of hybrid corn, and burgeoning demands of a livestock feeding industry developed by Farr Farms and others.[75] In the seventies, expansion of corn and ensilage harvests indicated the extent to

This farmer is cutting and chopping corn for silage. Corn became the largest crop in northeastern Colorado following the establishment of the livestock feeding industry in the 1960s. (Courtesy Bureau of Reclamation.)

which cropping patterns in the District had begun to change, and the Farr family was instrumental in agricultural innovation. They had been in livestock feeding since long before construction of the C–BT, but W. D. "Bill" Farr pioneered a special arrangement in the sixties that guaranteed farmers that if they agreed to plant feed crops, he would commit to purchasing their produce to feed his cattle. Although sugar beets remained the crop of highest value in the NCWCD area through 1974, Farr's program resulted in greater security for District farmers at a time when agriculture was at best an unstable industry.

An NCWCD Board member since 1955 and chairman of the Greeley Water Board, Farr was recognized by the Weld County Board of Realtors as the 1970 Citizen of the Year.[76] This was only one of many honors for his commitment to domestic and international agriculture, high-altitude water storage, and the free-market economy. Farr also embodied the NCWCD's juxtaposed drives for economic growth and environmentally sensitive irrigated agriculture. He had been an implacable supporter of the C–BT since its inception during the Great Depression. At the same time, he served on many regional and national boards and committees[77] that kept him better informed about environmental issues than others with a more limited sense of social and economic responsibility. As a presidential appointee on Nixon's Water Pollution Control Advisory Board, Farr traveled across the country to inspect lakes and rivers polluted by industry, cities, and agriculture. He became convinced that land- and water-use planning was inevitable, especially in Colorado, where the population growth rate was twice the national rate. He was not sure whether responsibility for planning should lie with the state or the counties, but he was certain that good environmental planning should be executed in Colorado on a regional basis.[78]

Exceptionally visionary in his concern for northern Colorado's economy, Farr's leadership resulted in several key accomplishments. The superiority of Greeley's water system, the city's "near-infinite capacity for growth,"[79] and the organization of the Municipal Subdistrict to build the Windy Gap project testify to his foresight. The awards he received repeatedly recognized his unselfishness; his interest in bringing the federal government, agriculture, and the general public to the bargaining table; and his talent for pioneering innovative and successful communication of complex ideas. Although he warned against rapid implementation of environmental controls that might limit fertilizer use or fence streams from livestock,[80] he also recognized environmental problems within the District and praised the efforts of Larimer and Weld counties to address these matters jointly.

Like other community builders, Farr took great pride in the steady growth of northern Colorado's economy. In addition to the remarkable increase in corn and ensilage harvests, 1970 was notable as the first year in which the District's revenue from ad valorem property taxes surpassed revenue from water assessments. Census data for 1970 also revealed that population in the District's major municipalities had grown by 69 percent since 1960. A quarter of the state's entire growth during the sixties' boom had taken place within the NCWCD boundaries.[81] Of the state's $1.2 billion agriculture and livestock production in 1970, 80 percent was attributable to livestock marketing, half of which emanated from northeastern Colorado.[82]

As required by Article 33 of the Repayment Contract, annual NCWCD reports between 1957 and 1974 provided abundant agricultural data. Information from county agents, Great Western Sugar Company, and the Colorado Department of Agriculture revealed the importance of diverse economic growth in Weld, Boulder, and Larimer counties, which had produced an average of 80 percent of all District ad valorem taxes. From 1965 through 1970, average annual incremental increases showed Boulder County at 12 percent, Larimer County at 8.2 percent, and Weld County at 7 percent. Annual reports also estimated that approximately 720,000 acres were under agricultural production, although the exact amount was difficult to determine because of return flows and temporary and seasonal water rentals. In sum, from 1957 to 1974, the combination of industrial, municipal, and agricultural expansion produced a 150 percent overall increase in District valuation, part of which resulted from a 272 percent increase in the value of harvested crops. Annual reports specified problems with inflation, commodity prices, and a general cost-price squeeze on farmers across the nation; but data also showed improved agricultural efficiency and record production during the last three years of Barkley's administration. By 1974 ad valorem and water rental revenues had reached nearly $1.5 million.[83] This level of prosperity and growth placed the District in a position to plan for the last ten years of debt obligations to the United States under terms of the 1938 Repayment Contract.

Barkley wanted to amend Article 15 of the Repayment Contract, under which excess revenues could be invested in treasury certificates purchased through local banks. According to the original contract, however, excess revenues were to be escrowed with the secretary of the treasury and invested only in bonds. Barkley believed the District could do better.[84] At a Washington luncheon meeting with Commissioner Floyd E. Dominy, he explained the advantage of depositing this money in higher yielding funds, albeit with some limitations imposed by the secretary of the interior. Dominy agreed. On October 29, 1964, the United States executed Supplement No. 3 of the Repayment Contract, which amended Article 15 to allow deposit of excess revenues into a member agency of the Federal Reserve system until the account totaled $11 million.[85] Convinced of the need to include the new account as a component part of the budget procedure, Barkley prepared a chart that showed what amount of annual deposits over the next twenty-seven years would result in the required payments of $1,125,775 in ten annual installments beginning in 1992. Board member Moffit urged Directors to inform the public of these steps in order to protect District allottees and taxpayers.[86] During the last ten years of Barkley's administration, and especially after 1970, steady agricultural, industrial, and municipal growth made it possible to budget substantial amounts for deposit in the new escrow account. At a time when reclamation projects were criticized for failing to pay their way, productivity and overall growth within the District allowed the accumulation of large sums for retiring the construction debt during the last ten years of the Repayment Contract. With only 12 percent of C–BT water being used for municipal and domestic purposes in 1974,[87] agriculture remained the principal beneficiary and primary reason for economic stability in northeastern Colorado.

Agriculture had problems, both nationally and statewide, but occasionally a silver lining was visible. Although the U.S. Department of Agriculture documented a declining farm population; a reduction in the number of farms in the country (about the same number of farms in 1967 as in 1876); a net farm income drop averaging 1.4 percent per year; inflationary rises in the cost of chemicals, pesticides, machinery, labor, interest, and taxes; and an increase in the average size of farms,[88] the early seventies still provided room for optimism. Data from 1973 revealed the highest one-year gain in farm income since 1916. Agricultural exports had increased 175 percent since 1968, and farmers were able, even with inflation, to net the highest share of their gross returns since 1958.[89]

Colorado trends were similar. The number of farms had declined, and the average farm size had increased from 942 acres in 1958 to 1,353 acres in 1975.[90] The smaller number of farms was directly related to mechanization of farm equipment and its high cost. Even in productive Weld County, fewer farms were being worked, and those that survived were larger and frequently managed by tenant operators.[91] Net farm income had dropped steadily as the cost-price squeeze worsened, causing a reduction in on-farm population of more than 22 percent between 1940 and 1968, a trend that continued into the seventies at an annual rate of from 4 percent to 5 percent.[92]

The good news was that those who continued to farm began experiencing better times starting in 1970, what *Colorado Rancher and Farmer* considered the "banner year," when the index for all crop production reached 119 percent of the 1957–1959 base. Along with the "spectacular efficiency and increased productivity" of Colorado farmers, as noted by the American Farm Bureau, ample evidence revealed that by 1975 Colorado had experienced five years of record agricultural production and some improvement in net income.[93] The same boast could be made for gross crop production values within the District. From the approximately 640,000 acres under cultivation during the 1970–1975 period, gross returns from agriculture rose steadily to new records. Since 1958, feed grain and forage harvests had increased five-fold, providing an annual cash increment of more than 12 percent, while livestock production and marketing remained consistently strong. Farmers' successes were translated into increased property valuations that, in turn, improved District revenues and deposits in the Repayment Contract escrow fund.[94]

By any standard, the combination of Front Range population growth and reliable supplemental water in a free market made inclusion in the NCWCD an attractive option for communities concerned about the future. As rural domestic water companies incorporated and planned to purchase C–BT units for delivery to clients, the Board reminded hopeful petitioners that under the Water Conservancy District Act, C–BT water could not be delivered outside District boundaries. Rules existed for the inclusion of new areas into the District, but the Board had no set policy prior to June 1966 as to how much or in what direction to expand. Between 1937 and 1953, when the District comprised 1,482,000 acres, inclusions were made largely to correct original boundaries; Boulder's addition in 1953 resulted in more than 30,000 new acres. More lands were included to assist rural domestic associations and to make water exchanges possible, but the Board had no formal inclusion policy as of 1966. Consequently, Sayre recommended a policy that reflected the District's position vis-à-vis the increasing interest of old communities and new subdivisions in acquiring a stable water supply.[95] Very little happened for a few years. Estes Park made a strong case for the inclusion of suburbs based on increased numbers of retirees and other year-around residents who were winterizing homes in new subdivisions outside municipal limits. During discussions, the Board adopted a revised inclusion policy that opposed expansion of 1959 boundaries to the north and to the southeast, with the exception of areas that were "substantially surrounded by previously included lands." In such cases the Board would only consider "the supplying of domestic water service through facilities of existing water distribution entities that [were] present allottees of the District." Back taxes, equivalent to what would have been paid annually since 1937, would have to be collected. After considering Estes Park's petition, the Board agreed in 1967 to its inclusion if the municipality would pay $57,444 in back taxes over a ten-year period at an interest rate of 4.5 percent.[96]

Far more pressure was exerted on the District by small communities east of Boulder, located south of the District's southeastern boundary. The Board's difficulty in adhering to a policy was exemplified in the case of the "Little Red School House," located just outside the District, approximately 5 miles south of the town of Kersey, near Greeley, Colorado. The Valley View School's problem involved well water for drinking that, according to chemical analysis, contained more than twice the amount of nitrates allowed by the U.S. Public Health Department. Colorado State University's Department of Chemistry judged this water "no good" for household use.[97] The attorney for the school district, Ralph Waldo, asked the Board to consider inclusion of 296 square feet of property so that higher quality C–BT water could be delivered to the school by the Central Weld County Water District.

The Board denied the request. Referring to the policy resolution of June 10, 1966, Barkley told Waldo the Board's dilemma. Several persons and organizations were situated in locations like that of Valley View School. Should the Board make exceptions to policy, petitions for inclusion would pour in, with no way to determine where to stop once the boundary was crossed. Furthermore, he emphasized, the Board remained concerned that continued and uncontrolled expansion would "dilute the originally intended benefits of District water service operation." Singled out specifically as municipalities the District would never include were Fort Lupton and Brighton.[98] Waldo requested a hearing in which he emphasized the school children's plight and asked Barkley to check whether there was, in fact, another case similar to that of Valley View School; whether there was or not proved irrelevant. As Boulder extended service closer and closer to Louisville and Lafayette and as both towns petitioned for inclusion to become eligible for C–BT water, pressure increased for the Board to stand firm on the 1966 resolution. Consequently, the children of the "Little Red School House" lost in the Board's struggle to enforce a policy of keeping District boundaries intact.[99]

This policy required further refinement in 1972 as new subdivisions came together west of the District's 1959 western boundary in Boulder and Larimer counties. The Board amended the June 10, 1966, resolution to state that inclusions would be considered only if the lands involved were annexed to a municipality from which water service could be provided. This amendment also stated that any lands not within the corporate or service areas of a municipality would receive C–BT water only as a result of contracts between the District and existing beneficiaries.[100] In other words, the District wanted to retain control of water deliveries to newly included areas. A year later the Board adopted a formula to determine the tax amounts a petitioner would pay as a result of authorized inclusion.[101] In addition to Boulder (1953), Firestone (1963), Dacona (1967), Frederick (1973) and its suburb of Evanston (1974), Estes Park (1967), the Left Hand Water District (1967), and the Baseline Heights Water and Sanitation District (1971) had been included in the District along with numerous privately owned parcels in Boulder, Larimer, and Weld counties.[102]

Related to this policy issue was the augmented cost of pumping additional water from Flatiron Reservoir through Carter Lake to these newly included areas. Although Barkley and Dille had urged the Bureau many years earlier to consider a gravity-flow system to Carter Lake from Bald Mountain, the Bureau had insisted on using the power head to raise revenue. Because no one in 1937 anticipated that the area around Boulder would grow exponentially in the sixties, the pumping costs from servicing these areas resulted in a net diminution of the Bureau's marketable power and caused the United States to demand financial assistance from the District. Region 7 director H. P. Dugan explained the Bureau's position to the Board in no uncertain terms: He would sit on any further inclusion applications until a contract was signed to compensate the United States for this "power interference." He defended this position by opening up an old scar; the District had a very favorable Repayment Contract, he noted, and the Bureau needed revenues from power generation to repay part of the irrigation construction costs. Furthermore, present congressional policy required higher payment for municipal and industrial water uses. Thus, it was unfair for the District to acquire additional revenues from higher water uses while reducing net power revenue to the Bureau because of an inclusion policy that increased pumping costs to Carter Lake from Flat-iron.[103]

Some Board members and Boulder representatives steamed over the Bureau's blatant use of leverage; others recognized that some sort of deal was necessary. When Dugan left, the Board agreed that Barkley, Sayre, and President J. Ben Nix would leave for Washington to confer with their ally, Commissioner Dominy. At the next month's Board meeting, Barkley reported a successful meeting with Dominy and Assistant Commissioner Gilbert G. Stamm, who agreed to use actual water deliveries from Carter Lake between 1962 and 1966 to determine real pumping costs. They also agreed to limit revenue recovery by the United States to the amount necessary to keep its power revenue intact. Stamm informed Barkley that Dugan had been advised to release those inclusion applications detained pending settlement of this dispute.[104] The contract took a year for approval by the secretary of the interior, but on June 18, 1968, the Board passed a resolution authorizing execution of Supplement No. 4 to the Repayment Contract.[105]

Not surprisingly, discussions leading to creation of a Municipal Sub-district took place while the power interference debate raged. With seemingly endless inclusion requests, noteworthy agricultural productivity, municipal growth, and new industries along the Front Range — to say nothing of the possibility of water use restrictions imposed by federal and state environmental laws — representatives from six Front Range cities met in winter 1967 to discuss ways to increase C–BT deliveries to the full 310,000 acre-feet promised in Senate Document 80. The Windy Gap project emerged from these deliberations.

20 The Origins of Windy Gap and the Municipal Subdistrict

Construction of a dam at Windy Gap to collect unappropriated Colorado River water for the C–BT system was an idea the Bureau had explored and deemed infeasible in 1952. At that time, construction cost was evaluated as unjustifiable for irrigated agriculture in the NCWCD area. Within a few years, however, municipal growth on the East Slope fostered renewed interest, and by the early sixties municipal and District officials viewed a Windy Gap project as the only way to fully utilize the design capacity of the C–BT and to provide water for unremitting Front Range population pressures. The only alternative would witness further conversion of agricultural water to municipal and industrial use, and neither the Board nor the municipalities wanted that.

Both Senate Document 80 and the Repayment Contract had anticipated delivery of 310,000 acre-feet of water through the Adams Tunnel. Even though 1930s hydrology studies were only good faith estimates, NCWCD negotiations with the West Slope were based on the quid pro quo that in return for compensatory expenditures, the District would receive its full share of Colorado River water. According to J. R. "Bob" Barkley, however, District water deliveries averaged less than 260,000 acre-feet in the ten years after C–BT system completion in 1957.[1] One reason for this was the Bureau's decision not to spend an estimated $1.7 million to bring water from Strawberry and Meadow creeks into Lake Granby. Although construction of conduits from these streams to Lake Granby was included in the original Project plan, the Bureau's postwar penury and further studies showing that less than 10,000 acre-feet of divertible water were available resulted in the Bureau's decision not to proceed with construction. J. M. Dille and Barkley met frequently with the Bureau to register the District's disapproval. They agreed that the existing C–BT collection system could produce an average yearly supply of approximately 245,000 acre-feet, but they urged the Bureau to find ways to increase deliveries to the promised 310,000 acre-feet. The Bureau's South Platte project manager, James H. Knights, gave verbal consent to accomplish this objective[2] and proved to be a man of his word.

In December 1956 the Bureau completed a study entitled "Reconnaissance Report on the Western Slope Extension, Colorado–Big Thompson Project," which detailed how nearly 30,000 acre-feet of additional water could be added annually to the C–BT system. It focused once again on the Windy Gap area of the Colorado River. The development plan called for a dam and forebay .7 mile below the confluence of the Fraser and Colorado rivers. Unappropriated flows of approximately 30,000 acre-feet would be collected and pumped to Willow Creek Reservoir via a 2-mile tunnel. After some enlargement of existing conduits, this water would be delivered from Willow Creek Reservoir to Lake Granby.[3] Bureau personnel arrived at this 1956 plan after reanalysis studies of the Meadow and Strawberry creek drainages. Their review of hydrology and existing water rights revealed that the city of Englewood had purchased filings on Meadow Creek and that Denver had plans to fully utilize its rights in the Fraser River basin.[4] Water available to the C–BT system would obviously be depleted if these projects were fully developed.

A Windy Gap project was the only viable means of increasing C–BT water deliveries from the West Slope. Bureau data anticipated a yield of 31,500 acre-feet of water to the C–BT power system and 29,200 acre-feet to District irrigators. In monetary terms, the project would add approximately $613,000 annually in irrigation benefits and an increase of $168,000 annually in power revenues. The total estimated cost of $8.4 million would be divided between the Bureau and the District, with the former paying 25 percent and the latter 75 percent. If the Repayment Contract could be amended to increase the District's additional debt obligation, construction of a "Western Slope Extension" (Windy Gap) appeared sound from an engineering standpoint and economically and financially feasible. This 1956 Bureau report recommended approval and allocation of funds by the Department of the Interior.[5] Englewood's water rights had been adjudicated in October 1955. Six years later the District Board had established a precedent of great significance to the Windy Gap project: to permit the transport of approximately 6,000 acre-feet of water annually through the C–BT system. The secretary of the interior formally approved this Englewood carriage contract in July 1961, but the city never completed the project.[6]

Meanwhile, John P. Elliott's Four Counties Water Association was searching for a similar arrangement that would allow transmountain diversion of Yampa River water through the Adams Tunnel to Boulder, Adams,

Weld, and Larimer counties, where municipal growth caused the greatest concern among water planners.[7] Elliott failed to acquire the firm water rights that would have legitimized his proposal, but Barkley agreed with his need assessment for additional municipal water in the four counties. When representatives from Boulder, Longmont, Loveland, Estes Park, and Fort Collins finally met with the Bureau in winter 1967 to discuss augmentation of the C–BT system, Elliott's creative planning, the Bureau's Windy Gap studies, and the existence of a viable carriage contract with Englewood strongly influenced the course of discussions.[8] Fear of power shortages had already brought together Longmont, Estes Park, Loveland, Fort Collins, and Fort Morgan in 1964, when they explored how cooperation with the Bureau might mean acquisition of more electricity from the CRSP.[9] When those same cities, excluding Fort Morgan, met with Boulder in March 1967, they had a common objective regarding future water needs and they already had some informal experience working together.

At the Boulder meeting, Knights explained the Bureau's position. Although legislative attention was distracted by negotiations on the lower Colorado River basin bill, he favored a joint effort by the cities and the Bureau to build the Windy Gap project. The rate at which municipalities were purchasing agricultural water would only diminish, he pointed out, if the existing water supply were augmented by additions from the West Slope. Everyone agreed on the need to plan ahead; the existing growth rate was projected to continue. Total population for the Six Cities was estimated to rise from 217,000 in 1970 to 500,000 in 1990, a 130 percent increase. Most city officials had no doubt that they were preparing wisely for future water needs. Furthermore, filing quickly on surplus waters in the Fraser and Colorado River basin would preempt the five West Slope projects designated in the lower Colorado River basin bill when that legislation received congressional authorization.[10]

Longmont Mayor Ralph Price was very enthusiastic about the Windy Gap plan. As trustee for the informally organized Six Cities (Greeley was now included with Fort Collins, Loveland, Longmont, Boulder, and Estes Park), he drove to Hot Sulphur Springs (Water District No. 58) on July 17, 1967, and filed on 30,000 acre-feet of water at Windy Gap.[11] Over the next year and a half, while Barkley and John M. Sayre discussed the advantages of forming a Municipal Subdistrict of the NCWCD, the Six Cities agreed to formalize their own organization. On February 24, 1969, two representatives from each of the six municipalities met to form the Six-City Water Study Committee (better known as the Six Cities Committee). With approval from their respective city councils, the Six Cities

Committee immediately and unanimously approved action toward formation of an NCWCD Municipal Subdistrict (MSD). They organized committees to work with the NCWCD, selected a consulting engineer, and developed a presentation for voters of the Six Cities, who would be asked to approve or disapprove creation of an MSD.[12]

The 1937 Water Conservancy District Act had anticipated formation of subdistricts under parent districts. Given the NCWCD's long-standing relationship and contract with the Bureau for 310,000 acre-feet of water through the Adams Tunnel, its history as a proven legal entity, and the perceived tendency of six different municipalities to pursue their own agendas, organization of the MSD also made good sense.[13] Although the Subdistrict's function was "to represent the Six Cities in matters of planning, construction, and ultimate operation of the facilities needed to utilize these supplemental water supplies,"[14] the relationship between the Six Cities and the MSD suffered from occasional frictions. Apart from the cities' concern about excessive District aggressiveness, relations were sometimes strained by leadership disputes involving the strong personality of Boulder representative Charles Hallenbeck, who had been elected chairman by the Six Cities Committee following Mayor Price's unexpected death in August 1969.

Less than two years later, Judge Donald A. Carpenter appointed Hallenbeck to the NCWCD Board, where he automatically became a member of the MSD Board. On January 25, 1971, Hallenbeck was elected vice president of the MSD. Having originally opposed formation of a MSD, preferring instead that the Six Cities Committee execute a construction contract with the federal government, Hallenbeck knew that an informal municipal league would have no authority under state statutes to raise funds for a water project;[15] nevertheless, he wanted the Six Cities to have a say in making policy and procedural decisions. He insisted on their right to review construction plans and costs, and even proposed purchasing Elliott's Yampa River water decrees.[16] He pushed for more aggressive dealings with the Bureau when carriage contract negotiations were stalled;[17] and when water allotment contracts with the cities were finalized after dozens of changes, he urged additional revisions that would prevent the cities from transferring their allotments "prior to the incurrence of any debt by the Subdistrict [and] without any obligation to any future debt."[18] Barkley saw Hallenbeck as something of a "maverick." Because both the NCWCD and MSD had the same appointed Board, however, and because Sayre acted as counsel for both, Hallenbeck's outspoken commitment to preserving some authority for the Six Cities was commendable. A tough negotiator and a highly respected engineer, Hallenbeck eventually tired of delays imposed by environmental regulations and the West Slope and became impatient to get the Windy Gap project built. Although Sayre and others may have tired of his manner, the District's "Resolution of Appreciation" to Hallenbeck when he retired in 1974 singled out his "faithful and energetic" contributions to the Board, his "knowledge and experience," and his "leadership skills."[19]

Hallenbeck kept things stirred up from time to time, but the organization and operation of the MSD generally proceeded smoothly. The Water Conservancy District Act specified that petitions for a Subdistrict had to be signed by 25 percent of the owners of irrigated lands and 5 percent of the owners of nonirrigated lands or lands within the incorporated limits of a town or city.[20] After approval by city attorneys, petitions were circulated by firemen and school personnel and then filed on May 5, 1970, with the clerk of the District Court for Weld County. For three weeks, according to law, major newspapers in each of the three affected counties carried notices of a hearing date. When no protesting petitions were filed, Judge Carpenter entered an order on July 6, 1970, declaring the "Municipal Subdistrict, Northern Colorado Water Conservancy District" organized.[21] It was set up to use the same staff and Board as the parent. The Longmont newspaper questioned the legitimacy of organizing an MSD with taxing power when approval of only 5 percent of the urban population was required. Some critics saw taxation without representation and tyranny of the minority in the making; but fear of future water shortages ran so high that the newspaper reassured readers that if water costs were too high, no taxes would be levied on municipal residents.[22] In all likelihood, most citizens in the proposed Subdistrict area either were uninformed or were so concerned about Front Range growth predictions that they cared very little about how the water project was financed as long as supplemental water was delivered from somewhere soon.

With the organizational process under way, the Six Cities Committee hired Engineering Consultants, Inc. (ECI), of Denver to update the Bureau's hydrology studies at Windy Gap. ECI personnel visited the site, collected streamflow and diversion data for 1951–1967, and investigated adjudicated water rights that might affect a proposed Windy Gap project. Their conclusion was twofold: (1) 30,000 to 70,000 acre-feet of water could be diverted, depending on how much replacement storage was available on the West Slope;[23] and (2) the only competing water appropriation would be the CRWCD's proposed 80,000 acre-feet Azure Reservoir. There was water for the Windy Gap project "if the cities [could] afford it, [and] if they [could] arrange credit for Green Mountain Reservoir replacement water."[24] By summer 1970, therefore, the task at hand was how to finance the Windy Gap project and how to persuade the Bureau to accept a carriage contract with a modest charge per acre-foot of water through the C–BT system.

W. D. "Bill" Farr wanted to see the Eastman Kodak Company join with the Six Cities to build the Windy Gap project without assistance from the Bureau.[25] He knew that the Bureau was undergoing personnel and policy changes, that it was concerned about restrictive legislation imposed by the EPA, and that the national uproar over reclamation projects in general was causing caution among Bureau officials. South Platte project manager James H. Knights hoped for a partnership with the NCWCD, but by 1970 the Directors had found another way to finance construction. Within weeks after officially forming the MSD, the Six Cities finance committee recommended applying for funding to the Department of Housing and Urban Development (HUD), a federal agency that promoted "Federal Assistance of Public Works and Facility Type Projects."[26] The maximum grant available was $1.5 million, but HUD representatives indicated that additional funds might be awarded.[27] With Windy Gap project costs estimated at the incredibly low figure of $30.5 million, a HUD grant looked pretty inviting.[28]

No one anticipated the rash of costly obstacles imposed by the federal bureaucracy. Although each city had already paid $6,000 for expenses, HUD insisted that the project first be approved by the Front Range Council of Governments and then cleared by local planning groups, the State Planning Committee, and other interested agencies specified by the Bureau of the Budget. A full year after the application process had begun, HUD and the Bureau announced the need for an environmental impact statement (EIS).[29]

Planning coordinator and Windy Gap project manager Larry D. Simpson worked diligently to meet the government's demands. By fall 1971 the EIS was complete and regional organizations had expressed support for the project.[30] All required data were ready for submission to HUD, but emerging problems related to Windy Gap water filings caused Sayre to recommend a delay in the process. Making the application public, he warned, could have an adverse effect on the Subdistrict's adjudication hearings in the West Slope's Division 5 Water Court.[31]

Concerns about inflation, water rights, West Slope opposition, and government red tape made all delays seem intolerable. In addition, HUD announced a low priority for the Windy Gap project because of no immediate need and because a $1.5 million grant would consume 25 percent of

Windy Gap site prior to reservoir construction, looking west down the Colorado River. (Photograph by Nancy Fisher Frazier.)

the agency's six-state allocation for the central Rockies.[32] With the Six Cities' total investment at $90,000 by the end of 1972, mounting criticism from the CRWCD, Longmont's threat to withdraw from the coalition, and the possibility of extensive and costly litigation, District staff came up with a simple plan and an amendment to state statutes for funding through the sale of revenue bonds.[33] Meanwhile, however, the Bureau stalled approval of the Windy Gap project's linchpin: a carriage contract to bring additional water through the Adams Tunnel to the Front Range municipalities. The first draft of the contract was submitted to the Bureau in August 1970.[34] Although the previously mentioned contract with Englewood established a precedent, Region 7 officials did not indicate that they would respond to the Windy Gap proposal until May 1971. Barkley threatened to appeal to his good friend, Assistant Commissioner Gilbert G. Stamm in Washington. Everyone knew, however, that the reorganization within the Bureau, the recent appointment of Commissioner Ellis Armstrong, and concerns about the EPA's role made for the federal bureaucracy's hesitancy and indecision.[35] Barkley's trip to Washington brought minimal results. During 1972 and most of 1973 the original draft went through many revisions. The Bureau's Washington office required a three-party contract between the

District, the Subdistrict, and the United States, as well as an EIS. Not until October 3, 1973, did the Department of the Interior finally execute a carriage contract — more than three years after the District submitted its initial draft.

During this period the CRWCD's opposition to the Windy Gap project became increasingly obvious. When the CRWCD asked the Bureau to inform them of carriage contract negotiations, the District bluntly retorted that this process was "of no concern to the CRWCD";[36] and although CRWCD attorney Kenneth Balcomb persuaded the secretary of the interior of his right to comment on the proposed contract,[37] the Bureau's legal department ruled that contract negotiations were of no concern to the West Slope.[38] Less than a year after a carriage contract was signed, the CRWCD filed a suit in Federal District Court to set aside the agreement. West Slope opposition to the Windy Gap project was entirely predictable. William H. Nelson, the *Grand Junction Sentinel*'s associate editor, believed that the Subdistrict's Windy Gap plan violated agreements reached during Fry-Ark discussions. At that time a pledge had been made to the West Slope that no further *federally financed* transmountain diversions would be implemented until water needs of the West Slope had been determined.[39] By 1971 Nelson and his colleagues felt deceived. In 1963 Barkley had assured him in writing that the District would make "no attempt to increase the average take of water [from 245,000 acre-feet] to meet the envisioned 310,000 [acre-feet]. We do not intend to do so," he wrote, reminding Nelson that he had given the same assurances to the CRWCD board members three months earlier.[40]

Much had changed on the East Slope since that commitment had been made. Three years after writing Nelson, Barkley told developer John Elliott that the growth potential of Front Range municipalities was so dynamic that a probable need now existed for "importation of [an] additional water supply."[41] When Mayor Price filed for Windy Gap water in 1967, therefore, the West Slope once again concluded that the East Slope was untrustworthy. CRWCD leaders thus prepared to do everything possible to forestall awarding either a carriage contract or a conditional water decree. Moreover, West Slope critics raised some visceral questions for Windy Gap promoters. How could additional C–BT water be transferred to municipalities when the Project's purpose was to supplement irrigated farming? Why were the Six Cities reluctant to explore more efficient use of existing water? And what was being done to conserve and recycle the supplies om hand?[42] From Grand County's point of view, the East Slope appeared profligate. As the Denver metropolitan area coordinated efforts to increase its water supply and as the CCWCD revived its claims on the Blue River,[43] the proposed Windy Gap project appeared to be just another of the East Slope's never-ending raids on West Slope water. Nelson argued opposition at every opportunity because the project violated the "spirit" of Senate Document 80[44] and because it was proposed when the West Slope's oil shale industry was showing signs of commercial development.

Overlapping the West Slope's protest of Windy Gap water rights filings was the federal government's determination to protect water claims in the newly created wilderness areas as well as in the naval oil shale lands; consequently, litigation involving the MSD occurred on two fronts. Sayre appeared in Division 5 Water Court for arguments over U.S.–implied reserved rights claims. In the same court, the CRWCD opposed Windy Gap adjudication hearings. West Slope arguments stated that the MSD was not entitled to a conditional decree because the Windy Gap replacement water plan was inadequate and because the federal government should have jurisdiction.[45] With so many groups involved in litigation, the Water Court consolidated all claims for water rights in Water Division 5 into one proceeding. The Colorado Supreme Court then appointed a master-referee to handle the actual hearings.

In Federal District Court, meanwhile, the CRWCD filed suit against the secretary of the interior to challenge the legality of the carriage contract. In both cases, claims of the federal government and the West Slope caused numerous annoying and costly delays, and the longer resolution took, the higher the eventual cost of Windy Gap project water. In 1973 Simpson estimated the cost per acre-foot of delivered water at $37;[46] each year of delay increased this estimate by at least 10 percent. In addition, added legal expenses worried MSD and Six Cities officials. Although Sayre expressed willingness to stick with both cases to the end, "without pay if necessary,"[47] the organizations worried about litigation costs and how long individual cities would continue voluntary contributions.[48] But there was no realistic shortcut in the litigation process. In spring 1974, as a result of a partial master-referee report on the Windy Gap filing, the MSD received approval of a conditional water right for 48,600 acre-feet.[49] Almost immediately, the CRWCD appealed the ruling to the Colorado Supreme Court and filed suit against the District in U.S. District Court, claiming that West Slope interests were not being protected as required in the 1937 Water Conservancy District Act.[50] Simultaneously, attorney Balcomb sent a letter to Barkley requesting negotiations.

At first, the District believed that the CRWCD lawsuit created "an untenable atmosphere" for negotiations. Barkley was "shocked" and "disappointed" that the CRWCD's "overture of good will" came at the same time as their complaint "for filing in Federal District Court against, among others, this Municipal Subdistrict." In a letter to CRWCD manager Roland C. Fischer, he said that the lawsuit created "a climate within which there can be no meaningful discussions related to mutuality of interest in the joint venture to which you referred."[51] After receiving another request five months later "to discuss a possible amicable solution to the legal controversies created by the adjudication and the carriage contract suit,"[52] Sayre told the Board that the District should enter into discussions. Following an initial meeting early in 1975, the Directors decided that negotiations should be pursued. The first step was a meeting with the board of the Middle Park Water Conservancy District (MPWCD) to elicit modifications in the Windy Gap project that might benefit Middle Park's attempt to attract tourism. By contrast, the CRWCD was more interested in preserving water for a prospective oil shale industry. Recognizing the potential difficulty of an internal conflict on the West Slope, the Directors said that they would have to return to litigation if no progress were made in a reasonable amount of time.

Unfortunately, progress did not result. Throughout the year, the District exchanged letters with Balcomb and Robert Delaney, the latter acting as counsel for both the CRWCD and the MPWCD. Neither attorney was in a hurry to detail specific proposals or to respond to those of the NCWCD. At the same time, correspondence from District president J. Ben Nix expressed urgency regarding the District's concern about inflation. West Slope attorneys missed deadlines, ignored informal opportunities for discussion, and replied to specific proposals in general terms. The Board felt subjected to delaying tactics by people who really did not want to negotiate in good faith.[53] After Barkley stepped down as secretary-manager in 1974, the Directors proceeded with litigation of both the carriage contract suit and the water adjudications. In response, the CRWCD moved to introduce additional opposing evidence to the Windy Gap decree in a forthcoming hearing.[54] Both sides tried intermittently to reopen discussions in 1976, but Sayre and Nix were convinced that the West Slope still lacked motivation. Successful negotiations did not occur until 1979, twelve years after Mayor Price had filed for a conditional water decree. These meetings came about largely because of the increasingly high cost of litigation and because the Colorado Supreme Court ruled on appeal that "in its opinion the provisions for protection of the western slope. . . had not been complied with" and instructed the Water Court "to proceed with such additional hearings, as necessary."[55] This decision, which dealt a blow to the

NCWCD, set the stage for a 1980 "Settlement Agreement," about which more will be said in Part V.

Throughout years of legal haggling, the Six Cities held together remarkably well. Longmont hesitated in 1973, fearing that the Windy Gap project would never be built;[56] however, the city water board favored participation and persuaded the city council to reinstate itself as a full participant.[57] Fort Collins hesitated because the city water board recommended giving Joe Wright Reservoir construction top priority. This $5 million investment would store nearly 6,600 acre-feet of water,[58] thus quelling the urgency of Fort Collins's growth situation. As Fort Collins and Longmont considered ways of withdrawing from the Windy Gap project, Boulder was willing to contract for twice its $1/6$ water allotment. Other bodies, including the town of Windsor, expressed a formal interest in purchasing any Windy Gap units not committed to the original Six Cities.[59]

The most persistent applicant was the Platte River Power Authority (PRPA), which at first expressed interest in obtaining only rights to return flows from the individual cities.[60] As construction estimates of the Windy Gap project climbed to $20 million, however, and Fort Collins, Estes Park, and Loveland publicly expressed interest in transferring some or all of their rights to another entity,[61] PRPA sent a delegation to the MSD to discuss a proposal to purchase the uncommitted units of Windy Gap water. Because PRPA proposed a facility to meet the power needs of Fort Collins, Loveland, Estes Park, and Longmont by 1982, the authority hoped to find 15,000 acre-feet of new cooling water. The organization was willing to contract either with the MSD or with the Six Cities to purchase Windy Gap units and was open to allowing the cities reuse rights of the purchased water.[62]

The most difficult question for the MSD was whether to allow water to be transferred directly to PRPA from the MSD or to allow passage from the MSD to the cities and thence to PRPA. Fort Collins argued in favor of a direct transfer to avoid a city election,[63] but Sayre recommended to the Board that each city take its full allotment and then transfer any portion thereof to PRPA. The Six Cities Committee and the MSD board agreed to this plan.[64] In July 1975 allotments of 80 units of Windy Gap water (a 1/6 share) were formally assigned to each of the Six Cities. At the same meeting, Estes Park and Loveland each transferred 40 units and Fort Collins transferred all of its 80 units to PRPA.[65] Allotment contracts with each of the Six Cities required almost as much preparatory work for District staff as other organizational tasks. Wording was critical, not only to the special requirements of six different municipalities (three of which were home-rule cities)[66] but to the Bureau, the West Slope, and the New York City bond counselors, whose endorsement was critical to the success of revenue bond sales.

After extensive investigation of alternatives, the Subdistrict and Six Cities boards had decided that financing the Windy Gap project would come from the sale of bonds, not from municipal taxpayers or the federal government.[67] Frustrations with HUD's seemingly endless obstacles made it readily apparent that reclamation projects were no longer favored by the federal bureaucracy. If the Windy Gap project were to be, the only viable plan that would avoid an ad valorem mill levy on MSD residents was issuing revenue bonds. Sayre advised the Board that such bonds could be legally issued by a quasi-municipal corporation without a vote of the electorate, but the New York firm of Mudge, Rose, Guthrie and Alexander advised the District that certain changes would be required in the Water Conservancy District Act.[68] With the assistance of Loveland State Senator Fred Anderson, the Colorado General Assembly passed the necessary amendments to the Local Governments Act and the Water Conservancy District Act.[69] In 1977 the first of four series of revenue bonds was marketed in the amount of $3 million.[70]

Following his retirement in fall 1974, Barkley worked briefly as a consultant to locate an engineering firm for feasibility studies, site investigations, and, most probably, final design and construction of Windy Gap. International Engineering Company (IECO) was finally selected by the MSD from twenty-two firms invited to bid, and Dames and Moore, Inc., was chosen to prepare the environmental assessment. If both firms met their objectives on schedule, the Board predicted that construction would begin in spring 1978.[71] This optimistic estimate did not consider unresolved legal problems that required five months of intense negotiations with the West Slope. The 1979 meetings continued what had been started and discontinued in 1975 because of no progress. They were prompted by the CRWCD's conviction that Windy Gap would jeopardize development of a viable oil shale industry. Keenly sensitive to events following the 1973 oil embargo and aware of Senate Document 80's commitment to preserve water in the Colorado River basin for shale oil development,[72] West Slope representatives felt they were in a strong position to block Windy Gap if they chose.

The amount of water that the oil shale industry would require was open to question. During discussions of the Fry-Ark project with Governor Stephen McNichols, CRWCD counsel Frank Delaney had stated that if and when production started, water demand would run so high that insufficient quantities would remain for transmountain diversions.[73] CWCB Director Felix "Larry" Sparks doubted the state's ability to proceed with certain other water projects due to the quantity of water required to run an oil shale retort operation.[74] Others warned of salinity and pollution problems that would be created by the U.S. claim to 200,000 acre-feet of Colorado River water for shale processing and for serving the new communities that would emerge.[75] Environmentalists were concerned about high concentrations of ammonia, carbonic acid, and suspended solids that would leave a surface film on the river and on shoreline deposits in the riparian corridors.[76]

At the May 1970 Board meeting, several years before the oil embargo focused national attention on Colorado's oil shale, NCWCD Directors were told that the CRWCD had put out a news release asking for participants in a computer simulation study of the upper Colorado and White rivers (CORSIM).[77] Aimed at determining water availability and water rights under a variety of circumstances, the CORSIM plan immediately appealed to the District, which sought ways to prove that a Windy Gap project could be built without detriment to the West Slope. By creating hypothetical scenarios for the CORSIM model, the District hoped to show that adequate water was available below the Windy Gap site to meet all industrial, domestic, and agricultural needs. The Board voted to participate in the study for a three-year period at a cost of $350,000. At the CORSIM organizational meeting in Denver's Mobil Oil conference room, ten oil companies, two municipalities (Denver and Colorado Springs), the two water districts (NCWCD and CRWCD), and the Public Service Company agreed to share costs. Barkley was elected chairman of the Specifications and Selection Committee, whose function was to locate qualified engineering and computer firms. After trips to Denver, San Francisco, Houston, Chicago, and New York, Barkley's committee finally selected the New York firm of Parsons, Brinkerhoff, Quade and Douglas and the David E. Fleming Company of Denver. The contract specified a total of $475,000, to be paid over a two-year period in return for developing a comprehensive computer model of the Colorado River and all its tributaries, except the Gunnison River, from the headwaters to approximately the Utah state line.[78]

A demonstration run was made for all participants that included a ten-year record of all water decrees on the system and showed what would occur with hypothetical calls under the 1922 Colorado River Compact. Six months later all work was completed, and a management and operation contract was drawn up between the fifteen participants and the joint-venture companies.[79] For nearly twenty years the CORSIM model proved

The current NCWCD headquarters building in Loveland was constructed in 1971. (Courtesy NCWCD.)

a useful tool for planning on the Colorado River; in 1987 the participants unanimously agreed to maintain and update the data system. Barkley, who took pride in the CORSIM development, was pleased to see it in operation as he neared retirement. He believed that the collection of water rights and water flow data would help with future West Slope negotiations, especially Windy Gap, and he hoped the information would ease the work load that had steadily increased in the District since organization of the MSD. In fact, the Windy Gap project, the growth of Front Range municipalities, extensive maintenance requirements on the C–BT system, and the formation of twenty-four rural domestic water companies between 1960 and 1970 challenged NCWCD employees to meet their most basic responsibilities. The District needed more people and a new building.

Barkley had been interested in expanding District offices as early as 1962, but serious discussions with the Board did not take place until 1968 when concerns about Front Range industrialization coincided with formation of the MSD.[80] As soon as the owner of adjoining land to the west offered to sell eleven acres, the Board agreed to offer $3000 an acre, with the understanding that purchase would be subject to the city of Loveland's approval of a rezoning petition.[81] A year later, the municipality approved architects' plans for a new building at an estimated cost of $278,000.[82] Because inflation was increasingly worrisome, everyone hoped that construction would begin early in 1970; however, architectural and construction delays raised costs to $400,000. Construction, which finally began in the summer, was completed in nine months. The District and MSD held their first meeting in April 1971 at 1250 North Wilson Avenue, the building that remains as their principal place of business. At the same time, the Bureau also moved to Wilson Avenue, a block south of the District, as part of a long-range plan to establish remote control of the C–BT reservoirs and power plants.[83]

Some staff increases followed. As previously mentioned, Simpson joined the District as planning coordinator to advise Barkley and the Board about incipient regional land and water programs. Due to rapid inflation of salaries and wage payments — caused by Kodak, IBM, Hewlett Packard, and other corporations that needed well-trained clerical, stenographic, and maintenance people — Barkley feared that it might be difficult to replace several staff members who had already served almost twenty years with the District and who qualified for retirement. When O&M superintendent Dennis Walker and treasurer James C. Nelson died unexpectedly in 1971 within four months of each other, Barkley hired Robert R. "Smitty" Smith to be the new O&M superintendent. Earl F. Phipps, Walker's predecessor, had been transferred from O&M to assistant manager in 1964, where he stayed until replacing Barkley as manager in 1974. Leona M. Schwab, who had been secretary, receptionist, and finally administrative secretary since 1954, shared what had been Nelson's responsibilities with Minerva G. Lee; Schwab retired in 1975. Since Barkley had moved to secretary-manager in 1958, the District staff of ten had grown to nine administrative and eight O&M employees.[84]

In addition to new staffing arrangements, Barkley addressed the ever-present problem of telling the public what the NCWCD was doing and how and why taxpayers' money was being spent — never an easy task. The 1963 meeting with municipal and water entity officials proved a step in the right direction, although the average citizen was still ignorant of the District's obligations under Senate Document 80 and the Repayment Contract. Some state legislators wanted conservancy district board members elected in order to encourage better communication with the voters.[85] Others, like Mrs. Donald E. Clusen of the League of Women Voters, pointed out that water experts were not providing the public with facts in an understandable format. Citizens ought to be presented with choices rather than the opportunity to approve or oppose a ready-made plan. She urged leaders in the water community to consider the "social values" of water projects and to include environmental impact in their future explanations.[86] Sayre totally agreed. "We've got to meet with those who don't understand us and tend to oppose us," he said. "We've spent too many years talking to ourselves."[87] Barkley responded appropriately. By 1970 he had begun to distribute the *Annual Report* to a much wider audience, including municipalities, water entities, and various school libraries. The pamphlet entitled "With Water Enough . . . A Wonderland" was updated and reprinted with the new title, "With Water Enough . . . A Better Land." It covered the NCWCD's historical background, arrangements for financing, the C–BT system engineering, and the benefits that supplemental water had brought to northeastern Colorado. As the number of immigrants to northeastern Colorado increased, taxpayers untutored in water matters also grew. Barkley looked for a way to release NCWCD information to the media on a sustained basis.

Journalist and long-time South Platte Valley resident Merritt Lewis suggested monthly articles for local newspapers. Lewis noted that as with the East's general disenchantment with the Bureau, local criticism of the District stemmed from a lack of information or from repetition of misinformation regarding water projects. With the Board's approval Lewis contracted for a maximum of ninety hours a year to write stories on the District and on MSD. For a brief time, he prepared interesting commentaries for the press; however, his wife's illness forced him to leave Colorado,[88] and he was not replaced. The problem of inadequate public education remained.

An area of serious concern to both the public and the District was the steadily increasing money spent on litigation and related preparations. The budget for legal fees and administrative costs had actually declined from 16.7 percent in 1958 to 14.3 percent in 1974; however, the public perceived a more than threefold increase in dollars spent — from $13,000 in 1958 to $45,000 in 1974. Actually, the dramatic growth in legal expenditures did not come until 1980, after Barkley's retirement, when 31.3 percent of the District budget was allocated to legal costs, including litigation with the West Slope over Windy Gap.[89]

During Barkley's administration and following principal counsel Jack Clayton's unexpected death in 1964, John M. Sayre from Ryan, Sayre, Martin and Brotzman of Boulder had ably represented the District. When Sayre transferred to the Denver law firm of Davis, Graham and Stubbs in 1966 to head their division of natural resources, he knew that legal costs were rising precipitously; but he insisted on District representation in U.S. claims for what the government called its "federal reserved rights" along the Colorado River.[90] Some Board members explored ways to reduce legal costs, including full-time employment of in-house legal counsel, but staff recommended the status quo due to legal work irregularities during most years.[91] To meet expected litigation with the West Slope and the United States, Barkley set up a new account for "special legal services" to cover charges for required court appearances. To put the District's legal expenses in perspective, he noted that the Southeastern Colorado Water Conservancy District (SECWCD) had budgeted $55,000 for 1975 and the CRWCD had estimated $85,500; the District's total legal expenses for 1975 were $37,647.[92]

The litigation and Barkley's contacts with state, regional, and national organizations gave the NCWCD a national and international reputation. Visitors from around the world came to study the construction and operation of the C–BT system. Even during the height of the Cold War, Russians wanted to learn about possibilities of diverting water from the Caucusus Mountains into Armenia. The Spanish minister of public works sought help for a transbasin diversion project for irrigated agriculture. Other interested dignitaries — many sponsored by the Administration for International Development (AID) — from Taiwan, Mexico, Yugoslavia, Thailand, Venezuela, Brazil, Pakistan, Afghanistan, and many other countries viewed the Project as successful and hoped to learn useful engineering and management information for their own countries.

Barkley was largely responsible for the NCWCD's excellent reputation. For sixteen years he had run an efficient operation, earned the respect of employees and colleagues in the water business, and received offers from other water entities that admired his leadership and experience. The DWB invited him to become planning coordinator; the Bureau wooed him as chief of the Division of Irrigation Operations in the chief engineer's office. He refused both offers.[93] When J. E. Whitten retired as state engineer in 1965, officials in several of the state's water districts asked Barkley to consider the job. He again refused, noting the lack of statutory machinery, inadequate personnel, and the paucity of legislative support. While Governor John Love pressured Barkley to change his mind, the Board told him to follow his personal views. Barkley concluded that functioning effectively as state engineer would consume more time than working with organization representatives toward legislative changes so that the state engineer's office could actually administer the state's water rights.[94] Thank you very much, but he would stay with the District.

Barkley's decision to stay with the District says as much about him as anything. He was not a self-promoter. He was modest about his accomplishments, and he did not covet the limelight or the power of the state engineer's office to satisfy his ego. By retirement, his record was filled with evidence of professional success. As an active member of the NRA, Barkley represented the District in 1958 in its efforts to explain the reclamation program to the eastern states. Ten years later he was elected Colorado director when the NRA was renamed the National Water Resources Association (NWRA), signifying a broader interest in weather modification, desalinization, electrical power programs, and water quality problems associated with urban communities.[95] As a result of his valuable contributions on several committees, Barkley was elected NWRA president for 1974. At thirty straight NRA/NWRA conventions Barkley also contributed his expertise as chairman of the Colorado River Advisory Committee of the CWCB and as president of both the CWC and the Four States Irrigation Council. The breadth of his interests was recognized by many requests to testify in Washington, memberships on national water committees, and frequent trips to national and international meetings.

Eight months prior to his official retirement at a May 31, 1974, open house in the Loveland Community Building, NCWCD employees surprised Barkley with a farewell party that caught him off guard. He might have preferred no fanfare for his twenty-nine years of District service, but as Nix noted, his accomplishments deserved commendation. The District had developed policies and procedures that were the envy of other water organizations. Furthermore, it was financially secure and able to meet obligations under several contracts to the United States. More than anything else, however, Nix stressed Barkley's management abilities. Although prone to occasional loquaciousness and very occasional angry outbursts, he led by example. With a great capacity for work, a keen sense of humor, patience with others' imperfections, a fantastic memory, and the ability to mediate between disputing parties, Barkley was greatly admired as something of a water statesman — "a manager in the finest sense of the word."[96] "We'll miss you, Bob," said the Board's formal resolution, "and many thanks for a job exceptionally well done."[97] Signed by the new secretary-manager, Earl F. Phipps, these words conveyed a sense of Barkley's indelible mark on the District.

Phipps was well qualified to fill his predecessor's managerial shoes. Barkley officially retired in January 1975, but Phipps took over for the last two months of 1974. Because of the pending Windy Gap situation, the amount of unresolved litigation, and the leadership transition, the Board agreed to sign a consulting contract with Barkley, whose services water districts, law offices, and government agencies promptly requested. Because he feared conflicts of interest and tired of refusing requests, Barkley headed for Arizona to detach himself from day-to-day affairs of the water business. Colorado and the District eventually wooed Barkley back, but meanwhile, Phipps was left to confront the anti-reclamation policies and the "hit list" attitude of President Jimmy Carter.

Part V: *District Management in an Era of Environmental Activism (1974–1990)*

21 *The National Picture*

From the mid-seventies through the 1980s the District faced unrelenting pressures from national and state regulatory agencies. Restrictions on water development combined with a general rise in environmental consciousness from coast to coast. Simultaneously, growth of municipal water needs along the Front Range threatened to preempt existing agricultural water supplies. The Windy Gap project was built to address this problem during these tumultuous years. During the long struggle to complete financing, carriage contract negotiations, and construction, the District and Subdistrict coped with a legion of new regulations, environmentalist activism, a highly sensitive and sometimes frightened Bureau, and a plethora of legal challenges. The District successfully survived hundreds of tests of its perseverance and grew in size, power, and influence. Staff and Board members more actively influenced state legislation while ties were strengthened with federal agencies and the Colorado delegation in Washington. The District sought cooperation from other water entities to present a united front against a perceived conspiracy of no-growth forces. As the DWB began to lose strength as the state's preeminent water broker, the NCWCD not unwillingly moved into a leadership position.

This was a critical time in the NCWCD's evolution. The policies of Presidents Nixon, Ford, Carter, and Reagan required major adjustments by water organizations accustomed to the hands-off approach of previous administrations. Rising inflation and national deficits meant that every request for federal funds underwent seemingly endless scrutiny and delays. Previously authorized projects were denied funding. Growth-sensitive planners were branded as environmentally insensitive developers, and all water use was subjected to criticism from individuals and organizations concerned about pollution, congestion, and protection of the natural environment. While Congress responded by withdrawing substantial support for traditional reclamation projects, the federal government once again sought to quantify its water rights on federal lands in a challenge to the states' traditional rights to assert control over their waters.

A review of federal policies from Nixon's to Reagan's presidency illuminates the kinds of pressures the NCWCD felt during the administrations of both Earl F. Phipps (1975–1982) and Larry D. Simpson (1982–). Although they responded differently, both men understood that the District's future would be markedly affected by shifts in national priorities, statutory changes emanating from Congress, and White House directives. From the energy crisis of 1973 to the EPA's 1990 veto of Denver's Two Forks Dam project, NCWCD concerns increasingly reflected the revolution in national land and water policy. Some saw these policies as a direct challenge to the constitutionally sanctioned principles of Colorado water law while others felt that the old states' rights battle was being refought by federal agencies trying to centralize power in their respective bureaucracies. To those in the water business, erosion of reclamation support had a long historical taproot that finally surfaced in the early 1970s.

Nixon's confused domestic policy was evidenced in the performance of his Interior secretaries and the Bureau. Neither Walter Hickel nor Rogers C. B. Morton was highly regarded by Nixon's inner circle.[1] The president's development of a supercabinet, his reliance on the Office of Management and Budget (OMB) to undermine existing legislation and withhold funds from authorized projects, and the responsibility given to the Department of Agriculture for protection of the nation's natural resources undermined the Interior Department's traditional role as guardian of the nation's waters. Nixon espoused creation of a Department of Natural Resources to absorb the Department of the Interior and to eliminate the intragovernmental conflicts that impeded progress in environmental concerns. "One department's watershed project," said Nixon, "threatens to slow the flow of water to another department's reclamation project downstream."[2] But Vietnam and the Watergate crisis aggravated Nixon's domestic problems. The Department of Natural Resources was never established, and environmental protection was frequently delegated to the states.

Not that the Nixon years were bereft of significant water-policy developments. The National Water Commission (NWC) was created in response to anxieties about degradation and overuse of water in the Colorado River basin. During four years of study, the commission investigated many of the nation's water problems and looked for ways to balance efficiency and conservation of existing and proposed water supplies, innovative methods for developing the "highest economic use of water," the economic and social consequences of water development, and aesthetic values affecting the quality of life of the American people.[3] Foremost in the commissioners' minds was ensuring that public policies reflected public preferences, a new twist that signaled an end to unfettered water development and that alerted water agencies like the NCWCD to greater public criticism of existing water projects. Although 1972 marked the largest congressionally approved dollar appropriation for the Bureau, Commissioner Ellis Armstrong mistakenly concluded that he could begin construction of many previously authorized projects.[4] The president's Water Resources Council (WRC) guideline, however, proposed new water projects that echoed new reclamation trends. These included higher interest rates, elimination of secondary benefits in project feasibility, and closer scrutiny of cost-benefit ratios. Irrigation projects received low priority. Responding to the administration's directives, a national energy crisis, and the need for greater emphasis on environmental problems,[5] the Bureau's water development program had to focus more on oil shale, coal, and municipal water supplies. WRC policy directives reached the District by January 1975. On behalf of the Directors and staff, Bureau project manager Robert L. Berling wrote the Bureau's regional director to express great difficulty in interpreting a requirement that federal water projects prepare a water-use plan. He complained that literal interpretation of this order "would tend to place an unnecessary burden on existing projects, such as the Colorado–Big Thompson Project, and could bankrupt projects of lesser financial stability. In addition," he added, "it would stifle the development of future irrigation and power projects." To Berling, the requirement simply created another costly "paper monster." If the directive became law, it "would impose a greater hardship on existing projects than the 1969 NEPA."[6]

Trends of the Nixon administration were continued under Ford. Policy statements from the Department of Interior stressed water conservation and quality while encouraging more efficient water use. Responding to criticism from Berling and others, the Department of the Interior stated that only *future* plans for water use and development would have to include environmental impact statements.[7] Federal involvement in existing water projects, however, was becoming increasingly noticeable.

Nixon and Ford administrations responded to significant numbers of environmental concerns addressed in congressional statutes. In addition to NEPA and the 1968 Wild and Scenic Rivers Act, legislators approved the Environmental Quality Improvement Act (1970), the Federal Water Pollution Control Act (1972), the Federal Environmental Pesticide Control Act (1972), the Endangered Species Act (1973), the Energy Reorganization Act (1974), the Safe Drinking Water Act (1974), the Federal Land Policy and Management Act (1976), and many other statutes of special interest to water-project managers.[8] Ford, particularly concerned with pollution and cleaning up the environment, also signed a bill for loan guarantees to communities that constructed municipal waste-water treatment plants. This was followed by the Land and Water Conservation Fund Act, designed to significantly expand recreational facilities, national parks, and wildlife sanctuaries in the United States.[9]

By 1976 a pattern of federal action had already been established that set the stage for Carter's 1977 "hit list." Even before his successful election bid, the natural resources section of the president's transition staff had prepared a fifty-page option paper that suggested comprehensive reform of the nation's water policy. When Carter spoke to the Congress three months later he announced a major review of federally funded water resource projects designed to protect the environment and to use taxpayers' money more responsibly. He doubted the wisdom of some 320 approved projects and stated that nineteen were insupportable on environmental, economic, or safety grounds. He recommended that Secretary of the Interior Cecil D. Andrus work with OMB and the Council on Environmental Quality (CEQ) to evaluate current water-resources policy and to present alternatives and suggestions for water-policy reform.[10] In a subsequent statement on May 23, 1977, Carter pledged support to change the federal government's traditionally uncoordinated approach to managing the nation's water resources. His objective was a comprehensive, unified federal water-management policy. OMB, CEQ, and WRC were given six months to undertake a study and to generate specific recommendations for reforming national water policy.[11] Two months later the government fired its first salvo when the Water Resources Council suggested using the Federal Water Pollution Control Act to impose instream flow requirements on states utilizing the prior appropriation doctrine.

While the environmental community cheered this radical departure from business-as-usual water politics and saw Carter's leadership as a rebuke to the traditional pork-barrel approach of western congresssmen and their constituencies, Colorado Governor Richard Lamm and several outspoken water officials were less than pleased. Noting that seven Colorado projects might not get administrative backing, Lamm advised the president to tread softly. "We are hoping President Carter will see the error of his ways," he said, but if necessary, "we will have to commit ourselves to educating the President about what water means to the West." Carter might believe that "all water projects are boondoggles," said Lamm, and "that may be the case in Georgia." What the president must understand is that "the West needs reclamation projects to utilize the water that it has. It doesn't rain every

Governor Richard Lamm was distressed by President Carter's "hit list," but he also recognized the need for Colorado to find better ways to finance its water projects. (Courtesy Colorado Historical Society.)

week."[12] Director Felix "Larry" Sparks of the CWCB cautioned Carter that "Hell hath no fury like that of a people betrayed."[13] Senator Gary Hart told Carter that his justification for elimination of water projects was "laughable."[14] Most of the Colorado delegation agreed. Representative Pat Schroeder, on the other hand, voted against funding for three Colorado water projects because her mail was running 70-30 against them.

Returning from a meeting of the NWRA, where Carter's "hit list" was the principal topic of discussion, NCWCD attorney John M. Sayre reported that the government's proposed changes in national water policy could greatly affect the District. He said that they had been hastily formulated and framed in an atmosphere hostile to water development. Because of the serious implications of Carter's own pronouncements and the published findings of the president's six-month task force, Phipps sent agency coordinator Ray Reeb to represent the District at a special water-policy hearing in Washington,[15] where he discovered that Carter's statements and tactics had unleashed a political firestorm. Even though Carter had recommended cancellation of only nineteen of 320 authorized projects, he had not consulted Congress. Senators and representatives were up in arms. The task-force study echoed advice contained in earlier reports from the Nixon and Ford eras, but Andrus threw out several important new warnings to managers of existing projects. He recommended that interstate cooperation and modernization of state water policies were essential to developing a national perspective on both water quantity and water quality. Indian water rights requirements, energy needs, and environmental degradation necessitated a new level of federal-state cooperation. To this end Andrus supported the task force's recommendations to quantify federally reserved water rights, to increase cost sharing by states and nonfederal water entities, to coordinate surface and groundwater policies, and to enforce acreage limitations and residency requirements in the 1902 Reclamation Act.[16] The District heard the message: expect a more visible federal presence in all matters pertaining to Colorado water.

Evidence of this trend appeared rather quickly. Although exempt from the acreage limitations of the Reclamation Act, NCWCD allottees worried about enforced residency requirements. Sayre supported the Directors' decision to contribute to the Farm Water Alliance, which was raising funds to fight the new water policies in Washington.[17] He also warned Directors of rising legal costs, not just to contest the "overwhelming" number of federal reserved rights claims filed in Division 1 Water Court but to counter the Environmental Defense Fund's recent suit against the EPA, the secretary of the interior, and the commissioner of reclamation for alleged failure to prevent salinity increases in the Colorado River.[18] Meanwhile, Reeb reported on hearings in Fort Collins on the Wild and Scenic Rivers Act. Success by the act's proponents, he felt, could mean that portions of the Poudre and Big Thompson rivers would come under federal control thereby halting further development possibilities.[19]

Meanwhile, Carter responded to criticism of his water policies; he had not consulted the states because of budget submission deadlines. The United States was in its ninth year of deficits, and he wanted to show his commitment to cutting waste and balancing the budget.[20] With deep concern over the relationship between low interest rates for federally funded water projects and the construction of unsafe dams in the West — a worry exacerbated by the 1976 collapse of Teton Dam in eastern Idaho — Carter opposed both uneconomical and unsafe water projects. He insisted that the federal government have a coherent water policy and reevaluate projects already authorized. He also promised to hold public hearings and consult Congress before making further decisions. A revised water-policy message to Congress on June 6, 1978, indicated that Carter had sidestepped some politically sensitive issues. Much to environmentalists' dismay, issues such as water quality, research, and planning coordination were discussed in only general terms.[21] At the same time, however, Carter reaffirmed the government's commitment to more efficient management of federal water

Gregory J. Hobbs, Jr., came to the District with an extensive background in water quality and other environmental regulations. (Courtesy NCWCD.)

resources, prevention of waste, and encouragement of cost-effective, safe, and environmentally sound projects. He also warned that the federal government would use its leadership to enforce environmental statutes, conserve water, and protect instream flows, fish and wildlife, and groundwater resources. He directed Andrus to require that new and renegotiated contracts include provisions to recalculate water rates every five years and to recover operation and maintenance costs.[22]

The tone of the administration's new water policy discouraged the Colorado delegation and Governor Lamm's office because it required front-end money from states for future projects. State Senator Fred Anderson joined with other Colorado lawmakers to search for alternate ways of financing water projects to avoid federal entanglements.[23] Feeling that Carter's policies were unacceptable "as currently proposed," the District Board passed two resolutions, one to accelerate studies on public lands to be opened to grazing, timber harvest, mineral exploration, and "water resource project investigation and development"; and the other opposing Carter's proposal for cost sharing by the states.[24] In June 1979 the law firm of Davis, Graham and Stubbs opened a Washington office to utilize the services of former Congressman Frank Evans. With no definite funding plan for the Windy Gap project, keeping a close eye on Washington had become a District imperative. Simultaneously, Sayre hired Gregory J. Hobbs, Jr., head of the Natural Resources Section of the Colorado Attorney General's Office. In October 1979 the District designated Hobbs its associate counsel.

Although Bureau Commissioner R. Keith Higginson conceded that Carter's emphasis on conservation would result in fewer recommendations for "major impoundment and distribution systems" (big dams?), he did not feel that the president's focus on environmental protection would cause major changes in the Bureau's manner of operation. Existing contracts would be honored, but new projects would include evaluations of nonstructural alternatives, conservation rather than storage and redistribution of water, and evidence of public support for projects. In summary, Higginson told a Senate Water Resources Subcommittee that although Carter's new national water policy would not have much impact on the Bureau,[25] its image needed changing. Effective November 6, 1979, the Bureau of Reclamation changed its name to the Water and Power Resources Service. "We need a name," said Higginson, "that signifies to all Americans our commitment to the responsible development and use of water resources and energy. . . . The name shows clearly that we are involved in the conservation and wise development of the nation's water and power resources."[26]

A year and a half later, President Reagan's secretary of the interior, James G. Watt, restored the Bureau's familiar name, as if Carter's new direction had been a major mistake that needed immediate rejection by the incoming administration. Indeed, the commotion caused by Carter's "hit list" proved that real water reform was still not politically viable. After three years of battling with Congress, Carter managed only miniscule savings.[27] Jittery water-project managers felt temporarily relieved when Watt assured them in a 1982 speech to the NWRA that the previous administration's policies threatened America's future. If executed, said Watt, they would have undermined American agriculture, industry, and the well-being of U.S. states and communities. The New Federalism proposed by the Reagan administration would counter Carter's anti-water project philosophy. A new partnership between the states and the federal government, based on the states' rights to allocate and manage their own water resources, would be worked out. As Watt explained, the Reagan administration wanted a return to building new projects that were economically and environmentally sound. "I am here to tell you," Watt said, "that the long dry spell is over."[28]

Whereas Carter had attempted major reclamation reform with little success, the Reagan administration returned to national resource development but also with little success. By the 1980s officials found both a public that was more committed to Carter's original objectives than to Reagan's and a Congress that still wanted financial control over water policy.

Through various forms of activism, including litigation, environmental organizations undercut Watt's pro-development rhetoric and forced water project managers to address concerns about clean water, clean air, point and nonpoint source pollution, and pristine wilderness. Upset with Carter and Andrus, Colorado water officials had hoped that the Reagan-Watt team signaled a return to easy federal money for reclamation.[29] Watt seemed determined to have his way, and Reagan wanted to reward southern and western allies. Bureau Commissioner Robert N. Broadbent assured everyone that the Reagan administration favored water development and that a serious water crisis would occur without efforts to develop the nation's water resources.[30] Both Simpson and Sayre reported to the District Board that the commissioner appeared disposed to resolve most of their concerns. [31] Meanwhile, the president was developing an Office of Water Policy (OWP) to accumulate and coordinate water interests of the states, Congress, and interested citizens. Charged with reporting to Reagan, the OWP was to plan and recommend new projects on the basis of cost sharing between federal and nonfederal entities.[32]

To Watt, cost sharing meant "up front" investment by nonfederal entities to relieve the burden on the federal budget. In a memorandum to the president, Watt recommended that water projects that provided municipal or industrial water should finance themselves 100 percent; irrigation projects would put up at least 35 percent, "depending on benefits to users."[33] Reagan agreed that "the traditional Federal role [was] no longer appropriate and that project beneficiaries must contribute a larger share of costs for water projects."[34] Although the cost-sharing approach was strongly endorsed by OMB director David Stockman, Reagan eventually dropped plans for uniform cost sharing in favor of negotiating individual agreements for each water project. As a consequence, Watt continued his push for more financial support from Congress until he was replaced by William P. Clark in 1983. Noting that the president had been denied a requested 23 percent increase in funding for water projects in 1983, Watt warned Congress somewhat melodramatically that "in the 1984 budget we are going to come back with even a greater increase, because we believe in the future of this land. We believe there must be change. And we are going to continue trying to bring [about] that change."[35] Broadbent tried to echo his boss regarding any conflict between the environment and growth. "My choice is going to be with the people. That doesn't mean we shouldn't be concerned about our environment, but somewhere along the line you have to make a judgement decision. . . . What comes first?"[36]

When Reagan signed the 1982 Reclamation Reform Act into law, he put federal water recipients on notice about a possible limit on how many acres they farmed and how far from their land they could live. This act caused no small concern in the NCWCD. Sayre warned that it might possibly force the District to amend the Repayment Contract with the United States.[37] Under the new law, two different limitations applied. The first expanded the land area owned by legal entities that benefited less than twenty-five people to 960 acres. The District's federally financed water supply was supplemental and, therefore, exempt from this provision. The second restriction placed a 50-mile limitation on the distance a landowner could live from his or her land. Eventually, Sayre could report that the residency requirements had been repealed and that the District's interests were protected.[38] But the Reclamation Reform Act, environmental pressures, national deficit problems, and an ongoing debate over the energy crisis all shocked the Bureau into announcing an image change in 1987. The statement came after Interior Secretary Donald P. Hodel ordered the Bureau to take a hard look at its past and its future. After seven months' soul searching, the Bureau announced in October its assumption of new responsibilities that would reflect the public's changing values. Recreation and environmental concerns would become primary areas of interest. Reorganization would mirror the agency's new role in water conservation, groundwater development, and resource management. In keeping with the Reagan philosophy, the Bureau would consider privatization of its facilities.

Cynics doubted the Bureau's sincerity. Some employees even charged that a contemplated move to Denver was meant to distance the Bureau from congressional scrutiny and to better empower major water users in the West. The District responded differently, however, by proposing to the Bureau that the NCWCD operate and maintain all C–BT water and power generation facilities. Negotiations were put on hold in 1987, but the proposal has not been formally rejected as of this writing.[39] Responding to twenty years of federal attempts to redirect the nation's reclamation policy and reeling from increasingly effective environmental restrictions on agricultural and municipal water use, District officials began looking for ways to lessen or eliminate their dependency on the United States. One alternative was to take over more of the operation, maintenance, and ownership of C–BT facilities. The struggle to implement the Windy Gap project served as a catalyst for these feelings. No other water project in the central Rockies better demonstrated the impact of twenty years of fluctuating presidential policies, congressional penury, and an environmentally sensitive public.

The Construction of Windy Gap:
Negotiation, Litigation, Negotiation

On a sunny June 29, 1985, with a mild breeze blowing up the Colorado River, a group of nearly 500 people gathered to witness the morning dedication of a water project that had been in planning and construction stages for twenty-one years. The sun's warmth and the happy occasion distorted memories of the stormy encounters that had plagued construction of what Subdistrict president W. D. "Bill" Farr described as the "last western slope water that will be brought to the eastern slope up north."[1] Farr, as ecstatic as anyone, had labored diligently to effect the compromises necessary to complete the Windy Gap project. At groundbreaking ceremonies four years earlier, he had spoken of overcoming the delays from the 1969 NEPA and the cooperation, "particularly [with] our West Slope friends,"[2] that had finally made construction possible. With his back to the Colorado River, Farr looked over the crowd to a 6-mile pipeline that was originally planned to deliver an average of 48,000 acre-feet of water annually to Lake Granby for use by Estes Park, Longmont, Boulder, Loveland, Greeley, and the Platte River Power Authority (PRPA). He spoke proudly of overcoming "tense moments" with the West Slope and of the satisfaction of maintaining the respect and friendship of those with whom the battle had been waged.[3]

Other speakers mentioned the spirit of cooperation, environmental mitigation, and mutual benefits of the Windy Gap project to both slopes. Congressman Hank Brown, who had also been at the 1981 ground breaking, recalled setting off the dynamite charges along the axis of what was now a completed dam on the Colorado River. Without the persistent dedication of leaders from Grand County, the CRWCD, and the NCWCD, he noted, the 48,000 acre-feet of water saved would have gone downstream to Arizona and California. Even as Brown noted the triumph of East and West Slope cooperation, he also recognized the angst of West Slope residents who viewed their loss of Colorado River water as an unfortunate fait accompli. "It is easy for those of us who live on the East Slope to be here today," he said. "It takes some vision and understanding for those on the West Slope to be here."[4] Instead of feeling too sorry for them, he noted that a settlement had been reached just three months earlier for payment of $10.2 million to the CRWCD for construction of its own compensatory storage reservoir on Muddy Creek, a tributary to the Colorado River north of Kremmling.

But a huge feast, commemorative medallions, and tours of what Farr called a "state-of-the-art" project could not conceal the fact that many delays — some expected and some not — had pushed Windy Gap's cost to $107 million, three times greater than estimates in the early 1970s.[5] As Brown suggested, the cost in human terms — struggles between MSD and CRWCD boards, staffs, and attorneys — had been titanic at times. With vivid memories of the long, strenuous negotiations leading to the construction of Green Mountain Reservoir as compensation for the C–BT Project, both sides had fought for their respective objectives in ways that would have elicited knowing smiles from Charles Hansen, J. M. Dille, Frank Delaney, Edward T. Taylor, and many others immersed in the transmountain diversion battles of the 1930s. Forty years later, stakes were just as high, the struggle just as furious; by 1985, however, it was probably correct to say, "no more." With so many federal and state statutes that had added environmental restrictions to existing East-West Slope tensions, Farr was probably safe in saying that the Windy Gap project was "the last transmountain water we will develop."[6] Perhaps Farr better than anyone at the dedication, remembered and comprehended the true cost of the "cooperation" that so many speakers referred to on that June day in 1985. This is the story of that struggle.

Eleven years before this dedication, the MSD had been "shocked and disappointed" by the CRWCD's decision to challenge its carriage contract with the Bureau and the application for a conditional water decree in Division 5 Water Court.[7] The MSD attempted negotiations with the West Slope in 1975 and 1976 that went nowhere. The River District and the MPWCD seemed to be stalling. The Subdistrict was impatient and frustrated with the West Slope. Officials firmly believed that they were entitled to Windy Gap water to fulfill the 310,000 acre-feet diversion through the Adams Tunnel established in Senate Document 80. Until 1979, when the Colorado Supreme Court returned the MSD's conditional water decree to the water court for clarification, the MSD appeared to have the advantage in these negotiations.[8]

West Slope concerns about the Windy Gap project that had been stated in 1974 during a meeting in Grand Junction included questions regarding increased salinity of the Colorado River, projections by the

Colorado Division of Planning for population growth in Grand and Summit counties,[9] Middle Park water shortages, protection of present and future water rights as specified in Senate Document 80 and the 1973 Colorado Revised Statutes,[10] environmental impact, and the loss of tax base. Except for the salinity question, responded Earl F. Phipps, most of these points were negotiable. "But unless there were apparent signs of progress within 60 days," he warned, "counsel [would] request the Federal [District] Court to reset the [carriage contract] case for hearing."[11] In other words, the MSD felt confident enough in 1975 to engage the West Slope in litigation; however, conciliation failed to develop. Instead, West Slope attorney Robert Delaney declared that the proposed project would require careful analysis and argued that construction of Windy Gap would cause "total depletion" and would elevate the salinity problem in the Colorado River to one of "grave concern" to water users.[12] Adequate compensatory storage had to be provided at no cost to the CRWCD or the MPWCD, and West Slope water users would have to be guaranteed protection from any possible "pollution" caused by the Windy Gap project.[13]

Because the MSD was already proceeding with water allotment contracts for the Six Cities, selection of engineering and environmental assessment firms, and plans to amend the Water Conservancy District Act so that the project could be financed by water revenue bonds, Delaney's perceived slow-down tactics were not well received. Phipps replied that the MSD was quite willing to negotiate, but Delaney's concerns could take years to resolve. Instead, he said that the MSD would pay its share of any added salinity to the Colorado River caused by the Windy Gap project; however, because the federal government had "unilaterally, through its agreement with Mexico and through the EPA, proposed salinity standards for the Colorado River," it should bear the burden of responsibility for water quality control. He also offered 5,000 acre-feet of water to the MPWCD, provided the West Slope withdrew opposition to the carriage contract and to the MSD's application for a conditional water decree. When the West Slope failed to return an affirmative response in five weeks, Phipps concluded that "we must assume that there is no basis for a negotiated agreement."[14] Phipps wrote Redwood Fisher, president of the MPWCD, to express his disappointment at the "complete lack of direct response to our letter of May 28, 1975." We still prefer negotiations, he said, but we are "fearful of the cost increases resulting from delay." The Board quickly decided to proceed with scheduled hearings in both state and federal courts if the West Slope did not respond to their offer by August 15, 1975.[15]

No letter arrived, but Sayre received a phone call from CRWCD attorney Kenneth Balcomb. What the West Slope wanted was a 28,000 acre-foot capacity reservoir at the Azure Dam site on the Colorado River and a second reservoir on Troublesome Creek, both to be built at no cost to the CRWCD and the MPWCD. Even with this capital cost, Balcomb argued, the MSD would have "the cheapest water in the world, namely $36.25 an acre-foot."[16] From Sayre's standpoint, the proposal was "unacceptable." Capital costs for building the reservoirs would exceed $30 million, doubling the cost of Windy Gap water to the Six Cities. Such expenditures "could well make the Windy Gap project infeasible to the cities." Concluded Sayre, the West Slope's counteroffer should be rejected as "unsatisfactory, and the MSD must proceed with litigation." Although Phipps's next letter to Delaney echoed these sentiments, he again stressed the hope that negotiations would continue.[17]

For the next six months, however, each side retreated from negotiations to pursue its own interests. Phipps reported that talks had broken down because the MSD feared inflation and rising costs of building materials.[18] While West Slope attorneys enlarged objections to a conditional Windy Gap water decree, Larry D. Simpson told the MSD Board that engineering studies predicted a yield of 48,000 acre-feet of deliverable water at Windy Gap. A suitable project, he said, could be built at a capital cost of approximately $30 million.[19] The negotiation door then opened a crack. Directors of all three boards met at different times during the winter of 1976 to explore possible agreements. Encouraged by signs of a more cooperative spirit, the MSD Board authorized Phipps to prepare a "document of intent" in March 1976 that would address some West Slope needs but carefully avoid mention of a compensatory storage reservoir. The offer contained a commitment to provide the MPWCD with the right to use up to 2,000 acre-feet of Windy Gap project water annually and a fund of $1 million for construction of water resource facilities in the MPWCD. The offer asked for a response prior to a scheduled March 24 hearing in Federal District Court, at which time the CRWCD's challenge to the carriage contract would be decided.[20]

Once again the time limit elapsed with no word from the West Slope. On March 24 the Federal District Court granted the MSD's motion for summary judgment against the CRWCD. East Slope negotiators now had less incentive for conciliation. The ruling might remove some impetus for negotiation, wrote Farr to Fischer, but the MSD would still seek a negotiated agreement because of a long-standing conviction that "costly and unproductive litigation [is] a poor substitute for mutually beneficial negotiated agreements."[21] As much as both sides wanted to negotiate, they began to drift apart. Feeling confident of their legal advantage, MSD Directors proceeded with financial planning associated with project construction. While Treasurer Minerva G. Lee wrestled heroically with unprecedented accounting problems, bond counsel Jim Ziglar, from the New York firm of Mudge, Rose, Guthrie & Alexander, explained the process of issuing water revenue bonds. By examining MSD records, he concluded that obtaining the conditional water decree from Division 5 Water Court remained the only obstacle.[22] The Six Cities Committee, which made suggestions to the MSD Board, reviewed budgets and reported to their respective city councils that they favored proceeding with construction.[23] But MSD Directors demurred. A legitimate conditional water decree was essential for favorable rates in the bond market. Meanwhile, with no water right or agreement with the West Slope, District staff (MSD and NCWCD staff were one and the same) started right-of-way acquisitions and work on the dredge-and-fill permit application required by the 1972 Water Pollution Control Act (Section 404). They also concentrated on environmental impact statements required by the EPA as well as on a number of issues raised by the CWQCC.

Concerning future distribution of Windy Gap water, PRPA's general manager, Al Hamilton, suggested that discussions begin soon with State Senator Fred Anderson to amend the Water Conservancy District Act. Changes were necessary so that Windy Gap water could be used anywhere within the parent (NCWCD) district. Because PRPA had purchased all of Fort Collins's Windy Gap units plus half of those assigned to Estes Park and Loveland (160 of the total 480 units), the Six Cities agreed to make PRPA a partner with an equal vote on the committee. Anderson accomplished the statutory amendments by May 1977.[24] This increased activity on the East Slope brought even more vocal protests from West Slope critics of the Windy Gap project. At a packed meeting in Hot Sulphur Springs, they complained about what diversion of another 48,000 acre-feet would do to their rafting industry, gold-medal fisheries, municipal water quality, and operation of ranchers' headgates. Some expressed concern about a lowered water table while others charged the MSD with misinforming the citizenry regarding the PRPA's role in the project: Windy Gap water was to be used for the six original municipalities, not for cooling water at PRPA's planned Rawhide Power Plant.[25] Although these accusations were not altogether accurate, they represented West Slope fears that resulted from past history and from the MSD's refusal to negotiate as long as the River District was unwilling "to seriously discuss these matters."[26] When the CRWCD asked for help to oppose the Vidler Water Tunnel Company and Golden's speculative Sheephorn project, the Subdistrict responded that in light of the CRWCD litigation and general unwillingness to cooperate, the Directors had decided not to join the protest.[27] The spirit of cooperation had drifted away.

At the heart of the matter was the River District's increasing desire for a compensatory reservoir at the Azure site on the Colorado River. The CRWCD had filed for a conditional decree at this site in 1962 but had not included a power plant; later attempts to attach one to the decree were now being opposed by the MSD. Sayre felt very strongly that construction of Azure Reservoir would "place an impossible burden on the allottees of the Subdistrict during the early years of the project." Even if capital could be raised, Azure without a power plant was unthinkable because the MSD would have no way to recover capital costs.[28] Then what was to be gained by blocking the CRWCD application to amend the 1962 decree? Sayre wanted to force the River District into negotiation. He may also have feared that if the CRWCD built the Azure project, its senior water decree could take priority over the Windy Gap project in dry years.[29] The possibility of standing the expense of Azure Reservoir and a power plant as compensation to the West Slope for the Windy Gap project did not seem realistic to the MSD. Negotiations seemed more likely.

Both sides met in Granby in March 1977, with Azure the principal topic. Farr told the River District that IECO had studied the site and concluded that preliminary cost projections showed power rates would have to be at least twice present market levels to amortize construction of a reservoir and power plant.[30] The River District offered to build both if the MSD would agree to buy power at market prices, but Farr vigorously opposed this suggestion. He was convinced that River District attorney Kenneth Balcomb was "nit-picking" the Windy Gap project just to collect fees.[31] Three months later the MSD Board unanimously agreed not to consider the Azure option any further but to seek other ways to continue negotiations with the West Slope.[32]

Events of the next nine months, however, were not propitious for productive give-and-take discussions. The Special Master's Report on conditional decrees for Windy Gap, published in November, recommended approval to District Judge Charles F. Stewart; but the judge, who had suffered a stroke the previous year, was complaining about enormous amounts of work on the federal government's reserved rights claims. Sayre spoke to several Colorado Supreme Court justices about expediting a conditional water decree decision. Early in 1978 the case was transferred to Judge George Lohr, who granted the conditional decrees on February 23, 1978. As expected, the CRWCD immediately appealed the ruling to the Colorado Supreme Court, but both Sayre and Phipps were optimistic that the court would uphold Lohr's ruling.[33] Forced to delay the decision for a year and a half because the lower court inexplicably lost the case records, the supreme court finally ruled on September 17, 1979, that the Six Cities and MSD had failed to demonstrate that taking Colorado River water at Windy Gap would not adversely affect "present or future uses" in the Colorado basin as stipulated in the Water Conservancy District Act of 1937.[34] The case was remanded to the water court with directions for further proceedings. The conditional water decree was not denied, but the court said that before validation, the impact of the Windy Gap project would have to specifically address the West Slope's present and anticipated future uses of Colorado River water under terms of Colorado's 1937 Water Conservancy District Act.

The impact of this unexpected decision on East Slope officials cannot be exaggerated. In control of the negotiation process to this point, they now had to consider major concessions to the West Slope if the project were to move forward. No one had paid much attention in 1977 when a Steamboat Springs Democrat had unsuccessfully tried to pass a law prohibiting transbasin diversion of water without a "preponderance of evidence" that the basin of origin would not suffer economic or ecological damage.[35] Instead, Subdistrict officials and staff had relied on the 1937 agreement with the West Slope in which Green Mountain Reservoir would protect "present and future" uses of Colorado River water for the West Slope. In return for this compensation, the C–BT was supposed to provide an annual average of 310,000 acre-feet of water through the Adams Tunnel. As long as all District and Subdistrict diversions remained within the 310,000 acre-feet allotment, argued the MSD, West Slope interests were protected.[36]

As logical as this argument seemed, the supreme court's ruling totally changed how the East Slope viewed its West Slope obligations. Working at times in executive session and in some secrecy over the next three months, the MSD hammered out an agreement acceptable to the the CRWCD, the MPWCD, Grand County, and a number of other West Slope entities. There was really no other alternative. The Six Cities opposed litigation. Even if the Azure project had to be built, Phipps argued that Windy Gap water would still be cheaper than C–BT water.[37] Furthermore, a draft EIS on the Windy Gap project had already been filed with the Bureau, and there had been public hearings on both slopes. Power discussions were under way with the Bureau, and progress was being made in a

The Azure project was designed to give compensatory water storage to the West Slope along with power generation through pump-back storage. (Courtesy NCWCD.)

dispute with the CWQCC and the Northwest Regional Council of Governments (NWRCOG) over the alleged contributions of the Windy Gap project to Colorado River salinity. Too much had been accomplished to abandon the project or to risk the delays and burdensome costs of litigation. On January 14, 1980, with Simpson and Sayre as the lead MSD negotiators and Hobbs providing the environmental and land use permitting analysis, the two sides achieved a milestone agreement that was officially ratified by all parties on April 30, 1980.

At the heart was the MSD's commitment to construct the Azure Reservoir and Power Plant as a compensatory storage facility. The reservoir would have an estimated capacity of 28,000 to 30,000 acre-feet of water that the CRWCD would market. A hydroelectric plant would generate electricity that the MSD would sell first to repay construction costs. Revenues would then be divided equally between the MSD and the CRWCD. One of the most important parts of the agreement had to do with the time limit for building at the Azure site. If the Azure project were found infeasible because of economic, environmental, or engineering concerns during the first fifteen years following the onset of construction of the Windy Gap project, the Subdistrict was obligated to build an alternate project or to make a cash payment of $10 million to the River District. This sum would be increased or decreased at the actual time of construction with reference to an acceptable engineering index. The MSD now estimated that Azure would cost $35 million over and above the $55 million estimated for the Windy Gap project and would generate approximately $4 million in revenues annually.[38] In addition to the dam and power plant, the MSD agreed to pay $420,000 to Hot Sulphur Springs for improving its water and sewage facilities and $25,000 to Grand County for salinity studies on the Colorado River. Unspecified additional funds would be paid to West Slope ranchers to help deliver water from the Colorado River to their meadows.[39]

In addition, a pioneering instream flow agreement was hammered out with the ranchers, Grand County, the Colorado Division of Wildlife (CDOW), and Trout Unlimited to protect fish flows for 24 miles of the Colorado River between Windy Gap and the mouth of the Blue River. Although the traditional water community viewed the action as heresy, the MSD subordinated its Windy Gap decrees to a junior CWCB instream flow water right over this 24-mile stretch. Finally, paragraph 25 clearly stated that the MSD agreed to "subordinate its Windy Gap decrees to all present and future in-basin irrigation, domestic and municipal uses, excluding industrial uses, on the Colorado and Fraser rivers and their tributaries above the Windy Gap reservoir site." This East Slope concession to the River District's interpretation of the Water Conservancy District Act, according to Hobbs, was necessary to any agreement with the West Slope.[40]

In return, the West Slope agreed to remove objections to the Windy Gap conditional decrees;[41] to support the MSD's application to the Federal Energy Regulatory Commission (FERC) for a power permit; to cooperate in obtaining all licenses, rights-of-way, and permits; and to allow immediate commencement of Windy Gap project construction. Everyone understood that no water could be delivered to the Six Cities prior to work on the Azure project or on some alternate facility. The handshake agreement of January 14 nearly collapsed when West Slope negotiators reported to the CRWCD board that River District engineers recommended increasing the $10 million figure to $14 million, but attorneys Balcomb and Delaney supported the agreement as presented. More than ten drafts were required before all parties accepted the language.[42] Following ratification, the document was delivered to the Colorado Supreme Court, which in turn ordered the district court to enter a conditional water decree consistent with the terms of the agreement. In the meantime, the MSD revised designs for the Windy Gap pumping system and expanded its water decree application from 400 cfs to 600 cfs to maintain the anticipated Windy Gap project yield and to satisfy the instream flow concessions to the West Slope.[43] District Judge Gavin D. Litwiller approved the Windy Gap Settlement

Agreement and the expanded conditional water decrees on October 27, 1980.[44] What Simpson, Sayre, and Hobbs characterized as a "last minute ambush" by the EPA was averted when the MSD agreed to build three islands in the Windy Gap Reservoir for waterfowl roosting. The EPA offered to provide funding for this project, but it was denied to avoid paper work and grant reporting requirements. With assistance from Senators Gary Hart and William Armstrong, the MSD finally obtained the required nonjeopardy endangered species opinion from the USF&WS.

Construction was now the primary objective. Both sides knew they had assumed certain risks by signing this agreement, but they had compromised without further litigation and with consideration for the principals of the prior appropriation doctrine. Each side had considered protection of the environment and future needs related to population growth as much as possible. They had also moved toward saving approximately 50,000 acre-feet of water annually from thirsty states of the lower Colorado River basin. Although negotiations had been difficult, no blood had been spilled, and any scars would heal. If they had to — and they would have to — both sides could negotiate again, but for now let the bulldozers and earthmovers begin.

IECO had been authorized in July 1976 to study hydrology and to prepare a final design for construction of the Windy Gap project and its integration with existing C–BT facilities. By simulating operations for over twenty-two years of past flow records on the Fraser River, IECO confirmed MSD staff estimates of an annual yield of 48,000 acre-feet of surplus water available for diversion to allottees on the East Slope. The water would be available during spring runoff, normally between April and July.[45] IECO had also prepared plans for an earthfill dam 25 feet high and 5,550 feet long on the Colorado River. A reservoir formed by the diversion dam would have a total live storage capacity under normal operations of 320 acre-feet over a surface area of 106 acres. A spillway designed for flood conditions was approved by the Dam Safety Branch of the Colorado State Engineer's Division of Water Resources. To satisfy downstream fish and irrigation flow requirements, IECO included a low-level bypass structure.[46] To pump surplus Colorado River water from the reservoir to Lake Granby, IECO designed a 9-foot diameter pipeline to extend along 30,000 feet of mainly private land. The pump plant would be located on the right abutment of the diversion dam, and four vertical shaft centrifugal pumps would be installed parallel to the flow of the Colorado River, 22 feet below the riverbed. To meet the 600 cfs terms of the conditional water decree, each pump would have a rating of 150 cfs at 600 rpm. Because pumps had to be specially ordered, the MSD invited bids early in 1981. The Subdistrict signed a contract with Hitachi America Incorporated when no U.S. companies entered the bidding.[47]

IECO estimated the project's capital cost at $46.8 million, based on May 1981 bids. With 51 percent of the estimated cost attributed to the pipeline and pump plant, the remainder would go into diversion dam construction, equipment, various energy uses, administration and management, inspection, and reclamation of damaged construction areas. Project financing was assured by the successful sale of a second series (Series B) of water revenue bonds. Series A bonds amounting to $3 million had been sold in 1977 to finance preconstruction costs, including engineering and environmental impact studies, right-of-way acquisitions, and legal and accounting expenses. Series B bonds worth $84,250,000 were sold to finance actual construction, to make deposits in various reserve funds, to defease (annul) Series A bonds, and to pay the cost of the most recent bond issue. Maturity for these bonds, which began in 1985, extended to the year 2014 at an interest rate ranging from 8.5 percent to 11.25 percent. They were sold to Dillon Reed and Company and Boettcher and Company, acting on behalf of themselves and certain investment dealers.[48] The successful sale was due mainly to the stability and technical feasibility of the Windy Gap project itself, though CWCB support merited a letter of sincere appreciation from Phipps.[49] With money in hand, there was a tendency to forget the year-long difficulties with the USF&WS, whose interpretation of the 1973 ESA had seriously threatened the MSD's ability to raise any money at all.[50]

The ESA provided for "the identification of endangered plant and animal species and the designation by the secretary of the interior of habitats critical to their preservation."[51] In September 1980, Simpson warned that construction delays might develop as a result of USF&WS concerns about the habitat of the Colorado River squawfish and humpback chub if the Windy Gap project were built as planned. He further noted that issuance of the Bureau's EIS, as well as other permits and licenses for construction, could be held up indefinitely by the Department of the Interior's decision to initiate a consultation process on new and existing water projects. A "non-jeopardy" opinion was necessary for construction work to begin.[52] At the very moment when East and West Slopes were to sign an agreement that allowed Windy Gap construction, the Department of the Interior's announcement seemed an unnecessary intrusion of the Carter administration into state water matters. Phipps was angry. He had already criticized Carter's "hit list" as a political maneuver to gain support from environmentalists, and he had blasted the Environmental Defense Fund, Trout Unlimited, and the Wilderness Society for trying to stop development of water projects.[53] Now he accused the United States of "regulatory and legislative excesses which have made the development of our water resource projects, even when financed by local capital, virtually impossible to achieve." In an impassioned letter to Colorado Senator William Armstrong, he especially singled out the "misuse" of the NEPA and the ESA. He pointed out that the Windy Gap project had been consistently stopped by "bureaucratic delay . . . [and] inept preparation of environmental statements by federal agencies who are afraid to process license applications and permits until all of the environmental processes are finished." Now he feared further delays because of harm to the habitat of two fish species. The "blizzard of regulations and restrictions" meant that the federal government was in effect abrogating the legitimate water laws of the State of Colorado.[54]

Obviously, Phipps had little patience with the intrusion of federal regulations on environmentally sensitive water projects. MSD president Farr, NCWCD president Gordon Dyekman, Sayre, Simpson, and others who shared some of his sentiments felt frustrated, but they believed in the project and wanted to negotiate a mutually acceptable program of mitigation. They understood that the USF&WS was required to make recommendations on the Bureau's EIS; however, they also knew that there was very little hydrologic data on which to base an opinion on the squawfish and humpback chub. The USF&WS was vulnerable to a legal challenge, but court action would only delay the project two to three years at an estimated cost increase of $5.5 million a year;[55] mitigation payments by the MSD seemed a far more realistic alternative.

After several intense meetings with USF&WS representatives, the MSD passed an acceptable resolution stating that the Subdistrict would contract with the USF&WS to sponsor a habitat manipulation project at a cost of $100,000. A second contract with the USF&WS would sponsor a biological investigation of Colorado River fishes at a cost not to exceed $450,000.[56] With this agreement signed, the Department of the Interior issued a nonjeopardy opinion, and the Bureau finalized its EIS.[57] The remainder of the permit process proceeded smoothly. Because the Fugitive Dust Permit was the only obstacle yet to overcome, ground breaking was optimistically scheduled for summer 1981.

The MSD had awarded contracts to Western States Construction Company of Loveland for general construction and to Johnson Brothers Corporation of Minnesota to lay the pipeline. With 175 people in attendance on July

11, 1981, Congressman Brown tripped the switch that set off dynamite charges on the diversion dam site. Farr spoke about the importance of Windy Gap water to the East Slope, where growing cities would no longer have to exchange or convert agricultural water to municipal water. He thanked the many organizations that had "set aside emotional feelings and negotiated with us in a fair minded spirit of cooperation and mutual benefit" and promised a "strong and diligent effort to construct the Azure Project for the benefit of the Western Slope as specified in the Windy Gap Settlement Agreement."[58] This was a moment of unparalleled satisfaction for proponents of the Windy Gap project, who had fought many battles during the previous fourteen years. Johnson Brothers bulldozers wasted no time in breaking ground on the 6-mile pipeline. Little did anyone expect that they would uncover reasons for another major delay, possibly one of the most important discoveries ever made in Colorado's archaeological history.

In conformance with the 1966 National Historic Preservation Act and the 1969 NEPA, the MSD contracted with Western Cultural Resource Management, Inc. (WCRM) of Boulder to do paleontological and archaeological analyses of the Windy Gap pipeline corridor. When work began in May 1981, the company had selected eight sites for testing. Field engineer John Eckhardt estimated a maximum mitigation cost of $120,000.[59] Two months later he advised the Subdistrict that the location of potentially significant additional sites would "almost assuredly" result in a cost far in excess of the budgeted amount. The reason was what WCRM project manager Chuck Wheeler called the "blockbuster": "mind boggling" results of early carbon dating at several of the forty-two sites identified along the proposed pipeline route. Bulldozer blades had unearthed the orange-colored remains of human habitation precisely where the pipe was to be laid. Evidence of wattle and daub residences and over 100 stone artifacts confirmed Wheeler's preliminary conclusions that intense and permanent occupation of the Windy Gap area went back as far as 8,000 years.[60] According to accepted belief, Middle Park was an area occupied irregularly by transients who had hunted prehistoric animals and mined jasper for spear points and stone tools; however, WCRM's initial discoveries suggested that humans had inhabited the area on a permanent basis at least 2,000 years earlier than previously imagined. Construction would have to be shut down.

Wheeler reported these findings to the MSD Board. Most of the sites were on MSD land that had formerly belonged to the Horn Ranch. He estimated that proper excavation would require $500,000 beyond the

$250,000 that the MSD had already spent. The Subdistrict authorized Wheeler to proceed but reserved the right to terminate the dig if funding were not available from private or public sources.[61] Board presidents Farr and Dyekman wrote directly to Secretary James Watt for assistance. They expected President Reagan to be more helpful than the Carter administration in regard to water projects. Senator Armstrong had conveyed that message to Phipps but also warned against expecting a blank check.[62] Optimism prevailed when Watt took a personal interest in the Windy Gap project. The Farr/Dyekman letter, which proposed a partnership "to forward the study of important human history together with the completion of a project critically needed for present-day human needs," also noted, not too subtly, that no recourse would be sought from the United States for construction delay "if we can excavate the archaeological resource in a timely fashion."[63]

During winter 1981–1982, WCRM moved into a heated structure, built with MSD funds over the most productive site; rumors circulated that the Windy Gap project might be canceled. When Watt unexpectedly failed to reply to the December 1981 Farr/Dyekman letter, the presidents wrote again. "Time was critical," they insisted, because the contractor was free to start work when the ground thawed. The MSD had absorbed another $70,000 of excavation expense "on the assumption that the request for funding by your Department would be favorably acted upon. It is our position that if [the Department of the Interior has] such jurisdiction, [it] can and should fund further archaeological efforts and is obligated to pay the costs of any construction contract delay or damages. If the Department has no jurisdiction, we must be left free to proceed in our best judgment. . . . We cannot justify the expenditure of any further funds for excavation."[64] On that same date the Subdistrict Board unanimously and inexplicably agreed to terminate the mitigation effort and begin construction. Delay penalties from the contractors were mounting. Watt responded almost immediately. Because most of the designated sites were on private land, the Department of the Interior could not fund ruins excavation, but he could request assistance from the Smithsonian Institute, the National Geographic Society, the National Science Foundation, and the National Academy of Sciences. At the same time, MSD representatives met with the Colorado Historical Society, the Federal Advisory Council on Historic Preservation, the USFS, and the BLM to work out a cooperative arrangement with all parties.[65] In addition, Undersecretary of the Interior Donald P. Hodel investigated the construction site and pledged to help raise private funding so that archeological activities could proceed expeditiously.

Some private money arrived. The National Trust for Historic Preservation donated $50,000, and the National Geographic Society provided $30,000. According to Arthur Townsend, Colorado's state historic preservation officer, $135,000 was still needed to meet the excavation budget.[66] Phipps's patience was wearing thin. He did not want to damage such an important archaeological site, he told the New York Times, but "the more we wait the more it costs our water users in construction delays. If someone doesn't come up with some funds to help pay for all this, we've got no choice but to go right ahead and build the pipeline."[67] By the end of July 1982 all available money had been expended. After building and firing a model wattel-and-daub house, archaeologists cleaned up their work sites and prepared to assess their evidence. At 10:14 A.M. on Monday, August 4, Cliff Lyons climbed into a bulldozer and plowed through the remains of what may have been one of the oldest civilizations in North America. As the machine crunched through the chunky soil, Wheeler and his colleagues pieced together the clues gathered during the previous year.[68] Although they had excavated only four sites, evidence tentatively described a "new montane archaic tradition" unique to the Colorado mountains. This find could have "major implications for the traditional interpretation of aboriginal occupation of these mountains." Middle Park, instead of being peripheral to other known culture areas, might have been a culturally distinct area.[69] Until more extensive excavation could be carried out, however, WCRM's hypothesis would remain tentative. The MSD agreed to cooperate with future archeological investigation along the pipeline route. In the meantime, construction work on the Windy Gap project moved ahead at full speed to make up for lost time.

For the first six months after August 4, 1982, Western States Contruction Company and Johnson Brothers Corporation made good progress until cold temperatures and heavy snow shut down all outdoor activity. They completed clearing, grubbing, and stripping for the dam and reservoir site and staked and graded islands for waterfowl. Concrete for the walls and floor of the pump house was poured, while IECO representatives and MSD staff met with Hitachi engineers at Hitachi City and Tsuchiura, Japan, to inspect pumps and motors. They witnessed hydrotesting of the pump casings and motors, cleared all pump drawings, discussed production schedules, and came away impressed with the quality of workmanship. By February 1983 the first pump was readied for shipment to Granby.[70] In the meantime, Johnson Brothers speeded up pipeline activities by moving to a six-day work week. They completed trenching from the pump house under Highway 40. Sixty percent of the 108-inch prestressed concrete pipe was placed along the 6-mile pipeline to Lake Granby before winter weather called a halt to these activities. Not far behind schedule, Johnson Brothers demobilized operations in December with plans to begin again in April 1983.[71]

As Farr had promised, the Subdistrict tackled the Azure project with equal tenacity. Suspecting that the West Slope still doubted the Subdistrict's sincerity, and concerned about starting construction prior to delivery of Windy Gap water, planning for Azure commenced with ground breaking on the Windy Gap project. Within months environmental studies and stream-gauging stations were operating in Gore Canyon. Sayre then launched inquiries with bond underwriting firms to determine the feasibility of financing an estimated $33 million of construction money.[72] Eckhardt, Hobbs, Simpson, and other staff members took a raft trip down the Colorado River to get a firsthand view of "one of the finest arch dam sites in Colorado."[73] Of immediate concern was the actively used railroad bed hugging the canyon wall and the BLM launch site for commercial and private rafting operations in the middle of the proposed reservoir site. In addition to great scenery, they encountered some unexpected opposition to the dam. Aurora and Colorado Springs were already opposed to Azure, believing that it would somehow have a negative impact on their Homestake project.[74] More vocal protests came from the Colorado River rafting industry, whose operation would have to move out of Gore Canyon to flatter water several miles downstream. At a meeting called by the MSD on January 29, 1983, in Kremmling, other opponents charged that the dam would increase traffic, inundate valuable cultural and archaeological sites, destroy endangered species, increase river sedimentation, and produce a negative impact on socioeconomic conditions in the valley.[75]

Ironically, most of this criticism resulted from Subdistrict investigations of a larger dam and reservoir site to accommodate the River District's desire for more compensatory storage. This would impound 85,000 acre-feet of water, as compared to 30,000 acre-feet, but would require rerouting the main line of the Denver and Rio Grande Western Railroad. The MSD had contracted with IECO to do feasibility studies of several options. By the end of 1982, Tom Pitts and Associates had studied environmental concerns and produced reports at a cost of $1.7 million that were available for public review.[76] These investigations did not support construction of the larger Azure project in any configuration. The dam in Gore Canyon, plus a reregulating reservoir near Radium, would require construction of 15 miles of railroad tunnel. Although the Denver and Rio Grande Western Railroad had no difficulty with rerouting the rails, they pointed out that such a long underground detour — 11 miles — would require engines with an alternate electrical power source. A smaller dam, 135 feet high and 350 feet long, however, would require no railroad relocation, although the reservoir capacity would be only 23,000 acre-feet. As part of this "small Azure" plan, water would be pumped uphill from Azure Reservoir to a 14,500 acre-feet storage facility in Trough Valley, where it would be released back into Azure Reservoir during periods of peak demand for power.[77] "This technique is known as pump-back storage. It is based on a typical power rate structure which enables a power entity to pump water up to a storage facility at cheaper off-peak rates and return the same water through generating turbines when a higher rate can be charged for electricity." IECO studies revealed that this pump-back storage design would have a potential cost-benefit ratio of 2.66:1,[78] but Subdistrict officials questioned whether the plan was financially feasible. Could they find markets for selling the generated hydropower quickly enough to pay off potential investors in a multimillion dollar bond issue?

Meanwhile, the River District grew anxious once again. Their people wanted the larger storage reservoir so that they could sell the water. From their attorney's point of view, the Subdistrict was obligated to construct the Azure project "regardless of what return is received by the hydrogeneration of electricity." Even though Balcomb recognized that the Windy Gap Settlement Agreement allowed for mutual abandonment of the Azure project "for engineering or *other reasons*" (emphasis added), he insisted that it made no provision for "financial feasibility."[79] Notwithstanding this criticism, the MSD was prepared by spring 1983 to apply for a license to FERC on the basis of a 23,000 acre-feet Azure Reservoir and a pump-back storage facility in Trough Valley. Because of the power features, FERC had to provide a license before construction could begin. Angered by the fact that revenues from hydroelectric generation were dictating the size and location of their storage reservoir, the CRWCD refused to sign as a partner on the license application.[80]

River District manager Fischer agreed with CRWCD attorneys that the "other reasons" phrase did not allow determination of financial feasibility. As he wrote to Sayre, the need for a power component was perfectly understandable, but "it was certainly not agreed that power should in any way reduce the amount of the compensatory storage of 28,000 to 30,000 acre-feet which we consider to be the Subdistrict's commitment under the Agreement." The CRWCD would not endorse a FERC application as long as that application indicated that "Azure Reservoir will be built only if it is self-financing with power revenues."[81] Once again the two sides were at odds. Negotiation or litigation? The Subdistrict finally applied for the FERC license alone. Other applications had been made in previous years for the same site, and there was a slight chance of an award to another entity.[82] As Simpson recalled, the MSD license application was flawed by an inadequate analysis of the power marketing potential;[83] however, the River District's resentment resulted more from the available "cost-free compensatory storage," which had been cut by two-thirds in the FERC application.[84] One of their attorneys further aired the differences between the CRWCD and the MSD in a letter to FERC.[85]

For the remainder of 1983 and 1984, the two sides tried to negotiate. Anticipating his retirement in two years at age sixty-five, Sayre assigned Hobbs to serve as Simpson's lead counsel in a committee including Board members Ray Joyce, William Bohlender, Ev Long and W. D. "Bill" Farr. A misunderstanding over the 28,000 acre-feet capacity in the proposed Azure Reservoir prevented another agreement. West Slope representatives argued that the Windy Gap Settlement Agreement promised them 28,000 to 30,000 acre-feet of stored water that would be available for sale; the MSD responded that the agreement only promised 28,000 to 30,000 acre-feet of "maximum feasible capacity" in a compensatory storage reservoir.[86] If the water had to be used for pump-back storage and to generate revenue from power sales, they could not sell it to River District customers. Although both sides nearly fell out over this disagreement, they both wanted what was spelled out in the 1980 agreement. Because the Six Cities insisted on negotiations, they continued to talk. River District officials asked for additional meetings, for MSD information to determine "maximum feasible capacity," and for time to study the data.[87] Simpson replied that two key reports would soon be available, at which time the Subdistrict would decide whether to proceed with the Azure project or to pursue an alternative as outlined in the 1980 Windy Gap Settlement Agreement.[88]

Reports published in September 1983 did not give the Azure project high marks. Because the MSD had already spent $3.5 million to purchase rights-of-way and $1.5–$2 million in feasibility studies,[89] the East Slope increasingly felt that money was being wasted. Because PRPA and Six Cities Committee representatives from Loveland and Boulder were asking hard questions, the Subdistrict asked the CRWCD to consider alternative sites or the possibility of a $10 million lump-sum payment.[90] In a cooperative effort, staffs of both districts made preliminary hydrologic evaluations of reservoir sites at Rock Creek and Wolford Mountain; both appeared more economical than construction at the original Azure site.[91] The River District proposed a cash settlement of $15 million, and the Subdistrict countered with $12 million and a commitment to subordinate Windy Gap water rights to either a Wolford Mountain or Rock Creek Reservoir.[92] Negotiating teams argued back and forth; attorneys argued in court to block each other's pet projects; angry moments developed when idle threats emerged over the lack of progress. Both sides were mindful of the costly alternative to successful negotiation, but a year passed before a satisfactory agreement could be signed. On March 29, 1985, representatives of the MSD, CRWCD, Grand County commissioners, NWRCOG, and the MPWCD signed a supplement to the original Windy Gap Settlement Agreement that provided a $10.2 million cash payment to the CRWCD "in complete satisfaction of any obligation Subdistrict has under the April 30, 1980 Agreement to construct the Azure Reservoir and Power project, or an alternate facility, for western Colorado." The supplement also provided 3,000 acre-feet of water from Lake Granby at no cost to MPWCD along with subordination of Windy Gap water rights to either Rock Creek or Wolford Mountain projects, as previously offered.[93] The River District was to retain water rights and engineering studies for the Azure Reservoir site.

Three months later to the day, Windy Gap project dedication ceremonies celebrated the end of construction. Work on the dam, pipeline, and pumps had proceeded, scarcely affected by the discord between MSD and CRWCD officials. In fact, major items of construction had been completed long before the supplemental agreement was signed. Johnson Brothers finished laying the 6-mile pipeline to Lake Granby in fall 1983, filled it with water in December, and successfully ran hydrostatic tests the following month. In spring 1984 Windy Gap Reservoir was regraded to approximately original contours, and the Bureau began filling it with releases from Willow Creek Reservoir and Lake Granby. Assembly work on the Hitachi pumps and motors continued as workers added finishing touches to the pump house and all electrical and mechanical systems. On October 10, 1984, one pump went through a twenty-four-hour test with 47 million gallons of water delivered from Windy Gap Reservoir to Lake Granby. By the end of November all pumps had been successfully tested and emergency shutdown tests performed. The project was ready for operation in January 1985, even though three additional months of negotiation were required before the Subdistrict and River District agreed to abandon the Azure project.

Building the Windy Gap water delivery system was a long and complicated process, but finding the power to drive the four Hitachi pumps proved equally difficult and potentially more significant to East Slope allottees.[94]

Late in 1982 the search began for a source of firm power that could be contracted and relied on for the three-month pumping season when surplus waters flowed in the Fraser River. Negotiation for this power was difficult because only a fixed amount was available and because local power companies owned the transmission lines. With no real competition, this was a seller's market. Early in 1983 the MSD Board encouraged staff to delay signing any contract until discussions could be held with a federal organization, the Western Area Power Administration (WAPA). WAPA was already dispatching and marketing power generated from the federally owned C–BT system. Sales were first made to "preference customers," such as rural electric associations (REAs), municipalities, and state and federal agencies at rates lower than they charged to nonpreference customers. After the MSD qualified as a preference customer, that group contracted for part of the energy needed to start one of the Windy Gap pumps. The "take-or-pay" contract required the Subdistrict to pay, whether or not the power was used. According to Simpson, "the United States should have given us all the energy [necessary] to pump Windy Gap, because they get twice as much energy out of this system by running [the water] through [their] power plants with no mess whatsoever," but the Bureau was adamantly opposed to this idea during the power negotiations, arguing that the NCWCD had gotten "a free ride on the C-BT Project, and now we're going to get some of it back." Both James E. Stokes, the Bureau's South Platte project manager, and Region 7 Director James M. Ingles firmly opposed free power for the Windy Gap project.[95] Clearly, the District's earlier success in limiting the Repayment Contract obligation to $25 million had remained a sore subject with the Bureau. To provide the necessary balance of power, the Subdistrict signed interim contracts with Tri-State Electric Company. As of this writing, final power agreements remain unconsumated. With competition from PRPA in the 1990s, the MSD has a good chance of reducing the enormous energy costs associated with pumping Windy Gap project water.[96]

Once Windy Gap water arrived in Lake Granby, the Subdistrict had to determine exactly where and when to use it. Colorado's Water Conservancy District Act restricted the use of Windy Gap water to areas included within the MSD or NCWCD but empowered the Board to extend these boundaries. Three water-related developments necessitated a clearer understanding of the eligibility question prior to the end of Windy Gap project construction: Denver's attempt to plan for future growth, the 1977 drought, and the PRPA's decision to build the coal-fired Rawhide Power Plant north of Fort Collins.

In 1975 a Denver metropolitan water study proposed new boundaries for the DWB service area that included all of Boulder County and portions of southern Weld County. Objecting to this proposal, the District told Denver to exclude the NCWCD area from the Metropolitan Water District. Furthermore, the District said it would "vigorously oppose the proposed use outside the boundaries of the NCWCD of any water derived under decrees held by the United States and allocated to users by contract with the District."[97] In the seventies the Denver metropolitan area was looking everywhere for more water to solve perceived growth problems; once again, Green Mountain Reservoir appeared vulnerable. When a serious drought threatened in 1977, Denver refused to release 28,622 acre-feet of water out of Dillon Reservoir pursuant to decrees adjudicated in the Consolidated Cases. Denver finally complied with the law after being defeated by an adverse decision in the Federal Court of Appeals. Several years later Governor Lamm organized the Metropolitan Water Roundtable to address these and other long-standing water conflicts between East and West Slopes, hoping to work out water exchange plans that would address Denver's needs.

The Windy Gap project fit because its water could be sold as reuse water anywhere in Colorado; thus, the MSD Board had to decide exactly who would have first-use rights as well as reuse rights, which they could implement or sell to others as legitimate Windy Gap allottees. First-use locations would determine the flexibility of subsequent uses. Subdistrict inclusion and allotment policies had to carefully protect established C–BT allottees and extant delivery systems while also addressing the Denver metropolitan area. Hobbs's representation on the Metropolitan Water Roundtable kept the channels of communication open. PRPA's inclusion as an equal partner and Windy Gap allottee with the Six Cities Committee further helped formulate Subdistrict allotment and inclusion policies. While the Rawhide Power Plant was being constructed in 1980, NCWCD Directors found temporary use of C–BT water by PRPA acceptable. Following the passage of appropriate amendments to the Water Conservancy District Act, the Board reaffirmed its 1973 inclusion policy, denying the use of C–BT water outside District boundaries "but [approving delivery] within Municipal Subdistrict boundaries now and in the future."[98] In other words, C–BT water could be used within the Subdistrict, with the Board's permission, and Subdistrict water could be used throughout the NCWCD without including the entire MSD area within the District.[99] Inclusion within the MSD also held out the potential of having the District Board transfer C–BT units from prior uses to accompany Windy Gap water in newly included areas of the Subdistrict.

The status of many populated areas annexed to the Six Cities since 1970 was still unclear. In 1983 the MSD Board's new policy stated that petitions for inclusion into the MSD had to be accompanied by a contract for purchase or lease of Windy Gap water. Petition review included careful evaluation of the C–BT delivery system and of the requirement that first use occur within the parent District or Subdistrict. If existing structures could handle Windy Gap water without prejudice to C–BT allottees or to original MSD allottees, petitions for change of Windy Gap allotments and inclusion of new areas were approved to communities north of the southern boundaries of the Boulder-Weld County lines.[100] The south-end delivery system and Boulder Reservoir were principal areas of concern. With the growth of metropolitan Denver moving toward District boundaries, limited storage and delivery capacity in this area forestalled any chance of using Windy Gap water to alleviate Denver's north metropolitan needs prior to, or in combination with, construction of the Two Forks Dam and Reservoir. Furthermore, the District's predilection toward keeping C–BT water from use in MSD areas not annexed to the NCWCD presented an additional obstacle to water management flexibility. Recognizing how important Windy Gap water had become to the future of the entire Front Range, especially between Denver and the NCWCD/MSD boundaries, the Subdistrict in 1985 organized a special team to see if a "short-term solution" could be found.[101]

With the EPA's 1990 defeat of Two Forks, Windy Gap and C–BT water became increasingly attractive to the bedroom communities surrounding the City and County of Denver. As of this writing, policies to balance Front Range needs against the contractual rights of District and Subdistrict allottees are still under review. Although the Windy Gap project has received its share of criticism, the twin objectives of lowering the price of C–BT water and slowing down the conversion of agricultural water to municipal use have been accomplished. Undoubtedly, this project would have difficulty being built today. As with the C–BT in the thirties, a window of opportunity opened in 1980 that allowed the Subdistrict to aggressively pursue construction and negotiations with the West Slope and with environmental organizations. Although unfulfilled, promises of a new reclamation era under President Reagan and Secretary James G. Watt gave the project new impetus. Costs of construction, mitigation, litigation, and bond interest ran much higher than anticipated by the Six Cities in 1970, but Windy Gap water remains competitive with C–BT water on a per-acre-foot basis. If a C–BT unit increases from its present value of $1,600 per acre-foot to $1,800 per acre-foot, Windy Gap water will actually be cheaper.[102]

A final observation seems appropriate. Litigating complicated water conflicts sets a potential trap for both public and private water entities. Old animosities die particularly slowly with out-of-basin water projects. Although the West Slope forced the Subdistrict to obtain its compensatory storage guaranteed by Colorado statutes, both the Subdistrict and the River District recognized the debilitating nature of long and costly courtroom litigation. Ultimately, negotiation produced benefits for both sides. Farr referred to this conciliation at the Windy Gap dedication ceremonies on June 29, 1985, when he lauded the "cooperative spirit" between East and West Slopes but downplayed the painful struggles endured along the way. Success did not come easily, and it had a considerable price. For men such as Phipps, who believed so totally in the District's entitlement to 310,000 acre-feet of water from the C–BT system, negotiations with the West Slope or the federal government were intolerable. The extensive negotiations to get Windy Gap built simply overwhelmed him and contributed to his untimely death in spring 1982.

23 The District Under Manager Earl F. Phipps

Since the District's 1937 founding, each manager has addressed unique problems and special circumstances. J. M. Dille presided over the District's organization and C–BT construction. J. R. "Bob" Barkley set policies for water distribution during a period of exponential postwar growth. Earl F. Phipps guided the District and Subdistrict into construction of the Windy Gap project while he simultaneously responded to years of severe drought, environmental issues, evolving federal and state water policies, and computerization complexities. If Dille got the Project built and Barkley put it on the map, Phipps somewhat reluctantly oversaw the NCWCD's transition from an important agricultural and quasi-municipal water entity on the Front Range to an aspiring water leader in Colorado and in the West.

Ironically, Phipps did not seek this role for himself and for the District. As a leader, he was not as outgoing and aggressive as either his predecessor or his successor, Larry D. Simpson; his strengths were in making the system work. Where Barkley was equally comfortable with both Washington politics and local ditch companies, Phipps was more adept at the details of daily operations. Given his agronomy training and nearly fifteen years' experience in the District's operations and maintenance department, Phipps's focus on neat and efficient water delivery naturally expressed his background and interests. Because of recent criticism of the District's expanded participation in water matters, and because Phipps's death in 1982 was to some extent related to pressures requiring him to change and compromise, his managerial style merits further comment.

Above everything, Phipps was totally committed to his work. He loved the District, served with enthusiasm and integrity for more than thirty years and never asked anyone to do a job he would not do himself. He was also a fiscal conservative who felt the need to count every penny spent. Departmental budgets had to be defended annually, and he praised those who found ways to cut expenses. Some employees remember him as obsessively preoccupied with all forms of spending. Because he had difficulty understanding double-entry bookkeeping, he kept his own set of

Earl F. Phipps, one of the District's first employees, was manager from 1974 until his death in 1982. (Courtesy NCWCD.)

records. Not a single expense item escaped his scrutiny. When the Subdistrict began work on Windy Gap, he worried about the municipalities' ability to pay the high construction costs, interest, and environmental mitigation. He was so concerned about spending that he planned to retire on his thirtieth anniversary with the District to save the taxpayers "a significant amount of money in terms of salary payment and insurance premiums."[1] Legal counsel John M. Sayre persuaded him otherwise, fearing that his retirement might somehow jeopardize efforts to promote and sell a Windy Gap bond issue. Phipps stayed on another year, concerned about the status of other employees who might want to continue working after "normal retirement," confused by feelings of inadequacy, and debilitated by his own declining health. On Easter, April 11, 1982, his wife found him dead in their garage, sitting behind the wheel with the car engine running.

To explain this tragedy requires some speculation that Phipps felt overwhelmed by forces over which he had lost control. The pain in his legs from shrapnel wounds brought increasing dependence on drugs and alcohol. Radical prostate surgery scared him and left questions about doctors' assurances that all the cancer had been removed. The proficiency and energy of assistant manager Simpson underscored his self-doubts about leadership, and the simple objective he embraced — providing water to farmers as efficiently and cheaply as possible while trying to meet increasing municipal demands — no longer seemed adequate in a complex world of environmentalism and government regulations. The manager's position became an intolerable pressure cooker. He worked nights and weekends to make sense out of the new order. The District "family" that he wanted to preserve was becoming more impersonal while the growing importance of litigation appeared to him a waste of energy and taxpayers' money. At his best, Phipps was a fine contract negotiator, winning praise from both Barkley and Sayre, but the strain of Windy Gap negotiations tired him because the simple world that he knew had come apart around him. He felt defeated, perhaps no longer needed. When he died, the District lost a dedicated servant.

One of Phipps's major frustrations was with environmentalists. He saw them as obstructionists with whom he preferred not to compromise. Sayre and the Board felt similarly aggravated, but they believed that C–BT and the Windy Gap operation might be severely restricted if environmentalists' interpretations of water quality and other federal legislation went unchallenged. A case in point was the debate over the deteriorating quality of Colorado River water. While the Subdistrict maintained that the Windy Gap project would contribute less than 1 percent to the river's salinity,[2] West Slope opponents pursued the old argument that "dilution is the solution to pollution." In other words, transmountain diversions deprived the Colorado River of the ability to dissolve salts and other minerals and flush them through the system. Three of the five projects promised to the West Slope in the 1968 central Arizona project legislation (Dallas Creek, Fruitland Mesa, and Savery–Pot Hook) were delayed pending completion of salinity studies. With the Windy Gap project threatening additional out-of-basin diversion in a few years, those projects had little chance of moving forward. CRWCD manager Roland C. Fischer insisted that the EPA require East Slope diverters to pay their fair share of costs to prevent further degradation of the Colorado River.[3] In total agreement, six West Slope counties represented by the NWRCOG asked Governor Richard Lamm for designation as an official management agency for control of transmountain diversion. Their studies indicated that the nineteen existing diversions from the West Slope were far more significant as causes of salinity than natural or artificial causes.[4]

Lamm was sympathetic. In 1977, with the state in the middle of a severe drought, he was looking for a way to reduce conflict over a limited water supply. In an open letter to the *Denver Post*, Lamm remarked that the West Slope felt incapable of fulfilling federal mandates to devise a water quality strategy when the East Slope was taking "fresh, high mountain water" from its river basins. He concluded that transmountain diversions were compromising the quality of the Colorado River.[5] Sayre objected to Lamm's conclusions. He blamed the NWRCOG for providing misleading information to the governor. "The figures expressed in the [NWRCOG] memorandum, are quite different from those which have been used by other parties reviewing this particular problem.... The thrust of the [NWRCOG] letter appears not to be for the preservation of water quality, but to prevent further transmountain diversions to areas needing the water.... I would hope that a statement such as you made would not be forthcoming again from your office."[6]

The EPA was slow to act on the Colorado River controversy. The Colorado River Salinity Forum presented data in 1977 showing that one-third of the salinity came from agricultural return flows and two-thirds from natural salinity sources. According to these numbers, transmountain diversion was practically blameless.[7] The EPA accepted these figures and issued rules for a new permit program that singled out agricultural point source discharges. The Environmental Defense Fund (EDF), with assistance from Trout Unlimited and the Wilderness Society, then filed suit against the EPA, the secretary of the interior, and the Bureau for allegedly neglecting their regulatory responsibilities. They asked the U.S. District Court to order a comprehensive EIS for the entire Colorado River basin, demanded state-line salinity standards, and insisted on a prohibition on construction and operation of existing water resource projects until the results were known.[8] Sayre immediately warned the Board that this litigation could have "serious ramifications" for those involved with water rights on the Colorado River.[9] If the plaintiffs succeeded, progress on the Windy Gap project could be halted. He expected all seven Colorado River basin states to intervene in the case and felt pleased when the Subdistrict Board unanimously agreed to join the suit and to contribute 15 percent of litigation costs.[10]

The Court ruled, however, that the Colorado River basin states were adequately represented by their attorneys general. No other parties were allowed to enter the EDF litigation except the Mountain States Legal Foundation. In 1979 a decision was handed down that upheld states' rights to set their own water quality standards. It also said that the seven-state Colorado River Basin Salinity Forum, functioning within the context of the Federal Salinity Control Project Act, was adequately addressing the issues involved in the case. Sayre was pleased by what he viewed as a "favorable" decision.[11] Both he and Phipps saw the attempted EDF injunction as the inspiration of powerful anti-western water sentiments within the administration of President Carter, whose "hit list," they believed, was "peanuts" compared to the potential threat of the EDF suit. Using even stronger language, CWCB Director Felix "Larry" Sparks referred to the environmentalists as an "idiot brigade."[12] If the EDF ruling cleared Colorado to determine its own water quality standards, then the CWQCC assumed greater authority, and Phipps soon learned that this organization also had teeth.

The Colorado Water Quality Control Act of 1973 was enacted to provide the CWQCC "with power to develop a comprehensive program for the prevention of stream pollution"[13] and to coordinate the state's antipollution efforts with the federally mandated 1972 Clean Water Act. Nothing in the Colorado legislation intended to undermine existing water rights or the prior appropriation doctrine. The CWQCC received responsibility for "both water quality protection and the development and maintenance of a comprehensive program for water pollution control."[14] Late in 1975 the NCWCD learned that the CWQCC had a plan to make transmountain diverters pay for Colorado River salinity control.[15] Because the commission had adopted the Colorado River Salinity Forum's report to the EPA, the District Board agreed not to respond immediately; but the salinity issue would not go away. The commission's technical secretary complained to Senator Gary Hart that industrial growth and energy development on the West Slope would increase salinity because of increased water consumption. Furthermore, he argued, water exported out of the Colorado River basin and fresh spring water stored in project reservoirs concentrated existing pollutants in the restricted flows. He urged Hart to consider these factors in any amendments to Public Law 92-500, the Federal Water Pollution Control Act.[16] The Colorado Water Quality Control Act also gave the CWQCC authority to classify streams according to four use categories: recreational, agricultural, aquatic, and municipal water supply. When the commission first published preliminary standards for each category, the District was shocked. W. D. "Bill" Farr successfully moved adoption of a resolution for concern over how the standards were being written and what time constraints were imposed relative to the distribution of standards for public comment and review.[17] Water users, representing 250,000 irrigated acres on the Front Range, supported the resolution and asked the CWQCC not to adopt its new proposals.[18] Phipps followed up with a letter to the CWQCC in which he suggested that the commission might have given insufficient consideration to the economic impact of these standards, the technical feasibility of attaining them, the possible conflict with federal law, and the logic of developing standards stricter than those of the United States without first conferring with water users and identifying specific pollutants. "With all due respect, it appears that [in the preparation of their data] the presence of practically oriented water users and waste treatment technicians was lacking."[19]

The District responded with litigation when the CWQCC formally adopted the regulations. The battle over water quality regulations and their impact on the exercise of water rights had come to a head. Joined by representatives from municipalities and industry, Simpson and associate legal counsel Gregory J. Hobbs, Jr., attended CWQCC hearings to persuade the nine commissioners that the South Platte River was primarily an agricultural waterway, not a fishery. They also endorsed recommendations in a Colorado Department of Agriculture report that urged the CWQCC not to classify irrigation ditches and canals for drinking water purposes and not to use water-quality regulations to establish minimum streamflows, a right legally available only to the CWCB after intense review of all relevant factors.[20] EPA regulations and CWQCC rules combined to leave water entities with the impression that water-quality laws, if misused, would represent a "monstrous overkill" while they simultaneously subjected water users to "bureaucratic tyranny."[21]

The main problem was that Windy Gap water would be pumped from the Colorado River below the wastewater treatment plants of several West Slope communities. The NWRCOG and environmental groups were suggesting that the Windy Gap pipeline might be a point source of pollution requiring a discharge permit that would have to be renewed every five years. The strain of meeting evolving state and federal regulatory conditions while operating the C–BT and moving the Windy Gap project forward was overwhelming. Furthermore, State Senator Fred Anderson noted that Colorado had a constitutional responsibilty to administer its own waters. The new rules and regulations on water quality seemed to subvert the very basis of Colorado water law.[22] Senator Hart threatened to introduce legislation to remove all EPA authority over water development issues if the agency did not drop the plan for a comprehensive water-resource development policy. The EPA, he concluded, was overstepping its authority.[23] A 1979 NCWCD resolution stated that the District was growing increasingly concerned about the federal government's attempts "to abolish or weaken productive, beneficial, and cost-effective programs such as the Soil Conservation Service snow surveys while, at the same time . . . by surreptitious interpretation of well intentioned laws, permitting and encouraging other wasteful and counterproductive programs administered by agencies such as the Environmental Protection Agency,

Health, Education and Welfare, Fish and Wildlife Service, Department of Labor, Bureau of Land Management, and others."[24]

   With the salinity issue still unresolved, environmental concerns began to focus increasingly on point and nonpoint sources of pollution.[25] The Colorado Water Congress had hoped that the EPA would exempt irrigated agriculture entirely from the 1972 Clean Water Act, but such a move was unthinkable. In fact, the EPA wanted to establish even greater control over irrigation by exploring ways of completely eradicating return flows on which many downstream South Platte River water users depended.[26] The Larimer-Weld Regional Council of Governments reacted immediately. They argued that irrigated agriculture had to be considered in all its complexity, and the historic use of return flows in the prior appropriation doctrine had to be protected.[27] At a Washington hearing, however, Phipps learned that agricultural return flows were identified as point sources of pollution requiring discharge permits similar to any city or industry.[28] This debate over whether agricultural return flows were point or nonpoint sources of pollution was of intense interest to the District because of 650,000 acres of land under irrigation from supplemental C-BT water and because of the implications to the proposed Windy Gap project. Colorado's discharge permit program for point source pollution was approved under the Federal Clean Water Act. To obtain federal approval, the state's permit programs had to resemble the National Pollutant Discharge Elimination System (NPDES) permit requirements. The EPA had ample authority to veto permits or to withdraw federal approval of the state program entirely if Colorado failed to comply with NPDES standards.[29] Perceiving this a potentially abusive use of federal power, the NCWCD Board told EPA officials that the rules seemed unjust. The Directors adopted a wait-and-see attitude pending implementation of enforcement policies and clarification of how agricultural return flows would be officially categorized.[30] In 1977 amendments to the Clean Water Act (CWA) specifically stated that return flows from irrigated agriculture would not require a state permit but that programs for control of nonpoint source pollution would have to be "developed and implemented in an expeditious manner."[31] District officials could clearly see that environmental concerns over agricultural pesticides, fertilizers, and salinity represented a national trend. Only imaginative programs would conform to the federal legislation.[32]

   Ironically, environmental struggles over water pollution were emerging at a time when Colorado's climate showed extremes in traditional moisture patterns. Even as the Carter administration threatened to withhold federal funding for all water projects and environmentalists acted to impose

The 1976 Big Thompson flood destroyed numerous residences and businesses and was responsible for at least 139 deaths. (Courtesy Bureau of Reclamation.)

restrictions on irrigation, northern Colorado experienced a severe flood followed by a major drought. The magnitude of these events put Colorado's water problems in a different perspective.

The 1976 Big Thompson flood caused 139 known deaths, left six people unaccounted for, caused over $35 million in property damage, destroyed hundreds of homes and businesses, and obliterated over 14 miles of U.S. Highway 34 within the Big Thompson Canyon between Loveland and Estes Park.[33] At some point late on July 31, an estimated 31,200 cfs[34] flood knocked out the south support of the Big Thompson Siphon carrying Hansen Feeder Canal water over the river to Horsetooth Reservoir. Because the National Weather Service's radar system was out of action, residents and travelers received no warning of the dangerous intensification of an immense storm over the north fork of the Big Thompson River. The first disaster news reached Bob Berling, project manager for the Bureau, just before midnight. His first move was to send his Flatiron foreman to verify loss of the Big Thompson Siphon. Radio reports confirmed the damage.

1976 Big Thompson flood aftermath showing destruction of U.S. Highway 34 and footings of the siphon that carried C–BT water across the canyon. (Courtesy Bureau of Reclamation.)

Earlier, the Bureau had shut off flows from Flatiron into the Hansen Feeder Canal, closed down the Adams Tunnel, and stopped releases at Olympus Dam, hoping that Lake Estes would contain rising flood waters. The Mary's Lake and Estes power plants immediately went off line. A maximum amount of water was then diverted out of Lake Estes through Pole Hill Tunnel into Flatiron Reservoir and Carter Lake. All of these actions were taken to decrease the flood potential in the Big Thompson watershed and to minimize the possibility of overtopping at Olympus Dam. The Bureau's main concern was that if the Flatiron pump to Carter Lake failed, a complete loss of power generation could occur. Without a reservoir to hold the water coming down the system from Lake Estes, electricity could not be generated.[35]

The District's major concern was Horsetooth Reservoir and the 600 water users along the north end of the system. Early on Sunday morning August 1, Phipps arrived at the Bureau office to ask what the District could do. Robert L. Berling recalled, "He was right there wanting to know what

Big Thompson Siphon after 1976 flood a quarter mile from its normal location. (Courtesy Bureau of Reclamation.)

[he] could do, because he knew we were in the middle of it and had our hands full."[36] While Governor Lamm, the sheriff, and other state and local officials inspected the area by helicopter, Phipps offered the District office as headquarters and command post for organizing disaster relief. With the media using much of the District's office space, the Salvation Army moved into the NCWCD garage. The Colorado National Guard and Larimer County Sheriff's office operated out of a mobile recreational vehicle. Telephones soon were so tied up with flood business that regular water orders had to be sent by radio to the District.[37] Recognizing the importance of initiating repairs immediately, Phipps offered to make $350,000 available from the District's contingency fund. Berling accepted, knowing that the Bureau would take longer to provide its share of the estimated $1.1 million in damages to the C–BT system.[38] The Board applied for federal disaster-assistance relief and received a check in November for $167,000 for flood damages.[39] Because the Big Thompson Siphon was critical, Berling was determined to replace it in ninety days, using the same engineering design that the Bureau had accepted forty years earlier. He rejected suggestions for placing the siphon under the river. Foundations for the supports were deepened and strengthened, and an order for new pipe

was placed with the Eaton Metal Works of Denver. The Bureau made only two changes in the old design. It followed the suggestion of a local environmental commission to paint the siphon sage green instead of the original aluminum color, and it raised the height of the siphon 10 feet in anticipation of possible future floods. In eighty-eight days, water once again flowed through the Hansen Feeder Canal to Horsetooth Reservoir.

While the Bureau worked on the siphon, Phipps volunteered to provide a temporary water supply into the Hansen Feeder Canal. A quick survey of 600 affected water users indicated that they had adequate supplies for one to two weeks in either canal siphons or in their own facilities. The Bureau agreed to furnish the necessary power from the Big Thompson Power Plant for an electric pump. After the Denver Pump Company was selected to provide a 300-hp motor to pump the water up to the canal, District O&M employees worked to excavate a site for the pump well to a depth of 8 feet. When the time came to pour concrete, the Eastman Kodak Company of Colorado contributed a 30-ton crane and a crew. The Big Thompson ran murky for a long time after the flood, but fresh water directed into the river from Carter Lake through Flatiron Reservoir and District personnel working overtime meant that the pump was installed and delivered an average flow of 7 cfs through a 14-inch pipeline to the canal by August 14. Filtration systems of domestic users eliminated remaining turbidity in the water.[40] Given that the pump was mistakenly sent to Salt Lake City, accomplishments of the District's O&M department were remarkable.

The significance of this catastrophe should not be minimized. First, the 12- to 13-inch rainfall in a concentrated area over a six-hour period was not so unusual when one compares the event to flooding on Cherry Creek (1864), the Arkansas River (1921), and the South Platte River (1965). East Slope flood plains are susceptible to these kinds of disasters, and those who build and rebuild residences and businesses in the watersheds are betting against climatological odds. Second, physical damage caused by the Big Thompson flood was partially mitigated by the C–BT Project. The Bureau's ability to capture some of the heavy rainfall in Lake Estes moderated flood water impact on the Big Thompson Canyon. Berling argued that a small dam at the canyon's mouth would have captured the water for future use and would have controlled the flood.[41] This may be true, but the wall of water that wiped out properties and lives in the Big Thompson Canyon could not have been contained by any structure; and if a dam had filled and burst, the damage downstream from the Narrows would have been even greater. Third, the close working arrangement between the Bureau and the District helped return the system to operation in record time. Calls for

Looking down on the Big Thompson Siphon crossing U.S. Highway 34 as it enters Big Thompson Canyon. The C–BT's Hansen Feeder Canal can be seen on either side above the siphon. (Courtesy Bureau of Reclamation.)

C–BT water from Poudre and South Platte allottees arrived at the NCWCD long before the Big Thompson Siphon was restored. Because District quota policies had established the importance of keeping Horsetooth Reservoir and Carter Lake as full as possible, water user needs were easily met. Horsetooth Reservoir was drawn down lower than it had been since 1962 but was still 83 percent of average at the end of the water delivery season.[42] What was far more disturbing and more significant for the future were data showing that overall Project storage was down while deliveries to water users ran well ahead of historic averages.[43]

By fall 1976, in fact, a severe drought was already underway. On both slopes of the Continental Divide the growing season had been warmer than usual in 1976, and river runoff was somewhere between 60 and 70 percent of average. By winter 1977 snowpack on the Colorado River watershed was down to 23 percent of average for that time of year. Conditions all over the state were considerably worse than they had been during the 1954 drought.

Horsetooth Reservoir looking south from Horsetooth Dam during 1977 drought. (Courtesy Bureau of Reclamation.)

By April 1977 runoff forecasts in the District service area predicted less than 50 percent of the average water supply. Worried by the trend, Governor Lamm created a Drought Council under CWCB director Sparks, who then asked the District to assume the role of lead agency in one of several subcouncils.[44] Cloud seeding quickly became one of the most popular topics of discussion. Encouraged by the Bureau's endorsement of this technique in 1975 when oil shale activities provoked estimates of West Slope water shortages, Governor Lamm signed legislation in February 1977 for emergency state funding. The act designated three geographical areas for cloud seeding: the Front Range, headwaters of the Arkansas River, and the San Juan Mountains.[45] Studies by the University of Colorado's Arctic and Alpine Research Institute, Colorado State University, and Fort Lewis College showed that cloud seeding was not harmful to the ecosystem and increased snowfall from 10 to 30 percent.[46]

Although legal questions remained unanswered, the Colorado Weather Modification Act of 1972 encouraged research and development of cloud-seeding activities by government and private enterprise. Moisture produced by cloud seeding was considered "developed water," eligible for an adjudicated decree and not subject to the vested rights of others.[47] The major problems were related to the developers' ability to prove the actual amount of developed water, carriage losses in stream basins, liability for damages resulting from weather modification, and obligations to interstate compacts. When the county jail in Silverton collapsed after 100 inches of snow fell, San Juan County prepared to sue Western Weather Consultants for repair costs.[48] The cloud seeders claimed they were working a different storm.

Even with potential liabilities, cloud seeding enjoyed great popularity during the 1977–1978 drought. The state budget for cloud seeding increased to $1 million for 1978. Officials planned to construct 100 ground stations to determine the impact of cloud seeding around the state.[49] When drought forecasts for the first three months of 1978 proved correct, the District willingly contributed $1,000 to the CWCB as a token of support for Sparks's leadership. Four months later the Board again voted to commit almost $30,000 to Western Weather Consultants for cloud seeding the following winter,[50] even though new data indicated that the drought had broken. Results were admittedly difficult to measure, but fear of future water shortages persuaded the District to join the DWB and other entities in structuring a standby cloud-seeding program at an annual cost of $6,500.[51] Directors also showed an interest in a five-year program suggested by the Department of the Interior that would increase Colorado River flows by 10 to 15 percent.[52] When Simpson described yet another proposal of Western Weather Consultants for winter 1981–1982, the Board again agreed to contribute in the amount of $18,000.[53] Clearly, the 1977 drought had motivated the District to do something about the capricious nature of the weather, precisely the same conditions that had inspired Hansen and others to pursue the C–BT Project fifty years earlier.

In addition to weather modification, the District became interested in other water matters that represented changes in state and federal water policies, although the impact of these changes on the C–BT was difficult to ascertain. Furthermore, the quality of leadership in Colorado was inconsistent. Phipps's stint as manager coincided with Lamm's first seven years in office (1975–1982), a time when the governor readily demonstrated his anger with federal policies and his desire to allocate Colorado's natural resources on a more equitable basis. Following the twin blows of Carter's "hit list" and the 1977 drought, Lamm pointed out that the state had entered a new era of water policies. Coloradans lived in a desert, he wrote in the *Denver Post*, and new answers had to be found for old questions about the future supply and distribution of water.[54] Although Lamm had questions about transmountain diversion, the District joined with the CWCB, the River District, and others to urge him to take positive steps in leading the state into a new era.[55] However, basic disagreements over the feasibility of Colorado water projects and how best to fund them as well as arguments over the wisdom of a state water plan deprived Lamm of the accord he sought with the water community.

Gubernatorial support for the Narrows project revealed a schism between Lamm and the NCWCD. Although approved earlier by Congress, this project had never received construction funding. Opponents argued that the proposed dam location was unsafe, environmentally damaging, and inferior to the Hardin site upstream. Even before the Narrows project appeared on Carter's "hit list," Lamm approved the state's formal request to become a party to litigation with those who demanded construction by the Bureau.[56] His motive may have been to preserve agricultural water for Morgan County farmers. Phipps made it clear that the District favored the Hardin site if any dam were built on the South Platte River.[57] This had also been Barkley's position, later endorsed by both Phipps and Simpson. As CWCB director, Sparks had refused to allow supporters of the Hardin site to present their evidence, but the state legislature passed a bill in 1981 that authorized feasibility studies of this location by the CWCB, which had just come under the direction of William J. MacDonald. MacDonald asked the District to join with the CCWCD (Greeley) and the LSPWCD (Sterling) to form a "central management committee" that would define the scope of services to be performed. Phipps and the Board agreed, and on December 31, the three entities jointly filed for a conditional decree for Hardin Reservoir.[58]

As expected, a negative response surfaced immediately from several quarters. Monfort Feedlots, the City of Thornton, Clear Creek Water Users Association, and others filed legal statements of opposition. The State of Colorado for the Division of Wildlife and the City of Broomfield also decided to enter appearances if litigation developed.[59] The Morgan County commissioners declared that they would withdraw from the District unless they got some indication that they would receive "value" in return for taxes paid to the NCWCD.[60] Nothing further happened at the Hardin site. The District came under intense criticism for not supporting the Narrows project, but the Directors knew that construction of either project would probably bankrupt farmers and municipalities along the lower South Platte River. To a certain extent, divisiveness among water users themselves was a godsend for the District. In addition, federal and state economic circum-stances and the debate over water priorities in a possible state water plan made the controversy moot.

Lamm's initial interest in reconstructing Colorado water policies was tempered by his desire to satisfy other state agency needs affected by population growth. His "Colorado Front Range project" is a case in point. Begun in 1979, this project consisted of five task forces charged to discuss the impact of a population increase of 1.25 million people by the year 2000 on thirteen Front Range counties.[61] The Natural Resources Task Force, with Phipps participating in the Subcommittee on Water,[62] reached some significant conclusions in its 1980 report. It considered the advantages and disadvantages of seven ways to increase the annual nonagricultural water supply by 65 percent. Conservation, better management of existing sup-plies, recycling, and reuse were the most strongly recommended suggestions for accommodating future needs. Purchase of agricultural water rights, additional transmountain diversions, mining of nontributary groundwater, and enlargement of existing storage reservoirs were also discussed as real-istic possibilities for narrowing the gap between anticipated demand and water supply. Weather modification, on the other hand, was not strongly endorsed. Although scientific knowledge had the potential to increase the water supply substantially, the unpopularity of weather modification with farmers and ranchers made it an unacceptable alternative.

What the report failed to mention was how the state government could establish a more equitable distribution of limited water supplies. While Lamm considered this vital, water users feared that any sort of state water plan threatened the doctrine of prior appropriation. The governor's posi-tion was that water and growth, which were interrelated, had to be under government control.[63] Senator Hart appeared to endorse this position when he told the Department of the Interior to delay evaluation of Denver's Foothills project until a Colorado water policy was firmly estab-lished.[64] After seeing the new federal policies of President Carter, Lamm realized that money for water projects would have to come from limited state resources. Some form of state funding and state control was essential if Colorado were to capture and protect all the water to which it was entitled.[65]

The problem was both financial and administrative. Lamm's Front Range study resulted in the imposition of spending restrictions on the state's Department of Natural Resources. The state's river commissioners were deprived of routine travel expenses. Lamm blamed the legislature for failing to create the necessary reserve funds,[66] but insufficient revenue was available for all state services, and no state agency had been established to align water project priorities or seek creative financing. Lamm wanted to allocate part of the state's general sales tax revenues to water projects. The legislature wanted to use money from severance taxes, mineral leases, and property taxes.[67] The CWCB voted to support creation of a state water project fund. When legislation was forthcoming, they drew up a policy giving preference to projects that would "increase the beneficial consumptive use of Colorado's compact entitled waters."[68] Because such a priority might reawaken difficulties between East and West Slopes at a time when the DWB was showing renewed interest in building Two Forks Dam and Reservoir, Lamm created the Metropolitan Water Roundtable, on which he served as chairman.

Thirty-one elected officials and private citizens, including NCWCD associate counsel Hobbs, began to meet in October 1981[69] to bring together "diverse and often adversarial interests from the Front Range, West Slope, environmental groups, housing developers, and water providers to discuss the contentious issues of providing future water to the Denver metropolitan area."[70] The Boettcher Foundation provided the initiative for the Roundtable by approaching the Rocky Mountain Center on the Environment (ROMCOE) as a possible mediator on the Two Forks issue.[71] Lamm seized the idea and created the Roundtable. Some of his own people said that traditional water opponents would never sit down together to work out disagreements,[72] but Lamm saw no other way to make sensible future plans. He scheduled meetings in Grand Junction and Denver approximately every other month until 1986, the end of his final year in office. Pleased with the Roundtable's accomplishments, Lamm credited it with speeding agreement on the Animas–La Plata project; laying the groundwork to establish nature conservancy districts and "natural areas"; helping the CWCB to construct more than fifty small water projects and initially plan thirty others; working out salinity control legislation for the Colorado River; and changing the "nature of water development decision-making, from a narrow, rather closed approach to an open and participatory approach that considered a wide range of options."[73]

Hobbs's appointment partially resulted from having known Lamm for the four years that he worked on air pollution, water, and other natural resource issues in the Colorado attorney general's office. Although he officially represented the public at large and not the District, Hobbs involved himself in issues relevant to the MSD and the NCWCD. In addition, he made regular reports on the Roundtable to District Directors. In retrospect, Hobbs saw the Roundtable as responsible for Denver's agreement with Summit County regarding water delivery out of Dillon Reservoir for snow making at the four ski areas above Dillon Reservoir. The Roundtable was also instrumental in the River District's acceptance of a joint-use reservoir on the West Slope, with construction financed by Denver metropolitan water interests. The 1986 Four-Party Agreement, involving Denver, the MSD, the NCWCD, and the CRWCD, further exemplified how the Roundtable functioned to bring adversarial interests together in settlement efforts.[74]

In 1981, however, the state still needed an agency with bonding power and the authority to contract feasibility studies and to build projects supported by the Roundtable. From the District's point of view, the CWCB was not prepared to meet this challenge. A new organization was needed, and the Colorado Water Resources and Power Development Authority (CWR&PDA) came into existence in June 1981 to address these funding problems. Loveland Senator Fred Anderson, who had already become the District's favorite water legislator, became its principal sponsor.[75] In winter 1980 Anderson had sponsored a bill that would enable the State Legislature to establish a water and power bond authority for the state. The effort was killed in the House Agricultural Committee, where members expressed concern that the bill might commit the state's credit to the success or failure of water projects, even though Anderson produced a legal opinion that the bill would not tie the state's assets to a water-bond issue.[76] Six months later Anderson drew up a similar bill that passed both houses after a year's debate and received Lamm's signature. The governor charged the CWR&PDA to develop all remaining water sources in the state as quickly as possible. A nine-person board, while not directly part of state government, would depend on the Legislature for authority and final approval of all fund expenditures. In 1982 the Legislature transferred $30 million from the CWCB construction fund to the CWR&PDA.[77]

Once again the close working relationship of NCWCD Directors and staff with other public and private water entities was revealed when Lamm named Farr to the CWR&PDA board as representative of the South Platte drainage basin. Believing that the CWR&PDA needed a professional water person as permanent director, Farr supported appointment of Ival Goslin as the organization's first executive director. Goslin's experience as executive director of the Upper Colorado River Commission made him an ideal choice; he knew how to compromise, and he was a skilled politician. His appointment coincided with the Reagan administration's announcement that the six-year freeze on new water project starts would continue indefinitely. Without federal assistance, the $30 million in the CWR&PDA's

escrow account could not be spent.[78] Nevertheless, CWR&PDA activities were noteworthy. In its first few years, the board studied the Narrows project; pursued funding possibilities for the Animas–La Plata project; evaluated projects proposed for the St. Vrain and Yampa rivers; and contracted with the Sutron Corporation for the purchase, installation, and maintenance of a complete satellite system for monitoring streamflows.[79] In 1984 the CWR&PDA received a request from the NCWCD to study the Cache La Poudre River basin. Because legislation was pending in Congress to designate portions of the river as wild and scenic, action was temporarily deferred. When a public meeting in Fort Collins late in the year revealed the existence of overwhelming local support for the study, the CWR&PDA agreed to begin its "first comprehensive basin-wide analysis and evaluation of water and hydroelectric water resources management alternatives for meeting the water needs of the entire basin through the year 2040."[80] Interest in what became known as the "Poudre Project" began in the sixties, experienced intense debates during Phipps's tenure as manager, and continues today after publication of the December 1990 report.[81]

On the heels of the 1977 drought, the Larimer-Weld Regional Council of Governments Drought Council formally asked the CWCB to request a Bureau feasibility study of the Grey Mountain Reservoir site on the Poudre River. The Fort Collins and Greeley water boards, along with the CLPWUA and the NCWCD, unanimously agreed to support this request.[82] When the Bureau indicated that it would take no action until the Poudre River became a higher priority, Simpson wrote Senator Hart to ask for assistance in getting "this study off dead center."[83] Accompanied by Phipps and Sayre, he went to Washington to meet with other members of the Colorado congressional delegation, but nothing came of their trip. When the Bureau pleaded insufficient funds, Poudre Canyon property owners, who had organized to fight the dam, breathed more easily but remained determined to organize again if the Poudre project ever came close to reality.[84] As expected, the idea did not go away. The District believed strongly in the efficacy of the Poudre project, although Phipps conceded that finding $1 million for feasibility and environmental impact studies would be difficult. He also believed that adequate storage was "the cornerstone of efficient water use in the semi-arid West." Grey Mountain seemed an ideal site to store water for drought years and to keep surplus water from flowing out of the state into Nebraska.[85] Simpson agreed. The Poudre project, he said, was economically feasible due to the growing importance and value of hydroelectric power as well as the increased storage benefits. Anticipating creation of the CWR&PDA in 1981, he indicated that the best way to fund the Poudre project would be to combine state monies with major bond funding by an organization that would include participation from northern Colorado's water entities.[86]

Criticism of the Poudre project surfaced quickly. Some argued that the addition of new regional water and power resources would accelerate urban growth, the loss of agricultural land and water rights, and environmental contamination. Representatives from Preserve Our Poudre charged that District association with a Poudre project study would be like "asking the fox if he wants more chicken coops in the canyon."[87] Although Phipps responded that the District would back off from the role of study sponsor and would reimburse the state for study costs (if that were the will of the state), the Upper Poudre Association questioned the project's compatibility with the possible wild and scenic designation of the Poudre River by the USFS.[88] The District's closest ally in the Poudre project was the CLPWUA, whose attorneys were infuriated by the USFS Poudre River study. It failed, they argued, to comply with federal statutes and was "legally inadequate. . . . It would be a tragedy if Congress were to foreclose all the possible future developments in the Poudre basin on the basis of a totally improper study."[89] The CLPWUA, which considered filing suit against the USFS, worked out an agreement with the District that the NCWCD would contribute up to a maximum of $10,000 to the litigation. Because Windy Gap project funding was at a delicate stage in 1981, the District simultaneously asked the CLPWUA to file for a conditional decree on the Grey Mountain site in the name of the CLPWUA for later assignment to the NCWCD. The filing would protect the water right while studies on construction and environmental impact were completed.[90]

The CLPWUA agreed to the filing, favoring any action that might keep the Poudre River from being designated wild and scenic.[91] Over objections from the CDOW, the water referee in Water Division 1 awarded a conditional decree to the CLPWUA for the Grey Mountain–Idylwilde project by early summer 1982. A year later, with Windy Gap construction proceeding as planned, the CLPWUA asked the District to assume the burdens of trial and any other efforts related to decree adjudication. The District accepted this responsibility and applied to the CWR&PDA for a study of the Cache La Poudre River basin.[92] At first the CWR&PDA deferred action because of pending wild and scenic designation by the USFS, but a meeting in Fort Collins revealed public support for the study, and a contract was signed with Harza Engineering Company to begin work in June 1985. During the course of the Harza study, President Reagan signed an amendment to the Wild and Scenic Rivers Act on October 30, 1986, setting aside five segments of the Poudre River as either "wild" or "recreational." Lower reaches of the river below Poudre Park were left untouched. An amendment to the original application for a conditional water decree would reflect loss of the Idylwilde site (designated "recreational"), but the Poudre project was still feasible. Harza's final recommendations included Glade Reservoir for off-channel water storage and a mainstem reservoir (Grey Mountain or the Poudre Dam site) to connect with Greyrock Mountain Reservoir via a pumped-storage hydropower facility.[93] Recognizing the high cost of constructing these facilities, the District looked for ways to scale down Harza's recommendations, with an eye to delaying some construction. After three years' study, the District's conclusions appeared in the December 1990 *Cache La Poudre Basin Study Extension*.

Because of public criticism and cost, the Poudre project may or may not be built. Simpson, who argues that northern Colorado still needs 200,000 acre-feet of water storage to meet future growth requirements, says that this amount could come from either the Poudre or St. Vrain rivers or possibly a combination of both. What will more likely delay the Poudre project is growing interest in integrating Windy Gap and C–BT water, in persuading farmers to purchase interruptible contracts for drought years, and in arranging more elaborate exchanges between agriculture and municipalities.[94] District Directors, who continue to study these options, are excited by alternatives to old reclamation policies that centered on dam building. Choices have come about because of public awareness of the need to conserve available water supplies, to efficiently distribute existing supplies, and to protect the environment. In contrast to earlier feasibility studies, the *Extension Report* also included careful study of how dams will affect recreation on the Poudre River. Fifty years ago the public did not anticipate such radical changes in how water projects might best serve the people. When the C–BT Project was proposed in the thirties, feasibility studies were concerned primarily with irrigated agriculture and hydroelectric power. Few if any considerations projected the value of benefits to the region and state from artificial, water-based recreation. As with many other developments during the Phipps administration, the recreational boom of the seventies and eighties gave new meaning to the C–BT system's role in northern Colorado. Recreation benefits, although difficult to quantify, have provided significant annual revenues to local and regional economies.

According to University of Colorado economist Charles W. Howe, the C–BT Project may not have paid for itself economically in national terms, but it has been enormously successful from a regional point of view.[95] When

Phipps became manager in 1974, visitors to Carter Lake in that year alone exceeded 250,000 and were expected to increase significantly the following year.[96] At Horsetooth Reservoir, recreational use was also rising rapidly. Until the Bureau joined with the Larimer County Parks and Recreation Department (LCPR) in the mid-seventies to fund a fifty-fifty recreational development plan, control and supervision of recreation on the reservoirs was infrequent at best. Starting with a $50,000 budget in 1974, the LCPR tried to keep up with exponential development of water-based recreation. Picnicking, camping, and boating facilities were constructed as rapidly as possible, but visitor use increased unexpectedly during midweek and during all daytime hours. The county budget expanded to $1.1 million by 1991. LCPR director John McFarlane now feels that unless Congress passes a bill to help defray operation and maintenance costs, the LCPR may not have the funds to continue supervision of reservoir recreation on the C–BT system.[97] Boulder experienced a similar dilemma when the basic recreational facilities at Boulder Reservoir deteriorated so badly that a bond issue was required to fund necessary refurbishment. With annual visitor attendance increasing from approximately 75,000 in 1970 to 120,000 in 1982, radical measures were necessary to maintain the quality of the recreational experience and to assure the city's income from fees that had soared from $67,000 to $192,000 during the same time period.[98]

West Slope reservoirs experienced the same impact. A short time after construction of Lake Granby and Shadow Mountain Reservoir, private individuals who wanted to capitalize on recreational opportunities threatened the health and safety of nearby communities when their uncontrolled businesses polluted the lakes. The Bureau responded by signing a memorandum of understanding with the NPS in 1952 to establish the Shadow Mountain Recreation Area (now known as the Arapahoe National Recreation Area). Following 1955 amendments to the agreement, the area surrounding the lakes came under control of the NPS until the USFS took over in 1979. Arapahoe National Forest and BLM lands were designated for recreational use and management around the lake shores. Between 1960 and 1974 visitors continued to increase from 748,000 to 2.2 million yearly,[99] and escalating numbers in succeeding years increased both the problems and potential benefits. Green Mountain Reservoir, at first under Bureau control and with no recreational facilities, was much slower to develop. In time the Bureau's policy improved slightly to provide minimum basic facilities. When the USFS took over, water-based recreation expanded from an estimated 20,000 users in 1960 to 230,000 in 1980.[100] This exponential use rate was attributable to the fact that Green Mountain

Reservoir was ideal for summer recreation. Operational policy dictated that it would remain full in summer and drawn down in winter.

Although data for all twelve storage reservoirs in the C–BT system are uneven due to the number of controlling agencies and different record-keeping systems, available information is not difficult to interpret in terms of general recreational trends. Since the first water entered the Adams Tunnel in 1947, land values have increased, income from property taxes has risen, retail sales and services around the lakes have skyrocketed, new recreation-based businesses have formed, and new jobs have appeared.[101] Motorboating, sailboating, windsurfing, waterskiing, fishing, and camping have consistently lured out-of-state tourists and locals to the reservoirs. From the perspective of former U.S. Bureau of Reclamation (USBR) Regional Manager Berling, visitors' recreational opportunities have become something of an inalienable right. People expect to enjoy water sports available to them on federally owned reservoirs. In contrast to this thinking, however, the primary objective of the C–BT Project continues to be delivery of supplemental water from the Colorado River to the East Slope for agricultural and municipal use.[102] Consequently, when Shadow Mountain Reservoir began showing heavy weed infestations because of relatively shallow water depth and warm summer sun, the recreational community demanded that something be done to ease the concern of motorboat operators. However, Shadow Mountain Reservoir was designed primarily as a canal in the C–BT system; as long as its basic function to maintain the level of Grand Lake was fulfilled, the weed situation remained of lesser importance to Bureau and C–BT officials.

From Phipps's viewpoint, this was only one of many problems that required imaginative, sensitive responses from the District. The times seemed to be changing terribly fast. Instead of just going about the business of distributing water, the NCWCD was once again caught up in technology advances, litigation, and outside pressures that required patience and improved public relations. Phipps endorsed the need for more aggressive water education and persuaded the Board to provide financial assistance to the River District's plans to make a new film about the Colorado River. He favored publishing a special newspaper insert that described District responsibilities and authorized employee presentations to public groups involved in debates over Lamm's Front Range project. He approved both a District newsletter and Board president Dyekman's suggestion that more women be involved in tours of the C–BT Project.[103] Phipps also supported the introduction of computer technology, although the cybernetic revolution proved far more difficult for him to accept.

One of the first tasks assigned John Eckhardt after his hiring in 1976 was to investigate the feasibility of computerizing water operations and record keeping for water allotment contracts. When the study was completed, he told the Board that the cost could not be justified.[104] However, three years later, Phipps attended a seminar to learn computer language and ordered installation of the first computer units. He was never comfortable with computers, but he had the foresight to see how computerization could make water distribution more efficient. He asked Eckhardt to make the computers function in the same way that things had been done prior to this technology.[105] Before Phipps died, Eckhardt and the newly hired computer staff had written programs for right-of-way contracts, water delivery reports, annual quotas, estimated electrical output at potential hydropower sites on the C–BT system, a supervisory control and data acquisition system for the Windy Gap project (SCADA),[106] and many database functions for office management. Like it or not, Phipps realized that this new technology was ideally suited for water engineering, water distribution, and water law. Especially noteworthy was the hiring of Gordon Huke, a computer specialist, who took Eckhardt's water account programs and streamlined them for more efficient use. Huke's employment signaled the beginning of professional computerization of District records and operations.

Legal problems were not solved as easily. With the Windy Gap project, the Poudre project, environmental legislation, and federal reserved rights challenges — to mention but a few of the matters with which Sayre and Hobbs had to deal — the work load and cost of legal work mounted steadily. As a percentage of administrative costs, legal fees jumped from 14 percent in 1974 to 35 percent in 1982. Fees soared from $45,000 in 1974 to $469,000 in 1982.[107] Understandably, the Board worried about this trend, and Sayre was also concerned. When appropriate, he recommended that the District refrain from litigation,[108] but it was difficult to follow this course. When opponents of the Animas–La Plata project threatened to file suit in 1982 over the constitutionality of the 1937 Water Conservancy District Act, Sayre persuaded the Board to intervene.[109] When the Board discussed a National Wildlife Federation suit a year later, Director Ray Joyce sounded an appropriate warning that the District could not be "all things to all people." Representing the District's interests where appropriate was a good idea, but spending money on all cases that might be relevant to NCWCD water interests was not.[110] The dilemma was clear. By 1982 the District was fast becoming one of the state's leading water entities. Increasingly, the DWB was losing prestige because of the controversy over

Two Forks Reservoir. Almost all litigation involving water issues in state and federal courts had some interest, tangential or otherwise, to NCWCD Board members. As the District grew in power and eminence it became involved in many kinds of litigation as plaintiff, defendant, or *amicus curiae*. In a certain sense, therefore, the price of protecting its domain was ever-increasing, costly litigation.[111]

Phipps did not actively seek this leadership role for the District, which developed despite his personal wishes for a more conservative operation. By 1980 the DWB was no longer the bully on the block. The organization had lost in its attempt to expand metropolitan water service into the District, had been forced to release water from Dillon Reservoir during the 1977 drought, and had had its attempts to reopen the Consolidated Cases denied by Federal District Court Judge Alfred J. Arraj. The NCWCD, meanwhile, had actively participated in Lamm's Drought Council, Metropolitan Water Roundtable, and the Front Range project. In 1981 Sayre had been elected NWRA representative from Colorado; Davis, Graham and Stubbs had opened an office in Washington; and a close contact had again been established with President Reagan's new secretary of the interior, James Watt, and his undersecretary, Donald P. Hodel.[112] In 1981 Simpson was elected president of the Colorado Water Congress, and Phipps recognized the District's close relationship with the CWCB when he thanked Director McDonald for his "continued cooperative attitude" toward the Poudre project feasibility study.[113] A District resolution that praised Senator Anderson for his supportive efforts for nine bills in the State Legislature reinforced still another important liaison.[114] This network with state and federal entities gave the District considerable clout in the future course of state and regional water developments. Although it had not become a water "empire," by 1982 the NCWCD was a power to be reckoned with in all aspects of Colorado water development, distribution, and conservation.

Not surprisingly, shortly after Simpson became District manager, Lamm asked him to help draw up a water exchange plan for Denver and the West Slope that involved Green Mountain Reservoir.[115] Unwittingly, but not unexpectedly, Phipps's legacy to his successor was a District that had become strong enough to act as a broker in Colorado's water affairs. In contrast to Phipps, Simpson was eager to expand the District's activities while preserving the excellent physical, administrative, and financial condition of the C–BT that had been handed to him by his predecessor.

24 *The District's Expanding Role Under Manager Larry D. Simpson*

Larry D. Simpson came to the NCWCD after ten years with the Los Angeles County Flood Control District. A native Coloradan, Simpson was born in Walden and raised in Eaton, where his father was an emergency welder for the Public Service Company. He learned about irrigated agriculture while working on a nearby farm that belonged to J. Ben Nix, NCWCD Director in 1945 and Board president from 1955 to 1976. While on a Colorado vacation in 1970, when manager J. R. "Bob" Barkley was looking for additional staff, Simpson agreed to Nix's request that he interview for work with the District. Simpson, who had a well-paid position in Los Angeles, was nevertheless eager to return home, even though he had to accept a considerable salary reduction to do so. Barkley offered him the position of planning coordinator, whose task it was to attend meetings of local, regional, and state water entities. Simpson accepted the offer and began work in July 1971. Although his primary function was that of Windy Gap project manager, Simpson first learned how C–BT operations were integrated with ditch companies, water boards, regional planning organizations, and the state engineer's office.[1] He also became familiar with a variety of water problems up and down the Front Range and on the West Slope.

Barkley liked Simpson's credentials. Thirty-four years old in 1971, he had graduated from the Colorado School of Mines with a professional degree in geological engineering and from California State University, Los Angeles, with a master's degree in finance. The Los Angeles County Flood Control District had hired him to design water conservation facilities,[2] knowing that at some time he would have to serve two years of active duty with the Army Corps of Engineers. With the Cuban missile crisis in the early sixties, Simpson received orders for Fort Lewis, Washington, where he commanded an assault bridge company with the 4th Infantry Division. The entire division, which was ordered to Germany, lined up on the Czechoslovakian border in anticipation of war with the Soviet Union. Simpson spent many restless days listening for Soviet tanks. When

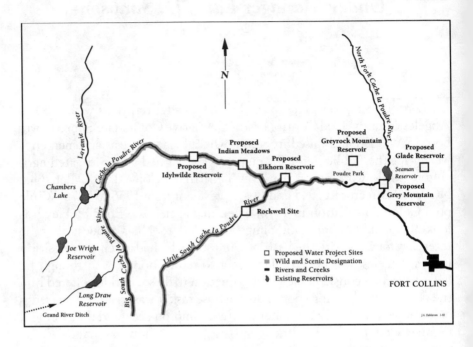

Proposed Poudre River Storage Sites.

Khrushchev finally agreed to call off the missile-bearing ships heading for Cuba, the 4th was rotated back to Fort Lewis, and Simpson was separated from military service.

In 1962 he returned to the design section of the Los Angeles County Flood Control District. Gradually working his way up the ladder to chief of operations in the hydraulics division and chief of permits in the project planning division, Simpson supervised other engineers; coordinated operations of dams, conservation facilities, and pumping plants; synchronized interagency activities; and prepared budgets in excess of a million dollars. His leadership strengths lay more in organizing and planning for the future than in fussing over daily administrative details. He liked people, felt confident and persuasive, and enjoyed the camaraderie of those who promoted water development. He reported for work at the District precisely when water management began to experience the impact of environmental activism, retrenchment of federal funding, and exponential regional growth.

When the Board selected Simpson to replace Earl F. Phipps in 1982, he was already familiar with the many local and regional organizations interested in NCWCD operations. Phipps had encouraged him to be out and about. As the District's fourth manager, Simpson soon involved himself and the Board in regional confrontations that his predecessor had avoided. Whatever Simpson lacked in preparation for the job, attorney John M. Sayre provided. The transition from Phipps to Simpson was smooth, but the focus of leadership was radically different.

Nineteen eighty-two was seen as a watershed year for reclamation projects. In October Congress passed the Reclamation Reform Act (RRA),[3] the first major revision of the 1902 Reclamation Act since 1939. Several articles revealed how Congress's thinking had changed in sixty years. Environmental and budgetary concerns dictated that new projects would pay interest on reimbursable costs as determined by the secretary of the treasury; irrigation water would not be delivered to farms in excess of 960 acres unless farmers agreed to pay full cost for that water; and any existing water district that amended its contract with the secretary of the interior would also be subject to these new provisions. For both proposed and existing projects, the act required a water conservation plan with "definite goals, appropriate water conservation measures, and a time schedule for meeting the water conservation objectives."[4] In other words, future irrigation projects would pay for the real cost of their water while existing water conservancy districts would develop conservation programs to decrease erosion, salinity, and toxicity in tailwater and return flows. With

Satellite-linked weather station near Brush, Colorado. One of many projects associated with the District's Irrigation Management Service. (Courtesy NCWCD.)

passage of the RRA, the Bureau's priorities became more consistent with environmental legislation of the seventies. The District took notice.

Established in 1981, the NCWCD's Irrigation Management Service (IMS) gained greater importance as a result of this act.[5] It was initially designed to help farmers improve water management and conservation at no cost to themselves. The idea was that farmers who knew when to irrigate and how much water to apply to their crops could produce more abundant harvests at less cost. The environment would be an additional beneficiary. For the first two years, the IMS progressed slowly. Farmers were reluctant to change old habits. Available scientific and technical information regarding soil properties, evapotranspiration rates for different crops, and irrigation patterns were inadequate. As of 1984, NCWCD employees were monitoring sugar beets, corn, alfalfa, barley, beans, and winter wheat on only 2,000 acres, primarily in Larimer and Weld counties. Seeing potential for growth of the program, however, NCWCD staff asked for budget increases to install weather stations and to enlarge the number of field tests throughout the District. By 1988 twenty farmers were involved on sixty-five different fields where tensiometers (to measure soil moisture) operated along with other instruments to help farmers optimize crop irrigation.[6] Participating farmers were pleased with the results, but District budgetary restrictions limited the number of water users who could participate. By 1989 the IMS program had expanded to include nitrogen fertilizer management to reduce nonpoint source pollution from irrigated agriculture.[7] In addition to helping farmers realize profits, the IMS had become a key factor in the District's response to charges that irrigated agriculture contaminated surface streams and underground aquifers. With nearly fifty farmers now participating (about 3 percent of all farmers in the District); weather stations located in Longmont, Greeley, Wiggins, Brush, Sterling, Loveland, Fort Collins, Ovid, and Crook; and a fertilizer management program partially funded by the CWQCC the IMS was successfully established in the agricultural community. A waiting list existed for farmers interested in direct participation.[8]

A more serious and complex problem for irrigated agriculture had emerged: conflicts between proponents of water storage and environmentalists concerned about the degradation of water quality in crop-producing areas. Whereas the NCWCD had long argued for reservoirs to catch spring runoff (opportunity water) and to stablize agricultural operations during dry years, federal agencies were under pressure from environmental groups to interpret and enforce the 1973 Endangered Species Act (ESA) and the 1977 CWA. Their objective was to decontaminate polluted surface waters and to preserve streams in their natural condition for domestic, aquatic, and recreational uses. They encountered strong opposition from proponents of Colorado water law, who felt that environmental legislation was used illegally to deter necessary water development and to undermine long-established state authority over Colorado waters. The District's interest in supporting the proposed construction of Wildcat Reservoir on the lower South Platte River and a storage reservoir higher up on the Poudre River exemplifies the character of this debate.

In the late seventies, Riverside Irrigation Company and Public Service Company of Colorado (PSC) had obtained from Division 1 Water Court a right for storage and use of 60,000 acre-feet of water on Wildcat Creek, a small tributary of the South Platte River near Brush, Colorado. Consumptive use of water in Wildcat Reservoir was expected to be 11,000 acre-feet annually for irrigation and power plant cooling.[9] Based on a USF&WS biological opinion, the Army Corps of Engineers determined that high water flows were needed 260 miles down the South Platte River in Nebraska to clear out woody vegetation in a 50-mile-long nesting area of the endangered whooping crane. Unless project sponsors provided 11,000 acre-feet of replacement water, the Corps concluded that Wildcat Reservoir could not be built under a temporary "nationwide" permit.[10] The Corps and the USF&WS determined that an individual, site-specific permit would be necessary but would only be issued with proof of no harm to the whooping crane habitat.

Immediately, Riverside and the PSC filed suit in Federal District Court.[11] Simpson expressed the consternation of water developers when he wrote Morgan Smith, executive director of the Colorado Department of Agriculture, that the NCWCD Board was "greatly concerned" about the Corps' assertion of federal authority to prohibit construction of Wildcat Reservoir. In addition to limiting agricultural production, he noted, the "real issue" was that the USF&WS "has explicitly stated that any additional consumptive use of water in the South Platte basin by Colorado water users shall not be allowed, despite the terms of the South Platte River Compact." This "highly questionable and destructive assertion of federal power," he concluded, must not go unchallenged.[12] In a related letter to Colorado's attorney general, State Engineer Jeris A. Danielson also expressed deep concern about this "blatant attack on the water rights structure of the State of Colorado by a Federal agency under the guise of Section 404 of the Clean Water Act."[13] Urging participation by Colorado in the Riverside litigation, Danielson decried the "unilateral abrogation of an interstate compact" that could be a "dangerous precedent to say the least."[14] The USF&WS changed its mind, claiming that release from storage of 11,000 acre-feet of water from Wildcat would have no impact on the whooping crane habitat. William Gianelli, assistant secretary of the Army, directed the Corps to defer to state authority "for setting and regulating quantities of water which may be diverted from a stream,"[15] but Federal District Judge John L. Kane, Jr., ruled that denial of a nationwide 404 permit by the Corps was a proper exercise of federal police powers. Project proponents, therefore, would have to proceed through the expensive, time-consuming individual permit application and review process.

Shocked by the judge's findings, the NCWCD Board agreed to contribute $5,000 to the CWC's endangered species study fund to monitor the activities and research of the USF&WS.[16] The Directors also agreed to pursue an appeal in the Riverside litigation. Attorney Gregory J. Hobbs, Jr., working with his colleague John M. Sayre and other appellants from the River District, the LSPWCD, the SWCD, and the State of Colorado, prepared briefs for the 10th Circuit Court of Appeals. Hobbs's legal arguments echoed the traditional fears of water developers and managers that the environmental community wanted to transform the purpose of the CWA "from a pollutant discharge control program [to] a national water law that would govern the allocation, diversion, storage and use of water."[17] He insisted that Riverside had every right to a nationwide 404 permit to discharge dredged or fill material in connection with the construction of Wildcat Reservoir and that the Corps had no right to impose conditions or require Riverside Irrigation Company to obtain an individual permit solely because of depletion effects that would allegedly occur downstream. Additionally, Hobbs made three points. First, Section 101(g) of the CWA clearly stated that a state's authority to allocate water was not to be superseded, abrogated, or impaired in any way. By this provision Congress had reaffirmed its policy of "cooperative federalism" in water allocation. Second, the 404 permit program was not a water quantity regulatory program; the Corps had no authority to regulate privately held water rights. Third, although Riverside did not seek an exemption from the ESA, Section 7 of that law could not be "triggered," as claimed by the United States, because it only applied to actions "authorized, funded, or carried out" by a federal agency.[18] Because this was a private project, the Corps' authority could not be expanded under the ESA.

The significance of this case became readily apparent. When the appeals court rejected Hobbs's arguments, the District concluded that it had suffered a major defeat. In what NCWCD minutes describe as an "adverse decision,"[19] the appeals court agreed with Judge Kane that Riverside should not be allowed to take advantage of a nationwide permit. The effects of downstream water depletion would have to be considered when deciding whether or not endangered species were affected by a water project. Additionally, the court noted that the Corps acted within its authority by requiring developers to proceed under individual permits. If problems existed between the state's interest in allocating water and the federal government's interest in protecting the environment, accommodation would be reached through the individual permitting process.[20]

As difficult as it was for the District to accept this decision in 1985, Hobbs came to feel that the appeals court had adroitly navigated some very troubled waters. Water users, he wrote, sometimes "protest too much about alleged interference with their water rights." Unless actually deprived of a water source, its priority, quantity, or beneficial use, the "reasonable measures" included in the individual permitting process proved the best way to accommodate federal environmental law and state water law.[21] He might also have noted that the decision actually saved the PSC from a bad investment by indefinitely postponing its commitment to build a second unit of the Brush Power Plant on the basis of the Riverside ruling. In view of the declining market for electrical power, PSC officials felt relieved. District officials further concluded that any dam or reservoir proposed for the South Platte River would face considerable, if not identical, limitations. Environmental objectives would affect every kind of water development; thus, the Narrows project 5 miles west of Fort Morgan, as well as the Poudre and Two Forks projects, would be more costly than previously estimated or nearly impossible to clear through the federal regulatory process. Permitting requirements and the power of national environmental groups, brought to light in the Wildcat Reservoir controversy, clarified this issue in a watershed case. The District and its supporters soon wished they had not called so much attention to northeastern Colorado in that litigation.

While preparations were underway for trying the Riverside case in 1983, the LSPWCD had asked the NCWCD Board to formally endorse the Narrows Dam and Reservoir. Having successfully sidestepped this issue for years because of local opposition and because the upriver Hardin site seemed more feasible, the Board wanted to complete a basin-wide study of the South Platte River prior to any commitments.[22] However, with thousands of acre-feet of "opportunity" water flowing into Nebraska during the wet years of 1983 and 1984, the Board formally announced support for the Narrows project under certain conditions: an operating plan would have to assure preservation of the rights of water users depending on C–BT return flows as well as those utilizing underground aquifers; another plan would show how the Department of the Interior would mitigate "any alleged damage to endangered species" without diminishing Colorado's entitlement under the South Platte River Compact; and finally, a standing committee would be organized to analyze and recommend modifications to water operations in the entire South Platte River basin.[23]

On the surface the LSPWCD had apparently obtained the District's endorsement for the Narrows project. What they failed to realize was that the Riverside litigation showed a need for environmental mitigation of any South Platte River project. Furthermore, a pronounced need existed for an in-depth study of the entire river system to gain some sort of integration and cooperation among entities up and down the river. But old patterns of behavior were difficult to change. When Narrows project diligence hearings began in water court in 1986, the District objected that the project's exact nature was still unclear.[24] What the District meant was that opposition to the Narrows project would continue until assurance was given that its Poudre River project was properly protected.[25] When the Bureau admitted "little or no chance" that the federal government would fund the Narrows project, LSPWCD and CCWCD officials formed a negotiating team with representatives from the NCWCD.[26] Urged on by Representative Brown, this team took the first steps toward a cooperative agreement for the entire South Platte River basin. They hoped to draw up a plan for future development of all basin waters;[27] thus, the yet-to-be-completed South Platte Basin Study was born.

Environmental activism regarding water quality and endangered species, litigation over Wildcat Reservoir, Narrows project diligence hearings, the growth and water needs of Denver's suburbs, and completion of the Windy Gap project (with its potential for providing an annual additional 48,000 acre-feet of potable water to the Front Range) — all of these developments demanded creative thinking from the water community. Barkley, Nix, Phipps, and W. D. "Bill" Farr had talked about regional water planning for many years, and Simpson was heir to their pioneering efforts. The eighties' uniqueness was that these circumstances began to dictate new thinking along with the gradual abandonment of territorial jealousies. Simpson's experience as planning coordinator showed him that all regional organizations were staffed by some officials who were interested in sharing information, research, and labor to assure adequate water for agriculture, municipalities, and industry. Cooperation appeared more attractive than ever. For example, Simpson recognized that fighting the Narrows project in court was counterproductive. Instead, the Narrows' conditional water decree could be preserved and the project redefined as part of a much broader, comprehensive, basin-wide plan that might even include a storage reservoir and power plant on the Poudre River. He also knew that accomplishing this goal meant confrontations with environmentalists who were determined to preserve the Poudre River without a storage dam. With fresh memories of successful negotiations that had produced a compromise Windy Gap Settlement Agreement, Simpson looked upon Poudre project discussions with some optimism.

As noted in previous chapters, a Poudre project had been considered since the 1960s. The Bureau had designed the Idylwilde Dam and Reservoir to be built in the Spencer Heights area just below Sleeping Elephant Mountain. From an engineering standpoint, this perfect location offered good storage, a re-regulation reservoir downstream, and a power plant through which water would pass into Grey Mountain Reservoir. According to Simpson, the Bureau had had local support in the sixties, and it might have been built if water users had been willing to sign a repayment contract.[28] But when it was discovered that the north end of the Idylwilde Dam site was undercut by a glacial moraine, cost estimates for a dam increased significantly. In addition, the Bureau had a surplus of power to sell in the sixties and was not enthusiastic about building another power project at that time.

Fort Collins and Greeley also had a dam site on the South Fork that they were reluctant to abandon when environmentalist groups sought special designation for the Poudre River under the 1968 Wild and Scenic Rivers Act. Water users were concerned that future basin water supply needs might be foreclosed by a wild and scenic designation. Representative Hank Brown again urged all parties to compromise on developmental and environmental issues. Simpson participated in the discussions with the Bureau, Fort Collins, the Colorado Environmental Coalition, Larimer County commissioners, and local citizen representatives. Participants eventually reached an agreement that they presented to Congress, but opposition by the Sierra Club and the American Rivers Council defeated the measure. Everyone involved with the compromise felt annoyed, but again negotiations resumed under Brown's urging, along with a CWR&PDA commitment to begin a thorough study of the Poudre River basin.[29] This time Brown assured both sides that his next bill would not be introduced unless it reflected their viewpoints. Anticipating the need for additional regional storage, the NCWCD, meanwhile, filed applications in water court for enlargements to previously designed forebay and afterbay dams as well as an application for Glade Reservoir for drought protection. A project below the town of Poudre Park would allow water users to abandon upstream reservoir sites. In less than six months the District had purchased some of the land required for the off-channel Glade Reservoir.[30] Not unexpectedly, opposition to the District's water rights filings came from Thornton and Aurora, the North Poudre Irrigation Company, and the CDOW.[31] Poudre Canyon residents and others who had hoped for a wild and scenic designation for the entire Poudre River complained even more vociferously.

Active and outspoken, Poudre River environmentalists wanted to leave the river alone because of its natural beauty and recreational importance, and they criticized plans for a Poudre project dam and power plant. If more storage were really necessary, they said, farmers should contribute by dredging their own reservoirs. They also objected that an appointed District Board might tax them to retire a bond issue for electrical power development for which there was no in-state market. Taxation without representation, they argued, and unnecessary taxation at that! Efforts of Energy Resource Development Associates (ERDA) to locate power project investors had not proved fruitful. The market for electricity was weak, and financial commitments were not secured.[32] Poudre project opponents were also angry about the Poudre basin study. Although they were represented on the CWR&PDA study team, they felt that the data had been biased by engineering consultants whose entire history was dedicated to constructing water projects; the CWR&PDA's recommendations, therefore, were suspect.[33] Poudre Canyon residents who wanted to sell their land were also unhappy with the District. They wanted assurance that they would receive fair market value for their property if the Poudre project were built. Although the Board passed two resolutions that committed the District to engage professional appraisers who would not discount property values "because of the imminence of a major water resources project," everyone who lived near the proposed dam and reservoir sites worried about losing equity in their land.[34]

With so much opposition to damming the Poudre River, therefore, Brown deserves credit for persuading environmentalists and water developers to meet and hammer out another compromise acceptable on local, state, and national levels. This time Congress passed the compromise agreement as an amendment to the Wild and Scenic Rivers Act.[35] Simpson and Hobbs had worked closely with environmental attorneys Barney White (for the Colorado Open Space Council and its successor, the Colorado Environmental Coalition), Maggie Fox (Southwest representative of the Sierra Club), Chuck Wanner (representing the group Preserve Our Poudre), and Gerry Horak (representing the Fort Collins City

Poudre River within wild and scenic segment. (Photograph by Kenneth Whitmore.)

Council).[36] The District's main objective was to preserve the lower 8 miles of the Poudre River Canyon for possible development. The Idylwilde, Elkhorn, and Indian Meadows sites further up the canyon could be abandoned if environmentalists would forego any restrictive designation on the lower canyon. On this basis they reached an accord that designated 75 of the Poudre River's 83 miles above the mouth of Poudre Canyon as "wild" or "recreational."[37] A water project site (Rockwell) was also left undesignated on the South Fork of the Poudre River for Fort Collins and Greeley. Soon after the legislation became law in fall 1986, and under permit from the FERC, the District began to finalize a plan for an off-stream Glade Reservoir to receive water through a tunnel from Grey Mountain Reservoir on the mainstem of the Poudre River. Grey Mountain Reservoir, to be located near the junction of the Poudre's North and South Forks, would extend to the beginning of the newly designated wild and scenic area at Poudre Park. Water would be pumped from Grey Mountain Reservoir to a smaller forebay reservoir and would be released through turbines to generate electrical energy during periods of peak demand. This pump-back storage plan, similar to that planned for Azure Reservoir on the West Slope, was designed for the District to generate power revenue sufficient to repay construction costs.

The Poudre River was the first and only river in Colorado to be added to the National Wild and Scenic River system. With the Nature Conservancy active in preserving Phantom Canyon on the North Fork, the Poudre River basin was turned into an environmental treasure as well as an intensely managed water supply resource. Whether or not dams, power plants, and reservoirs on the lower river are "inevitable," as Simpson and others believe, the upper Poudre River will not be subjected to further water resource development because of this designation.[38] A severe drought could have a profound impact on how dam opponents view the Poudre project, but conservation and regional cooperation over water exchanges may delay the project indefinitely. Negotiations leading up to the 1986 compromise legislation showed that entrenched differences over water use and distribution could be worked out at the bargaining table far more economically than in the courts. Decisive political leadership moved the process along expeditiously; without this, or with partisan disagreement on public display, motivation for settlement could have been undermined. Environmentalists' demands that the United States claim reserved water rights in wilderness areas as well as subsequent disputes over establishing more than half a million acres of new wilderness lands in Colorado show the difficulties of uniting the two sides of Colorado's soul — development and preservation — without strong and consistent political leadership.

In January 1984 the Sierra Club Legal Defense Fund filed a complaint for "declaratory and injunctive relief" in the Federal District Court for Colorado, saying that the departments of Agriculture and the Interior had failed to claim federal reserved water rights for the existing twenty-four wilderness areas in Colorado. They argued that the government's duty under the 1964 Wilderness Act was to administer these lands so as to leave them unimpaired for future use and enjoyment, which could only be accomplished by protecting the water resources with a federal water right.[39] Senators William Armstrong and Gary Hart were already considering a new wilderness bill and had reached a tentative understanding on boundaries, but progress came to a halt with the advent of the Sierra Club lawsuit. The NCWCD's participation in *Sierra Club* v. *Block* (John R. Block was secretary of agriculture) seemed necessary to the Board of Directors to avert the potential threat to transmountain diversion, Colorado water law, and use of the state's interstate compact water entitlements. Once again the rights of states versus those of the federal government in the allocation of Colorado's water were at stake.[40] The Board approved a substantial contribution to help the CWC pursue litigation, with Davis, Graham and Stubbs retained as primary counsel. Other contributors included the River District, the cities of Colorado Springs and Aurora, the SWCD, the SECWCD, the Rio Grande Water Conservation District, the Jackson County Water Conservancy District, and the Metropolitan Water Providers. This was all-out war in a showdown over what water developers perceived as intrusion by environmentalists into Colorado water law. As expected, Hobbs and Sayre filed a motion to intervene in the suit on behalf of the CWC.[41] The U.S. Justice Department tried to have the case dismissed, but Judge Kane denied the motion, arguing that "the United States has reserved water rights any time it withdraws land from the public domain," even though the water rights are unperfected.[42] Following arguments from both sides, eighteen months later, Kane ruled in favor of the Sierra Club. The federal government, he said, had failed to claim reserved water rights and had not produced a plan to protect wilderness water resources in violation of its duties under the terms of the 1964 Wilderness Act.[43] The defendants appealed. Kane gave the USFS eighteen months to show adherence to its statutory duty, but he agreed to waive this requirement pending a ruling in the 10th Circuit Court of Appeals.

In his brief before the Appeals Court, Hobbs noted that water users were agitated over the possibility of a federal reserved water right in wilderness areas, because Colorado would be deprived of its interstate water allocation under the 1922 Colorado River Compact. In tracing the historical intent of the wilderness legislation, he pointed out that the first wildernesss bill, introduced by Senator Hubert Humphrey in 1957, had shown no intent to create a federal reserved water right. When the California Department of Water Resources had learned that some sites for their State Water Plan might receive wilderness designation, their congressional delegation actually inserted protective language in the bill that "nothing in this Act shall constitute an express or implied claim on the part of the United States for exemption from state water law." Senator Humphrey endorsed this language,[44] which was included in the 1964 Wilderness Act. Hobbs also noted that the USFS was claiming a right to limit or deny access to build water facilities in Colorado's twenty-four wilderness areas when, in fact, the Wilderness Act required explicit authorization by the president of the United States.

While the Appeals Court pondered these issues, Hobbs participated in several meetings to obtain a "conceptual settlement" in March 1987. All parties agreed "to work for federal and state legislation that would provide for appropriation by the United States of water for Wilderness in Colorado, while also providing that federal reserved water rights claims for Wilderness would not be asserted in Colorado if the appropriation mechanism were available to the United States." A strong polarity of views still remained between environmentalists and water developers, with no strong political leadership to carry the process into law. While the Colorado Assembly continued to be suspicious of environmentalists' motivations, Senators Tim Wirth (Hart's successor in 1987) and Armstrong organized two negotiating teams to prepare suggestions for wilderness water legislation — a water rights team (developers) and a conservationists team (environmentalists).[45] Environmentalists insisted that the proposed federal legislation recognize an explicit federal reserved water right for all wilderness areas to protect their natural condition. Accommodation with state law did not seem to be an option. Water user groups, working with Armstrong, disclaimed the existence of a federal reserved water right and urged that the proposed legislation leave the matter of water in wilderness to the CWCB's instream flow program. As long as neither side would budge, reconciliation was impossible.[46] Colorado's congressional delegation was also divided in the House of Representatives, so efforts at compromise went awry.

In summer 1990 the Court of Appeals finally ruled — in what was then called *Sierra Club* v. *Yeutter* (Clayton K. Yeutter had replaced Block as secretary of agriculture) — to vacate Kane's decision and to reject Sierra Club views that the USFS needed implied federal reserved water rights in wilderness areas. The court concluded that the injury claimed by the Sierra Club was "hypothetical or speculative in nature . . . and because the Forest Service stated that there were 'no present or foreseeable future threats to the Wilderness resources which would diminish their Wilderness characteristics,' " the case was not ripe for judicial review. The District Court was given directions to dismiss the complaint.[47] Colorado environmental interests next attempted to get a ruling in favor of federal reserved water rights for the Holy Cross Wilderness in a case involving Colorado Springs. They failed, but debate over water rights in wilderness areas was just beginning. Kane's 1985 ruling now looked like a Pyrrhic victory. In 1990 environmentalists who celebrated what had been won in the lower court found that their argument for wilderness always needing federal reserved water rights had been discarded. As with the Riverside case, the Sierra Club case denied a clear victory to either side and returned debate to the political arena. When rival interest groups cancel each other out in matters of great importance, the public looks to political leaders for assistance. Unfortunately, that leadership is not always willing or able to meet the challenge of pleasing all interests.

Whether water should be preempted from the state appropriation system for wilderness purposes and the quantity of water that should be specified in light of the state's future water needs were very much at issue in the ten-year struggle to establish new wilderness areas in Colorado.[48] Armstrong and Wirth disagreed on how legislation should be written. Despite "suspicion about dealing with the conservationists in view of the litigation they have brought," Hobbs dispatched a four-point plan to the senators in summer 1988 based on agreements reached with the water rights negotiating team.[49] Essentially, he sought recognition of Colorado's system for water rights allocation and repeated his earlier demand that the CWCB provide the federal government with instream flow rights. Hobbs also warned both senators about the dangers inherent in designating wilderness areas downstream from existing ski area developments, which required diversions for snow-making programs to extend and stabilize Colorado's recreational economy. He urged congressional disclaimer on the federal-reserved water rights concept for wilderness areas.[50]

But the leadership required to get wilderness legislation for Colorado remained divided; Armstrong and Wirth in the Senate could not overcome partisan agendas. Colorado Representatives Pat Schroeder and David Skaggs supported the Sierra Club, the Wilderness Society, and the Colorado Environmental Coalition in their demand for a federal reserved water right for newly designated wilderness areas, but Congressman Ben Nighthorse Campbell, in whose district the newly proposed wilderness areas were located, wanted compromise. Environmentalists' opposition to compromise legislation sprang from seeing federal wilderness water rights created in New Mexico, Washington, Arizona, and Nevada prior to the reversal of Judge Kane's ruling. They were also disenchanted with a new Colorado law stating that federal reserved water rights would have to be purchased from senior appropriators and donated to the CWCB for instream flows.[51] Because chairmen of both the House Interior Committee and the Public Lands Subcommittee favored the environmentalists' position and Colorado's leadership remained divided, the desire of moderates in both camps to set aside nearly 640,000 acres of new wilderness was not realized.

The federal reserved water rights issue would not disappear. When the USFS sued in Colorado courts over "roughly half the stream flows in four national forests in northeastern Colorado," the District once again became involved.[52] This time, however, Hobbs delegated the litigation to his colleague, Robert Trout, an expert in complex trial court water proceedings. The government argued that unless withdrawals of water from the national forests were restricted, diminished stream channel capacities would cause severe flooding and greater deposits of sediment downstream.

The District's interest was awakened by two perceived threats: first, that a quantified water right in forest streams would impede the right to divert, store, and transport water along the Continental Divide, where transmountain diversion occurred; and second, that the USFS was demanding a priority right based on creation dates of the four forests (1892–1917). This early right could effectively preempt municipal and agricultural appropriators. The USFS, however, was responding to an environmental problem; both sides agreed that some water must remain in stream channels to address fisheries and to properly flush the system. The debate in court focused on water quantity and on the proper roles of state and federal authorities in water rights creation and administration.[53] Once again, litigation, not negotiated compromise, was necessitated by the absence of strong and united political leadership. During a costly year-long trial before Judge Robert Behrman, the U.S. Justice Department, the Colorado attorney general, and the District argued the complex legal and factual issues of federal supremacy versus state and local water administration.

From the source of the South Platte River and its tributaries to the Colorado-Nebraska border, the interplay of water quantity and quality issues grew in complexity by the mid-1980s. Whether headwater stream channels in Colorado or whooping crane habitats in Nebraska, environmental concerns had become a visceral element in water exchanges and allocations. Although more old water "buffaloes" were coming around to negotiate disagreements, the city of Thornton's quiet attempts to plan for future water needs through control of the WSSC revealed that powerful entities still believed advantage in the water business should be sought by whatever means necessary and be followed by litigation to preserve those spoils. In this instance, however, Thornton's disregard for Riverside, Sierra Club, the Poudre project, and wilderness water rights lessons proved the value of negotiated solutions. By 1985 — the year Thornton began to purchase farms and water rights in Weld and Larimer counties — the Windy Gap project had been completed; Denver had been struggling for four years to solve the "tap gap" problem through meetings of Governor Richard Lamm's Metropolitan Water Roundtable; and the District had reiterated its 1979 policy opposing any permanent water acquisitions that would remove water to areas outside the District, thus diminishing base water supplies or significantly altering return flow patterns.[54] Convinced that growth was certain, if not an economic necessity, and that the NCWCD and MSD would not extend boundaries into metropolitan Denver, the DWB revived plans for a dam at the junction of the two forks of the South Platte River, a project that had first been surveyed in 1896, vetoed in the 1920s, rejected in the 1950s, and struck down again in 1974.[55] This time Denver saw no alternative but to proceed with the permitting process. Metropolitan cities and their water districts agreed to share most of the costs and the water that resulted from this Two Forks project. Thornton was committed to 13 percent, more than any other metropolitan suburb. Mayor Margaret W. Carpenter believed that a proposed new highway and airport would create such rapid growth in unused lands within Thornton's city limits that water needs would more than double by 1992.[56] At that time, additional water sources from Clear Creek seemed unavailable.

Carpenter also sat on the steering committee of the governor's Metropolitan Water Roundtable and on a metropolitan providers group known as Water for Colorado. Meeting after meeting, she watched the growing strength of the Front Range Environmental Caucus in the Two Forks process and became convinced that environmentalists would either delay Two Forks indefinitely or make it prohibitively expensive. Thornton's water needs would have to be resolved in some other manner. The NCWCD showed no interest in selling C–BT or Windy Gap water outside District boundaries except on a temporary lease basis; Denver was pressuring the thirsty suburbs into paying for its schools, hospitals, libraries, and other urban programs; and continuing citizen outrage might mean that Two Forks Dam would never be built. A new plan was needed. Unhappy, debt-ridden farmers in the north might be persuaded to sell their rights to good, potable water. If Two Forks water were to cost upwards of $10,000 an acre-foot and farmers were persuaded to sell the same quality water at $4000 an acre-foot, Thornton could fill its needs more quickly through direct purchase. Even with construction of a pipeline from Fort Collins to Thornton utilizing Poudre River water, Carpenter reasoned, total costs would be lower than the DWB's Two Forks plan. Therefore, Thornton quietly began to buy WSSC water rights on farms between Fort Collins and Ault, using brokers who did not disclose the purchaser's identity. When farmers also wanted to sell their farms, the city through its agents developed a lease-back arrangement so that farmers could continue farming even as they used proceeds from land and water sales to pay their debts. By early summer 1986 Thornton had spent $60 million for approximately 21,000 acres of farmland and appurtenant water. When it was learned from newspaper stories that the city had purchased enough water rights to own nearly 50 percent of WSSC shares, northern Colorado reacted quickly, but with differing points of view.

The NCWCD Board believed that these moves directly attacked base water supplies that the District had sworn to protect. Simpson accused

Gordon Dyekman, president of the Northern Colorado Water Conservancy District from 1976–1991, regularly defended agricultural water rights. (Courtesy NCWCD.)

Thornton of ignoring the economic and engineering feasibility of its plan as well as the vested rights of return-flow users. The Directors instructed staff and counsel to obtain all information concerning Thornton's plan and to meet with cities, counties, ditch companies, districts, and water-user associations to coordinate opposition to what they considered a bold, pernicious water raid. At the same time, they went on record that they would be happy to meet with Thornton to address the city's "future water supply needs in a way which will not injure the base water supply and return flow patterns historically available for use within the District."[57] Because Thornton's water purchases from WSSC reduced or eliminated the base supply on lands that also received supplemental C–BT water, the Directors decided that water deliveries to WSSC should be restricted. Because Thornton, a nontaxable entity, now owned more than a thousand units of C–BT water that could no longer be secured by the required property lien, the city was given ninety days to "correct" the allotment contracts or to subject itself to the Board's judgment regarding the best disposition of this water.[58] Most water entities in the District agreed with this tough stance. City councils passed resolutions that condemned the "water grab"; WSSC authorized 300 shares of additional stock to weaken Thornton's chances of controlling the company; and other voices warned that Larimer and Weld counties would now experience the dewatering process that had dried up thousands of acres in Crowley, Otero, and Park counties in the Arkansas River valley.[59]

Such responses were predictable. What received less publicity was the fact that most farmers who sold their water were ecstatic. One man, whose family had been farming in the Ault area since 1914 and who had served on the Farm Bureau and on the CLPWUA board, wrote NCWCD Directors that he disagreed with their hard-line policy. "The District owes its existence to the fact that you are allowed to take 320,000 [sic] acre-feet [of water] and import it into your District. You are also the mechanical means of the Windy Gap project bringing 48,000 acre-feet [of water] from another district. Good sense tells me that you can't have your cake and eat it [too]."[60] The Thornton purchase was a "godsend" for him. Payments on farms were made for the first time in three years, and land and water prices had stabilized. Although no one liked change, he concluded, "if irrigated agriculture is going to exist from Denver north, it will be through a second use of water." In fact, Thornton's plans did indeed call for purchase of first-use rights; 40 percent would be returned as effluent "to the source [Black Hollow Reservoir] for agricultural use" after recycling.[61] On the surface, farmers appeared happy. Approximately 100 farms had been sold, only three sellers had retired from farming, and Thornton would pay any increase in water assessments should WSSC water rates charged to farmers exceed $550 a share. If Thornton did everything it meant to accomplish, the *Greeley Tribune* concluded that the city's plan would work.[62]

Unfortunately, Thornton had given too little thought to the actual quantity of water that could legally be removed from Larimer and Weld counties. The city also failed to accurately assess the NCWCD's fierce determination to prevent any water from leaving the District, to which Thornton did not belong. A costly court battle loomed. WSSC attorney Ward Fischer attempted to avoid litigation via a discussion paper in which he listed four issues he hoped the District would approve: that Thornton be represented on the WSSC board; that first-use water sold to the city be replaced in the same quantity, place, and time; that effluent water be returned with a quality suitable for agriculture, nonodoriferous, and non-hazardous to humans; and that the newly issued shares of WSSC be retired. He urged recognition of the legitimate needs of both Thornton and the WSSC and avoidance of costly litigation.[63] NCWCD Directors thanked Fischer for his efforts to achieve a negotiated settlement with Thornton, but they preferred reaffirmation of NCWCD rules and regulations, refusing delivery of water to an organization that directly or indirectly transferred that water outside the boundaries of the District or MSD.[64] Thornton had seemingly invaded the District's inner sanctum with impunity, asserting the very principles of Colorado water law that District managers and attorneys had fought to preserve from federal and environmental encroachments. While Hobbs and Simpson had at times preferred compromise over litigation, Thornton's cryptic methods, its questionable calculation of the quantity of water to which it was entitled, and the example the city was setting for other thirsty and powerful Denver metropolitan water entities required that the District fight back in a court battle that badly drained the financial resources of both sides.

Ironically, and precisely to avoid litigation, the NCWCD simultaneously was forging a compromise understanding with Denver and the River District over future water needs. The conceptual agreement, eventually signed by the DWB, the River District, NCWCD, and MSD (1986 Four Party Agreement), was a watershed event. Ed Marston, editor of *High Country News*, suggested that it was not too much of an exaggeration to compare it to the Treaty of Versailles.[65] Given that the agreement was made out of court and without attorneys, that it ended two lawsuits, and that its impact was felt throughout the entire Colorado River basin, the understanding was truly unusual, precedent-setting, and full of hope for those tired of relentless water litigation. However, five years of negotiation were required before the agreement was signed.

The process began in 1981, when Lamm realized that environmental groups would make the proposed Two Forks project a political nightmare. The governor asked the Metropolitan Water Roundtable to find alternatives that would ensure adequate water for the Denver metropolitan area. Thirty individuals represented interests from East and West Slopes, Denver and its suburbs, Colorado Springs, environmental groups, agriculture, and business. Motivation for participation varied. The DWB had lost three court cases (1955, 1964, and 1979) attempting to obtain water that was legally called past Dillon Reservoir and into Green Mountain Reservoir. Additionally, Denver's hard-fought battle over the Foothills Treatment Plant (1973–1979) clearly showed that environmental opposition to a Two Forks Dam and to development of the city's Eagle River rights on the West Slope would be costly and protracted. The West Slope was also anxious to talk. Summit County needed water for summer and winter recreation and municipal water supplies; EXXON had declared its intent to develop a million-barrel-per-day oil shale operation at Parachute Creek on the Colorado River. The District participated through Hobbs's appointment to the Metropolitan Water Roundtable, because the C–BT and Windy Gap projects were integrally involved in any exchange plans that might be proposed. Green Mountain Reservoir, which was key to the District's transmountain diversion, had to be protected against trades or exchanges that might compromise the system. If Denver were assisted in long-range planning, the District might get cooperation to alleviate water shortages along its southern boundary. In general terms, these motives were embraced by four participants who responded to Lamm's call for discussions about the future.

While the Metropolitan Water Roundtable studied Denver's population growth projections, conservation plans, and alternatives to the Two Forks project,[66] officials from the Bureau, the DWB, the NCWCD and the River District met in Silverthorne to discuss providing mountain ski areas with water out of Green Mountain Reservoir. Against Simpson's judgment that Senate Document 80 was not being respected, the Bureau persuaded the NCWCD Board to accept new operating criteria for Green Mountain Reservoir that allowed the River District to contract directly with ski areas for snow-making water.[67] The government, however, refused to approve the contracts for a firm and uninterruptible supply of water, forcing another approach. Meanwhile, the Board would be pleased to work with the Metropolitan Water Roundtable in support of a CWR&PDA study on the feasibility of either a joint-use reservoir or a larger water exchange involving Green Mountain and Dillon reservoirs.[68] Metropolitan Water Roundtable representatives had already agreed in principle to construction of a joint-use reservoir that would provide Denver with new water through Dillon Reservoir and the Roberts Tunnel, but progress was halted when attorneys tried to resolve complex legal questions. Suddenly, a startling change of procedure brought DWB, NCWCD, and CRWCD managers together to discuss mutual needs without benefit of counsel.

Although the new approach worked, it took three years to get all the signatures. The CWR&PDA feasibility study, formally requested in 1984, formed an important basis for several significant decisions and concluded that Denver's cheapest and most reliable water would come from a joint-use reservoir. A larger replacement reservoir could be built, allowing Denver to utilize all of the water in Green Mountain Reservoir, but the only site large enough to hold 152,000 acre-feet was at Wolcott, far downstream from the Blue River. The estimated cost of water from one gigantic replacement reservoir was two to three times greater than from a smaller, joint-use reservoir. In addition, agreement on a smaller reservoir would form the basis for future East-West Slope cooperation, with a key role to be played by the Bureau in permitting alternate operational plans at Green Mountain Reservoir.[69]

Other suggestions in the CWR&PDA study assisted the managers in reaching a momentous accord. On December 15, 1986, they signed the Four Party Agreement, which called for reservoir construction by the River District at Rock Creek or Muddy Creek. Denver would contract to lease 15,000 acre-feet of this water for replacement purposes in the Colorado River, thus allowing more water to be diverted at Dillon Reservoir through the Roberts Tunnel and replaced to the Colorado River from the River District's new reservoir. Denver agreed to reduce and delay its Eagle River plans and assured the NCWCD that should the city build an Eagle-Colorado project, it would be operated without impairing MSD diversions at Windy Gap. Meanwhile, the River District, NCWCD, and MSD would cooperate with Denver to find a suitable reservoir or combination of reservoirs to replace the 152,000 acre-feet decreed for Green Mountain Reservoir, with the understanding that Senate Document 80 would be a controlling document in this process. Once the replacement reservoir or reservoirs were built, Denver could pump water from Green Mountain Reservoir to Dillon Reservoir for delivery through the Roberts Tunnel.

This long-range project also received support from environmentalists who opposed the Two Forks project. Finally, all parties reiterated the importance of continued discussions of mutual water supply problems on the Front Range. The River District, NCWCD, and MSD agreed not to oppose the permitting for Two Forks Dam and Reservoir. Should unforeseen obstacles appear, the signatories would confer to effect the needed substitution agreements and arrangements for water that Denver would otherwise have to bypass from Dillon to Green Mountain Reservoir.[70]

How significant was this agreement? From an historical viewpoint, it may be too early to say, because much depends on individuals and on their sense of commitment to a conceptual agreement that they may or may not have negotiated or signed. Some were angered. Kenneth Balcomb, former attorney for the River District, was incensed over being left out of negotiations. Sayre was equally miffed. Confronted with the fait accompli at a 1986 NWRA meeting, he felt that Simpson had betrayed him. He had been informed in general terms during three years of discussions, but the managers had agreed to leave the attorneys out of direct negotiations, and Simpson had kept his word. Sayre was so much a part of the District after more than twenty years' service that he could not reconcile himself to being left out of the loop. He retired somewhat bitterly the following year.

DWB outside counsel Jack Ross was also unhappy. With the ink hardly dried on the Four Party Agreement, Denver attorneys filed applications for water rights on nine reservoir sites on the Colorado River between Glenwood Springs and the headwaters. Denver's intent was supposedly to take over those areas with appropriative rights of exchange that the city could later develop as replacement reservoirs, thus making possible full utilization of the water in Green Mountain Reservoir. When challenged in court, Ross claimed that Denver was unilaterally entitled under Colorado water law to make such applications and was not required to seek prior approval from the secretary of the interior. In fall 1991, however, the 10th Circuit Court ruled that Denver was obligated to first seek secretarial approval under terms of the 1964 stipulation regarding Green Mountain Reservoir.[71] Defeated once again on the Blue River and having seen the Two Forks project vetoed by the EPA, Denver found that it had also alienated the Denver Metropolitan Water Providers, who felt left out of the Four Party Agreement and angry that the DWB had chosen not to litigate the EPA's veto. They threatened to sue Denver, arguing that the city had no right to join in a Muddy Creek substitution agreement that might jeopardize plans for construction of some future Two Forks project.[72] Instead, some of the metropolitan water providers sued the EPA over the Two Forks veto.

Not everyone complained about the Four Party Agreement. The NCWCD felt relieved that the River District would probably begin work on a Muddy Creek reservoir with mitigation funds that the District had made available in 1985 during construction of the Windy Gap project.[73] Directors were pleased that money would be saved because of stipulations agreed on in two court cases and because Denver had agreed to work with the District on a better instream flow arrangement for the Colorado River. Whether the metropolitan suburbs located south of the District boundaries will benefit remains to be seen. Thornton's abandonment of the Two Forks scheme in April 1986 sowed distrust, especially when it was learned that Lamm's chief consultant on the Metropolitan Water Roundtable had known about Thornton's plans and had decided to remain silent.[74] Still, Thornton appeared to be an aberration, albeit one against which the District decided to fight.

So that other metropolitan water suppliers will not attempt to take control of northern Colorado ditch companies, the NCWCD Board has shown interest in finding a way to make Windy Gap water available to the Denver suburbs on an interim basis until the Two Forks project is built or an equivalent plan is in operation. As of this writing, the "new" DWB seems more conciliatory. Monte Pascoe, Malcolm Murray, and Hubert Farbes are more interested in cooperation than in confrontation. Charlie Jordan, an early Lamm staffer to the Metropolitan Water Roundtable, later hired by the DWB, has demonstrated a new attitude of openness. Vail's leaders are also pleased. The Eagle's Nest Wilderness Area has been saved by Denver's agreement to cut back its Eagle River projects. Because the Muddy Creek/Williams Fork Substitution Agreement was finally signed on December 30, 1991, by the Bureau, DWB, CRWCD, and NCWCD, authorizing Denver to take up to 30,000 acre-feet of Blue River water from Dillon Reservoir through the Roberts Tunnel,[75] the spirit of the 1986 agreement seems to have retained sufficient force to continue as a basis for significant accomplishments in the nineties. Water supply management links between the NCWCD/MSD, CRWCD, DWB, and the Bureau are being forged to replace more than forty years of legal wrangling. The DWB's appointment of Colorado Department of Natural Resource director Hamlet "Chips" Barry as manager points to a new, more cooperative era for all water entities on both East and West Slopes, and Governor Roy Romer has urged the Metropolitan Water Providers to forego expensive litigation of the Two Forks project in favor of alternate, less acrimonious solutions. At long last, a cooperative spirit seems to have a chance of replacing the tradition of adversarial combat in the state's courts.

Litigation has dominated in this description of Simpson's management period, not because the only meaningful events happened in the courts, but because one can see in the hard-fought legal battles a glimmer of attitude changes that bodes well for the future. Bloodied by adversarial confrontation, and somewhat embarrassed by the cost-benefit ratio of expensive litigation, Simpson and the Board have begun to look for better ways to manage the existing water supply. Accurate information is essential to this planning. Basin-wide water management studies have been completed on the Poudre and St. Vrain rivers, future needs of northern Colorado municipalities have been documented in a very detailed manner, methods to "share" existing supplies are being studied, and steps have been taken to analyze existing water rights and return flow patterns of the entire South Platte River basin from Brighton to the Nebraska line.[76] As the District continues to support free market water rights exchanges — the envy of other foreign and domestic water delivery systems — these kinds of management studies will be viewed in the future as having had as much substance and significance as all the fractious litigation of the last ten years.

25 Operation, Maintenance, and a Peek at the Future

On May 13, 1987, the Colorado General Assembly paid tribute to the NCWCD for outstanding achievements during a half century of existence. Exactly fifty years earlier, following protracted struggles with the West Slope and Congressman Edward T. Taylor, the assembly had authorized formation of water conservancy districts. The NCWCD — the first of its kind — was organized and in operation by fall 1937. Today Colorado has forty-six water conservancy districts; how well they have served the public might be the focus of another book. This book has shown the NCWCD to be the most powerful and the most active of the conservancy districts in determining the course of water-related events throughout Colorado and the West. The organization's present condition, vulnerabilities, and future concerns are the focus of this last chapter.

Few aspects of District affairs elicit more pride than the operation and maintenance of the water delivery system. The Bureau built the C–BT well, but the District's ability to deliver water consistently and safely since the fifties has resulted from its high standards of maintenance. At times, District O&M policies have caused difficulties with water users. For example, the Munroe Gravity Canal was built with District funds under an agreement that obligated the North Poudre Irrigation Company (NPIC) to assume the costs of annual maintenance. Several times during the sixties and seventies, District O&M personnel reported substandard repair and maintenance, a message that NPIC did not want to hear. Tensions developed, complicated by differences of opinion over whether or not NPIC should pay the higher assessment for that portion of the water it was delivering to municipalities. Earl F. Phipps worked up an operations contract, which was delivered to NPIC but never returned.[1] Dangerous seeps were also noted in the canal above the Kremers Ranch. By 1986 the Directors became sufficiently concerned to threaten taking over O&M responsibilities from NPIC. They feared possible U.S. charges that terms of the 1938 Repayment Contract were being breached by not maintaining the system to adequate standards. NPIC sought a restraining order,[2] and the District threatened countersuits. After several shouting matches, an agreement was reached, NPIC eventually took care of the canal problems, and relations with the District improved.

On the system's south end, maintenance had also caused major worry, with frustrations exacerbated by the District's contributing a majority of maintenance costs on the South Platte Supply Canal, although repairs were performed by two separate ditch companies. Rapid population growth in this part of the District necessitated proper maintenance, a critical issue in the canal's ability to deliver C–BT and Windy Gap water. Maintaining good relations with residents along the St. Vrain Supply Canal and the Boulder Feeder Canal was also important at a time when the entire area was growing more urbanized. When citizens' recreation needs emerged in an area where a ditch company superintendent was known for shoddy and sometimes insensitive operation and maintenance practices, the District became involved in uncharacteristic and bitter arguments with a land-owner. From this experience, the NCWCD learned something about the fragile condition of its rights-of-way.

When J. R. "Bob" Barkley was manager, he hired a new O&M super-intendent, Robert R. "Smitty" Smith, a maintenance and right-of-way expert from the Los Angeles Flood Control District. Larry D. Simpson had recommended Smith following the unexpected death of O&M superinten-dent Dennis Walker. The right-of way records were in deplorable shape: no maps, nothing recorded in county records, and no clear way to tell whether a canal bank had been taken over by the District as an easement or in fee-simple title. Frequently on his own time, Smith straightened out the records and set up a logical licensing process.

When landowner Paul Page began drifting some cattle back and forth on the St. Vrain Supply Canal in 1983 — claiming that because the District held only an easement, it could not dictate how he used his own land — the District went to court for a restraining order. Page got a lawyer.[3] To complicate matters, the Boulder County Department of Parks and Open Space asked the District's permission for a recreational trail designation on the Boulder Feeder Canal. The pending Page situation and canal residents' protests at a public hearing over the possibility of joggers, bikers, litter, and noise near their property caused the District to recommend a one-year trial program — and then only if certain safety conditions were met.[4] Mean-while, the Page situation turned ugly when he armed himself, threatened a District employee, and then, with a pistol in his shoulder holster, demanded a showdown with Simpson. Once calm had been restored, Page's property was shown to have been incorrectly certified in fee title. In addition to a large cash payment from the title insurance company, the District granted Page permission to construct a ditch and roadway across the canal for his cattle. But as more and more subdivisions sprang up in lands near the District's 100 miles of canals, careful maintenance and tactful public relations were required to keep the peace. Suburban residents used the canals for dumping trash, riding horseback, jogging, and other forms of recreation. Posting signs and building perimeter fences have had limited acceptance. The future will require better education so that the public understands and appreciates the District's mission as well as the dangers inherent in the canals.[5]

Another maintenance problem surfaced at Horsetooth Reservoir. As a result of the 1976 Teton Dam disaster, Congress had passed the Reclamation Safety of Dams Act in 1978, which authorized a nationwide review of Bureau structures. In 1983, one year after the collapse of Lawn Lake Dam in Rocky Mountain National Park, Simpson received a technical engineering analysis report on Horsetooth Dam, indicating that water would come close to overtopping the four Horsetooth dams and Satanka Dike under probable maximum flood (PMF) conditions (24 inches of rain in twelve hours).[6] The Bureau also noted that Dixon and Spring Canyon dams had settled almost 2 feet and that the District would have to pay 50 percent of the cost to modify all of the Horsetooth structures or be faced with restricted storage.[7] In fall 1984 the Bureau's regional director informed Simpson that "effective immediately" an operating restriction would be placed on Horsetooth Reservoir to protect everyone downstream.[8] Simpson responded angrily. He felt that PMF data had been conjured up by some computer whiz kid who had played with the concept of a thousand-year flood, using a super storm in Montana as a totally inapplicable model to reinvent the science of hydrology. He was equally convinced that the so-called "settling" of Dixon and Spring Canyon dams was in fact a Bureau surveying error resulting from the Bureau's use of different benchmarks during construction.[9] On the basis of these observations, he sent a letter to the commissioner of reclamation, noting that the operating restrictions were illegal under the Repayment Contract, that they controverted the tenets of Colorado water law, "in particular the basic need for water storage facilities,"[10] and that they would deprive the District of approximately 10,000 acre-feet of supplemental water per year. Senator William Armstrong asked the secretary of the interior for a review and reversal of the Bureau's decision, but the commissioner held his ground. He disputed Simpson's figures and responded that a water loss would only occur in wet years when water would be spilled at Lake Granby for lack of East Slope storage space.

Because wet years had only occurred in five of the past twenty-two years, the District's annual estimated water loss would be more like 2,230 acre-feet.[11] Unfortunately for the District, the only question that remained was how much the District should pay for the necessary repairs. The Bureau insisted on a fifty-fifty split of costs required to raise all dams to the same elevation. Although the District complained, the November 6, 1986, contract stated that the Bureau would lift the storage restriction on Horse-tooth Reservoir on completion of construction.[12] Work began in summer 1988 and was completed in two years.

Principal O&M concerns on the West Slope involved electrical pumps at both Granby and Windy Gap. Each problem was distinct. The aging of three 6,000 hp pump motors that lifted water from Lake Granby to Shadow Mountain Reservoir was a potential liability to the successful operation of the C–BT and Windy Gap systems and required prompt attention. Comparable to a human heart, these pumps were the driving force that enabled the C–BT's circulatory system to function. If they failed, the East Slope would get no water and the Bureau would have no revenue from hydroelectric power generation. After agreeing to split an estimated $600,000 rewinding cost with the Bureau,[13] the District began repairs in spring 1990 and finished all three pumps in fall 1991. The critical work had been done, but maintenance on other parts of the pumping system was still in a "catch-up" phase. Over $1 million had to be budgeted for the next six years to replace protective relays, meters, and voltage regulators; install emergency generators and switch gear; replace existing piping, valves, and sump pumps; upgrade computer systems; and do general rehabilitation. Combined with approximately $800,000 estimated for rehabilitation of the Willow Creek system, West Slope maintenance was destined to be a significant part of NCWCD budgets through the mid-1990s.[14] The Bureau should have done much of this work on a routine basis prior to transfer of West Slope O&M responsibilities to the District in June 1986,[15] but they had been limited by funding woes of their own.

Windy Gap pumps presented a different kind of problem. The four 12,000-hp motors had been built in Japan by Hitachi Corporation according to designs from Morrison-Knudsen Company's wholly owned subsidiary IECO. When they were first started in 1985, they created a voltage dip throughout the Granby and Grand Lake areas that caused television sets to flicker, cash registers to malfunction, and a local sewage treatmant plant to go off line.[16] A lot of people complained because their favorite Monday night football game had been interrupted. Who was to blame? Hitachi had delivered pumps as requested. IECO, on the other hand, had assumed that local transmission lines could handle a 10 percent voltage drop, but the impact of just one 26.5-ton rotor going from 0 to 600 rpm in thirty seconds caused an unexpected brownout. The local power supplier, Mountain Parks Electric, wanted to placate customers and therefore blamed the MSD, which had a contractual obligation to remedy the problem. The MSD sought relief from IECO. Morrison-Knudsen was willing to sign a tolling agreement to compensate the MSD for expenses, but a preliminary cost estimate of motor modification came to more than $2 million. Furthermore, Morrison-Knudsen's insurance company was unwilling to settle for such a large sum.[17] MSD attorneys filed a lawsuit. In the meantime, the Western Area Power Administration (WAPA), which had already agreed to provide the Windy Gap Pump Plant with 3.5 megawatts of firm power, upgraded one of the transmission lines into the plant, thus reducing the voltage dip to an acceptable 6 percent. An out-of-court settlement followed, and Monday night football returned to customary and acceptable levels of West Slope flickering.

WAPA's commitment to resolve the voltage dip problem was somewhat self-serving. Since its creation in 1977, this organization had moved toward takeover of all the C–BT joint works and power systems.[18] The District decided to block these efforts. In spring 1985 the Bureau and the District formed a negotiating team to study the transfer of West Slope operations and maintenance to the District. Simpson felt convinced that District maintenance would ultimately result in cost reductions and flexible operations, thus assuring water users that they would always get the water they were paying for. The Bureau had no reason to object, because the transfer process was anticipated in the original Repayment Contract. In addition, a Bureau feasibility study revealed undeniable economic advantages to both entities, including the District's willingness to hire Bureau personnel.[19] With the official transfer of O&M responsibilities at Granby and Willow Creek on June 1, 1986, the Bureau only retained operation and maintenance for Green Mountain Dam, Reservoir, and Power Plant, as well as for the Adams Tunnel and the communications system to the West Slope. Three months later the Board endorsed transfer of O&M responsibilities at Carter Lake and Horsetooth Reservoir to the District. This February 1987 agreement meant that all facilities formerly maintained jointly by the Bureau and the NCWCD were now under District control.

Simpson next suggested taking over operation and maintenance of the C–BT power system, excluding Green Mountain Dam and Power Plant. He argued that greater control over both water and power scheduling would mean that Windy Gap and C–BT operations could be more efficiently integrated and managed.[20] Opposition surfaced immediately from WAPA, REA officials, and other power entities in the West, whose officials objected to the District's proposed foray into the power business. Simpson's response was that Bureau maintenance standards were unacceptable — witness the condition of recently transferred West Slope facilities — and that a power system breakdown would delay or even halt water deliveries. He conceded that the Bureau was not directly to blame because the Bureau was getting insufficient funds from Congress for an adequate maintenance job. Although the Department of the Interior asked the District to bid on purchasing the entire C–BT system (power and water delivery), Simpson promised to back off if WAPA and the Bonneville Power Administration would lobby to establish a revolving fund from power revenues that would allow the Bureau to perform adequate maintenance before extracting profits for the United States. The plan was accepted verbally, but Simpson soon realized that WAPA and Bonneville officials were less than eager to uphold the bargain due to competitiveness for funds and interagency jealousies.[21] Nevertheless, the District showed no further interest in owning the Bureau's C–BT power facilities, and Simpson kept his word. Planning for the District's future during the last ten years of the Repayment Contract (1992–2002) would keep him and everyone connected with the District focused on far more challenging issues.

The C–BT's original mission was to supply supplemental water to agriculture within the NCWCD's boundaries. In 1957, the first full year of C–BT water deliveries, 720,000 acres of irrigated land in the District produced $68.7 million of harvested crops; by 1990 approximately 630,000 acres of cropland were harvested with a total crop value of $331 million. Aside from the decline in acreage under cultivation, the most significant change in thirty-four years was the transfer of C–BT units from agriculture to municipalities. In 1957 over 85 percent of C–BT units were owned by agriculture; in 1990, 57 percent of total C–BT units were owned by agriculture, 37 percent by domestic and municipal entities, and 6 percent by industrial and multipurpose water users.[22] Because of rental and lease agreements, however, 73 percent of 1990 C–BT units were still delivered to agriculture by means of yearly rental agreements. Municipalities purchased C-BT shares to prepare for future needs; until drought or population growth occur, farmers will continue to use the water. Another measure of the value of C–BT water to the Front Range north of Denver can be seen in Larimer, Weld, and Boulder counties, where deliveries have accounted for an average of 34 percent of all water used during drought years between 1958 and 1990.[23] Farmers have not consistently enjoyed great profits since

Rawhide Power Plant, owned and operated by Platte River Power Authority, uses Windy Gap water. (Courtesy Platte River Power Authority.)

1957, but supplemental C–BT water has made possible bumper crops for most of the thirty-four years.

The challenge of the 1990s for NCWCD and MSD leadership is determining how to preserve agriculture while serving the increasing needs of nonagricultural entities from Denver to northeastern Colorado in an environmentally sensitive manner. For example, when Anheuser-Busch opened a plant in Fort Collins, the company expected to receive C–BT water from the city; unfortunately, the company's plan called for a second use of this water, which violated District rules and regulations designed to protect return flows for the benefit of downstream water users in the District who had paid the mill levy since 1938. Eventually Anheuser-Busch agreed to acquire 4,200 acre-feet of PRPA's Windy Gap water — which included the right of reuse — but the company resisted this arrangement until its brewmaster was persuaded that Windy Gap and C–BT water were equal in quality.[24] PRPA's coal-fired Rawhide Power Plant also required water for steam generation and power-plant cooling. The PRPA successfully petitioned for inclusion within MSD boundaries in 1980, after which the group purchased one-third of the Windy Gap water supply (160 shares or 16,000 acre-feet per year) from three of the Six Cities (also PRPA members) that had second thoughts about water utilization and about

Windy Gap contruction debt. PRPA based this decision on two related observations: (1) power needs in the area would justify construction of additional units at the Rawhide site; and (2) PSC would build a second power plant at Fort St. Vrain, giving PRPA the chance to contribute Windy Gap water to the capital investment.[25] The calculations proved incorrect. Not until 1991 did PRPA begin to sell power locally. The one completed Rawhide unit used only 5,000 acre-feet of the total Windy Gap allotment, allowing PRPA to act as a water bank for municipalities by leasing what they could not use through the C–BT system,[26] a procedure that will only work on a regular basis if C–BT storage reservoirs have sufficient space for water coming through the Adams Tunnel. Integration of C–BT and Windy Gap water will facilitate this procedure.

A second challenge for the future results from the difficulties of getting water to major growth areas and to sites where contaminated groundwater cannot legally be used for domestic purposes under environmental laws. The District's inclusion policy prevents delivery of C–BT and Windy Gap water outside NCWCD/MSD boundaries except on a lease or exchange basis. As shown in the recently completed *Regional Water Supply Study*, the largest growth increments in the 1980s were located outside these boundaries in the area between Denver and the District's southern limits. From 1990 to 2020, population is expected to increase 75 percent along the northern edge of the Denver metropolitan area, where water needs will increase by 130,000 acre-feet annually. "Without additional supplies or regional integration of available supplies," the *Study* concluded, water shortages from Denver throughout northeastern Colorado during a year of moderate drought would reach 191,000 acre-feet. With complete integration of all water supplies, no additional water would be needed until 2015.[27] Other towns, like Lafayette, Louisville, Fort Lupton, Wiggins, Brush, and Fort Morgan, need to replace a nitrate-saturated domestic supply with potable water that will pass inspection under the Federal Safe Drinking Water Act as administered by the Colorado Department of Health. Even if the inclusion policy becomes more flexible, some combination of institutional integration and increased structural capacity will be necessary to solve these problems.

In 1984 water broker Craig Harrison completed a three-dimensional, raised-relief map showing all water delivery systems between Denver and the Colorado-Wyoming border. With a computerized listing of all water rights, Harrison Land and Cattle Company (now Harrison Resource Corporation) prepared to make real estate deals based on growth projections and water rights. Harrison's overview approach, which made sense to water

Craig Harrison's map of the Front Range, showing Colorado Springs, Denver, Fort Collins, and other communities. (Photograph by Tim O'Hara.)

users, was viewed with great interest by the NCWCD Board.[28] In 1987 the Directors resolved to operate C–BT and Windy Gap project water in an integrated manner.[29] Hydrosphere Resource Consultants undertook a study of the integration concept. Based on 1950 to 1989 hydrology records, the study concluded that the integrated water supply and storage of the C–BT and Windy Gap projects were sufficient to meet Windy Gap yields of 48,000 acre-feet per year and the full quota of the C–BT allottees as set by the Board. Hydrosphere also examined the integrated operation of the two projects under a 1-in-100 year drought hydrology scenario. During four of the seven drought years, Windy Gap deliveries would be reduced to 60 percent of full demand. During the entire seven-year period, with unlimited Windy Gap borrowing, C–BT shortages would increase by approximately 100,000 acre-feet.[30] On March 1, 1990, the Bureau signed an amended carriage contract with the Subdistrict and the District to implement the principle of integrated operations: Windy Gap participants who borrowed C–BT water would have to obtain a back-up water supply on call by the District Board.[31] As Hydrosphere's study also noted, such borrowing would help to optimize water yields and reduce Lake Granby spills during wet years because reservoirs would be maintained at lower levels.

With a plan to maximize water deliveries through integration, along with sufficient information about future water needs, the Board focused on the plight of Broomfield, whose water supply allegedly had been contaminated by radioactive wastes from the Rocky Flats nuclear weapons facility. In sharp contrast to Thornton's purchase of land and water rights in the District, Broomfield petitioned for District membership after contracting for 4,300 acre-feet of Windy Gap water from Boulder. Following extensive discussions with the District, which assured Broomfield that this water would be delivered in a drought at least as severe as those expected every fifty years, the two entities signed a contract in fall 1991. Windy Gap water would be delivered out of Carter Lake via a pipeline to be constructed and owned by the District, paid for by Broomfield, reimbursed by the Department of Energy, and completed if possible by January 1995.[32] How large a pipeline was constructed and its location depended on how many contracts the District signed with other communities for potable water. All C–BT and Windy Gap allottees were eligible to participate. By the end of 1991 what came to be known as the Southern Water Supply project had been planned to build a pipeline south out of Carter Lake to serve Broomfield, via Longmont, with an additional pipeline east to Platteville, and then south to Fort Lupton. Further extension of the pipeline to Fort Morgan and Brush was in the developmental stage.[33]

Cooperation, better management, and environmental sensitivity are essential to the future health of the District and to the economic stability of agriculture, municipalities, and industry along the Front Range corridor. Greater efforts to complete the ten-year-old South Platte Basin Study from Brighton to the Nebraska line will be rewarded if Denver supports a similar study of the river basin from Brighton to the river's headwaters. The more hydrologic and water-use information that is available, the easier and more efficient will be the methods of water distribution. Less competition and more cooperation between the NCWCD and the DWB seem promising under the DWB's new manager, Hamlet "Chips" Barry. The DWB's old adversarial style may have changed in 1991, coincidentally, the same year that its most venerable and intractable warrior, Glenn G. Saunders, died.

As the *Regional Water Supply Study* noted, however, moving beyond old rivalries and knee-jerk water litigation — a legacy of the prior appropriation doctrine — will require new leadership and possibly a new regional water authority.[34] W. D. "Bill" Farr has expressed a desire to see the NCWCD assume this role. Following in the tradition of other planners like Charles Hansen, Frank Delaney, Clifford Stone, J. R. "Bob" Barkley, and J. Ben Nix, Farr imagines the Front Range's future with an optimism matching the "axis of global intensity" theory of William Gilpin, Colorado's first territorial governor.[35] Farr envisions that Denver's new airport will become an international hub; that water for the Front Range area can be pooled and managed on a "volumetric"[36] rather than a priority basis; that irrigated agriculture will respond to international markets; and that dams on the Poudre and Little Thompson rivers, constructed by Denver money to provide greater water management flexibility through storage reservoirs, will also keep surplus water from passing to Nebraska.[37] Water management of this complexity, including attention to groundwater and environmental regulations, will require a level of cooperation not seen since the first mutual ditch companies were organized in simpler times. Concluding that the Front Range has no shortage of water for the foreseeable future, Farr believes that with sophisticated computer modeling, a creative system of water exchanges can be formulated to serve the needs of the water users of the future. Enlightened management is the key.

To some extent Simpson agrees, but he has expressed concern about the District assuming a leadership burden that could jeopardize its primary responsibility of serving the needs of its tax-paying water users. The "kiss of death," he says, would be for the District to mirror the way Denver tried to influence and direct water users in the greater metropolitan area. Instead of organizing a centralized water management organization for the Front

Range, Simpson argues the need to be more receptive to the District's constituency — anticipating changing circumstances and responding to them before they reach the controversial stage.

Colorado State University sociologist Evan Vlachos spoke to these issues at the NCWCD's fall 1991 water-users meeting.[38] He described how a more complex world has caused people to embrace an "apocalyptic" view of society. Many fear that humans have not cared for planet earth well and that the greenhouse effect has resulted from this irresponsibility. Future water managers, he said, will have to deal with many different constituencies that promote various solutions to the sometimes conflicting needs of humans and their land. Resultant pressures will tempt water managers to go with the quick fix to avoid "gridlock." The federal government's attempts to solve environmental problems with ever-more-complex legislation will increase the tendency toward litigated settlements. The solution must be to release water across district boundaries as new demands develop so that agriculture, industry, and municipalities can prosper without further environmental degradation.[39] Planners must look further ahead, and their meetings must involve all groups with vested interests in water. This will be very stressful, because old habits are hard to break: people recoil from change; data are interpreted differently by people with different viewpoints; and leaders with fresh ideas are often branded visionaries by Cassandras who see a glass of water half empty rather than half full. Organization managers who want cooperation among all water users on the Front Range will need common sense, a willingness to adapt plans to rapidly changing circumstances, and high levels of enthusiasm and fair dealing to win the trust of all.

If it can accept this mandate, the District can easily respond to the popular groundswell that urges more democratic representation on the Board. If it can use the IMS and other programs as management tools to help farmers produce better crops more efficiently with less stream degradation, if it can continue to seek negotiation instead of litigation, if it can enhance existing educational programs to describe its mission to the public, and if it can accept the reality of the environmental revolution begun by NEPA in 1969, the NCWCD will be in an excellent position to continue serving the people of northeastern Colorado for a long time to come. That was the original intent of Charles Hansen, "Godfather of the Big T," when he began working toward a transmountain diversion project in 1933. It should be no less than the objective of present and future NCWCD/MSD Board members and staff who hope to better manage limited supplies of water for the future of northern Colorado.

Acronyms and Abbreviations

AAA	Agricultural Adjustment Act
af	acre foot
AFL	American Federation of Labor
BLM	Bureau of Land Management
BSFW	Bureau of Sports Fisheries and Wildlife
Bureau	Bureau of Reclamation
CAL Papers	Charles A. Lory Papers
CAP	Central Arizona Project
C–BT	Colorado–Big Thompson Project
CCC	Civilian Conservation Corps
CCWCD	Central Colorado Water Conservancy District
CEQ	Council on Environmental Quality
cfs	cubic foot per second
CIO	Congress of Industrial Organizations
CLPWUA	Cache la Poudre Water Users Association
Corps	Army Corps of Engineers
CORSIM	Colorado River Simulation Model
CRS	Colorado Revised Statutes
CRSP	Colorado River Storage Project
CRWCD	Colorado River Water Conservation District (same as River District)
CRWCDA	Colorado River Water Conservancy District Archives
CSPC	Colorado State Planning Commission
CSUA	Colorado State University Archives
CWA	Clean Water Act
CWC	Colorado Water Congress
CWCB	Colorado Water Conservation Board

CWIC	Colorado Water Investigation Commission
CWQCC	Colorado Water Quality Control Commission
CWR&PDA	Colorado Water Resources and Power Development Authority
District	Northern Colorado Water Conservancy District (same as NCWCD)
DWB	Denver Water Board
DWD	Denver Water Department
ECI	Engineering Consultants, Inc.
EDF	Environmental Defense Fund
EIS	Environmental Impact Statement
EPA	Environmental Protection Agency
ERDA	Energy Resource Development Associates
ESA	Endangered Species Act
FERA	Federal Emergency Relief Administration
FERC	Federal Energy Regulatory Commission
FLPMA	Federal Land Policy and Management Act
Fry-Ark	Fryingpan-Arkansas Project
GPO	Government Printing Office
H.B.	House Bill No.
H.D.	House Document No.
H.R.	House Report No.
HUD	Housing and Urban Development
IECO	International Engineering Company
I.O.O.F.	Independent Order of Odd Fellows
IMS	Irrigation Management Service
LCPR	Larimer County Parks and Recreation Department
L.Ed.	Lawyers' Edition
LSPWCD	Lower South Platte Water Conservancy District
MPWCD	Middle Park Water Conservancy District
MSD	Municipal Subdistrict, Northern Colorado Water Conservancy District (same as Subdistrict)
MVA	Missouri Valley Authority
NCWCD	Northern Colorado Water Conservancy District
NCWCDA	Northern Colorado Water Conservancy District Archives
NCWUA	Northern Colorado Water Users Association

NEPA	National Environmental Protection Act
NIRA	National Industrial Recovery Act
NPIC	North Poudre Irrigation Company
NPS	National Park Service
NRA	National Reclamation Association
NWC	National Water Commission
NWRA	National Water Reclamation Association
NWRCOG	Northwest Regional Council of Governments
O&M	Operations and Maintenance
OMB	Office of Management and Budget
OWP	Office of Water Policy
P.L.	Public Law
PMF	Probable Maximum Flood
PRPA	Platte River Power Authority
PSC	Public Service Company
PWA	Public Works Administration
REA	Rural Electrification Association
RFC	Reconstruction Finance Corporation
River District	Colorado River Water Conservation District (same as CRWCD)
RMNP	Rocky Mountain National Park
RRA	Reclamation Reform Act
S.	Senate
S.B.	Senate Bill
S.Ct.	Supreme Court
SCWSC	Six-City Water Study Committee
S.D.	Senate Document
SECWCD	Southeastern Colorado Water Conservancy District
S.R.	Senate Report
Stat.	United States Statutes
Subdistrict	Municipal Subdistrict, Northern Colorado Water Conservancy District (same as MSD)
SWCD	Southwestern Water Conservation District
TVA	Tennessee Valley Authority
UCRC	Upper Colorado River Commission
USBR	United States Bureau of Reclamation

USC	United States Code
USDA	United States Department of Agriculture
USFS	United States Forest Service
USF&WS	United States Fish and Wildlfe Service
USGS	United States Geological Survey
WAPA	Western Area Power Administration
WCRM	Western Cultural Resource Management
WFA	War Food Administration
WMC	War Manpower Commission
WPA	Works Progress Administration
WPB	War Production Board
WRC	Water Resources Council
WSPA	West Slope Protective Association
WSSC	Water Supply and Storage Company

Glossary

Absolute decree: The final water decree that defines a party's right to a specified amount of water under specific conditions with a specified priority date. The decree is handed down by one of seven Colorado district courts with jurisdiction over water matters and can be granted only after water has been captured, possessed, controlled, and put to beneficial use.

Acre-foot: The common measure of water when discussing municipal, industrial, and agricultural water supplies. It is the amount of water needed to cover an acre of land to a depth of one foot. An acre-foot contains approximately 326,000 gallons, which is the amount of water used by an average urban family of four in one year.

Ad valorem tax: A property tax charged under the terms of the Water Conservancy District Act to property owners within the boundaries of a water conservancy district. The tax helps support the district's operation and retire capital expenditure debts incurred in building water projects.

Adjudication: The judicial process for determining water right decrees. Adjudication confirms the existence of an appropriation and its priority date for purposes of administration vis-à-vis other water rights. Water court decrees are subject to appeal to the Colorado Supreme Court before they become final.

Afterbay: A water body located just below a point of industrial application, for example, just below a hydroelectric power plant. See also Tailrace.

Allotment contract: A contractual right for the beneficial use of water issued by a water conservancy district under specific terms and provisions. There are approximately 2,500 allotment contracts for the C–BT's 310,000 units.

Appropriation: The establishment of a water right through the intent and activities that demonstrate intent to capture, possess, and control water for beneficial use. The appropriation must be adjudicated to establish priority for the purposes of water rights administration.

Appropriator: The entity or person who has made an appropriation.

Aquifer: An underground bed of saturated sand, gravel, or porous rock through which water may move by gravity, and which is usually surrounded by impervious materials.

Augmentation: The addition or replacement of water for the benefit of a senior water user who would otherwise be injured by a junior water user taking water to which he would not otherwise be entitled.

Azure project: A project originally proposed by the Municipal Subdistrict as mitigation to the West Slope for building Windy Gap. The proposed location would be on the Colorado River in Gore Canyon. Wolford Mountain Reservoir on Muddy Creek was selected by the Colorado River Water Conservation District in lieu of the Azure site.

Basin of origin: The watershed or basin in which developed water originates. Colorado water law allows water to be removed from its basin of origin under certain conditions.

Beneficial use: Diversion of a reasonable and appropriate amount of water used under reasonably efficient practices to accomplish without waste the purpose for which the appropriation is lawfully made. Beneficial uses in Colorado include agricultural, municipal, mining, manufacturing, recreational, aquacultural, and flood control uses.

Bifurcation: Separating or branching into two parts. Refers in this case to a water supply canal or conduit.

Bypass structure: An auxillary passage structure for water.

California Doctrine: A legal concept retaining aspects of both riparian rights and the principles of prior appropriation.

Call: The request by a senior appropriator for water to which a person is entitled by decreed priority. A call will force those users with junior decrees to cease or diminish their diversions and pass the requested amount of water to the downstream senior user making the call.

Carriage contract: A contract allowing water to be delivered through an existing project's facilities. The Subdistrict has such a contract with the United States and NCWCD for transportation of Windy Gap water through the existing facilities of the C–BT Project.

Cloud seeding: A technique that adds substances (most commonly silver iodide) to clouds in order to alter their natural development and promote precipitation in a designated area.

Cofferdam: A temporary watertight enclosure from which water is pumped to expose the bottom of a body of water thus permitting construction of a larger, permanent dam structure in the channel of a stream or river.

Colorado Doctrine: See prior appropriation doctrine.

Colorado River Basin Project Act, 1968: An act passed authorizing construction of the Central Arizona project (CAP) and simultaneous development of five Colorado projects: Animas–La Plata, Dolores, Dallas Creek, West Divide, and San Miguel.

Colorado River Compact: A 1922 interstate agreement to apportion the waters of the Colorado River among seven western states, with 7.5 million acre-feet of water reserved for the upper basin states (Colorado, New Mexico, Utah, Wyoming) and 7.5 million acre-feet of water reserved for the lower basin states (Arizona, California, Nevada). The dividing point of the upper and lower basins is at Lee Ferry, Arizona, on the Colorado River.

Colorado River Storage Project Act, 1956: An act passed following the 1922 Colorado River Compact and the 1948 Upper Basin States Compact authorizing specified reclamation projects for development of waters in the upper basin of the Colorado River. Examples include Glen Canyon, Navajo, Curecanti, and Flaming Gorge reservoirs. This act was intended to enable the upper basin states to utilize their entitlements under the Colorado River Compact.

Compact: A contract or agreement between two or more states entered into with the consent of the federal government. In the matter of water, compacts define the relative rights of two or more states on an interstate stream to use the waters of that stream.

Compensatory storage: Provisions for water storage to make water available for present and prospective beneficial uses in the basin of origin in association with an out-of-basin diversion.

Conditional decree: The first legal definition of a water right issued after a party applies for a decree but has not yet constructed the necessary water works to perfect the appropriation. The decree must be protected by proving that the applicant is working diligently toward full development of the appropriation. The value of a conditional decree is that if the appropriation is completed within a reasonable time, the priority date reverts back to the date of the appropriation's initiation. A conditional decree becomes perfected and can be confirmed by an absolute decree when water is captured, possessed, controlled, and actually applied to beneficial use.

Conservancy district: Established by decree of a court under the Water Conservancy District Act of 1937. A conservancy district can obtain rights-of-way for works; contract with the United States or otherwise provide for the construction of facilities; assume contractual or bonded indebtedness; administer, operate, and maintain physical works; have authority to conserve, control, allocate, and distribute water supplies; and have contracting and limited taxing authority to derive the revenues necessary to accomplish its purposes. There are currently forty-six conservancy districts in Colorado.

Conservation district: Established under specific statutes by the Colorado General Assembly. There are currently three conservation districts in Colorado: the Colorado River Water Conservation District, the Southwestern Water Conservation District, and the Rio Grande Water Conservation District. Their mission is to oversee the conservation, use, and development of water in large geographical areas of the state.

Consolidated cases: The water adjudication proceedings involving the Blue River, Colorado River, and Green Mountain Reservoir, which pitted the United States, NCWCD, and the CRWCD against Denver for nearly fifty years.

Consumptive use: The portion of water consumed during use that does not become return flow available for further use.

Continental Divide: The physical divide in North America separating streams that flow into either the Pacific or Atlantic drainages.

Cubic feet per second: Sometimes referred to as "second feet," cfs is the basic measurement of flowing water. A cubic foot per second is approximately 7.48 gallons per second, which is 646,317 gallons per day. Thus a flow of or right to 1 cfs is a flow of or right to 646,317 gallons in twenty-four hours, which is almost 2 acre-feet.

Dead storage: The capacity of a water storage reservoir that exists below the level of the outtake structures.

Decree: An official document issued by the court defining the priority, amount, use, and location of a water right or plan of augmentation.

Delaney Resolution: A 1935 resolution drawn up by West Slope representatives and presented to a meeting of the Colorado State Planning Commission, which agreed to transmountain diversion provided that adequate surveys of West Slope hydrology would first be conducted to determine the West Slope's present and future water needs.

Depletion: Use of water in a manner that makes it no longer available for other uses in a hydraulically connected water system.

Desalinization: Removal of salt, in this case from water.

Developed water: Water that is produced or brought into a water system that would not have entered the water system without dams, reservoirs, conduits, tunnels, or other water facilities.

Diligence: Action taken toward the perfection of a conditional water right. In Colorado, when a conditional right is granted by the court, the applicant must demonstrate every six years that steps have been taken toward perfecting that right. If diligence in perfecting an appropriation is not demonstrated, the conditional right is canceled. Due diligence is activity that a water court recognizes as satisfactory effort by an applicant wanting to perfect an absolute decree from a conditional decree.

Direct-flow water: Water diverted for use without interruption between diversion and use, except for purposes incidental to the use such as settling or filtration.

Ditch: A narrow trench cut into the surface of the ground to convey water from a stream to the location of use.

Diversion: Removal of water from its natural course or location — or controlling water in its natural course or location — by means of a ditch, canal, flume, reservoir, bypass, pipeline, conduit, well, pump, or other structure or device.

Division engineer: The subordinate officer under the state engineer for each of the seven water divisions or major streams in Colorado who performs the functions of the state engineer in those water divisions.

Duty of water: The total volume of water reasonably required for a beneficial use, normally referring to irrigation water required to be conveyed to and mature a particular variety of crop.

East Slope: The portion of Colorado east of the Continental Divide.

Environmental Impact Statement: A report analyzing the potential impact on land and water use in terms of environmental, engineering, aesthetic, and economic aspects of a proposed project and its alternatives.

Evapotranspiration: The combined processes by which water is transferred from the Earth's surface to the atmosphere: evaporation of liquid or solid water plus transpiration from plants.

Federal reserved water right: A claim by the federal government, based on the Winters Doctrine, that argues for a federal water right on federal lands in a quantity sufficient to maintain the purpose for which the reservation was established.

Feeder canal: A canal that feeds water into a reservoir.

Firm power: A contract for electrical power that is not interruptible.

First-use right: Associated with use of C–BT water. Under the 1938 repayment contract between the United States and the NCWCD, allottees have the right to one use of the C–BT water with all return flows dedicated back to the river system and available for downstream uses within the District.

Floodplain: An area adjacent to a stream or other water course that is subject to flooding.

Flume: An inclined channel used to convey and/or measure water.

Forebay: A reservoir or canal from which water is immediately taken to produce hydropower.

Foreign water: See Developed Water.

Front Range: The portion of Colorado situated immediately east of the Rocky Mountains, generally extending east to the edge of the piedmont and from Fort Collins south to Trinidad.

Fryingpan-Arkansas project: Built in the 1960s, this project diverts water from the West Slope to the Arkansas River valley much like the C–BT Project, which diverts water from the West Slope to the South Platte River valley. The compensatory storage for the Fryingpan-Arkansas project is Ruedi Reservoir.

Futile call: A condition that arises when a junior appropriator's cessation of diversions would not result in a significant increase in water being made available to a downstream senior appropriator. In such cases the call need not be honored.

Grand Lake Committee: An outgrowth of the Greeley Chamber of Commerce committee established to study a transmountain diversion project from the Colorado River basin. In 1933 this committee officially became the Northern Colorado Water Users Association.

Grand Lake Project: The original name of the Colorado–Big Thompson Project. The name was officially changed to the C–BT in July 1936.

Gravity canal: A canal that conveys water by gravity without mechanical pumping or other powered forces.

Groundwater: Water in an aquifer. Although all aquifer water is technically groundwater, Colorado law treats water in an aquifer tributary to a river as surface water. Water experts generally consider nontributary groundwater to be confined to a sealed aquifer that has no connection to flowing surface water.

Headgate: A device used to divert or channel water from a river into a ditch or from a large ditch into a smaller ditch. A headgate also controls the amount of water diverted.

Historic use: The documented diversion and use of water by a water right holder over a period of years.

Hydroelectric: A term relating to the production of electricity by waterpower.

Inclusion: A method by which owners of land may petition the NCWCD Board or a court that their lands be included within the NCWCD. Once included, property owners are subject to the 1 mill ad valorem tax set forth in the Water Conservancy District Act.

Instream flow right: A water right that is used to maintain water in the stream channel to preserve the environment for fish, wildlife, and aesthetic purposes. In Colorado an instream flow right may be appropriated only by the Colorado Water Conservation Board "to preserve the environment to a reasonable degree."

Integrated operations: Operation of the C–BT and Windy Gap projects under the amended carriage contract with the United States allowing use of District and Subdistrict water between allottees of either or both, so long as no injury occurs to C–BT allottees.

Irrigation: The distribution of water on the land surface to establish a crop or to increase crop yield where the natural precipitation is inadequate.

Junior decree: A decree for water in a hydraulically connected stream system that is subject to the call of senior rights. It is also used generically to describe rights that are subject to full or partial curtailment when the available supply cannot fill all the rights or when comparing two or more decrees, i.e., junior and senior decrees.

Lateral: A smaller ditch that carries irrigation water from a primary supply ditch or canal to the location of use.

Lower basin states: Arizona, California, Nevada, as stipulated by the 1922 Colorado River Compact.

McCarran Amendment, 1952: An act of Congress allowing the states to require the United States to make its water right claims in state court.

Mill: One one-thousandth of a dollar of assessed value. A mill levy is a tax on property based on this formula.

Miner's inch: An antiquated water measurement, still used by many irrigation ditch companies, roughly equivalent to cubic inches per second (cis). To translate it to acre-feet, divide the number of miner's inches by 38.4, then divide that result by 2 to arrive at the number of acre-feet of flow over a twenty-four-hour period. The original miner's inch was the size and volume of a man's thumb: about 1 inch in diameter and 4 inches long.

Minimum streamflow requirement: Water right decreed to the Colorado Water Conservation Board requiring that a set amount of water be maintained in a water course between two specified points for the purpose of maintaining the environment to a reasonable degree. The minimum streamflow right takes its place in the appropriation system in the manner of another junior water right, although capture, possession, control, and diversion of the water is not required.

Mutual ditch companies: Owner-operated and -financed irrigation companies that distribute water according to the ownership of shares in the company. Shareholders hold in common an ownership in the water rights and the water facilities of the company.

Nonjeopardy opinion: A formal opinion issued by the USF&WS that a proposed project will not cause jeopardy or increase jeopardy to an endangered species or damage its critical habitat.

Nonpoint source pollution: Environmental pollution that cannot be identified as coming from one specific source. Some examples of nonpoint sources include mine drainage, urban storm runoff, and agricultural runoff.

Open-rate contracts: Those C–BT water allotments that are subject to a rate fixed annually by the Board. Approximately 49 percent of the 310,000 acre-foot units are open rated; 51 percent are fixed rated at $1.50 per acre-foot.

Opportunity water: Snowmelt runoff water that fills streams and rivers during the two- to three-month runoff period.

Parent district: A term used by the Municipal Subdistrict when referring to the Northern Colorado Water Conservancy District.

Peaking power: Electric power production in response to maximum demand.

Plan for augmentation: A detailed program to increase the supply of water available for beneficial use by the development of new or alternate means or points of diversion; by a pooling of water resources; by water exchange projects; by providing substitute supplies of water; by the development of new sources of water; or by other appropriate means.

Point of diversion: The specific location of a headgate or water diversion structure for capturing, possessing, and controlling water.

Point source pollution: Pollution that can be traced to a specific source.

Preferred water use: Domestic use has priority over all other uses. Agricultural use has preference over water used for manufacturing. In Colorado these preferences apply only in condemnation actions or when a contract or other legal arrangement gives them preference over other uses.

Prior appropriation doctrine: A legal concept in which the first person to appropriate water and apply it to a beneficial use has the first right to use that amount of water from that source. Each successive appropriator may only take a share of the water remaining after all senior water rights are satisfied. This is the historical basis for Colorado water law and is sometimes known as the Colorado Doctrine or the principle of "first in time, first in right."

Priority: The relative seniority of a water right for purposes of administration as determined by its adjudication and appropriation dates.

Public domain: Land owned by the federal government but not reserved for specific uses.

Pump-back storage: A term that describes a water project with two reservoirs and a pump/hydroelectric system whereby water can be pumped to the uppermost reservoir at times of low electrical demand and later released to the lower reservoir to generate electricity during times of peak electrical demand.

Quasi-municipal: Governmental entities — such as fire, water, and sanitation districts — that maintain some aspects of a municipality (taxing authority) yet remain separate from them. They are not general government; they provide only certain services to the public.

Reclamation Act 1902: Also known as the Newlands Act, this established the United States Reclamation Service, which built water projects in the western United States. Money was initially provided through the sale of public lands and later by general fund appropriations.

Reclamation Reform Act 1982: A revision of the Reclamation Act, which identified the number of acres a landowner could own and still receive Bureau of Reclamation water at less than a full-cost rate.

Reclamation Service: Former name for the Bureau of Reclamation.

Repayment Contract: Document signed on July 5, 1938, between the Northern Colorado Water Conservancy District and the United States, establishing the conditions for construction and operation of the C–BT and requiring the Northern Colorado Water Conservancy District to repay the United States for a portion of the C–BT construction costs.

Replacement storage: See Compensatory storage.

Reserved water right: See Winters Doctrine.

Reservoir: Surface water impounded behind a dam as a source of water for multipurpose use.

Return flow: Water that, once diverted from its natural streamflow and used for irrigation or other purposes, naturally finds its way back toward the stream either as surface runoff or via an aquifer.

Riparian rights doctrine: A legal concept in which owners of lands along the banks of a stream or water body have the right to reasonable use of the waters and a correlative right protecting against unreasonable use of the waters by others that substantially diminishes either the quantity or quality of water in the stream or water body. The right is appurtenant to the land and does not depend on prior use. Riparian rights are not recognized in Colorado but are common in the eastern United States. They are utilized in California along with prior appropriation rights.

Runoff: The flow of precipitation into streams and rivers. In Colorado the term is used primarily to describe the two- to three-month period (April-May-June) in the spring when the mountain snowpack melts. Colorado obtains most of its water from spring runoff.

Rural domestic water districts/associations: Water supply entities that sprang up in the late 1950s and 1960s to meet the domestic water supply needs of residents outside of city water service areas.

Salinity: The amount of dissolved solids in water, sometimes referred to as Total Dissolved Solids (TDS).

Second foot: Verbal shorthand for "cubic feet per second."

Section 404 permit: A permit issued by the U.S. Army Corps of Engineers under the Clean Water Act for the discharge of dredged or fill materials into U.S. waters. Permit issuance can be vetoed by the EPA. A Section 404 permit is usually a prerequisite for construction of a water project.

Senate Document 80: This document outlines the plan of development, operation, and cost estimates for the C–BT Project. Presented to Congress by Alva B. Adams in June 1937, Senate Document 80 is often referred to as the "Bible" of the C–BT Project.

Senior decree: A decree that is filled before others when the available supply is not sufficient to fill all water rights in a hydraulically connected water system. Generally used when discussing the relative seniority/priority of two or more decrees.

Shoshone Power Plant: The priority call on the Colorado River with a date of 1902 for 1250 cfs of water. This is the key senior call on the river and thus must be met before any water is diverted to the East Slope.

Six Cities Committee: Formed in 1969 by six northern Front Range communities interested in pursuing construction of the Windy Gap project. These included Fort Collins, Greeley, Loveland, Longmont, Boulder, and Estes Park.

Spillway: A passage or channel for excess water over or around a dam, usually designed to accommodate flood events.

State Engineer: The chief executive officer in the Colorado Division of Water Resources, whose office administers the decrees of courts and issues water well permits.

Storage right: A right defined in terms of the volume of water that may be diverted from or controlled in the channel of a stream, stored in a reservoir, and then withdrawn or released for subsequent beneficial use.

Supplemental water: Water that is in addition to an already existing base supply. The C–BT Project provides supplemental Colorado River water to augment northeastern Colorado native South Platte basin water supplies held by ditch companies, cities, and businesses.

Supply canal: A canal that supplies water to a river.

Surge tank: A standpipe or storage reservoir at the downstream end of a closed aqueduct or feeder pipe, used to absorb sudden rises in pressure and to furnish water quickly during a drop in pressure.

Surplus water: Water that is available above that necessary to meet demand. See also Opportunity Water.

Tailrace: A channel for conveying water away from a point of industrial application.

Tailwater: Water in a tailrace, below a dam, or below a field after irrigation.

Take or pay contract: A contract that requires payments to be made whether or not the water or other service is actually ordered or needed in any given year.

Transmountain diversion: The diversion of water from a watershed on one side of a mountain range to another watershed or basin on the other side.

Tributary: A tributary is generally regarded as a surface water drainage system that is interconnected with a river system. Under Colorado law, all surface or groundwater, the withdrawal of which would affect the rate or direction of flow of a surface stream within 100 years, is considered to be tributary to a natural stream.

Trifurcation: The separating or branching into three parts. Refers in this case to a water supply canal or conduit.

Upper basin states: Colorado, New Mexico, Utah, Wyoming, as stipulated by the 1922 Colorado River Compact.

Water commissioner: The public official under the direction of the division engineers who carries out the detailed administration of a portion of the waters of each water division.

Water conservancy district: A special unit of local government with authority to tax and incur bonded indebtedness in order to provide water supply services for persons or entities within its boundaries under Colorado's 1937 Water Conservancy District Act.

Water conservation: The efficient use of water by methods ranging from improved efficient practices in farm, home, and industry to capturing water for beneficial use through environmentally sensitive water storage or conservation projects.

Water court: A specific district court that has exclusive jurisdiction to hear and adjudicate water matters within each of Colorado's seven water divisions.

Water division: A major watershed of the state such as the South Platte River valley, which is Water Division No. 1. There are seven such divisions within Colorado. The water divisions are used for purposes of water rights administration by the state engineer and by courts for water rights adjudication.

Water right: The right to use a certain portion of the state's waters for beneficial purposes. A water right is a real property right entitling the owner to capture, possess, control, and apply water to beneficial use. As with other real property, it may be bought and sold, leased, exchanged, or traded subject to not injuring other water rights.

Watershed: The land area or basin drained by a specific river or river system.

West Slope: The portion of Colorado that lies west of the Continental Divide.

Winters Doctrine: The doctrine enunciated by the United States Supreme Court in the 1908 *Winters* v. *United States* decision, affirming that tribal Indians on reservations have federal water rights that are superior to appropriative or riparian rights that came into existence after the date the reservation was created.

Notes

The NCWCDA has a complete set of the minute books of both the NCWUA and the NCWCD. Roll no. 1 of the microfilm begins in April 1934 and ends on December 12, 1980. Roll no. 2 begins with the meeting in January 1981 and goes through December 1986.

CHAPTER 1

1. *Time Capsule/1933: A History of the Year Condensed From the Pages of Time* (New York: Time Inc., 1967), p. 16.
2. Henry Steele Commager, ed., *Documents of American History*, 2 vols. (New York: Meredith Publishing Company, 1963), 2, pp. 239–242.
3. Arthur M. Schlesinger, Jr., *The Age of Roosevelt: The Coming of the New Deal* (Boston: Houghton Mifflin, 1965), p. 1.
4. Ibid., p. 7.
5. Ibid., p. 10.
6. *Time Capsule/1933*, p. 19.
7. Ibid., p. 21.
8. Schlesinger, *The Age of Roosevelt*, p. 21.
9. *Fort Collins Express-Courier*, 5 March 1933.
10. In the *Fort Collins Express-Courier*, March 5, 1933, for example, equal space was given to the inaugural activities in Washington and the new water diversion plan proposed by the Colorado delegation at a meeting with Wyoming officials in Cheyenne. This eleven-point plan featured diversion of water from the Yampa River in exchange for North Platte water diverted to the Cache la Poudre, basing the amount diverted on the quantity of water supplied by the Yampa to the North Platte. After many years of trying to persuade Wyoming to agree to a larger diversion out of the North Platte system, this Yampa plan appeared, for the time being, to have tentative approval on both sides.
11. Colorado, Department of the State Engineer, *Preliminary Engineering Report: Northern Transmountain Diversion*, by Royce J. Tipton (Denver: December 1933), p. 25. (Cited hereafter as the Tipton Report.)
12. Ibid., p. 33.
13. In preparing a statement on events leading up to the organization of the Northern Colorado Water Conservancy District, Senator Fred Norcross recollected that by 1933 the land under ditch in northern Colorado had known water shortages for more than twenty years, but the worst period had been since 1929. "Genesis of the Colorado–Big Thompson Project," *Colorado Magazine* 30:1 (January 1953), p. 30. Charles Hansen echoed these views in letters to Senators Edward P. Costigan and Alva Adams, June 11, 1934, in which he noted the extreme shortage of irrigation water over the past three years, making it "imperative to find new sources of supply." Charles Hansen Files, NCWDCA.

14. U.S. Department of Agriculture, "Irrigation in Northern Colorado," by Robert G. Hemphill, Bulletin 1026 (Washington: May 16, 1922), pp. 10, 13, 81.

15. Tipton Report, pp. 6, 7, 11–13.

16. Ibid., p. 13.

17. Colorado, State Board of Immigration, *Colorado Year Book, 1933–1934* (Denver: September 1934), pp. 14, 96. According to U.S. Department of Agriculture data cited in the *Colorado Year Book* (p. 99), the value of Colorado sugar beet harvests declined from 34.94 percent of the total national production to 22.28 percent in 1933. Likewise, the quantity of beets produced declined from 35.71 percent to 23.71 percent, and the acreage planted was reduced from 30.57 percent to 21.24 percent.

18. James F. Wickens, *Colorado in the Great Depression* (New York: Garland, 1979), p. 409. Wickens cites *Colorado Agricultural Statistics, 1942*, p. 10 in his Appendix I, entitled "Colorado Farm Income, 1929–1942."

19. Workers of the Writers' Program of the Works Progress Administration in the State of Colorado, *Colorado: A Guide to the Highest State*, American Guide Series, sponsored by the Colorado State Planning Commission (New York: Hastings House, 1941), p. 65. The authors also note that whereas beets were grown on only 10 percent of all irrigated land in the sixteen leading beet counties from 1929–1939, the average crop value totaled 40 percent of the value of all principal crops grown on irrigated land in the state.

20. From a chart entitled, "Sugar Beet Production, 1905 to 1935 Inclusive," *Colorado Agricultural Statistics, 1935* (Denver: Colorado Cooperative Crop and Livestock Reporting Service, 1935), p. 61.

21. Richard Lowitt and Maurine Beasley, eds., *One Third of a Nation: Lorena Hickok Reports on the Great Depression* (Urbana: University of Illinois Press, 1981), p. 283. Lorena Hickok, an astute observer of the social and economic consequences of the drought and depression in the West, was quick to criticize Great Western Sugar for making huge profits at the expense of small farmers and Mexican laborers. To her, GW was the "arch villain."

22. Herbert E. Dyer and Robert Barkley, Table VI, "Percent of Total Value of Principal Crops Harvested Under Irrigation (Avge. 1929–1938 Incl.)," in "Agricultural Production in Northern Colorado Water Conservancy District as Related to National Defense" (Denver: Colorado Water Conservation Board, December 1941), p. J.

23. Ibid., Table V. By county, the average value of crops produced under irrigation between 1929 and 1938 was as follows: Weld, $14,210,110; Larimer, $3,222,980; Morgan, $3,092,120; Logan, $2,403,160; Boulder, $1,948,140; Sedgwick, $688,980; and Washington, $207,600.

24. Tipton Report, p. 24. Data are for 1930.

25. U.S. Department of the Interior, Water and Power Resources Service, Bureau of Reclamation, *Project Data, 1981* (Denver: GPO, 1981), p. 558.

26. *Congressional Record*, 69th Cong., 1st sess., 1926, 67, pt. 10: 10831. In his letter to the chairman of the House Committee on Irrigation and Reclamation, Secretary Work notes the dates of the Bureau of Reclamation and Department of Agriculture studies. The feasibility study of 1920 came to light at the January 13, 14, and February 1, 1928, hearings on the Casper-Alcova project before the Senate Committee on Irrigation and Reclamation. On June 7, 1924, the secretary of the interior was directed to submit all reports, along with cost estimates, to Congress for the purpose of planning the construction of Casper-Alcova and two other projects. See 43 Stat. 668, June 7, 1924.

27. The Nebraska Compact limited Colorado's unconditional right to the South Platte to the period from October 15 to April 1. From April 1 to October 15, only pre-1897 rights of Colorado irrigators would be recognized if the flow of the river dropped below 120 cfs at the state line. See George E. Radosevitch and Donald H. Hamburg, eds., *Colorado Water Laws, Compacts, Treaties and Selected Cases* (Denver: Colorado State Division of Water Resources, 1971), pp. 119–122.

28. *Congressional Record*, 69th Cong., 1st sess., 1926, 67, pt. 8:8469–8470.

29. Ibid., pt. 10:10830–10831.

30. 16 January 1926 and 2 April 1926, *Congressional Record*, 69th Cong., 1st sess.

31. U.S. Senate, *Hearings Before the Committee on Irrigation and Reclamation, January 13, 14, and February 1, 1928 on S. 1136*, 70th Cong., 1st sess.

32. Ibid.

33. U.S. *Congressional Record*, 70th Cong., 1st sess., S.R. 1184, May 18, 1928; H.R. 1749. Department of the Interior, Bureau of Reclamation, "Report on the North Platte River Basin," (Denver: June 1957), p. 108.

34. U.S. House of Representatives, 71st Cong., 3d sess., H.D. No. 674. This document is composed of two reports: the "Land Classification and Economic Report, Wyoming," by W. W. Johnston, associate reclamation economist, February 1930; and the "Engineering Report on the Casper-Alcova Irrigation project, Wyoming," by J. R. Iakisch, engineer, Bureau of Reclamation. Both reports were referred to the Committee on Irrigation and Reclamation on December 8, 1930.

35. Opinion of the Supreme Court delivered by Mr. Justice Douglas in *Nebraska v. Wyoming*, 1945 (325 U.S. 589, 65 S.Ct. 1332, 89 L.Ed. 1815), in which it is noted that the North Platte flowed at the following percentages of the mean for the 1904 to 1930 period: 1931 (55%), 1932 (116%), 1933 (89%), 1934 (30%), 1935 (54%). See Frank J. Trelease and George A. Gould, *Water Law Cases and Materials*, 4th ed. (St. Paul, Minn.: West Publishing Company, 1986), p. 290.

36. "Water Distribution Affected by Grand Lake Tunnel Project Explained by Local Engineer," *Greeley Tribune*, 26 August 1933.

37. Bureau of Reclamation, "Report on the North Platte River Basin," pp. 50–51; U.S. House of Representatives, H.D. 775, Letter, 16 February 1931, President Herbert Hoover to the Speaker of the House, Serial Set No. 9380, V. 30, 71st Cong., 3d sess.

38. *Fort Collins Express-Courier*, 17 March 1933.

39. Ibid., 10 April 1933. On April 13 the newspaper reported that Fort Collins irrigators were blaming Hinderlider's order for their inability to fill their reservoirs, which in turn had "choked off credit for the 1933 crop by banks because of lack of storage." On June 8 the *Express-Courier* noted that Hinderlider misunderstood the exchange system in the valley, resulting in "intense feeling against the State Engineer's Office." Some were looking for a way to run him out of office under civil service regulations.

40. Ibid., 12 March and 12 April 1933. Charges against Hinderlider and Johnson of being water dictators appeared in the *Greeley Tribune* on March 18, April 11, and April 12, 1933. Hinderlider's restriction on filling reservoirs led Frank B. Davis of Greeley, one of the original members of the Grand Lake Committee, to complain that representatives from Morgan and Logan counties were blocking bills in the State Assembly that would put reservoir water on an equal basis with direct-flow water. See *Greeley Tribune*, 13 April 1933. Hinderlider's order to cease storing water in reservoirs was reported rescinded on April 22, 1933. See *Greeley Tribune*, 22 April 1933.

41. *Fort Collins Express-Courier*, 12, 19 March 1933.

42. Ibid., 17 April 1933.

43. Ibid., 18 April 1933.

44. Ibid., 14 June 1933.

45. Ibid., 6 June 1933.

46. Samuel I. Rosenman, comp., *The Public Papers and Addresses of Franklin D. Roosevelt*, introduction and notes by Roosevelt (New York: Random House, 1938).

47. *Fort Collins Express-Courier*, 15 June 1933.

48. Ibid., 25 June 1933. The seven directors of this association were listed as C. A. Bartels (Fort Collins), W. W. Brown (Eaton), C. G. Carlson (Eaton), Roy Portner (Fort Collins), Frank B. Davis (Greeley), E. F. Monroe (Fort Collins), T. J. Warren (Fort Collins).

49. Ibid., 20 June 1933.

50. Ibid., 16 July 1933.

51. *Greeley Tribune*, 29 July 1933. *Fort Collins Express-Courier*, 2 August 1933. The PWA actually funded three projects at the same time: Grand Coulee Dam, the Mississippi River Canal, and Casper-Alcova.

52. *Fort Collins Express-Courier*, 5 September 1933. When the tri-state delegates returned to Washington a few weeks later to discuss cooperation with government assistance, Ickes called the meeting to order and then retired from the room. See Ibid., 22 September 1933.

53. *Greeley Tribune*, 29 July 1933.

54. *Greeley Tribune*, 4 August 1933.

55. *Fort Collins Express-Courier*, 6 August 1933.

56. Ibid. *Greeley Tribune*, 7 August 1933.

57. *Fort Collins Express-Courier*, 6 August 1933.

58. Proponents of an agreement on the North Platte hoped to reopen State Engineer Hinderlider's plan of bringing 50,000 acre-feet of water from Douglas Creek into the Laramie River above the Pioneer Ditch and then to work out a water exchange with Wyoming. See *Fort Collins Express-Courier*, 14 August 1933.

59. Ibid., 22 September 1933.

60. Ibid., 4 December 1933.

CHAPTER 2

1. "A Conversation with William R. Kelly, Esquire," transcript of interviews with Lee G. Norris, which took place between 1977 and 1981. This typescript, dated November 3, 1982, is in the possession of Professor James E. Hansen II, Colorado State University. Pages iv through viii include a brief memorial to Kelly presented to the Weld County Bar Association on September 11, 1981. Kelly died on January 20, 1981, one month shy of his ninety-eighth birthday.

2. *Greeley Tribune*, 29 July 1933.

3. Ibid.

4. This amount includes the Laramie River and all the tributaries flowing out of Colorado into both the Laramie and the North Platte.

5. *Greeley Tribune*, 29 July 1933.

6. *Fort Collins Express-Courier*, 24 August 1933.

7. Ibid.

8. Quoted by Kelly in the *Fort Collins Express-Courier*, 12 October 1933. Kelly also criticized the failure of the State Assembly to pass a measure to organize a conservancy district for the purpose of facilitating grants of federal funds.

9. Letter, 5 July 1940, William R. Kelly to George Irvin, President, Greeley Chamber of Commerce, Charles Hansen files, NCWCDA. See also Lee Norris, ed., "A Conversation With William R. Kelly, Esquire," pp. 315–317.

10. *Denver Post*, 18 June 1952, p. 48.

11. Mills E. Bunger, "Early History, Colorado–Big Thompson Project, 1889–1935." Four-page typescript with exhibits, bound in *Colorado–Big Thompson Project, Early History, Tipton Report, 1933: Colorado Water Conservancy District Law*, p. 1, NCWCDA.

12. Colorado, Office of the State Engineer, *Fifth Biennial Report, 1889–1891* (Denver, 1891), pp. 596–597.

13. Ibid., pp. 597–598.

14. Ibid., p. 599. S.B. 248 ("A bill for an act to provide for the diversion of unappropriated waters at or near the sources of the Grand, Laramie and North Platte River systems and their tributaries, and cause the same to flow eastward") was passed by the Senate on March 29, 1889, and submitted to the governor for his signature on April 1 by the Joint Committee on Enrollment. See Colorado, *House Journal*, 7th sess., 1889, 2:2360, 2633.

15. U.S. House of Representatives, Committee on Irrigation of Arid Lands, *Hearings, January 28 to February 9, 1901* (Washington: GPO, 1901), pp. 88–93, 99–108.

16. *Colorado–Big Thompson Project, Technical Record of Design and Construction, Volume I: Planning, Legislation, and General Description* (Washington: U.S. Department of the Interior, Bureau of Reclamation, April 1957), pp. xix, 13.

17. U.S. House of Representatives, 59th Cong., 1st sess., H.D. 86, Department of the Interior, U.S. geological Survey, *Fourth Annual Report of the Reclamation Service, 1904–1905*, F. H. Newell, Chief Engineer (Washington: GPO, 1906), p. 124.

18. Ibid., pp. 125, 127.

19. Ibid., p. 127. One cubic foot per second is the equivalent of 1.9835 acre-feet per day.

20. U.S. Department of the Interior, U.S. Geological Survey, Water Supply and Irrigation Paper 133, "Report of Progress of Stream Measurements for the Calendar Year 1904," prepared under the direction of F. H. Newell by M. C. Hinderlider, G. L. Swendsen, and A. E. Chandler. Part X: Colorado River and the Great Basin Drainage (Washington: GPO, 1905), pp. 130–137.

21. U.S. Department of the Interior, U.S. Geological Survey, Water Supply Paper 395, "Colorado River and Its Utilization," by E. C. La Rue (Washington: GPO, 1916), p. 11.

22. Ibid., p. 156. La Rue refers to the Shoshone Plant, whose need for a minimum flow in the Colorado River figured strongly in the decision to build Green Mountain Dam.

23. The six diversions are Grand River (11,400 af), Busk-Ivanhoe (3,710 af), Ewing (2,000 af), Tarbell (2,000 af), Berthoud (685 af), and Boreas Pass (600 af).

24. U.S. Department of the Interior, "Upper Colorado River and Its Utilization," by Robert Follansbee, Water-Supply Paper 617 (Washington: GPO, 1929), pp. viii, xii.

25. Ibid., p. 54.

26. Ibid., p. 60.

27. Colorado, Department of the State Engineer, "Report on the Water Resources of the South Platte Basin in Colorado and Present Utilization of Same Together With Present and Future Transmountain Diversions," prepared under the direction of M. C. Hinderlider, State Engineer, in cooperation with the Platte Valley Water Conservation League and the U.S. Army Engineers (Denver: 1931), p. 255. The "open cuts" referred to the Grand River Ditch (12,300 af), Church Ditch or Berthoud Pass Diversion (685 af), and the Boreas Pass Diversion from the Blue River (600 af). The report also noted that work was being done on the Grand River Ditch to nearly double the carriage.

28. Ibid., p. 257.

29. Ibid., p. 262.

30. Ibid.

31. Ibid., pp. 266–267. Table 12 on page 266, entitled "Summary Mean Monthly Possible Transmountain Diversions From Upper Colorado River Into South Platte River Basin-Acre-Feet," shows that a total of 491,860 acre-feet could be diverted into the South Platte basin without infringing on existing Colorado River water rights. The totals are as follows: Grand Lake (178,080 af), Grand River Ditch (12,560 af), Fraser River (Moffat Tunnel) (90,450 af), Williams River (25,570 af), and Blue River (185,200 af).

32. *Greeley Tribune*, 15 August 1933.

33. Ibid.

34. *Fort Collins Express-Courier*, 15 August 1933.

35. *Greeley Tribune,* 16 August 1933.

36. Ibid., 18, 19 August 1933.

37. This delegation was made up of Fort Collins city engineer Burgis G. Coy (tunnel expert who had supervised construction of the Moffat Tunnel, the Laramie-Poudre Tunnel, and some New York City subways), T. J. Warren (secretary of the Cache la Poudre Water Users Association), and irrigation engineers A. L. Marhoff and James R. Miller. See *Fort Collins Express-Courier,* 29 August 1933.

38. Ibid., 25 August 1933.

39. Fort Collins only subscribed $750. Some irrigation men were disappointed that $1,000 was not approved. See *Fort Collins Express-Courier,* 7 September 1933.

40. *Greeley Tribune,* 29 August 1933.

41. Colorado, Department of the State Engineer, *Preliminary Engineering Report: Northern Transmountain Diversion,* by Royce J. Tipton (Denver: 1933), p. 1.

42. Ibid., p. 14.

43. Ibid., p. 16.

44. Ibid., p. 18.

CHAPTER 3

1. James F. Wickens, *Colorado in the Great Depression* (New York: Garland, 1979), p. 180.

2. William R. Kelly, "Colorado–Big Thompson Project Initiation," unpublished memorandum, 3 June 1952, p. 10, in "C–BT History" box, NCWCDA. A version of this was published in *Colorado Magazine* 34 (January 1957), pp. 66–74.

3. Wickens, *Colorado in the Great Depression,* p. 180.

4. Ibid., p. 196. Even the Pioneer Bore of the Moffat Tunnel, proposed by the Denver Water Board in July 1933, met the usual delays.

5. "A Conversation with William R. Kelly, Esquire," transcript of interviews with Lee G. Norris, November 3, 1982, p. 188, Professor James E. Hansen II, Colorado State University. According to J. R. Barkley, some of Kelly's trips to Washington were attempts to gain financing for the Laramie-Poudre Irrigation Company and the Greeley-Poudre District. He was Weld County attorney at the time, and the county was in receivership.

6. Articles in the *Greeley Tribune* reported Ickes's opposition to any program of public works involving transmountain diversion because it was against the public interest and because he was against a tunnel under Rocky Mountain National Park. See *Greeley Tribune,* 12, 16 September 1933.

7. Wickens, *Colorado in the Great Depression,* p. 191.

8. Ibid., pp. 40, 70.

9. James E. Hansen II, "Charles A. Lory and the Challenges of Colorado's Semi-Arid Frontier" (Paper presented in San Diego, August 1980, p. 4). Grand Lake Project, Development Correspondence, 1936, in folder dealing with Northern Colorado Water User's Association, NCWCDA.

10. "A Conversation with William R. Kelly," p. 189.

11. Hansen, "Charles A. Lory," p. 5. See also Michael C. Robinson, *Water For The West: The Bureau of Reclamation, 1902–1977* (Chicago: Public Works Historical Society, 1979), p. 45.

12. Letter, 19 February 1935, Elwood Mead to Charles Hansen, Charles Hansen Files, NCWCDA.

13. Letter, 16 May 1934, Charles Lory to Elwood Mead, miscellaneous correspondence in CRWCDA files. Because "Northern [Colorado] Transmountain Diversion" did not locate the project properly, Porter J. Preston, senior engineer for the Bureau of Reclamation in Denver, won approval from

Commissioner Mead to change the name to "Grand Lake–Big Thompson Transmountain Project." See Letter, 20 February 1935, Porter Preston to Charles Hansen, Charles Hansen Files, NCWCDA.

14. Letter, 23 January 1936, Charles Hansen to Fred Cummings, Charles Hansen Files, NCWCDA. Hansen also mentioned his hope that Charles Lory would be considered for commissioner when Mead stepped down.

15. Robinson, *Water For the West*, p. 47.

16. Fred N. Norcross, "Genesis of the Colorado–Big Thompson Project," *Colorado Magazine* 30 (January 1953), p. 32.

17. "Colorado Irrigation Men Bury Ax to Get U.S. Cash," *Rocky Mountain News*, 28 September 1933.

18. Letter, 10 April 1934, Charles Hansen to Walter Walker, editor of the Grand Junction *Sentinel*, NCWCDA. The two sessions of the legislature that Hansen mentioned most likely refer to the "Twiddling Twenty-Ninth," which showed no political leadership, wanted only to balance the budget, and could not locate the matching funds necessary to keep the Federal Emergency Relief Administration (FERA) payments coming into the state. By 1934, when an estimated 250,000 people in Colorado needed some form of financial relief, unemployed men staged two riots in Denver, followed by an invasion of the State Capitol and the Senate chambers, until Governor Ed Johnson finally agreed to a relief bill to raise enough money for FERA payments to continue. See Wickens, *Colorado in the Great Depression*, pp. 61–73.

19. Letter, 10 April 1934, Charles Hansen to Walter Walker, editor of the Grand Junction *Sentinel*, NCWCDA.

20. Telegram, 5 March 1936, Edward T. Taylor to Edward D. Foster, Director, Colorado State Planning Commission, Charles Hansen Files, NCWCDA.

21. *Congressional Record*, 75th Cong., 3d sess., 1938, Appendix, 83, pt. 11:2412. Taylor went on to explain that he doubted the East Slope's ability to match in compensatory reservoir capacity whatever water they might be able to catch and take across the divide in the flood season; but he was more sanguine regarding their ability to match whatever waters they took away in the irrigation season. His 1938 views, however, had mellowed significantly when compared to the hard line he took in 1933. Under the headline "Colorado Irrigation Men Bury Ax to Get U.S. Cash," the *Rocky Mountain News* reported on the terms of the resolution in its September 28, 1933, issue.

22. *Rifle Telegram*, 14 October, 1926.

23. Minutes, NCWUA, April 6, 1934.

24. Memorandum, n.d. Edward D. Foster to Luke J. Kavanaugh, n.d. in Minutes, NCWUA, April 6, 1934. Governor Johnson signed the executive order in accordance with H.B. 394, creating a State Planning Commission and designating the commissioner of the State Board of Immigration, the state engineer, and the state highway engineer as ex officio members of said commission, and providing for the appointment of nine members, who represented the major segments of the state.

25. Richard Lowitt, *The New Deal and the West* (Bloomington: Indiana University Press, 1984), pp. 44, 55, 79.

26. Letter, 30 January 1935, Edward D. Foster to C. A. Watson, Fowler, Colorado, CSPC records, NCWCDA.

27. Letter, 16 January 1936, Edward D. Foster to J. M. Dille, ibid.

28. Report of John T. Barnett, CSPC, written between February 28 and March 17, 1936, Minutes, NCWUA.

29. Letter, 8 June 1936, Edward D. Foster to J. M. Dille, CSPC records, NCWCDA.

30. Letter, 14 January 1936, Edward D. Foster to all Colorado senators and congressmen, ibid.

31. Wickens, *Colorado in the Great Depression*, pp. 40–41.

32. Ibid., p. 32.

33. Ibid., p. 44.

34. Speech of Representative Fred L. Crawford, 1 March 1935, *Congressional Record*, 74th Cong., 1st sess., 1935, 79: 2900. Before moving to Michigan, Crawford lived in Texas, where he engaged in the manufacture and marketing of sugar-beet related products.

35. Speeches of Senator Edward P. Costigan, 11, 12 March 1935, *Congressional Record*, 74th Cong., 1st sess., 1935, 79, pt. 3:3449, 3451, 3358.

36. Notice of the Greeley Chamber of Commerce, n.d., in Minutes, NCWUA, April 6, 1934.

37. Ibid.

38. "NCWUA Articles of Incorporation," NCWCDA. Article 3 provided in part that the purpose of the corporation is to acquire water from natural streams in Colorado, enter into compacts with other water users, negotiate for and obtain moneys from the United States government for "construction of an irrigation works project and to carry water from the Western Slope to the Eastern Slope of the Rocky Mountains in the State of Colorado."

39. Biographical data form prepared by Charles Hansen for the Colorado Historical Society, Denver, on October 6, 1942.

40. *Greeley Tribune*, 10 October 1930.

41. Charles Hansen, "The Greatest Enterprise: The Laramie Poudre Project," *Greeley Tribune*, Great Prosperity edition, 21 October 1908.

42. Ibid.

43. Ibid.

44. *Greeley Tribune*, 25 May 1953.

45. "Charlie Hansen Godfather of Project," *Rocky Mountain News*, 1 November 1955, says that Hansen and Taylor launched their careers together as cub reporters on a Grand Rapids, Michigan, newspaper.

46. Minutes, NCWUA, May 4, 1935.

47. Letters, 10, 19 May 1935, Charles Hansen to Fred Cummings, and telegram, 15 May 1935, Charles Hansen to Fred Norcross, in "Washington trip re appropriations, May, June and July 1937 and May 1935" folder, NCWCDA.

48. Donald C. Swain, "The National Park Service and the New Deal, 1933–1940," *Pacific Historical Review* 41 (August 1972), p. 314.

49. Ibid., pp. 315, 319.

50. Letter, 22 March 1935, A. E. Demaray to Committee, Bureau of Reclamation, in "Northern Colorado Water Users Association" box in "Grand Lake Project" folder, NCWCDA.

51. Swain, "The National Park Service and the New Deal," p. 322. The Federal Water Power Act is 14 Stat. 1353.

52. Letter, 2 April 1935, Thomas A. Nixon to the NCWUA, in "Thomas A. Nixon" folder in "Administration, C–BT Construction" document drawer, NCWCDA. The act creating Rocky Mountain National Park is 38 Stat. 690.

53. *Statutes at Large*, Chap. 19, Sec. 1, Vol. 38 p. 798, Act of January 26, 1915. The solicitor general agreed with Nixon's assessment of the situation in an opinion rendered on July 19, 1935.

54. Minutes, NCWUA, April 15, 1935.

55. Letter, 6 May 1935, Alva Adams to Charles Hansen, Charles Hansen Files, NCWCDA.

56. William R. Kelly, "Colorado–Big Thompson Initiation, 1933–1938," *Colorado Magazine* 34 (January 1957), p. 73. It should be noted that Hansen had made a second trip to Washington in June to attend a hearing called by Secretary Ickes regarding the objections of the NPS. Finally, Ickes agreed to let the Bureau proceed as long as issues were worked out satisfactorily with the NPS. See Minutes, NCWUA, July 6, 1935.

57. Report, Water Resources Advisory Committee, June 15, 1935, Charles Hansen Files, NCWCDA. The Committee of Seventeen represented both slopes of Colorado: from the West Slope (J. A. Clay, Durango; George J. Bailey, Walden; Milton Welch, Delta; F. I. Huntington, Hot Sulphur Springs; D. W. Aupperle, Grand Junction; Frank Delaney, Glenwood Springs; Clifford Stone, Gunnison); from the East Slope (Charles M. Rolfson, Julesburg; Charles Hansen, Greeley; A. D. Wall, Denver; Malcolm Lindsey, Denver; M. M. Simpson, McClave; John W. Beatty, Manzanola; D. H. Ernest, Trinidad); and from the San Luis Valley (Ralph Carr, Antonito; John I. Palmer, Saguache). Royce J. Tipton represented the state engineer and S. P. Howell represented the attorney general.

58. Phyllis Kaplan, *Guide to the Frank L. Delaney Papers, 1914–1978*, ed. John A. Brennan (Boulder: Western Historical Collections, University Libraries, University of Colorado, 1985). Pages ix and x provide a brief biographical sketch.

59. Resolution 1, presented by Frank Delaney, Glenwood Springs, as printed in Minutes of Board Meetings, 1935–1938, NCWCDA.

60. In an angry telegram dated March 5, 1936, Taylor accused the State Planning Commission of abandoning the September 27, 1933, agreement. "If the Eastern Slope people had frankly kept their agreement," Taylor said, "Colorado's water development would have been advanced more than a year. . . . You people now repudiate your agreements so that no 'understandings' about future understandings will be considered by me at all." See Charles Hansen Files, NCWCDA. Foster's moderated response by mail explained the Commission's even-handed approach to all water projects. 6 March 1936, ibid.

61. Letter, 11 March 1936, Frank Delaney to Dan Hughes, Montrose, Delaney Papers, CRWCDA.

62. Resolution 17, presented by Charles Hansen, Greeley, as printed in Minutes of Board Meetings, NCWUA, July 6, 1935, NCWCDA.

63. Minutes, June 13, 1935, Water Resources Advisory Committee, Charles Hansen Files, NCWCDA.

64. Letter, Edward T. Taylor to the *Grand Junction Sentinel*, 23 December 1935, Charles Hansen Files, NCWCDA.

65. Letter, 28 September 1936, NCWUA to Carl R. Gray, President, Union Pacific Railroad, Charles Hansen Files, NCWCDA.

66. Letter, 24 December 1935, Charles Lory to Charles Hansen, Charles Hansen Files, NCWCDA.

67. Telegram, 8 January 1936, Alva Adams to Edward D. Foster, in "C–BT History" box, NCWCDA. Adams further informed Foster that the Colorado delegation favored efforts to "furnish the necessary supporting data in order that we may, in so far as possible, meet the executive requirements."

68. Letter (unsigned), 21 January 1936, Charles Hansen to Edward T. Taylor, Charles Hansen Files, NCWCDA.

69. Letter, 15 January 1936, Edward T. Taylor to Edward D. Foster, in "Grand Lake Project: Development Correspondence, 1936" folder, NCWCDA.

70. Minutes, NCWUA, February 1, 1936, in "Minutes of NCWUA Board Meetings, 1935–1938" notebook, NCWCDA.

71. Letter, 21 February 1936, Edward T. Taylor to D. W. Aupperle, CRWCDA.

72. *Congressional Record*, 74th Cong., 2d sess., 1936, 80, pt. 3:2900–2901.

73. The Gila River project required withdrawal of 2,000,000 acre-feet of water per year from the mainstream of the Colorado River, taken from the east end of the Imperial Dam of the All-American Canal for the irrigation of 585,000 acres of land in the valley of the Gila River. Total cost was estimated at $80,000,000. See ibid., 80, pt. 9:9390.

74. Ibid., 80, pt. 3:3341. Two months later, Taber asked: "Should we not stop the expenditures for these tremendous items? The Grand Lake–Big Thompson Project . . . will probably run $35–$40 million and has never been properly investigated by even the Bureau of Reclamation. . . . Why

should we authorize something that the Secretary of Interior himself says we should not embark on unless he has the discretion to stop it?" Ibid., 80, pt. 7:7640.

75. Telegram, 5 March 1936, Edward T. Taylor to Edward D. Foster, Charles Hansen Files, NCWCDA.

76. Telegram, 4 March 1936, Fred Cummings to Charles Hansen, Charles Hansen Files, NCWCDA.

77. Colorado, House Joint Resolution 1, signed March 31, 1936, printed in *Senate Journal of the Second Extraordinary Session of the Thirtieth Legislature*, pp. 56–58.

78. In a letter to Charles Hansen dated June 5, 1936, Edward D. Foster mentions having received this information from Senator Adams. Charles Hansen Files, NCWCDA.

79. *Congressional Record,* 74th Cong., 1st sess., 1936, 80, pt. 9.

80. The name change was not officially accepted in Congress until the Senate Committee on Irrigation and Reclamation reported back S. 2681 with a proposed amendment that "Colorado" be inserted in place of "Grand Lake." This insertion was agreed to. See *Congressional Record*, 75th Cong., 1st sess., 1937, 81, pt. 6:6293.

81. As reported by Bureau engineer R. J. Tipton to Charles Hansen after returning to Colorado from a trip to Washington. See Minutes, NCWUA, November 7, 1936.

82. Letter, 16 November 1936, Alva Adams to Ebert K. Burlew, Administrative Assistant and Budget Officer, Department of the Interior, Charles Hansen Files, NCWCDA. Adams admitted that his information came from a citizen of northern Colorado. He wrote Burlew, who he said was the most influential man in the Department of the Interior next to Ickes, asking if inquiries could be made about the foundation of this report.

83. Minutes, NCWUA, September 19, 1936.

84. U.S. House of Representatives, *A History of the Committee on Appropriations, House of Representatives,* by Edward T. Taylor, 77th Cong., 1st sess., H.D. 299, p. 72.

85. Letter, 13 April 1937, Fred Cummings to Charles Hansen, Charles Hansen Files, NCWCDA. Taylor was, in fact, getting quite sick at this point. His doctor had told him to "stay out of all hearings that would tend in any way to cause him to become excited." 29 April 1937, ibid.

86. Letter, 20 April and 4 May 1937, Fred Cummings to Charles Hansen, Charles Hansen Files, NCWCDA.

CHAPTER 4

1. Report of the State Planning Commission, January 1, 1936, Charles Hansen Files, NCWCDA.

2. *Session Laws of Colorado,* 1935, Ch. 145, Sec. 3 (b) (6) S.B. 116. The bill provides that the District should be divided "as nearly as possible" into three subdivisions "so that the population within each subdivision shall be as nearly as possible equal to that of each of the other subdivisions within the District."

3. Ibid., Sec. 5.

4. Ibid., Sec. 8.

5. Letter, 31 January 1936, Spencer L. Baird to Edward D. Foster, Director, Colorado State Planning Commission, Charles Hansen Files, NCWCDA.

6. Letter, 21 January 1936, Charles Hansen to Congressman Edward T. Taylor, Charles Hansen Files, NCWCDA.

7. Memorandum, 10 January 1936, Ray F. Walter to Edward D. Foster, J. M. Dille, R. J. Tipton, and Malcolm Lindsey, in "State Planning Commission" folder, NCWCDA.

8. Letter, 14 January 1936, Edward D. Foster to all Colorado senators and congressmen, in "State Planning Commission" folder, NCWCDA.

9. Letter, 2 February 1937, Charles Hansen to Carl Gray, Charles Hansen Files, NCWCDA. The railroads took a special interest in this matter because they were property owners in the proposed district where taxes would increase if the proposed district contracted to build the Colorado–Big Thompson Project.

10. William R. Kelly, "Colorado–Big Thompson Project Initiation," speech given June 3, 1952, pp. 22–23. Copy in the author's possession.

11. *People ex rel. Rogers, Atty. Gen.* v. *Letford et al.*, No. 14254, Supreme Court of Colorado, in 79 *Pacific Reporter*, 2d series, p. 280.

12. Ibid., p. 281.

13. Ibid., p. 282. Specific citations for these acts are as follows: Metropolitan Water Districts Act, *Utah Session Laws*, 1935, Ch. 110; Metropolitan Water Districts Act and California Bridges and Highway Districts Act, *California Amended Statutes*, 1929, p. 1613. See William R. Kelly, "Water Conservancy Districts (Quasi-Municipal Corporations With General Taxing Powers)," *Rocky Mountain Law Review* 22 (1950), p. 437, n. 7.

14. *Rocky Mountain Law Review* 22 (1950), p. 440, n. 7a.

15. Recollections of William Kelly, in "C–BT Project Initiation, William Kelly" folder in "C–BT History" box, NCWCDA. The Water Conservancy District Act is officially H.B. 714 (*Session Laws of Colorado*, 1937, Ch. 266).

16. *Session Laws of Colorado*, 1937, Ch. 266, pp. 1309–1359.

17. Ibid., Sec. 4. The legislature later changed these provisions to a $200,000 total of irrigated land valuation on a petition signed by 25 percent of the irrigated landowners and 5 percent of the nonirrigated landowners. See *Session Laws of Colorado*, 1939, Ch. 174, and *Session Laws of Colorado*, 1949, Ch. 250.

18. Ibid., Sec. 3.

19. Ibid., Sec. 7.

20. In civil law, a quo warranto suit is a legal proceeding brought by the sovereign in which a person or corporation must show by what authority he or it holds office. The proceedings in which the Colorado Supreme Court upheld the legality of the Northern Colorado Water Conservancy District were entitled *People ex rel. Rogers* v. *Letford* (102 Colo. 284, 79 P.2d 279 [1938]). The suit was filed on November 6, 1937, and on May 2, 1938, the demurrer of the relator was overruled and the writ discharged.

21. *Session Laws of Colorado*, 1937. Ch. 266, Sec. 25.

22. Statement by Frank Delaney, in stenographic notes of the Minutes of the WSPA, March 24, 1937, CRWCDA. Delaney further noted that while he favored Denver having adequate water for domestic purposes without the requirement of compensatory storage, "they are now filing decrees for municipal, agricultural, and industrial uses, and we are now in court with them. In addition, they are making claims on the Blue River."

23. Letter, November 1934, Edward T. Taylor to D. W. Aupperle, CRWCDA. The full text of this paragraph reads as follows:

    I am more positive than ever that our only salvation in our fight with eastern Colorado is to make a defiant and determined stand on the proposition of their building and maintaining compensatory reservoirs and not permit any subterfuge to sidestep that. It is a subterfuge for them to talk about making Grand Lake a storage reservoir. They very adroitly are scheming to avoid spending any money to build reservoirs for us, and I am going to very vehemently insist in Washington that that Board [PWA Board] must recognize and adher [sic] to it, before the Government puts any money into those blue sky transmountain diversion promotion schemes.

24. Letter, May 1936, D. W. Aupperle to County Clerks of 21 western Colorado counties, CRWCDA. In a letter to the author, February 5, 1988, Lee Harris, CRWCD public affairs consultant, states

that his archives contain no information on the WSPA from its initial meeting on June 29, 1933, until the meeting on April 27, 1934.

25. Letter, 29 April 1933, D. W. Aupperle to Edward T. Taylor, CRWCDA.

26. President D. W. Aupperle of the WSPA called this matter to the attention of the WSPA directors, noting that even after constant urging by the county commissioners to get all water rights on the West Slope established and fixed "at the highest possible duty, very little has been done." He suggested making an abstract of all filings in the state engineer's office, followed by a classification as to their current status. "The facts which such records will disclose," said Aupperle, "will no doubt show the Eastern Slope people that liberal provision for replacement storage must be made for their own protection if they expect to be benefitted by diversion works." See letter 18 December 1934, CRWCDA. A year later Aupperle was still urging his people to adjudicate their water rights. See letter, 2 January 1936, Aupperle to WSPA "NCWUA," NCWCDA.

27. Minutes, NCWUA, April 6, 1934.

28. Letter, 21 April 1934, Charles Hansen to D. W. Aupperle, CRWCDA.

29. Minutes, NCWUA, April 6, 1934.

30. Letter, 10 April 1934, Charles Hansen to D. W. Aupperle, CRWCDA.

31. Letter, 14 April 1934, Walter Walker to D. W. Aupperle, CRWCDA.

32. Letter, 14 April 1934, Walter Walker to Charles Hansen, CRWCDA. As already noted in Chapter 1, Hinderlider also created controversy on the East Slope when he ordered an end to filling reservoirs in 1933 due to the extreme drought.

33. Letter, 17 April 1934, D. W. Aupperle to Edward T. Taylor, CRWCDA.

34. Letter, 17 April 1934, D. W. Aupperle to Charles Hansen, CRWCDA. Aupperle was probably referring to Article 3 of the 1922 Colorado River Compact in which 7.5 million acre-feet of water per annum were apportioned to both the upper and lower basin of the river. He was concerned about what might happen in a dry year if the lower basin did not receive its apportionment. The compact can be found in H.D. 605, 67th Cong., 4th sess., pp. 7–12.

35. Letter, 21 April 1934, Charles Hansen to D. W. Aupperle, CRWCDA.

36. Letter, 23 April 1934, Charles Hansen to J. M. Dille, "Northern Colorado Water Users Association," NCWCDA.

37. Letter, 30 April 1934, Charles Hansen to D. W. Aupperle, CRWCDA.

38. Ibid.

39. Letters, 5, 6 May 1934, Charles Hansen to J. M. Dille and Dille to Hansen, "Northern Colorado Water Users Association," NCWCDA. Dille reported that while he found Silmon Smith "passively favorable" to the Project, he needed evidence proving that clear water rather than silt could be stored in the compensatory reservoirs. He also met with Aupperle, who reiterated his mistrust of State Engineer Hinderlider. Lunching at the Lion's Club in Grand Junction, Dille was introduced as a "man stealing our water." In Glenwood Springs he contacted Frank Delaney, who was "friendly but non-committal."

40. Letter, 30 April 1934, Charles Hansen to D. W. Aupperle, CRWCDA.

41. Letter, 21 May 1934, D. W. Aupperle to Edward T. Taylor, CRWCDA.

42. Minutes, meeting of the Colorado Delegation on Colorado River Matters, June 28, 1934, Frank Delaney Papers, Norlin Library, University of Colorado, Boulder, Colorado.

43. Resolution, June 30, 1934, Charles Hansen Files, NCWCDA. "Northern Colorado Water Users Association," NCWCDA. Minutes, WSPA, December 28, 1934, Delaney Papers, Norlin Library, University of Colorado, Boulder, Colorado. Article 5 of the 1922 Colorado River Compact obligated the state engineer, in cooperation with the Bureau of Reclamation and the Geological Survey, to determine the "flow appropriation, consumption and use of water in the Colorado River Basin." This mandate was spelled out further in the 1929 Boulder Canyon Act. See Note 56 in this chapter.

44. Letter, 16 November 1934, D. W. Aupperle to Directors of the WSPA, CRWCDA.

45. President Aupperle, Secretary Silmon Smith, Senator Roy Chapman, Engineer F. C. Merriell, County Commissioners John Heuschkel and C. G. Kendall (acting on behalf of Frank Delaney), James F. Shults, and Directors Frank I. Huntington, B. M. Long, and M. R. Welch were present. See Minutes, November 27, 1934, WSPA, CRWCDA.

46. Ibid.

47. Ibid.

48. Ibid.

49. Letter, 18 December 1934, D. W. Aupperle to Directors of the WSPA, CRWCDA. Aupperle states that Colorado had never received money for these kinds of projects. Both the Caddoa Dam and Rio Grande projects were less likely to be funded; thus, "The Grand Lake Diversion Project" appeared to be in the most favorable position. Furthermore, except for Taylor, Colorado's delegation in Washington was in favor, as was the assistant secretary of the interior and Colorado's own Josephine Roche (the first woman assistant secretary of the treasury), "who isn't a 'dead one' either."

50. Ibid.

51. Minutes, WSPA meeting, December 28, 1934, CRWCDA.

52. Ibid. Of this sum, Aupperle said that it was "neither ample nor appropriate," but he agreed to continue on for another thirty days. The WSPA also organized an executive committee (not named) to work with the president and secretary for the financial stability of the organization.

53. Minutes, January 28, 1935, WSPA, CRWCDA.

54. Ibid.

55. Minutes, January 29, 1935, WSPA, CRWCDA. President Aupperle pointed out that "it should be realized by western Colorado that we furnish from western Colorado 65 percent of all the water passing Lee Ferry, and that our best safeguard is to have the water definitely not only used but decreed."

56. Section 15 of the Boulder Canyon Project Act provided that

    The Secretary of the Interior is authorized and directed to make investigation and public reports of the feasibility of projects for irrigation, generation of electric power, and other purposes in the States of Arizona, Nevada, Colorado, New Mexico, Utah, and Wyoming for the purpose of making such information available to said States and to the Congress, and of formulating a comprehensive scheme of control and the improvement and utilization of the water of the Colorado River and its tributaries. The sum of $250,000 is hereby authorized to be appropriated from said Colorado River Dam fund, created by Sec. 2 of this Act, for such purposes.

    See *Statutes at Large,* Vol. 45, Part 1, p. 1065.

57. See letter, 2 April 1935, Edward T. Taylor to Secretary Ickes, Charles Hansen Files, NCWCDA, in which he mentioned two speeches he had made on this subject that were printed in the Congressional Record. Letter, 3 July 1934, Michael C. Hinderlider to various people, Charles Hansen Files, NCWCDA.

58. Letter, 9 August 1935, R. F. Walter, Chief Engineer of the Denver Bureau of Reclamation, to Charles Hansen, Charles Hansen Files, NCWCDA. Reference is to the solicitor general's opinion of July 19, 1935.

59. Letter, 20 August 1935, Charles Lory to Ralph Parshall, Senior Engineer, Charles Hansen Files, NCWCDA.

60. Mimeographed letter, 27 November 1935, N. R. McCreery, District Manager of Great Western Sugar Company, to Colorado managers, Charles Hansen Files, NCWCDA.

61. Minutes, WSPA, March 20, 1935, CRWCDA.

62. Letter, 19 December 1935, Edward D. Foster to D. W. Aupperle, CRWCDA.

63. Minutes, Statewide Water Conference, Grand Junction, February 27, 28, 1936, Delaney Papers, Norlin Library, University of Colorado, Boulder, Colorado.

64. Letter, 21 February 1936, Edward T. Taylor to D. W. Aupperle, Delaney Papers, Norlin Library, University of Colorado, Boulder, Colorado.

65. Article 3, Draft Resolution, 1934, Charles Hansen Files, NCWCDA.

66. U.S. Senate, "Synopsis of Report on Colorado–Big Thompson Project, Plan of Development and Cost Estimate Prepared by the Bureau of Reclamation, Department of the Interior," 75th Cong., 1st sess., June 15, 1937. (Cited hereafter as S.D. 80.) Section 5 (i) was reinterpreted in Section 501 (e) of the Colorado River Basin Project Act and signed by President Lyndon B. Johnson on September 30, 1968. The wording in this statute recognized the applicability of the doctrine of prior appropriation to the construction of future West Slope projects authorized in this legislation or in the 1956 Colorado River Storage Project Act. A fuller account of this matter can be found in Part IV, Chapter 18.

67. Deposition of Silmon Smith, Grand Junction, Colorado, November 3, 1961, in the matter of U.S. District Court, Civil Nos. 2782, 5016, 5017, NCWCDA. Stanley W. Cazier of Granby, Colorado, called this document to my attention.

68. Letter, 11 March 1936, Frank Delaney to Dan Hughes, Delaney Papers, Norlin Library, University of Colorado, Boulder, Colorado.

69. Letter, 22 July 1936, Edward T. Taylor to D. W. Aupperle, CRWCDA.

70. Letter (unsigned copy), 24 December 1936, Frank Delaney to Thomas A. Nixon, Charles Hansen Files, NCWCDA.

71. Memorandum, 3–4 January 1937, Denver, Shirley-Savoy Hotel conference, Charles Hansen Files, NCWCDA.

72. Minutes, meeting of March 24, 1937, Directors of the WSPA, County Commissioners of western Colorado, and other interested water users and citizens, Grand Junction. These stenographic minutes constitute forty-seven pages of text available in the Delaney Papers, Norlin Library, University of Colorado, Boulder, Colorado, and in the CRWCDA. Further citations by Delaney in the text of this chapter are taken from these same minutes.

73. Letter, 17 March 1937, Charles Hansen to Fred Cummings, NCWCDA. Dille made his remarks after the March 24 meeting. See letter, 31 May 1937, J. M. Dille to Charles Hansen, Charles Hansen Files, NCWCDA.

74. Minutes, March 24, 1937, Delaney Papers, Norlin Library, University of Colorado, Boulder, Colorado.

75. Ibid. As special representative of the Grand County Natural Resources Association, Breeze carried Grand County's complaints to Greeley and to Washington. He fought hard for adequate compensation for the loss of tax revenues that resulted from building C–BT reservoirs. In an interview with the author in 1988, he remembered Hansen, Dille, and Nixon as fair and honest negotiators.

76. Ibid.

77. Minutes, NCWUA, April 3, 1937, NCWCDA.

78. Letter, 26 April 1937, J. M. Dille to Edward D. Foster, State Planning Commission Files, NCWCDA. Dille reported that the Bureau had completed the surveys for the Colorado–Big Thompson Project and had found everything practical and feasible. The Project had received approval by the National Resources Committee and was recommended to President Roosevelt.

79. Telegram, 27 May 1937, Charles Hansen to J. M. Dille, NCWCDA. Breeze came to believe that the agreement with the East Slope was a good one, but in 1988 he spoke strongly against the proposed Two Forks project on the South Platte. Interview, Carl Breeze, 25 June 1988.

80. Letter, 7 April and 7 May 1937, Fred Cummings to Charles Hansen, Charles Hansen Files, NCWCDA.

81. Letter, 19 May 1937, Charles Hansen to J. M. Dille, in "Washington Trip re Appropriations, May, June, and July 1937 and May 1935" folder, NCWCDA.

82. Letter, 4 June 1937, Charles Hansen to J. M. Dille, ibid. This controversy was ultimately settled by the language in S.D. 80 that allowed the secretary of the interior to make a ruling after the C–BT had been in operation for a while. This ruling came in the form of a "Fish Release Schedule," 1961.

83. *Session Laws of Colorado*, 1937, Ch. 265, pp. 1300–1308.

84. Ibid., Ch. 220, pp. 997–1030.

85. Statement of Accounts, WSPA, September 24, 1938, showing the life of the WSPA from June 19, 1933, to August 11, 1938, CRWCDA.

86. Letter, 6 June 1937, Thomas A. Nixon to J. M. Dille, NCWCDA.

87. Telegram, 12 June 1937, Charles Hansen to J. M. Dille, NCWCDA.

CHAPTER 5

1. Ironically, on July 22, 1937, the same day that S. 2681 (the authorization bill for the Colorado–Big Thompson Project) was debated in the House of Representatives, the Senate "recommitted the original [Supreme Court] reorganization bill to the Judiciary Committee where it died." See Richard B. Morris, *Encyclopedia of American History*, rev. ed. (New York: Harper and Row, 1965), p. 357.

2. Letters, 20 April and 7 May 1937, Fred Cummings to Charles Hansen, Charles Hansen Files, NCWCDA.

3. Letter, 6 May 1937, Ed Johnson to Charles Hansen, ibid.

4. During the July 22, 1937, debate in the House on the addition of $900,000 for the C–BT in the Interior Department appropriation bill, Congressman Robert F. Rich of Pennsylvania challenged the Democrats by pointing out that FDR had asked Congress to cut down on expenses while spending $10.4 million a day more than was spent in 1936. See *Congressional Record*, 72nd Cong., 1st sess., 75, pt. 6:7413. As late as December 16, 1937, Secretary Manager F. O. Hagie of the National Reclamation Association noted in a letter to Clifford Stone that there was an "economy move" and a "broad, general desire to balance the budget" in Washington. See Charles Hansen Files, NCWCDA.

5. Telegram, 12 June 1937, Charles Hansen to J. M. Dille, in "Washington Trip, re Appropriations, May, June, and July 1937 and May 1935" folder, NCWCDA.

6. U.S. Department of the Interior, "Synopsis of Report On Colorado–Big Thompson Project, Plan of Development and Cost Estimate Prepared by the Bureau of Reclamation, Department of the Interior," presented by Mr. Adams, 75th Cong. 1st sess., June 15, 1937, S.D. 80.

7. *Congressional Record*, 75th Cong., 1st sess., 81, pt. 6:5953.

8. This was "An Act making appropriations for the Department of the Interior for the fiscal year ending June 30, 1938, and for other purposes" (50 Stat. 564), which appropriated $900,000 for the C–BT. Adams was afraid that the C–BT funds would get knocked out of this appropriation bill if the C–BT lacked legislative authorization. Hansen made the same point in a letter to J. M. Dille, saying that Adams feared that the appropriation might be ruled out on a "point of order that the project was not authorized." See letter, 24 June 1937, Charles Hansen to J. M. Dille, Charles Hansen Files, NCWCDA.

9. *Congressional Record*, 75th Cong., 1st sess., 81, pt. 10: 1725.

10. Ibid., pt. 6:6016, 6293. The Senate Committee on Irrigation and Reclamation reported S. 2681 with its Report No. 775.

11. As reported by Charles Hansen in a letter to Dille, June 24, 1937, NCWCDA.

12. The House Committee on Irrigation and Reclamation reported S. 2681 favorably with its Report No. 1180, July 6, 1937, noting that the Senate had passed an amendment to the Interior

Department appropriation bill in the 74th Congress, but the House had rejected the amendment because of the lack of agreement between East and West Slopes.

13. Letter, 1 July 1937, Charles Hansen to J. M. Dille, NCWCDA.

14. Letter, n.d., J. M. Dille to Charles Hansen, Charles Hansen Files, NCWCDA.

15. *Congressional Record*, 75th Cong., 1st sess., 81, pt. 10:1722.

16. Ibid., p. 1725.

17. Letter, 12 July 1937, Charles Hansen to J. M. Dille, NCWCDA.

18. Ibid., 10 July 1937. Although Hansen said that an agreement had been reached between the NPS and the Bureau (discussed later in this chapter), his frustration with 1930s "environmentalists" showed when he referred to the park attorneys, including Ed Taylor's son, as a group that did not "know a water right from a side of bacon." Also, the head of the Natural Resources Committee was one of FDR's relatives, Frederick A. Delano.

19. *Congressional Record*, 75th Cong., 1st sess., 81, pt. 7:7414.

20. Ibid., p. 7410.

21. Ibid., pp. 7408–7409.

22. Ibid., p. 7412.

23. Ibid., p. 7415.

24. *Statutes at Large*, Vol. 50, Part I, p. 564.

25. John Marr Dille, *A Brief History of Northern Colorado Water Conservancy District and the Colorado–Big Thompson Project* (Loveland, Colo.: NCWCD, 1958), p. 20.

26. *United States Code*, title 16, sec. 191, being Chap. 19, sec. 1 of 38 Stat. 798.

27. Letter, 16 November 1937, Walter Woodman Wright to Senator Bankhead, Legislative Files, House and Senate Committees on Irrigation and Reclamation, 75th Cong., 1st sess. Other letters echoing the same theme came from the Pennsylvania Federation of Sportsmen's Clubs, June 19, 1937; the Robert E. Farley Organization, June 26, 1937; the Dublin New Hampshire Garden Club, July 8, 1937; and the American Planning and Civic Association, June 19, 1937.

28. Ibid., the author's summary of many letters.

29. House of Representatives, *Hearings Before the Committee of Irrigation and Reclamation, on S. 2681*, 75th Cong., 1st sess., 30 June and 2 July 1937, p. 58.

30. Ibid., p. 62.

31. Ibid., pp. 66–68.

32. Letter, 12 October 1937, Harold Ickes to Charles Hansen, Charles Hansen Files, NCWCDA. Under the terms of the Reclamation Act, June 17, 1902, the secretary of the interior, not Congress, had complete power to approve or disapprove reclamation projects. See *Statutes at Large*, Vol. 32, Part I, pp. 388–390.

33. Letter, 3 July 1937, Charles Hansen to J. M. Dille, NCWCDA.

34. Letter, 9 July 1937, John C. Page to Fred Cummings, Charles Hansen Files, NCWCDA. It was also agreed that "if and when the owners of the Grand River Ditch so desired, the project will transport the water of this ditch through the tunnel and thus permit the elimination of this canal from the Park."

35. *Hearing before the Secretary of the Interior on the Colorado–Big Thompson Water Diversion Project, Colorado. 1937.*

36. Ibid.

37. Ibid. Ickes's dilemma was no less agonizing than that of Governor Roy Romer of Colorado in June 1988. After committing himself to a successful campaign for the construction of a new airport in Adams County, Romer had three weeks to decide whether or not to approve the Two Forks Dam project on the South Platte. He made his decision in the face of conflicting advice, overwhelming amounts of data, and strongly worded arguments both in favor — from such diverse groups as the

Denver Water Board and the NCWCD — and against — from groups such as the National Audubon Society and Sierra Club. See Daniel Tyler, "Big Thompson to Two Forks," *Rocky Mountain News,* 26 June 1988.

38. Letter, 16 December 1937, F. O. Hagie, Secretary Manager of the National Reclamation Association to Clifford Stone, Charles Hansen Files, NCWCDA. The letter states that Ickes would send a letter of justification to the president "at an opportune time" and that his delay was because Roosevelt was "greatly disturbed over the Japanese situation and over the conduct of Congress." "Colorado–Big Thompson Project Comparison of 1937 and 1947 Plans and Costs," by Bureau, 1947, Charles Hansen Files, NCWCDA, comparing the years 1937 and 1947, notes that President Roosevelt approved the finding of feasibility on December 21, 1937. Ickes himself, in a December 28, 1937, statement to Congress, noted that the finding of feasibility was the "final step preliminary to the start of construction." See *Congressional Record,* 75th Cong., 3rd sess., 83, pt. 9:6.

39. Article 2, Sec. 3, Colorado Water Conservancy District Law (*Session Laws of Colorado,* 1937, Ch. 266), H.B. No. 714. Additional quotes in this paragraph are from Sections 4–8.

40. Dille, *A Brief History,* p. 24.

41. Letter, 26 June 1937, J. M. Dille to Charles Hansen, Charles Hansen Files, NCWCDA.

42. Letter, n.d., J. M. Dille to Charles Hansen, Charles Hansen Files, NCWCDA. Letter, 2 July 1937, J. M. Dille to Charles Hansen, in "Administration, C-BT Construction" drawer, NCWCDA.

43. Letter, 10 June 1937, J. M. Dille to Charles Hansen, Charles Hansen Files, NCWCDA. Dille praises Lory in this letter. Attorney William R. Kelly remembered the "outstanding service" of several Greeley Chamber of Commerce men, especially Farr and Smith, in Brief Statement by Kelly to George Irvin, President of the Chamber of Commerce, August 14, 1940, in Charles Hansen Files, NCWCDA.

44. Letter, 12 June 1937, J. M. Dille to Charles Hansen, Charles Hansen Files, NCWCDA.

45. Letter, n.d., J. M. Dille to Charles Hansen, ibid.

46. Letter, 16 June 1937, J. M. Dille to Charles Hansen, ibid.

47. Letter, 2 June 1937, J. M. Dille to attorney Tom Nixon, in "Washington Trip, re appropriations May, June, and July 1937 and May 1935" folder, NCWCDA.

48. Ibid.

49. Telegrams, 4 June 1937, Thomas A. Nixon to J. M. Dille and Charles Hansen to Dille, ibid.

50. Letter, 4 June 1937, Charles Hansen to J. M. Dille, ibid.

51. Letter, 6 June 1937, Thomas A. Nixon to J. M. Dille, ibid.

52. Minutes, June 5, 1937, NCWUA, NCWCDA. The town of Platteville was included in the original court order.

53. Minutes, November 6, 1937, and February 5, 1938, NCWUA, NCWCDA.

54. Minutes, May 1, 1937, NCWUA, NCWCDA.

55. Letter, 2 June 1937, J. M. Dille to Thomas A. Nixon, in "Washington Trip re appropriations, May, June and July 1937 and May 1935" folder, NCWCDA.

56. Dille, *A Brief History,* p. 24.

57. Ibid.

58. Petition to the District Court of Weld County, July 19, 1937, regarding the matter of the Northern Colorado Water Conservancy District, in "Fred Cummings" folder, NCWCDA.

59. Letter, 22 November 1937, Thomas A. Nixon to Charles Hansen, in "Thomas A. Nixon" folder, NCWCDA.

60. Minutes, September 29, 1937, NCWUA, NCWCDA.

61. Ibid.

62. The last entry of the NCWUA minutes is dated July 5, 1938, when the association assigned maps and statements on Lake Granby and the C–BT, along with its right, title, and interest in all water

appropriations, to the United States. See Minutes, July 5, 1938, NCWUA, NCWCDA. The NCWUA continued on the District's books until March 1953, when as part of a new accounting policy, the Board voted to remove it from the records. In 1955 Norcross mistakenly wrote that he was still secretary of the NCWUA, although activities had ceased with the signing of the Repayment Contract. See Fred N. Norcross, "Genesis of the Colorado–Big Thompson Project," *Colorado Magazine* 30 (January 1955), p. 37.

63. Minutes, NCWCD, March 21, 28, 29, 1938.

64. Charles A. Lory participated in seventy-two formal hearings and thirty special conferences arranged by this commission, which was organized by Secretary Ickes on November 30, 1937. The objective was to develop ways to make loans and to repay them without repeating the high rate of default that occurred in the 1920s. See James E. Hansen II, "Charles A. Lory and the Challenges of Colorado's Semi-Arid Frontier" (Paper presented at the Pacific Coast Branch meeting of the Organization of American Historians, San Diego, August 1980). Hansen refers to an article by John C. Page in *Reclamation Era* 27 (December 1937).

65. Letter, 5 December 1938, Robert G. Smith to Ralph G. Crosman, University of Colorado, NCWCDA. The author discusses the possibility of giving an honorary degree to Nixon, whose role was vital in drawing up this contract. "I am informed," wrote Smith, "that the Interior Department is using it as a basis for similar projects in the other states of the Union."

66. Letter and memorandum, 8 May 1938, Royce J. Tipton to Charles Hansen, Charles Hansen Files, NCWCDA.

67. Minutes, NCWCD, May 23, 1938. In the minutes of June 20, 1938, eight days before the special election, Dille noted that the District's share of construction costs had been "reduced" to $22 million and that "in no event can the District's costs under the contract exceed $25,000,000."

68. Letter, 23 June 1939, Royce J. Tipton to Charles Hansen, Charles Hansen Files, NCWCDA.

69. Dille, *A Brief History*, p. 27.

70. "Contract Between the United States and Northern Colorado Water Conservancy District, Providing For the Construction of Lake Granby, Continental Tunnel, and Related Works." Contract ILR-1051, NCWCDA.

71. Minutes, NCWCD, July 5, 1938.

72. Ibid.

73. *Congressional Record*, 75th Cong., 3d sess., 83, pt. 6:6876, 7713, and pt. 7:8323. The exact wording was: "That the excess land provisions of the Federal reclamation laws shall not be applicable to lands which now have an irrigation water supply from sources other than a Federal reclamation project and which will receive a supplemental supply from the Colorado–Big Thompson project." In *Rivers of Empire* (New York: Pantheon Books, 1985), Donald Worster shows how the 160-acre limitation was also removed or circumvented in other Bureau of Reclamation projects. See pp. 173, 212, 289, 294, 302.

74. *Congressional Record*, 75th Cong., 3d sess., 83, pt. 7:7215, 8459, and pt. 8:8832, 9131–9132, 9346, 9352, 9545.

75. Letter, 12 February 1938, Fred Cummings to Charles Hansen, Charles Hansen Files, NCWCDA.

76. Ibid., 19 February 1938.

77. *Congressional Record*, 75th Cong., 3rd sess., 83, pt. 11:2412.

78. Letter, 21 December 1940, Charles Hansen to Edward T. Taylor, in "Edward T. Taylor" folder, NCWCDA.

79. Letter, 26 June 1941, Edward T. Taylor to Charles Hansen, Charles Hansen Files, NCWCDA. Hansen accepted this responsibility in a very personal manner, as events of 1948 would reveal. See Chapter 12.

80. Letter, 29 July 1937, Charles Hansen to D. W. Aupperle, in "Grand Lake Project: Development Correspondence, 1936" folder, NCWCDA.

81. Oral discussion of the origins of Green Mountain Reservoir, Colorado Water Conservation District, 1938, Glenwood Springs, Colorado, CRWCD.

CHAPTER 6

1. James MacGregor Burns, *Roosevelt: The Lion and the Fox* (New York: Harcourt, Brace and World, 1956), p. 318.
2. As quoted in *This Fabulous Century*, vol. 4, 1930–1940 (New York: Time-Life Books, 1970), p. 136.
3. Stanley J. Bastian, "The Northern Colorado Water Conservancy District: A Political System" (M.A. thesis, Colorado State University, 1970), pp. 91–93.
4. T. M. Callahan from Boulder County and Burgis Coy and Charles Lory from Larimer County, though members of the NCWUA, were not appointed to the first NCWCD Board of Directors.
5. Minutes, NCWCD, November 6, 1937, and July 5, 1938. Financial woes plagued the District in spring 1938. A $10,000 loan had to be secured from the First National Bank of Longmont at 5 percent interest to meet the estimated $5,500 cost of the Repayment Contract election. See Minutes, NCWCD, August 3, 1938.
6. Water Conservancy District Act, *Colorado Revised Statutes*, 1973, v. 15, 37-45-125.
7. Minutes, NCWCD, February 4, 1938. Class D allotments, the first offered to District residents, were contracts between the District and owners of farmlands in which landowners agreed that annual installments and charges for operation and maintenance "shall become a tax lien upon the lands for which such water is petitioned and allotted."
8. A warning reported in the *Fort Collins Express-Courier*, January 27, 1938, by Mills E. Bunger, Bureau of Reclamation engineer whose final report on the C-BT Project became S.D. 80.
9. Ibid., 5 March 1938.
10. Ibid., 13, 22 February, 1938.
11. Ibid., 20 April 1938. The Board took no formal action on the water petitions until January and February 1939, when Dille announced public hearings on 1,934 petitions for C–BT water, calling for an allotment of 158,187 acre-feet. After reviewing all petitions, the Board adopted a resolution on April 8, 1939, allotting water on 1,035 Class D petitions for a total of 77,179 acre-feet. On August 5, 1939, the Board adopted another resolution and order allotting 55,967 acre-feet, making a total of 133,146 acre-feet allotted on 1,732 Class D petitions, all recorded in their respective counties and in the "Water Allotment Record" of the District. See NCWCD *Secretary-Manager's Report*, 1939, p. 2.
12. Interview, J. R. Barkley, Denver, 23 August 1988. An article in the *Montrose Daily Press*, January 1, 1938, described Stone as one of the "Four Horsemen" of the West Slope, along with Hughes, Smith, and Delaney, all of whom had stood like Gibraltar against transmountain water diversion. The author lamented the fact that Stone, as CWCB director, had sold out to the East Slope people, concluding, "Verily, the mighty hath fallen."
13. Minutes, CWCB, January 15, 1941.
14. Minutes, NCWCD, March 28, 1938.
15. Ibid., April 15, 1938.
16. Ibid., April 25, 27, and May 23, 1938. See also Repayment Contract Between United States of America and Northern Colorado Water Conservancy District For the Construction of the Colorado–Big Thompson Project, executed July 5, 1938. Article 5 limits the District's obligation to $25 million.
17. *Denver Post*, 28 July 1938.

18. U.S. Senate, Colorado–Big Thompson Project, Synopsis of Report, 75th Cong., 1st sess., S.D. 80, Sec. 5 (h).

19. U.S. Department of the Interior, Bureau of Reclamation, *Annual Project History, Colorado–Big Thompson Project, Colorado*, Vol. 1, 1938, p. 68.

20. Minutes, NCWCD, November 4, 1938, including a letter from Tipton to the Board dated November 1, 1938. Tipton recommended that the Bureau update the Board on its current estimates for the remainder of the Project.

21. Ibid., December 3, 1938.

22. Minutes, NCWCD, November 1, 1938.

23. Interview, Bill Farr, Loveland, 8 July 1988.

24. *Project History*, 1938, p. 56.

25. *Fort Collins Express-Courier*, 28 August 1938.

26. Letter with attachments, 4 October 1938, Turner W. Battle, Assistant Secretary of Labor to John C. Page, Commissioner, Bureau of Reclamation, as printed in *Project History*, 1938, Appendix.

27. *Project History*, 1938, Appendix, pp. 2, 3.

28. Minutes, NCWCD, February 23, 1939.

29. *Fort Collins Express-Courier*, 15 March 1939.

30. *Denver Post*, 15 March 1939.

31. Opinion of attorney Porter Preston of the Bureau of Reclamation as reported in the *Fort Collins Express-Courier*, 20 March 1939.

32. *Greeley Tribune*, 28 March 1939. Attorney Nixon also pointed out that some of the men working at Green Mountain had come directly from Shasta Dam in California for the purpose of causing trouble.

33. *Fort Collins Express-Courier*, 30 March 1939.

34. Ibid., 3 April 1939.

35. Ibid., 6 April 1939.

36. Minutes, NCWCD, April 8, 1939. According to *The Summit County Journal*, April 14, 1939, the Workers Association, a nonprofit organization designed to protect every workman from organized labor, charged dues of a dollar a year and invited membership from both union and nonunion workers.

37. *The Summit County Journal*, 3 June 1939.

38. Ibid., 5 July 1939.

39. *Greeley Tribune*, 21 July 1939.

40. *Fort Collins Express-Courier*, 19 July 1939.

41. *The Middle Park Times*, 3 August 1939.

42. *Fort Collins Express-Courier*, 2 August 1939.

43. In addition to the *Middle Park Times*, mentioned in the previous note, see the *Fort Collins Express-Courier*, 2, 3 August 1939, *Denver Post*, 3 August 1939, and *Rocky Mountain News*, 3 August 1939.

44. *Fort Collins Express-Courier*, 9 August 1939.

45. Ibid., 13, 15 August 1939.

46. Ibid., 18, 20 August 1939.

47. Ibid., 20, 21 August 1939.

48. Ibid., 22 August 1939. *Greeley Tribune*, 22 August 1939. In the *Fort Collins Express-Courier* of August 23, 1939, the editor of the *Middle Park Times* was quoted as saying that Kremmling citizens

felt that they would not have an opportunity for jobs at Green Mountain under closed shop conditions.

49. *Fort Collins Express-Courier*, 5 September 1939.

50. Ibid., 25 August 1939 and 2 September 1939.

51. Ibid., 8 September 1939. In the NCWCD, *Secretary-Manager's Report* for 1939, Dille noted tersely that Secretary Ickes had announced that the District had no right to claim job preferences on the C–BT for its own people — that work should go to union men from the cities. At the April 13, 1940, Board meeting, Directors of the NCWCD finally accepted the fact that it "should refrain from any active participation on labor problems or controversies." See Minutes, NCWCD, April 13, 1940.

52. *Project History*, 1939, p. 22.

53. Ibid., pp. 52–54.

54. Ibid., pp. 71–76.

55. Minutes, NCWCD, July 5, 1939.

56. NCWCD, *Secretary-Manager's Report*, 1939, pp. 8–9.

CHAPTER 7

1. *Greeley Tribune*, 1 October 1940.

2. Ibid., 28 September 1938.

3. Ibid., 1 October 1940.

4. Letter, 11 October 1948, Charles Hansen to Claude C. Coffin, Charles Hansen Files, NCWCDA.

5. Water Conservancy District Act, *Colorado Revised Statutes*, 1973, v. 15, 37-45-122.

6. Minutes, NCWCD, February 4, April 8, and June 3, 1939. Special ownership taxes were collected by the county clerk and apportioned to the state and its political subdivisions by the county treasurer. The District was legally described as a quasi-municipality in the Letford case. See *Fort Collins Express-Courier*, 9 March 1939.

7. Unidentified newspaper, 29 September 1941, under headline, "Water District Not Entitled to Part of Automobile Tax," in NCWCD Newspaper Clippings Book, 1938–1944.

8. Article 20 of the Repayment Contract required the District to purchase all rights-of-way at prices satisfactory to the secretary of the interior with title taken by the Bureau in the name of the United States. When all deeds, contracts, and other papers were found satisfactory, the United States was obligated to reimburse the District for purchase price and expenses. In the event of a dispute between landowners and the District, the District was authorized to enter into condemnation suits.

9. NCWCD, *Secretary-Manager's Report*, 1939, p. 9.

10. *Greeley Tribune*, 19 September 1940.

11. Right-of-way expense estimates increased in NCWCD budgets from $5000 in 1939 and $4,000 in 1940 to $16,000 in 1941. See Minutes, NCWCD, September 2, 1939; September 14, 1940; and September 6, 1941. Payments to Grand County to compensate for lost tax revenue were set out in paragraph 5, subsection (k), S.D. 80, and were reinforced in Article 7 of the Repayment Contract.

12. Unidentified newspaper, January 1940, under headline "Institute Hears Hansen Report on G-L Project," in NCWCD Newspaper Clippings Book, 1938–1944. See also Minutes, NCWCD, October 7, 1939.

13. Minutes, NCWCD, November 6, 1937; March 5, 1938; April 13, 1940. The canals that were eventually built are now called the Boulder Feeder Canal and the Boulder Creek Supply Canal. When Carter Lake was constructed, the St. Vrain Supply Canal was added.

14. The District instituted nine condemnation suits in 1939, two in 1940, and one in 1941; five were settled out of court. See NCWCD *Secretary-Manager's Report* for 1939, 1940, and 1941.

15. Minutes, NCWCD, January 8, 1938.

16. *Greeley Tribune*, 8 October 1938.

17. *Fort Collins Express-Courier*, 13 October 1938. "It has been agreed between the Conservancy District and the Federal Government that the return flow water will go into the rivers to be administered by the state engineer the same as is return flow water from existing irrigation ditches."

18. Minutes, NCWCD, April 15, 1939. Nixon cited *Windsor Reservoir and Canal Company* v. *Lake Supply Ditch Company*, 44 Colo. 214, and *Holbrook Irrigation District* v. *Ft. Lyon Canal Company*, 84 Colo. 174.

19. Minutes, NCWCD, July 5, 1939. See also NCWCD, *Secretary-Manager's Report*, 1939, p. 10.

20. Letter, 26 June 1941, Edward T. Taylor to Charles Hansen, Charles Hansen Files, NCWCDA. This letter responds to one from Hansen written three days earlier in which Hansen thanked Taylor for all he had done on behalf of the C–BT. Taylor expressed his appreciation for Hansen's sentiments and compared his governmental service to that of Benjamin Franklin, reiterating his many years of loyalty to the proponents of the C–BT. Time and age have a way of distorting the collective memory.

21. *Denver Post*, 28 June 1940. The Blue River struggle continued well past the postwar period. In 1943 Denver introduced "Statement of Claim" No. 1709 into the District Court of Summit County, defending its claim to 1600 cfs on the Blue River and noting that project construction began on March 21, 1914; that the beneficial use of water was for municipal and other uses; and that a map and statement of the project had been filed with the state engineer on May 31, 1923. This information was found in Folder 775, Box 220, Bureau of Reclamation Archives, Denver Federal Center.

22. *Rocky Mountain News*, 4 September 1940.

23. *Fort Collins Express-Courier*, 24 June 1940. Lory served on the board of the NCWUA from 1935 to 1938, was appointed Director of the NCWCD in 1940 and reappointed until 1954, at which time he was made Director emeritus.

24. Article 16 of the Repayment Contract specified that the "use of water made available by the Project shall be primarily for irrigation and domestic uses; and that the manner of delivery shall be to this end." The implication was that generation of power was secondary.

25. They argued that crop losses occurred annually because of water shortages; that pumping plants were being constructed wasting local capital; that demand for electric energy in the area was increasing; that early completion of the Project was desirable to provide the United States with an appropriate return on its investment; that population decreases had occurred because of water shortages; and that government investments should not be abandoned. See unidentified article, 2 December 1940, with headline "Irrigation Advocate Concerned Lest Non-Defense Saving Slash Expenditures For Reclamation," in NCWCD Newspaper Clippings Book, 1938–1944.

26. Ibid., 9 December 1940, "Big Thompson Project Power Report Shortly: $5,125,000 to Carry Work on Grand Lake Diversion Next Fiscal Year."

27. Ibid., 5 January 1941, "Thompson Project to be Continued: Defense Program Demands Power."

28. Ibid., 13 February 1941, "Big Thompson Project Classed by Ickes As One To Be Pushed To Supply Power For Defense." The *Fort Collins Express-Courier*, 13 February 1941, quoted Ickes as saying that power production on the C–BT and the "Colorado [Blue River]" would need to be increased by a total of 105,000 kilowatts.

29. Memorandum, Clifford Stone to Royce J. Tipton, Charles Hansen, and J. M. Dille, 18 February 1941, Charles Hansen Files, NCWCDA.

30. *Rocky Mountain News*, 12 June 1941.

31. *Ft. Collins, Express-Courier*, 23 July 1941.

32. Letter, 28 July 1941, Charles Hansen to Ed Johnson, Charles Hansen Files, NCWCDA.

33. Letter, 19 February 1942, Eugene D. Millikin to J. M. Dille, Eugene D. Millikin Files, NCWCDA.

34. Minutes, NCWCD, December 5, 1941.

35. R. J. Tipton, "Analysis of Power Features of Colorado–Big Thompson Project With Recommended Construction Schedule," prepared for the CWCB with assistance from H. S. Sands (Denver: CWCB, January 5, 1942).

36. *Greeley Tribune*, 28 December 1938. An estimated $60 million a year was needed to sustain existing reclamation projects. According to an article in the *Denver Post*, 8 February 1938, the curtailment of oil production in Wyoming — the "principal revenue producer for the fund" — was causing the immediate crisis.

37. J. M. Dille, *A Brief History of Northern Colorado Water Conservancy District and The Colorado–Big Thompson Project* (Loveland, Colo.: NCWCD, 1958), p. 70. NCWCD Minutes for March 1, 1941, confirm this figure and further indicate that as of February 1, 1941, $1,680,000 of the appropriated moneys had not been spent.

38. Letter, 12 September 1940, Charles Hansen to Alva Adams, Alva B. Adams Files, NCWCDA. Three large projects already funded from the general fund were Casper-Alcova, Central Valley, and Grand Coulee.

39. Minutes, NCWCD, May 3 and 31, 1941.

40. See U.S. House of Representatives, Department of the Interior Appropriations Act, (Public Law 136, Chapter 259), H.R. 4590, 77th Cong., 1st sess., p. 33. Also see Dille, *Brief History*, p. 70. Dille did not mention appropriations for fiscal 1942, but H.R. 4590 stated that the C–BT received $3 million from the general fund and $1 million from the reclamation fund. Dille noted that with the exception of $800,000 received from the reclamation fund in 1946, all funding after 1941 came from the general fund.

41. NCWCD *Secretary-Manager's Report*, 1941, p. 6.

42. *Project History*, 1940, p. 69.

43. *Greeley Tribune*, 24 June 1940.

44. Newspaper article unidentified and undated with headline "Secretary Ickes Says Colorado–Big Thompson Project Shows U.S. Democracy is Functioning," in NCWCD Newspaper Clippings Book, 1938–1944.

45. *Project History*, 1940, p. 76. Other data dealing with the construction on both ends of the tunnel are also taken from this source.

46. NCWCD *Secretary-Manager's Report*, 1941, p. 9.

47. *Project History*, 1941, p. 53.

48. "Long John" Austin — a celebrated "hard rock wizard" with a passion for tunnels — was 6 feet, 8 inches tall, with a driving spirit, an outstanding safety record, and a tolerance for alcohol and hard work that won his men's respect. He was not without prejudices. The only time he was ever hurt on the job, he confessed, was when he violated mining tradition by letting a woman into a tunnel he was building for the Louisville and Nashville railroad. He was equally superstitious about singing and whistling in a tunnel because he believed that accidents always followed. On the same job, a shift was ready to enter the tunnel when two blacks ambled by, twanging a banjo. Knowing that the men would refuse to go to work unless he did something, Long John "broke the banjo over one Negro's head and broke his own hand on the singer's skull." The blacks made tracks, and the men went to work. Austin did note that one man was killed the next day. See *Denver Post*, 12 September 1942, and *Time*, 5 July 1943.

49. NCWCD *Secretary-Manager's Report*, 1941, pp. 7–8.

50. Some Bureau people considered pumping directly from Lake Granby to Grand Lake; however, Francis J. Thomas's report, incorporated into the NCWCD Minutes of September 6, 1941, noted that without Shadow Mountain Reservoir's accumulated natural runoff, more water would have to be pumped electrically out of Lake Granby, increasing operation costs to the District.

51. *Project History*, 1941, pp. 49–50.

52. Letter, 23 September 1941, J. M. Dille to Alva Adams, Alva B. Adams Files, NCWCDA.

53. Letter, 27 September 1941, Alva Adams to J. M. Dille, ibid.

54. Letter, 5 December 1938, Robert G. Smith to Ralph L. Crossman, Charles Hansen Files, NCWCDA.

55. Unidentified newspaper, 1 December 1941, with headline "Senator Adams Dies of Heart Attack Caused by Overwork," in NCWCD Newspaper Clippings Book, 1938–1944.

56. Minutes, NCWCD, December 5, 1941.

CHAPTER 8

1. Minutes, NCWCD, January 10, 1942.

2. Letter, 13 March 1941, Leland Olds to Clifford Stone, in "Washington Trips re Appropriations" folder, NCWCDA.

3. Titles are: "Agricultural Production in Northern Colorado Water Conservancy District as Related to National Defense," by E. Herbert Dyer and Robert Barkley, December 1941 (hereafter referred to as "1941 Agriculture Report"); "Statement Concerning 1942 Sugar Beet Production in Northern Colorado Water Conservancy District and its Relation to the Colorado–Big Thompson Project, Supplementing the Report of December 1941," unspecified author, March 1942 (hereafter referred to as "1942 Sugar Beet Report"); and "Analysis of Power Features of Colorado–Big Thompson Project With Recommended Construction Schedule," by R. J. Tipton and H. S. Sands, January 5, 1942 (hereafter referred to as "1942 Power Report").

4. Letter, 25 March 1943, J. M. Dille to Charles Hansen, in "Washington Trips re Appropriations" folder, NCWCDA.

5. "1941 Agricultural Report," in which the authors mention USDA quotas that increased production as follows: sheep and lambs on feed, 7.3 percent; cattle and calves on feed, 11.2 percent; pigs, 30 percent; milk produced on farms, 5.2 percent; oats, 8.6 percent; barley, 6.5 percent; potatoes, 19.3 percent; sugar beets, 30.3 percent; green peas, 11 percent; green peas for processing, 20.7 percent; snap beans, 1 percent; cabbage, 11.5 percent; onions, 12 percent; miscellaneous truck crops, .3 percent; and a 9 percent *decrease* in wheat production. All of this could be accomplished, concluded the authors, by a 5 percent increase in the 1929–1938 acreage or by importing additional water to existing acreage.

6. "1942 Sugar Beet Report."

7. As quoted from the 1942 supplement to the "1941 Agricultural Report."

8. "1942 Power Report." Specifically, this report called for "$24,005,000 for fiscal 1943, $23,069,000 for fiscal 1944, and $6,876,000 for fiscal 1945.

9. Minutes, NCWCD, February 14, 1942. Minutes, CWCB, February 26 and 27, 1942.

10. *Fort Collins Express-Courier*, 24 March 1942.

11. *Denver Post*, 9 July 1942.

12. *Fort Collins Express-Courier*, 11 August 1942.

13. See Unidentified newspaper, 3 March 1942, with headline "Tunnel Now Half Drilled, Harper Says," in NCWCD Newspaper Clippings Book, 1938–1944. Also see Minutes, NCWCD, September 5, 1942, and USBR, *Annual Project History*, 1942, pp. 3–33, 53.

14. Memorandum, 28 October 1942, Ernest Kanzler, Director General for Operations, War Production Board, to Honorable Eugene D. Millikin, NCWCDA.

15. *Fort Collins Express-Courier*, 28 October and 9 December 1942.

16. Letters, 16 November and 1 December 1942, Eugene D. Millikin to Clifford Stone. Also see telegrams, n.d. and 29 December 1942, Millikin to Stone in "Eugene D. Millikin," folder, NCWCDA.

17. Letter, 5 December 1942, F. Eberstadt, Vice Chairman of the WPB, to Eugene D. Millikin, ibid.

18. Letter, 30 December 1942, Eugene D. Millikin to J. M. Dille, ibid.

19. Minutes, NCWCD, Nov. 6, 1942.

20. Ibid., December 5, 1942. The Bureau was hoping to find a cheaper way to deliver both power and irrigation water by taking Colorado River water from Estes Park east into new reservoirs, thus avoiding risks associated with the Big Thompson Canyon route. To Dille, the plan had three principal flaws: it would take longer to build, thus delaying water to northern Colorado crops; it would cause problems with the allotment system through which allottees had already been promised water via specific tributaries of the South Platte; and it emphasized the use of water for power. See memoranda of November 1942 and November 1943 in "Office Memorandums, Office Reports, Relating to Project Water Deliveries, Dille or Barkley" notebook, NCWCDA.

21. Minutes, NCWCD, January 9, 1943.

22. "Colorado–Big Thompson Project: Present Status and Suggested Plan for Continuation of Work," January 1943 and February 20, 1943, signed by Dille and Stone (Denver: Colorado Water Conservation Board, January 1943), in "Early History, Tipton Report, 1933, Colorado Water Conservancy District Law, etc." volume (hereafter referred to as "NCWCD, Early History"), NCWCDA. In a letter to Congressman Lawrence Lewis, September 8, 1943, Dille explained that the modified plan was conceived in January 1943 "in view of the extreme importance of the additional food that can be produced." He emphasized that this plan eliminated for the present additional power plants and storage reservoirs and included only the completion of the Continental Divide Tunnel, the North Fork Dam, and a temporary conduit to convey the water from the East Portal down to the Big Thompson River, thus permitting the delivery of 100,000 acre-feet of water annually. See "Lawrence Lewis" folder, NCWCDA.

23. Letter, 2 March 1943, Harold Ickes to Claude R. Wickard, Food Administrator, United States Department of Agriculture, NCWCDA.

24. Letter, 14 March 1943, J. M. Dille to Charles Hansen, NCWCDA. In other correspondence, Commissioner Page told Hayden that he expected the WPB to realize that the food crisis confronting the United States could be addressed by unfreezing the stop work orders affecting Bureau irrigation projects now under construction. See Ibid., 24 February 1943.

25. Letter, 22 April 1943, Eugene D. Millikin to Clifford Stone, ibid.

26. Minutes, NCWCD, April 3, 1943.

27. Letter, 25 May 1943, Eugene D. Millikin to Clifford Stone, in "Eugene Millikin" folder, NCWCDA. In Book Three of *Virgin Land* (Cambridge, Mass.: Harvard University Press, 1950), Henry Nash Smith describes how U.S. citizens historically have looked at the West as "The Garden of the World." In a *Rocky Mountain News* article, "West Must Feed the World, Reclamation Group Told," 27 October 1943, National Reclamation Association secretary F. O. Hagie reportedly said that the global war effort was so immense that "it has taken twelve months to acquaint our military and wartime leaders with the part which agriculture in general, and irrigation agriculture in particular, must play in a global war." They had to convince the Department of Agriculture that irrigation agriculture in the West would be the surest means of increasing production to meet unprecedented demands for high-protein foodstuffs for the United States, its allies, "and eventually to help feed the millions of now subjugated, hungry, and starving people throughout the world."

28. Letter, 21 June 1943, Donald M. Nelson to F. D. Roosevelt, in "Eugene Millikin" folder, NCWCDA. The eight projects were Yakima-Rozas in Washington, Newton in Utah, Anderson

Ranch in Idaho, Klamath-Modoc in Oregon and California, Mancos and C-BT in Colorado, Rapid Valley in South Dakota, and the Friant Kern Canal in California. Dille believed that Ickes and the Federal Power Commission were competing to see who would control future hydroelectric power. Sometime in early 1943 the battle lines extended to the WPB, whose policies generally received the president's blessing. Nelson's willingness to review the status of the C–BT may have resulted from these political maneuverings. See letters, 6 April 1941, and 9 March 1943, J. M. Dille to Charles Hansen, ibid.

29. Letter, 25 June 1943, F. D. Roosevelt to John C. Vivian, ibid.

30. Letter, 7 May 1943, J. M. Dille to Eugene D. Millikin, ibid.. See also Minutes, NCWCD, April 3, 1943.

31. Letter, 15 June 1943, Eugene D. Millikin to Clifford Stone, and telegram, 18 June 1943, Eugene D. Millikin to J. M. Dille, in "Eugene Millikin" folder, NCWCDA. The committee actually approved $3.5 million on June 17, 1943.

32. Letter, 4 August 1943, Acting Commissioner of the Bureau H. W. Bashore to the Office of the Commissioner of the War Manpower Commission, ibid.

33. *Greeley Tribune*, n.d., in NCWCD Newspaper Clippings Book, 1938–1944. Mussolini resigned on July 25, 1943.

34. Letter, 4 August 1943, Acting Commissioner of the Bureau H. W. Bashore to the Office of the Commissioner of the War Manpower Commission, in "Eugene Millikin" folder, NCWCDA, and memorandum, 8 July 1943, P. L. Slagsvold, Production Programs Branch of USDA, to N. E. Dodd, Chief of the AAA, ibid.

35. Letter, 6 January 1943, J. M. Dille to Eugene D. Millikin, ibid.

36. *Project History*, 1943, pp. 60–62.

37. Ibid., pp. 34, 35. In order to keep workers on the job, time and a half was paid for all work in excess of eight hours. Since 1940, wage rates on the Continental Divide Tunnel had risen 48.7 percent for contractors' employees and 28.1 percent for government employees. Most contractors wanted to extend the work week to fifty-four hours because they were unable to hire men on a forty-hour basis, a request that was approved by the secretary of interior on May 27, 1942. See correspondence, Folder 151, Box 211, Record Group 115, USBR records, National Archives, Denver Federal Center.

38. *Fort Collins Express-Courier*, 4 July 1943. C–BT Project manager C. H. Howell, who requested Japanese American labor in 1944, was told that they might be used at Shadow Mountain Reservoir. The following year, Region 7 Director E. B. Debler told Howell that the U.S. Employment Service could probably furnish Japanese American labor from the internment camp at Granada, Colorado. See letters from Howell to Debler, April 5, 1944, and Debler to Howell, March 31, 1945, in Box 211, Record Group 115, USBR records, National Archives, Denver Federal Center,.

39. *Project History*, 1943, pp. 61, 62. November 6, 1943, NCWCD minutes note that Austin's men were still working on the fire at Moffat Tunnel No. 10.

40. *Project History*, 1943, pp. 53–66.

41. Ibid., p. 8.

42. *Project History*, 1944, pp. 44–45.

43. Minutes, NCWCD, June 3, 1944. The minutes make no further mention of the holing through.

44. Unidentified newspapers, 10 and 12 June 1944, in NCWCD Newspaper Clippings Book, 1938–1944. *Fort Collins Express-Courier*, 9, 11 June 1944.

45. *Project History*, 1944, p. 44.

46. Letter, 7 February 1942, Ed Johnson to Charles Hansen, Charles Hansen Files, NCWCDA.

47. Letter, 11 and 16 February 1942, Charles Hansen to Ed Johnson, ibid.

48. Letter, 20 February 1942, Ed Johnson to Charles Hansen, ibid. Dille met Johnson on one of his trips to find construction money for the C–BT. Johnson bemoaned his predicament, saying that Mrs. Adams and her sister maintained that Senator Adams's last wish was to have the C–BT named after him; because the Senate's memorial service was pending, he had to have a decision soon. See Letter, 14 March 1942, Dille to Hansen, NCWCDA.

49. Minutes, NCWCD, April 4, 1942.

50. Letter, 17 March 1942, Charles Hansen to Ed Johnson, Charles Hansen Files, NCWCDA.

51. *Project History*, 1944, p. 41. Anyone who has had trouble navigating a boat under the narrow green bridge between Grand Lake and the connecting channel will now know that the citizens of Grand County are to blame, not the District or the Bureau.

52. Letter, 13 March 1943, Commissioner John C. Page to Eugene D. Millikin, in "Eugene Millikin" folder, NCWCDA.

53. A letter from J. E. Whitten to engineer S. O. Harper, April 6, 1943 (ibid.), says that 550 cfs from Grand Lake to the Big Thompson would not create any problems. The Bureau began photographing the Big Thompson in 1945 but terminated this project when the war ended. See *Project History*, 1945, p. 26.

54. NCWCD, *Secretary-Manager's Report*, 1944, p. 13.

55. Ibid. Bureau engineer S. O. Harper estimated a water delivery date of July 24, 1945, if three shifts of men could be used; and September 17, 1946, if one shift were available. See letter, 18 November 1944, Harper to John E. Gross, Regional Director XI, War Manpower Commission, Box 211, Record Group 115, USBR records, National Archives, Denver Federal Center.

56. Letter, 11 November 1944, Wilson Cowen, Assistant Administrator, War Food Administration, to Paul V. McNutt, Chairman, War Manpower Commission, Box 211, Record Group 115, USBR records, National Archives, Denver Federal Center. Letter, 27 November 1944, C. H. Howell to L. A. West, State Manpower Director, ibid. Letter, 30 November 1944, J. M. Dille to L. A. West, ibid. Dille's letter notes that the modified plan was supported by the WFA and the WPB at a time when "the problem of food to support the war effort loomed larger in importance, or at least in general opinion, than it seems now." He also noted that the country was very fortunate to have had two boom crop years in 1943 and 1944 because of near-perfect growing conditions. But what about next year, he asked. What would be the feeling if the Project were shut down and another year like 1934 came along?

57. Letter, 6 December 1944, L. A. West to S. S. Magoffin, ibid. Harper was informed of this decision a few days later.

58. Letter, 14 December 1944, L. A. West to L. R. Douglas, Bureau of Reclamation, Denver, ibid. See also letter, 21 December 1944, Walker R. Young, Acting Chief Engineer of the Bureau, to Commissioner Harry Bashore, ibid.

59. Letter, 15 December 1944, E. B. Debler to John E. Gross, Regional Director, War Manpower Commission, ibid.

60. Letter, 9 January 1945, L. A. West to S. S. Magoffin, ibid. Telegram, 10 January 1945, C. H. Howell to Stiers Brothers, ibid.

61. Letter, 11 January 1945, Walter R. Young to John E. Gross, ibid. NCWCD, *Secretary-Manager's Report*, 1945, p. 14.

CHAPTER 9

1. NCWCD, *Secretary-Manager's Report*, 1942, p. 14.

2. J. M. Dille, "Project Water Delivery," memo, November 1942, to District Directors, in "Office Memorandums, Office Reports, Relating to Project Water Deliveries, Dille or Barkley" notebook, NCWCDA.

3. Ibid.
4. Ibid., and following table entitled "Recap of Water Distribution."
5. Ibid. The Blue River project was Denver's plan to bring water from the Blue River into the South Platte River by way of a tunnel under the Continental Divide. Dillon Reservoir and the Roberts Tunnel were the fulfillment of this plan.
6. Ibid.
7. Minutes, NCWCD, June 12, 1943. Section 4 of the Repayment Contract provided for changes in the nature and/or location of features mentioned in S.D. 80 and detailed in Section 4 of the Repayment Contract with the approval of the secretary of the interior.
8. Ibid., July 31, 1943.
9. Ibid., October 16, 1943. In addition to Flatiron and Rattlesnake, these included capacity expansion at Reservoir No. 6 west of Wellington, Cobb Lake south of Wellington, and Boyd Lake northeast of Loveland.
10. NCWCD, *Secretary-Manager's Report*, 1943, p. 10.
11. *Fort Collins Express-Courier*, 28 December 1943.
12. Special Memo to Directors, 1 December 1943, in "Office Memorandums, Office Reports, Relating to Project Water Deliveries, Dille or Barkley" notebook, NCWCDA, p. 3.
13. Ibid., p. 4.
14. Ibid., pp. 4, 5. Capacity of the Adams Tunnel is 550 cfs.
15. *Fort Collins Express-Courier*, 28 December 1943.
16. U.S. Senate, Colorado–Bit Thompson Project, Synopsis of Report, 75th Cong., 1st sess., S.D. 80, pp. 23, 24. The capacity of Horsetooth Reservoir, originally estimated at 96,756 acre-feet, was described in this document as "necessary," because irrigation use "requires that the entire amount of supplemental water be delivered at a rate that would supply it in 60 days."
17. Special Memo to Directors, 1 December 1943, in "Office Memorandums, Office Reports, Relating to Project Water Deliveries, Dille or Barkley" notebook, NCWCDA, pp. 5–7.
18. Ibid., p. 9.
19. Ibid.
20. Ibid., Suggested Construction Schedule.
21. Michael C. Robinson, *Water for the West: The Bureau of Reclamation, 1902–1977* (Chicago: Public Works Historical Society, 1979), pp. 76, 77.
22. Minutes, NCWCD, July 8, 1944.
23. Ibid., December 2, 1944.
24. NCWCD, *Secretary-Manager's Report*, 1944, p. 11.
25. Robinson, *Water for the West*, p. 83.
26. Ibid.
27. Minutes, NCWCD, August 12, 1944.
28. Ibid., September 8, 1945.
29. Minutes, CWCB, June 9, 10, 1942.
30. Ibid.
31. Ibid., May 10 and 11, 1943.
32. "Utilization of Waters of Colorado and Tijuana Rivers and of the Rio Grande," in *Treaties and Other International Agreements of the United States of America, 1776–1949*, compiled by Charles I. Bevans (Washington: Department of State, 1972), vol. 9, pp. 1166–1192. Article 10 pertains to the Colorado River.

33. Unidentified newspaper, 13 January 1944, "Hansen Tells Progress on Big Thompson," in NCWCD Newspaper Clippings Book, 1938–1944. See also Minutes, NCWCD, March 4, 1944. In a letter to Hansen, March 6, 1944, J. F. McGurk, Chief, Division of Mexican Affairs, State Department, acknowledged the telegram's message that ratification of the treaty would "determine for all time the extent of the burden on the Colorado River." McGurk expressed his appreciation for the support. See Charles Hansen Files, 1938–1945, NCWCDA.

34. Letter, 4 March 1944, J. M. Dille to Senator Eugene Millikin, in "Eugene Millikin" folder, NCWCDA.

35. Letter, 6 March 1945, L. A. West to John Austin, S. S. Magoffin, and J. F. Shea Co., Inc., in Folder 150, "Colorado–Big Thompson, Administration and Planning, March 1, 1945–December 31, 1949," Box 211, Record Group 115, USBR records, National Archives, Denver Federal Center.

36. Letter, 9 March 1945, Walter R. Young to Harry Bashore, ibid.

37. Telegram, 12 March 1945, Harry Bashore to Young, ibid.

38. USBR, *Annual Project History,* January 1, 1945, to December 31, 1945, p. 32.

39. Minutes, NCWCD, June 9, 1945.

40. Ibid., August 4, 1945.

41. Ibid., April 28, 1945. Memorandum, December 1945, J. M. Dille to Directors, in "Office Memorandums, Office Reports, Relating to Project Water Deliveries, Dille or Barkley" notebook, NCWCDA.

42. Memorandum, 21 February 1946, J. M. Dille to E. B. Debler, in "Office Memorandums, Office Reports, Relating to Project Water Deliveries, Dille or Barkley" notebook, NCWCDA. The Bureau implied that if the Denver Water Board succeeded in building the Blue River project, residents of the District's south end could request from that system supplemental water flowing in the South Platte River.

43. Memorandum, November 1945, J. M. Dille to Directors, ibid.

44. Ibid.

45. When the Bureau favored a gravity-flow canal instead of a pump plant, the North Poudre Irrigation Company made its second application for 40,000 acre-feet of supplemental water from the C–BT. The company filed the first petition in 1938, but the Board did not act due to the ambiguity of language in the petition and the uncertainty of operational costs of a pump plant. On December 8, 1945, the Board agreed to execute the contract with North Poudre, subject to building a diversion canal. See Minutes, NCWCD, December 8, 1945.

46. Ibid., January 5, 1946.

47. Ibid., June 9, 1945.

48. NCWCD *Secretary-Manager's Report,* 1945, p. 7. Dille's letter to Debler, dated August 8, 1945, said: "Therefore, they [the Directors] make the suggestion — and it is more than a suggestion, — that you consider whether it would not be better for all interests concerned to abandon the emergency program for delivery of water in 1946 and concentrate the energies of the Bureau personnel and the funds available toward the completion of the final Project as originally planned." One year later Dille asked for renewal of the modified plan.

49. Minutes, CWCB, September 13, 14, 1945.

50. NCWCD *Secretary-Manager's Report,* 1945, p. 5. Of the total amount appropriated, "about" $23 million had been expended as follows: "about" $8.3 million for the Green Mountain Dam and power project; $11.2 million for the Adams Tunnel to date; and $800,000 for Shadow Mountain Dam and spillway.

51. Minutes, NCWCD, May 4, 1946.

52. The Bureau estimated that labor rates increased 79 percent between 1940 and the end of 1946. See *Annual Project History,* 1946, pp. 45, 46. In July 1946, Region 7 director Debler estimated total cost of the Project at $110 million. He thought that the Bureau could not pay its share of $85

million by the generation of hydroelectric power, and he hoped for a revision in the Repayment Contract. See notes of July 6, 1946, meeting between Debler, Tipton, Stone, Bob Barkley, Dille, and the Directors regarding Project costs, in "Meetings and Conferences, 1946–1953" notebook, NCWCDA.

53. Minutes, NCWCD, June 8, 1946.

54. Ibid., July 6, 1946.

55. Notes on meetings, September 20 and 28, 1946, Greeley, Colorado, in "Meetings and Conferences, 1946–1953" notebook, NCWCDA.

56. Ibid., July 6 and August 10, 1946. Precipitation fell 40 percent below normal during the first four months of 1946, and a late freeze hurt crops that did germinate. From May to August moisture registered normal, but an early snow caught 50 percent of the best crop in the ground. See NCWCD, *Secretary-Manager's Report*, 1946, p. 2.

57. Minutes, NCWCD, September 21, 1946.

58. July 6, 1946, meeting of NCWCD Board with Bureau of Reclamation officials, in "Meetings and Conferences, 1946–1953" notebook, NCWCDA.

59. Notes taken by Bob Barkley, October 10, 1946, Omaha, Nebraska, in "Meetings and Conferences, 1946–1953" notebook, NCWCDA. Unless otherwise noted, further discussion of this meeting comes from this source.

60. Recalling this meeting forty-one years later, Barkley concluded that Commissioner Straus "gave up" after Hansen finished speaking. Although the Bureau continued to urge renegotiation on the District, Barkley believed that this showdown persuaded the commissioner that the Repayment Contract would have to be honored as written. Telephone conversation, Bob Barkley, 3 November 1988.

61. Minutes, NCWCD, Omaha, Nebraska, October 11, 1946. The Bureau had simply offered to bring water to the East Portal, where the District and the users would determine use.

62. In fall 1945 Dille and Hansen were looking for an engineer to operate the completed Project. Dille knew Barkley's CWCB work before he had entered active duty in 1942. When Barkley returned to Denver in October 1945, Dille asked him to work for the NCWCD. Barkley decided the C–BT might be more interesting than the CWCB, so he became the District's third employee, along with Dille and Sadie Johnson. The Board approved his appointment in November at a salary of $275 a month. Interview, Bob Barkley, Denver, 23 August 1988, and Minutes, NCWCD, November 3, 1945, and January 5, 1946.

63. Notes taken by Bob Barkley, October 17, 1946, Greeley, Colorado, NCWCDA. Directors of the new company who were present were Charles Swink and James Stewart (Greeley-Loveland), Clarence Svedman (Louden), L. A. Benson (South Side), and D. R. Pulliam (Home Supply).

64. Minutes, NCWCD, November 16, 1946, and January 11, 1947.

65. NCWCD, *Secretary-Manager's Report*, 1946, p. 10.

66. Notes taken by Bob Barkley at a meeting between District and Bureau officials, November 8, 1946, Denver, in "Meetings and Conferences, 1946–1953" notebook, NCWCDA.

67. Memorandum, 9 January 1947, Region 7 Director to NCWCD Board of Directors, in "C–BT–1937–1947" folder, NCWCDA.

68. *Congressional Record*, 80th Cong., 1st sess., 93, pt. 8:9573. Congress established the fifty-year payback period in the Boulder Canyon Project Act, which included a ten-year development period and a forty-year repayment period.

69. Section 9 (a) (4) of the Reclamation Project Act of 1939 authorized the secretary of the interior to make findings on "the part of the estimated cost which can be properly allocated to power and probably returned to the United States in net power revenues." See *Statutes at Large*, Vol. 53, pt. 2, p. 1187, Reclamation Act of 1939 (codified in *United States Code*, Title 43, Chap. 16, 1939). In an interview on August 3, 1987, Barkley explained that building costs on the C–BT water distribution system were roughly $63 million, including the government's share of the joint

features used for both power and irrigation. The cost of the total power "was right at the $100 million, but in setting up the repayment schedule out of the power revenues, the Bureau allocated $100 million against irrigation features and $63 million against the power features." The District would pay $25 million of this, so the Bureau in effect gave itself an interest-free loan of $75 million.

70. NCWCD, *Secretary-Manager's Report*, 1946, p. 5.

71. Ibid., pp. 6–9.

72. *Annual Project History*, 1947, p. 4.

73. Hatfield Chilson (Paper delivered to the Loveland Rotary Club, March 12, 1985). Judge Chilson acted as the company's secretary and attorney.

74. Ibid.

75. *The Middle Park Times*, 26 June 1947.

76. *Fort Collins Coloradoan*, 23, 24 June 1947.

77. Interview, Bill Farr, Loveland, 8 July 1988.

78. Of the many people in this audience, probably none was more pleased by the occasion's triumph than Fred Cummings, who received an invitation from Charles Hansen and wrote, "Dear Charley: Yours of the 16th received. Thanks for the invitation and free grub. I had not forgotten appointment made several years ago. Will be there with my bottle and expecting you with yours." See "Adams Tunnel Ceremonies" folder, NCWCDA. Another celebration was held on August 11, 1947, at Loveland when the first water was actually diverted for use, with the Colorado Air National Guard, "The Minute Men," and Secretary of the Interior Fred A. Seaton.

79. *Fort Collins Coloradoan*, 23, 24 June 1947.

80. In a letter to Dille, July 7, 1947, Congressman William S. Hill reported that he and Straus had returned to Washington together. He also noted that the commissioner had indicated that because he was "under the thumb" of the chairman of the House Appropriations Committee, he had to "advocate or insist on a new contract with the District." See "Adams Tunnel Ceremonies" folder, NCWCDA.

81. Ibid., 24 June 1947.

82. Ibid.

83. See "Northern Colorado Water Conservancy District and Colorado–Big Thompson Project Supplemental to the 1950 Progress Report" (Greeley, Colo.: *Greeley Tribune*, January 1952).

CHAPTER 10

1. USBR, *Annual Project History*, 1938, pp. 42, 43, 62.

2. *Annual Project History*, 1939, p. 46.

3. *Annual Project History*, 1940, p. 49.

4. Letter, 11 January 1944, J. M. Dille to Thomas J. Barbre, in " 'Green Fields' Project film" folder, NCWCDA. The cost included a 16mm projector.

5. Minutes, NCWCD, November 6 and December 4, 1943; February 5 and May 6, 1944.

6. Letters, 10 November 1949, Clare S. Merman, Acting Administrative Officer, Bureau of Reclamation, Denver, to J. R. Barkley, and 10 February 1953, J. M. Dille to H. S. Varner, Jr., Administrative Officer, Bureau of Reclamation, Denver, in " 'Green Fields' Project film" folder, NCWCDA.

7. Interview, Bill Bohlender, in *Without a Drought*, NCWCD newsletter, October 1988.

8. Frank Davis, representing a Chamber of Commerce group from Greeley, expressed amazement that the city had contracted for so much water. "It is far more than we will ever need," he told the

Board. See handwritten notes, February 9, 1946, in "Meetings and Conferences, 1946–1953" notebook, NCWCDA.

9. The District's carefully prepared data showed that the average annual crop loss from water shortage between 1929 and 1939 was $6,253,000; the average annual water shortage for these years was 503,000 acre-feet. Even this information failed to change the most skeptical minds. The District's public relations job loomed increasingly important.

10. Minutes, NCWCD, November 16, 1946.

11. In July 1945, seven groups of men from different sections of the District toured the East Portal. At this stage, women were not invited. See Minutes, NCWCD, July 7, 1945.

12. See NCWCD, *Secretary-Manager's Reports*, 1939–1947. The largest sums of money were disbursed for "Rights of Way Projects" and "Rights of Way Expenses," but this money was reimbursed to the District by the United States in conformity with Section 20 of the Repayment Contract.

13. *Annual Project History*, 1939, 1940, 1941, 1942, 1943, 1944, 1945, 1946, 1947. Civil Cases Nos. 5016 and 5017 were consolidated for this trial. On October 12, 1955, Federal District Judge William Lee Knous signed the Order, Findings, Judgment and Decree that recognized the priority date of August 1, 1935, for Green Mountain Reservoir. See Chapters 12 and 13 for additional discussion of the Blue River Decrees.

14. Minutes, NCWCD, March 23, 1946.

15. Ibid., April 13, 1946.

16. Minutes, CWCB, February 1, 1940, and January 15, 1941.

17. Ibid., November 7 and 8, 1940, and September 16, 1942. Section 13 of the Water Conservancy District Act (*Session Laws of Colorado*, 1937, Ch. 266) was amended by H.B. 331 and approved April 20, 1943.

18. Minutes, CWCB, September 13, 14, 1945.

19. NCWCD, *Secretary-Manager's Report*, 1947, p. 15.

20. Memorandum, November 1942, J. M. Dille to NCWCD Directors, in "Office Memorandums, Office Reports, Relating to Project Water Deliveries, Dille or Barkley" notebook, NCWCDA. At a July 6, 1946, meeting of the Board with Bureau and CWCB representatives, Dille pointed out that contracts had been made with seven municipalities, one irrigation district, two mutual companies, and 1,800 individuals (Class D allotments). See "Meetings and Conferences, 1946–1953" notebook, NCWCDA.

21. Letters to J. M. Dille from several Federal Land Bank officials, February 1938 to July 1939, in "Federal Land Bank of Wichita" folder, Administration, C–BT Construction, NCWCDA.

22. NCWCD, *Secretary-Manager's Report*, 1947, p. 16.

23. Minutes, NCWCD, April 13, 1946.

24. NCWCD, *Secretary-Manager's Report*, 1948, p. 5.

CHAPTER 11

1. Unidentified newspaper clippings, NCWCD Newspaper Clippings Book 4, pp. 93, 96.

2. Elmo Richardson, *Dams, Parks and Politics: Resource Development in the Truman-Eisenhower Era* (Lexington: The University Press of Kentucky, 1973), pp. 14, 21.

3. Ibid., pp. 14, 15.

4. Ibid., p. 16.

5. Ibid., p. 19.

6. Ibid., pp. 22, 23. Straus was actually a Roosevelt appointment. He has also been viewed as Ickes's alter ego, "a newspaperman, a liberal, a fighter, a curmudgeon." Rude, arrogant, cavalier, and

mendacious, Straus was also an idealist, who "bore a ferocious grudge against the private utilities of the West" and, like any stalwart liberal in the New Deal tradition, "believed in bringing the fruits of technology to the common man." The Colorado River storage project was his idea. See Marc Reisner, *Cadillac Desert: The American West and Its Disappearing Water* (New York: Viking Penguin, 1986), pp. 142–145.

7. Richardson, *Dams, Parks and Politics*, p. 23.

8. Ibid., p. 24. See also undated newspaper editorial, c. December 1946, in which Straus is quoted as defending the Missouri Valley Authority and the three-man board that would govern all projects including the C-BT. Editorial is in Charles A. Lory Papers (cited hereafter as CAL Papers), Colorado State University Archives (CSUA).

9. Memorandum, 20 July 1945, J. M. Dille to "Dear Sir," in "Professional Correspondence, 1949" folder, CAL Papers, CSUA.

10. Memorandum, 18 March 1946, J. M. Dille to Directors of the NCWCD, ibid.

11. Donald R. McCoy, *The Presidency of Harry S. Truman* (Lawrence: The University of Kansas Press, 1984), pp. 66, 91.

12. Richardson, *Dams, Parks and Politics*, pp. 26, 27.

13. Memorandum, 3 December 1946, J. M. Dille to the Board, in "Professional Correspondence, 1949" folder, CAL Papers, CSUA.

14. Memorandum, 28 February 1947, J. M. Dille to the Directors, ibid.

15. Ibid. J. M. Dille further noted that the total estimated cost of the C–BT stood at $128,000,000. Under present reclamation laws, he added, "all reimbursable costs of multiple purpose projects above the ability of the water users to pay may be allocated to be repaid by power in addition to actual power costs."

16. Memoranda, 1, 27 April 1947, J. M. Dille to Directors; 7 May 1947, J. R. Barkley to Directors, ibid. *Denver Post*, 16 May 1947.

17. Notes taken by Bob Barkley at a meeting with Avery Batson and other Bureau representatives, September 15, 1947, in "Meetings and Conferences, 1946–1953" notebook, NCWCDA.

18. Minutes, NCWCD, November 15, 1947. Both Tipton and Stone recommended that the Board agree to cooperate in the restudy.

19. Letter, 6 October 1947, Avery Batson to NCWCD Board, NCWCDA. Field work for this report was done under the supervision of Mills E. Bunger; the economic study was carried out by Ralph L. Parshall, senior irrigating engineer, Bureau of Agricultural Engineering, U.S. Department of Agriculture.

20. Ibid. Batson quoted the report of the House Committee on Appropriations on the Interior Department Appropriation Bill, 1948. He interpreted this language as an "order" to C–BT Directors to revise their Repayment Contract. See Bob Barkley's notes on meeting, September 15, 1947, between Region 7 and NCWCD officials in "Meetings and Conferences, 1946–1953" notebook, NCWCDA.

21. "Colorado–Big Thompson Project: Comparison of 1937 and 1947 Plans and Costs," 1947, NCWCDA.

22. Ibid. This valuable report describes changes made by the Bureau in each of the C–BT's features, beginning with Green Mountain Reservoir and touching on each of the works moving from west to east over the entire Project.

23. In March 1947, after discussing the repayment matter with Judge Stone of the CWCB, the Board passed a resolution endorsing legislation then pending in Congress (S. 539 and H.R. 1886) that would extend the repayment periods of reclamation contracts and reduce the interest rate on power costs. Other bills were introduced in 1947, and Stone made it clear that the House Interior Appropriations Subcommittee would continue to oppose large payments to the Bureau until legislation was passed to clarify the proposed amendments to the 1939 Reclamation Act. See Minutes, NCWCD, March 8 and April 12, 1947.

24. Memorandum, January 1947, J. M. Dille to Directors, in "Joint O and M Replacement Reserve" folder, NCWCDA.

25. J. R. Barkley, "Facts Relating to the Twenty-Five Million Dollar Obligation of Northern Colorado Water Conservancy District," June 1946, in "Office Memos and Reports relating to Repayment Matters" notebook, NCWCDA.

26. Interview, Bob Barkley, Denver, 3 October 1989.

27. Ibid.

28. U.S. Senate, Colorado–Big Thompson Project, Synopsis of Report, 75th Cong., 1st sess., 80, item (c), p. 13.

29. USBR "Colorado–Big Thompson Project: Comparison of 1937 and 1947 Plans and Costs," p. 2.

30. Notes taken by Bob Barkley at a meeting of the NCWCD Board with Avery Batson, director of Region 7 of the Bureau, March 5, 1949, in "Meetings and Conferences, 1946–1953" notebook, NCWCDA. A marginal note in Barkley's handwriting says, "power people told to design for 310,000."

31. According to ample evidence, the Bureau was very supportive of Denver's search for additional water supplies, through expansion of the collection system for the Moffat Tunnel and through the city's plan to bring Blue River water under the Continental Divide into the South Platte. See letter, 1 March 1950, Sam Y. West, Jefferson County Planning Commission, to J. R. Barkley, NCWCDA, in which he states that the Blue-Platte project is being carried in the plans of the Bureau of Reclamation.

32. Notes taken by Bob Barkley at a meeting, June 15, 1950, in "Meetings and Conferences, 1946–1953" notebook, NCWCDA.

33. Ibid., June 1, 1950.

34. Ibid., December 16, 1950.

35. Interview, Bob Barkley, 3 October 1989. Barkley also noted that the District later claimed that it had lived up to its obligation under S.D. 80 to build Green Mountain Reservoir. The CRWCD, beneficiaries of Green Mountain, had no right to oppose NCWCD plans to pursue the remainder of the 310,000 acre-feet in the Windy Gap project; however, events proved that there was considerable opposition.

36. Richardson, *Dams, Parks and Politics*, p. 28.

37. Article in unidentified newspaper, 30 May 1948, NCWCD Newspaper Clippings Book 4, p. 136.

38. Minutes, NCWCD, February 14, March 6, and June 12, 1948.

39. Articles in unidentified newspaper, 26, 28 September 1948, NCWCD Newspaper Clippings Book 4, pp. 140, 141.

40. As reported in the *Denver Post*, 26 January 1949.

41. Leslie Miller, "The Battle That Squanders Billions," *Saturday Evening Post*, 14 May 1949.

42. *Denver Post*, May 14, 1949.

43. See miscellaneous letters to Dille and the Board from local citizens Allyn H. Tedmon of Littleton, August 15, 1946, and Parker D. Shepperd of Denver, April 3, 1947, NCWCDA.

44. See "Professional Correspondence," 1947–1949, CAL Papers, Box 4, CSUA.

45. *Denver Post*, 22 May 1949.

46. Unidentified newspaper clippings 2, 5 July and 2 August 1949, NCWCD Newspaper Clippings Book 4, pp. 186–190.

47. Unidentified newspaper, 3 February 1949, ibid., p. 157.

48. Reisner, *Cadillac Desert*, pp. 144–145.

49. Ibid., p. 154.

50. Unidentified newspaper, 9 July 1948, NCWCD Newspaper Clippings Book 4, p. 132.

51. The *Denver Post* ran an article by staff writer Robert Steinbruner in the April 25, 1948, issue, showing that the Colorado River was bankrupt even if the upper basin states took only their 7.5 million acre-feet. A few months later, the newspaper noted that the upper basin states were unable to break a deadlock on their Colorado Compact quota, with Colorado asking for 56 percent of the 7.5 million acre-feet.

52. Downey and Knowland were also the individuals most instrumental in trying to remove Commissioner Straus. The Upper Colorado River Basin Compact was formally signed on October 12, 1948, in Santa Fe, New Mexico, at the Palace of the Governors. Arizona's legislature was the first to ratify.

53. S.D. 80, p. 24.

54. Letter, 18 February 1946, E. B. Debler to J. M. Dille, NCWCDA.

55. Minutes, NCWCD, February 14, 1948.

56. Ibid., September 11, 1948.

57. Ibid., December 4, 1948, and March 5, 1949.

58. Ibid., March 5, 1949.

59. Notes taken by Bob Barkley, April 29, 1949, in "Meetings and Conferences, 1946–1953" notebook, NCWCDA.

60. Ibid., July 6, 1949.

61. Ibid.

62. Minutes, NCWCD, March 18, 1950.

63. At least this is the opinion of Senator Clinton P. Anderson (D-N.M.), as recorded in an unidentified newspaper, 13 November 1949, NCWCD Newpspaper Clippings Book 5, p. 7.

64. Richardson, *Dams, Parks and Politics*, p. 36.

65. Minutes, NCWCD, May 8, 1950.

66. See J. M. Dille's memoranda to Directors, April 22, 1950, and June 13, 1950, and Dille's statement, Hearing on North Poudre Contract, which provides a history of how the contract was finally signed. "Professional Correspondence" folder, December 1950, CAL Papers, CSUA.

67. Minutes, NCWCD, July 7, 1950 and September 8, 1950.

68. Notes taken by Bob Barkley at meeting with Bureau, February 8, 1951, in "Meetings and Conferences, 1946–1953" notebook, NCWCDA. See also Minutes, NCWCD, February 10, 1951.

69. Notes taken by Bob Barkley at meeting with Bureau, February 10, 1951, in "Meetings and Conferences, 1946–1953" notebook, NCWCDA.

70. Notes taken by Bob Barkley at meeting with Bureau, April 24, 1951, and August 7, 1951, ibid.

71. Munroe, who was appointed to the original NCWCD Board in 1937, served for four years, until 1940. Reappointed by Judge Coffin in 1944, he continued on the Board until 1958 when he was made Director emeritus.

72. NCWCD, *Secretary-Manager's Report*, 1950, p. 18. Even before the communist invasion of South Korea, Secretary Chapman spoke at an American Legion banquet on the booming growth in the West and on the need to support this expansion with new sources of power. Senator Joseph O'Mahoney (D-Wyo.), who appeared on the same program, said that Americans must unite just as they did in wartime to maintain a prosperous and free economy. "The alternative," he said, "was to be overrun by Communism." Chapman also urged creation of the Missouri Valley Authority and a similar authority for the Colorado River. See unidentified newspaper article, 1 March 1950, NCWCD Newspaper Clippings Book 5, p. 29.

73. S.D. 80 called for a canal of 1,000 cfs capacity to divert the flow of Willow Creek from an interception point near Dexter, Colorado, to Lake Granby. Notes taken by Bob Barkley at meeting in the District office with Bureau officials, January 20, 1950, in "Meetings and Conferences, 1946–1953" notebook, NCWCDA.

74. Ibid., April 25, 1950.

75. Ibid., June 1, 1950.

76. Ibid., April 6, 1950.

77. NCWCD, *Secretary-Manager's Report,* 1950, p. 1.

78. Memorandum, 13 April 1950, J. R. Barkley to the NCWCD Board of Directors, in "Letter Drafts for Negotiations of Completed Project" folder, NCWCDA.

79. Minutes, NCWCD, June 3, 1950. The resolution was approved by Board members on November 10, 1950.

80. S.D. 80 called for a feeder canal of 300 cfs to be built from Carter Lake to the St. Vrain. Nothing else was said about extensions into Boulder Creek or to the South Platte River because in 1937 no one expected that allotments would be contracted that far south.

81. Letter, 21 February 1946, J. M. Dille to E. B. Debler, and memoranda 15, November 1945, and March 1949, in "Office Memos, Office Reports, Relating to Project Water Deliveries" notebook, NCWCDA.

82. Minutes, NCWCD, March 18, 1950.

83. Ibid., September 8, 1950. Notes taken by Bob Barkley at a meeting in Boulder for a discussion of City of Boulder and Public Service Company water needs, August 2, 1950, in "Meetings and Conferences, 1946–1953" notebook, NCWCDA. See also NCWCD Newspaper Clippings Book 5, p. 48.

84. Letters, 5 July 1950, Charles Lory to Charles Hansen, and 14 July 1950, Hansen to Lory, in "CAL Professional Correspondence, 1950" folder, CAL Papers, CSUA.

85. Notes taken by Bob Barkley, June 15 and June 21, 1950, in "Meetings and Conferences, 1946–1953" notebook, NCWCDA.

86. Ibid., July 21, 1950. These "improvements" now included a Soldier Canyon Outlet at Horsetooth Reservoir, Poudre Supply Canal, Dille Tunnel, Horsetooth Feeder Canal turnouts, Poudre Supply Canal turnouts, and enlargement of the St. Vrain Supply Canal.

87. The rest of the south-end story is chronicled in Chapter 4.

88. Notes taken by Bob Barkley, September 27, 1950, and December 11, 1950, in "Meetings and Conferences, 1946–1953" notebook, NCWCDA.

89. Ibid., March 9, 1951.

90. Contract No. 181r-1414 (12-15-50).

CHAPTER 12

1.   *United States* v. *Northern Colorado Water Conservancy District,* United States District Court for Colorado, Case No. 2782, June 10, 1949.

2.   *United States* v. *Fallbrook Public Utility District,* 101 F. Supp. 298 (S.D. Cal. 1951). The United States brought action against the Fallbrook Public Utility District, a public service corporation of California, to establish the plaintiff's right to the entire and undiminished flow of the Santa Margarita River through lands acquired for the establishment of Camp Pendleton. The U.S. District Court held that the United States was entitled to a determination in Federal District Court as to its claimed rights. The suit was entered by U.S. attorney William H. Veeder, who was then with the Lands Division of the Justice Department. California water users were so upset by the federal government's attempt to adjudicate state water rights that they produced a color movie, "The Fallbrook Story," showing the United States knocking down water users with a hammer. Interview, Bob Barkley, 3 October 1989. See also Carl G. Mueller, Jr., "Federal Ownership of Inland Waters: The Fallbrook Case," *Texas Law Review* 31 (April 1953), pp. 404–417.

3. E. S. Toelle, pamphlet entitled "Irrigation and Bureaucracy," 1949, in "Miscellaneous Correspondence and Data, F–J" folder, NCWCDA. Toelle, secretary-treasurer of the Association of Water Users for State Control, Greeley, Colorado, wrote several letters detailing his conspiracy theory to staff members of the NCWCD.

4. *Greeley Tribune*, 18 February 1952.

5. Minutes, CRWCD, April 16, 1946. With the advice of Delaney, the CRWCB board increased the budget for legal fees to $5,000 and contemplated a mill levy increase in order to fight against Denver's claims to the Blue River.

6. Denver claimed a March 23, 1914, date to the Blue River, based on Denver City Planning Commission employee Ralph Meeker's three-day visit to the drainage areas of the Fraser, Williams, and Blue rivers. He took a few pictures, wrote a reconnaissance report, and recommended diversions without any details on the quantity of water available. After reviewing the evidence, Judge William H. Luby, Summit County District Court, issued a "proposed decree" in November 1951 giving Denver a 1946 priority date on the Blue River and Colorado Springs a 1948 priority date. The proposed decree also placed the rights of Green Mountain Reservoir ahead of those of Denver and denied the claims of the CRWCD. A conditional decree, issued in March 1952, gave Denver 788 cfs and Colorado Springs 400 cfs from the Blue River with priority dates as mentioned. This decree was upheld by the Colorado Supreme Court on October 18, 1954.

7. *Year Book of the State of Colorado, 1948–1950* (Denver: The Colorado State Planning Commission, 1951). Unless otherwise noted, all growth data come from this volume.

8. *Report of the Board of Water Commissioners, Denver, Colorado*, years ending December 31, 1946, and 1947.

9. Ibid., December 31, 1948.

10. Ibid.

11. Ibid., December 31, 1950.

12. Ibid., December 31, 1953.

13. *Greeley Tribune*, 15 November 1951. During 1954's severe drought, *Cervi's Journal* not only harangued Denver for not building Two Forks, but accused the DWB of sitting on its hands, of opposing the city's growth with its "blue line," and of allowing the water system's fate to be controlled by Glenn G. Saunders, "who has been building the City's water supply on paper and in lawsuits for years without delivering an acre-foot of wetness." The journal recommended sending Denver's best-equipped spokesmen to Washington to acquire the Two Forks site from the Department of the Interior. See *Cervi's Rocky Mountain Journal*, 26 July 1954.

14. In a November 1951 interview, William H. Veeder, special assistant to the attorney general in Washington, said that Denver's claims on the Colorado River, if recognized, could very well destroy the C-BT. See unidentified newspaper clipping, in NCWCD Newspaper Clippings Book 5, p. 110.

15. On January 19, 1944, the United States and the NCWCD filed a joint application and claim in Summit County District Court for adjudication of Green Mountain Reservoir and Power Plant water rights in Water District No. 36. Denver's 1942 suit in Summit County District Court asked for a March 23, 1914, conditional decree to all water that entered the Blue River from Tenmile Creek and Snake River at Dillon. The CRWCB's Delaney argued that Denver's decree, if granted, would impair the operation of Green Mountain Reservoir. See Minutes, CRWCB, July 15, 1947, and USBR, *Annual Project History: Colorado–Big Thompson Project*, 1950, p. 48.

16. *Denver Post*, 28 June 1940.

17. See *Report of the Board of Water Commissioners, Denver, Colorado*, years ending December 31, 1946, 1947, 1948, 1949. The CRWCB noted that Denver was spending "token money" of $250,000 on both ends of the proposed tunnel and that Denver and the Bureau had agreed to limit the project to 400,000 acre-feet. See Minutes, CRWCB, April 15, 1947.

18. Minutes, CRWCB, April 20, 1948. The NCWCD was at odds with Denver because Section IV, General Powers (37-45-118) of the 1937 Water Conservancy District Act required the District

to operate the C–BT so that the "present appropriations of water" and "prospective uses of water for irrigation and other beneficial consumptive use purposes . . . will not be impaired or increased in cost at the expense of the water users in the natural basin [of the Colorado River]." Denver has not considered itself limited by the same restrictions.

19. Ibid.

20. Ibid.

21. Ibid., July 20, 1948.

22. Minutes, NCWCD, October 19, 1948. Denver did not seriously commit to limitation of use until 1955.

23. Ibid., November 6, 1948.

24. Ibid., September 11 and October 19, 1948.

25. Memorandum, 20 November 1947, William R. Kelly and E. Tyndall Snyder for Northern Colorado Water Conservancy District on Suit Proposed by Attorney General of the United States To Be Brought by the United States and by the Conservancy District in United States District Court Against Various Appropriators of Water on the Colorado River and the Thompson River and Tributaries, pp. 14, 15. (Hereafter, this memorandum referred to as "Kelly Memo, 1947.")

26. Ibid., pp. 19, 21.

27. Ibid., p. 23.

28. Minutes, NCWCD, January 10, 1948.

29. Ibid., July 17, 1948.

30. In a June 26, 1941, letter to Hansen, Taylor wrote,

> I earnestly hope that the Northern Colorado Water Conservancy District will stand by that agreement [S.D. 80] and help protect the Western Slope in the rights we established by that agreement. The consideration of that agreement was really the construction of the Green Mountain Reservoir to stabilize the flow of waters of the Colorado River. Now, Denver, a lot of promoters, real estate men, engineers, and lawyers are trying to promote a scheme to take "all of the water'"of the Blue River at a point above that reservoir. . . . While the whole matter is such a preposterous and brazen conception, nevertheless its backing is very dangerous to the Western Slope. I earnestly hope and believe that you people are still with us and will prevent that outrage which will practically amount to a destruction of the beneficial purposes of Green Mountain Reservoir.

In conclusion, he hoped that Hansen would serve notice on the "Denver bunch" that the District wanted Blue River water conserved for the Green Mountain Reservoir. See Charles Hansen Files, NCWCDA.

31. Resolution No. 17, 1935, Charles Hansen Files, NCWCDA. See also memorandum, October 1948, William Kelly to Directors on Adjudication, in "Professional Correspondence, April-September, 1948" folder, CAL Papers, CSUA.

32. Colorado, Department of the State Engineer, *Preliminary Engineering Report, Northern Transmountain Diversion*, by Royce J. Tipton (Denver: 1933), pp. 68–77.

33. William R. Kelly, Confidential Memorandum Report to Northern Colorado Water Conservancy District, Colorado–Big Thompson Project, Water Adjudication, Lake Granby and Green Mountain Reservoir, 5 pp. (Supplied to author by Gregory J. Hobbs, Jr., of Davis, Graham and Stubbs.)

34. Letter, 24 July 1948, Royce J. Tipton to Charles Hansen, NCWCDA.

35. Letter, 6 June 1990, Gregory J. Hobbs, Jr., to the author.

36. Minutes, NCWCD, August 14, 1948.

37. Ibid.

38. Ibid. The clear implication was that Kelly would obey the Board but not Hansen.

39. Memorandum, 26 August 1948, William R. Kelly to Charles Hansen and the NCWCD Board of Directors, CAL Papers, CSUA.

40. Ibid.

41. Letter, 28 September 1948, Claude C. Coffin to NCWCD Directors and officers, Charles Hansen Files, NCWCDA.

42. Letter, 2 October 1948, Charles Hansen to Claude C. Coffin, Charles Hansen Files, NCWCDA. Hansen, who was so disturbed by the need to defend his interpretation of S.D. 80 and the spirit of agreements made with the West Slope, asked Coffin in the rough draft of this letter to relieve him of further service as a Director. See "Miscellaneous Undated Documents" folder, Charles Hansen Files, NCWCDA.

43. Ibid. The remainder of the citations relating to Hansen's response to Coffin come from the same letter.

44. Letter, 4 October 1948, Claude C Coffin to Charles Hansen, Charles Hansen Files, NCWCDA.

45. Memorandum, October 1948, J. M. Dille to Directors on Adjudication, in "Professional Correspondence, October 1948" folder, CAP Papers.

46. Ibid. Dille also recommended that the federal government be allowed to take responsibility for the adjudication of project water rights. Because the CWCB and the Bureau were working to develop a compromise satisfactory to all interests on the Blue River, while at the same time assuring the NCWCD that its interests would be completely protected, Dille urged the Board to advise the Bureau "what we expect in results. Offer to cooperate in any way that is helpful, but leave to them, as they actually have, the full responsibility for final results."

47. Minutes, NCWCD, October 9, 1948.

48. Ibid. Hansen referred to S.D. 80, page 10, which set forth the summary and conclusions of the land classification studies and which showed only 32,800 acres for potential irrigation along the lower main stem of the river, which had an annual flow of 3,000,000 acre-feet of Colorado River water.

49. Minutes, NCWCD, October 19, 1948.

50. Minutes, NCWCD, November 6, 1948.

51. Minutes, NCWCD, October 9, 1948.

52. See letter, 24 January 1990, Gregory J. Hobbs, Jr., to the author.

53. Kelly made his initial request for a salary increase in April 1948. See Minutes, NCWCD, April 10, 1948. Minutes of January 15, 1949, show that Kelly and Clayton were to receive a salary of $500 a month, retroactive six months. In a letter to Hansen in May 1948, Kelly noted that his firm had spent 130 days during 1947 on NCWCD business; that he had traveled to Boulder, Denver, Grand Junction, and most of the counties within the District; and that he had not taken any vacation. He explained that only $33,000 of the $48,000 that the firm received from the District in 1947 was net as compensation for services. Because salaries had remained fixed since 1941 while inflation and increasing costs ate into profits, Kelly asked Hansen "to do what is fair in view of changing conditions." See letter, 27 May 1948, William R. Kelly to Charles Hansen, Charles Hansen Files, NCWCDA.

54. For example: disputes arising over the North Poudre Gravity Canal (Minutes, NCWCD, September 13, 1949); reallocation and transfer procedures (Notes taken by Bob Barkley, July 27, 1948, "Meetings and Conferences, 1946–1953" notebook, NCWCD); the agreement to send water south, in Kelly's words, to "that bunch of thieves" in the Boulder area (Interview, Bob Barkley, 11 August 1989); water allotments to farmers and municipalities (Minutes, NCWCD, June 6, 1953, and February 3, 1955); and Kelly's expressed dissatisfaction with the Board's decision to move headquarters from Greeley to Loveland following Hansen's death in 1953 (Minutes, NCWCD, May 8, 1953).

55. Interview, Bob Barkley, 3 October 1989.

56. See Minutes, NCWCD, February 7, March 7, 1953; September 29, 1955; and January 1, 1956.

57. Interview, Bob Barkley, 11 August 1989.

58. Minutes, NCWCD, July 13, 1956. Nix told Barkley that, as president of the Board, he had to stop by Kelly's house and tell him that he had been fired. On hearing the news, "Ben said that Kelly threw up his hands, turned red as a beet, and screamed like a mashed cow: 'They can't do this to me,' and slammed the door in Nix's face." Interview, Bob Barkley, 3 October 1989.

59. Minutes, NCWCD, August 10, 1956.

CHAPTER 13

1. Minutes, CRWCD, January 18, October 18, 1949, and February 19, 1951.

2. *Session Laws of Colorado*, Ch. 192, Sec. 1 (b), 1943. The language used in this act is almost identical to Section IV, General Powers (37-45-118), of the 1937 Water Conservancy District Act.

3. Congressional approval of the Upper Colorado River Basin Compact in April 1949 was the green light for planning the CRSP. Although the upper basin states had been slow to plan for development of the 7.5 million acre-feet authorized in the Colorado River Compact of 1922, Bureau personnel had already drafted plans for the largest power and reclamation project ever conceived, including dams identified as Echo Park, Flaming Gorge, Glen Canyon, Navajo, Cross Mountain, Crystal, Curecanti, Gray Mountain, Split Mountain, and others. See John Upton Terrell, *War for the Colorado River*, 2 vols. (Glendale, Calif.: The Arthur H. Clark Company, 1965). Volume Two contains a legislative history of the CRSP as well as a description of each project.

4. As reported by the *Grand Junction Sentinel*, 26 April 1949, one-time Bureau Commissioner Page told an audience in Grand Junction that they could do little about their destiny and "may as well stop trying"; the *Sentinel* called Page an "Apostle of Futility." But Delaney sensed that the West Slope was falling behind in the race for water utilization. With Denver claiming 166,000 acre-feet from the Blue River and Colorado Springs hoping for 20,000 acre-feet from the same stream, while the South Platte Water Users Association planned to develop 70,000 acre-feet from the Blue River and Williams Fork, Delaney noted that the only identifiable West Slope scheme at the time was the 14,000 acre-feet Paonia project. See Minutes, CRWCB, January 17, 1950.

5. It is not clear whether these industrial uses were contemplated in Bureau studies completed prior to construction of Green Mountain Reservoir. Paragraph (c), "Manner of Operation," S.D. 80, states that the 100,000 acre-feet stored in Green Mountain Reservoir for power purposes would also be available for future domestic use, irrigation, and "the development of the shale oil or other industries." In 1949 Tipton advised Barkley that in his view future industrial developments along the Colorado River would not be entitled to water from Green Mountain Reservoir. In a memorandum written a few years later, Barkley implied that the West Slope could be assured that future use of Green Mountain water for domestic, irrigation, and industrial developments would not be jeopardized by East Slope transmountain diversions. See notes taken by Bob Barkley, June 18, 1949, in "Meetings and Conferences 1946–1953" notebook, NCWCD, and memorandum, September 1955, NCWCD, Utilization of Blue River Water Supply and Green Mountain Reservoir in Fulfillment of Obligations Under Senate Document No. 80, in "Office Memos and Reports Relating to Repayment Matters" notebook, NCWCDA.

6. Minutes, CRWCB, January 22 and July 12, 1952. Delaney pointed out that the Army Corps of Engineers had reported on coal and oil shale development in the Colorado River basin. They estimated construction of thirty-five shale plants on the Colorado River by 1960 and fifty-nine plants by 1975, each of which would require from 1,190 to 1,470 acre-feet of water for yearly operation. The water supply work on this report was done by Royce J. Tipton and Associates.

7. Minutes, CWCB, February 16, 1953.

8. Ibid., February 22, 1951.

9. In 1953 Bureau officials reported completion of some surveys, but they needed another five years to finish work on the West Slope. See Minutes, CWCB, February 16, 1953.

10. *Grand Junction Sentinel,* 10 March 1953. The author also echoed the old West Slope complaints that the decision "involves in various ways justice and fairness in highways, freight rates, tunnels through the Continental Divide, taxes, and business relations." Denver was brandishing the big club, he said, but failing to speak softly.

11. From 1940 to 1950 Director Stone of the CWCB made personal and official commitments to protect economic development in the "natural basin" of the Colorado River. See Minutes, CRWCD, July 28, 1949, and Minutes, CWCB, August 15, 1947, and June 15, 1950.

12. Unidentified newspaper, 30 December 1953, NCWCD Newspaper Clippings Book 6, p. 61. Thornton was keenly interested in Colorado's unification on water matters. Without harmony between East and West Slopes, he feared that Congress would never fund the CRSP. As chairman of the CWCB, he was identified in the minds of certain West Slope individuals with the group that had already capitulated to the DWB. In fact, Thornton was upset with Saunders and the DWB because he felt that focus on lawsuits kept the state disunified and thereby delayed congressional support for the CRSP.

13. NCWCD Scrapbook 6, February 16, 1954, p. 72.

14. Ibid., December 31, 1953, p. 63.

15. This is a reference to the Delaney Resolution. *Longmont Daily Times-Call,* 13 August 1955.

16. *Greeley Tribune,* 19 May 1953. See also Minutes, CWCB, April 27, 1953.

17. Notes taken by Bob Barkley, June 18, 1949, in "Meetings and Conferences, 1946–1953" notebook, NCWCDA. Saunders meant that the 100,000 acre-feet in Green Mountain Reservoir should be available to vested rights on either side of the Continental Divide, loosely construing paragraph (c) in the Manner of Operation section of S.D. 80. At a later date (August 1955), Saunders changed directions and argued that Senate Document 80 was not law. He compared it to the "hundreds of monographs which are each year printed in the government printing office for convenient reference by congressional committees and by the members of each house of Congress." See Brief of Defendant, City and County of Denver, August 19, 1955, filed in *United States v. NCWCD,* Civil Action Nos. 5016 and 5017, U.S. District Court.

18. *Denver Post,* 18 November 1951; Minutes, CWCB, February 16, 1953.

19. Letter of Governor Johnson to the Denver Chamber of Commerce saying that he hoped the Chamber could control its own officials, as reported in the *Longmont Daily Times-Call,* 2 May 1955.

20. *Report of the Board of Water Commissioners, Denver Colorado,* year ending December 31, 1952.

21. Kelly was present at the 1949 opening session of Summit County District Court on July 11 to announce that the NCWCD was joining the United States in withdrawing from the claim in state court. Minutes, NCWCD, August 13, 1949.

22. Kelly's opinion as reported in Minutes, NCWCD, October 1, 1952.

23. The South Platte Water Users Association had sought a decree of 3,300 cfs with a date of October 27, 1942, plus certain storage priorities. The landmark Colorado Supreme Court case that rejected Denver's claimed priority dates is reported as *City and County of Denver* v. *Northern Colorado Water Conservancy District,* 130 Colo. 375, 276 P. 2d 992 (1954).

24. *Rocky Mountain News,* 4 January 1955. Denver helped wage a successful campaign to defeat Judge Mortimer Stone, who was replaced by Henry S. Lindsley in the next election.

25. *Greeley Tribune,* 13 December 1954.

26. Unidentified newspaper, 11 March 1955, NCWCD Newspaper Clippings Book 7, p. 22.

27. *Report of the Board of Water Commissioners, Denver, Colorado,* for the year ending December 31, 1954. Based on studies of Alvord, Burdick & Howson, Consulting Engineers, Chicago, Illinois, attorneys for the DWB estimated quite accurately that by 1960 Denver would be serving a metropolitan population of 680,000 and would need 184,590 acre-feet of raw water diversion. The average annual yield from the South Platte, Fraser, and Williams Fork rivers was calculated at

120,000 acre-feet, leaving a deficit of almost 65,000 acre-feet. See Brief of Defendant, City and County of Denver, August 19, 1955, filed in *United States* v. *NCWCD*, Civil Action Nos. 5016 and 5017, U.S. District Court.

28. *Greeley Tribune*, 9 March 1954.

29. Both Denver and Boulder implemented water restrictions and conservation practices. In 1954 Boulder limited lawn sprinkling and reported a high level of citizen cooperation. In 1955 Denver introduced various conservation devices and reported that, while 7,016 additional taps were installed, 22 percent less water was consumed and the average consumption per capita of 147 gallons was the lowest recorded since 1918. See Report of the *Board of Water Commissioners, Denver, Colorado*, for year ending December 31, 1955. See also various newspaper clippings, in NCWCD Newspaper Clippings Book 6, January–August 1954.

30. *Denver Post*, 6 October 1954.

31. Minutes, CWCB, February 16, 17, 1953. See also article by Gene S. Breitenstein, "The Colorado — River of Controversy," NCWCD Newspaper Clippings Book 6, pp, 76, 77.

32. See unidentified newspaper article, 1 January 1953, in NCWCD Newspaper Clippings Book 6, p. 156. Other newspaper articles written in 1952 and 1953 strongly suggest that the Bureau's tactic vis-à-vis the CRSP was to convince Congress that the dams and power plants had to be authorized quickly, both because of the estimated twenty-five years required to build them and because increased power and food production would make the United States less vulnerable during the Cold War.

33. The CRSP was introduced in the House after Eisenhower had been in office barely three months. He made bold promises about what the Republicans would do in the field of water and power development, and his administration gave a very clear signal that the president supported authorization and funding, even though he may have had very little information on the feasibility of the CRSP. See Terrell, *War for the Colorado River*, 2, pp. 15, 16.

34. Unidentified newspaper, 7 January 1954, NCWCD Newspaper Clippings Book 6, p. 65.

35. Minutes, NCWCD, December 7, 1951.

36. Unidentified newspaper, 26 May 1954, NCWCD Newspaper Clippings Book 6, p. 89. Some referred to the resignations as Black Friday for the CWCB.

37. Even Kelly saw that Roberts was entitled to "large credit" for the results that were ultimately attained. See letter, 18 October 1955, William R. Kelly to NCWCD Directors, NCWCDA.

38. The Henrylyn Irrigation District was one of several entities cooperating in a plan to bring water from the West Slope to the South Platte Valley. Mills Bunger, one of the Bureau engineers who designed the C–BT, drew up a plan to provide domestic water for an estimated population of 1.5 million. The objective was to create a conservancy district adjoining the NCWCD to the south in which an additional 155,000 acre-feet could be added to Denver's extant supply along with 268,000 acre-feet of supplemental water for farmers in the South Plate Valley. Hudson was located in the geographic center of the proposed district, with Denver at the south end, Prospect Valley on the east, Frederick, Erie, Lafayette, and Louisville on the west, and the NCWCD on the north. This information was supplied to the author by Karen L. Rademacher, water resources engineer for the Central Colorado Water Conservancy District.

39. Notes taken by Bob Barkley, December 29, 1954, in "Meetings and Conferences, 1946–1953" notebook, NCWCDA.

40. Minutes, NCWCD, December 18, 1954.

41. Notes taken by Bob Barkley, December 29, 1954, in "Meetings and Conferences, 1946–1953" notebook, NCWCDA.

42. Barkley's studies of 1953 and 1954 Blue River flows indicated that the NCWCD's replacement obligations would not be hindered even if Denver diverted "all the water available on her 1946 decree out of the Blue River. . . . As a summary conclusion," Barkley wrote, "there is no foreseeable method of operation by the City and County of Denver which is prejudicial to the District's fulfillment of its obligation to make replacement from Green Mountain Reservoir, or, further,

which would require direct releases from Granby and Willow Creek reservoirs in order to supplement from Green Mountain." See memorandum, Northern Colorado Water Conservancy District, Utilization of Blue River Water Supply and Green Mountain Reservoir in Fulfillment of Obligations Under Senate Document No. 80, p. 9, in "Office Memos and Reports" notebook, NCWCDA.

43. Notes taken by Bob Barkley, December 29, 1954, "Meetings and Conferences, 1946–1953" notebook, NCWCDA.

44. Ibid.

45. *Denver Post*, 23 February 1955. Denver based its argument on Article IV (b) of the 1922 Colorado River Compact, that "subject to the provisions of this compact, water of the Colorado River System may be impounded and used for the generation of electrical power, but such impounding and use shall be subservient to the use and consumption of such water for agricultural and domestic purposes and shall not interfere with or prevent use for such dominant purposes."

46. The McCarran Amendment, adopted by Congress on July 10, 1952, located in Section 208 (a), (b), (c), and (d) of the 1953 Justice Department Appropriation Act, now provides for the joinder of United States water claims in state court. See *Statutes at Large*, Vol. 66, p. 560. Department of Justice Appropriation Act of 1953 (codified in *United States Code*, Title 43, Chap. 666, 1953). See also Memorandum of Points and Authorities in Opposition to Motions of the City and County of Denver and Colorado Springs to Remand, Civil Action Nos. 2782, 5015, 5017, May 31, 1955. Prior to the McCarran Amendment, the United States had not waived its sovereign immunity.

47. Notes taken by Bob Barkley, December 29, 1954, in "Meetings and Conferences, 1946–1953" notebook, NCWCDA.

48. *Greeley Tribune*, 10 May 1955. Attorneys for the United States had petitioned that the federal power water rights issue be removed to Knous's Federal District Court. This petition was granted, and on April 27, 1955, "an alias notice and summons" in Civil Action Nos. 1805 and 1806 was served upon the attorney general of the United States. Over objections by Denver and Colorado Springs, a trial date was set for October 5, 1955.

49. Minutes, NCWCD, September 8, 1955.

50. Such releases would violate S.D. 80. For information on this meeting, see notes taken by Bob Barkley, September 2, 1955, in "Meetings and Conferences, 1946–1953" notebook, NCWCDA.

51. Interview, Bob Barkley, 11 August 1989.

52. *Rocky Mountain News*, 14 September 1955.

53. Minutes, NCWCD, September 29, 1955.

54. *Rocky Mountain News*, 6 October 1955.

55. In 1977, another dry year on the Front Range, Denver refused to release 28,622 acre-feet of water from Dillon Reservoir to satisfy the senior call of Green Mountain Reservoir. Proceedings of the Federal District Court and the U.S. Court of Appeals for the 10th Circuit ordered Denver to release the water and ruled that Denver had no right, title, or interest in the waters of Green Mountain Reservoir. See *United States v. Northern Colorado Water Conservancy District*, 608 F.2d 422 (10th Cir. 1979).

56. Ibid. See also letter, 18 October 1955, William R. Kelly to NCWCD Board of Directors. Findings of Fact and Conclusions of Law, U.S. District Court for Colorado, Consolidated Case Nos. 5016 and 5017, issued by Judge William Lee Knous, October 12, 1955.

CHAPTER 14

1. All Project features were completed by summer 1956 except the last power plant being built on the Big Thompson River.

2. Seaton also noted that the Central Valley project in California and the Columbia basin project in Washington were larger but still incomplete. The best description of the Loveland dedication can be found in the *Loveland Reporter-Herald,* 12 August 1956.

3. *Denver Post,* 12 August 1956.

4. *Denver Post,* American Weekly Section, 7 October 1956. Responses to Wylie's article appeared in several newspapers, including the *Rocky Mountain News,* 8 October 1956, and the *Greeley Tribune,* 12 October 1956.

5. Leslie Miller, "The Battle that Squanders Millions," *Saturday Evening Post,* 14 May 1949. Speaking around the country, Miller stressed the need to curb waste in reclamation spending.

6. Bernard DeVoto, "Shall We Let Them Ruin Our National Parks?" *Saturday Evening Post,* 22 July 1950. DeVoto, who usually articulated his vision of the West from his "Easy Chair" column in *Harper's Magazine,* routinely lashed out against subsidies and giveaways of federal lands.

7. NCWCD, *Secretary-Manager's Report,* 1948, p. 23. R. L. Parshall of the Soil Conservation Service and Director Lory expressed concern about the Bureau's costly designs in their 1949 communications with Dille. Dille responded that the District's policy was not to interfere "unless we catch some matter which we can call to their attention informally." See "Professional Correspondence, 1949," CAL Papers, CSUA. Barkley also recalled that Bureau engineers constantly developed fancy designs "that practically drove the contractors crazy." Interview, Bob Barkley, 3 October 1989.

8. USBR, *Annual Project History,* 1949, p. 5.

9. Ibid., 1951, p. 79; 1952, p. 87. These leaks were of concern to Granby citizens who appeared before the CWCB to express their fears. Following an inspection by State Engineer J. E. Whitten (who replaced M. C. Hinderlider in 1951), J. H. Knights, South Platte District manager, and R. J. Tipton, the CWCB's consulting engineer, assured them that the grouting process would adequately eliminate all danger. See Minutes, CWCB, December 20, 1951, and May 5, 1952.

10. *Annual Project History,* 1948, p. 59. NCWCD, *Secretary-Manager's Report,* 1947, 1948.

11. Unidentified newspapers, 20 July 1951, NCWCDA Newspaper Clippings Book 5, p. 84.

12. Minutes, NCWCD, January 10, 1948.

13. Letters, April–June, 1949, Mrs. Enos A. Mills and others to Charles Lory, in "CAL Correspondence, 1949," CAL Papers, CSUA.

14. *Annual Project History,* 1949, pp. 100–104. NCWCD, *Secretary-Manager's Report,* 1949, p. 13.

15. *Annual Project History,* 1950, p. 77; 1951, p. 84; 1952, pp. 93–95; and 1953, p. 72. NCWCD, *Secretary-Manager's Report,* 1950, p. 9; 1951, pp. 13, 14; 1952, p. 17; 1953, p. 12.

16. USBR, *Colorado–Big Thompson Project: Technical Record of Design and Construction,* 4 vols. (Denver: USBR, 1957), 3, pp. 36, 38. 17.

17. NCWCD, *Secretary-Manager's Report,* 1953, p. 12. Based on recorded flows between 1900 and 1936, Bureau engineers in 1937 estimated an annual average of 55,400 acre-feet from Willow Creek. See S.D. 80, pp. 13, 14. Present-day NCWCD records show that annual net deliveries to Lake Granby between 1957 and 1988 averaged 33,412 acre-feet.

18. *Colorado–Big Thompson Project: Technical Record,* 1, p. 88.

19. Ibid., p. 91.

20. Ibid., p. 99; 3, p. 59.

21. NCWCD, *Secretary-Manager's Report,* 1950, p. 10. *Annual Project History,* 1950, pp. 86, 87.

22. NCWCD, *Secretary-Manager's Report,* 1951, p. 14.

23. Ibid., 1948, p. 9.

24. Unidentified newspaper, 6 June 1949, NCWCD Newspaper Clippings Book 4, p. 181. Commissioner Straus did not attend, but sent a congratulatory letter. At other talks delivered during the summer, Straus predicted that the Bureau would work on multiple-basin projects and would do as much construction in 1950 as had been done in the first thirty years under the Reclamation Law.

25. J. R. Barkley, speech given June 5, 1949, in "Office memos and Reports Relating to Repayment Matters" notebook, NCWCDA.

26. NCWCD, *Secretary-Manager's Report*, 1948, p. 15.

27. Ibid. Dille's prediction reflected his concern about Congress withholding funds for commencement of new work. If legislators continued in this vein, the Project would be delayed by several years.

28. The first water deliveries were made to shareholders in the Ish Reservoir. The other ditches that benefited are mentioned in the NCWCD, *Secretary-Manager's Report*, 1953, p. 16. Cal Maier, commissioner of Water District No. 5, had suggested the Hell Canyon delivery route in 1950 when the Boulder area was suffering one of its frequent water shortages. See NCWCD, Minutes, September 8, 1950.

29. President Eisenhower issued a directive in October 1950 that required reductions in federal expenditures. In compliance, Secretary Chapman ordered a $2 million cutback in C–BT funding and froze an additional $2.5 million; however, because the Project was nearing completion and offered the potential of power production to improve national strength, Congress provided adequate funding during the war years. Compared to average annual appropriations of $1.9 million from 1938 through 1948, Congress appropriated an annual average of $19.67 million between 1949–1953. See NCWCD, *Secretary-Manager's Report*, 1952, p. 13.

30. NCWCD, *Secretary-Manager's Report*, 1949, p. 11.

31. Ibid., 1951, p. 16.

32. *Annual Project History*, 1952, p. 117.

33. *Rocky Mountain News*, 27 February 1954.

34. The two-part contract was let in 1952, with canals and tunnels by the Winston Brothers Company and the Little Thompson Siphon by the Adler Construction Company. Delays in completion of the St. Vrain Supply Canal were partly due to major landslides that caused the contractor to excavate more material than expected. See NCWCD, *Secretary-Manager's Report*, 1952, p. 19.

35. *Annual Project History*, 1950, pp. 6, 7, 12.

36. *Greeley Tribune*, 21 July 1951. *Fort Collins Coloradoan*, 22 July 1951.

37. NCWCD, *Secretary-Manager's Report*, 1954, p. 1.

38. *Annual Project History*, 1948, pp. 74, 75.

39. NCWCD, *Secretary-Manager's Report*, 1952, p. 3.

40. When fully constructed, this trifucation structure made possible C–BT water movement in three directions: through the Big Thompson Siphon and the Horsetooth Feeder Canal, through the Big Thompson Power Plant and into the Big Thompson River, or directly into the Big Thompson River.

41. *Annual Project History*, 1949, pp. 80–90; 1950, pp. 2–8, 110.

42. This conclusion is drawn from the *Annual Project History* for these years. The Bureau noted some work stoppage at Mary's Lake and Estes Park power plants in 1949 and again in 1950 with strikes that lasted one or two months. See *Annual Project History*, 1949, pp. 2, 3; 1950, pp. 4, 5. Other strikes mentioned lasted a week or so.

43. Minutes, NCWCD, February 7, 1953. The State Assembly's 1951 decision made this possible, amending Section 29 of the 1937 Water Conservancy District Act to permit inclusion of towns, cities, and other lands as well as individual tracts of land into a conservancy district. *Session Laws of Colorado*, 1951, Ch. 294. Before the act passed, Hansen and other members of the Board opposed any changes in the Water Conservancy District Act "which would permit Conservancy Districts to sell rented water outside of its boundaries." In contrast, Dille reported to the Directors that the attorneys "seemed to favor amending Section 29 to permit inclusion of municipalities and also were very anxious to *remove* the restrictions in the present Act to a district selling water outside the boundaries" (emphasis added). See Minutes, NCWCD, February 10, 1951, and memorandum, 29 January 1951, J. M. Dille to Directors, in CAL Papars, CSUA.

44. The Longmont office, which opened in January 1953 on the second floor of the Longmont City Hall under District employee Earl F. Phipps, received petitions for allotments from farm owners in the St. Vrain, Boulder Creek, and South Platte valleys. See *Boulder Daily Camera,* 8 January 1953.

45. Minutes, NCWCD, May 8, 1948.

46. Ibid., July 9, 1949 and March 18, 1950. Notes taken by Bob Barkley July 5, 1950, in "Meetings and Conferences, 1946–1953" notebook, NCWCDA.

47. Notes taken by Bob Barkley in Royce Tipton's office with representatives from the City of Boulder, August 2, 1950, in "Meetings and Conferences, 1946–1953" notebook, NCWCDA. See also unidentified newspapers, NCWCD Newspaper Clippings Book 5, pp. 45, 48.

48. Minutes, NCWCD, December 9, 1950.

49. *Boulder Daily Camera,* 2 May 1951.

50. Minutes, NCWCD, October 5, 1951. Barkley recalled that Kelly's interests in acquiring water for the Laramie-Poudre and Greeley-Poudre irrigation companies made him somewhat antagonistic to Boulder's request. See interview, Bob Barkley, 11 August 1989.

51. Minutes, NCWCD, April 5, 1952.

52. Notes taken by Bob Barkley, December 18, 1952, in "Meetings and Conferences, 1946–1953" notebook, NCWCDA. Minutes, NCWCD, August 2, 1952.

53. Minutes, NCWCD, January 3, 1953. This proposal was consistent with Section 13 (f) of the Water Conservancy District Act. The first unit, therefore, included the original allottees who paid $1.50 per acre-foot unit for C–BT water.

54. See NCWCD resolution of January 10, 1953. An Operating Agreement was signed on August 24, 1953, and a Supplemental Agreement on February 6, 1954. To comply with state engineer requirements regarding flood control, Boulder Reservoir capacity was increased to 13,100 acre-feet. On May 14, 1965, a Second Supplemental Agreement was signed to define land areas, structures, and facilities that would be controlled, operated, and maintained by both parties. A Filter Plant Operating Agreement was negotiated on May 9, 1969. These contracts were all voided by the agreements of March 14, 1975, August 10, 1979, and May 27, 1980.

55. Newspaper articles in February 1953 pointed to a possible water shortage. While Boulder tried once again to purchase water from Denver, newspaper data pointed to very low flows on tributaries of the South Platte River, snow accumulation at 60 to 90 percent of normal, and a 37 percent decline in the storage capacity of Front Range reservoirs. See NCWCD Newspaper Clippings Book 6, pp. 3–6, and *Denver Post,* 11 February 1953.

56. *Boulder Daily Camera,* 1 April and 1–8 June 1953. Minutes, NCWCD, July 2, 1953.

57. Notes taken by Bob Barkley at meetings with ditch officials, October 28, November 16, December 9, 14, 1953, in "Meetings and Conferences, 1946–1953" notebook, NCWCDA. At the NCWCD Board meeting of June 12, 1954, Directors agreed to ditch company demands as well as the Platte Valley Irrigation Company's request for 10,329 acre-feet of Project water. Contracts with all three companies were validated on June 30, 1954. See Minutes, NCWCD, July 8, 1954.

58. Minutes, NCWCD, September 8, 1954. NCWCD, *Secretary-Manager's Report,* 1955, p. 9.

59. Barkley reported to the Board on November 9, 1956, that the District's share of one-third of the cost of Boulder Reservoir would amount to approximately $372,000. Minutes, NCWCD, March 6, April 10, 1954, and November 9, 1956. The District was committed to pay $9,289 a year through 1994 plus interest at 2.463 percent on the unpaid balance.

60. *Annual Project History,* 1955, pp. 7, 13.

61. Ibid., 1954, p. 7; 1955, pp. 7, 8; 1956, p. 10.

62. Ibid., 1956, p. 16.

63. The new contract executed September 10, 1956, was requested by the commissioner of the Bureau because revenues anticipated in the December 15, 1950, interim contract had not been realized.

With this objective in mind, Barkley persuaded the government to approve early commencement of the "second" period which included: (1) automatic beginning of the construction repayment period; (2) establishing two reserve funds; (3) distributing revenues to the government over a five-year period for recovery of money expended on Project additions and improvements; and (4) activating the 1-mill ad valorem tax and special assessments on allotment contracts. See Supplement No. 2 of contract Ilr-1051, September 10, 1956.

64. NCWCD, *Secretary-Manager's Report*, 1956, p. 6.

65. Walter Prescott Webb, "The American West, Perpetual Mirage," *Harper's Magazine* (May 1957), pp. 25–31.

CHAPTER 15

1. As defined in the Repayment Contract (Article 9 [d]), "the operation of the Project shall be divided into two periods: (1) the period ending with December 31 two years prior to the initial repayment installment provided in the first paragraph of Article 6 and (2) the period after such date." Basically, the first period was construction; the second period was to begin when the physical system was complete and the District could assess a 1-mill ad valorem tax along with assessments for water allotments.

2. Minutes, NCWCD, March 10, 1951.

3. *Wyoming* v. *Colorado,* 259 U.S. 419 (1922). *Nebraska* v. *Wyoming and Colorado* 325 U.S. 589 (1945). Previously, Carpenter had been instrumental in bringing about the South Platte River Compact, April 27, 1923, effective March 8, 1926.

4. Letter, March 1, 1951, Clifford Stone to Judge Donald Carpenter (son of Delph Carpenter), Miscellaneous Correspondence, NCWCDA.

5. *Denver Post,* 22, 23 October 1952. A short biography of Stone is in *The Reclamation Era,* 39:1 (January 1953), pp. 5, 6, 9.

6. The CWCB also passed a resolution that noted Stone's death as an "irreparable loss" and suggested that he was so devoted to his work that he died of exhaustion. See Minutes, CWCB, October 1952.

7. Minutes, NCWCD, May 5, 1951.

8. Ibid., March 7, 1953. On this same date, the Board also agreed to clear the NCWUA account off District books.

9. Letter, 31 March 1953, Charles Lory to Charles Hansen, CAL Papers, CSUA.

10. Letter, 14 June 1953, William R. Kelly to Charles Lory, ibid.

11. Thomas Hornsby Ferril, Colorado's poet laureate, wrote that Hansen was the "quietest evangelist I ever knew. . . . He would talk in a low voice to anyone who would listen; then he would take you down in the basement of the *Tribune* and show you the worksheets, the preliminary drawings, the calculations. You would come away convinced that the C–BT Project would somehow, some day, come into being, and it did." See Ideas and Comment column, *Rocky Mountain News,* 5 November 1955.

12. Coffin and Kelly played the critical role orienting the Board to S.D. 80 and Colorado water law as the quintessential guidelines for making policy decisions. Letter, 24 January 1990, Gregory J. Hobbs, Jr., to the author.

13. Minutes, NCWCD, September 9, 1954.

14. Ibid., March 6 and April 10, 1948.

15. Ibid, July 8 and September 29, 1955.

16. Memorandum, May 1948, "Discussion of Allotments and Reallocations," by J. M. Dille, NCWCDA.

17. Ibid. The Water Conservancy District Act authorized the District to make water allotments.

18. Ibid.

19. Minutes, NCWCD, December 6, 1947. Transfers were defined as the removal of water from the originally described land to another area where a new lien was required. A reallocation occurred when water was divided on the originally described land under the same lien.

20. Interview, Bob Barkley, 3 October 1989.

21. Memorandum, May 1948, "Discussion of Allotments and Reallocations," by J. M. Dille, NCWCDA.

22. Ibid.

23. Notes taken by Bob Barkley, July 27, 1948, at a meeting in the District office between Hansen, Dille, Clayton, and Kelly, in "Meetings and Conferences, 1946–1953" notebook, NCWCDA.

24. Ibid.

25. *Boulder Daily Camera*, 8 January 1953.

26. This total includes the 208,476 acre-feet mentioned above plus 6,000 acre-feet allocated to the Bijou Irrigation Company and 600 acre-feet to the town of Johnstown.

27. Minutes, NCWCD, June 6, 1953.

28. Ibid., October 2, 1953.

29. *Loveland Reporter-Herald*, 11 February 1955.

30. Minutes, NCWCD, February 24, 1955. Of the 310,000 total acre-foot units available to the Project, 245,106 were already allotted and 64,894 remained for the Board's action on February 24. Of those units already allotted, 133,146 were individual farm contracts (Class D); 44,950 were municipal contracts, including Fort Collins, Greeley, Loveland, Longmont, Boulder, Berthoud, Johnstown, Mead, and Lyons; and 67,010 were Section 25 corporate contracts, including Great Western Sugar, North Poudre Irrigation Company, the State Board of Agriculture, and Bijou Irrigation Company.

31. Minutes, NCWCD, February 3, 1955. Hatfield Chilson was the only Director to vote with Kelly.

32. Ibid., July 8, 1955.

33. Ibid., February 10, 1956.

34. Ibid., March 9, 1956.

35. Ibid., December 14, 1956. Readers should note that the *involuntary* request for transfer or reallocation meant that at least one of the lien holders did not agree with the petition for change. To address this frequently occurring problem, the April 13, 1955, rules and regulations were enforced so that everyone would have an opportunity to express an opinion in front of the District Board, which acted as the final arbiter. A *voluntary* request was one in which all lien holders agreed on the change; in these cases, a hearing was unnecessary.

36. Ibid., January 11, 1957.

37. Ibid., June 6, 1953.

38. Ibid., August 5, 1953.

39. Report of the committee to the Board, August 7, 1953, signed by J. Ben Nix, chairman, and Hatfield Chilson, NCWCDA.

40. *Greeley Tribune*, September 8, 1953.

41. Letter, 3 November 1953, James M. Hunter to J. M. Dille, NCWCDA.

42. The *Greeley Tribune* of May 26, 1954, noted that Barkley would be moving his family to Loveland by June 10 but that Dille would stay in his home at Fort Morgan.

43. Minutes, NCWCD, July 8, 1954.

44. *Loveland Reporter-Herald*, 18 September 1954. The Bureau's original announcement was made on July 26, 1954. Avery Batson informed the District in 1947 that Loveland was the logical place for

the Bureau to have a project office, but a prohibitive cost of an estimated $500,000 meant that personnel would remain divided between Denver and Estes Park. See notes taken by Bob Barkley, October 4, 1947, "Meetings and Conferences, 1946–1953" notebook, NCWCDA.

45. Minutes, NCWCD, April 10, 1948.

46. Letters, 5 August 1948, Kenneth W. Chomers, state conservationist, USDA, to J. R. Barkley and 9 August 1948, Barkley to Chomers, Miscellaneous Correspondence, NCWCDA. Both letters note the scarcity of available engineers; Chomers estimated ten engineering jobs for every man to fill them.

47. Letter, 15 June 1950, Charles Lory to Charles Hansen, CAL Papers, CSUA.

48. Minutes, NCWCD, February 10, 1951.

49. NCWCD, *Secretary-Manager's Report*, 1951, pp. 30–31. Phipps was expected to work with water users, ditch companies, and water commissioners to facilitate distribution of C BT water under the December 15, 1950, interim contract. At the close of the water season (April 1–October 31), he returned to Greeley to help with administrative work.

50. Ibid., 1951, 1952.

51. Minutes, NCWCD, November 6, 1952. In August 1956 the Board approved a retirement and insurance plan with Mutual of New York.

52. NCWCD, Tentative Organization, 1953, CAL Papers, CSUA.

53. Letter, 20 November 1952, Ed Johnson to Charles Lory, CAL Papers, CSUA.

54. Minutes, NCWCD, May 8, 1954. Upon termination, Sadie Johnson set herself up as a public stenographer who worked out of her Greeley home. She died in 1958 at the age of eighty-two.

55. Article 8 (B), Repayment Contract, July 5, 1938, between the United States and the NCWCD.

56. NCWCD, *Secretary-Manager's Report*, 1953, pp. 18–19. In 1953, 178,463 acre-feet of Project water were delivered at an overall cost per acre-foot of approximately seven cents. See also Minutes, NCWCD, March 7 and September 4, 1953.

57. Kenneth L. Whitmore joined the maintenance crew in 1954 and retired on December 31, 1990. He has pointed out that, during the early years of operation, no effort was spared to develop good relations with landowners and to deliver at least 1 percent more water to the water users than was called for in their contracts. Interview, Kenneth L. Whitmore, 11 January 1990.

58. NCWCD, *Secretary-Manager's Report*, 1955, p. 28; 1956, p. 12.

59. Minutes, NCWCD, March 6, 1948.

60. Ibid., July 7, 1950.

61. Ibid., February 6, 1954.

62. St. Vrain Water Users Association and the Big Thompson Water Users Association. See Ibid., September 9 and October 7, 1954.

63. Ibid., November 4, 1954.

64. Ibid., May 11, 1956.

65. Ibid., August 10, 1956.

66. Ibid., October 5, 1956.

67. Ibid., March 8, 1957.

68. At the January 11, 1957, Board meeting, Director Herbert H. Vandemoer noted that taxpayers in Logan County were paying their 1-mill tax under protest. They did not directly blame the District for inadequate return flows but felt it important to protest their situation. Some of the farmers discussed "exclusion" from the District, but Dille pointed out that this procedure applied only to specific tracts of land and depended on an approval order from the Board. Barkley had already informed the Bureau that east end residents feared the Project, not so much because it might not deliver supplemental water but because government intervention could deprive them

of free access and use of underground water. See notes taken by Bob Barkley, November 15, 1946, in "Meetings and Conferences, 1946–1953" notebook, NCWCDA.

69. This model, set up at the Denver Federal Center, was moved to the Loveland Museum in 1957, where it is still on display.

70. *Loveland Reporter-Herald*, 16 January 1956.

71. Letter, 4 November 1957, R. J. Walter to J. M. Dille, NCWCDA.

72. "The Green Echo of Snow," three-quarters sponsored by the Bureau and one-quarter by the District, was produced by Rainbow Pictures of Denver during 1975 and was shown for the first time in Loveland on July 30, 1976. Suggested alternate titles included "Water Wonderland," "Look Again, Major Long," "Power and Plenty," "Notice: Water at Work," "Water Be Dammed," "The Parting of the Waters," and many others.

73. Minutes, NCWCD, November 15, 1947, November 6, 1948, October 8, 1949, and October 5, 1951. This restriction is not applicable under current Colorado law because of the District's contractual obligations to the federal government.

74. Ibid., September 9, 1954. See NCWCD, *Secretary-Manager's Report*, 1954, for District valuations.

75. Interview, Bob Barkley, 11 August 1989.

76. Minutes, NCWCD, December 7, 1951.

77. Letter, 16 February 1952, R. L. Parshall to Charles Lory, CAL Papers, CSUA.

78. Letter, 7 February 1953, Committee of Concerned Citizens to NCWCD Board, ibid.

79. Letter, 18 September 1954, Charles Lory to W. A. Dexheimer, ibid.

80. After Judge Coffin's death in 1954, Buck became district judge. He appointed Dudley Hutchinson, Sr., of Boulder and John G. Nesbit of Fort Collins in 1954, but these were nominees of his predecessor. In 1955 he added Andrew D. Steele of Boulder to replace Jacob Schey, Gordon Dyekman of Larimer County to replace Hatfield Chilson, and W. D. Farr from Weld County to replace Marvin J. Collins. In 1956 he appointed Herb Vandemoer of Logan County to replace William E. Blair and, in 1957, R. J. Lamborn of Morgan County to replace J. C. Howell. In his reflections on the Board's changing composition, Barkley singled out Buck's appointments of Clyde Moffit, W. D. Farr, John Moore, and Dudley Hutchinson, none of whom had close connections with the old ditch companies. See interview, Bob Barkley, 3 October 1989.

81. Even before Buck became district judge, he asked Dille if he could make a trip over the Project to familiarize himself with all its features. See letter, 2 September, 1953, William Buck to J. M. Dille, Miscellaneous Correspondence, NCWCDA.

82. Coffin mentioned this view to Hansen in a September 20, 1951, letter, Charles Hansen Files, NCWCDA. In a 1955 paper presented to a group of North Dakotans interested in the operation of Colorado's conservancy districts, Barkley noted that Director appointments were conducted on a nonpartisan basis and that the district court had chosen to rotate the appointment of Directors in each division of the District "and to appoint men of variable background and experience in order to give the Board as a whole a wider representation." See "Office Memoranda and History" notebook, NCWCDA.

83. *Greeley Tribune*, 28 February 1955. See also unidentified newspaper, 30 May 1948, NCWCD Newspaper Clippings Book 4, p. 129.

84. *Greeley Tribune*, 19 May 1953.

85. Minutes, NCWCD, February 8 and November 15, 1957.

86. Unidentified newspaper, 16 February 1955, NCWCD Newspaper Clippings Book 7, p. 15.

87. Minutes, NCWCD, July 2, 1953, and January 6, 1955.

88. Interview, Bob Barkley, 11 August 1989.

89. Minutes, NCWCD, September 6 and November 6, 1952. As of 1992, annual payments to the United States increased to $1.1 million for ten years.

90. NCWCD, *Secretary-Manager's Report*, 1957.

91. J. M. Dille, A *Brief History of Northern Colorado Water Conservancy District and the Colorado–Big Thompson Project* (Loveland, Colo.: NCWCD, 1958.)

92. Dille used this phrase in a speech to the NRA in 1949. See *Fort Collins Coloradoan*, 22 November 1949. Quotes on the award ceremony came from the *Greeley Tribune*, 13 March 1956, and the *Loveland Reporter-Herald*, 3 May 1956.

CHAPTER 16

1. Bob Barkley, "Manager-Director Relations," speech to the Four States Irrigation Council, January 15, 1959, Barkley Box, NCWCDA.

2. Robert L. Branyan and Larson H. Lawrence, *The Eisenhower Administration, 1953–1961: A Documentary History* (New York: Random House, 1971), pp. 43, 45.

3. Michael C. Robinson, *Water for the West. The Bureau of Reclamation 1902–1977* (Chicago: Public Works Historical Society, 1979), p. 80.

4. An example of the kind of criticism the Bureau was experiencing came from University of Chicago Professor Charles Hardin. Speaking at the Western Resources Conference in Boulder, Colorado, Hardin noted that irrigation of semiarid land yields a smaller return than irrigation of more humid areas; that water used by cities and industry yields a greater return than water devoted to marginal crop land; that irrigation produces surplus crops other countries can produce more cheaply; that reclamation has become too costly because most of the feasible projects have already been built; and that reclamation is subsidized by partial cost write-offs or by higher prices to power consumers. See *Denver Post*, 15 July 1959.

5. When Barkley became secretary-manager, the District's operating budget was approximately $825,000 with nearly $475,000 raised from annual charges for existing water allotment contracts and $350,000 from the 1-mill ad valorem tax. The District was committed to repaying $26,031,000 over a forty-year period. Beginning in 1962, payments were calculated at $475,775 for 20 years; during the next ten years, payments would reach $525,775 annually; and in the final ten years, the District would make annual payments of $1,125,775.

6. Minutes, NCWCD, March 13, 1959.

7. Quoted in the May 27, 1959, *Greeley Tribune* is Barkley's report prepared for the Board, in which he estimated that by the year 2001, District operating costs would approach $2 million while projected revenues would only reach $1.5 million. Open-rated contracts would allow the District to eliminate this potential ten-year deficit of $5 million.

8. Minutes, NCWCD, April 3, 1959. Barkley's plan to amend the Repayment Contract (Article 15), allowing the District to invest its excess income, was effected in 1964. See Supplement No. 3, October 29, 1964, of the Repayment Contract, July 5, 1938, between the United States and the NCWCD.

9. On at least two separate occasions, Barkley reminded the Board that the study he had done prior to suggesting the open-rate procedure did not intend a rate increase on Class D contracts until such time as a definite need for revenue arose or until a high percentage of Class D contracts had been serviced. Although some Board members wanted to see these rates raised just to establish the precedent, the majority favored leaving Class D water at $1.50 (Unit 1) and $2.00 (Unit 2), until additional income was needed. See Minutes, NCWCD, January 6 and March 10, 1961.

10. Raymond L. Anderson, *Urbanization of Rural Lands in the Northern Colorado Front Range, 1955 to 1983* (Fort Collins, Colo.: Department of Agriculture and Natural Resource Economics, Extension Service, Colorado State University, 1984), p. 12.

11. United States Census reports, as quoted in *Colorado Year Book, 1959–1961* (Denver: State Planning Division, 1962), pp. 282–283.

12. Minutes, NCWCD, November 10, 1961. Saunders is quoted in the *Fort Collins Coloradoan*, 15 June 1960. Interestingly, five months earlier, while the Roberts Tunnel was still being built, the

DWB lifted its nine-year freeze on extending service beyond a "Blue Line" and accepted applications from organized water districts.

13. Minutes, NCWCD, November 9, 1962.

14. *Fort Collins Coloradoan*, 16 January 1959 and 3 July 1960.

15. *Boulder Daily Camera*, 31 August 1961. *Fort Collins Coloradoan*, 19 October 1961.

16. The average farm used between 8,000 and 10,000 gallons of water a month. Highly mineralized underground water not only corroded equipment, but also damaged the soil and prevented adequate weight gaining by livestock and dairy cattle. See *Denver Post*, 14 November 1960. Studies by economist Raymond L. Anderson showed that twelve rural domestics in the NCWCD area as of 1982 had a bonded indebtedness ranging from $97,000 (North Carter Lake Water District) to $5.1 million (Central Weld County Water District) and held a total of 18,881 shares of C–BT water. See *Expansion of Water Delivery by Municipalities and Special Water Districts in the Northern Front Range, Colorado, 1972–1982*, technical report no. 46 (Fort Collins, Colo.: Colorado Water Resources Research Institute, 1984), pp. 32, 40.

17. Interview, Bob Barkley, 9 May 1990.

18. Minutes, NCWCD, December 9, 1960, and January 12, 1962.

19. Interview, Bob Barkley, 31 May 1990.

20. Joseph L. Sax, "Selling Reclamation Water Rights: A Case Study in Federal Reclamation Policy," *Michigan Law Review* 64:1 (November 1965), pp. 13–46. Barkley replied to Sax that all forms of federal subsidization resulted in increased incremental values. Why, he asked, should reclamation projects be singled out when they were only one area of a vast and complex system of federal subsidy? Furthermore, pursuing Sax's proposals would freeze water allocations, and cities would not get the water they needed. See *Boulder Daily Camera*, 8 May 1966. As of 1992 Sax taught at the University of California, Berkeley.

21. Minutes, NCWCD, December 9, 1960. An excellent economic analysis of the efficiency of water transfers in the NCWCD area can be found in Chapter 5 of L. M. Hartman and Don Seastone, *Water Transfers: Economic Efficiency and Alternative Institutions* (Baltimore, Md.: The Johns Hopkins Press, 1970). One of Seastone's Colorado State University students, S. Lee Gray, presented a master's thesis in 1965 entitled "The Effect of the Northern Colorado Water Conservancy District on Water Transfer." Gray found the NCWCD open-market system the best among several he studied "because water has been transferred to its highest-valued and lowest-consumptive uses and return flows available for secondary appropriation have been increased." See p. 122.

22. The second quota was first announced in 1960. In the first ten years of C–BT operation, 100 percent quotas were set in 1958, 1963, and 1966.

23. Article 16 of the Repayment Contract gives the United States the right to "a minimum *annual* transmountain flow of 255,000 acre-feet" (emphasis added).

24. J. R. Barkley, "Agricultural Uses of Snow Surveys and Seasonal Water Forecasts," speech to Soil Conservation Society of America, August 27, 1959.

25. NCWCDA contains an entire folder of articles and letters from C. O. Plum to the District and to various newspapers, urging better use of C–BT water in development of agricultural lands in the Nunn area.

26. Responding to a farmer who asked whether transferring Project water to municipalities was decreasing the amount of water for agricultural operations, Barkley replied that the quota was the same for all water users, regardless of the class of service and that the transfer of water to municipalities had no bearing whatsoever on the quota itself. See Minutes, NCWCD, August 9, 1968.

27. According to the *Grand Junction Sentinel*, 18 January 1965, Colorado had 17,000 underground wells, 5,000 of which operated on the South Platte River. In 1964 alone, 1,660 new wells were registered. The volume of groundwater pumped annually for irrigation between 1959 and 1964

ranged from 1,600,000 to 2,180,000 acre-feet. See *Colorado Year Book, 1962–1964* (Denver: State Planning Division, 1965), p. 514.

28. George Vranesh, *Colorado Water Law* 3 vols. (Boulder, Colo.: Design Press, 1987), 1, pp. 244, 245. Vranesh cites the *Colorado Revised Statutes*, section 147-18-4 (1953).

29. Ibid., pp. 246, 247.

30. *Denver Post*, 13 April 1958. *Fort Collins Coloradoan*, 4 June 1958.

31. As quoted in Vranesh, *Colorado Water Law*, 1, p. 250. The court cited and agreed with an article by William R. Kelly entitled "Colorado Ground Water Act of 1957: Is Ground Water Property of the Public?" *Rocky Mountain Law Review* 31 (1959), pp. 165, 171.

32. Vranesh, *Colorado Water Law*, 1, pp. 256, 257.

33. The Colorado Water Congress came into being to a great extent because of Clayton's interest. See *Greeley Tribune*, 27 February 1958.

34. Minutes, NCWCD, November 10, 1961.

35. Ibid., February 10, 1961.

36. Ibid., April 2 and August 13, 1965

37. *Denver Post*, 24 February 1958.

38. Minutes, CRWCD, June 3, 1958.

39. Ibid. This committee worked with Governor McNichols to hammer out compromises suitable to both slopes. It divided the state into nineteen districts, gave western Colorado nine members on the Rules Committee, and stipulated that any three members of this committee could bar from the floor discussion on any controversial subject. Further, if East Slope members of the CWC tried to abrogate these safeguards, West Slope representatives could withdraw from the CWC.

40. These "objectives" were quoted by the *Longmont Daily Times-Call*, 22 April 1959, from a speech given by John Barnard, Jr., first assistant Colorado attorney general. Speaking in Loveland a year later, Barnard pointed out that Governor McNichols's Washington trip to appeal for action on the Fry-Ark project convinced him that Colorado needed an organization exclusively to promote water planning and resolve interbasin conflicts. See *Boulder Daily Camera*, 16 July 1960.

41. Minutes, NCWCD, June 13, 1958.

42. *Fort Collins Coloradoan*, 4 June 1958.

43. *Greeley Tribune*, 13 October 1960.

44. Minutes, NCWCD, July 11, 1958, and May 8, 1959.

45. *Denver Post*, 26 October 1959.

46. Ibid., 17 January 1960.

47. *Greeley Tribune*, 8 November 1961

48. *Fort Collins Coloradoan*, 9 January 1960. The three judges were Dale E. Shannon, Donald A. Carpenter, and William E. Buck. To further represent urban growth in the District's south end, the district court ordered appointment of a third Director from Boulder County, increasing the Board members to twelve. Dudley I. Hutchinson was the first appointee.

49. Constitutional Amendment 1, Senate Concurrent Resolution 12, 43d General Assembly, 1961, *Session Laws of of Colorado*, Ch. 313.

50. *Fort Collins Coloradoan*, 21 December 1962.

51. Resolution Passed at Regular Meeting of Board of Directors of The Cache la Poudre Water Users' Association, June 3, 1963, NCWCDA

52. Miscellaneous Correspondence, NCWCDA.

53. Enacted by the legislature, the Cache la Poudre Water Users' Association Amendment became Section (1) (c) of 37-45-114.

54. *Greeley Tribune*, 27 July 1963. *Boulder Daily Camera*, 27 July 1963. *Fort Collins Coloradoan*, 26 July 1963. At the Fort Collins meeting, Charles Boustead, manager of the Southeastern Colorado Water Conservancy District, expressed a related concern when he suggested clarifying the portion of the Water Conservancy District Act that refers to election of Directors in lieu of appointment by the court. See Minutes, NCWCD, August 9, 1963, and Section 37-45-114 (2) of the Water Conservancy District Act. C. O. Plum, the District's gadfly, complained that the existing Board served the purposes of the few while opposing the best interests of the allottees and taxpayers. See his letter to the *Greeley Tribune*, 8 October 1963.

55. *Fort Collins Coloradoan*, 9 August 1966.

56. *Grand Junction Sentinel*, 5 October 1966.

57. Ibid., 5 February 1967.

58. Minutes, NCWCD, February 10, 1967.

59. *Denver Post*, n.d. September 1967, NCWCD Newspaper Clippings Book 17, 1967.

60. Minutes, NCWCD, July 14 and August 11, 1961. "With Water Enough, A Wonderland" was the single-page flyer published in 1962 and reprinted in 1970 under the title "With Water Enough . . . A Better Land." In 1968 the Bureau published its own flyer, "The Colorado–Big Thompson Project," which announced availablity of "The Barrier Between," a color-sound, 16mm movie lasting 27 minutes, first premiered in 1958 and replaced in 1976 by "Green Echo of Snow."

61. Minutes, NCWCD, Special Meeting, March 26, 1963.

62. Ibid., February 13, 1970.

63. Ibid., February 8, 1974.

64. Ibid., July 12 and November 8, 1974.

65. University of Colorado economist Charles W. Howe has estimated that between 1960 and 1980, the value of C–BT recreation benefits in 1960 dollars was $91.7 million, nearly twice the original cost estimate for building the entire system ($44 million) in 1937 dollars. See Charles W. Howe, "Project Benefits and Costs from National and Regional Viewpoints: Methodological Issues and Case Study of the Colorado–Big Thompson Project," *Natural Resources Journal* 27 (Winter 1987), pp. 5–20.

66. Minutes, NCWCD, September 12 1958.

67. *Denver Post*, 28 September 1958.

68. Minutes, NCWCD, May 13, 1960.

69. Ibid., January 10, 1964.

70. As reported in the *Fort Collins Coloradoan*, 5 March 1961 and 19 January 1964.

71. *Grand Junction Sentinel*, 24 January 1964. *Greeley Tribune*, n.d. August 1964, NCWCD Newspaper Clippings Book, 12 1963.

72. Boulder City Manager E. Robert Turner told reporters that telling farmers whose crops were burning up that "we are going to keep water in the reservoirs for water skiers" would be difficult. See *Boulder Daily Camera*, 17 April 1963.

73. *Fort Collins Coloradoan*, 14 August 1963.

74. Ibid., 16 August 1959.

75. *Greeley Tribune*, 12 September 1961.

76. *Denver Post*, 14 February 1961.

77. Minutes, NCWCD, May 11, 1962.

78. *Greeley Tribune*, 28 March 1963.

79. Minutes, NCWCD, October 5, 1962.

80. Ibid., April 15, 1963.

81. *Greeley Tribune,* 19 August 1963. The Bureau's feasibility report estimated that 16,000 acre-feet would be used for the municipalities of Fort Collins and Greeley, enabling them to reach a total population of 175,000 by the year 2000.

82. Minutes, NCWCD, September 13, 1963.

83. *Fort Collins Coloradoan,* 9 December 1965. Farr believed that the Bureau's lack of support came from its failure to identify "a market for pumped back peaking power." See letter, 18 December 1990, W. D. Farr to the author, property of the author.

CHAPTER 17

1. Minutes, CWCB, April 25, 1949. An excellent study of the Narrows can be found in Marc Reisner's *Cadillac Desert: The American West and Its Disappearing Water* (New York: Viking Penguin, 1986), pp. 428–451.

2. This was the view of J. H. Knights, Region 7 engineer for the Bureau of Reclamation, as reported in unidentified newspaper, 30 May 1948, NCWCD Newspaper Clippings Book 4, p. 129.

3. Minutes, NCWCD, September 29, 1955.

4. *Fort Morgan Times,* 8 September 1951.

5. Views presented by Bob Barkley and Larry Simpson at a staff meeting of the NCWCD, n.d., ca. 1984. The Bijou Irrigation Company on the south side of the South Platte River irrigated much of the good land south of Fort Morgan and Brush. The Riverside Irrigation Company served a system 80 miles long on the north side of the river. Both systems could be served by a dam at the Hardin site. State Engineer Clarence Kuiper, who opposed the dam against the politicians' wishes, was convinced that the Narrows Dam would never hold water because of 300 feet of alluvial material underneath the chosen site. He feared a repeat of Wyoming's Teton Dam disaster. See Reisner, *Cadillac Desert,* pp. 437ff.

6. *Greeley Tribune,* 19 May 1953.

7. The Water Users Protective Association of Sterling made this request to the NCWCD and urged the Bureau to consider construction of a delivery system. See *Greeley Tribune,* February 1955, NCWCD Newspaper Clippings Book 7, p. 18, and Minutes, NCWCD, July 8, 1954, and January 6, and February 24, 1955.

8. Minutes, NCWCD, August 4, 1955.

9. Ibid., January 11, February 8, and November 15, 1957.

10. Don Hamil, first president of the Lower South Platte Water Conservancy District, said that Barkley opposed the Narrows because he was a disciple of Dille. He also identified Director R. J. Lamborn, a Weldon Valley resident, as an outspoken opponent. Hamil hoped that the NCWCD would take responsibility for building a dam on the lower South Platte so that the taxpayers in these counties would receive the return flow benefits promised in the 1938 Repayment Contract. Interview, Don Hamil, 15 May 1990.

11. *Greeley Tribune,* 12 June 1963. Minutes, NCWCD, February 14, 1969.

12. Recollections of Bob Barkley presented at NCWCD staff meeting, n.d., ca. 1984.

13. Minutes, NCWCD, October 13, 1961, and February 9, 1962.

14. *Fort Morgan Times,* 25 February 1963.

15. Minutes, NCWCD, September 10, 1964.

16. *Fort Morgan Times,* 13 December 1963. As with all new conservancy districts, opponents who wanted to challenge formation had to get signatures from 20 percent of the irrigated landowners (with assessed valuation of $50,000) and 5 percent of the nonirrigated landowners (with assessed valuation of $20,000) in the proposed district area; they failed.

17. *Fort Morgan Times,* 12 September 1964. See also Minutes, NCWCD, October 9, 1964.

18. By mid-1970 the Denver Water Board viewed Two Forks Dam as "an absolutely necessary part of Denver's long range water requirements." *Denver Post*, 14 June 1970. Since 1961, the Bureau had been studying the possibility of building two dams on the South Platte, one at the Narrows or Hardin area and the other at Two Forks. John Spencer, director of the Bureau's Region 7, described the Narrows and Fry-Ark projects as the most feasible multipurpose reclamation programs in the West. See *Denver Post*, 28 July 1961.

19. Minutes, NCWCD, January 9, 1970.

20. Ibid., November 8 and December 13, 1968.

21. Minutes, NCWCD, April 3, 1970.

22. *Fort Morgan Times*, 31 May 1968, 28 January 1969, and 23 March 1970.

23. Ibid., 10 June, 4 August, and 1 September 1970.

24. Ibid., 28 January 1972, 30 January 1973.

25. Ibid., 9 November and 15 December 1972.

26. Ibid., 14 May 1974.

27. At a meeting of the NCWCD staff, ca. 1984, Barkley stated that "in the early 1960s the Lower South Platte formed their own conservancy district in the area below Narrows and on down to the Nebraska line with boundaries that are exactly the same as the Northern District. Well, very frankly, this gave to the Board of Northern Colorado the best out they ever had, because in effect they were saying, 'We want our own district and we're going to build our own reservoirs.' Our Board was in the position to say, 'Fine, you want your own district and your own reservoirs? Have at it!' "

28. Ibid.

29. Minutes, CRWCD, April 15 and July 15, 1958.

30. Minutes, CWCB, February 22, 1951. During Fry-Ark discussions eleven months earlier, West Slope representative to the CWCB, Judge Dan Hughes of Gunnison, brought up the basin-of-origin protection language in Chapter 191 of *Session Laws of Colorado, 1943*. He cautioned fellow board members not to compromise the "present and potential" development of West Slope water and "called attention to the need for surveys, investigations, and studies in the natural basin of the Colorado River in Colorado to determine potential water development in the area before large exportation from the basin was undertaken. He deplored the slow progress that had been witnessed in the past in carrying on and completing such surveys and investigations." See Minutes, CWCB, June 15 and December 18, 1950.

31. *Session Laws of Colorado, 1943*, Articles 1 and 15, Ch. 192, Reference to Aspen Reservoir reflects early views on where compensatory storage would be located. Ruedi Reservoir on the Fryingpan River was the final site selection.

32. Minutes, CWCB, February 16, 1953.

33. *Grand Junction Sentinel*, 30 December 1953.

34. *Fort Collins Coloradoan*, 11 December 1956.

35. *Longmont Daily Times-Call*, 21 August 1958.

36. *Greeley Tribune*, 1 May 1959.

37. *Colorado Electric News*, February 1962, NCWCDA.

38. *Longmont Daily Times-Call*, 7 June 1962.

39. Phrase coined by John P. Saylor (R) of Pennsylvania, who had fought against the C-BT thirty years earlier, as quoted in the *Fort Collins Coloradoan*, 13 June 1962.

40. Minutes, NCWCD, May 11, 1962.

41. *Fort Collins Coloradoan*, 6 August 1962.

42. Minutes, NCWCD, February 9, 1962. See also letter, 30 January 1962, J. R. Barkley to Charles H. Boustead, Executive Secretary, Southeastern Colorado Water Conservancy District, NCWCDA.

43. Minutes, CRWCB, October 20, 1959, and March 8, 1960. The four sites were North Park, Kremmling, Dotsero, and Rifle.

44. Letters, 9 April 1960, John P. Akolt to John M. Spencer, Director, Region 7, and 8 July 1960, John P. Akolt to Felix L. Sparks, NCWCDA. The CWCB's endorsement of Crown Zellerbach's plan was made at a meeting in Alamosa, Colorado, August 15, 1960.

45. Letter, 16 August 1960, Glenn G. Saunders to Jack Clayton and Bob Barkley, NCWCDA. See also letter, 27 April 1960, Jack Clayton and J. R. Barkley to Secretary of the Interior Fred A. Seaton, NCWCDA, which noted that Denver changed its position from denying any responsibility under S.D. 80 during negotiations for the 1955 Blue River decrees to claiming that the city was an intended beneficiary of S.D. 80.

46. Letter, 27 April 1960, Jack Clayton and J. R. Barkley to Fred A. Seaton, NCWCDA.

47. Ibid., to John N. Spencer, August 11, 1960.

48. Ibid.

49. Letters, 10 March and 22 March 1961, ibid.

50. Letter, 16 March 1961, John R. Akolt to John N. Spencer, NCWCDA.

51. Letter, 23 March 1961, John Barnard to John N. Spencer, NCWCDA.

52. Letter, 22 March 1961, Jack Clayton and J. R. Barkley to John N. Spencer, NCWCDA.

53. Ibid., 22 August 1961.

54. Letter, 15 December 1961, J. R. Barkley to John N. Spencer, NCWCDA.

55. Letter, 4 January 1962, John N. Spencer to Jack Clayton and J. R. Barkley, NCWCDA.

56. Minutes, NCWCD, February 9, 1962.

57. Minutes, NCWCD, May 14, 1965.

58. Ibid., April 11, 1958.

59. Ibid., May 13, 1960.

60. Interview, Bob Barkley, 9 May 1990.

61. Ibid. According to Barkley, the Board knew very well what it was doing at the time, and the Directors were glad to give Englewood a helping hand because Saunders had not always been a close friend of the District.

62. Minutes, NCWCD, September 9, 1960.

63. Ibid., December 9, 1960, and January 6, 1961. Westminster and Broomfield hoped to utilize the Elliott water through an exchange between the Lower Boulder Canal and Baseline Reservoir.

64. Ibid., April 7, 1961. Barkley stated that the flexibility of Boulder Reservoir would allow release of water on exchange to Englewood and that the District could expect to make $35,000 to $45,000 annually on this basis.

65. Memorandum, 2 December 1960, "Statutory Powers of District to Transport Other Than Project Water," NCWCDA. In addition to citing the Water Conservancy District Act as amended (149-6 CRS 1953), this memorandum recommended a system of six priorities for future users of the "unused capacity" of the C–BT system: (1) the NCWCD; (2) municipal corporations within the boundaries of the District; (3) public corporations within the boundaries of the District; (4) municipal corporations outside the boundaries of the District; (5) public corporations outside the boundaries of the District; and (6) all others.

66. Contract No. 14-06-700-3123 approved by resolution, August 11, 1961. The City of Englewood passed Ordinance No. 23, August 7, 1961, NCWCDA.

67. Letter, 15 September 1961, William R. Kelly to J. R. Barkley, NCWCDA.

68. Letter, 21 September 1961, J. R. Barkley to William R. Kelly, NCWCDA.

69. Telephone conversation June 29, 1990, with W. W. "Pete" Wheeler, retired president of W. W. Wheeler and Associates, which made hydrology studies on the Fraser River and McClellan Reservoir.

70. Letter, 26 July 1961, Jack Clayton to J. R. Barkley, NCWCDA. Clayton's letter reported a July 4 telephone conversation with Elliott, who said that he had "talked to 'over fifty attorneys' who had all informed him that the best way to obtain a decree was to put his water to beneficiary [sic] use and then go in for a conditional decree. He stated that to do otherwise he would 'be over 110 years old' before he ever obtained a conditional decree. . . . I pointed out to him that we felt that it was reasonable to require at least a conditional decree with any part[y] with whom we negotiated." Elliott responded that the District's position was "grossly unfair" and "gave indications that he might endeavor to obtain a contract between himself and the government which we would have to recognize. . . . Needless to say, Mr. Elliott was extremely displeased with our conversation."

71. Minutes, NCWCD, January 12, 1962. Three months later the CRWCD passed a resolution informing the secretary of the interior and the CWCB that approval of any contract between the Bureau and John Elliott would violate a resolution of the CWCB opposing further federally funded transmountain diversion projects until the needs of the West Slope had been determined and protected. See Minutes, CRWCD, April 17, 1962. A letter from Barkley to Elliott, December 21, 1962, NCWCDA, however, makes clear that Elliott's project was still open for discussion.

72. Minutes, NCWCD, May 10, 1963.

73. Ibid., April 2, 1965.

74. Ibid., February 11, 1966. In addition to Boulder and Fort Collins, the towns of Lafayette, Erie, Broomfield, Thornton, and Fort Lupton sent letters of intent to use Elliott's water to the Four Counties Water Association. See *Denver Post*, 11 October 1965.

75. On April 13, 1966, the *Grand Junction Sentinel* editorialized that water taken from the Yampa and Colorado rivers meant that more must be reserved from other streams to meet the state's commitment to both upper and lower basin states; implied was the growing excitement about a major oil shale development along the Colorado River. In addition, the CCWCD, with Mills Bunger and David Miller leading the charge, was attempting to revive the old Blue River/South Platte project. From the West Slope's vantage point, the East Slope's acquisitive interest in their water had no end. See *Grand Junction Sentinel*, 3, 4, 5 January 1966.

76. *Grand Junction Sentinel*, 4 July 1965.

77. *Denver Post*, 17 June 1966.

78. Minutes, NCWCD, July 8, 1966, and April 5, 1968.

79. Ibid., February 10, 1967.

80. Letter, 9 July 1937, John C. Page to Congressman Fred Cummings, Charles Hansen Files, NCWCDA.

81. Ibid., 8 September 1961. Interview, Bob Barkley, 9 May 1990. When the city of Thornton purchased one-half of WSSC's water supply many years later, the decision not to approve a carriage contract for Grand River Ditch water through the C–BT system was magnified in importance.

82. Memorandum, 22 August 1963, Felix Sparks to CWCB and Colorado Water Investigation Commission, NCWCDA.

83. Letter, 10 October 1963, Bob Barkley to William H. Nelson, Associate Editor of the *Grand Junction Sentinel*, NCWCDA. Barkley mentions Sparks's memorandum of September 11, 1963.

84. Minutes, NCWCD, July 12, 1963.

85. Letter, 16 September 1963, William H. Nelson to Felix Sparks, NCWCDA.

86. Letter, 26 September 1963, J. R. Barkley to William H. Nelson, NCWCDA. Barkley's letter also noted that the Elliott proposal was far different in specifics from that of Fort Collins and would indeed require the CWCB's consent.

87. Letter, 3 October 1963, William H. Nelson to J. R. Barkley, NCWCDA.

88. *Loveland Reporter-Herald*, 9 December 1964.

CHAPTER 18

1. U.S. Senate, Colorado–Big Thompson Project, Synopsis of Report, 75th Cong., 1st sess., S.D. 80, Article 5 (l), "Manner of Operation of Project Facilities and Auxiliary Features."

2. NCWCD, *Annual Report, Fiscal Year 1957–58*, pp. 12, 39.

3. Ibid., and Minutes, NCWCD, January 10 and February 14, 1958.

4. Minutes, NCWCD, August 8 and September 12, 1958.

5. Ibid., February 13, 1959.

6. Ibid., October 9, 1959.

7. Ibid., February 12 and December 9, 1960.

8. The final agreement, known as "Principles to govern the Release of Water from Granby Dam to provide Fishery Flows immediately Downstream in the Colorado River," January 19, 1961, is signed by the Bureau of Sports Fisheries and Wildlife, the commissioner of the Bureau of Reclamation, the assistant secretary of the interior for fish and wildlife, the assistant secretary of the interior for water and power, and the secretary of the interior, NCWCDA.

9. Minutes, NCWCD, February 10, 1961.

10. Interview, Bob Barkley, 29 June 1990.

11. Barkley made the first mention of this situation to the Board at the August 4, 1959, meeting. Shortly thereafter, Glenn Saunders commented that the water from Green Mountain reservoir "should be made available to all vested rights and not to just a few." See *Greeley Tribune*, 14 August 1959.

12. *Denver Post*, 22 January 1958.

13. Letter, 14 June 1956, J. R. Barkley to Harold D. Roberts, DWB, NCWCDA.

14. Minutes, CWCB, August 16 and October 11, 1960.

15. Letter, 26 April 1960, Robert S. Millar, DWB, to Secretary of the Interior Fred A. Seaton, NCWCDA. Assistant Secretary of the Interior Fred G. Aandahl replied on May 16, 1960, that the request would be given "careful consideration." Minutes, CWCB, October 11, 1960.

16. Minutes, CWCB, October 11, 1960.

17. Letter, 8 November 1960, Jack Clayton to J. R. Barkley, NCWCDA. Clayton reported that the Justice Department stated that it had "much in common" with the NCWCD.

18. *Longmont Daily Times-Call*, 19 November 1959.

19. NCWCD, *Annual Report, Fiscal Year 1959–60*, p. 32.

20. What is known as the Cameo Call, a total of 2,260 cfs. See also Minutes, NCWCD, December 11, 1959.

21. NCWCD, *Annual Report, Fiscal Year 1959–60*, p. 33.

22. Minutes, NCWCD, April 1, 1960.

23. Ibid., November 4, 1960. Clayton wrote to Barkley, January 5, 1961, that the hearing would be on Denver's motion "for injunction and for remand to State Court" (of Case No. 2782, one of the three "Consolidated Cases"). See "Consolidated Cases, Phase II," NCWCDA.

24. Minutes, NCWCD, July 13, 1962.

25. Letter, 2 August 1962, Robert S. Millar to Secretary of the Interior Stewart L. Udall, and reply dated 9 November 1962, NCWCDA.

26. As reported in the *Fort Collins Coloradoan*, 2 October 1961.

27. *Denver Post*, 23 May 1962 and 7 July 1963. Dillon Reservoir was designed to hold 262,000 acre-feet of water, nearly doubling Denver's existing storage capacity in other reservoirs.

28. *Denver Post*, 28 April 1963.

29. *Fort Collins Coloradoan*, 7 August 1963.

30. *Denver Post*, 1 April 1962.

31. *Longmont Daily Times-Call*, 6 April 1962. See also *Chicago Daily News*, special to the *Denver Post*, 2 January 1963, in which Professor Terah L. Smiley, University of Arizona, blamed the new passion for air-conditioned environments for diminishing water resources.

32. *Loveland Reporter-Herald*, 3 October 1963.

33. *Greeley Tribune*, 13 May 1963. State Engineer J. E. Whitten refused to accept the filing, but the Colorado Groundwater Commission immediately hired two experts to look into the situation.

34. NCWCD, *Annual Report, Fiscal Year 1962–63*, pp. 5–6.

35. *Denver Post*, 15 May 1963.

36. Ibid., 19 January 1964. Denver's freeze on additional water contracts ended in 1960 after nine years of "Blue Line" restrictions. Enlargement of the DWB's service area coincided with major progress in the Roberts Tunnel. See Ibid., 3 January 1960.

37. *Longmont Daily Times-Call*, 7 September 1963.

38. *Grand Junction Sentinel*, 13 September 1963.

39. *Greeley Tribune*, 5 September 1963. Minutes, NCWCD, September 13, 1963.

40. NCWCD, *Annual Report, Fiscal Year 1962–63*, p. 38.

41. Letter, 21 September 1963, Ramsey Clark to Judge Arraj, NCWCDA.

42. Letter, 26 September 1963, Glenn G. Saunders, Jack Ross, John Dickson, and attorneys from Colorado Springs to Judge Arraj, NCWCDA.

43. Minutes, NCWCD, December 13, 1963.

44. *Rocky Mountain News*, 19 November 1963.

45. Minutes, NCWCD, February 14, 1964.

46. *Denver Post*, 23 December 1963.

47. John M. Sayre, an attorney with the firm Ryan, Sayre, Martin and Brotzman of Boulder, Colorado, was appointed in 1960 to represent Boulder County. The day following Clayton's death, the Board named Sayre special counsel to aid the junior members of the Clayton and Arnold law firm. In July 1964 the Board completed legal matters with Clayton and Arnold and retained Ryan, Sayre, Martin and Brotzman for the District, with Sayre acting as principal counsel.

48. Interview, Bob Barkley, 9 May 1990.

49. *Rocky Mountain News*, 12 April 1964.

50. NCWCD, *Annual Report, Fiscal Year 1963–64*, p. 4. See also Consolidated Cases (Civil Nos., 2782, 5016, 5017), Decree, stipulated April 16, 1964.

51. Letter, 28 April 1964, John M. Sayre to NCWCD Board of Directors, NCWCDA.

52. Helen M. Ingram, *Patterns of Politics in Water Resource Development: A Case Study of New Mexico's Role in the Colorado River Basin Bill* (Albuquerque: The University of New Mexico Press, 1969), pp. 21–23.

53. Frank Welsh, *How to Create a Water Crisis* (Boulder, Colo.: Johnson Books, 1985), p. 79. The author also noted that the Bureau estimated a 30 percent loss in cultivated acreage without construction of the Central Arizona project (CAP), although from 1947 to 1981 lands under cultivation actually increased from approximately 800,000 to over 1.35 million acres.

54. Rich Johnson, *The Central Arizona Project* (Tucson: The University of Arizona Press, 1977), p. 32.

55. Philip L. Fradkin, *A River No More: The Colorado River and the West* (Tucson: The University of Arizona Press, 1968), p. 250. A most thorough and readable account of the Colorado River Compact and Arizona's troubles with California can be found in Norris Hundley, Jr., *Water and the West: The Colorado River Compact and the Politics of Water in the American West* (Berkeley: University of California Press, 1975). See especially Chapter 9.

56. Minutes, NCWCD, March 14, 1958.

57. Simon H. Rifkind, Special Master, Draft Report, May 5, 1960, No. 9, Original in the Supreme Court of the United States, October Term, 1959, *Arizona v. California*, 373 U.S. 546(1963), decree entered by *Arizona v. California*, 376 U.S. 340 (1964), decree amended by *Arizona v. California*, 383 U.S. 268 (1966).

58. *Denver Post*, 9 January 1962.

59. Ibid., 13 June 1963.

60. Salinity results when minerals — mainly calcium, chloride, bicarbonate, magnesium, sodium, and sulfate — are dissolved in water. Salt measurement is either in parts per million or milligrams per liter, both of which count total dissolved solids. The sources of salinity in the Colorado River basin are divided fairly evenly between natural and human causes, with irrigation being "by far the largest man-caused source of salinity." By 1961, salinity levels rose to 2,700 milligrams per liter because agricultural waste waters were dumped into the river just above the border. See Fradkin, *A River No More*, pp. 297, 302.

61. Ibid., pp. 302–303.

62. *Denver Post*, 29 January 1962.

63. Fradkin, *A River No More*, p. 303.

64. Minutes, NCWCD, May 10, 1963.

65. *Greeley Tribune*, 8 February 1964.

66. Minutes, Colorado Advisory Committee, December 10, 1965, NCWCDA.

67. *Denver Post*, 11 January 1966.

68. Johnson, *The Central Arizona Project*, p. 178.

69. *Boulder Daily Camera*, 4 April 1969.

70. *Longmont Daily Times Call*, 26 October 1964.

71. Johnson, *The Central Arizona Project*, p. 176.

72. Minutes, NCWCD, May 13, 1966.

73. *Denver Post*, 17 February 1970, and *Boulder Daily Camera* 17 June 1973.

74. Testimony, J. R. Barkley, at a hearing before the Subcommittee on Irrigation and Reclamation of the Committee on Interior and Insular Affairs of the House of Representatives, on H. R. 4671 and similar bills, 89th Cong., 1st sess., August 23 to September 1, 1965.

75. Carol Edmonds, *Wayne Aspinall: Mr. Chairman* (Lakewood, Colo.: Crownpoint, 1980), p. 120.

76. Ibid., p. 125, 127.

77. Ibid., p. 131. On May 8, 1966, the *Grand Junction Sentinel* reported that cost per acre-foot for the Dolores project was $630; for the Dallas Creek project, $1,140; for the West Divide project, $1,710; and for the San Miguel project, $1,310.

78. *Grand Junction Sentinel*, 23 February 1966.

79. Edmonds, *Wayne Aspinall*, p. 131.

80. Johnson, *The Central Arizona Project*, p. 214.

81. Colorado Coordinator of the Division of Natural Resources Richard T. Eckles angered Aspinall when he referred to the five projects as "those five dogs on the western slope"; as Barkley recalled later, however, "Wayne knew it as well as anyone else. He felt that he had to include them knowing full well that when they were examined by the Bureau for authorization they would never make

it." Interview, Bob Barkley, 13 June 1990. See also Edmonds's notes in *Wayne Aspinall*, pp. 131 ff.

82. *Denver Post*, 2 February 1966.

83. S.D. 80, p. 5. The "Manner of Operation" was that part of S.D. 80 that was hammered out by NCWUA representatives and the WSPA. Bureau Commissioner John C. Page actually drew up the language. See deposition of Silmon Smith taken November 3, 1961, by John B. Barnard, attorney at law, Granby, Colorado, NCWCDA.

84. Hansen's memorandum summarized this meeting between Frank Delaney, Silmon Smith, Clifford Stone, Dan Hughes, and C. H. Stewart of the West Slope and Hansen, Dille, Tom Nixon, and William Kelly of the East Slope, with Mills Bunger and Porter Preston representing the Bureau. The West Slope demanded that any "turn down" of water to the lower basin states, resulting from a Colorado River Compact call "would have to be entirely borne out of the transmountain diversions to the Eastern Slope." See Charles Hansen Files for 1937, NCWCDA.

85. Interview, Kenneth Balcomb, 25 April 1990. See also *Grand Junction Sentinel*, 9 February 1966, in which Balcomb states that he and the CRWCD opposed any interpretation of S.D. 80 by means of legislation.

86. *Grand Junction Sentinel*, 13 April 1966.

87. Ibid., 30 January 1972.

88. Minutes, NCWCD, September 10 and November 19, 1965, and January 14, 1966. See also interview, Bob Barkley, 31 May 1990.

89. *Denver Post*, 30 January and 2 February 1966. *Grand Junction Sentinel*, 9 February 1966. David Miller of the CCWCD wanted to add something in the legislation to enable his organization to get federal funds for feasibility studies for future East Slope projects.

90. Colorado River Basin Project Act, Pub. Law 90-537, 90th Cong., S.1004, September 30, 1968.

91. Interview, Bob Barkley, 13 June 1990.

92. *Greeley Tribune*, 18 September 1968.

93. Letters, 22 May 1968, Felix Sparks to J. Ben Nix, and 22 June 1968, J. R. Barkley to John Love, NCWCDA.

CHAPTER 19

1. Robert G. Athearn, *The Mythic West* (Lawrence: University of Kansas Press, 1986), p. 213. This reference is from Chapter 9, "Wilderness Evangelists," written by Elliott West at Athearn's request.

2. Minutes, NCWCD, February 13 and March 13, 1959.

3. *Denver Post*, 23 November 1959.

4. Ibid., 18 November 1958, 7 December 1958, and 18 February 1960.

5. Ibid., 21 January 1962.

6. *Greeley Tribune*, 9 May 1962. The five areas in Colorado were Maroon Bells/Snowmass, Mt. Zirkel/Dome Peak, Rawah, West Elk, and La Garita on the Rio Grande.

7. *Grand Junction Sentinel*, 10 January 1964.

8. Carol Edmonds, *Wayne Aspinall: Mr. Chairman* (Lakewood, Colo.: Crownpoint ,1980), p. 157.

9. By the beginning of 1989 — the silver anniversary of the Wilderness Act — 90,760,106 acres were included in 474 units of the Wilderness Preservation System. See *Wilderness* (Spring 1989), p. 6. In Colorado approximately 18 percent of all national forest land is designated wilderness.

10. Minutes, NCWCD, October 9, 1970, and September 14, 1973.

11. Ibid., October 12, 1973.

12. *Grand Junction Sentinel*, 8 July 1974. *Longmont Daily Times-Call*, 5 August 1974.

13. On March 24, 1971, U.S. Supreme Court Justice William O. Douglas handed down a decision in *United States* v. *District Court in and for Eagle County*, 401 U.S. 520 (1971) for a unanimous Court. The verdict stated that the United States, like any other water user on the Eagle River, must go to district court to have water rights adjudicated. The complex litigation that followed can best be traced by referring to W-467 and W-469 in District Court for Water Division 5. Eventually, many cases were consolidated and submitted to a master-referee for hearings on nineteen separate occasions, resulting in approximately 10,000 pages of transcript. On April 16, 1976, the master-referee submitted a report of over 1,000 pages entitled "Partial Master-Referee Report Covering All of the Claims of the United States of AMERICA."

14. The reserved rights doctrine, established by the U.S. Supreme Court in *Winters* v. *United States,* 207 U.S. 564 (1908) states that any lands reserved by the federal government are entitled to enough water to sustain the purpose of the reservation. In *Arizona* v. *California*, 373 U.S. 757 (1963) the federal government successfully applied the reserved rights doctrine to non-Indian federal reservations. Since then, the Department of the Interior has used the Winters Doctrine to acquire water rights for national parks and national monuments. As of this writing, the Forest Service has not won a reserved water rights case in court and has sustained a major setback in *United States* v. *New Mexico*, 438 U.S. 696 (1978).

15. The Municipal Subdistrict, NCWCD was formed by the district court under the Water Conservancy District Act on July 6, 1970. Members of the Subdistrict initially included Boulder, Greeley, Loveland, Longmont, Fort Collins, and Estes Park — the Six Cities. Platte River Power Authority became a member of the Six Cities in 1975.

16. Sayre also reported that he was trying to coordinate the interests of other Front Range conservancy districts so that they all might be represented by a single attorney. He noted that Colorado had not joined in opposition to the United States' claims, fearing that its entire water rights system might be challenged. See Minutes, NCWCD, September 8, 1972.

17. *Grand Junction Sentinel*, 8 July 1974. The Consolidated Cases were not tried immediately in state district court. In addition to being tried separately because of the many issues involved, some cases still have not reached final judgment.

18. Samuel P. Hays, *Beauty, Health, and Permanence: Environmental Politics in the United States, 1955–1985* (Cambridge: Cambridge University Press, 1987), p. 77.

19. Secretary of the Interior Stewart Udall predicted in 1960 that the population of the United States would reach 383 million by the year 2000. Five years later, a Senate subcommittee report on pollution in the nation's ninety major rivers noted that industry was the culprit because of secrecy regarding the nature of wastes being dumped into waterways. See the *Fort Collins Coloradoan*, 19 October 1961; *Boulder Daily Camera*, 29 March 1961 and 5 September 1965; and *Denver Post*, 28 July 1961. According to Professor John C. Ward of Colorado State University, Colorado cities by the year 2000 would be forced to desalt drinking water and to reuse sewage for domestic purposes. See *Denver Post*, 1 March 1970.

20. Hays, *Beauty, Wealth and Permanence*, p. 77. *Grand Junction Sentinel*, 5, 23 April 1965.

21. *Fort Collins Coloradoan*, 15 July 1965.

22. As quoted in Hays, *Beauty, Wealth and Permanence*, p. 78.

23. Walter A. Rosenbaum, *The Politics of Environmental Concern*, 2d ed. (New York: Praeger, 1977), p. 158.

24. Minutes, NCWCD, July 13, 1973.

25. Ibid., April 5, 1974. *Fort Collins Coloradoan*, 27 December 1973.

26. Ibid., 5 April 1968. Barkley reported to the Board on his meeting with the U.S. Committee on Irrigation and Drainage in Phoenix, where he learned about the problems developing in the Central and San Joaquin valleys.

27. Ibid., 13 March and 10 July 1970.

28. Speaking to the Four States Irrigation Council in January 1960, Bureau Commissioner Floyd Dominy said that water irrigation uses would be difficult to defend as long as waste continued to

be "as outrageous as it is." Two years later, speaking to the same group, Gilbert G. Stamm, then chief of the Bureau's Irrigation and Land Use section, noted that a 50 percent water efficiency rate on farms was all too common. One of the most important policies for the future, he said, would be the "conservation and efficient use of existing supplies of water." See *Greeley Tribune*, 15 January 1960 and *Denver Post*, 12 January 1962.

29. *Denver Post*, 11 January 1965. *Greeley Tribune*, 18 January 1966.

30. Comment attributed to Felix Sparks, director, CWCB, as published in the *Boulder Daily Camera*, 14 January 1971.

31. *Denver Post*, 14 May 1967.

32. *Grand Junction Sentinel*, 16 June 1968.

33. *Denver Post*, 1 March 1970. *Loveland Reporter-Herald*, 11, 12 July 1970. A July 24, 1970, article from the Loveland newspaper noted that water from the C–BT is the best in Colorado, coming from Grand Lake with a low mineral quality.

34. *Session Laws of Colorado*, 1973, Ch. 210, approved July 6, 1973. Sections 25-8-102 and 25-8-104 are discussed in George Vranesh, *Colorado Water Law*, 3 vols. (Boulder, Colo.: Design Press, 1987), 3, pp. 1296ff.

35. As quoted in David H. Getches, *Water Law in a Nutshell* (St. Paul, Minn.: West Publishing Company, 1984), p. 369.

36. Minutes, NCWCD, July 13, 1973.

37. NCWCD, *Annual Report, 1971–1972*, pp. 1, 19.

38. *Grand Junction Sentinel*, 7 November 1971.

39. The 1970 Census provided statistical proof that the Front Range was one of the fastest growing areas in the U.S. Preliminary data showed that population increases in major municipalities in the District averaged 69 percent, compared with 11.7 percent nationally. Colorado was ranked as the sixth fastest growing state in the nation, with a 25 percent jump in population since 1960. See NCWCD, *Annual Report, 1969–1970*, p. 1.

40. Minutes, NCWCD, May 10, 1968.

41. The U.S. Public Health Service identified "severe pollution and serious degradation of water quality" in the South Platte basin, with the biggest pollution source being waste products of sugar beet processors. See *Greeley Tribune*, 29 October 1963. Three years later, Great Western estimated a cost of $30 million to reduce pollution in the South Platte River from its ten factories; in the view of company officials, Great Western's compliance would result in a "profitless industry." See *Fort Collins Coloradoan*, 28 April 1966.

42. Interview, Bob Barkley, 13 June 1990.

43. *Greeley Tribune*, 6 October 1970.

44. Minutes, NCWCD, March 12, 1971. Simpson took a cut in salary from $20,000 to $16,000.

45. *Boulder Daily Camera*, 3 October 1971.

46. Minutes, NCWCD, August 13, 1971.

47. *Grand Junction Sentinel*, 21 November 1971.

48. *Fort Collins Coloradoan*, 12 January 1972. *Loveland Reporter-Herald*, 22 March 1972.

49. *Grand Junction Sentinel*, 8 October 1972.

50. Ibid., 1 October 1972.

51. Robert G. Athearn, *The Coloradans* (Albuquerque: University of New Mexico Press, 1976), pp. 361–362.

52. NCWCD, Minutes, March 9, 1973.

53. Ibid., May 11, 1973.

54. *Grand Junction Sentinel*, 1 March 1973.

55. *Greeley Tribune,* 25 January 1974.

56. Ibid., 15 December 1966.

57. Minutes, NCWCD, December 11, 1970, and April 2, 1971.

58. *Denver Post,* 31 January 1971.

59. Minutes, NCWCD, July 9, 1971.

60. Ritter, who focused on Sections 1 and 3 of the CRSP, told defendants that their claim of immunity was invalid because the suit was specifically directed against Secretary Rogers C. Morton and Commissioner Ellis L. Armstrong. See *Friends of the Earth* v. *Armstrong,* 360 F.Supp. 165 (D. Utah, 1973) at 168, 185.

61. *Federal Reporter,* 2d series, Vol. 485 F.2d 1 (1973), pp. 3–6.

62. Minutes, NCWCD, March 9 and August 10, 1973, and February 8, 1974. *Greeley Tribune,* 3, 23 May 1973.

63. *Grand Junction Sentinel,* 9 February 1970. Aspinall reportedly said that the Nixon administration and the country were on an "emotional binge relative to environmental quality, ecology, and anything to enhance the land."

64. Ira G. Clark, *Water in New Mexico* (Albuquerque: University of New Mexico Press, 1987), p. 586. The act specifically stated that the Federal Power Commission "shall not license the construction of any dam, water conduit, reservoir, powerhouse, transmission line, or other project works under the Federal Power Act, as amended, on or directly affecting any river which is listed in section 5, subsection (a), of this Act." See Public Law 90-542, October 2, 1968.

65. *Boulder Daily Camera,* 9 August 1965.

66. The mainstem of the Poudre River to below Poudre Park and most of the South Fork were designated wild and scenic through the passage of H.R. 3547 on October 30, 1986.

67. The Council on Environmental Quality, *Twentieth Annual Report to the President of the United States,* 1990, pp. 2–3.

68. Minutes, NCWCD, March 13, 1970.

69. *Grand Junction Sentinel,* 28 February 1970.

70. *Denver Post,* 17 February 1970. *Fort Collins Coloradoan,* 10 February 1970. *Boulder Daily Camera,* 3 February 1970.

71. Minutes, NCWCD, May 11, 1973. *Grand Junction Sentinel,* 20 January 1973. *Greeley Tribune,* 10 January 1973.

72. *Colorado River Water Conservation District* v. *Colorado Water Conservation Board,* 197 Colo. 469, 594 P.2d 570 (1979).

73. Minutes, NCWCD, July 13, 1973.

74. Richard L. Berkman and W. Kip Viscusi, *Damming the West* (New York: Grossman Publishers, 1973). This work is popularly known as Ralph Nader's Study Group Report on the Bureau of Reclamation.

75. See NCWCD *Annual Report* for the years under consideration and letter, 18 December 1990, W. D. Farr to the author.

76. *Greeley Tribune,* 23 November 1970. In reciting Farr's credits, attorney James Shelton noted that Farr had been selected for the award because he had given so freely of his own personal time on numerous boards and agencies along the Front Range.

77. The following gives just a sampling of Farr's far-ranging activities by 1974. He was chairman of the Greeley Water Board and the force behind dam site studies on the upper Poudre River in the 1950s. He was elected director of Great Western Sugar Company; the Greeley National Bank; the U.S. National Bank; Mountain States Telephone Company; the Greeley Home, Light, and Power Company; and the Foundation for American Agriculture. He became president of the National Cattleman's Association, vice president of the Colorado Cattle Feeders Association, a member of the U.S. Department of Agriculture's National Cattle Advisory Committee of the

United States Chamber of Commerce, and a member of President Nixon's Food-Industry Advisory Committee. He represented the United States in France, Spain, and Italy as spokesman for the U.S. Department of Agriculture, and he received awards from the National Cattleman's Association, the American Meat Institute, Colorado State University, the National Western Stock Show, and the American Polled Hereford Association.

78. *Greeley Tribune*, 24 April 1972.

79. John C. Bromley, "A Proud Legacy: Water and W. D. Farr," *Colorado Heritage* (Autumn 1990), pp. 2–13.

80. Minutes, NCWCD, April 2, 1971.

81. The NCWCD *Annual Report, 1969–1970* shows gross receipts from water rentals at $608,331.80 and from ad valorem taxes at $644,598.45. See pp. 1, 28.

82. NCWCD, *Annual Report, 1969–1970*. Ad valorem revenue for this year was $644,598, and water rental revenue was $608,331.

83. These data are derived from NCWCD *Annual Reports*, 1957–1974.

84. Interviews, Bob Barkley, 9, 31 May and 29 June 1990.

85. Supplement 3, Repayment Contract, 1938. The last two sentences of Article 15 were deleted and replaced by a paragraph that stated in part: "The District shall continue to make the minimum levies and assessments as provided for in this article only until (A) the escrow account has reached $11,000,000, or (B) the commencement of the last ten-year repayment period, whichever event occurs first." As of 1990 the account had sufficient funds to retire the entire construction debt due to the Board's ability to take advantage of rising rates during a 1980s inflationary period.

86. Minutes, NCWCD, January 8, 1965.

87. NCWCD, *Annual Report, 1973–1974*, p. 11. Barkley noted in 1968 that even with municipal growth taking agricultural land out of production, only 12 percent of C–BT deliveries that year were for municipal and industrial uses. See *Longmont Daily Times-Call*, August 13, 1968.

88. A sampling of newspaper articles based on USDA statistics appears in the *Grand Junction Sentinel*, 4 August 1963; the *Boulder Daily Camera*, 2 January 1966; the *Fort Collins Coloradoan*, 28 March 1968; and the *Greeley Tribune*, 3 October 1969 and 19 January 1973.

89. See the *Greeley Tribune*, 19 January 1973, 10 January 1974, and 2 August 1974.

90. *Colorado Agricultural Statistics*, 1957 and 1973 Final, 1958 and 1974 Preliminary. Colorado Department of Agriculture.

91. *Greeley Tribune*, 28 October 1960.

92. *Fort Collins Coloradoan*, 12 May 1968. *1975 Agricultural Statistics*. Colorado Department of Agriculture, p. 67.

93. *Colorado Rancher and Farmer* (January 1971). *Fort Collins Coloradoan*, 29 August 1971 and October 21, 1973. *Greeley Tribune*, 19 October 1972 and 8 December 1973.

94. NCWCD, *Annual Report*, 1972–1973, 1973–1974, 1974–1975. A chart on page 14 of the 1976 *Annual Report* shows that from 1974 to 1976, the District made payments into the escrow account that exceeded the amounts Barkley had projected as necessary ten years earlier.

95. Minutes, NCWCD, October 9, 1964. See also draft of letter, 26 October 1966, J. R. Barkley to H. P. Dugan, NCWCDA.

96. Minutes, NCWCD, 10 June 1966 and 9 June 1967.

97. Report of William W. Allison, Water Analyst, Department of Chemistry, Colorado State University, October 5, 1967, Inclusion Records, NCWCDA.

98. Letter, 4 August 1967, J. R. Barkley to Ralph J. Waldo, Jr., Inclusion Records, NCWCDA. See also Minutes, NCWCD, April 10, 1967, which note that the District was unable to serve all of eastern Colorado's needs and that all water had been allotted since 1955. Kenneth Whitmore provided assistance in gathering the information on the Valley View School. In a draft letter to J. K. Headley, secretary of the Central Weld County Water District, October 7, 1966, Barkley said

that Frederick and Dacono would be eligible for inclusion, but Fort Lupton and Brighton were "beyond the limits to which this District wishes to expand."

99. Barkley's letter to Waldo on August 4, 1967, states the Board's policy. See Inclusion Records, NCWCDA. See also Minutes, NCWCD, June 14, 1968, and June 18, 1970, regarding Louisville and Lafayette.

100. Minutes, NCWCD, August 11, 1972.

101. Ibid., February 9, 1973. The formula involved dividing the total accumulated ad valorem tax revenues of Weld, Boulder, and Larimer counties paid since 1937 by the current valuations of the District within the three counties. The resulting fraction, or ratio, was then multiplied against the current valuation of the property to be included. The District was to recompute the ratio annually.

102. Ibid., May 11, 1973. *Longmont Daily Times-Call,* 13 July 1973. Except for the Wagner Water District, no other municipal inclusions were made from 1973 until 1990, when Fort Lupton, Nunn, and Hudson were approved.

103. Minutes, NCWCD, March 10, 1967.

104. Ibid., April 7, 1967.

105. Ibid., June 14, 1968. Articles 4.B.(3-11) described a complex system of debits and credits relating to the percentage of water delivered to Carter Lake and to the Big Thompson River.

CHAPTER 20

1. Minutes, NCWCD, January 10, 1969. This figure is high; more commonly, District officials used 245,000 acre-feet. In fact, deliveries through the Adams Tunnel between 1957 and 1968 averaged 221,541 acre-feet. See "Tables of Nine," NCWCDA.

2. See notes taken by Bob Barkley, 1946–1953, on meetings with the Bureau's Region 7 staff, NCWCDA. The 245,000 acre-feet annual average yield seems accurate.

3. USBR, Region 7, Denver, Colorado, "Reconnaissance Report on the Western Slope Extension, Colorado–Big Thompson Project" (December 1956), p 2.

4. Ibid., p. 32.

5. Ibid., pp. 63, 75, 85, 86, 88. When finally completed with a different design, the Windy Gap project cost in excess of $50 million.

6. Ibid., Part IV, Ch. 2.

7. *Denver Post,* 17 June 1966. The Elliott story is further discussed in Chapters 17, and 18.

8. Minutes, NCWCD, June 9, 1967.

9. *Fort Collins Coloradoan,* 9 July 1964.

10. Interview, Bob Barkley, 13 June 1990. According to U.S. Census figures, the Six Cities population actually reached a total of 303,260 by 1988. At that same growth rate, the 1990 total would be 312,842. Thus, the twenty-year combined growth rate was only 44 percent rather than 130 percent. See U.S. Department of Commerce, Bureau of the Census, Local Population Reports, Colorado, March 1990, pp. 19–23; and NCWCD, *Annual Report,* 1968–1969, p. 21. The *Final Environmental Statement* for the Windy Gap project estimated a 397,600 population for Boulder, Estes Park, Greeley, Longmont, and Loveland by the year 2000. See U.S. Department of the Interior, Water and Power Resources Service, Lower Missouri Region, *Final Environmental Statement,* Colorado–Big Thompson Windy Gap projects Colorado, 1981, p. 1–3.

11. See *Fort Collins Coloradoan,* 19 July 1967, and *Longmont Daily Times-Call,* 26 January 1974, which note that the filing was later increased to 54,000 acre-feet out of the Colorado River.

12. Minutes, Six-City Water Supply Study Committee (SCWSC), February 24, 1969. The original Six-City Water Study Committee members were: Boulder (Charles Hallenbeck, Ted Tedesco); Estes Park (Clarence Graves, Ernest Hartwell); Fort Collins (Tom Coffey, Norm Evans, Harvey

Johnson, Owen Moore); Greeley (Bill Farr, O. L. Shafer); Longmont (Frank Humphrey, Ralph Price); and Loveland (Lynn Hammond, Don Hataway).

13. See John M. Sayre, "The Windy Gap Project: A Case Study" (Paper presented to the Natural Resources Law Center, University of Colorado School of Law, June 9, 1982); interview, Bob Barkley, 9 May 1990; and Minutes, NCWCD, July 14, 1967.

14. NCWCD, *Annual Report,* 1969–1970, p. 19.

15. Interview, Bob Barkley, June 13, 1990.

16. Minutes, SCWSC, May 26, 1969, and November 25, 1974.

17. Minutes, NCWCD, October 8, 1971.

18. Minutes, Municipal Subdistrict, NCWCD, May 9, 1975.

19. Ibid., October 11, 1974.

20. Sections 150-5-15 and 150-5-3, C.R.S. 1963.

21. Findings and Decree, July 6, 1970, District Court Weld County, Colorado, No. 9454–S1, signed by Judge Donald A. Carpenter.

22. *Longmont Daily Times-Call,* 26 January 1970. For anyone surprised by the 5 percent figure, recall that the Water Conservancy District Act was passed in 1937 when post–World War II municipal growth was inconceivable.

23. Minutes, NCWCD, January 14, 1969. Minutes, MSD, September 29 and November 3, 1969.

24. Ibid., September 29, 1969. Engineering Consultants, Inc., expected the MSD to compensate the West Slope by storing additional water in Green Mountain Reservoir.

25. Minutes, NCWCD, November 8, 1968.

26. Minutes, MSD, October 9, 1970. Minutes, Six-Cities Committee, July 27, 1970.

27. Minutes, Six-Cities Committee, April 26, 1971.

28. Estimate made by Six-Cities Committee representative from Boulder, Ted Tedesco, in *Longmont Daily Times-Call,* 28 July 1970.

29. Minutes, Six-Cities Committee, July 27, 1970, and August 12, 1971. Minutes, MSD, April 2 and July 9, 1971.

30. These organizations include the Denver Regional Council of Governments, the Larimer-Weld Regional Planning Commission, and the State Planning Office. See Minutes, MSD, August 13 and November 17, 1971.

31. Ibid., January 14, 1972.

32. *Fort Collins Coloradoan,* 27 April 1971. Minutes, MSD, April 7, 1972.

33. *Loveland Reporter-Herald,* 8 September 1972. Memorandum, 27 February 1973, C.V. Hallenbeck to the city councils of the Six Cities, NCWCDA. *Greeley Tribune,* 16 March 1973.

34. Minutes, NCWCD, August 14, 1970.

35. Ibid., July 9, 1971. Minutes, MSD, May 14 and June 11, 1971. Hallenbeck, however, believed that delays were also due to "vigorous, repeated, unyielding and successful attempts by Subdistrict staff to obtain regional agreement [from the Bureau] on reduced [carriage] charges." See Hallenbeck, Memorandum, 27 February 1973, NCWCDA.

36. Minutes, NCWCD, May 12, 1972.

37. Minutes, MSD, April 6, 1973.

38. Minutes, NCWCD, December 8, 1972.

39. *Grand Junction Sentinel,* 31 October 1971.

40. Letter, 26 September 1963, J. R. Barkley to William H. Nelson, NCWCDA. This letter responded to Nelson's letter to Felix L. Sparks, Colorado Water Conservation Board director, in which Nelson had objected to the NCWCD's apparent willingness to carry water from the Mitchell Ditch in Water District No. 51 through the Adams Tunnel to Fort Collins.

41. Draft of letter, 18 March 1966, J. R. Barkley to John P. Elliott, NCWCDA.

42. *Grand Junction Sentinel,* 31 October 1971.

43. Ibid., 3, 4 August 1967. Mills Bunger had been trying to persuade the Denver Water Board to grant carriage rights through the Roberts Tunnel so that the CCWCD could develop West Slope water.

44. Ibid., 31 October 1971.

45. Minutes, Six-Cities Committee, June 7, 1972.

46. Ibid., December 17, 1973. Simpson based his estimate on a yearly indebtedness of $1,769,526 for twenty years (for 480 units). A 1/6 share equaled $294,000 for 1/6 of 48,600 acre-feet (80 units) of delivered water. Thus one unit roughly equaled $37 ($24 for capitalization, $6 for operation, and $7 for the carriage contract).

47. Minutes, MSD, January 12, 1973.

48. Ibid., May 11, 1973. Longmont announced on May 8, 1973, that no further financial contributions would be made to the Six Cities Committee.

49. Minutes, Six Cities Committee, April 29, 1974. Minutes, MSD, January 11, 1974.

50. Section 37-45-118 (b) IV, known as the "basin of origin" protection provision, says that "Any such works or facilities shall be designed, constructed, and operated in such a manner that the present appropriations of water, and in addition thereto prospective uses of water for irrigation and other beneficial consumptive use purposes . . . will not be impaired nor increased in cost at the expense of the water users within the natural basin."

51. Minutes, MSD, June 14, 1974. Letter (unsigned draft), n.d., J. R. Barkley to Roland Fischer, in response to Roland Fischer's letter of 10 May 1974.

52. Minutes, MSD, November 8, 1974.

53. Ibid., May 9, 1975. Correspondence between East and West Slope attorneys was graciously provided by Stanley W. Cazier, MPWCD attorney since the mid-seventies.

54. Ibid., December 12, 1975.

55. Sayre, "The Windy Gap Project," p. 6.

56. James C. Klein, "The Windy Gap Project, 1964–1982: A Chronological Description and Promotional Analysis" (Paper presented as partial fulfillment of a master's degree in public policy, University of Colorado, December 18, 1982).

57. Minutes, MSD, February 8, 1974.

58. Ibid., February 8 and March 8, 1974.

59. Ibid., October 12, 1973, and January 11, 1974. Director Milt Nelson noted that municipalities, rural domestic associations, and industries had expressed a "strong desire" to participate in Subdistrict activities. Barkley specifically added the towns of Erie, Louisville, Lafayette, Windsor, and Fort Lupton, also noting the interests of several water districts, Eastman Kodak, and Public Service Company of Colorado.

60. Ibid., June 14, 1974.

61. *Fort Collins Coloradoan,* 21 July 1974. *Estes Park Trail-Gazette,* 24 July 1974.

62. Minutes, MSD, July 12, 1974.

63. City attorney Art March pointed out that Fort Collins could not give up a water right, once acquired, without an election. Other members of the Six Cities also preferred "transfer by preassignment," but all agreed that each city should feel free "to use its share of Windy Gap Project water for whatever purpose it felt was necessary." See Minutes, MSD, August 9, 1974.

64. Ibid., MSD, September 13, 1974.

65. Ibid., July 11, 1975.

66. Greeley, Boulder, and Fort Collins were home-rule cities that were required to hold elections before they were legally able to sign allotment contracts for Windy Gap water. See ibid., MSD, May 10, 1974.

67. Abandonment of HUD came in fall 1972 when the MSD engineered a new plan and new financing objectives. See *Loveland Reporter-Herald*, 8 September 1972, and Minutes, MSD, June 9, 1972.

68. Minutes, MSD, September 13 and December 13, 1974.

69. Ibid., February 14 and March 14, 1975.

70. Bond issues began in 1977 in the amount of $3 million, followed by three other issues in June 1981 ($84 million), April 1983 ($107 million), and July 1986 ($94 million).

71. Minutes, MSD, September 12, 1975. Ground breaking actually occurred in July 1981.

72. S.D. 80, Section 5 (c), page 4, says that "Water not required for the above purposes shall be available for disposal to agencies for the development of the shale oil or other industries."

73. Minutes, CRWCD, July 15, 1958.

74. *Grand Junction Sentinel*, 20 July 1964. Sparks was more worried about having sufficient water for the proposed West Divide and Yellow Jacket projects.

75. Minutes, NCWCD, February 9, 1973, and February 8, 1974.

76. Andrew Gulliford, *Boomtown Blues: Colorado Oil Shale, 1885–1985* (Niwot: University Press of Colorado, 1989), p. 109.

77. Minutes, NCWCD, May 8, 1970.

78. Ibid., August 13, 1971. See also CORSIM correspondence in Davis, Graham and Stubbs, file 14-026-19-01.

79. Minutes, NCWCD, February 9, 1973, and January 11, 1974.

80. Ibid., August 9, 1968.

81. Ibid., November 8, 1968.

82. Ibid., November 14, 1969.

83. *Loveland Reporter-Herald*, 27, 28 March 1971.

84. NCWCD, *Annual Report*, 1974–1975. When Nelson died in 1971, Leona Schwab took over allotment contract work and Minerva G. Lee, an employee since 1962, assumed Nelson's financial responsibilities.

85. *Denver Post*, September 1967 (included in NCWCD Newspaper Clippings Book 17). Senator James Thomas was speaking before the Legislative Council Committee in support of a bill to have conservancy district board members elected; the committee defeated the bill.

86. *Denver Post*, 26 August 1969.

87. Ibid., 23 October 1969. Sayre was speaking at the NWRA convention in Seattle, Washington.

88. Minutes, NCWCD, July 12 and November 8, 1974. See also Barkley interview with the author, 9 May 1990.

89. NCWCD, *Annual Reports*, 1958–1974. Curiously, CRWCD legal expenses jumped between 1973 and 1974, increasing 81 percent to a total of $107,252, and they actually declined from $135,271 in 1979 to $128,190 in 1980. This information provided courtesy of Roland C. Fischer, CRWCD secretary-engineer, May 16, 1990.

90. Minutes, NCWCD, October 9, 1970, and March 10, 1972.

91. Ibid., September 13 and October 11, 1974.

92. Ibid., October 11, 1974.

93. Ibid., November 4, 1960, and February 9, 1968.

94. Ibid., May 14, 1965.

95. *Denver Post*, 24 October 1969.

96. Remarks of J. Ben Nix, May 31, 1974, "Barkley Papers and Speeches" folder, NCWCDA.

97. Minutes, NCWCD, November 8, 1974.

CHAPTER 21

1. Richard P. Nathan, *The Plot That Failed: Nixon and the Administrative Presidency* (New York: John Wiley and Sons, 1975), p. 78. For Hickel's relationship with Nixon, see Walter J. Hickel, *Who Owns America?* (Englewood Cliffs, N.J.: Prentice Hall, 1971), p. 7.

2. Richard M. Nixon, *A New Road for America* (Garden City, N.J.: Doubleday and Company, 1972), pp. 418–419.

3. Charles F. Luce, *Review Draft: A Proposed Report of the National Water Commission*, vol. 1, Arlington, Virginia (Distributed by National Technical Information Service, United States, Department of Commerce, 1972), p. v.

4. Ellis L. Armstrong, "A Hopeful Year," *Reclamation Era* (February 1972), p. ii.

5. David W. Carle, "75 Years of Reclamation Leadership," *Reclamation Era* 63:1, 2 [75th Anniversary of the USBR, n.d.], pp. 93–94. According to the author, Armstrong (1970–1973) was the first commissioner of the Bureau who opened channels with environmental interest groups, but his successor, Gilbert G. Stamm (1973–1976), further recognized the Bureau's need to modernize its policies to reflect a changing emphasis on economic, environmental, and social values. Stamm believed that water management should not give exclusive priority to any one function but should represent the needs of population distribution, national security, food production, fish and wildlife enhancement, energy generation, fossil fuel development, and humanitarian obligations. See also "Introducing Gilbert G. Stamm," ibid., 59:4 (Autumn 1973) and "The National Conference on Water," ibid., 61:2 (Summer 1975).

6. Letter, 22 January 1975, Robert L. Berling to Regional Director, USBR, NCWCDA.

7. U.S. Department of Interior, "Water Resources: Use and Management Policy Statement," August 21, 1975.

8. Warren Freedman, *Federal Statutes on Environmental Protection: Regulation in the Public Interest* (New York: Quorum Books, 1987). The primary environmental acts that affect the use of water in the West are The National Environmental Policy Act (NEPA), 42 U.S.C., section 4321; The Clean Water Act (CWA), 33 U.S.C., section 1251; The Endangered Species Act (ESA), 16 U.S.C., section 1531; and the Federal Land Policy and Management Act (FLPMA), 43 U.S.C., section 1701.

9. U.S. President, *Public Papers of the Presidents of the United States* (Washington: Office of the Federal Register, National Archives and Records Service, 1976–1977), Gerald R. Ford, Book III, July 10, 1976–January 20, 1977, pp. 2356–2357.

10. Ibid., Jimmy Carter, 1977, Book I, January 20–June 24, 1977, pp. 207–208.

11. Milton H. Jamail, John R. McCain, and Scott J. Ullery, *Federal-State Water Use Relations in the American West: An Evolutionary Guide to Future Equilibrium* (Tucson: University of Arizona, Office of Arid Land Studies, 1978), p. 40.

12. *Greeley Tribune*, 9 March 1977. *Boulder Daily Camera*, 20 March 1977.

13. *Grand Junction Sentinel*, 21 March 1977.

14. *Fort Morgan Times*, 29 March 1977. Senator Hart demanded and obtained retraction of a Region 8 EPA policy that attempted to implement the WRC instream flow policy. See Gregory J. Hobbs, Jr., and Bennett W. Raley, "Water Quality Versus Water Quantity: A Delicate Balance," *Rocky Mountain Mineral Law Institute* 34 (1988), section 24.03, p. 18–24.

15. Minutes, NCWCD, July 8 and August 12, 1977. From its inception, the District has kept a close eye on congressional and state legislation. Attorneys have served as District watchdogs, occasion-

ally sounding alarms when threats were distant or imagined. Since the 1970s, this protective role of counsel has been viewed by critics as legal paranoia.

16. Jamail, *Federal-State Water Use Relations*, pp. 41–48. See also U.S. President, Executive Order, "Water Resources Council: Water Resource Policy Study," *Federal Register*, July 15, 1977, vol. 42, no. 136, pp. 36788–36795.

17. Minutes, NCWCD, September 9, 1977, and July 14, 1978.

18. Ibid., and February 10, 1978. In December 1977 the federal government filed more than 400 applications for water rights in Division 1 Water Court alone on behalf of the BLM, the USFS, the NPS, and the Air Force. Some of these filings sought rulings that would protect stream flow in rivers and streams for their scenic appeal. See *Greeley Tribune*, 15, 30 December 1977.

19. *Greeley Tribune*, 13 January 1978.

20. U.S. President, *Public Papers of the Presidents of the United States*, Book I, January 20–June 24, 1977, pp. 287–288. The last years of government surpluses were 1960 and 1969; from 1961 to 1980 the annual federal deficit increased from $3.3 billion to $73.8 billion. See U.S. President, OMB, *Historical Tables: Budget of the United States Government*, Fiscal Year 1986 (Washington: GPO, 1985).

21. Some environmentalists concluded that Carter had abandoned the philosophy announced in the 1977 "hit list" and that his 1978 statement was a "reaffirmation of traditional pork-barrel politics concerning water policy." See Jamail, *Federal State Water Use*, pp. 53–54.

22. "Federal Water Policy," Message to the President, June 6, 1978, *Public Papers of the Presidents*, pp. 1043–1051.

23. *Loveland Reporter-Herald*, 18 December 1978.

24. Minutes, NCWCD, December 8, 1978, and July 13, 1979.

25. U.S. Congress, Senate, Committee on Environment and Public Works, "To Establish a National Water Policy," *Hearings Before the Subcommittee on Water Resources.* 95th Cong., 2d sess., August–December, 1978.

26. "New Name for Bureau of Reclamation," *Reclamation Era* 65:2 [n.d.], p. 1.

27. Daniel McCool, *Command of the Waters: Iron Triangles, Federal Water Development, and Indian Water* (Berkeley: University of California Press, 1987), p. 208.

28. Remarks by Secretary Watt to the NWRA, Salt Lake City, October 26, 1982, NWRA files, NCWCDA.

29. Toward the end of the Carter administration, the West Slope pro-growth organization, Club 20, called a convention in Denver where forty-four water organizations met to resolve the long-standing feud between East and West Slopes and to settle on a strategy for combating federal policies. The conference condemned federal water quality and environmental laws as a "monstruous overkill." *Grand Junction Sentinel*, 17 September 1979.

30. McCool, *Command of the Waters*, p. 208.

31. Minutes, NCWCD, October 9, 1981.

32. U.S. Congress, Senate, Committee on Environment and Public Works, *Water Resources Policy Issues: Hearings Before the Subcommittee on Water Resources*, 97th Cong., 1st sess., April 21–23 and June 8, 12, 1981.

33. Memorandum, 15 June 1982, James G. Watt, chairman pro tem, Cabinet Council on Natural Resources and Environment, to the president, Miscellaneous Correspondence, NCWCDA.

34. U.S. President, *Public Papers of the Presidents of the United States*, Reagan, Book II, June 29–December 31, 1985, p. 996.

35. U.S. Congress, House, Committee on Interior and Insular Affairs, *Briefing by the Secretary of the Interior: Oversight Hearing Before the Committee on Interior and Insular Affairs*, 98th Cong., 1st sess., January 26, 1983.

36. *Reclamation Era* 66:2, 3 (Spring/Summer 1981), p. 2.

37. Minutes, NCWCD, January 8, 1982.

38. *Reclamation Era* 67:4 [n.d.], p. 20.

39. *High Country News*, 9 November 1987. See also U.S. Congress, House, *Reorganization of the Bureau of Reclamation, Oversight Hearing Before the Subcommittee on Water and Power Resources of the Committee on Interior and Insular Affairs*, 100th Cong., 1st sess., October 29, 1987.

CHAPTER 22

1. *Greeley Tribune*, 30 June 1985.

2. W. D. Farr, speech given June 11, 1981, "Windy Gap Groundbreaking," NCWCDA.

3. "Windy Gap Inauguration," June 29, 1985, NCWCDA.

4. Ibid.

5. Series C water revenue bonds were issued to refund earlier bond issues at a lower interest rate and to complete construction. The total amount of the aggregate principal was $107,445,000; the Windy Gap dedication ceremony cost the MSD $18,150.

6. *Greeley Tribune*, 30 June 1985.

7. Letter, 21 May 1974, J. R. Barkley to Roland C. Fischer, CRWCD, NCWCDA. Barkley's letter responded to Fischer's letter of May 10, 1974, which called for discussions of a joint venture between the CRWCD and the MSD to construct a dam and reservoir at the Azure site on the Colorado River.

8. The Colorado Supreme Court overruled the water court by finding that the conditional water right could not be granted until the MSD defined a plan to adequately mitigate the potential harm to prospective water users within the upper Colorado River basin. Colo. Rev. Stat. § 37-45-118 (1) (b) (IV) said that

   > any works or facilities planned and designed for the exportation of water from the natural basin of the Colorado River and its tributaries in Colorado, by any district created under this article, shall be subject to the provisions of the Colorado River Compact and the Boulder Canyon Project Act. Any such works shall be designed, constructed, and operated in such manner that the present appropriations of water, and in addition thereto prospective uses of water for irrigation and other beneficial consumptive use purposes, including consumptive uses for domestic, mining, and industrial purposes, within the natural basin of the Colorado River in the state of Colorado, from which water is exported, will not be impaired nor increased in cost at the expense of the water users in the natural basin.

9. "Statistical Information, Population Projections for Colorado Planning Regions, 1970–2000, February 22, 1974," Colorado Division of Planning, Demographic Section. Information collected was based on county commissioners' responses to questionaires, along with University of Colorado Division of Business Research and U.S. Census information.

10. CRWCD attorney Kenneth Balcomb angered the NCWCD's John Sayre and Earl Phipps by pressing the Bureau for a more flexible interpretation of S.D. 80's guidelines for utilization of Green Mountain Reservoir water. Believing that West Slope population would expand, Balcomb asked for expansion of "domestic" use, as expanded in S.D. 80, to include industrial and municipal uses. After seeing a copy of Balcomb's letter to the Bureau, Sayre stated:

    > Frankly I am getting extremely tired of Mr. Balcomb's attempts to thwart interested parties in proceeding [to do] the best job they can. Any group that has to operate a project must make interpretations of basic documents. If some other party is dissatisfied with the interpretation or operation, that party should seek judicial relief rather than write letters in muddy waters. In fact, there is a great deal of evidence to indicate that Mr. Balcomb thinks his interpretation of Senate Document 80 carries more weight than anyone else's

and that we should all agree with him and bow to his wishes. Our District does not intend to do this. We are willing to cooperate with all parties in interest, including the Colorado River Water Conservation District, but we refuse to have the Colorado River Water Conservation District try to dictate its interpretations upon other parties.

See Letter, 5 April 1976, John M. Sayre to John Little, Regional Solicitor, Bureau of Reclamation, NCWCDA.

11. Letters, 31 January 1975, and 20 March 1975, Earl F. Phipps to Roland C. Fischer, NCWCDA.

12. Letter, 6 May 1975, Frank Delaney to Earl F. Phipps, NCWCDA.

13. Letter, 8 May 1975, Frank Delaney to John M. Sayre, NCWCDA.

14. Letter, 28 May 1975, Earl F. Phipps to Frank Delaney, NCWCDA.

15. Letter, 14 July 1975, Earl F. Phipps to Redwood Fisher, NCWCDA.

16. Memorandum, 4 August 1975, John M. Sayre to NCWCD Board, NCWCDA.

17. Ibid. See also letter, 19 August 1975, Earl F. Phipps to Frank Delaney, NCWCDA.

18. *Triangle Review*, 1 October 1975.

19. Minutes, Municipal Subdistrict, December 12, 1975.

20. Letter, 16 March 1976, Earl F. Phipps to Redwood Fisher, NCWCDA. The "document of intent" combined what the MSD had offered on May 28, 1975, and what Grand Junction attorney Edward Currier had suggested in a March 10, 1976, letter to Phipps, written on behalf of Fisher.

21. Letter, 26 March 1976, W. D. Farr to Roland C. Fischer, NCWCDA.

22. Minutes, MSD, March 12, 1976, and April 1, 1977.

23. Minutes, Six Cities Committee, February 23, 1977. Minutes, MSD, April 1, 1977.

24. Minutes, Six Cities Committee, February 23 and July 26, 1976, and January 31, 1977. To amend the Water Conservancy District Act, Anderson sponsored S.B. 166, which provided that water developed by a principal (parent) district, or a subdistrict of a conservancy district, would only be made available for use within the boundaries of the principal district, the subdistrict, or both.

25. *Sky-Hi News*, 6 August 1976. *Middle Park Times*, 9 December 1976 and 4 August 1977.

26. Letter, 24 May 1976, John M. Sayre to Roland C. Fisher, NCWCDA.

27. Letter, 25 May 1976, Earl F. Phipps to CRWCD, NCWCDA.

28. Minutes, MSD, August 13 and December 10, 1976, NCWCDA.

29. This opinion is suggested in a seven-page letter from Roland C. Fischer to John D. Vanderhoof, president of Club 20 and ex-governor of Colorado, February 23, 1977. Fischer commented on a February 4, 1977, letter from Farr to Vanderhoof that accused the River District of failing to cooperate in Windy Gap discussions, CRWCD.

30. Ibid., April 1, 1977.

31. Letter, 4 February 1977, W. D. Farr to John Vanderhoof. In this "personal" letter, provided to the author courtesy of the CRWCD, Farr sought Vanderhoof's assistance in progress with the stalled negotiations.

32. Ibid., July, 8, 1977.

33. Minutes, Six Cities Committee, May 22, 1978. *Triangle Review*, 15 March 1978.

34. *Greeley Tribune*, 17 September 1979. See also Note 8 in this chapter.

35. *Longmont Daily Times-Call*, 17 March 1977.

36. The C–BT was producing an annual average of 245,000 acre-feet. Forty-eight thousand acre-feet from the Windy Gap project would make a total of 293,000 acre-feet.

37. Minutes, Six Cities Committee, April 28, 1980.

38. *Greeley Tribune*, 6 May 1980.

39. Manager Larry D. Simpson estimated that the total cost of modernizing rancher diversions was $750,000. Interview, Larry Simpson, 8 August 1991.

40. Letter, 19 June 1980, Greg Hobbs Jr., to Roy Howard, Longmont City Manager, NCWCDA.

41. Part VI, paragraph 34 (p. 22) of the April 30, 1980, Windy Gap Settlement Agreement states that the "Subdistrict may divert under its decrees an amount of water not in excess of 90,000 acre-feet in any one year, and not to exceed an average of 65,000 acre-feet per year in any consecutive ten-year period." The long-term annual yield of water to the Subdistrict "will be approximately 54,000 acre-feet."

42. Letter, 26 March 1980, Scott Balcomb to A. Allen Brown, President, CRWCD, CRWCDA.

43. See Part V, paragraph 24, Windy Gap Settlement Agreement, April 30, 1980.

44. On June 22, 1967, the initial Windy Gap project filing applied for a 300 cfs water decree, a 1,546 acre-feet storage reservoir on the Colorado River, and an 11,291 acre-feet Jasper Reservoir. Subsequently, the water decree application was increased by 100 cfs on July 9, 1976. Finally, the MSD filed for an additional 200 cfs on May 7, 1980, making a total of 600 cfs approved as a conditional decree by Water Judge Gavin D. Litwiller on October 27, 1980. The 1980 Windy Gap settlement agreement was included by court stipulation as part of the decree.

45. Letter, 1 June 1981, R. B. Christensen, Executive Vice President, IECO, to MSD President Bill Farr and Board of Directors (hereafter referred to as IECO Letter, 1981), NCWCDA.

46. Ibid. As completed, Windy Gap Dam reached a height of 27 feet. The other data are consistent with final construction.

47. Minutes, MSD, June 18, 1981.

48. Ibid. On April 29, 1983, the MSD Board approved a resolution that endorsed the sale of Series C revenue bonds for $107,445,000. They were issued to refund existing bonded debt at lower rates of interest (7% to 9.25%) and to provide an additional $5.2 million to complete construction of the Windy Gap project.

49. Letter, 2 June 1981, Earl F. Phipps to J. William McDonald, Director, Colorado Water Conservation Board, NCWCDA.

50. Minutes, MSD, January 9, 1981. The Subdistrict's financial advisor and bond counselor, James Ziglar, felt that consultations between the USF&WS and the MSD should be completed prior to issuing a new series of bonds.

51. Quoted in George Vranesh, *Colorado Water Law*, 3 vols. (Boulder, Colo.: Design Press, 1987), 2, p. 811.

52. Minutes, Six Cities Committee, September 23, November 24, 1980. Minutes, MSD, November 14, 1980.

53. *Longmont Daily Times-Call*, 1, 2 July 1978, *Loveland Reporter-Herald*, 22 July 1978.

54. Letter, 12 February 1981, Earl F. Phipps to Senator William L. Armstrong, NCWCDA.

55. Letter, 10 March 1981, Earl F. Phipps to Senator Gary Hart.

56. Minutes, MSD, March 3, 1981.

57. In August 1981, U.S. District Judge Alfred A. Arraj ruled that the secretary of the interior could not enforce the endangered species designation for the squawfish and humpback chub because he failed to give proper notice and to allow public participation in discussion of case facts.

58. *Sky-Hi News*, 9 July 1981.

59. Letter, 13 May 1981, Rich Drew, Assistant Engineer, MSD, to Michael S. Burney, President, WCRM, NCWCDA. See also WCRM, *Windy Gap Archaeological Report*, Final Draft, April 15, 1984, p. 1, NCWCDA. Eckhardt's estimate is in Minutes, MSD, May 8, 1981.

60. *Sky-Hi News*, 17 September 1981. *Windy Gap Archaeological Report*, Final Draft, p. 345.

61. Minutes, MSD, January 8, 1982.

62. Letter, 20 January 1981, Ellis Armstrong to Earl F. Phipps, NCWCDA.

63. Letter, 11 December 1981, W. D. Farr and Gordon Dyekman to James Watt, "Subdistrict Outgoing Correspondence, 1981–1983," NCWCDA.

64. Letter, 12 March 1982, ibid.

65. *Loveland Reporter-Herald,* 31 March 1982.

66. *Middle Park Times,* 23 April 1982.

67. *New York Times,* 4 April 1982.

68. *Rocky Mountain News,* 3 August 1982.

69. WCRM, *Windy Gap Archaeological Report,* Final Draft, pp. 340–346.

70. International Engineering Company, Windy Gap Project, Phase IV Construction, Progress Report 20, "IECO Files," NCWCDA.

71. Ibid., Progress Report 18, 20.

72. Minutes, MSD, August 13, 1982.

73. Larry D. Simpson, "The Azure Project," speech given May 1985, "Simpson Speeches," NCWCDA.

74. Minutes, MSD, May 14, 1982.

75. Letter, 1 March 1983, Mark J. Bernhardt to Rich Drew, Azure project manager, MSD, NCWCDA. Bernhardt complained about a Subdistrict plan to build a much larger project with two dams and a reservoir holding 85,000 acre-feet. His sentiments were echoed by Joseph E. Kelso, Colorado River Runs, Inc., in a March 9, 1983, letter to the Subdistrict. Kelso asked the Subdistrict not to build the $800 million hydroelectric project.

76. Affidavit, Larry D. Simpson, December 1982, before the Federal Energy Regulatory Commission (FERC), NCWCDA.

77. Informational outline, 17 May 1983, Gregory A. Llafet, Public Information Officer, MSD/NCWCD, to Doug Freeman, Timber Rafters, Winter Park, Colorado, "Municipal Subdistrict, Outgoing Correspondence, 1981–1983," NCWCDA.

78. Minutes, MSD, November 12, 1982. A rule of thumb for pump-back storage projects is that water pumped uphill during the night costs one-third of what the returns for power sold during periods of peak demand. This 3:1 ratio works for pump-back storage projects as long as a market exists for the power.

79. Memorandum, 27 January 1983, Donald H. Hamburg, General Counsel, to Azure Committee, CRWCD board, CRWCDA.

80. Minutes, MSD, March 11, 1983.

81. Letter, 18 March 1983, Roland C. Fischer to John M. Sayre, NCWCDA. John Eckhardt tried to deliver the FERC license application to the River District, but they would not accept it.

82. The Vidler Water Tunnel Company application to FERC for a project to bring water from the Colorado and Yampa rivers to the East Slope represented the biggest threat to the MSD application. In fall 1984, however, the Colorado Supreme Court decided that the Vidler filing was speculative and ordered dismissal of Vidler's water rights application. See *Colorado River Water Conservation District* v. *Vidler Tunnel Water Company,* 594 P.2d 566 (Colo. 1979).

83. Simpson, "The Azure Project," NCWCDA.

84. Letter, 6 April 1983, Roland C. Fischer to John M. Sayre, NCWCDA.

85. Letter, 12 April 1983, John M. Sayre to Roland C. Fischer, NCWCDA. The letter in question was written by Robert L. McCarty to FERC on April 5, 1983.

86. Ibid. Sayre referred to Part V, Paragraph 6, of the 1980 Windy Gap Settlement Agreement.

87. Letter, 20 April 1983, Roland C. Fischer to John M. Sayre, NCWCDA.

88. Minutes, MSD, August 12, 1983. Simpson mentioned the Definite Project Report being prepared by IECO and Stone and Webster's Market Demand Study.

89. Paper prepared by MSD staff for meeting with CRWCD, September 28, 1983, "Windy Gap: Azure Settlement Agreement Negotiation Correspondence, 1980–1985," NCWCDA.

90. Minutes, Six Cities Committee, October 12, 1983. Letter, 11 October 1983, Larry Simpson to Roland C. Fischer, NCWCDA.

91. Unidentified report, December 5, 1983, that showed a firm yield of 18,500 acre-feet at both sites and a cost ranging between $11.4 million for Rock Creek Reservoir and $13.2 million for Wolford Mountain Reservoir, NCWCDA.

92. Letter, 3 February 1984, Rial R. Lake, President, CRWCD, to W. D. Farr, NCWCDA. Letter, 16 March 1984, Gregory J. Hobbs to CRWCD attorneys, NCWCDA.

93. Supplement to Agreement of April 30, 1980, paragraphs 1–3, NCWCDA. This supplement was approved by Division 5 Water Court, then set aside on a motion by Kenneth Balcomb representing clients other than the River District, and then reinstated by the court when District lobbyist Fred Anderson obtained passage of an act in the Colorado General Assembly that recognized the right of water courts to approve plans and amendments to plans under the Colorado Water Conservancy District Act's Colorado River protective provision.

94. Minutes, MSD, November 11, 1983. Simpson told the Board that power contracts could be the "most important financial factor to the participants in the operation of the Windy Gap Project."

95. Interview, Larry D. Simpson, 8 August 1991.

96. Ibid. Simpson explained that simply turning on the first pump for one minute costs $30,000 to $40,000 for electric capacity, "whether we pump another time that month or not"; one minute costs the same as thirty days. In addition, power companies levy a charge for kilowatt hours of energy.

97. Minutes, NCWCD, January 10 and November 7, 1975. See also letter, 11 November 1975, Raymond O. Reeb, NCWCD agency coordinator, to Lenny Arnold, Legislative Council Staff, Committee on Denver and Metropolitan Water District, NCWCDA. This letter mentions earlier District Board resolutions of 1966, 1972, and 1973 that froze District boundaries.

98. Minutes, NCWCD, March 14, 1980.

99. Minutes, MSD, November 5, 1976. Minutes, NCWCD, November 16, 1979.

100. Minutes, MSD, September 9, 1983.

101. Ibid., April 5, 1985.

102. C–BT water was selling at $3,400 per acre-foot in 1980. With Windy Gap project completion and revised predictions of population growth, sales and prices fell dramatically. According to Simpson, calculations of the capital, carriage, and pumping costs from Windy Gap project water reveal that the per-acre-foot value is now (1991) very close to that of C–BT water. Interview, 8 August 1991.

CHAPTER 23

1. Letter, 2 June 1981, Earl F. Phipps to John M. Sayre, NCWCDA.

2. Minutes, Six Cities Committee, February 23, 1976.

3. *Grand Junction Sentinel*, 16 July 1975. *Sky Hi News*, 21 January 1977.

4. *Denver Post*, 6 October 1977. The NWRCOG represented six counties: Eagle, Grand, Jackson, Pitkin, Routt, and Summit.

5. *Denver Post*, 18 October 1977.

6. Letter, 21 October 1977, John M. Sayre to Richard Lamm, NCWCDA.

7. Minutes, NCWCD, August 8, 1975.

8. See *Greeley Tribune*, 25 July 1978. *Environmental Defense Fund* v. *Costle*, 657 F.2d 275 (Dist. Ct. App. 1981), was filed in the U.S. District Court for the District of Columbia. The litigation

essentially challenged the Colorado River Salinity Forum's and EPA's standards for salinity control in the Colorado River.

9. Ibid., 13 May 1977.

10. Minutes, MSD, July 14, 1978. Minutes, NCWCD, December 9, 1977.

11. Minutes, NCWCD, October 12, 1979. The decision of the Court of Appeals for the District of Columbia Circuit is reported as *Environmental Defense Fund* v. *Costle*, 657 F.2d 295 (D.C. Circuit 1981).

12. *Loveland Reporter-Herald*, 22 July 1978.

13. George Vranesh, *Colorado Water Law*, 3 vols. (Boulder, Colo.: Design Press, 1987), 3, p. 1298.

14. Ibid., p. 1299.

15. Minutes, NCWCD, November 7, 1975.

16. Letter, 11 October 1977, Evan D. Dildine, Technical Secretary, CWQCC, to Senator Gary Hart, "Correspondence Files," NCWCDA.

17. Minutes, NCWCD, November 5, 1976.

18. *Loveland Reporter-Herald*, 4, 5 December 1976.

19. Letter, 7 December 1976, Earl F. Phipps to the CWQCC, "Correspondence Files," NCWCDA.

20. Minutes, NCWCD, August 8, 1980. Testimony of Larry D. Simpson before the CWQCC, 1980. Colorado Department of Agriculture, *Agricultural Lands Conversion in Colorado*, 2 vols., NCWCDA.

21. *Grand Junction Sentinel*, 17 September 1979. Letter, 15 March 1979, Larry Simpson to Gary Hart, NCWCDA.

22. *Loveland Reporter Herald*, 6 November 1979.

23. *Longmont Daily Times-Call*, 7 April 1980.

24. Minutes, NCWCD, April 6, 1979. The District successfully participated in a case that ruled that the Northwest Regional Colorado Council of Governments, in conducting planning activities for water quality management under the CWA, did not become an agency of the United States. The court held that NWRCOG would have only the powers it was given under Colorado law. See *Northern Colorado Water Conservancy District* v. *Board of County Commissioners of Grand County*, 482 F.Supp. 1115 (D. Colo. 1980). Two years later the District participated in a federal case brought by the National Wildlife Federation in which the Court of Appeals held that dams were not point sources of pollution and therefore did not require EPA discharge permits. See *National Wildlife Federation* v. *Gorsuch*, 693 F.2d 156 (D.C. Circ. 1982).

25. As defined in the Clean Water Act, a point source is "any discernible, confined and discrete conveyance, including but not limited to, any pipe, ditch, channel, conduit, well, discrete fissure, container, rolling stock, concentrated animal feeding operation, or vessel or other floating craft, from which pollutants are or may be discharged." See Vranesh, *Colorado Water Law*, 3, p. 1307. The Clean Water Act did not define a nonpoint source of pollution, which was generally considered to be "diffuse surface runoff."

26. *Longmont Daily Times-Call*, 7 March 1976. *Loveland Reporter-Herald*, 19 May 1976.

27. *Fort Collins Coloradoan*, 17 October 1976.

28. Minutes, NCWCD, November 7, 1975.

29. Vranesh, *Colorado Water Law*, 3, p. 1300.

30. Minutes, NCWCD, March 12 and July 9, 1976. The Clean Water Act of 1977, Pub. L. No. 95-217, 91 Stat. 1566, amended by P.L. 97-117, 95 Stat. 1623 (1981) (codified at 33 U.S.C. §§ 1251 et seq., 1982). Section 33 (c)(1) of the 1977 amendments excluded irrigation return flows from point source regulations.

31. Clean Water Act of 1977, Pub. L. No. 95-217, 91 Stat. 1566, § 33 (c) (1), December 27, 1977. See also Section 101 (g), the Wallop Amendment to the CWA. The Wallop Amendment,

co-sponsored by Wyoming Senator Malcolm Wallop and Colorado Senator Hart, was a water rights protective provision that resulted from a general concern in the West that the CWA might be used to usurp state water law.

32. In 1981 the District began the Irrigation Management Program to instruct farmers "in the practical application of sound irrigation principles and technologies to improve water management and conservation." In 1989 the IMS program was expanded to include nitrogen fertilizer management "in order to reduce and/or prevent nonpoint source pollution from irrigated agriculture." See Mark A. Crookston, "Irrigation Management Service," March 29, 1991, "IMS Files," NCWCDA.

33. David McComb, *Big Thompson: Profile of a National Disaster* (Boulder, Colo.: Pruett Publishing Company, 1980), p. 17. "Cleaning Up After the Big T Flood," *Rocky Mountain Construction*, August 27, 1976, p. 16, NCWCDA.

34. The Big Thompson River's normal flow for that time of year is 165 cfs to 200 cfs.

35. *Fort Collins Coloradoan*, August 1976, Special Report on the Big Thompson Flood.

36. Interview, Bob Berling, 2 July 1991.

37. Interview, Jim Wooldridge, District O&M, with Greg Silkensen, August 1991.

38. Minutes, NCWCD, August 13, 1976.

39. Ibid., November 5, 1976.

40. Larry Simpson, "Damage Assessment, Start of Repair Simultaneous at NCWCD," in Grant Judkins, ed., *The Big Thompson Disaster* (Loveland, Colo.: Lithographic Press, n.d.).

41. Interview, Bob Berling, 2 July 1991.

42. Minutes, NCWCD, October 8, 1976.

43. Ibid., July 9, 1976.

44. Ibid., February 11, 1977.

45. *Boulder Daily Camera*, 5 February 1977.

46. *Fort Collins Coloradoan*, 1 August 1976.

47. Colo. Rev. Stat. §§ 36-20-101 through 36-20-126, as quoted in Vranesh, *Colorado Water Law*, 1, pp. 367–368.

48. *Boulder Daily Camera*, 19 October 1979.

49. *Greeley Tribune*, 4, 6 October 1977.

50. Minutes, NCWCD, August 11, 1978.

51. Ibid., October 12, 1979.

52. Ibid., January 11, 1980.

53. Ibid., September 11, 1981.

54. *Denver Post*, 18 October 1977.

55. Minutes, NCWCD, August 8, 1980.

56. *Loveland Reporter-Herald*, 27 January 1977.

57. *Greeley Tribune*, 7 January 1982. Because the two biggest ditch companies on the lower South Platte River had their headgates above the Narrows location, they would not benefit from a dam at this site.

58. Minutes, NCWCD, June 10, 1981, and January 8, 1982.

59. Ibid., March 12, 1982.

60. Letter, 19 October 1983, Morgan County Commissioners to Gordon Dyekman, NCWCD President, "Correspondence Files," NCWCDA.

61. The five task forces were Patterns of Development (to study trends and forces affecting development), Transportation (to compile a report on present and expected transportation needs and problems), Governmental Services (to consider the growing problem of financing and providing

services to an expanding population base), Natural Resources (to study the effects of increased population on land, air, energy, and water), and Visions (to consider alternatives for the future and to develop option statements for a desirable future). See State of Colorado, Governor's Office, *Task Force Reports to the Conference*, September 26–27, 1980. Lamm's more comprehensive approach to land use planning and expanded state authority over natural resources were frustrated by a Republican legislature. The Front Range project study gained notoriety as the "Human Settlements Policy," evoking overtones of World War II and dooming reasoned public debate.

62. Minutes, MSD, December 14, 1979. Phipps's name does not appear in the final report of members of the Natural Resources Task Force.

63. *Boulder Daily Camera*, 27 October 1976. Minutes, NCWCD, October 8, 1976.

64. *Grand Junction Sentinel*, 16 July 1976.

65. Richard Lamm, State of the State, January 1982, as reported in *Longmont Daily Times-Call*, 7 January 1982.

66. *Longmont Daily Times-Call*, 18 March 1982.

67. *Loveland Reporter-Herald*, 3–4 February 1979.

68. CWCB, draft memorandum, 10 March 1981, NCWCDA.

69. Hobbs was invited to serve on the Governor's Advisory Committee in a personal capacity, not as an official representative of the District. See Minutes, NCWCD, November 13, 1981.

70. Richard D. Lamm, "The Lamm Administration: A Retrospective," unpublished doc., December 1986, NCWCDA.

71. "Metropolitan Water Roundtable," *Resolve* (Summer 1982).

72. Former gubernatorial advisor Charlie Jordan told Lamm that the DWB, suburbs, West Slope, and environmentalists could never communicate with each other. See *Western Colorado Report*, 11 October 1982.

73. Lamm, "Retrospective."

74. Telephone conversation, Greg Hobbs, 25 September 1991.

75. Minutes, NCWCD, July 10, 1981. The Board passed a resolution of appreciation for Anderson's action on nine different bills.

76. *Denver Post*, 10 March 1980.

77. CWR&PDA, *Annual Report*, 1982, p. 1.

78. *Grand Junction Sentinel*, 8 November 1982.

79. CWR&PDA, *Annual Report* for 1982, 1983, and 1984.

80. Ibid., 1985, p. 16.

81. NCWCD, *Cache La Poudre Basin Study Extension*, December 1990, NCWCDA. This report addressed recommendations made by Harza Engineering Company, which had been contracted by the CWR&PDR to do a two-part study on the Poudre River basin. Work on phase 1, which began in June 1985, was completed in January 1987 in a report entitled *The Cache La Poudre Basin Water and Hydropower Resources Management Study*. The District's *Extension* study examined the alternatives suggested by Harza Engineering Company and suggested how to scale down the Harza recommendations to a manageable process.

82. *Fort Collins Coloradoan*, 13 April 1978. Minutes, NCWCD, March 10, 1978.

83. Letter, 30 March 1979, Larry Simpson to Gary Hart, NCWCDA.

84. *Triangle Review*, 22 April 1979.

85. *Boulder Daily Camera*, 25 February 1980. *Greeley Tribune*, 27 June 1980.

86. *Greeley Tribune*, 22 January 1980. *Rocky Mountain News*, 23 June 1982.

87. *Greeley Tribune*, 24 March 1981.

88. Ibid., 22 January 1980.

89. Minutes, CLPWUA, August 4, 1980.

90. Ibid., December 15, 1980.

91. Ibid., April 25, 1983.

92. Ibid., June 27 and December 1, 1983. CWR&PDA, *Annual Report*, 1984, pp. 17–18.

93. Information provided courtesy of Karl Dreher, senior engineer, NCWCD. As of fall 1991 the District and the CLPWUA were still applicants on the original water decree; the District was the only applicant for the Glade Reservoir and Grey Rock Reservoir pump storage.

94. Interview, Larry Simpson, 8 August 1991.

95. Charles W. Howe, "Project Benefits and Costs from National and Regional Viewpoints: Methodological Issues and Case Study of the Colorado–Big Thompson Project," *Natural Resources Journal* 27 (Winter 1987), pp. 5–20.

96. *Loveland Reporter-Herald*, 16, 17 August 1975. Bureau data for 1970 show visitor use at Green Mountain Reservoir (73,123), Lake Granby (1,029,353), Shadow Mountain Reservoir (67,871), and Horsetooth Reservoir (71,000), as cited in NCWCD, *Waternews*, Fall 1988, p. 15.

97. Interview, John McFarlane, 31 July 1991. McFarlane pointed out that Bureau projects constructed after 1965 have cost-sharing agreements that help pay for recreation. A bill is needed that will address the problems of projects built prior to 1965.

98. Boulder County, County Parks and Open Space Department, Statement of "Revenue vs. Expenses and Attendance," 1991.

99. Rocky Mountain National Park, Superintendent's Monthly Reports, Shadow Mountain National Recreation Area, 1967–1978.

100. USBR, Recreation and Wildlife Summary, Annual Reports. Review of this information and additional data were provided by Jerry A. Westbrook, Head, Land and Water Contract Services Department, NCWCD.

101. J. Gordon Milliken and H. E. Mew, Jr., *Economic and Social Impact of Recreation at Reclamation Reservoirs: An Exploratory Study of Selected Colorado Reservoir Areas* (Denver: Denver Research Institute, University of Denver, 1969), pp. 92–108.

102. Interview, Bob Berling, 2 July 1991.

103. Minutes, NCWCD, November 10, 1978; May 11, September 14, November 16, and December 14, 1979; May 8 and July 10, 1981.

104. Minutes, NCWCD, June 11, 1976.

105. Interview, John Eckhardt, 26 July 1991.

106. John Eckhardt, "The Windy Gap Project SCADA System," *Journal of Water Resources Planning and Management* 112:3 (July 1986), pp. 366–381.

107. NCWCD, *Annual Report*, 1974–1982.

108. Minutes, NCWCD, January 11, 1980, and February 13, 1981.

109. Ibid., April 2, 1982.

110. Minutes, MSD, February 11, 1983.

111. In *Rivers of Empire* (New York: Pantheon Books, 1985), historian Donald Worster argues that hydraulic societies tend to create empires that ultimately decline because people no longer tolerate their leaders' abuse of power or because irrigation systems poison the very land they serve. While it is too early to determine whether his deterministic analysis applies to the NCWCD/MSD, costly litigation, increasing urbanization, public criticism of an appointed Board of Directors, and the potential of severe pollution from irrigated agriculture will require constant vigilance to assure that C–BT and Windy Gap waters continue to be distributed in a fair and environmentally sound manner.

112. Minutes, NCWCD, April 3, 1981.

113. Letter, 2 June 1981, Earl F. Phipps to Larry McDonald, NCWCDA.

114. Minutes, NCWCD, June 10, 1981.

115. Letter, 25 August 1983, Richard Lamm to Larry Simpson, NCWCDA. Previously, a letter had been sent to Lamm "requesting the appointment of Larry Simpson to the Green Mountain Exchange Committee with a strong endorsement from the Board of Directors of the Northern Colorado Water Conservancy District and that Mr. Sayre also be appointed as the legal adviser serving with Mr. Simpson." See Minutes, NCWCD, July 8, 1983.

CHAPTER 24

1. As NCWCD manager, Simpson later recognized the importance of liaison activities by employing two men as full-time planning coordinators.

2. Interview, Larry Simpson, 22 November 1991. Simpson took special pride in developing an inflatable rubberized dam that diverted water from a canal or deflated during flood conditions. Before going on active duty, he designed a rubber dam 250 feet long and 15 feet high. In addition to being the largest hydraulic "diaphragm" of its kind, Simpson's design has since been copied by Orange County, California.

3. Reclamation Reform Act of 1982, Title II, Pub. L. No. 97-293, 96 Stat. 1293 (codified in *United States Code*, Title 43, Chap. 390aa et seq., 1982).

4. Ibid., Sec. 210(b).

5. Minutes, NCWCD, March 9 and June 8, 1984.

6. Memorandum, IMS, 19 October 1988, NCWCDA.

7. Mark A Crookston, Senior Water Resources Engineer, NCWCD, "Irrigation Management Service," abstract of a paper presented at the 1991 regional meeting of the U.S. Committee on Irrigation and Drainage, Denver, Colorado, NCWCDA.

8. Christine Anderson, "Chalking Up Water Savings," *Colorado Rancher and Farmer*, October 1, 1989, pp. 15–16.

9. Gregory J. Hobbs, Jr., "Federal Environmental Law and State Water Law: Accommodation or Preemption," *Natural Resources & Environment* 1:4 (Winter 1986), pp. 23–26, 57–59.

10. As defined in the 1972 Federal Water Pollution Control Act, a nationwide permit could only be issued if a project were located on a headwater stream with a flow of less than 5 cfs, if the dam discharge had no impact on threatened or endangered species as identified in the ESA, and if there were only minimal adverse effects and minimal accumulative effects on the environment. In the event of conflict, the law provided for accommodation through the individual, site-specific permit system. Nationwide permits had to be renewed or revised every five years. See *Riverside Irrigation District v. Andrews*, 758 F.2d 508 (10th Cir. 1985).

11. *Riverside Irrigation District v. Stipo*, 658 F.2d 762 (10th Cir. 1981) on remand to *Riverside Irrigation Dist. v. Andrews*, 568 F.Supp. 583 (D. Colo. 1983) and judgment affirmed by *Riverside Irrigation Dist. v. Andrews*, 758 F.2d 508 (10th Cir. 1985).

12. Letter, 25 June 1980, Larry Simpson to Morgan Smith, Riverside Case, NCWCDA. Article 7 of the 1923 South Platte River Compact states that "compliance by Colorado with the provisions of this compact and the delivery of water in accordance with its terms shall relieve Colorado from any further or additional demand or claim by Nebraska upon the waters of the South Platte River within Colorado."

13. Section 404 of the CWA requires a federal permit for the discharge of dredged or fill material into navigable waters. The permit is issued by the Army Corps of Engineers, with the EPA having veto authority and the USF&WS having a key consultation role. For a brief review of the CWA, its most significant sections, and the Water Quality Act of 1987, see Warren Freedman, *Federal Statutes on Environmental Protection: Regulation in the Public Interest* (New York: Quorum Books, 1987), pp. 27–32.

14. Letter, 11 June 1980, Jeris A. Danielson, State Engineer, to the Honorable J. D. MacFarlane, Attorney General of Colorado, Riverside Case, NCWCDA.

15. Memorandum, 18 November 1981, William R. Gianelli, Assistant Secretary of the Army, to Directors of Civil Works, U.S. Army Corps of Engineers, Riverside Case, NCWCDA.

16. Minutes, NCWCD, November 11, 1983.

17. See testimony of the National Water Resources Association (NWRA) regarding S. 1081, by Gregory J. Hobbs, Jr., before the Senate Environment and Public Works Committee, Subcommittee on Environmental Protection, July 29, 1991. Hearing before the Subcommittee on Environmental Protection of the Committee on Environmental and Public Works. U.S. Senate, 102d Cong., 1st sess. on S. 1081 (A bill to amend and reauthorize the Federal Water Pollution Control Act), May 21, June 13, July 9, 17, 18, 1991.

18. Section 7 of the ESA requires federal agencies to "insure that any action authorized, funded, or carried out by such agency is not likely to jeopardize the continued existence of any endangered species . . . or result in the destruction or adverse modification of habitat of such species which is determined . . . to be critical." 16 U.S.C. Section 1536(a)(2) (1982 Supp.) as quoted in *Riverside* v. *Andrews*, Appeal from the United States District Court for the District of Colorado, Judge John L. Kane, "Opening Brief of Plaintiff-Intervenor-Appellants, State of Colorado, Northern Colorado Water Conservancy District, Colorado Water Conservation District, and Lower South Platte Water Conservancy District, In the United States Court of Appeals for the Tenth Circuit, May 3, 1984."

19. Minutes, NCWCD, April 5, 1985.

20. *Riverside Irrigation District* v. *Andrews*, 758 F.2d 508 (10th Cir. 1985).

21. Gregory J. Hobbs, Jr., and Bennett W. Raley, "Water Rights Protection in Water Quality Law," *University of Colorado Law Review* 60:4 (1989), pp. 869–871. He also noted that "agencies and the courts must guard against administrative abuse of the 404 permit process, so that the public's interest in a stable, secure, and clean water supply for beneficial use is not undermined by one-dimensional second-guessing of the state's water allocation determination" (p. 870). See also Gregory J. Hobbs, Jr., and Bennett W. Raley, "Water Quality Versus Water Quantity: A Delicate Balance," *Rocky Mountain Mineral Law Institute* 34 (1988).

22. Minutes, NCWCD, February 11, 1983.

23. Ibid., Narrows Project Resolution, April 6, 1984. The standing committee would be composed of representatives from NCWCD, LSPWCD, CCWCD, the Bureau, CWCB, CWR&PDA, Colorado Division of Water Resources, Groundwater Appropriators of the South Platte Basin, and others.

24. Ibid., August 8, 1986.

25. Ibid., April 3, 1987.

26. Ibid., November 14, 1986.

27. Ibid., July 10, 1987.

28. Interview, Larry D. Simpson, 1 November 1991.

29. Ibid. According to the *Annual Report of Colorado Water Resources and Power Development Authority*, 1985, "The Cache La Poudre Pre-Feasibility Water Resources Management and Development Project Study" was authorized by the CWR&PDA in March 1985. The NCWCD had requested the report in February 1984, but legislation in Congress regarding the Poudre River's possible wild and scenic river status delayed action. The first stage appeared in January 1987 under the title "Cache la Poudre Basin Study, Summary Report," with a "Cache la Poudre Basin Study Extension, Executive Summary" completed in December 1990. The 1987 report, prepared by Harza Engineering Company of Denver, defined a combination of "water and hydropower resource management alternatives, both structural and non-structural which will provide for the efficient and environmentally sound development of the water and hydropower resources of the Cache la Poudre Basin." The 1990 report, jointly prepared by Harza Engineering Company and five

environmental firms, focused on refining the environmental, economic, and engineering analyses presented in the earlier study.

30. Resolution, Minutes, NCWCD, October 12, 1984.

31. Minutes, NCWCD, December 13, 1985.

32. In an October 3, 1986, letter to Simpson, James D. Pendergrass, general manager of Platte River Power Authority (PRPA), wrote that "ERDA will have a very difficult time getting contracts for *anyone* to purchase pumped storage capacity. There is no market in this area at all and the California markets have declined so much that the Bonneville Power Administration is having trouble marketing surplus conventional hydro." See Poudre project Correspondence, 1984–1990, NCWCDA.

33. The local group opposing the Poudre project was first named "Preserve Our Poudre," which was reorganized in 1986 as "Friends of the Poudre." Their criticism of the Poudre project is taken from several informational bulletins and newsletters issued between 1986 and 1990.

34. Minutes, NCWCD, June 13, 1986, and June 12, 1987.

35. Wild and Scenic Rivers Act, Amendments, P.L. 99-590, October 30, 1986.

36. Greg Hobbs credited Wanner with being the principal broker between two ideological positions. He and his citizen constituents insisted on a wild and scenic designation for the river, but they were willing to fight for a compromise. Hobbs, conversation with the author, 12 December 1991.

37. Under federal law the "wild" designation is for rivers that are free of impoundments and generally inaccessible except by trail, with essentially primitive watersheds, shorelines, and unpolluted waters. The "scenic" designation applies to similar rivers except that watersheds and shorelines might be accessible in places by roads. "Recreational" designates readily accessible rivers that may have shoreline development and may have some impoundments and diversions.

38. As quoted in Howard Ensign Evans and Mary Alice Evans, *Cache La Poudre: The Natural History of a Rocky Mountain River* (Niwot: University Press of Colorado, 1991), p. 238. Most NCWCD Board members agree with Simpson's assessment.

39. Complaint for Declaratory and Injunctive Relief, January 3, 1984. *Sierra Club* v. *Block*, 615 F.Supp. 44 (D. Colo. 1985). *Sierra Club* v. *Yeutter*, 911 F.2d 1405 (10th Cir. 1990). The idea of federal reserved rights came from the 1908 *Winters* v. *United States* decision, which stated that an Indian reservation was entitled to enough water to sustain the reservation's purpose. The Sierra Club attempted to have the court apply the same rule to creation of the Forest Reserves (National Forests).

40. Minutes, NCWCD, October 12, 1984. Sayre told the Board that support for litigation was advisable if the District wanted to protect the Indian Meadows reservoir site on the Poudre River.

41. Ibid., November 9, 1984. In Colorado 2.8 million acres of national forest lands (18 percent of all USFS lands in the state) had already been designated wilderness. More than 500,000 additional acres were being considered for designation, and the BLM was studying approximately 500,000 acres for possible designation at lower altitudes near Colorado and New Mexico state lands.

42. Memorandum and Order, Judge John Kane, July 29, 1984, *Sierra Club* v. *Block*, 622 F.Supp. 842 (D. Colo. 1985).

43. Memorandum Opinion and Order, Judge John Kane, November 25, 1985, *Sierra Club* v. *Block*.

44. Brief filed in the 10th Circuit Court of Appeals, May 28, 1986.

45. For the water rights negotiating team, Hobbs exerted leadership and represented the NCWCD and the CWC; other members of the team included Sam Maynes (Southwestern Water Conservation District and Rio Grande Water Conservation District); Harold Miskel (Colorado Springs, Aurora, and Pueblo, the Southeastern Colorado Water Conservancy District, the Denver Water Providers, the Metropolitan Denver Water Authority); Keith Probst (Colorado Farm Bureau); Carl Trick (Colorado Cattlemen's Association); and Bill McDonald (CWCB). The conservationists' negotiating team was composed of Chris Meyer (National Wildlife Federation); Maggie Fox (Sierra Club); Charles B. "Barney" White, David Getches, and Glen Porzak (Colorado Mountain

Club); Francis Green (Holy Cross Wilderness Defense Fund); Darrell Knuffke (The Wilderness Society); and Lori Potter (Sierra Club Legal Defense Fund).

46. Letter, 30 March 1987, Gregory J. Hobbs, Jr., to "colleagues," *Sierra* v. *Block* file, NCWCDA. In an August 1, 1987, letter from Wirth and Armstrong to Hobbs, the senators expressed their hope that suggestions from both teams would help them "proceed with negotiations to find a sound compromise."

47. *Sierra Club* v. *Yeutter*, Appeal from the United States District Court for the District of Colorado (D.C. No. 84-M-2), August 10, 1990, 911 F2d. 1405 (10th Cir. 1990).

48. The meaning of the *Sierra Club* v. *Yeutter* decision is discussed in Hobbs, "Federal Appellate Court Vacates Judge Kane's Wilderness Water Rights Decision," *Colorado Water Rights* (a publication of the Colorado Water Congress) 9 (Summer/Fall 1990), p. 3.

49. Letter, 25 August 1988, Gregory J. Hobbs, Jr., to Ellis Armstrong, Davis, Graham and Stubbs, Denver, Colorado. In sum, the four principles demanded protection for existing water-rights holders, protection of the priority system, observation of existing interstate water compacts, and either the exclusion of nonheadwater stream segments in future wilderness designations or water amounts designated by the CWCB for instream flows.

50. Letter, 18 April 1989, Gregory J. Hobbs, Jr., to Tim Wirth, Davis, Graham and Stubbs, Denver, Colorado. Hobbs believed that the areas most vulnerable to federal reserved wilderness water rights were downstream, below Colorado cities, farms, and areas with recreational development potential. A downstream federal water rights call would place Colorado's water future in the hands of Washington, D.C., officials and with national environmental interests, whose leaders insisted that state water interests wanted to "gut" the wilderness preservation system.

51. *Rocky Mountain News*, 18 May, 1 December, and 8 November 1991. Shortly after Brown became a senator in March 1990, he and Wirth effected a compromise. Passed in fall 1990, their bill contained no federal water rights but protected streams in wilderness by barring dams, by letting the state guarantee minimum flows, and by authorizing the federal government to buy water rights. A similar bill is sponsored by Representative Ben Nighthorse Campbell in the House.

52. *High Country News*, 10 September 1990.

53. A decision from Judge Robert A. Behrman, Division 1 Water Court in Greeley, is expected sometime in 1992.

54. Minutes, NCWCD, Resolution of July 13, 1979, reaffirmed May 9, 1986, following revelations of Thornton's water purchases. The "tap gap," as described by Hobbs in 1985, noted that Denver would need at least 7,000 water taps per year for the next ten years; required water supplies could be obtained from the Two Forks project. Without new water, Denver could not issue new permits for water taps. See Minutes, MSD, February 8, 1985.

55. The Two Forks project called for a dam in Cheesman Canyon, just upstream from Strontia Springs Reservoir. At its largest, the $1 billion reservoir would hold 1.1 billion acre-feet of water. Denver planned to utilize West Slope water rights to fill the reservoir by way of the Roberts Tunnel and undeveloped South Platte River water rights, but the environmental objections to flooding a beautiful canyon, as well as concerns about sandhill and whooping crane habitats and other endangered species on the South Platte River, pressured the DWB to scale down the project or to come up with an alternative site. Denver agreed to a smaller 400,000-acre-foot reservoir, but the EPA had already reached a decision to veto any configuration of the Two Forks project.

56. *Rocky Mountain News*, 10 April 1986.

57. Minutes, NCWCD, May 9, 1986.

58. Ibid., July 11, 1986. Letter, 19 March 1987, Larry Simpson to Mayor Carpenter, Thornton files, NCWCDA.

59. Letter, 16 April 1986, Richard Hamilton, River Basin Authority, to Larimer County Administrator Arlen Stokes. See also Memorandum, 18 June 1986, WSSC, to all shareholders, Thornton files, NCWCDA.

60. Letter, 15 May 1986, A. L. Anderson, Jr., to Board of Directors, NCWCD, Thornton files, NCWCDA.

61. City of Thornton, Fact Sheet, "Cooperative City-Farm Water Program," April 23, 1986. The amount of water to be returned to agriculture was calculated on the basis that 60 percent of the purchased water was customarily consumed in farming. Therefore, if 20,000 acre-feet were purchased, 8,000 acre-feet would be returned to Black Hollow Reservoir.

62. *The Greeley News*, 14 November 1986.

63. Letter, 29 September 1986, Roland C. Fischer to John M. Sayre, with accompanying document entitled "Issues Arising as a Result of Recent and Expected Water Acquisitions by Thornton and Others, and Potential Resolution of Such Issues," Thornton files, NCWCDA.

64. Minutes, NCWCD, October 10, 1986.

65. Ed Marston, "Treaty Ends Colorado Water Wars," *High Country News*, 22 December 1986.

66. See particularly John R. Morris and Clive V. Jones, "Water for Denver. An Analysis of the Alternatives," prepared with a grant from the Environmental Defense Fund, Inc., 1980, NCWCDA.

67. Minutes, NCWCD, April 1, June 10, July 8, and September 9, 1983. Simpson and Sayre both insisted that the agreement include statements that protected all C–BT decrees.

68. Minutes, NCWCD, November 11, 1983. The joint-use idea involved building a West Slope reservoir from which Denver could lease a certain percentage of stored water. With the $10.2 million that the River District already had from the 1985 Supplemental Windy Gap agreement, construction could be initiated. The balance of funds would come from a bond issue to be retired by income received from Denver.

69. See CWR&PDA, *Annual Report*, 1985, 1986, 1987, 1988. The joint-use reservoir was estimated to provide an annual firm yield for $180 to $260, compared to $520 to $790 for the Green Mountain Reservoir exchange project.

70. Memorandum of Agreement between CRWCD and NCWCD, December 15, 1986, NCWCDA.

71. On appeal from Federal District Court, the 10th Circuit Court of Appeals ruled that Denver seek consent from the secretary of the interior before any water applications involving Green Mountain Reservoir operations can be filed. See *City and County of Denver* v. *United States*, 935 F.2d 1143 (10th Cir. 1991).

72. Denver's suburbs were counting on Two Forks to help them achieve independence from the DWB. The Metropolitan Water Providers were committed to paying 40 percent of an EIS estimated to cost $35 million; they wanted something for their money. The EIS, which actually cost $45 million, was the most expensive ever prepared.

73. Although $10.2 million was insufficient to build a Muddy Creek Reservoir in 1986, the River District would get additional funds from Denver from a contract to lease the stored water. The District's main concern was to see this money used so that no one would further question the fulfillment of its plan for basin-of-origin protection under the Water Conservancy District Act.

74. Jim Monaghan was a private consultant and chief negotiator at the Metropolitan Water Roundtable. His critics contend that the Thornton deal violated a preliminary agreement made by participants in 1982. When Thornton pulled out, the Roundtable never really recovered. See Bryan Abas, "No Consultation Without Representation," *Westword* 9:4 (June 11–17, 1986), pp. 8, 10, 13, 16, 18.

75. The Muddy Creek/Williams Fork Substitution Agreement will place in operation a lease agreement between Denver and the River District, paving the way for construction of Wolford Mountain Reservoir on Muddy Creek north of Kremmling. Under this agreement, Denver hopes to obtain firm delivery of 15,000 acre-feet of water per year, with expectations that the city may be able to take up to 30,000 acre-feet during wet years through a combination of Muddy Creek and Williams Fork exchanges.

76. Completed studies are as follows: CWR&PDA, "St. Vrain Basin Reconnaissance Study" (Denver: R. W. Beck and Associates, Dames and Moore, 1986); CWR&PDA, "Cache La Poudre Basin Study: Summary Report" (Denver: Harza Engineering Company, 1987); NCWCD, "Regional Water Supply Study: Draft Report" (Denver: BBC, Inc., and Camp, Dresser & McKee, Inc; Aurora: Black and Veatch, 1991).

CHAPTER 25

1. Interview, Larry Simpson, 22 November 1991.

2. Minutes, NCWCD, June 13 and July 11, 1986.

3. Ibid., October 14, 1983.

4. Ibid., July 13, 1984.

5. Interview, Larry Simpson, 22 November 1991. Simpson noted that fencing alone is not the answer, as shown by an Arizona case in which parents won a liability suit against the Salt River project because they could not climb a protective safety fence to rescue their children, who drowned in a canal.

6. Minutes, NCWCD, June 10, 1983.

7. Memorandum, December 1983, Bureau of Reclamation, Lower Missouri Region, Denver, Colorado, *Modification of Horsetooth Reservoir Dams*, NCWCDA.

8. Letter, 12 September 1984, B. E. Martin to Larry Simpson, NCWCDA.

9. Interview, Larry Simpson, 1 November 1991.

10. Letter, 9 January 1985, Larry Simpson to Commissioner of Reclamation Robert N. Broadbent, NCWCDA.

11. Letter, 20 October 1984, Robert N. Broadbent to Ellis Armstrong. Letter, 9 July 1985, Acting Commissioner James E. Cook to Larry Simpson, NCWCDA.

12. Total costs were estimated at $3.6 million, including $940,000 for raising Dixon and Spring Canyon dams and $2,660,000 for raising all crests to a 5,443-foot elevation.

13. Minutes, NCWCD, January 9, 1987.

14. O&M rehabilitation costs for Willow Creek and Granby pump plants are spread out through 1997, and the Bureau is committed to paying 50 percent.

15. Multipurpose works transferred by the Bureau on June 1, 1986, include: Granby Pumping Plant, Granby discharge line and Pump Canal, Granby Dam, Willow Creek Pumping Plant, Willow Creek Pump Canal, Willow Creek Dam, Shadow Mountain Dam, and Shadow Mountain connecting channel.

16. Interview, Craig McKee, NCWCD engineer, 8 November 1991.

17. Minutes, MSD, March 13, 1987.

18. Interview, Larry Simpson, 1 November 1991. See also Missouri Basin States Association, "The Missouri River Report," October 1991, NCWCDA.

19. Interview, Larry Simpson, 1 November 1991. Minutes, NCWCD, October 11, 1985.

20. A press release went out on September 16, 1987, stating that both the Bureau and District would "work diligently to have the transfer completed by April 1, 1988." For Simpson's goals, see Minutes, Six Cities Committee, October 7, 1987.

21. Interview, Larry Simpson, 1 November 1991. Simpson stated that both WAPA and Bonneville have revolving funds, but they are reluctant to help the Bureau because of interagency fights.

22. Figures prepared by the NCWCD for Colorado Representative David Skaggs, June 13, 1990. Crop values and acreages are prepared annually by the District for the Bureau and for the Colorado Department of Agriculture.

23. Data provided by Roger A. Sinden, Head, Distribution Systems, Operations and Maintenance Branch, NCWCD. Sinden identified the drought years as 1958, 1963, 1964, 1966, 1976, 1977, 1981, and 1989.

24. Interview, Larry Simpson, 22 November 1991. See also Minutes, NCWCD, April 3, 1987.

25. Interview, Brian Blakely, attorney, PRPA, 4 November 1991. Blakely also noted that power estimates made in 1979 and 1980 were high and that only recently had Rawhide energy been called for in the immediate service area.

26. In 1991 C–BT allottees needed water. Approximately 10,000 acre-feet was leased by various entities for $21 an acre-foot. The income helped PRPA pay the $3 million annual cost of its one-third share of the Windy Gap project.

27. NCWCD, *Regional Water Supply Study* (Draft Report, May 1991), pp. 20–21, NCWCDA.

28. Minutes, NCWCD, September 14, 1984.

29. Ibid., June 12, 1987.

30. "CBT/Windy Gap Operations Study, Final Report," prepared for the NCWCD Municipal Subdistrict by Hydrosphere Resource Consultants, November 1990, NCWCDA. This report also evaluates the merits of adding additional storage facilities on East and West Slopes.

31. Availability of Windy Gap water prior to the integrated arrangement depended on pumping decisions made during the thirty to forty days of high spring runoff. A borrowing system makes more storage available in the system, which allows larger quantities of water to be pumped during the brief period of high flows.

32. Because of Rocky Flats's contracts with the Department of Energy, Broomfield's funds for this construction would come from the United States: $13 million to guarantee the Windy Gap yield and $18.38 million for the capital cost of facilities to transport the water from Carter Lake to Broomfield. NCWCD will own, operate, and maintain the project, and Broomfield will pay a pro-rata share of O&M, depending on the number of other entities that the pipeline will serve.

33. Southern Water Supply project, Status Report, November 15, 1991, NCWCDA. The city of Fort Morgan and others have expressed interest in continuing the pipeline east to Brush.

34. *Regional Water Supply Study*, p. 19.

35. See William Gilpin, *The Central Gold Region: The Grain, Pastoral and Gold Region of North America* (Philadelphia: Sower, Barnes and Co.; and St. Louis: E. K. Woodward, 1860). Gilpin predicted that the Mississippi Valley, with Denver as its capital, would be the future center of civilization.

36. This concept embraces a system that would reflect variable climatological conditions up and down the Front Range by converting cfs flow rates to acre-foot volumes; thus, exchanges of water quantities could be better managed among all water-using entities.

37. W. D. Farr, "The Future of Northern Colorado Water Supplies," speech given at the Fort Collins Water Symposium, October 21, 1991. Other references to Farr's views are taken from an interview with the author, September 19, 1991.

38. Evan Vlachos, "The Changing World of the Water Manager," NCWCD Fall Water Users Meeting, November 21, 1991.

39. This idea is suggested by Marc Reisner in "The Next Water War: Cities Versus Agriculture," *Issues in Science and Technology* (Winter 1988–1989), pp. 98–102.

Bibliography

Research for this book was facilitated by an excellent archival collection at the NCWCD organized and arranged by Brian Werner and partially computerized by David Ayers and Brad Leach. Although large quantities of correspondence and other records were destroyed in the 1970s, a sufficient variety of materials was available for most segments of this history. The author also reviewed and/or used archival collections of the CWCB, the CRWCD, Norlin Library at the University of Colorado, the Greeley Museum, the Bureau of Reclamation collections at Billings, Montana, and the Denver Federal Center, the DWB, the CWR&PDA, several ditch companies, and the photographic collections of the Colorado State Historical Society and the Western History Department of the Denver Public Library. The University of Wyoming archives contain several collections of personal papers that have a tangential bearing on the C–BT. The citations selected herein are representative of the most important sources used in the writing of this history. The notes contain additional references that may be of further use to investigators. Abbreviations of organizations will be found in the list of acronyms.

BOOKS

Anderson, Raymond L. *Urbanization of Rural Lands in the Northern Colorado Front Range, 1955 to 1983*. Fort Collins, Colo.: Department of Agriculture and Natural Resource Economics, Extension Service, Colorado State University, 1984.

Athearn, Robert G. *The Coloradans*. Albuquerque: University of New Mexico Press, 1976.

———. *The Mythic West*. Lawrence: University of Kansas Press, 1986.

Berkman, Richard L., and W. Kip Viscusi. *Damming the West*. New York: Grossman Publishers, 1973.

Bevans, Charles I., comp. *Treaties and Other International Agreements of the United States, 1776–1949*. Washington: Department of State, 1972.

Branyan, Robert L., and Larson H. Lawrence. *The Eisenhower Administration, 1953–1961: A Documentary History*. New York: Random House, 1971.

Buchholtz, C. W. *Rocky Mountain National Park: A History*. Boulder: Colorado Associated University Press, 1983.

Burns, James MacGregor. *Roosevelt: The Lion and the Fox*. New York: Harcourt, Brace and World, 1956.

Clark, Ira G. *Water in New Mexico*. Albuquerque: University of New Mexico Press, 1987.

Colorado Water Conservation Board, and Colorado Agricultural and Mechanical College. *A Hundred Years of Irrigation in Colorado, 1852–1952*. Denver: Colorado Water Conservation Board, 1952.

Commager, Henry Steele, ed. *Documents of American History*, 2 vols. New York: Meredith Publishing Company, 1963.

Dickerman, Alan R., Kenneth Nobe, and George E. Radosevich. *Foundations of Federal Reclamation Policies: An Historical Review of Changing Goals and Objectives*. Fort Collins, Colo.: Department of Economics, Colorado State University, 1970.

Dille, J. M. *A Brief History of Northern Colorado Water Conservancy District and the Colorado–Big Thompson Project*. Loveland, Colo.: NCWCD, 1958.

Dunbar, Robert G. *Forging New Rights in Western Waters*. Lincoln: University of Nebraska Press, 1983.

Edmonds, Carol. *Wayne Aspinall: Mr. Chairman*. Lakewood, Colo.: Crownpoint, 1980.

Evans, Howard Ensign, and Mary Alice Evans. *Cache La Poudre: The Natural History of a Rocky Mountain River*. Niwot: University Press of Colorado, 1991.

Expansion of Water Delivery by Municipalities and Special Water Districts in the Northern Front Range, Colorado, 1972–1982. Technical Report No. 46. Fort Collins: Colorado Water Resources Research Institute, Colorado State University, [1984].

Fischer, Ward H. *A Guide to Colorado Water Law*. Fort Collins: Colorado Water Resources Research Institute, Colorado State University, 1978.

Fradkin, Philip L. *A River No More: The Colorado River and the West*. Tucson: The University of Arizona Press, 1984.

Freedman, Warren. *Federal Statutes on Environmental Protection: Regulation in the Public Interest*. New York: Quorum Books, 1987.

Getches, David H. *Water Law in a Nutshell*. St. Paul, Minn.: West Publishing Company, 1984.

Gilpin, William. *The Central Gold Region: The Grain, Pastoral and Gold Region of North America*. Philadelphia: Sower, Barnes, and Co. and St. Louis: E. K. Woodward, 1860.

Gulliford, Andrew. *Boomtown Blues: Colorado Oil Shale, 1885–1985*. Niwot: University Press of Colorado, 1989.

Hansen, Charles. *My Heart in the Hills*. Philadelphia: Dorrance and Company, 1925.

Hartman, L. M., and Don Seastone. *Water Transfers: Economic Efficiency and Alternative Institutions*. Baltimore, Md.: The Johns Hopkins Press, 1970.

Hays, Samuel P. *Beauty, Health, and Permanence: Environmental Politics in the United States, 1955–1985*. Cambridge: Cambridge University Press, 1987.

Hickel, Walter J. *Who Owns America?* Englewood Cliffs, N.J.: Prentice Hall, 1971.

Howe, Charles W., and K. William Easter. *Interbasin Transfers of Water: Economic Issues and Impacts*. Baltimore, Md.: The Johns Hopkins Press, 1971.

Hundley, Norris, Jr. *Water and the West: The Colorado River Compact and the Politics of Water in the American West*. Berkeley: University of California Press, 1975.

Ingram, Helen M. *Patterns of Politics in Water Resource Development: A Case Study of New Mexico's Role in the Colorado River Basin Bill*. The Institute for Social Research and Development. Albuquerque: The University of New Mexico Press, 1969.

Jamail, Milton H., John R. McCain, and Scott J. Ullery. *Federal-State Water Use Relations in the American West: An Evolutionary Guide to Future Equilibrium*. Tucson: University of Arizona, Office of Arid Land Studies, 1978.

Johnson, Richard. *The Central Arizona Project*. Tucson: The University of Arizona Press, 1977.

Judkins, Grant, ed. *The Big Thompson Disaster*. Loveland, Colo.: Lithographic Press, n.d.

Kaplan, Phyllis. *Guide to the Frank L. Delaney Papers, 1914–1978*. Boulder, Colo.: Western Historical Collections, University Libraries, University of Colorado, 1985.

Kinney, Clesson S. *A Treatise on the Law of Irrigation Rights*. San Francisco: Bender-Moss Co., 1912.

Lee, Lawrence B. *Reclaiming the American West*. Santa Barbara, Calif.: ABC-Clio, 1980.

Lowitt, Richard. *The New Deal and the West*. Bloomington: Indiana University Press, 1984.

Lowitt, Richard, and Maurine Beasley, eds. *One Third of a Nation: Lorena Hickok Reports on the Great Depression*. Urbana: University of Illinois Press, 1981.

Maass, Arthur, and Raymond L. Anderson. . . . *and the Desert Shall Rejoice: Conflict, Growth, and Justice in Arid Environments*. Cambridge, Mass.: MIT Press, 1978.

Marston, Ed, ed. *Western Water Made Simple*. Washington: Island Press, 1987.

McComb, David. *Big Thompson: Profile of a National Disaster*. Boulder, Colo.: Pruett Publishing Company, 1980.

McCool, Daniel. *Command of the Waters: Iron Triangles, Federal Water Development, and Indian Water*. Berkeley: University of California Press, 1987.

McCoy, Donald R. *The Presidency of Harry S. Truman*. Lawrence: The University of Kansas Press, 1984.

Milliken, J. Gordon, and H. E. Mew, Jr. *Economic and Social Impact of Recreation at Reclamation Reservoirs: An Exploratory Study of Selected Colorado Reservoir Areas*. Denver, Colo.: Denver Research Institute, University of Denver, 1969.

Morris, Richard. *Encyclopedia of American History*. Rev. ed. New York: Harper & Row, 1965.

Munroe, Gladys. *Documentary and Life of Edward F. Monroe*. Fort Collins, Colo.: Robinson Press, 1985.

Nathan, Richard P. *The Plot that Failed: Nixon and the Administrative Presidency*. New York: John Wiley and Sons, 1975.

Nixon, Richard M. *A New Road for America*. Garden City, N.J.: Doubleday and Company, 1972.

Norris, Jane E., and Lee G. Norris. *Written in Water: The Life of Benjamin Harrison Eaton*. Athens, Ohio: Swallow Press/Ohio University Press, 1990.

Pabor, William E. *Colorado as an Agricultural State*. New York: Orange Judd Co., 1883.

Radosevich, George E., et al. *Evolution and Administration of Colorado Water Law, 1876–1976*. Fort Collins, Colo.: Water Resources Publications, 1976.

Radosevich, George E., and Donald H. Hamburg, eds. *Colorado Water Laws, Compacts, Treaties and Selected Cases*. Denver: Colorado State Division of Water Resources, 1971.

Reisner, Marc. *Cadillac Desert: The American West and Its Disappearing Water*. New York: Viking Penguin, 1986.

Reisner, Marc, and Sarah Bates. *Overtapped Oasis: Reform or Revolution for Western Water*. Washington: Island Press, 1990.

Richardson, Elmo. *Dams, Parks and Politics: Resource Development in the Truman-Eisenhower Era*. Lexington: The University Press of Kentucky, 1973.

Robinson, Michael C. *Water For the West: The Bureau of Reclamation, 1902–1977*. Chicago: Public Works Historical Society, 1979.

Rosenbaum, Walter A. *The Politics of Environmental Concern*. 2d ed. New York: Praeger, 1977.

Rosenman, Samuel I., comp. *The Public Papers and Addresses of Franklin D. Roosevelt*. Introduction and notes by Roosevelt. New York: Random House, 1938.

Schlesinger, Arthur M., Jr. *The Age of Roosevelt: The Coming of the New Deal*. Boston: Houghton Mifflin, 1965.

Smith, Henry Nash. *Virgin Land*. Cambridge, Mass.: Harvard University Press, 1950.

Steinel, Alvin T. *History of Agriculture in Colorado, 1858–1921*. Fort Collins, Colo.: State Agricultural College, 1926.

Terrell, John Upton. *War For the Colorado River*. 2 vols. Glendale, Calif.: The Arthur H. Clark Company, 1965.

This Fabulous Century. Vol. 4, 1930–1940. New York: Time Life Books [1970].

Time Capsule/1933: A History of the Year Condensed From the Pages of Time. New York: Time Inc. [1967].

Trelease, Frank J., and George A. Gould. *Water Law Cases and Materials*. 4th ed. St. Paul, Minn.: West Publishing Company, 1986.

Veblen, Thomas T., and Diane C. Lorenz. *The Colorado Front Range: A Century of Ecological Change*. Salt Lake City: University of Utah Press, 1991.

Vranesh, George. *Colorado Water Law*. 3 vols. Boulder, Colo.: Design Press, 1987.

Warne, William E. *The Bureau of Reclamation*. Boulder, Colo.: Westview Press, 1985.

Welsh, Frank. *How to Create a Water Crisis*. Boulder, Colo.: Johnson Publishing Company, 1985.

Whitney, Gleaves. *Colorado Front Range: A Landscape Divided*. Boulder, Colo.: Johnson Publishing Company, 1983.

Wickens, James F. *Colorado in the Great Depression*. New York: Garland, 1979.

Works Progress Administration Writer's Program. *Colorado: A Guide to the Highest State*. New York: Hastings House, American Guide Series, 1941.

Worster, Donald. *Rivers of Empire*. New York: Pantheon Books, 1985.

JOURNAL ARTICLES

Abas, Bryan. "No Consultation Without Representation." *Westword* 9 (June 11–17, 1986).

Anderson, Christine. "Chalking Up Water Savings." *Colorado Rancher and Farmer* (October 1, 1989): 15–16.

Anderson, Raymond L. "Emerging Nonirrigation Demands for Water." *Economics Research* 17 (October 1965): 116–121.

———. "Windfall Gains From Transfer of Water Allotments Within the Colorado–Big Thompson Project." *Land Economics* 43 (August 1967): 265–273.

Armstrong, Ellis L. "A Hopeful Year." *Reclamation Era* (February 1972): ii.

Bromley, John C. "A Proud Legacy: Water and W. D. Farr." *Colorado Heritage* (Autumn 1990): 2–13.

Carle, David W. "75 Years of Reclamation Leadership." *Reclamation Era* 63 (Winter and Spring 1978): 86–96.

"Cleaning Up After the Big T Flood." *Rocky Mountain Construction* (August 27, 1976): 16–18.

Cole, Donald Bernard. "Transmountain Water Diversion in Colorado." *The Colorado Magazine* 25 (March [and] May 1948): 118–135.

Colorado Electric News (February 1962), NCWCDA.

Colorado Rancher and Farmer 25 (January 1971): 15–16.

DeVoto, Bernard. "Shall We Let Them Ruin Our National Parks?" *Saturday Evening Post* 223 (July 22, 1950).

Dunbar, Robert G. "The Adaptability of Water Law to the Aridity of the West." *Journal of the West* 24 (January 1985): 57–65.

———. "The Origins of the Colorado System of Water-Right Control." *The Colorado Magazine* 27 (October 1950): 241–262.

———. "The Significance of the Colorado Agricultural Frontier." *Agricultural History* 34 (July 1960): 119–125.

———. "Water Conflicts and Controls in Colorado." *Agricultural History* 22 (July 1948): 180–181.

Eckhardt, John. "The Windy Gap Project SCADA System." *Journal of Water Resources Planning and Management* 112 (July 1986): 366–381.

Hobbs, Gregory J., Jr., "Federal Appellate Court Vacates Judge Kane's Wilderness Water Rights Decision." *Colorado Water Rights* 9 (Summer/Fall 1990): 3.

————. "Federal Environmental Law and State Water Law: Accommodation or Preemption." *Natural Resources & Environment* 1 (Winter 1986): 23–26, 57–59.

Hobbs, Gregory J., Jr., and Bennett W. Raley. "Water Rights Protection in Water Quality Law." *University of Colorado Law Review* 60 (1989): 869–871.

Hobbs, Gregory J., Jr., and Bennett W. Raley. "Water Quality Versus Water Quantity: A Delicate Balance." *Rocky Mountain Mineral Law Institute* 34 (1988): 24-1 to 24-64.

Howe, Charles W. "Project Benefits and Costs from National and Regional Viewpoints: Methodological Issues and Case Study of the Colorado–Big Thompson Project." *Natural Resources Journal* 27 (Winter 1987): 5–20.

Hutchins, Wells A. "Background and Modern Development in Water Law in the United States." *Natural Resources Journal* 2 (December 1962): 416–444.

Jenkins, Mark. "Rescuing the Poudre: A Wild Northern Colorado River Faces Yet Another Threat." *Backpacker* 19 (September 1991): 13.

Keleta, Ghebreyohannes, Robert A. Young, and Edward W. Sparling. "Economic Aspects of Cost-Sharing Arrangements for Federal Irrigation Projects: A Case Study." Report Number: COMPLE-TION-118; W83-02327; OWRT-A-015-COLO(2). Washington: Office of Water Research and Technology. December 1982.

Kelly, William R. "Colorado-Big Thompson Project Initiation." *The Colorado Magazine* 34 (January 1957): 66–74.

————. "Colorado Ground Water Act of 1957 — Is Ground Water Property of the Public?" *Rocky Mountain Law Review* 31 (1959): 165–171.

————. "Water Conservancy Districts (Quasi-Municipal Corporations with General Taxing Powers)." *Rocky Mountain Law Review* 22 (June 1950): 432–452.

Knight, Oliver. "Correcting Nature's Error: The Colorado–Big Thompson Project." *Agricultural History* 30 (October 1956): 157–169.

"Metropolitan Water Roundtable." *Resolve* (Summer 1982).

Miller, Leslie A. "The Battle that Squanders Billions." *Saturday Evening Post* 221 (May 14, 1949): 30.

Mueller, Carl G., Jr. "Federal Ownership of Inland Waters: The Fallbrook Case." *Texas Law Review* 31 (April 1953): 404–417.

"New Name for Bureau of Reclamation." *Reclamation Era* 65:2: 1.

Norcross, Fred N. "Genesis of the Colorado-Big Thompson Project." *The Colorado Magazine* 30 (January 1953): 29–37.

Page, John C. "The Relationship Between the Bureau of Reclamation and its Water Users." *Reclamation Era* 27 (September 1937): 197–198, 201.

Pisani, Donald J. "Enterprise and Equity: A Critique of Western Water Law in the Nineteenth Century." *Western Historical Quarterly* 18 (January 1987): 15–37.

————. "The Irrigation District and the Federal Relationship. Neglected Aspects of Water History in the Twentieth Century." In *The Twentieth Century West*, edited by Gerald D. Nash and Richard W. Etulain. Albuquerque: University of New Mexico Press, 1989, pp. 257–292.

Reclamation Era 39 (January 1953). Entire issue.

Reisner, Marc. "The Next Water War: Cities Versus Agriculture." *Issues in Science and Technology* (Winter 1988–89): 98–102.

Sax, Joseph L. "Selling Reclamation Water Rights: A Case Study in Federal Reclamation Policy." *Michigan Law Review* 64 (November 1965): 13–46.

Swain, Donald C. "The Bureau of Reclamation and the New Deal, 1933–1940." *Pacific Northwest Quarterly* 61 (1970): 137–146.

———. "The National Park Service and the New Deal, 1933–1940." *Pacific Historical Review* 41 (August 1972): 312–332.

Vlachos, Evan C., Paul C. Huszar, George E. Radosevich, and Gaylord V. Skogerboe. "Consolidation of Irrigation Systems: Phase II — Engineering, Economic, Legal and Sociological Requirements." Report Number: COMPLETION-94; W80-06321; OWRT-B-083-COLO(10). Washington: Office of Water Research and Technology. May 1980.

Weatherford, Gary D., Dean N. Birch, Lee Brown, Charles T. DuMars, and Robert M. Hagan. "Western Water Institutions in a Changing Environment. Volume I. Analysis of the Role of Water Institutions in the Conservation and Reallocation of Agricultural Water." Report Number: NSF/PRA-7817903/1. Washington: National Science Foundation. December 15, 1980.

Webb, Walter Prescott. "The American West, Perpetual Mirage." *Harper's Magazine* (May 1957): 25–31.

Western Colorado Report (October 11, 1982). Entire issue.

Wilderness (Spring 1989). Entire issue.

Wilkinson, Charles F. "Colorado Water and the Lords of Yesterday." *Trail & Timberline* (November 1987): 244–251.

———. "Law and the American West: The Search for an Ethic of Place." *University of Colorado Law Review* 59 (Summer 1988): 401–425.

Without a Drought. NCWCD Employee Newsletter. 1986–1991.

Young, Robert A. "Economic Impacts of Transferring Water from Agriculture to Alternative Uses in Colorado." Report Number: COMPLETION-122; W83-03303; OWRT-048-COLO(1). Washington: Office of Water Research and Technology. April 1983.

NEWSPAPERS

Boulder Daily Camera: 1951, 1953, 1960–1961, 1963, 1965–1966, 1969, 1970–1971, 1976–1977, 1979–1980.

Chicago Daily News: 1963.

Denver Post: 1938–1940, 1942, 1947–1949, 1951–1954, 1956, 1958–1967, 1970–1971, 1977, 1980.

Estes Park Trail-Gazette: 1974.

Fort Collins Coloradoan: 1947, 1949, 1956–1966, 1968, 1970–1973, 1976, 1978.

Fort Collins Express-Courier: 1933, 1938–1943.

Fort Collins Triangle Review: 1975, 1978–1979.

Fort Morgan Times: 1951, 1963–1964, 1968–1970, 1972–1974, 1977.

Grand Junction Sentinel: 1949, 1953, 1963–1968, 1970–1977, 1979, 1982.

Greeley Tribune: 1908, 1930, 1933, 1938–1940, 1951–1956, 1958–1964, 1966, 1968–1970, 1972–1974, 1977–1982, 1985–1986.

High Country News: 1986–1987, 1990.

Longmont Daily Times-Call: 1955, 1958–1959, 1962–1964, 1968, 1973–1974, 1976–1978, 1980, 1982.

Loveland Reporter-Herald: 1954–1956, 1963–1964, 1970, 1972, 1975–1979, 1982.

Middle Park Times: 1939, 1947, 1976–1977, 1982.

Montrose Daily Press: 1938.

New York Times: 1982.

Rifle Telegram: 1926.

Rocky Mountain Journal: 1954.

Rocky Mountain News: 1933, 1939–1941, 1954–1956, 1963–1964, 1982, 1986, 1991.

Sky-Hi News: 1976–1977, 1981.

Many of the newspaper articles used for this research were found in the NCWCD Newspaper Clippings Books, 1938–1986, located in the NCWCD Archives.

FEDERAL/STATE LAWS AND LEGAL CASES

Animas–La Plata Project Compact 1968. C.R.S. 1973, 37-64-101; 82 Stat. 885.

Arizona v. California. 373 U.S. 757 (1963).

Arkansas River Compact 1949. C.R.S. 37-69-101; 63 Stat. 145.

Boulder Canyon Project Act 1928. 43 U.S.C. 617(q); 45 Stat. 1065.

California v. United States. 438 U.S. 645, 662 (1978).

Clean Water Act 1977. 33 U.S.C. 1251(g); 91 Stat. 1567.

Coffin v. Left Hand Ditch. 6 Colo. 443, 447 (Colorado 1882).

Colorado–Big Thompson Project 1938. 43 U.S.C. 386; 52 Stat. 764.

Colorado River Basin Project Act 1968. 43 U.S.C. 1551; 82 Stat. 885.

Colorado River Basin Salinity Control Act 1974. 43 U.S.C. 1591; 88 Stat. 270.

Colorado River Compact 1922. C.R.S. 1973, 37-61-101; 42 Stat. 171.

Colorado River Storage Project Act 1956. 43 U.S.C. 620(m); 70 Stat. 110.

Colorado River Water Conservation District v. Colorado Water Conservation Board. 594 P.2d 570 (Colorado 1979).

Colorado River Water Conservation District v. United States. 424 U.S. 800 (1976).

Colorado River Water Conservation District v. Vidler Tunnel Water Company. 197 Colo. 413, 594 P.2d 566 (1979).

Colorado v. New Mexico. 459 U.S. 176 (1982).

Colorado v. New Mexico. 467 U.S. 310 (1984).

Colorado Water Conservancy Act 1937. C.R.S. 1973, 37-45-101.

Colorado Water Right Determination and Administration Act 1969. C.R.S. 1973, 37-92-101.

Colorado Wilderness Act 1980. 16 U.S.C. 1132; 94 Stat. 3265.

Endangered Species Act 1973. 16 U.S.C. 1531; 87 Stat. 884.

Environmental Defense Fund v. Costle. 657 F.2d 275 (D.C. Cir. 1981).

Federal Land Policy and Management Act 1976. 43 U.S.C. 1701; 90 Stat. 2744.

Federal Power Act 1920. 16 U.S.C. 802(b), 821; 41 Stat. 1077.

Federal Water Pollution Control Amendments 1972. 33 U.S.C. 1251; 86 Stat. 816.

Friends of the Earth v. Armstrong. 360 F. Supp. 165 (D. Utah 1973).

Fryingpan-Arkansas Project 1962. 43 U.S.C. 616(d); 76 Stat. 392.

Kansas v. Colorado. 185 U.S. 125 (1902).

Kansas v. Colorado. 206 U.S. 46 (1907).

McCarran Amendment 1952. 43 U.S.C. 666; 66 Stat. 560.

Mexican Water Treaty 1944. Treaty Series 994; 59 Stat. 1219.

National Environmental Policy Act 1970. 42 U.S.C. 4321; 83 Stat. 852.

National Forest Organic Act 1897. 16 U.S.C. 481; 30 Stat. 36.

National Wilderness Preservation Act 1964. 16 U.S.C. 1131; 78 Stat. 890.

National Wildlife Federation v. *Gorsuch*. 693 F.2d 156 (D.C. Cir. 1982).

Nebraska v. *Wyoming and Colorado*. 325 U.S. 589 (1945).

Northern Colorado Water Conservancy District v. *Board of County Commissioners of Grand County*. 482 F. Supp. 1115 (D. Colorado 1980).

People ex rel. Rogers, Atty. Gen. v. *Letford*, 102 Colo. 284, 79 P.2d 279 (1938).

Reclamation Act 1902. 43 U.S.C. 372, 383; 32 Stat. 388.

Riverside Irrigation District v. *Andrews*. 758 F.2d 508 (10th Cir. 1990); vacated *Riverside Irrigation District* v. *Stipo*. 658 F.2d (10th Cir. 1981).

Sierra Club v. *Block*. 622 F. Supp. 842 (D. Colorado 1985); vacated *Sierra Club* v. *Yeutter*. 911 F.2d 1405 (10th Cir. 1990).

South Platte River Compact 1923. C.R.S. 1973, 37-64-101; 44 Stat. 195.

United States of America v. *Bell*. 724 P.2d 631 (Colorado 1986).

United States of America v. *Northern Colorado Water Conservancy District et al*. Civil No. 2782 (1949).

United States v. *City and County of Denver*. 656 P.2d 1 (Colorado 1983).

United States v. *District Court in and for Eagle County*. 401 U.S. 520 (1971).

United States v. *New Mexico*. 438 U.S. 696 (1978).

Upper Colorado River Compact 1948. C.R.S. 1973, 37-62-101; 63 Stat. 31.

Wild and Scenic Rivers Act 1968. 16 U.S.C. 1271; 82 Stat. 906.

Winters v. *United States*. 207 U.S. 564 (1908).

Wyoming v. *Colorado*. 259 U.S. 419 (1922)

COLORADO STATE GOVERNMENT DOCUMENTS

Colorado Revised Statutes. 1973, 1985.

Cooperative Crop and Livestock Reporting Service. *Colorado Agricultural Statistics, 1935*. Denver: 1935.

Department of Agriculture. *Colorado Agricultural Statistics*. 1957 to 1973 Final; 1958 to 1974 Preliminary. 1975.

Department of the State Engineer. *Analysis of Power Features of Colorado–Big Thompson Project With Recommended Construction Schedule*. Denver: January 1942.

Department of the State Engineer. *Preliminary Engineering Report: Northern Transmountain Diversion*. By Royce J. Tipton. Denver: December 1933.

Department of the State Engineer. *Report on the Water Resources of the South Platte Basin in Colorado and Present Utilization of Same Together With Present and Future Transmountain Diversions*. Prepared under the direction of M. C. Hinderlider, State Engineer. Denver: 1931.

House. *Joint Resolution No. 1*. March 31, 1936.

Office of the State Engineer. *Fifth Biennial Report, 1889–1891*. Denver: 1891

Senate. *Session Laws of Colorado*. 1935, 1937, 1939, 1943, 1949, 1961, 1973.

State Board of Immigration. *Colorado Year Book, 1933–1934*. Denver: September 1934.

State Planning Commission. *Year Book of the State of Colorado, 1948–1950*. Denver: 1951.

State Planning Division. *Colorado Year Book, 1959–1961*. Denver: 1962.

State Planning Division. *Colorado Year Book, 1962–1964*. Denver: 1965.

UNITED STATES GOVERNMENT DOCUMENTS

Statutes at Large

The Act Creating Rocky Mountain National Park. Statutes at Large. Vol. 38 (1915).

Boulder Canyon Project Act. Statutes at Large. Vol. 45, part I (1927–1929).

Colorado–Big Thompson Project Act. Statutes at Large. Vol. 50 (1937).

Department of Justice Appropriation Act, 1953. Statutes at Large. Vol. 66 (1952).

Department of State, Justice, Commerce, and the Judicial Appropriation Act, 1953. Statutes at Large. Vol. 66 (1952).

Reclamation Project Act of 1939. Statutes at Large. Vol. 53, part I (1939).

Other Federal Documents

Council on Environmental Quality. *Twentieth Annual Report to the President of the United States*. 1990.

U.S. Congress. *Congressional Record*. 69th Cong., 1st sess., Vol. 69, pt. 8. 1925–1926.

U.S. Congress. *Congressional Record*. 72nd Cong., 1st sess., Vol. 75, pt. 6. 1931–1932.

U.S. Congress. *Congressional Record*. 74th Cong., 1st sess., 1935. Vol. 79, pt. 3; Vol. 80, pts. 3, 7, 9.

U.S. Congress. *Congressional Record*. 75th Cong., 1st sess., 1937. Vol. 81, pts. 6, 7, 10.

U.S. Congress. *Congressional Record*. 75th Cong., 3d sess., 1938. Vol. 83, pts. 2, 6, 11.

U.S. Congress. *Congressional Record*. 80th Cong., 1st sess., 1947. Vol. 93, pt. 8.

U.S. Congress. House. *A History of the Committee on Appropriations, House of Representatives*. Prepared by Edward Taylor. 77th Cong., 1st sess., 1941. H.D. 299.

U.S. Congress. House. *Briefing by the Secretary of the Interior: Oversight Hearing Before the Committee on Interior and Insular Affairs*. 98th Cong., 1st sess., January 26, 1983.

U.S. Congress. House. *Department of the Interior Appropriations Act*. P.L. 136. 77th Cong., 1st sess., 1941. H.R. 4590.

U.S. Congress. House. *Fourth Annual Report of the Reclamation Service, 1904–1905*. Prepared by F. H. Newell, Chief Engineer, U.S. Geological Survey. 59th Cong., 1st sess., 1905. H.D. 86.

U.S. Congress. House. *Hearings Before the Committee on Irrigation and Reclamation*. 75th Cong., 1st sess., June 30, July 2, 1937.

U.S. Congress. House. *Hearings Before the Committee on Irrigation of Arid Lands*. January 28 to February 9, 1901.

U.S. Congress. House. *Land Classification and Economic Report, Wyoming*. Prepared by W. W. Johnston, Associate Reclamation Economist. *Engineering Report on the Casper-Alcova Irrigation Project, Wyoming*. Prepared by J. R. Iakisch, Engineer, Bureau of Reclamation. 71st Cong., 3d sess., 1931. H.D. 674.

U.S. Congress. House. Letter from Secretary Hubert Work to Addison T. Smith, Chairman of House Committee on Irrigation and Reclamation. 69th Cong., 1st sess. *Congressional Record*, Vol. 67, pt. 10. 1925–1926.

U.S. Congress. House. *Reorganization of the Bureau of Reclamation*. Oversight Hearing before the Subcommittee on Water and Power Resources of the Committee on Interior and Insular Affairs. 100th Cong., 1st sess., October 29, 1987.

U.S. Congress. House. *Report on the North Platte River Basin*. Prepared by Department of Interior, Bureau of Reclamation. 70th Cong., 1st sess., 1928. H.R. 1749.

U.S. Congress. *Memorial Services, House/Senate: Alva B. Adams*. 77th Cong., 2d sess. Washington: GPO, 1944.

U.S. Congress. *Memorial Services, House/Senate: Edward T. Taylor*. 77th Cong., 2nd sess. Washington: GPO, 1944.

U.S. Congress. Senate. *Colorado–Big Thompson Project, Synopsis of Report*. 75th Cong., 1st sess., 1937. S.D. 80.

U.S. Congress. Senate. *Hearings Before the Committee on Irrigation and Reclamation*. 70th Cong., 1st sess., January 13, 14, and February 1, 1928.

U.S. Congress. Senate. *Hearings Before the Subcommittee on Water Resources*. 97th Cong., 1st sess., April 21–23 and June 8, 12, 1981.

U.S. Congress. Senate. *Report on the North Platte River Basin*. Prepared by Department of Interior, Bureau of Reclamation. 70th Cong., 1st sess., 1928. S.R. 1184.

U.S. Congress. Senate. *Synopsis of Report on Colorado–Big Thompson Project, Plan of Development and Cost Estimate Prepared by the Bureau of Reclamation, Department of the Interior*. 75th Cong., 1st sess., June 15, 1937.

U.S. Department of Agriculture. *Irrigation in Northern Colorado*. Prepared by Robert G. Hemphill. Bulletin 1026. Washington: GPO, May 16, 1922.

U.S. Department of the Interior. Bureau of Reclamation. *Annual Project History, Colorado–Big Thompson Project, Colorado*. 1938–1983.

U.S. Department of the Interior. Bureau of Reclamation. *Colorado Big–Thompson Project: Technical Record of Design and Construction*. 4 vols. Denver: Bureau of Reclamation, 1957.

U.S. Department of the Interior. Bureau of Reclamation. *Recreation and Wildlife Summary*. Annual Reports.

U.S. Department of the Interior. Bureau of Reclamation. *The Story of the Colorado–Big Thompson Project*. Washington: GPO, 1968.

U.S. Department of the Interior. Bureau of Reclamation. Water and Power Resources Service. *Project Data, 1981*. Denver, 1981.

U.S. Department of the Interior. *Colorado River and Its Utilization*. By E. C. La Rue. Water Supply Paper 395. Washington: GPO, 1916.

U.S. Department of the Interior. *Colorado–Big Thompson Project, Technical Record of Design and Construction, Vol. I: Planning, Legislation, and General Description*. Washington: Bureau of Reclamation, April 1957.

U.S. Department of the Interior. U.S. Geological Survey. *Report of Progress of Stream Measurements for the Calendar Year 1904*. Prepared under the direction of F. E. Newell by M. C. Hinderlider, G. L. Swendsen, and A. E. Chandler. Water Supply and Irrigation Paper 133, ser. P, no. 10. Washington: GPO, 1905.

U.S. Department of the Interior. *Upper Colorado River and Its Utilization*. Prepared by Robert Follansbee. Water Supply Paper 617. Washington: GPO, 1929.

U.S. Department of the Interior. Water and Power Resources Service, Lower Missouri Region. *Final Environmental Statement: Colorado–Big Thompson, Windy Gap Projects, Colorado*. 1981.

U.S. Department of the Interior. *Water Resources: Use and Management Policy Statement*. August 21, 1975.

President. Executive Order. "Water Resources Council: Water Resource Policy Study." *Federal Register*. July 15, 1977. Vol. 42, no. 136, pp. 36788–36795.

President. Office of Management and Budget. *Historical Tables: Budget of the United States Government*. Fiscal Year 1986.

President. *Public Papers of the Presidents of the United States*. Washington: Office of the *Federal Register*, National Archives and Records Service. Gerald R. Ford, 1976.

President. *Public Papers of the Presidents of the United States*. Washington: Office of the *Federal Register*, National Archives and Records Service. Jimmy Carter, 1977, 1978.

President. *Public Papers of the Presidents of the United States*. Washington: Office of the *Federal Register*, National Archives and Records Service. Ronald Reagan, 1985.

Wild and Scenic Rivers Act. Amendments. P.L. 99-590. October 1986.

OTHER PRIMARY SOURCES

All materials listed here are located in the NCWCD Archives (NCWCDA) unless otherwise indicated.

Personal Files

Barkley, J. R.

Delaney, Frank. Norlin Library, University of Colorado. Boulder, Colorado.

Dille, J. M.

Hansen, Charles A.

Kelly, William R.

Lory, Charles A. Morgan Library, Colorado State University. Fort Collins, Colorado.

Nixon, Thomas A.

Interviews With the Author (unless otherwise indicated)

Anderson, Fred. November 1991.

Balcomb, Kenneth. April 1990.

Barkley, J. R. August, October 1988; August, October 1989; May, June 1990.

Berling, Robert. July 1991.

Blakely, Brian. November 1991.

Eckhardt, John. July 1991.

Farr, W. D. July 1988, September 1991.

Fischer, Roland. April 1990.

Gerk, Wes. May 1990.

Hamil, Donald. May 1990.

Harrison, Craig. November 1991.

Hobbs, Gregory J., Jr. November, December 1991.

McFarlane, John. July 1991.

McKee, Craig. November 1991.

Otsuka, Kish. May 1990.

Osborne, Cecil. May 1990.

Simpson, Larry. August, November 1991.

Smith, Robert. November 1991 (telephone interview).

Watson, Elton. May 1990.

Whitmore, Kenneth L. January 1990.

Wooldridge, Jim. By Greg Silkensen, August 1991.

Minutes

CLPWUA: 1980, 1983.

CRWCD: 1934–1935, 1946–1953, 1958–1960.

CWCB: 1941–1943, 1947, 1949–1953, 1960.

MSD: 1969–1990.

NCWCD: 1938–1990.

NCWUA: 1934–1938.

Six Cities Committee: 1976–1990.

WSPA: December 1934, March 1935.

Miscellaneous Papers/Reports/Studies

Allison, William W. "Water Analysis Report." Department of Chemistry, Colorado State University. Fort Collins, Colo., October 5, 1967. CSUA.

Anderson, Raymond L., and L. M. Hartman. "Introduction of Supplemental Irrigation Water: Agricultural Response to an Increased Water Supply in Northeastern Colorado." Colorado Agricultural Experiment Station, Colorado State University. Fort Collins, Colo., 1965. CSUA.

Anderson, Raymond L., C. W. DeRemer, and R. S. Hall. "Water Use and Management in an Arid Region (Fort Collins, Colorado and Vicinity)." Environmental Resources Center, Colorado Water Resources Research Institute, Information Series #26. Colorado State University. Fort Collins, Colo., 1977.

Barkley, J. R. "Agricultural Uses of Snow Surveys and Seasonal Water Forecasts." Speech given to the Soil Conservation Society of America. August 27, 1959.

Barkley, J. R. "Manager-Director Relations." Speech given to the Four States Irrigation Council. January 15, 1959.

Barkley, J. R. Testimony at Hearing before the Subcommittee on Irrigation and Reclamation of the Committee on Interior and Insular Affairs. House of Representatives, 89th Cong., 1st sess., August 23–September 1, 1965.

Barnett, John T. Report written between February 28 and March 17, 1936.

Bunger, Mills E. "Early History, Colorado–Big Thompson Project, 1889-1935." In *Colorado–Big Thompson Project, Early History, Tipton Report, 1933: Colorado Water Conservancy District Law*.

"Cache La Poudre Basin Study Extension Executive Summary." Prepared for the CWR&PDA. December 1990.

"Cache La Poudre Basin Water and Hydropower Resources Management Study." Prepared for the CWR&PDA. January 1987.

"C–BT/Windy Gap Operations Study, Final Report." Prepared for the Municipal Subdistrict, NCWCD. November 1990.

Chilson, Hatfield. Paper delivered to the Loveland Rotary Club. March 1985.

"A Conversation With William R. Kelly, Esquire." Transcript of interviews between Kelly and Lee G. Norris between 1977 and 1981. Colorado State University Archives, Morgan Library. Fort Collins, Colo.

Crookston, Mark A. "Irrigation Management Service." Abstract of a paper presented at the 1991 regional meeting of the United States Committee on Irrigation and Drainage. Denver, Colo.

Crookston, Mark A. "Irrigation Management Service." NCWCD. March 29, 1991.

CWR&PDA Annual Reports. 1981–1988.

Denver Board of Water Commissioners. Report. Denver, Colo. 1946–1950, 1952–1955.

Dille, J. M. "Discussion of Allotments and Reallocations." Paper. May 1948.

Dyer, Herbert E., and J. R. Barkley. "Agricultural Production in Northern Colorado Water Conservancy District as Related to National Defense." Colorado Water Conservation Board. Denver, Colo. December 1941.

Farr, W. D. "The Future of Northern Colorado Water Supplies." Speech given at the Fort Collins Water Symposium. October 21, 1991.

Hamburg, Donald H. Report to Azure Committee, CRWCD Board. January 27, 1983. CRWCDA.

Hansen, James E., II. "Charles A. Lory and the Challenges of Colorado's Semi-Arid Frontier." Paper presented at the 1980 meeting of the Pacific Coast Branch of the American Historical Association. August 1980. CSUA.

International Engineering Company. "Windy Gap Project, Progress Reports." July 1981–January 1985

Kelly, William R. "Colorado–Big Thompson Project Initiation." Speech given June 3, 1952. CSUA.

Lamm, Richard D. "The Lamm Administration: A Retrospective." December 1986.

Luce, Charles F. "Review Draft: A Proposed Report of the National Water Commission." Vol. 1. Arlington, Va.: U.S. Department of Commerce, n.d.

Missouri Basin States Association. "The Missouri River Report." October 1991.

Morris, John R., and Clive V. Jones. "Water For Denver: An Analysis of the Alternatives." Prepared with a grant from the Environmental Defense Fund, Inc. 1980. Davis, Graham and Stubbs. Denver, Colo.

NCWCD Annual Reports. 1957–1983 (fiscal year).

NCWCD Secretary-Manager's Reports. 1939–1967.

"Principles to Govern the Release of Water from Granby Dam to Provide Fishery Flows Immediately Downstream in the Colorado River." Final Agreement. January 19, 1961.

"Regional Water Supply Study." NCWCD Draft Report. May 1991.

Rocky Mountain National Park. Superintendents' Monthly Reports, Shadow Mountain National Recreation Area (non-NCWCDA). 1967–1978.

"Southern Water Supply Project, Status Report." November 15, 1991.

"Statistical Information, Population Projections for Colorado Planning Regions, 1970–2000, February 22, 1974." Colorado Division of Planning, Demographic Section. CSUA.

"Statutory Powers of District to Transport Other Than Project Water." Unpublished memorandum. December 2, 1960.

"St. Vrain Basin Reconnaissance Study." Prepared for the CWR&PDA. February 1986.

Toelle, E. S. "Irrigation and Bureaucracy." 1949.

Vlachos, Evan. "The Changing World of the Water Manager." NCWCD Fall Water Users Meeting. November 21, 1991.

Windy Gap Archaeological Report. Final Draft. April 15, 1984. Western Cultural Resources Management. Boulder, Colo.

Windy Gap Settlement Agreement. April 30, 1980.

Theses, Dissertations

Bastian, Stanley J. "The Northern Colorado Water Conservancy District: A Political System." Master's thesis, Colorado State University, 1970.

Bradt, Russell N. "Foreign Water in the Cache La Poudre Valley." Master's thesis, University of Northern Colorado, 1948.

Gray, Sanford Lee. "The Effect of the Northern Colorado Water Conservancy District on Water Transfer." Master's thesis, Colorado State University, 1965.

Hickey, Jeffrey S. "An Uneasy Coexistence: Rocky Mountain National Park and the Grand River Ditch." Master's thesis, University of Colorado, 1988.

Michelsen, Ari M. "Economics of Optioning Agricultural Water Rights for Urban Water Supplies During Drought." Ph.D. diss., Colorado State University, 1988.

Stefanec, Kharol E. "Federal Water Recreation in Colorado: Comprehensive View and Analysis." Master's thesis, Colorado State University, 1978.

Subramaniam, Janakiram. "Water Resources Institutions and Development." Master's thesis, Colorado State University, 1977.

Memoranda

Barkley, J. R., to NCWCD Directors, April 1950.

Dille, J. M., to NCWCD Directors, November 1942; November 1945; March, December 1946; January 1947; October 1948; April 1950.

Gianelli, William R., Assistant Secretary of the Army, to Directors of Civil Works, November 18, 1981.

IMS, October 19, 1988.

Kanzler, Ernest, to Eugene Millikin, October 28, 1942.

Kelly, William R., to President Hansen and the NCWCD Board, August 26, 1948; October 18, 1955.

Kelly, William R., and E. Tyndall Snyder, to NCWCD, November 20, 1947.

Project Water Delivery, to District Directors, November 1942.

Sayre, John, to NCWCD Board, August 4, 1975.

Sparks, Felix, to CWCB and Colorado Water Investigation Commission, August 22, 1963.

U.S. Bureau of Reclamation, Lower Missouri Region. "Modification of Horsetooth Reservoir." Denver, Colorado, December 1983.

Walter, Ray F., to Edward D. Foster, J. M. Dille, Royce J. Tipton, and Lindsey, January 10, 1936.

Watt, James, to President Reagan, June 15, 1982.

WSSC, to all shareholders, June 18, 1986.

Letters/Telegrams

Aandahl, Fred G., to Robert S. Millar, May 16, 1960.

Adams, Alva B., to Ebert K. Burlew, November 16, 1936.

Adams, Alva B., to J. M. Dille, September 27, 1941.

Adams, Alva B., to Edward D. Foster, (telegram) January 8, 1936.

Adams, Alva B., to Charles Hansen, May 6, 1935.

Akolt, John P., to Felix Sparks, July 8, 1960.

Akolt, John P., to John N. Spencer, April 9, 1960; March 16, 1961.

Anderson, A. L., to NCWCD Board, May 15, 1986.

Armstrong, William, to Earl F. Phipps, January 20, 1981.

Aupperle, D. W., to County Clerks of 21 Western Colorado Counties, May 6, 1936.

Aupperle, D. W., to Directors of the Western Colorado Protective Association, November 16, December 18, 1934 (CRWCDA).

Aupperle, D. W., to Charles Hansen, April 17, 1934.

Aupperle, D. W., to Edward T. Taylor, April 29, 1933; April 17, May 21, 1934.

Balcomb, Scott, to Hank Brown, March 26, 1980.

Barkley, J. R., to Charles H. Boustead, January 30, 1962.

Barkley, J. R., to Kenneth W. Chomers, August 9, 1948.

Barkley, J. R., to Roland C. Fischer, May 12, 1974.

Barkley, J. R., to William R. Kelly, September 21, 1961.

Barkley, J. R., to John Love, June 22, 1968.

Barkley, J. R., to William H. Nelson, September 26, October 10, 1963.

Barkley, J. R., to Harold Roberts, June 14, 1956.

Barkley, J. R., to John N. Spencer, December 15, 1961.

Barkley, J. R., to Ralph Waldo, August 4, 1967.

Barnard, John, to John N. Spencer, March 23, 1961.

Bashore, H. W., to Office of the Commissioner of the War Manpower Commission, August 4, 1943.

Batson, Avery, to NCWCD Board, October 6, 1947.

Berling, Robert, to Project Manager USBR, January 22, 1975 (USBR).

Bernhardt, Mark, to Rich Drew, March 1, 1983.

Broadbent, Robert N., to William Armstrong, October 20, 1984.

Buck, William E., to J. M. Dille, September 2, 1953.

Chomers, Kenneth W., to J. R. Barkley, August 5, 1948.

Christiansen, R. B., to W. D. Farr, June 1, 1981.

Clark, Ramsey, to Alfred A. Arraj, September 21, 1963.

Clayton, John, to J. R. Barkley, November 8, 1960; January 5, July 26, 1961.

Clayton, John, and J. R. Barkley, to Fred A. Seaton, April 20, 1960.

Clayton, John, and J. R. Barkley, to John N. Spencer, August 11, 1960; March 10, 22, August 22, 1961.

Coffin, Claude C., to Directors and Officers of NCWCD, September 28, 1948.

Coffin, Claude C., to Charles Hansen, October 4, 1948.

Cook, James E., to Larry D. Simpson, July 9, 1985.

Cowen, Wilson, to Paul V. McNutt, November 11, 1944.

Cummings, Fred, to Charles Hansen, (telegram) March 4, 1936; April 7, 13, 20, 29, May 4, 7, 1937; February 12, 19, 1938.

Danielson, Jeris A., to John MacFarlane, June 11, 1980.

Debler, E. B., to John M. Dille, February 14, 1948.

Debler, E. B., to John E. Gross, December 15, 1944.

Delaney, Frank, to Charles Evans Hughes, March 11, 1936 (CRWCDA).

Delaney, Frank, to Earl F. Phipps, May 6, 1975.

Delaney, Frank, to John M. Sayre, May 8, 1975.

Demaray, A. E., to Committee, USBR, March 22, 1935.

Dildine, Evan, to Gary Hart, October 11, 1977.

Dille, J. M., to Alva B. Adams, September 23, 1941.

Dille, J. M., to Thomas J. Barbre, January 11, 1944.

Dille, J. M., to E. B. Debler, February 21, 1946.

Dille, J. M., to Federal Land Bank of Wichita, 1938–1943.

Dille, J. M., to Edward D. Foster, April 26, 1937.

Dille, J. M., to Charles Hansen, May 6, 1934; June 10, 12, 16, 26, July 2, 1937; March 14, 25, 1943.

Dille, J. M., to Eugene D. Millikin, January 6, May 7, 1943; March 4, 1944.

Dille, J. M., to Richard M. Nixon, June 2, 1937.

Dille, J. M., to H. S. Varner, Jr., February 10, 1953.

Drew, Rich, to Michael S. Burney, May 13, 1981.

Eberstadt, F., to Eugene D. Millikin, December 5, 1942.

Farr, W. D., to Redwood Fisher, March 26, 1976.

Farr, W. D., to John Vanderhoof, February 4, July 8, 1977.

Farr, W. D., and Gordon Dyekman, to James Watt, December 11, 1981; March 12, 1982.

Fischer, Roland, to John M. Sayre, March 18, April 6, 20, 1983; September 29, 1986.

Fischer, Roland, to John Vanderhoof, February 23, 1977.

Foster, Edward D., to D. W. Aupperle, December 19, 1935 (CRWCDA).

Foster, Edward D., to Colorado Senators and Congressmen, January 14, 1936.

Foster, Edward D., to J. M. Dille, January 16, June 8, 1936.

Foster, Edward D., to Charles Hansen, June 5, 1936.

Foster, Edward D., to C. A. Watson, January 30, 1935.

Hagie, F. O., to Clifford Stone, December 16, 1937.

Hamilton, Richard, to James E. Stokes, April 16, 1986.

Hansen, Charles, to Alva B. Adams, September 12, 1940.

Hansen, Charles, to D. W. Aupperle, April 10, 21, 30, 1934; July 29, 1937.

Hansen, Charles, to Claude C. Coffin, October 2, 11, 1948.

Hansen, Charles, to Fred Cummings, May 10, 19, 1935; January 23, 1936; March 17, 1937.

Hansen, Charles, to J. M. Dille, April 23, May 5, 1934; May 19, (telegram) May 27, June 4, (telegram) June 12, June 24, July 1, 3, 10, 12, 1937.

Hansen, Charles, to Carl Gray, February 2, 1937.

Hansen, Charles, to Edwin C. Johnson, July 28, 1941; February 11, 16, March 17, 1942.

Hansen, Charles, to Fred Norcross, (telegram) May 15, 1935.

Hansen, Charles, to Edward T. Taylor, January 15, 21, 1936; December 21, 1940.

Hansen, Charles, to Walter Walker, April 10, 1934.

Hill, William S., to J. M. Dille, June 24, July 7, 1947.

Hobbs, Gregory J., Jr., to William Armstrong, August 25, 1988.

Hobbs, Gregory J., Jr., to "colleagues," March 30, 1987.

Hobbs, Gregory J., Jr., to CRWCD attorneys, March 16, 1984.

Hobbs, Gregory J., Jr., to Roy Howard, June 19, 1980.

Hobbs, Gregory J., Jr., to Daniel Tyler, January 4, 24, 1990.

Hobbs, Gregory J., Jr., to Tim Wirth, April 18, 1989.

Howell, Cleves H., to Stiers Brothers, January 10, 1945.

Hunter, James M., to J. M. Dille, November 3, 1953.

Ickes, Harold, to Charles Hansen, October 12, 1937.

Ickes, Harold, to Claude R. Wickard, March 2, 1943.

Johnson, Ed, to Charles Hansen, May 6, 1937; February 2, 20, 1942.

Kelly, William R., to George Irvin, July 5, 1940.

Lake, Rial, to W. D. Farr, February 3, 1984.

Lamm, Richard, to Larry D. Simpson, August 25, 1983.

Lory, Charles A., to Charles Hansen, December 24, 1935.

Lory, Charles A., to Elwood Mead, May 16, 1934 (CRWCDA).

Lory, Charles A., to R. L. Parshall, August 20, 1935.

Martin, B. E., to Larry D. Simpson, September 12, 1984.

McCreery, N. R., to Colorado Managers, November 27, 1935.

Mead, Elwood G., to Charles Hansen, February 19, 1935.

Merman, Clare S., to J. R. Barkley, November 10, 1949.

Millar, Robert S., to Fred A. Seaton, April 26, October 11, 1960.

Millar, Robert S., to Stewart Udall, August 2, 1962.

Millikin, Eugene D., to J. M. Dille, February 19, December 30, 1942; (telegram) June 18, 1943.

Millikin, Eugene D., to Clifford Stone, November 16, December 1, 29, 1942; April 22, May 25, June 15, 1943.

Morgan County Commissioners to Gordon Dyekman, October 19, 1983.

Nelson, Donald M., to J. R. Barkley, October 3, 1963.

Nelson, Donald M., to Franklin D. Roosevelt, June 21, 1943.

Nelson, Donald M., to Felix Sparks, September 26, 1963.

Nixon, Thomas A., to J. M. Dille, (telegram) June 4, 6, 1937.

Nixon, Thomas A., to Charles Hansen, November 22, 1937.

Nixon, Thomas A., to NCWUA, April 2, 1935.

Olds, Leland, to Clifford Stone, March 13, 1941.

Page, John C., to Fred Cummings, July 9, 1937.

Page, John C., to Eugene D. Millikin, March 13, 1943.

Pendergrass, James D., to Larry D. Simpson, October 3, 1986.

Phipps, Earl, to William Armstrong, February 12, 1981.

Phipps, Earl, to CRWCD, May 25, 1976.

Phipps, Earl, to CWQCC, December 7, 1976.

Phipps, Earl, to Frank Delaney, May 28, August 19, 1975.

Phipps, Earl, to Roland C. Fischer, January 31, March 20, 1975; March 16, 1976.

Phipps, Earl, to Redwood Fisher, July 14, 1975.

Phipps, Earl, to Gary Hart, March 10, 1981.

Phipps, Earl, to William J. McDonald, June 2, 1981.

Phipps, Earl, to John M. Sayre, June 2, 1981.

Reeb, Raymond, to Lenny Arnold, November 11, 1975.

Roosevelt, F. D., to John C. Vivian, June 25, 1943.

Saunders, Glenn, to Jack Clayton and J. R. Barkley, August 16, 1960.

Saunders, Dickenson, et al., to Alfred A. Arraj, September 26, 1963.

Sayre, John, to Roland C. Fischer, April 12, 1983.

Sayre, John, to Redwood Fisher, May 24, 1976.

Sayre, John, to Richard Lamm, October 21, 1977.

Sayre, John, to John Little, April 5, 1976.

Sayre, John, to NCWCD Board of Directors, April 28, 1964.

Simpson, Larry, to Robert N. Broadbent, January 9, 1985.

Simpson, Larry, to Delph Carpenter, March 19, 1987.

Simpson, Larry, to Roland C. Fischer, October 11, 1983.

Simpson, Larry, to Gary Hart, March 15, 30, 1979.

Simpson, Larry, to Morgan Smith, June 25, 1980.

Smith, Robert G., to Ralph L. Crossman, December 5, 1938 (CRWCDA).

Sparks, Felix, to J. Ben Nix, May 22, 1968.

Spencer, John M., to Jack Clayton and J. R. Barkley, January 4, 1962.

Stone, Clifford H., to Delph Carpenter, March 1, 1951.

Taylor, Edward, to D. W. Aupperle, November 1934; February 21, July 22, 1936 (CRWCDA).

Taylor, Edward, to Colorado State Planning Commission, September 27, 1933.

Taylor, Edward, to Edward D. Foster, January 15, 1936.

Taylor, Edward, to Charles Hansen, June 26, 1941.

Taylor, Edward, to Harold L. Ickes, April 2, 1935.

Taylor, Edward, to the *Grand Junction Sentinel*, December 23, 1935.

Tipton, Royce, to Charles Hansen, May 8, 1938; June 23, 1939; June 26, 1941.

Udall, Stewart, to Robert S. Millar, November 9, 1962.

Walker, R. F., to Charles Hansen, April 14, 1934.

Walter, R. F., to Charles Hansen, August 9, 1935.

Walter, R. J., to J. M. Dille, November 4, 1957.

West, L. A., to John Austin, S. S. Magoffin, and J. F. Shea Co. Inc., March 6, 1945.

West, L. A., to L. R. Douglas, December 14, 1944.

West, L. A., to S. S. Magoffin, December 6, 1944; January 9, 1945.

Whitten, J. E., to Sinclair O. Harper, April 6, 1943.

Wright, Walter W., to John Bankhead, November 16, 1937.

Young, Walter, to Harry Bashore, March 9, 1945.

Young, Walter, to John E. Gross, January 11, 1945.

Index